Family Communication

Cohesion and Change

Family Communication

Cohesion and Change

Eighth Edition

KATHLEEN M. **GALVIN**

Northwestern University

CARMA L. **BYLUND**

Memorial Sloan-Kettering Cancer Center

BERNARD J. **BROMMEL**

Northeastern Illinois University

Allyn and Bacon

Boston   Columbus   Indianapolis   New York   San Francisco   Upper Saddle River   Amsterdam
Cape Town   Dubai   London   Madrid   Milan   Munich   Paris   Montreal   Toronto   Delhi
Mexico City   São Paulo   Sydney   Hong Kong   Seoul   Singapore   Taipei   Tokyo

Editor in Chief, Communication: Karon Bowers
Project Editor: Toni Magyar
Editorial Assitant: Megan Sweeney
Director of Marketing: Megan Galvin-Fak
Marketing Manager: Wendy Gordon
Production Manager: Raegan Keida Heerema
Associate Managing Editor: Bayani Mendoza de Leon
Managing Editor: Linda Mihatov Behrens
Project Coordination: Electronic Publishing Services Inc., NYC
Text Design and Electronic Page Makeup: TexTech
Cover Design Manager and Designer: Anne Bonanno Nieglos
Cover Photo: © Monalyn Gracia/Corbis
Image Permission Coordinator: Annette Linder
Photo Researcher: Jodie Hein
Manufacturing Manager: Mary Ann Gloriande
Printer and Binder: STP Courier
Cover Printer: STP Courier

Library of Congress Cataloging-in-Publication Data

Galvin, Kathleen M.
   Family communication/Kathleen M. Galvin,
Carma L. Bylund, Bernard J. Brommel.—8th ed.
      p. cm.
   Includes bibliographical references and index.
   ISBN 978-0-205-71893-1
   1. Communication in the families—United States. 2. Interpersonal communication—United States. I. Bylund, Carma Lee. II. Brommel,
   Bernard J., 1930- III. Title.
   HQ734.G19   2012
   306.87—dc22   2010047072

1 2 3 4 5 6 7 8 9 10   CRS   14 13 12 11

Allyn & Bacon
is an imprint of

PEARSON

www.pearsonhighered.com

ISBN-13: 978-0-205-71893-1
ISBN-10:   0-205-71893-0

To my family: the Galvins, Wilkinsons, Nicholsens, and Sullivans, plus the special friends I consider as my family. *KMG*

To the many people I am privileged to call family, especially Greg, Thurman, and Nicholas. *CLB*

To my 6 children, 16 grandchildren, and friends that are also family. Thanks to my clients who have provided many valuable insights. *BJB*

CONTENTS

PREFACE

It is with a deep sense of gratitude that we introduce the eighth edition of *Family Communication: Cohesion and Change*. The first edition, published almost 30 years ago, served as the first textbook to examine the family from a communication perspective. At that time few classes even addressed the subject, and only a small number of communication scholars researched the issues. Today, most colleges and universities offer one or more courses on the subject at the undergraduate and graduate levels; increasing numbers of family communication scholars conduct research programs in this area. Over these years we have moved from an era in which marital communication dominated the research agenda, to an explosion of research programs representing every area of family life. The authorship team has also changed over time. Bernard J. Brommel served as a co-author on the first five editions; Carma L. Bylund has acted in that role for the last three editions.

Historically, family interactions received scholarly attention from family therapists, who addressed family problems, and sociologists, who studied family issues at the macro level. Today, communication scholars address family interactions within a wide range of functional family structures, life stages, and cultures using theories developed within the social sciences as well as by family communication scholars. Family communication scholars conduct research using multiple quantitative and qualitative methods that have grown increasingly sophisticated with each passing decade. As greater numbers of communication scholars focus on family interaction, their findings have provided increased depth and insight to each edition of the book.

Our basic premise remains the same—communication processes create and reflect family identity. Relying on a range of theoretical perspectives, we consider the communication processes within the family and how these patterns affect, and are affected by, members' actions as well as by changes in the larger social systems. Our focus remains descriptive rather than prescriptive because we believe there is no one right way to be a family. We continue to build upon a framework of primary family functions—regulating cohesion and flexibility, and secondary family functions—developing appropriate family images, themes, boundaries, and biosocial beliefs. Throughout the book we present highly adapted, de-identified versions of first-person examples provided by our students, clients, friends, and family members in order to ground the theory and research in real-life experiences.

NEW TO THIS EDITION

We have made some significant changes in this edition based on feedback from instructors using this book and from the thoughtful reviewer feedback that prompted these changes. We have removed the previous Chapter 11 (Contextual

Dimensions of Family Communication) because feedback indicated many instructors did not assign the chapter.

The following chapters were thoroughly revised to keep pace with changes in the discipline and with what instructors are covering in their courses, including:

- Chapter 1: Developed a new "Current Status of Families" section
- Chapter 3: Added Communication Privacy Management Theory
- Chapter 4: Reconfigured it to address family identity
- Chapter 5: Reconfigured it to address relational maintenance
- Chapter 6: Developed a new chapter solely on partner and family intimacy
- Chapter 12: Developed a new section on Difficult Conversations about genetics, money, and digital media

FEATURES

As in earlier editions, the first three chapters establish the theoretical foundations of the text. Chapter 1 presents an introduction to communication and family concepts as well as an overview of the current state of the family in the United States. Chapter 2 details our framework for analyzing family communication, a framework that threads through the remaining chapters. It also includes a discussion of family-of-origin patterns because they are related directly to the framework patterns. Chapter 3 examines a number of key theories focusing specifically on systems theory, which undergirds the text, as well as relational dialectical theory, narrative theory, social construction, and symbolic interaction. This edition includes communication privacy management theory for the first time. Chapter 4 addresses the communicative construction of family identity through family patterns and meanings, including discussion of communication, rules, secrets, networks, and narratives. Chapter 5 explores partner and family relational maintenance, including confirmation, rituals, and relational currencies. Chapter 6 focuses on commitment, self-disclosure, sexuality, forgiveness, and barriers to intimacy. Chapter 7 includes a discussion of the nature of family roles and family typologies. Chapter 8 focuses on power and decision making, while Chapter 9 presents models of conflict as well as a treatment of conflict patterns, both destructive and constructive. Chapters 10 and 11 focus on both predictable and unpredictable family stresses. Predictable stress includes communicatively managing family developmental stages and the transitions between these stages; unpredictable stress refers to the unforeseen, and usually negative, stresses including death, illness, and divorce as well as supportiveness. Finally, Chapter 12 examines family well-being in terms of physical and psychological issues. The first section examines communication about family health, followed by a discussion of the capacity to hold difficult dialogues, and, finally, psychological well-being and approaches to improving family communication.

ACKNOWLEDGMENTS

We are grateful to the Allyn and Bacon editors and editorial staff, specifically Jeanne Zalesky, Toni Magyar, Raegan Heerema, and, as always, Karon Bowers. We are thankful for the suggestions we received from our insightful reviewers,

Marcia S. Dixson, Indiana University–Purdue University Fort Wayne; Jane P. Elvins, University of Colorado–Boulder; Maureen Keeley, Texas State University; and Esther Rumsey, Sul Ross State University, and for the contributions of those who reviewed earlier editions. Lauren Grill, University of Illinois, provided another fine edition of the online Instructor's Manual for which we are most appreciative. In addition, we relied heavily on the amazing support of Rebecca Otto and Kathryn Johnstone, Northwestern University students. Finally, we remain thankful for all our students, colleagues, and friends who continue to expand our horizons on the fascinating subject of family communication.

Our own family lives have changed significantly over the past three decades, a reality that continually teaches us the importance of communication patterns, relationship maintenance and intimacy, developmental changes, and unpredictable stresses. To our growing number of family members, related to us by biological, legal, and linguistic ties, we express our continued gratitude for their patience, support, and unwitting contributions to our writing and teaching. From them and through our own research we continue to learn about family interaction patterns in multiple contexts. As time passes we increasingly appreciate what it means to be a member of a family system.

It is our hope that you will be captured by the importance and complexity of the field of family communication and that you will find the study of family interactions to be a thought-provoking and meaningful experience.

KATHLEEN M. GALVIN
CARMA L. BYLUND

Family Communication

Cohesion and Change

Introduction to the Family

"Families are made up of bonded relationships. The bonds
may be as binding as blood or as warming as a loving hug.
What makes a family 'family' is the sense of 'home' felt and
shared among individuals."

—Charles Wilkinson

Angela and her sister Gwen were born to Staci and Mike soon after he returned from combat in
Vietnam. Mike was ten years older than Staci and uncertain about fatherhood. She persuaded
him that children would bring joy and meaning to their lives and he reluctantly agreed to her
dreams of having children. Soon after the marriage, Angela was born, followed quickly by Gwen.
At this time Mike was struggling with uncertainty about his career path and confronting periods
of severe depression. Within five years he asked Staci for a divorce, citing her complete devotion
to the girls and distance from him, as well as his need for independence. After two years Staci
started to date Adam, a colleague at work who had never married. Six months later Staci and
the girls moved in with Adam; Mike seldom contacted the girls, who became attached to Adam
and his extended family. Staci and Adam worked long hours while Adam's mother cared for the
girls when they were not in school. Staci's career flourished and she moved quickly up the corporate ladder. After two years Adam proposed, indicating how much he loved Staci and the girls
and how he happily anticipated adding more children to their lives. He was devastated to hear
that Staci had no interest in having more children and, although they tried to continue their
living arrangement, Adam's pressured pleas for a new family led Staci to announce that she
and the girls were leaving. The girls were distraught at losing Adam and, although he tried
to maintain contact, Staci discouraged the connection. After six years of career success and
struggles as a single parent, Staci married Angelo, a widower with two grown sons whom she
met online. Although he treated the girls well, it was clear he could not wait until they would
leave home so he and their mother could begin a life involving just the two of them.

Last week Lacy's boss announced a company-wide cutback in hours and selected benefits
due to poor sales figures in the faltering economy. Lacy felt like she had been punched in the

stomach. As a 27-year-old wife, the mother of an autistic son (Sean), and an economic support for her mother who suffered from multiple sclerosis, any drop in income would create major family challenges. Her husband Will's position at a local factory paid less than her income; both incomes were necessary to keep the family afloat. On top of the income loss, the company dropped the tuition benefit that Lacy had used to take classes in respiration therapy at the local community college. She had four more classes to complete before finishing the program and starting on a career track. Eventually Lacy hoped to get her RN and work in pediatrics. Graduation would represent a major life milestone; she had been struggling to complete the program for five years as she attempted to balance Sean's needs and therapy, her work, and school, with little support. A teenage pregnancy had derailed her successful high school career, although she received her GED and took college classes whenever possible. Although Lacy could not bear to tell her mother the news, she decided to talk with her godmother, Belle, a preschool teacher who had been married to her Uncle Jack. Although Jack died in a car accident more than a decade ago, Belle remained strongly connected to Lacy, serving as a loving aunt and sounding board for her as she grew up. Whenever things piled up, Lacy knew she could count on Belle to talk her through the problem and to give her pragmatic advice. After two hours of talking and five cups of coffee, Lacy left with some ideas about government-supported tuition programs and the promise of loans to finish her course work.

We are born into a family, mature in a family, form new families, and leave our families upon death. Family life is a universal human experience. Yet, no two people share the exact same experience, partly because of the unique communication patterns in each family system. Because the family is such a powerful influence on our lives, we need to examine family relationships to understand ourselves better as members of one of the most complex and important societal groups. Family communication patterns serve to construct as well as reflect familial experience. We create our families just as we are created by these families.

As you read this text, you will examine a subject in which you have some expertise, because you have spent your life in some type or types of family arrangements. Yet, because you have lived in only one or a small number of family structures, your experience is limited compared to the range of potential family experiences. Your reading should expand your understanding of many families' communication patterns and life experiences, such as the families you encounter in the opening of each chapter.

You will encounter a framework for examining communication within families. Eventually, you should be able to apply this framework to an unknown family and analyze it as a communication system. We also hope that you will apply what you learn about communication dynamics to your own family or others' family experiences.

Throughout this book, you will find some material written in the first person and set off from the text. These selections, reconstructions of examples provided by friends, students, and clients, illustrate many of the concepts discussed in the text. They should enable you to understand the concepts more completely. Some comments will remind you specifically of your own family experiences, whereas others will seem quite different from your background. Yet, as the following portrays, there are different ways to live a functional family life.

I guess you could say I've had three "moms" and two-and-a-half "dads." My parents divorced when my twin brother and I were about three years old. My dad remarried and, after two more sons, got divorced again. Then he remarried and now I have a baby sister young enough to be my daughter. My mom remarried and got divorced again when we were about seven. The "half-father" that we had was a man who lived with us for 10 years who recently moved out at my mother's request. The reason my brother and I are still sane is because our mom and dad have always remained friends. We were never treated like pawns in the middle of a battle.

As family members, teachers, and family researchers, we hold certain basic beliefs that undergird our writings. Our backgrounds have given us particular perspectives that affect how we view families and their communication patterns. Our perspectives may be very similar to or quite different from yours. Because our backgrounds influence our thinking and writing, we wish to share these beliefs with you in order to establish a context for understanding.

1. There are many ways to be a family. Family life is as diverse as the types of persons who create families. There are many types of family structures and numerous ways to relate within each family type. Families are human systems created by ordinary people; the "perfect" family does not exist. Each family must struggle to create its own identity as it experiences good times and stressful times over many years. All families are influenced by the larger context in which they exist.

2. Communication serves to *construct* as well as *reflect* family relationships. It is through talk that persons define their identities and negotiate their relationships with other family members and with the rest of the world. Talk also serves to indicate the state of family relationships to family members and, sometimes, to others.

3. Communication serves as the process by which family members create and share their meanings with each other. Members develop a relational culture, or a shared worldview, that contributes to the creation of a relatively unique communication system.

4. Families involve multigenerational communication patterns. Members are influenced by the patterns of previous generations as they create their own patterns which, in turn, will influence future generations. The family serves as each person's first communication classroom, teaching members about managing relational closeness and distance in relationships, as well as change.

5. Families provide members with ways to make sense out of the world. Families socialize members to their underlying values and beliefs about significant life issues, such as gender, health, and religion, to name a few.

6. Families reflect cultural communication patterns. Racial and ethnic backgrounds influence lifestyle and behavior, as well as norms for communication that affect future generations unless they are consciously altered.

7. In well-functioning families members work at understanding and managing their communication patterns, recognizing that developing and maintaining relationships takes effort. Members develop the capacity to adapt, create connections, and manage conflict. Members are self-aware; they value the goal of effective communication.

This text avoids presenting prescriptive solutions for family problems; rather, it introduces you to the diverse world of families and their complex communication patterns. We believe the ideas and examples presented will help you develop your observational and analytical skills. We hope your increased understanding of family communication will result in an increased appreciation for complexities and variations inherent in today's diverse family forms. We also hope you will find the study of family communication as fascinating and challenging as we do.

As an introduction to the family, this chapter will discuss definitional issues and family status. The next section establishes an understanding of the concept of the family that will be used throughout the rest of the book. We invite you to read these pages with your heart as well as your head.

FAMILIES: DEFINITIONAL ISSUES

What does the word *family* mean to you? Reaching agreement on the meaning of the word *family* presents a greater challenge than you might suspect. In the following section, you will encounter the variations implied in the simple term *family*.

Family Types

Essentially, no widely agreed-upon definition of the term *family* exists. Families have been described according to blood ties and legal ties, as networks of persons who live together over periods of time supporting each other, and as groups of people who have ties of marriage and kinship to one another. In their attempt to identify the essence of family, Fitzpatrick and Badzinski (1985) suggested that the only universal family type is a small, kinship-structured group whose primary function is the nurturing socialization of newborn children. This position describes a *family realm*, created through the birth process and the establishment of ties across generations (Beutler, Burr, Bahr, & Herrin, 1988), the core aspect being biological, emotional, social, and developmental processes inherent in procreation and the nurturing of dependent children. This definition includes both intergenerational issues and multiple family forms. Decades later, after asserting that the question of how best to define family conceptually remains inherently problematic, Floyd, Mikkelson, and Judd (2006) offered three frames or lenses for crafting family definitions—a role lens, a sociolegal lens, and a biogenetic lens. Looking through the role lens, "relationships are familial to the extent that relational partners feel and act like family" (p. 27), establishing social behavior and emotion as the defining characteristics. The sociolegal lens relies on the enactment of laws and regulations, defining family relationships as those formally sanctioned by law. The biogenetic lens depends on two criteria: the extent to which the relationship is directly reproductive, at least potentially, and whether or not the relational partners share genetic material (p. 33). The latter point reflects findings that humans have an evolved motivation to be conscious of their levels of genetic relatedness with others. These approaches represent the complexity of family definition that challenges everyone, from researchers to each individual family's members.

The American family does not exist. Family historian Tamara Harevan (1982) expressed her concern with this idealized family, claiming that U.S. society always has contained "great diversities in family types and family behavior that were associated with the recurring entrance of new immigrant groups into American society. Ethnic, racial, cultural class differences have also resulted in diversity in family behavior" (p. 461). Another family historian, Stephanie Coontz (1999), believes that most Americans move in and out of a variety of family experiences across their lifetimes. In other words, "Families change their size and shape throughout their histories . . . but throughout these changes we recognize them still as families, and as whole ones at that" (Stewart, Copeland, Chester, Malley, & Barenbaum, 1997, pp. 245–246). Today, individual educational levels significantly affect the different paths of family formation and dissolution (Cherlin, 2010).

provide example of each

Today, families define themselves, for themselves, through their interactions. At the same time, longevity, legal flexibility, personal choice, ethnicity, gender, geographic distance, and reproductive technology impact traditional biological and legal conceptions of family. Society has passed the point of seeing the traditional versus nontraditional family categories as functional, because nontraditional families are not alternative but rather are emerging as normative family forms

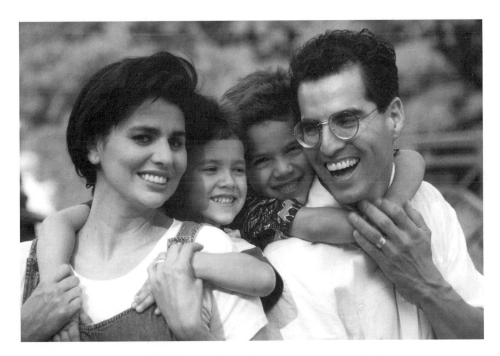

❙ Two-parent biological families are one of many forms.

(Le Poire, 2006). Fitzpatrick (1998) argued that society needs to "employ definitions of the family that depend on how families define themselves rather than definitions based on genetic and sociological criteria" (p. 45). From this perspective "families are constituted by the very communication processes one seeks to study as being 'within a family'" (Steier, 1989, p. 15). Many scholars are concerned with how family members define themselves as families—in other words, how they use communication to define their family for themselves. This *constitutive* approach to creating family challenges the conception of one dominant form of family life.

Today, a family may be viewed more broadly as a group of people with a past history, a present reality, and a future expectation of interconnected mutually influencing relationships. Members often, but not necessarily, are bound together by heredity, legal marital ties, adoption, or committed, voluntaristic ties. Wamboldt and Reiss (1989) developed a process definition of the family as "a group of intimates who generate a sense of home and group identity; complete with strong ties of loyalty and emotion, and experience history and future" (p. 728). In her essay on redefining families, Minow (1998) argued that it is not important whether a group fits a formal legal definition; instead what is important is "whether the group of people function as a family: do they share affection and resources, think of one another as family members, and present themselves as such to neighbors and others?" (p. 8). Clearly, these definitions emphasize the personal, voluntarily connected relationships among family members instead of relying solely on blood ties or legal agreements as the basis for a family.

Contemporary families depend, in part or in whole, on communication to define themselves and that although "discourse-dependency is not new; what is new is that the discourse-dependent families are becoming the norm" (Galvin, 2006a, p. 9). The more discourse-dependent a family is, the more members rely on communication strategies for external or internal boundary management. *External boundary management* involves utilizing communication strategies to reveal or conceal information about the family to outsiders. These strategies include labeling, explaining, legitimizing, and defending. In contrast, *internal boundary management* refers to the use of communication strategies to maintain members' internal sense of we-ness. These strategies include naming, discussing, narrating, and ritualizing. (Figure 1.1)

Figure 1.1

Discourse-Dependent Families: Constructing and Deconstructing Family Identity

External Boundary Management

When families appear different to outsiders, questions and challenges arise. Members reveal or conceal relevant family information.

Labeling

Titles and positions provide an orientation to a situation; labeling frequently involves identifying the familial tie when introducing or referring to another person.

• I want you to meet . . . My (options) stepfather, Bill, my mother's husband, my pops
• Maggie is . . . (options) My mother's friend, my mother's partner, my stepmother

Explaining

Explaining involves making a labeled family relationship understandable, giving reasons for it, or elaborating on how it works. Usually this is a response to non-hostile inquiry.

• My sister used a sperm donor and her eggs. I was the gestational carrier.

• We adopted him from Vietnam when he was eight months old.

Legitimizing

Legitimizing invokes the sanction of law or custom: it positions relationships as genuine and conforming to recognized standards.

• My mother and Don have been together for 14 years. He functions as my father.

• I adopted my husband's son after his former wife died. He calls me "Moms."

Defending

Defending involves shielding oneself or a familial relationship from attack, justifying it or maintaining its validity against opposition. This is a response to hostility or a direct challenge.

• My mother gets enraged when people ask if I'm her "real daughter."

• When someone tells me my mothers will go to hell, I tell them off.

Internal Boundary Management

Naming

Naming plays a significant role in the development of internal family identity as members struggle to indicate their familial status and connections.

• We call my birth mother Aunt Carrie or Carrie.

• My step-grandmother goes by "Nona Pat."

Discussing

Discussing reflects the degree of difference among family members that affects the amount of ambiguity in their family situation. This occurs when members see few role models for their family form.

• We talk about Karin's anonymous sperm donor and his musical talents.

• Jack asked us how he thought he should address his birth mother whom he located.

Narrating

Narrating involves the emergence of family stories; they represent the family's definition of itself. Members tell and retell, to themselves and to others, the story of who they are and how they got there.

• Let's get out the scrapbook with your adoption story.

• Tell Uncle Jack about the first time I introduced you to your stepmother.

Ritualizing

Ritualizing allows families to accomplish their "emotional business" as they enact their identity. Family rituals include major celebrations and mundane routines.

• Our family celebrates "Gotcha Days," or the days on which they adopted each of us.

• My father and stepfather agreed to walk me down the aisle together.

Adapted from: Galvin, K. M. (2006). Diversity's impact on the family: Discourse-dependence and identity. In L. H. Turner & R. West (Eds). *The Family Communication Sourcebook* (pp. 3–19). Thousand Oaks, CA: Sage.

As we talk about families, we will take a broad, inclusive view. Therefore, if the members consider themselves to be a family, and function as a family, we accept their self-definition. Generally, we will refer to families as *networks of people who share their lives over long periods of time bound by ties of marriage, blood, law, or commitment, legal or otherwise, who consider themselves as family and who share a significant history and anticipated future of functioning as a family.* Such a definition encompasses countless variations of familial forms and numerous types of interaction patterns.

In contemporary society, family diversity abounds. One indication of the complexities of today's families may be found in a review of current literature, which includes such categories as large, extended, blood-related groups; formal and informal communal groups; stepfamilies; single-parent families; and gay and lesbian partnerships. These families reflect multiple cultural and socioeconomic situations.

We, your authors, represent three very different family experiences. One grew up in New York City as an only child of Irish immigrants. After her parents died, she acquired an adoptive Norwegian-German family with three siblings. Currently she is married, a parent to three adult children, one of whom was adopted from Korea, and a grandmother of two. Another is the oldest of seven children and grew up in a university town in Missouri. After a short first marriage she is currently married and the mother of two energetic young boys. Finally a co-author on the first five editions grew up on an Iowa farm in a German-Irish family of nine children, married, fathered six children, divorced, and is now the grandfather of 16. Although blood relatives are important to each of us, we each have friends who are considered to be family members.

You may have grown up in a small family or a large four-generation household. Your brothers and sisters may be blood related, step, or adopted. Some of you may be single parents, stepparents, or foster parents. And some of you may have experienced one committed marriage or single lifestyle, whereas others may have experienced divorce and remarriage, or life in a committed partnership. No simple pattern exists.

My family consisted of a mother and brother only, but lacked a father. Due to this fact, my mother brought us together ideologically with a strong focus on being one as a group, but lacking strength when separated. Her comments strongly suggested this when, in time of crisis, she always said, "As long as we pull together and believe in one another, we'll be okay." Physical proximity also played a role in this togetherness through attending church together on Sundays, and trying to speak to our mother at least once a day. Due to the fact that she worked 13-hour days, she normally arrived home after we had fallen asleep.

This diverse family reality creates a challenge for texts such as this one. We wish to represent the multiple ways families are formed, yet much of the research still refers to discrete family categories. In the following pages we will note some of the traditional structures when talking about families because that reflects the research. However, we recognize that families represent overlapping structural forms. Our category system encompasses the following styles of family formation: the two-parent biological family, single-parent family, blended family, extended or intergenerational family, and committed partners or small groups. These are not discrete categories; many families encompass more than one. There is no longer a majority family form in the United States.

A *two-parent biological family* consists of parents and the children who are from the union of these parents. Thus, full blood ties characterize this family; the majority of parents are married but many are cohabiters.

A *single-parent family* consists of one parent and one or more children. This formation may include an unmarried man or woman and his or her offspring; a man or a woman who lost his or her partner through death, divorce, or desertion, and the children of that union; a single parent and his or her adopted or foster children or a child conceived with technological assistance. For some children, life in a single-parent system is temporary until the parent marries or remarries; however, many children will live with one parent until the age of 18.

Although the term *single parent* is commonly used, we will alternate that term with *primary parent* occasionally, recognizing Walsh's (1993) point that "single parent" describes one parent carrying out all parental obligations while ongoing involvement with the other parent is precluded. This occurs most frequently in cases of death and abandonment and single-parent adoption. When two parents take some, usually unequal, responsibility for children, the custodial parent is referred to as the primary parent. Both adults may be referred to as co-parents. The term *solo mother* refers to a mother rearing her children from birth without the support and assistance of the father (Gringlas & Weinraub, 1995).

The *blended family* consists of two adults and their children, all of whom are not from the union of their relationship. Most are families blended through remarriage or re-partnering, a situation that brings two previous systems into new family ties. You may have witnessed the common pattern in which a two-parent biological family becomes a single-parent family for a period of time, after which certain members become part of a stepfamily. Families may also be blended through the addition of adopted or foster children.

The stepfamily has been compared to a challenging and complex chess game, a delicate and intricate spiderweb, a second chance, and a time bomb. No matter what the analogy, the stepfamily is a complex, growing, and little-understood segment of American family life. Characteristics of stepfamilies include:

- Some or all members bring past family history from a relationship that has changed or ended. These members carry with them a sense of loss. They often hold unrealistic expectations for the stepfamilies.
- The couple does not begin as a dyad but, rather, the parent-child relationship predates the partnership bond.
- One or two biological parents (living or dead) influence the stepfamily.
- The family has a complex extended family network and children may function as members of two households.
- No legal relationship automatically exists between the stepparent and stepchild.

- Many of these family relationships began as "not-so-freely-chosen" or involuntary relationships, as children or stepparents may not choose each other. (Bray & Kelly, 1998; Braithwaite, Schrodt, & Baxter, 2006; Coleman, Ganong, & Fine, 2004; Pasley & Lee, 2010)

Although most stepfamilies are formed after the dissolution of a parent's first marriage, they also include single parents marrying or gay and lesbian stepfamilies.

Adoption creates another type of blended family—a family "that is *connected* to another family, the birth family, and often to different cultures and to different ethnic and national groups as well" (Bartholet, 1993, p. 186). This legally constructed family "does not signal the absolute end of one family and the beginning of another, nor does it sever the psychological tie to an earlier family" (Reitz & Watson, 1992, p. 11). We think of it as expanding family boundaries for everyone.

Constructing families through adoption is a centuries-old process, evolving from a responsibility managed within family bloodlines to practices of matching personal characteristics, such as ethnicity or religion, to an open style of connections crossing religious, racial, and international lines. In contrast to earlier practices, in recent decades an increasing number of adoptions are transnational, transracial, pertain to older children or children with disabilities, and involve single parents or gay male and lesbian parents (March & Miall, 2000). Many adoptions are "open," reflecting direct long-term connections between birth mothers and adoptive parents, creating new types of extended families with communication challenges (Galvin, 2006b).

Although an *extended* (or *intergenerational*) *family* traditionally refers to that group of relatives living within a nearby geographic area, it may be more narrowly understood as the presence of blood relatives, other than the parents, in the everyday life of a child. For example, this may take a cross-generational form, including grandparents who live with a parent-child system or who take on exclusive parenting roles for grandchildren. Given increasing longevity, more families will include four and five generations of relatives who may maintain active contact, as the following indicates.

I grew up in an extended family. My great-grandparents were the dominant figures. Most of us lived with our grandparents at one time or another. There were six different households in the neighborhood I grew up in. My great-grandmother, referred to as "Mother," babysat for all the kids while our parents were at work.

The intentional family involves a pair or a group of people, some or all of whom are unrelated biologically or legally, who share a commitment to each other, may live together, and consider themselves to be a family. These relationships are sometimes called *fictive* or *voluntaristic*. Formal examples of these family types are found in communal situations such as a kibbutz. Other extended families are informally formed around friendship or common interests or commitments. Two neighboring families may share so many experiences that, over time, both sets of children and parents begin to talk of each other as "part of the family." Families formed through many of these ties are highly discourse dependent; members rely heavily on the strategies described earlier in Figure 1.1.

Committed partners may include married couples who choose to remain child-free or are infertile, cohabiting heterosexual couples, and gay male and lesbian partners who consider themselves a family. Members of such partnerships continue to serve as children to the previous generation and as siblings and extended family members to other generations, while providing loyalty and affection to one another.

Most people experience family life in an evolutionary manner, moving through different family forms over time, experiencing changes due to aging and unpredictable stresses. In addition, most persons experience life with one or more biological, adopted, or stepsiblings, the longest-lasting family relationships due to age similarity. Sibling relationships are significant sources of information on communication patterns such as family stories, rituals, and memories, specifically in adulthood (Mikkelson, 2006).

I never consider Max a stepbrother—he is a brother to me. If I need him, he's there. If I ask him for advice, he listens without judgment. If I want to practice basketball or go for a run, he will drop whatever he's doing. Sure we have moments when we fight, but that's healthy. There is a mutual love and respect all the time. He's my brother.

It is important to distinguish between two types of family experiences: current families and families-of-origin. Families in combination beget families through the evolutionary cycles of coming together and separating. Each person experiences family life differently, starting with his or her family-of-origin. *Family-of-origin* refers to the family or families in which a person is raised. Pioneering family therapist Virginia Satir (1988) stresses the importance of the family-of-origin as the *blueprint for people making,* stating, "Blueprints vary from family to family. I believe some blueprints result in nurturing families, some result in troubled ones" (p. 210). Multigenerational patterns, those of more than two generations, are considered as part of the blueprint (Hoopes, 1987). As you will discover, family-of-origin and multigenerational experiences are crucial in the development of communication patterns in current families.

FAMILIES: CURRENT STATUS

Demographic Trends

The composition and shape of the contemporary family is constantly changing. In order to understand family interaction fully, it is necessary to examine the current status of family life in the United States. No matter how old you are, you have lived long enough to witness major changes in your family or in the families around you—changes that reflect an evolving national picture. American families continue to reflect greater racial and ethnic diversity with each passing decade, and many families face increasing economic stress or poverty. Although there are numerous similarities in family communication patterns across large groups, differences in family forms, composition, and culture affect members' interactions. As you read about the current trends, try to imagine their implications for family communication. A key baseline is the average number of people per household— 2.56 in 2008 (U.S. Census Bureau, 2010). Although research figures shift constantly and various sources provide slightly different numerical data, the overall point is clear: As you read the following trends, imagine how they might affect the ways in which family members communicate with each other.

The American family continues to undergo dramatic changes in the twenty-first century, as indicated by the following trends.

- *The majority of Americans will marry at least once.* Married couples with a spouse present account for 50.7 percent of the population's lifestyle. Americans today are less likely to marry than in previous decades (Wilcox, 2009). The number of legal marriage commitments has declined almost 50 percent from 1970 to 2007 and most people live together before they marry for the first time (Wilcox, 2009). Current trends indicate that first marriages are taking place later in life. Men marry at slightly older ages. For example, the median age for women at first marriage was 24 in 1994, 25 in 1997, and 25.6 in 2008. For men, it was 26.5 in 1992, 26.7 in 1997, and 27.4 in 2008. The average length of a first marriage ending in divorce is 8 years; approximately 15 percent of marriages involve one partner remarrying while the other is marrying for the first time (Kreider, 2005). Due to rising life expectancies American marriages are more likely to reach a fortieth wedding anniversary than ever before.
- *The divorce rate is stabilizing.* The divorce rate continues to drop: in 2007 it was 5.7 per 1,000 in the population (U.S. Bureau of Labor, 2010). These divorce rate figures vary by race and age. They also reflect the longevity of people in today's society. In earlier times, when more people died at a younger age, many unsatisfactory marriages were ended by death rather than divorce.
- *Remarriage rates, although high, are dropping* The majority of divorced individuals form new partnerships either through remarriage or through cohabitation. About five out of six men and three out of four women eventually remarry after a first divorce. The mean length of time between divorce and remarriage is four years; 30 percent remarry within a year (Kreider, 2005). Multiple remarriages are becoming more common. Approximately 50 percent of former partners marry in three to four years (Kreider, 2005). The divorce rate has hovered around 60 percent for second marriages, although remarriages of persons over age 40 tend to be more stable than first marriages. Twelve percent of men and 13 percent of women had married twice, while 3 percent of each had married three or more times (U.S. Census Bureau, 2007).
- *Age and parenting responsibility affect remarriage.* Childless divorced women less than 30 years old are most likely to remarry, followed by divorced women under age 30 with children. Older women are the least

likely to remarry. The incidence of re-divorce continues to rise as individuals remarry more often. For older divorced men and women, the rates of cohabitation are increasing.

- *Stepfamilies continue to increase through remarriage and cohabitation.* The stepfamily remains a vital family form, although exact figures are difficult to use because of variations in custodial arrangements. Thirteen hundred stepfamilies are forming every day according to Stepfamily Solutions (2010). In 2000, there were 4.4 million stepchildren in the United States (Kreider, 2003). Most children in remarried households live with their biological mother and stepfather. Many stepfamilies, approximately 25 percent, are formed by cohabiting couples, since cohabiting couples are more likely to enter a new union involving children than are remarrying couples (Coleman, Ganong, & Fine, 2000).

- *The number of single-parent families continues to increase.* Americans are witnessing the continuing rise of single-parent or primary parents systems. Single parents maintained 25 percent of U.S. households with children under 18. This does not include parents living with a partner but not married (U.S. Census Bureau, 2009a). Forty-three percent of all women who never married are mothers (Mother's Day, 2002). Yet, today the number of births to unmarried teenagers has declined slightly and some single parents marry after bearing children. Although rates of births to single mothers are increasing across the population, it is also clear that some of these children are living with a cohabiting mother, creating two-adult households (Primus, 2002).

  These figures vary by ethnicity. For example, only 34.5 percent of black children live in married households (Wilcox, 2009). In 2000, 77 percent of white non-Hispanic children lived with two parents, compared to 38 percent of African American children and 65 percent of children of Hispanic origin.

  > *ethnicity*

- *Fewer families have children under 18.* As the large baby boomer population ages and fertility rates decline, the percentage of families with their own child living at home decreased to 46 percent in 2008 (Edwards, 2009).

- *Families continue to be constructed through adoption.* In 2007, 2 percent of children, or 1.8 million, under 18 were adopted; approximately one-quarter of adoptions involve relatives (Vandivere & Malm, 2009). Adoption may include "related" and "nonrelated" children. The past decades have witnessed a significant increase in transnational and transracial adoption. Currently, the most common form of adoption is *open adoption*, involving some level of interaction among biological parent(s), adoptive parent(s), and the adoptee.

- *Some families are constructed or expanded through scientific technologies.* Although the numbers are small, some individuals and couples are achieving parenthood through anonymous or known donor insemination due to lifestyle choice or infertility. Two percent of women of reproductive age seek help for infertility each year. Infertility affects 7.3 million women and their partners each year—about 12 percent of the reproductive-age population (CDC, 2009). Although success rates remain low for infertile individuals, multiple attempts and scientific advances are making this possibility more viable although the overall impact is limited (Smock & Greenland, 2010). Often this process remains shrouded in secrecy (McWhinnie, 2001).

■ *More adult children are living at home.* Adult children are remaining at home until an older age and children are more likely to return after departures from the parental home. About 40 percent of 2008 college graduates still live with their parents and are often referred to as *boomerang kids* (Vogt, 2009). Although reasons vary, common explanations for this change include growing economic pressures, cultural norms, and returning young divorced mothers with small children.

■ *The number of cohabiting partners is growing rapidly.* In 2003, there were 4.6 million households classified as "unmarried partners," where two members of the opposite sex were living together (Fields, 2004). This represents another increase in the growing trend of cohabitation. For never-married young adults it is frequently a stage before marriage, but for others it is an end in itself. Cohabitation is frequently perceived as less of an investment in the relationship due to the lack of a formal ceremony and legal complications (DeMaris, 2001). Yet, cohabiters today are more likely to bear children than in previous times—a reality that involves commitment and legal ties. In 2009, over 6.5 million unmarried couples were together. Two-and-a-half million had a biological child of either partner (U.S. Census Report, 2009a).

■ *Families of lesbians and gay males are increasing.* Gay and lesbian committed couples are becoming more visible due, in part, to a greater willingness of same-sex partners to identify their lifestyle. Census data do not include gay and lesbian partners, although the 2000 data on unmarried partner households indicated that over half a million households were headed by same-sex partners, representing 1 percent of all coupled households (Simmons & O'Connell, 2003). According to the 2000 census, 33 percent of women in same-sex partnerships lived with children, as did 22 percent of men in same-sex partnerships. The 2008 American Community Survey, the first time the Census Bureau released official estimates for same-sex spouses, reported an estimated 150,000 same-sex couples reported one partner as a husband or wife and an estimated 415,000 self-identified as unmarried partners. These numbers are predicted to increase in the next decade.

Twenty-eight percent of lesbians, gays, and bisexuals report living with a partner as if they were married. Eight percent of lesbians, gays, and bisexuals are parents or legal guardians of a child who lives in their home; half of those who do not have a child under 18 would like to adopt a child someday (Kaiser Family Foundation, 2001). In 2009, 53 percent of Americans opposed allowing gays and lesbians to marry legally whereas 39 percent supported same-sex marriage (Pew Research Center, 2009a).

■ *Extended families continue to flourish.* U.S. households are increasingly multigenerational. In 2008, 16 percent of the population lived in a family household that contained at least two adult generations (Pew Research Center, 2010). Many other families are surrounded by relatives in nearby neighborhoods or communities. As American families become more culturally diverse through immigration, the extended family has reemerged in importance (Bush, Bohon, & Kim, 2010). The African American tradition of extended kinship, as well as the values of recent Asian immigrants, reinforces the central importance of biological or fictive kin (Lee & Mock, 2005; Hine & Boyd-Franklin, 2005).

Grandparents play a significant role in the family households of many children even when a parent is present. Ten percent of children who lived with a single mother were grandchildren of the householder, compared with 8 percent of children who lived with single fathers. When children lived in households without either of their parents, very often close to half lived in their grandparent's household.

■ *Families increasingly represent four and five generations.* Individuals continue to live longer. According to the CDC, U.S. life expectancy in 2007 was 77.9 years. Gender differences do exist, however. U.S. males have a life expectancy of 75.3 years, whereas women have an expectancy of 80.4 years (CDC, 2010).

This longevity results in four- and five-generation households. Increasing numbers of children are living in grandparent-headed households with or without a parent. In addition, more middle-aged persons are taking on care-giver roles for elderly parents and grandparents. Considering that most people marry for the first time before age 30, a continuous marriage might well be expected to last 45 to 50-plus years. The number of married couples without children at home continues to rise as people live longer and as women bear a smaller number of children in the early years of marriage. On a somber note, widowhood has become an expected life event for older married women, since more than two-thirds of persons who die at age 85 or older are females. Connections to siblings are becoming a central family concern for older persons.

These family descriptors do not fully capture the intentional family commitments made by individuals or groups that are not recorded in census or related data. You can imagine how family interactions might differ given these trends. Some family forms tend to encourage secrets or avoidance of family composition; others tend to require consistent renegotiation of members' roles. Some families encourage members to talk about their lives with outsiders, whereas others discourage such openness. Many current families engage in role negotiation regularly.

Economic Issues

All these demographic changes are intertwined with economic and cultural realities. Working mothers are commonplace. Many couples view a dual income as a necessity or highly desirable. Currently, almost half of parents who live with their children feel they spend too little time, and desire to spend more time, with their children (EHRC, 2009); more fathers report their greater commitment to family than in previous decades (Duckworth & Buzzanell, 2009). In many cases, dual-earner couples with children are working shift schedules for economic or personal reasons. Such arrangements tend to strengthen parent-child bonds but limit couple contact significantly. Due to these changes, family members experience great pressures.

Some preteens and teenagers are expected to contribute to the successful running of the household. Young children may spend many of their waking hours with babysitters or in day-care centers, encountering their parents only a few hours a day. Counselors report concerns that the pressures of work, long hours, and downsizing have created enormous stressors for families (Bonebright, Clay, & Ankenmann, 2000). Research on negative spillover between work and family concludes that negative stress from work-family overlap begins in young adulthood and continues through midlife (Grzywacz, Almeida, and McDonald , 2002).

Another economic reality with a direct impact on family life is poverty. In 2008, 19 percent of children (0–17) lived in poverty and 41 percent lived in low-income families (Wight, Chau, & Aratani, 2010). Children have replaced seniors as the poorest segment of the population. One-third of the homeless are families with children—a figure that is rising rapidly. It should be noted that 1 in 50 children, or over 1.5 million children, experiences homelessness each year. Although a large number of poor families contain two parents, about one quarter of single-parent families have incomes below the poverty level (Grall, 2009). Economic pressures add significant stress to the lives of poor family members, and this stress affects the ways family members relate to each other. Other factors cause economic stress in families. For example, families with members with a disability have lower median incomes than other families; when heads of households are disabled, they are more likely to be out of work than nondisabled counterparts (Wang, 2005). In good economic times, there are positive effects of male and female earnings and employment on marital quality, stability, and children's lives in general (White & Rogers,

The stresses of poverty increase family tensions.

2002). The recent economic downturns have affected family members of all ages and varying economic levels. A 2009 Pew Research study found that among 22- to 29-year-olds, 1 in 8 reported returning to live with their parents because of the recession (Pew Research Center, 2009b).

Racial/Ethnic Issues

No examination of family status is complete without a discussion of the effect of ethnicity on family functioning. Within the past decades, several forces have combined to bring ethnic issues to the attention of family scholars. First, the overall ethnic composition of U.S. families is changing as the number of African American, Hispanic American, and Asian American families increases. Second, scholars are recognizing the long-term effect of ethnic heritage on family functioning. Finally, there is an unequal impact of poverty across racial and ethnic groups.

American society represents a rapidly changing and diverse set of ethnic and cultural groups. In 2000, the U.S. Census reported that the population was 75.1 percent white, 12.3 percent black or African American, 3.6 percent Asian, 0.9 percent American Indian and Alaskan Native, and 0.1 percent Native Hawaiian and Other Pacific Islander, with 5.5 percent listed as some other race and 2.4 percent as two or more races. It then categorized the entire U.S. population as Hispanic or Latino (12.5 percent) and non-Hispanic or Latino (87.5 percent). The Hispanic figure reached 15.4 percent in 2008 (American Community Survey, 2008). Hispanics now make up 22 percent of all children under 18. This figure is projected to reach 30 percent by 2025 (Fry & Passel, 2009).

There is considerable difference in family structure by race and ethnicity. Asians report one of the highest percentages of currently married individuals and the lowest proportion of separated or divorced individuals. Black men and women reported the lowest percentage of currently married, although there were distinct gender differences—42 percent of black men were married, while 31 percent of black women were married. American Indians and Alaska natives reported the highest divorce rate, whereas, among women, blacks and Hispanics had the highest separation rates (Kreider & Simmons, 2003). Families with children vary greatly by ethnicity. Entering the second decade of the twenty-first century, Hispanics represent the largest minority group at 15 percent of the population. African Americans are the second largest group followed by Asians. Small percentages of American Indians and Alaska Natives and Native Hawaiians and Other Pacific Islanders round out the population (U.S. Census Bureau, 2009b). Whereas 35 percent of black children under two years old and 42 percent of black adolescents lived with a solo parent, findings for Asian children indicate 1 percent for toddlers and 9 percent for teenagers. These figures were six percent for white children, 17 percent for white teenagers, 10 percent for Hispanic children, and 22 percent for Hispanic teenagers, respectively (Kreider & Elliott, 2009). "The proportion of married couples with children under 18 ranged from 35 percent for residents born in Europe to 73.4 percent for those from Latin America" (Scott, 2002, p. A18). In 2000, 28.4 million foreign born, or 10.4 percent of the population, resided in the United States. One-half were born in Latin America, while one-third were born in Asia (Lollock, 2000). Traditionally, these families report strong grandparent and extended family ties.

Increasingly, single men and women or gay and lesbian partners are having or adopting children.

As a result of current Hispanic and Asian immigration patterns, many family members have difficulty speaking English or do not speak English at home. The number of people, ages five and older, who speak a language other than English at home has more than doubled in the past three decades although the majority of these individuals report speaking English "very well" (Shin & Kominski, 2010). Approximately 17 percent of school-aged children do not speak English at home. The majority of these children are of Hispanic or Asian origin.

In general, classification systems are becoming less useful as people marry and adopt across cultures. In the future, categorization of family race and ethnicity will have to change as intermarriage, adoption, and cohabitation increase the population of mixed-ethnicity families. In 2000, interracial couples accounted for 1.9 percent of married couples and 4.3 percent of unmarried couples (Simmons & O'Neill, 2001). Between 2003 and 2006, 24 percent of couples cohabiting were mixed-race couples (Morgan, 2009). The number of African American and white interracial married couples has almost doubled in the past two decades. Over 4 percent of U.S. children are of mixed race, and that figure is rapidly rising; over 22 percent of Americans report having a relative in a mixed-race marriage (Pew Research Center, 2006).

Although generalizations about cultural groups must always be accompanied by an indication of their many exceptions, a consideration of family ethnicity provides a critical perspective from which to examine communication patterns. This perspective will receive increased attention because, by the middle of the twenty-first century, Americans of European ancestry will be in the minority. This shift will influence underlying assumptions about what it means to be a family.

It is important to consider ethnicity in families because, contrary to popular myth, Americans have not become homogenized in a "melting pot"; instead, various cultural and ethnic heritages are maintained across generations. There is increasing evidence that ethnic values and identification are retained for many generations after immigration and play a significant role in family life and personal development throughout the life cycle, as second-, third-, and even fourth-generation Americans reflect their original cultural heritage in lifestyle and behavior (McGoldrick, Giordano, & Garcia-Preto, 2005) as indicated by the following comment.

My parents' marriage reflected an uneasy blend of Italian and Norwegian cultures. My mother included her Italian relatives in on many issues my father considered private. He was overwhelmed by her family's style of arguing and making up and would retreat to the porch during big celebrations. I came to realize that cultural tension was reflected in many of their differences, including their child-rearing patterns. I carry pieces of those conflicting patterns within me today.

Ethnicity may affect family life through its traditions, celebrations, occupations, values, and problem-solving strategies. There are strong variations across cultures and familial issues, such as age at first marriage, single parenthood, older marriages, changing marital partners, and male-female roles (McGoldrick, Giordano, & Garcia-Preto, 2005). The definition of the concept *family* may differ across ethnic groups. For example, whereas the majority "white Anglo-Saxon" definition focuses on the intact nuclear unit, African American families focus on a wide kinship network, and Italians function within a large, intergenerational, tightly knit family that includes godparents and old friends. Chinese family members are likely to include all ancestors and descendants in the concept of family. Each of these views has an impact on communication within the family.

Families are more likely to be poor if they are of African American, Hispanic, or Native American background. In 2004, black households had the lowest median income, followed by Hispanic households. Asian households had the highest median income (U.S. Census Bureau, 2005). Pressures that plague higher percentages of certain ethnic groups, such as unemployment, low wages, and poverty discourage or erode marriage, further confounding economic well-being (Simms, Fortuny, & Henderson, 2009).

Changes in family forms accompanied by economic and cultural variations have implications for the ways family members communicate with each other. For example, the rise of two-career families alters the amount of time parents and children are in direct contact. Economic stress frequently results in escalating family stress. The high divorce rate increases the chances that family members of all ages will undergo major stressful transitions, including changes in their communication patterns. The growth in single-parent systems and dual-career couples increases a child's interpersonal contact with a network of extended family or professional caregivers. Most children in stepfamilies function within two different family systems, each with its own communication patterns. As U.S. families reflect greater ethnic diversity, family life will be characterized by a wider range of communication patterns.

FUNCTIONAL FAMILIES

It is important to forecast the families we will discuss in the upcoming chapters. Historically, most literature on family interaction has focused on struggling or pathological families (Fincham & Beach, 2010). Early studies examined families with one or more severely troubled member—a trend that was followed by attempts to characterize "normal" families. As you may imagine from the previous description of the definitions and the status of families, there is little agreement on what is "normal." Currently many studies focus on the characteristics of well-functioning families.

The following four perspectives on so-called normal families represent the evolution of family studies on family functioning (Walsh, 1993, pp. 5–7):

1. *Normal Families as Asymptomatic Family Functioning.* This approach implies there are no major symptoms of psychopathology among family members.
2. *Normal Families as Average.* This approach identifies families that appear typical or seem to fit common patterns.
3. *Normal Families as Optimal.* This approach stresses positive or ideal characteristics often based on members' accomplishments.
4. *Normal Family Processes.* This approach stresses a systems perspective focusing on functional adaptation over the life cycle and as well as functional adaptation to stresses and diversity contexts.

The first three perspectives quickly prove unworkable because of the static nature of each explanation. The fourth perspective provides a sense of variation and adaptation that captures the dynamic nature of family experiences.

Recent studies of well-functioning families highlight the tremendous diversity of families that appear to be functional, even as they struggle with predictable and unpredictable changes (Fincham & Beach, 2010; Price, Price, & McKenry, 2010). A recent call for a focus on "*relationship flourishing*" reflects the current focus on well-functioning families that exhibit relationship strengths and how they harness such strengths in face of life stresses (Fincham & Beach, 2010). Characteristics of such families include intimacy, growth, and resilience as well as a balance between focusing on familial relationships and engaging the larger community.

In this text, we will focus on communication within functional families, because this constitutes the primary experience for most individuals, most of the time. We hold two basic assumptions about families: (1) there is no one right way to be a family and (2) there is no one right way to communicate within a family. The following pages will reflect a wide variety of family lifestyles and communication behaviors. Our goal is to increase your understanding of the dynamics of family communication, not to suggest specific solutions to family problems. Hence, we will focus on a descriptive, rather than a prescriptive, approach.

We hope you experience some personal, rather than just academic, gain from reading these pages. Most of you come from families that have experienced their share of pain and problems as well as joys and satisfactions. We hope that you will gain a new insight into the people with whom you share your lives as well as others who live in your communities. As you read these pages, think about your own family and other real or fictional families with which you are familiar. We also hope you choose to apply what you learn to your own family or families, although it may be difficult at times. The words of one previous reader describe this process better than we can:

> Analyzing my own family has not been an easy process. As I began, my entire soul cried out, "How do I begin to unravel the web of rules, roles, and strategies that make up our family system?" I do not claim to have all possible answers; certainly my opinions and attitudes are different from those of the others in my family. I also do not claim to have the answers to all our problems. But I have tried to provide answers to my own confusion and to provide some synthesis to the change and crises that I have experienced. And I have grown from the process.

CONCLUSION

This chapter provides an overview of what it means to be a family and illustrates the enormous diversity of family life. We shared some basic beliefs about families and communication, and provided an examination of family definitions. We also examined the current status of the American family in an overview of issues such as trends in marriage and partnering, divorce, and remarriage and the formation of families though birth, adoption, and stepfamily relations, as well as ongoing single-parent families. Additionally, issues such as economic pressures and cultural diversity were raised. The chapter concluded with a discussion of issues related to "normal" family functioning. Each of these issues will thread through the following chapters.

In Review

1. At this point in your life, what is your definition of a family? How does a good friend define family?

2. What is your reaction to the family categories described in the chapter? Describe how you might alter these categories, giving reasons for your choices.
3. What recent national or international events created stress for your family or a family you know? How were member communications affected?
4. Identify the family systems of three friends and describe them in terms of family types as well as socioeconomic and ethnic status. If possible, elaborate on how these descriptors have affected members' interactions.
5. At this point in your life, how would you describe a well-functioning family?

KEY WORDS

Blended family   9
Committed partners   11
Constitutive approach   6
Discourse-dependent family   6
External boundary management   6
Family   4

Family-of-origin   11
Internal boundary management   6
Legitimizing   7
Open adoption   13
Primary parent systems   9
Relationship flourishing   20

Framework for
Family Communication

"In their mutual interaction, the family members develop more or less adequate understanding of one another collaborating in the effort to establish consensus and to negotiate uncertainty. The family's life together is an endless process of movement in and around consensual understanding, from attachment to conflict to withdrawal—and over again. Separateness and connectedness are the underlying conditions of a family's life, and its common talk is to give form to both."

—Robert D. Hess and Gerald Handel, *Family Worlds*

Bruce grew up in a household where he learned not to trust anyone who was not a member of the family because "There's always somebody out to get you." His grandfather, swindled twice by trusted business partners, taught his children to be wary of outsiders, a belief passed down to his son, and eventually to his grandchildren. When Bruce finished high school he joined the family business in order to keep the company run by relatives. At age 22 he met and married Melissa, a warm, friendly, and trusting person. Unfortunately, their core worldview differences haunted their marriage. Bruce would tell the children, "Keep your hand on your wallet at all times," "Don't depend on anyone else; take care of it yourself," and "You can only depend on your family." Melissa, a rather naïve young woman, thought Bruce would realize how narrow his perspective was as he grew older and got to know others outside the family. She had grown up in a family surrounded by the warmth of adult friends and close neighbors; she made good friends in high school that she remained close to even though Bruce did not like them. Although Bruce was a distant son-in-law, somehow they created a good life despite their fundamental worldviews—until the children arrived.

As the children aged, Bruce insisted that they could not sleep over at other people's houses, join organized sports, or loan money to anyone. Close friends were discouraged; siblings and cousins were expected to meet each other's needs for companionship. Although Melissa tried to convince him that he was overreacting, his position never changed. In fact, he became increasingly angry when she would get involved with neighborhood female friends or with friends at work. After years of struggling with her husband about his need for total control, her need for friends, and that of the children's for outside companionship and participation in a larger world, Melissa chose to end the marriage.

Mark grew up in a family where his father worked outside the home while his mother stayed home to raise Mark and his two younger sisters. Mark's father was in the insurance industry and traveled a lot for work. Consequently, Mark didn't see his father much. Mark's father was the disciplinarian in the family. Whenever Mark or his sisters were misbehaving, his mother would say things like, "You better stop it, or I will tell your father." The threat of having his father discipline him was often enough to make Mark shape up. When he was young, his father would spank him; as he became older, his father would ground him or take away other privileges. Mark's father tended towards bursts of anger and verbal attacks, using words like "dumb," "bad," "irresponsible," and "worthless." After such incidents, Mark's father would never apologize, but seemed to go out of his way to be nicer toward him. Mark assumed his father loved him, even though he never said the words.

Later in life, Mark married Julie and a few years later their first child, Alex, was born. Mark loved being a father. But as Alex entered the "terrible twos," he became a challenging child to raise. Mark relied on what he had learned from his father about discipline, spanking Alex and calling him a "bad boy." Such behavior caused a great deal of tension between Mark and his wife Julie. Julie had been raised in a family where milder disciplinary tactics were used; neither she nor her siblings had ever been spanked. Her parents were soft-spoken, patient people who doled out more love and empathy than punishment. Julie preferred these tactics and was shocked the first time Mark spanked their son. It wasn't until Mark and Julie began marital counseling that Mark realized he had "become" his father—that he was recreating the unhealthy communication pattern he had had with his own father in his relationship with Alex.

Families repeat themselves within and across generations. Members become caught up in predictable and often unexamined life patterns that are created, in part, through their interactions with other family members. This text explores the family as a communication system, concentrating on processes by which communication patterns serve to create and reflect family relationships. Within the framework of shared cultural communication patterns, each family has the capacity to develop its own communication codes based on the experiences of individual members as well as the collective family experience. Individuals develop their communication skills within the family context, learning both the general cultural language(s) and specific familial communication patterns. Since most people take their personal backgrounds for granted, you may not be aware of the context your family provided for learning communication. For example, when you were a child, your family members taught you acceptable ways of expressing intimacy and conflict, how to relate to other family members, how to make decisions, and how to share information inside and outside the family boundaries. Other families may have taught their members different lessons. From our perspective families are defined primarily through their interaction patterns rather than through their structures (Whitchurch & Dickson, 1999). In other words, "Through their communicative practices, parties construct their social reality of who their family is and the meanings that organize it" (Baxter & Braithwaite, 2002, p. 94). This position establishes communication as *constitutive* of the family, thereby placing communication at the core of familial experience.

In order to understand the family as an interactive system, you need to explore key communication concepts and understand how they can be applied to family patterns. This chapter will (1) provide an overview of the communication process, including the development of interpersonal meanings; (2) explain a set of primary and secondary family functions that influence communication; (3) introduce the concept of transgenerational patterns; and (4) present a framework for examining family communication.

THE COMMUNICATION PROCESS

Communication may be viewed as a *symbolic, transactional process of creating* and *sharing meanings.* The claim that communication is *symbolic* implies that symbols are used to create meaning and messages. Words or verbal behavior represent the most commonly used symbols, but the whole range of nonverbal behavior—including facial expressions, eye contact, gestures, movement, posture, appearance, and spatial distance—also occurs symbolically. Symbols may represent things, feelings, or ideas. Families may use kisses, special food, teasing, or poems as symbols of love, and silence or yelling as symbols of anger. The symbols must be mutually understood for the meanings to be shared. For example, if family members do not agree on how much is "a lot" of money or how to express and recognize anger, confusion will result. If meanings are not mutually shared, messages may not be understood, resulting in the following example of misunderstanding.

In my first marriage, my wife and I often discovered that we had very different meanings for the same words. For example, we agreed we wanted a "large" family but I meant three children and she meant seven or eight. I thought "regular" sex meant once a day and she thought it meant once a week. I thought spending a "lot of money" meant spending over $1,000; she thought it meant spending over $100. In my second marriage, we talk very frequently about what our words mean so we don't have so many disagreements.

To say that communication is *transactional* means that communication consists of mutual interaction. Thus, in relationships, participants are both affecting and being affected by others simultaneously. The focus is placed on the relationship, not on the individual participants. Participation in an intimate relationship transforms fundamental reality definitions for both partners and in so doing transforms the partners themselves (Stephen & Enholm, 1987). Joint actions of partners contribute to the development of private relational realities that are dependent on the uniqueness of the pair acting together. Siblings may create patterns of teasing that allow them to feel connected, but no one else could joke that way without creating tension. Family members are engaging in symbolic interaction or creating joint meanings within their relationships.

A transactional communication perspective and a family systems perspective complement each other because they share a relational focus. In other words, relationships take precedence over individuals. A transactional communication perspective focuses on the interaction between two or more persons. Each individual communicates within an interpersonal context, and each communication act reflects the nature of those relationships. As two people interact, each creates a context for the other and relates to the other within that context. For example, you may perceive a brother-in-law as distant and relate to him in a very polite but restrained manner. In turn, he may perceive your politeness as formal and relate to you in an even more reserved manner. A similar situation is demonstrated here.

My father and brother had a very difficult relationship with each other for many years, although both of them had an excellent relationship with everyone else in the family. Daniel saw Dad as repressive and demanding, although I would characterize him as serious and concerned. Dad saw Daniel as careless and uncommitted, although no one else saw him that way. Whenever they tried to talk to each other, each responded to the person he created, and it was a continual battle.

In the previous example, knowing Daniel or his father separately does not account for their conflictual behaviors. Each influences the other's reactions and interactions. Each creates a context for the other and relates within that context. It is as if one says to the other, "You are sensitive," or "You are repressive," or "You are lazy," and "that's how I will relate to you." The content and style of messages vary according to how each person sees himself or herself and how each predicts the other individual will react.

The transactional perspective stresses the importance of the communicators' perceptions and actions in determining the outcome of interactions. Thus, the relationship *patterns,* not specific acts, become the focal point. One's perception of another and one's subsequent behavior can actually change the behavior of the other person. An aunt who constantly praises her nephew for his thoughtfulness and sensitivity and notices the good things in his efforts may change his perception of himself and his subsequent behavior with her and other relatives. A husband who constantly complains about his wife's parenting behavior may lower her self-esteem and change her subsequent behavior toward him and the children. Thus, in relationships, each person: (1) creates a context for the other, (2) simultaneously creates and interprets messages, and, therefore, (3) simultaneously affects and is affected by the other.

To say that communication is a *process* implies that it is continuously changing. Communication is not static; rather, it develops over time. Relationships, no matter how committed, change continuously, and communication both affects and reflects these changes. The passage of time brings with it predictable and unpredictable crises, which take their toll on family regularity and stability. Yet, everyday moods, minor pleasures, or irritations may shift the communication patterns on a day-to-day basis. As time passes, family members subtly renegotiate their relationships. Today, you may be in a bad mood and people respond to that personal state. Next week, a major job change may affect all your relationships. Over time, families change as they pass through stages of growth; members are born, age, leave, and die, and their communication patterns impact and reflect these developments in family life.

As indicated earlier, communication may be viewed as a symbolic, transactional process of creating and sharing meanings. Communication serves to create a family's social reality. Successful communication depends on the members' shared reality, or sets of meanings (Bochner & Eisenberg, 1987).

Meanings and Messages

How often do people in close and committed relationships find themselves saying, "That's not what I mean" or "What do you mean by that?" Even in the most mundane interchanges, participants' messages imply their visions of the nature of social and physical reality as well as their values, beliefs, and attitudes. These are referred to as their *meanings*. Communication involves the negotiation of shared meanings; if shared meanings are not held by interactants, confusion or misunderstanding results. A primary family task involves "meaning making," or the "cocreation of meanings." In their classic work, Berger and Kellner (1964) capture the sense of creating meanings within a marriage, suggesting, "Each partner's definition of reality must be continually correlated with the definitions of the other" (p. 224). Such correlation requires regular communication and ongoing coordination of meanings. Symbolic interaction, a theory discussed in Chapter 3, provides one lens through which family communication will be viewed. This meaning-centered theory holds communication to be central to the process of creating a family's social reality.

Worldviews reflect one's fundamental beliefs about issues, such as the nature of change and the nature of human beings; in other words, these are the unspoken presuppositions a person brings to each interpersonal encounter.

My mother and stepfather clash regularly because, deep down, they hold very different beliefs about human beings. My stepfather believes people are always out for themselves and he is generally suspicious of most people. My mother trusts everyone and sees only the good in people. Over the past five years each has moved a little closer toward a middle ground but it's hard to alter such fundamentally different worldviews.

The meaning-making tasks of family members serve to create a relational culture or worldview that characterizes the family system.

Family members negotiate meanings in a variety of family activities.

Development of Meanings   How does a person develop a set of meanings? Basically, your views of the world result from your perceptual filter systems. For example, imagine each person has lenses, or filters, through which he or she views the world. Everyone views the world within contexts such as age, race, ethnicity, gender, health status, religion, and national culture. In addition, views of reality are affected by sibling position as well as family history and traditions across generations. These factors combine uniquely for each individual, impacting how that person perceives and interacts with the world in general, and more specifically with the members of his or her family system. Although this sounds like a very individualistic process, remember the transactional perspective. Each communicator constantly affects and is affected by the other; thus, perceptions are *co-created* within the context of a relational system and are constantly influenced by that system.

Meanings emerge as information passes through each person's filter system. One's physical state, based on human sensory systems of sight, hearing, touch, taste, and smell, constitutes the first set of filters. Perceptions are also filtered through the social system including the way a person's language usage, accepted worldview, family culture, class status, and the socially agreed-upon conventions that characterize parts of his or her world. Eventually, a person shares common meanings for certain verbal and nonverbal symbols with those around him or her. An individual may share some general experiences with many people and more specific experiences with a smaller group of individuals.

Social experiences frame your world. The language you speak limits and shapes your meanings. For example, the move to replace the term "stepfamilies" with "blended" or "remarried" families reflects a belief that "step" terms are generally negative. Stepmothers, in particular, face negative images of themselves due to the historically "wicked" word association. Current terminology limits easy discussion of increasingly complex family relationships, such as "my half-brother's grandfather on his mother's side." Yet, although language may limit meanings, people are capable of broadening such perspectives by creating and learning new terminology and opening themselves to new experiences.

The immediate groups to which one belongs exert a strong influence on an individual's perceptual set. The family group provides contextual meaning and influences the way meaning is given to sensory data. If one considers handmade gifts as a special sign of caring, a hand-knitted scarf may be valued, whereas an expensive necklace may not convey affection. Although physical and social systems combine to provide perceptual filters, specific constraints and experiences influence an individual's meanings. Individual constraints refer to the interpretations you create for your meanings based on your own personal histories. Although you may share similar histories with others, each person develops a unique way of dealing with sensory information, and therefore develops an individual way of seeing the world and relating to others in it. This concept is captured in the expression, "No two children grow up in the same family." For example, many siblings disagree on the kind of family life they experienced together. One sister may state, "Mom was very nurturing," whereas her brother asserts, "Mom only really cared about her work." Specific events and people affect your meanings. Each person experiences family differently, as indicated in the following example.

In our house, my sister Diane was considered the "problem child." As far as psychologists can determine, her emotional difficulties stemmed from an unknown trauma when she was age three, when they suggest she was rejected by my parents at a time when she needed love. The reality was that Diane functioned as a scapegoat for all of us. Although Diane and I are close in age, we experienced a different family because of the way she perceived the family and was perceived by other members.

Over time, individuals negotiate their shared meanings. "People may not see the same meanings, but meanings do become coordinated, so that meaning for one family member elicits complementary meanings for other family members" (Breunlin, Schwartz, & Kune-Karrer, 2001, p. 52). The greater the repetition of interaction the greater the probability of a similar assigned meaning. Enduring relationships are characterized by agreements between members as to the meaning of things. These persons develop a relationship worldview reflecting the members' symbolic interdependence.

Eventually you learn to interpret and understand your meanings within your family. As a child, when you heard your mother yell "Jonathan" or "Kyung Chu," you were able to tell from her tone of voice just what to expect. Today, if you hear your younger sister say, "I just hate that Brett Holland," you know that she has just found a new boyfriend. Meanings are renegotiated over time as children move into adolescence, as adults witness the death or decline of their parents and grand-parents, and as world events force people to reevaluate their values and beliefs. For example, after 9/11 some long-term cohabiting couples decided to marry and certain individuals attempted to repair ruptured family ties.

Levels of Meaning and Metacommunication Meaning occurs on two levels: content and relationship. The content level contains information, whereas the relationship level indicates how the information should be interpreted or understood. The relationship level is more likely to involve nonverbal messages. When your older sister says, "When are you going to pick up those clothes?" it appears to be an informational question, but there may be another level of meaning. It is up to you to determine if, by her tone of voice, she is really questioning at what time of day you will remove the dirty socks and jeans, or if she is telling you to remove them in the next 30 seconds. Relational pairs develop their own interpretation of symbols. When a father puts his arm on his daughter's shoulder, it may mean "I support you" or "Slow down, relax." Usually his daughter will understand the intended message.

Metacommunication This occurs when people communicate about their communication—for example, when they give verbal and nonverbal indications about how their messages should be understood. Such remarks as "I was only kidding," "This is important," or "Talking about this makes me uncomfortable" signal to another about how to interpret certain comments. Nonverbal cues, such as facial expressions, gestures, or vocal tones, may indicate if a comment is humorous or serious. On a deeper level, many family members spend hours talking about how they might fight or express affection in a more desirable way. Metacommunication serves an important function within families because it allows members to state their needs, clarify confusion, and establish more constructive relational patterns. Meanings serve a central function in all family communication processes.

The ways in which people exchange messages influence the form and content of their relationships. Communication among family members shapes the structure of the family system, providing the family with its own set of meanings. Although we have used many family examples in describing the communication process, we have not explored the role of communication within the family. The next section examines the role communication plays in forming, maintaining, and changing family systems as families enact key functions.

COMMUNICATION PATTERNS
AND FAMILY FUNCTIONS

When you encounter other families, you often note how their communication practices differ from those of your family. Everyday ways of relating, making decisions, sharing feelings, and handling conflict will vary from your own personal experiences. Communication provides form and content to a family's life as members engage in family-related *functions*. From a technical perspective, a function is simply something a system must do, of an operation it must perform, in order to avoid a breakdown. The following section examines two primary family functions and four supporting functions that affect and are affected by communication and taken together form a family's collective identity.

Primary Functions

In their attempt to integrate the numerous concepts related to marital and family interaction, researchers Olson, Sprenkle, and Russell developed what is known as the circumplex model of marital and family systems (Olson, 2000; Olson, Russell, & Sprenkle, 1983; Olson, Sprenkle, & Russell, 1979). This model bridges family theory, research, and practice. Two central dimensions of family behavior, or family operations are at the core of the model: *family cohesion* and *family adaptability*. Each of these dimensions is divided into four levels matched on a grid to create 16 possible combinations. The four types in the center of the grid are called *balanced;* the types at the extremes are seen as *dysfunctional*. The theorists suggest moderate scores represent reasonable functioning, whereas the extreme scores represent family dysfunction.

Over time the model evolved to include three dimensions: (1) cohesion, (2) adaptability, and (3) communication. The two central dimensions remain family cohesion and family adaptability, which are perceived as the intersecting lines of an axis. The third dimension is *family communication,* a facilitating dimension that enables couples and families to move along the cohesion and adaptability dimensions, but because it is a facilitating dimension, it is seldom included in the model diagrams. We do not present the entire circumplex model here, rather we have adapted the dimensions of cohesion and adaptability as primary family functions.

In this text, the concepts of cohesion and change form a framework in which to view communication within various types of families. From this perspective, two primary family functions involve: (1) establishing a pattern of *cohesion,* or separateness and connectedness, and (2) establishing a pattern of *adaptability,* or change. These functions vary with regularity as families experience the tensions inherent in relational life.

Cohesion   From the moment of birth, you have been learning how to manage issues of distance and closeness within your family system. You were taught directly or subtly how to be connected to, or separated from, other family members. In other words, every family socializes its members about the extent to which closeness is encouraged or discouraged. *Cohesion* is defined as the emotional bonding that family members experience with each other and includes concepts of "emotional bonding, boundaries, coalitions, time, space, friends, decision-making, interests and recreation" (Olson, 2000, p. 145).

Although differing in terminology, the issue of cohesion has been identified by scholars from various fields as central to the understanding of family life (Pistole,

1994). Family researchers Kantor and Lehr (1976) viewed "distance regulation" as a major family function; family therapist Minuchin (1967) talked about "enmeshed and disengaged" families; sociologists Hess and Handel (1959) described the family's need to establish a pattern of separateness and connectedness. There are four levels of cohesion ranging from extremely low cohesion to extremely high cohesion. These levels are:

Disengaged. Family members maintain extreme separateness and independence, experiencing little belonging or loyalty.

Connected. Family members experience emotional independence as well as some sense of involvement and belonging.

Cohesive. Family members strive for emotional closeness, loyalty, and togetherness with emphasis on some individuality.

Enmeshed. Family members experience extreme closeness, loyalty, dependence, and almost no individuality. (Olson, DeFrain, & Skogard, 2008).

Through their communication family members develop, maintain, or change their patterns of cohesion. Because a father may decide that it is inappropriate to continue the physical closeness he has experienced with his daughter now that she has become a teenager, he may limit his playful roughhousing. This nonverbal message may be confusing or hurtful to his daughter. She may become distant, find new ways of being close, develop more outside friendships, or attempt to force her father back into the old patterns. A husband may demand more intimacy from his wife as he ages by asking for more serious conversation, making more sexual advances, or sharing more of his feelings. His wife may ignore this new behavior or increase her intimate behaviors. Balanced families generally are found at connected or cohesive levels; such families tend to be more functional.

In enmeshed families, those with extremely high cohesion, members are so intensely bonded and overinvolved that individuals experience little autonomy or fulfillment of personal needs and goals. Total loyalty is expected. Family members appear fused or joined so tightly that personal identities do not develop appropriately; thus, members are highly interdependent, as indicated by the following example.

My mother and I are "best friends," a mixed blessing. I relied on her heavily in high school and college when I had a lot of problems with other girls who hated my successes. She cried on my shoulder about my dad and her hard life. Now that I'm entering the entertainment industry, my mother has positioned me at the center of her life—her dreams and plans are totally intermeshed with mine. This level of "togetherness" has cost me romantic partners and created problems in my career.

In disengaged families, found at the other end of the continuum, members experience extreme emotional separateness; each member has high autonomy and individuality. Individual interests and priorities predominate.

Throughout this book, we will examine ways families deal with issues of coming together or staying apart and how they use communication in an attempt to manage their separateness and/or togetherness. Families do not remain permanently at one point on the cohesion continuum. Because there are widely varying cultural norms for acceptable or desirable cohesion, what seems balanced for one family may be quite distant for another. For example, Latino families may find acceptable cohesion at a point that is too high for families with a northern European background.

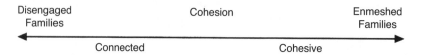

Cohesion continuum

Flexibility When you think of the changes in your own family over the past 5 or 10 years, you may be amazed at how different the system and its members are at this point. A family's experience changes as members move through developmental stages and deal with stresses that arise in everyday life, such as adapting to an illness or a job transfer of one of its members. Even everyday living involves relational tensions with which family members struggle.

Flexibility is defined as the amount of change in a family's leadership, role relationships, and relationship rules. It includes concepts of "leadership (control, discipline), negotiation, styles, role relationships and relationship rules" (Olson, 2000, p. 147). *Family flexibility,* or *adaptability,* focuses on how family systems manage stability and change. (We will continue to use the terms *adaptability* and *flexibility* interchangeably.)

There are four levels of adaptability ranging from extremely low adaptability to extremely high adaptability. These can be described as:

Rigid. Family members experience very low levels of change, as well as authoritarian leadership and strict roles and rules.

Structured. Family members experience more moderate levels of change as well as limited shared decision making and leadership and relatively stable roles and rules.

Flexible. Family members experience high levels of change, shared decision making, and shifting rules and roles.

Chaotic. Family members experience very high levels of change as well as nonexistent leadership, confused and very variable rules and roles. (Olson, DeFrain, & Skogard, 2008)

Each human system has both stability-promoting processes (morphostasis, or form maintaining) and change-promoting processes (morphogenesis, or form creating). Such systems need periods of stability as well as change in order to function. Chaotic families have little structure and few rules and roles. Due to almost total unpredictability and stress, members cannot maintain predictable relationships and common meanings. At the other extreme, rigidity characterizes families that resist change and growth, leaving members living in old patterns. Balanced families are generally found at structured or flexible levels.

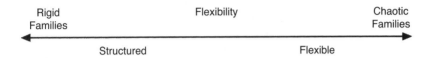

Flexibility continuum

Although most scholars consider either an excess or a lack of change to be dysfunctional, they see the ability of a system to change its structure as generally necessary and desirable. Again, issues of ethnicity and socioeconomic status affect a family's experience of change. For example, families confronting poverty and relying on social welfare agencies often experience life as more chaotic than those for whom a secure economic situation makes it easier to manage outside stresses.

Family systems constantly restructure themselves as they pass through predictable developmental stages such as pregnancy or launching children. Likewise, when positive or negative stresses arise involving such issues as money, illness, or divorce, families must adapt. Finally, family systems must adapt both structurally and functionally to the demands of other social institutions as well as to the needs of their own members, as evidenced here.

My son and daughter-in-law adopted an older child and had to adapt their communication patterns to accommodate her. Although lying was forbidden in their family, when they adopted Shirley they had to reassess this position, because she had learned to lie for most of her life. My son and daughter-in-law had to learn to be more tolerant of this behavior, particularly when she first joined the family, or they would have had to send her back to the agency.

Communication is central to the adaptive function of a family. Any effective adaptation relies on shared meanings developed within the family. Through communication, family members learn to regulate their adaptive behaviors, thereby affecting the system as a whole. Olson and his colleagues hypothesize that where there is a balance between change and stability within families, there will be more mutually assertive communication styles, shared leadership, successful negotiation, role

TABLE 2.1

Levels of Couple and Family Communication

Characteristic	Poor	Good	Very Good
Listening skills	Poor listening skills	Appear to listen, but feedback is limited	Give feedback, indicating good listening skills
Speaking skills	Often speak for others	Speak for self more than for others	Speak mainly for self rather than for others
Self-disclosure	Low sharing of feelings	Moderate sharing of feelings	High sharing of feelings
Clarity	Inconsistent messages	Clear messages	Very clear messages
Staying on topic	Seldom stay on topic	Often stay on topic	Mainly stay on topic
Respect and regard	Low to moderate	Moderate to high	High

sharing, and open rule making and sharing. The functions of cohesion and adaptability combine to create the two major functions family members continuously manage.

Communication does not appear on the various visual representations of the cohesion/flexibility model, yet it remains a critical factor in how families manage cohesion and flexibility. Communication serves as the "grease that smoothes frictions between partners and family members" (Olson, DeFrain, & Skogrand, 2008, p. 88). Olson and his colleagues depict the following six dimensions used to assess family communication: listening skills, speaking skills, self-disclosure, clarity, staying on topic, and respect or regard (see Table 2.1). Although communication does not emerge as a centerpiece of this model, Schrodt (2005) suggests that communication impacts the way families manage the dimensions of cohesion and flexibility, saying: "Whereas positive communication skills, including clarity, empathy, and effective problem solving, are believed to facilitate healthy levels of family cohesion and flexibility, lack of communication skills is believed to inhibit the family system's ability to change when needed" (p. 360).

Applying the work of Olson and his colleagues, you can visualize the mutual interaction of flexibility and cohesion within families by placing them on an axis (Figure 2.1a). By adding the extremes of cohesion (disengagement and enmeshment) and flexibility (rigidity and chaos), you can picture where more or less functional families would appear on the axis (Figure 2.1b).

The central area represents balanced or moderate levels of flexibility and cohesion, seen as a highly workable communication pattern for individual and family development, although there may be instances when a different pattern could aid a family through a particular developmental point or through a crisis. The outside areas represent the extremes of cohesion and flexibility, less workable for consistent long-term communication patterns.

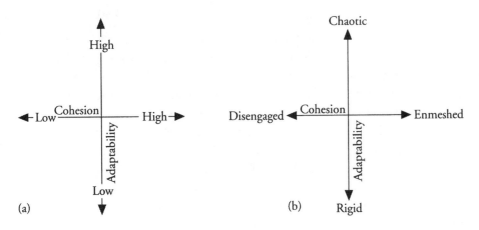

FIGURE 2.1

Family Cohesion–Adaptability Axes

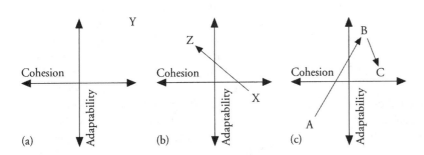

FIGURE 2.2

Application of Family Cohesion–Adaptability

Most well-functioning or balanced families are found short of the extremes, except when they are under high levels of stress. In those situations, placement at the extreme may serve a purpose. This idea will be developed in Chapter 11. If a family member dies, for example, a highly cohesive communication pattern may be critical for mourning purposes. At the time of a family death, members may find themselves at point Y (Figure 2.2a). Such a family may be experiencing extreme closeness among remaining members but chaos in terms of dealing with the changes in roles or in everyday activities. In contrast, a family with an acting-out teenager may find itself shifting from point X to point Z on the axis, as the adolescent demands greater freedom and less connectedness from the family, forcing changes in the system (Figure 2.2b).

The situation in the following quotation may be graphed as three moves (Figure 2.2c).

As a small child I lived in an active alcoholic family in which people kept pretty much to themselves. We did not talk about the problems caused by our parents' drinking and we acted as if things were fine. Yet we were very rigid because we never could bring anyone into the house, and we never let outsiders know about the drinking. My older sister always took care of me if there was a problem, while my older brother locked himself in his room. Thus, we were at point A. When my parents finally went into treatment, the house was crazy in a different way for a while, since no one knew exactly how to act, but we did get closer and we were all forced to discuss what was going on. I guess we got closer and almost too flexible or unpredictable (point B). Now, five years later, I'm the only child left at home and my sober parents and I have a relatively close and flexible relationship (point C).

If you think about stages in your family life, you should be able to envision how the family shifted from one point to another on the cohesion–adaptability axis.

Families at different developmental stages may appear more functional in different quadrants of the model, reflecting their life-stage demands. For example, young couples without babies function best in either the upper right or lower left quadrants. Families with adolescents function best in the central, or balanced, area; older couples relate best in the lower right quadrant. Adolescents function best when they have average cohesion, being neither enmeshed with parents or disengaged, and when their adaptability is midway between rigidity and chaos. Obviously, these results indicate adolescents' need for a family system without rigid rules. Older couples function best when cohesion is high but adaptability is low. Possible explanations for these findings will become clearer in the chapter on developmental changes. Although results may differ for families from varying ethnic origins, these findings support maintaining a flexible attitude toward well-family functioning.

When viewing an entire family system, there may be individual members who would be graphed in a different place if they were to be pictured separately. These models attempt to represent the whole family group on the axes. Throughout the text, the cohesion–flexibility framework will be used as a backdrop for understanding family communication.

Dialectical Interplay Most long-term intimate relationships are built on a history of struggle, as well as pleasure, and a continued interplay between opposing tendencies. Baxter and Montgomery (1996) refer to this tension as "relational dialectics." *Dialectic* implies opposition, polarity, and interconnection. *Relational dialectics* refers to the "both/and" quality of relationships or the need for partners to simultaneously experience independence and connection or openness and privacy. (Dialectical theory will be developed in detail in Chapter 3.)

How much closeness or distance do family members need in order to function effectively? How can individuals live in intimate connections without hurting each other too much? These questions are indicators of the tensions all relationships face. They reflect *dialectical tensions* and are managed through communication. As family members interact, they encounter tensions and struggles in managing the mutual needs of persons in a relationship. Dialectics recognizes the tension between relational partners as they negotiate and renegotiate what it means to be in a functional relationship.

From a dialectical perspective, cohesion and adaptability may be viewed as both family functions and dialectical tensions due to their importance and inescapable presence within the family. In discussing the cohesion function, Sabourin (1992) suggests:

> The dialectical perspective is useful in explaining how difficult achieving balance can be. It is a contradiction to need both autonomy and connection with others. . . . The dialectical perspective incorporates both. . . . Hence some families emphasize togetherness at the expense of developing personal identities. (p. 5)

Most families find they struggle over time with the issues of closeness and distance both between members and between the family system and outside persons or groups. The following quote from a young wife captures this dialectical tension.

> On the one hand it is like, sure, I can go on my own. And on the other hand, I want him to go with me. . . . I want to do things with him, and I think it is okay if he doesn't want to go and then it actually upsets me a lot if he doesn't go. (Hoppe-Nagao & Ting-Toomey, 2002, p. 146)

This is also true for flexibility. Family members struggle with how predictable or unpredictable members may be before creating tensions or difficulties for other members.

Although the issues related to cohesion and flexibility/change are viewed as the primary functions, these functions do not provide a complete picture. There are additional family functions—supporting functions—that contribute to an understanding of family interaction.

Supporting Functions

In conjunction with cohesion and adaptability, four supporting functions give shape to family life. Hess and Handel (1959) identified five processes, or family functions, that interact with the development of a family's message system. Because one of these processes relates to cohesion, we will list only the remaining four. The supporting family functions include:

1. Establishing a satisfactory congruence of images.
2. Evolving modes of interaction into central family themes.
3. Establishing the boundaries of the family's world of experience.
4. Managing significant biosocial issues of family life, such as gender, age, power, and roles. (p. 4)

Each of these processes interacts with a family's point on the cohesion-flexibility axis and influences a family's communication pattern. Each process is based on principles of symbolic interaction, since their underlying thread is the role of subjective meanings (White & Klein, 2002).

Family Images Relationship patterns can be viewed as metaphors, which allow people to understand one element in terms of another. We can also talk about root metaphors, which assume a connection between a way of talking about the world and a major analogy or metaphor. A simple metaphor may be "My sister is a butterfly. You can never get her to settle down." A root metaphor for a family would capture an overarching image of life in that family. Identifying small and simple metaphors is relatively easy; identifying an overarching root metaphor usually takes a good deal of thought and analysis.

If you had to create a mental image or a root metaphor for your family, what would it be—a nest, a broken wagon wheel, a corporation, a rowing team, or a schoolroom? Every family operates as an image-making or metaphor-creating entity. These metaphors reflect the family's worldview as they represent the family's collective experience (Pawlowski, 1996a). Each member develops images of what the family unit and other family members are like; these images affect his or her patterns of interaction with the others. An image of one's family embodies what is expected from it, what is given to it, and how important it is (Hess & Handel, 1959). Thus, the image has both realistic and idealized components that reflect both the imagined and the imaginer. The following root metaphor conveys a good deal of information about this two-parent family with four adolescent children.

My family is like a Navy fleet. In the center are my parents, both upon the carrier. My mother is the executive officer (XO). The XO is the bad guy who runs the ship, keeps things in order, and intercepts messes before they reach the commanding officer. My father is the commanding officer (CO). He decides the general direction the family heads but is more concerned with navigating than maintaining everyday life on board. My siblings and I are the small ships in the group. We can go off but must return to refuel. I am the cruiser and have more responsibilities and provide services, such as information. Jon and Stephanie are both destroyers, who are freer to range around. Michael is the airplane who sits on top of the mother ship. He has a short range and endurance away from the carrier. The destroyers like to intimidate him but would never really fire on him. We all know our places and positions and defend each other from any threat. We are close, but not too close. We all follow orders from the CO but spend much of our lives interacting more easily with the XO.

A less complicated example follows.

My family is a basketball team, with my dad as a player-coach. We all work together for the survival of our team, and we all contribute. Each one of us has strengths and weaknesses, yet there is always that force driving us to achieve more together. As the player-coach, my dad has the responsibility of guiding our performances and our practices; as the scorekeeper, my mother keeps the records and memories.

Family images differ significantly. One study of college students' family metaphors revealed 138 options for one's family-of-origin. Images such as rock, tree, circus, security blanket, safety net, and basketball team appeared more often than others (Pawlowski, Thilborger, & Cieloha-Meekins, 2001). Thilborger (1998) reported feminine metaphors for families-of-origin emphasize team/group, nature, and healing/nourishment. Male metaphors emphasize nature, particularly animals, and foundational objects such as brick walls or concrete structures. Sometimes images reflect a family's humor.

My family is like a Ferrero Rocher chocolate. On the outside we are a little bumpy with different personalities, health issues, and minor conflicts. We are also covered in gold foil that shows our respectability and success as a group. We are sweet and supportive and a little nutty.

If you think about metaphors within interactive systems, relationships may be viewed metaphorically. One set of siblings may be seen as "two peas in a pod"; another set may be "oil and water." If two people's images of each other are congruent and consistent for a period of time, a predictable pattern of communication emerges in which both are comfortable. For example, if a mother sees her son as a helpless and dependent creature, she may exhibit many protective behaviors, such as keeping bad news from him. If the son's image of his mother is as a protector, the congruence of the images will allow harmonious communication; but if the son sees his mother as a jailer, conflict may occur. If one child sees her mother as a jailer and her siblings see their mother as an angel, the inconsistent images may result in strong alliances among those with congruent images. A husband and wife are likely to experience conflict if their family images conflict; for example, if one sees the family as a "nest" involving nurturing, emotion, and protection, and the other sees it as a "corporation" involving a strong power structure and good organization. Yet, since complete consensus is improbable and change inevitable, the patterns will never become totally predictable. In an interpretation of his grandmother's role in the family, Trujillo (1998) developed images of his grandmother as the giver, server, and body, acknowledging that other family members may have seen her differently. Yet, as one would imagine, the greater the level of congruence is, the more effective the communication within the family. The family metaphor serves as an indicator of a family's collective identity. Because communicating feelings in some families remains difficult, metaphors may serve as an effective way to convey feelings (Pawlowski, Thilborger, & Cieloha-Meekins, 2001).

Family Themes As well as having images for the family and for every member, each family shares themes—or takes positions that affect every aspect of its functioning. A *theme* may be viewed as a pattern of feelings, motives, fantasies, and conventionalized understandings grouped around a particular locus of concern, which has a particular form in the personalities of individual members (Hess & Handel, 1959). Essentially, themes represent a fundamental view of reality and a way of dealing with this view. Through its theme, a family responds to the questions, Who are we? What do we do about it? and How do we invest our energies? Sample family values include physical security, strength, dependability, inclusion, separation, and kindness. To demonstrate the viability of themes in a family, we view them as statements that actualize the values and collective identity:

> The Nielsens play to win.
> We have responsibility for those less fortunate than us.
> You can sleep when you die.
> Happiness is homegrown.
> You can depend only on your family.
> You can always depend on your family.
> The Garcias never quit.
> Love sees no skin color.
> Life is a challenge: Always have Plan B.
> You can always do better.
> Seize the moment.
> Be happy with what you have.
> Respect La Via Vecchia (the old way).
> We are survivors.

Some families have the theme "Working together keeps us together."

Themes capture the beliefs that guide family members' actions; thereby you may predict a family's themes by watching how members live their lives. Living according to a theme necessitates the development of specific patterns of behavior for interacting with each other and the outside world. For example, a family with the theme "*We have responsibility for those less fortunate than us*" might be a flexible system open to helping extended family members and those outside the family. Members might give to charity, raise foster children, or work with the homeless. Yet, it may be difficult for family members to accept help from an outside source because of its caregiving theme. Members may tend to put themselves second. A mother who lives according to this theme may spend hours working at an adolescent drop-in center and be unaware of the problems her own teenage children face. Family themes undergird everyday life, as the following portrays.

I grew up with the theme "We'll love you anyway." This conveys the idea that the family will always forgive you and be there for you regardless of mistakes in judgment or action. Even when it's a shameful situation, such as getting kicked out of school or fired, or thrown in jail, the family stands behind that member. No members are rejected or cut off.

Family themes may be complex and subtle, involving worldviews that are not immediately obvious. It is important to identify a family's main theme(s) in order to fully understand the meanings and communication behavior of its members. Clearly the opening example of Bruce and Melissa demonstrates how difficult it is to live together with disparate strongly held core themes.

Boundaries Families create boundaries between and among members and between the family and the outside world. The *boundary* of a system is what separates it from its environment. The boundary defines the family system as an entity by creating a permeable separation between its interior (members) and the environment. You can imagine boundaries as physical or psychological limits that regulate family members' access to people, places, ideas, and values. Anything inside the boundary involves members; anything outside is part of the environment. All families establish some boundaries as they restrict their members from encountering certain physical and psychological forces. Most frequently, family boundaries regulate access to people, places, ideas, and values.

Outside World (Family   Outside World ¦ Family   Outside World ⦙ Family

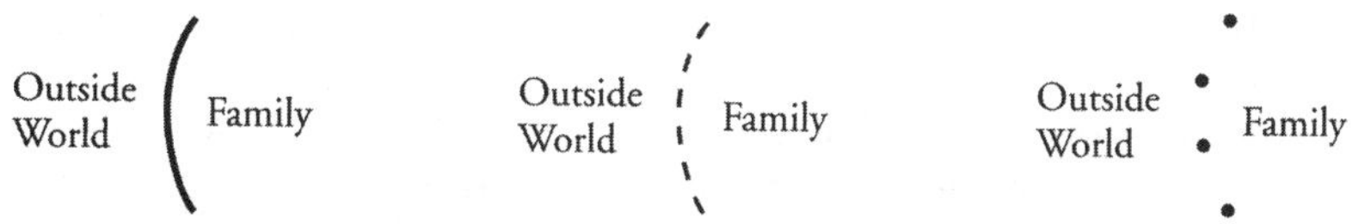

FIGURE 2.3
External Boundaries

In Communication Privacy Management Theory, Petronio (2002) described how people manage private information through a boundaries metaphor, saying, "Regulating boundary openness and closedness contributes to balancing the publicness or privacy of individuals. The regulation process is fundamentally communicative in nature" (p. 8). Some family boundaries are highly permeable, or flexible, allowing easy movement across them. These open boundaries support the flow of information or people from the external environment (Breunlin, Schwartz, & Kune-Karrer, 1997). Closed boundaries resist flow across them due to their rigidity and inflexibility (Figure 2.3). Finally, others are so invisible or diffuse as to be nonexistent.

External boundaries establish the level of connections between family members and the rest of the world. Certain families permit or encourage their children to make many different kinds of friends, explore alternative religious ideas, and encounter controversial ideas through the media; such permeable boundaries permit new people, ideas, and values to enter the family. Other families retain rigid control of their children's activities to prevent them from coming into contact with people or ideas considered to be "undesirable." Families expect members to internalize the family boundaries, as does the grandfather in this example.

My grandfather says "The family does not end at the front step." When you are a Cammastro, you represent the entire family (your aunts, uncles, cousins, grandparents, and your heritage), so you never make a fool of yourself. This means that one must be at one's best whenever in public and never tell family stories or secrets.

Extremes of such expectations result in the creation of rigid boundaries around the family system. Rigid boundaries protect secrets, known to and guarded by members (Vangelisti & Caughlin, 1997).

Finally, some families provide no boundaries—no sense of membership identity and no control of their contact with people, places, ideas, or values. Members of such systems experience little sense of "family," since there appears to be no collective identity.

Families are not always able to control their own boundaries. Many examples of everyday intergroup interactions occur between family members and the societal systems that affect families (Socha & Stamp, 2009). Outside agencies, such as schools, may require parents to share private family information, purchase school uniforms, or volunteer as a room parent in order for their children to be enrolled. Families formed through transracial/transnational adoption may confront invasive questions or comments from medical or educational professionals because of the visual dissimilarity of family members (Suter & Ballard, 2009).

Family boundaries vary according to members' personalities, the types of experiences to which members are exposed, and the freedom each member has to enact a personal value system. Although a parental subsystem may set strong boundaries, a strong, self-assured member may challenge rigid positions on certain issues and reject the established traditional boundaries. An intensely emotional or sensitive child may explore ideas never imagined by other family members. A child may push far beyond the geographic limits or aspirational limits held by other family members or explore the Internet world outside a parent's reach. According to Beavers (1982), optimal family members can switch-hit, flexibly identifying with the larger world at times and yet maintaining individual boundaries.

Internal boundaries help keep family members appropriately placed in relationship to each other. Functional families establish internal boundaries to protect members' self-identities and the identity of generational groups. If the boundaries between individuals are diffuse, or nonexistent, members may experience psychological problems, such as overinvolvement, codependency, or a loss of physical boundaries, such as occurs in incest. If the internal boundaries are too rigid and strong, members will feel disengaged and out of touch. Imber-Black (1998) suggests a patterned "family dance" occurs when members maneuver around the internal boundaries surrounding individual or subgroup secrets.

Most families experience boundaries between generations, which establish subsystems of generational hierarchy. Generations establish their boundaries based on behaviors appropriate for their age and role. Yet, the term "helicopter parent" depicts adults who "hover" over their adolescent or young adult children, resisting the development of age-appropriate boundaries that would separate (Lum, 2006). Parents usually provide nurture and control for their children, gradually withdrawing from certain roles and responsibilities. It is unusual for children to nurture or control their parents intensively unless the parents have become dysfunctional or ill. In two-parent families, the adult subsystem represents a significant bounded dyad. Usually, partners share unique information and interact in special emotional and physical ways. Children are not allowed to share in all aspects of the partnered relationship. Sometimes even adult children can be separated from the marital relationship, as noted below.

My parents had used illnesses not only as intra-family secrets but also as punishment. My father had surgery at one time and needed to stay at the hospital for a short visit. My mother decided to keep this a secret and not tell anyone, even their adult children. When we figured it out and called to check in on my parents to see how they were, my father became angry that no one came to see him at the hospital and then refused to speak with us for weeks. All five of us children felt that, because we were not told about any of their illnesses, we were considered outsiders.

Conversely, conflicts arise if the family's interpersonal boundaries, particularly the marital or partnership boundaries, are too permeable and children are expected to fulfill some functions of the spousal role. For example, troubled families, such as those with an alcoholic or drug-addicted parent, may experience shifts in the marital boundary as the functional parent relies on children for assistance. If a depressed husband cannot provide the interpersonal support needed by his wife, she may co-opt one of the children into the marital subsystem by expecting the child to act as an adult confidant and emotional partner. When boundaries are inappropriately crossed, roles become confused and pain may result for all members.

Internal boundary membership differs across cultural groups. Given the high degree of interdependence among extended family members in many ethnic cultures, the family may have less rigid boundaries, as members are part of multiple households with strong emotional ties and mutual assistance. When new immigrant families face issues such as language barriers or limited outside social support networks, these extended family ties become even more critical and intense (Bush, Bohon, & Kim, 2010).

Boundary issues may be played out across a series of generations. Although many adults enact family boundaries similar to those in their families-of-origin, a daughter whose mother invaded her personal life may determine not to act in the same way toward her children, and actually distance herself from them. Her children, in turn, may resolve to develop closeness with their offspring and end up invading their children's lives. The physical and psychological boundaries set by each family strongly influence the interpersonal communication that occurs within the system.

Biosocial Issues All families operate within a larger community and cultural sphere that provides conventional ways of coping with biosocial issues of gender, age, power, and roles. Each family creates its own answers within the larger framework. Hess and Handel (1959) identified the following biosocial issues: male and female identity, authority and power, shaping and influencing children, and children's rights. Families differ in the extent to which criteria such as gender, age, and position/role in the family, for example, oldest brother, youngest sister, or grandfather, determine the power and responsibilities of members. Position-oriented families allocate rights and responsibilities according to their criteria; person-oriented families tend to rely more on individuals' interests, talents, and availability. In the latter case, a teenage male may choose to cook dinner regularly whereas his twin sister may purchase and maintain the family computers.

The family serves as a primary source of gender identity (Wood, 2007a). Gender identity and physical development issues affect styles of interaction and vice versa. A family that assigns responsibilities based on a member's gender differs from one that uses personal interest or preference as the basis for assigning responsibilities. Usually it is more acceptable for girls to act masculine than it is for boys to act feminine: The most fundamental requirement for manhood is not to think, act, or feel like a female because aggression, sexuality, success, and self-reliance are prized (Wood, 2011). But emerging views of masculinity challenge some previously held beliefs. Conversely, females may still feel pressures from expectations regarding appearance, sensitivity, and superwoman powers even as such expectations continue to shift.

Gendered familial expectations may be subtle and surprising. In their study of parental attitudes and infidelity, Fenigstein and Peltz (2002) found that both mothers and fathers regarded sexual infidelity as more distressing when committed by a daughter-in-law than by a son-in-law. In contrast, they found emotional infidelity was more distressing when it involved a son-in-law. Such traditional gender beliefs are often unrecognized but operational.

Gender experiences vary across cultural groups. For example, in Hispanic and African American families, collectivistic values affect gendered family roles. Such a cultural perspective is displayed in the following comment.

My mother has characteristics of both the Korean attitude and the Western point of view toward women. She fulfills the Korean view of what a woman should be by being the primary nurturer of the family. She is the parent who drove us to piano lessons and took care of us when we were sick. She is the parent that we talk to first when we have a relational problem. In addition to being the nurturer of the family, she also meets the Western view that women should have careers. She is an equal financial contributor to our family. This helps us relate to her even more.

Other value decisions relate to the use of power within the family structure. To what extent are decision making and authority issues resolved according to traditional gender and role configurations? Some flexible families engage in ongoing negotiations regarding power and decision making in the system. The social sphere also involves attitudinal issues related to roles and responsibilities that may be exemplified in parent-child relationships. Parent-child interactions reflect members' beliefs and attitudes. If a parent views children as a temporary responsibility, his or her interactions will be immensely different from those of a parent who envisions a prolonged responsibility for offspring, far beyond the adolescent years. Complicated gender issues may arise as new family configurations form as noted in the following quote.

For the first 11 years of life, my stepson, Travis, was raised in a household that catered to his every need. He was encouraged both to be dependent and to remain a little boy in many ways. His mother, Martha, could not have more children, so she doted on him. Before he died, Martha's first husband treated her and Travis as fragile. When I married Martha, my two daughters came to live with us. They had been raised to be self-sufficient and independent. I have found myself becoming very impatient with Travis and pushing him to act like my children. As a result, Martha and I have had many fights over the children's responsibilities.

Family images, themes, boundaries, and responses to biosocial issues interact with the functions of cohesion and adaptability. Flexible families will experience greater variety in images, themes, boundaries, and responses to biosocial issues than will rigid ones. These factors also affect the family's acceptable levels of cohesion and adaptability. For example, a family with strong boundaries and themes supporting strong family dependence will develop extremely high cohesion and low adaptability in contrast to the family with flexible boundaries and themes supporting independence. This entire process is reflected in the family members' communication behaviors. Communication serves as the means by which families establish their patterns of cohesion and adaptability, and develop their images, themes, boundaries, and responses to biosocial issues.

Family-of-Origin Influences

"My son's a Kaplan, all right. He'll walk up and talk to anyone without a trace of shyness." "My grandparents and parents always fought by yelling at each other and then forgetting about it. My wife doesn't understand this." These statements indicate family-of-origin influences on the communication patterns of the next generation. The term family-of-origin refers to the family or families in which a person is raised. One's family-of-origin is generally considered to be the earliest and most powerful source of influence on one's personality (Bochner & Eisenberg, 1987) and a primary source of expectations for how families should function. The opening vignette describing Mark and his father's patterns of discipline provides an example of this concept.

The term *family-of-origin influences* refers to how current relational experiences reflect: (1) unique multigenerational transmissions and (2) the members' ethnic heritages. The multigenerational and ethnic background that each person brings to a partnered relationship creates a significant social influence on their interpersonal interactions and interactions with any children of that relationship. You may desire to create an adult family life different from the one you experienced as a child, yet you find yourself recreating similar patterns in your adult familial relationships. Parental socialization serves as a major factor in determining children's family-formation behavior. People often create relationships and marriages similar to that of their parents because they enact a family pattern. For example, research indicates that links between family-of-origin experiences of hostility and positive engagement during adolescence is a predictor of later marital hostility and positive behavior of offspring (Whitton, Wakdinger, Schulz, Allen, & Crowell, 2008); research also indicates links between family-of-origin attachment styles and behavior during adolescence with romantic relationship behaviors in young adulthood (Dinero, Conger, Shaver, Widaman, & Larsen-Rife, 2008). Finally, Amato and Cheadle's (2005) analysis of links between the grandparent and grandchild generation report that divorce in the older generation has consequences later for the grandchildren in terms of marital discord and strength of family ties.

Multigenerational Transmissions   Families-of-origin provide blueprints for the communication of future generations. Initially, communication is learned in the home, and,

Messages and meanings pass from one generation to the next.

throughout life, the family setting provides a major testing ground for new communication skills or strategies. Each young person who leaves the family-of-origin to form a new system takes with him or her a set of conscious and unconscious ways of relating to others based on the socializing influence of his or her family (DeGenovaa & Rice, 2005). For example, the idiosyncrasies and culturally based communication patterns of the current Watson family may be passed on to generations of children. Even language may cross generations as the following quote suggests.

My husband gets crazy with all the odd words my family uses, especially around children. I came from a family of 12 kids and there were always words someone couldn't say or codes for things. So I talk to our kids about "Sea Friends" (bath toys), doing a "zipperino" (getting dressed), or "Letter Letter M's" (M&M's). Their cousin calls candy, "M-de-M's" and says "Almost yet" (yet).

Just as simple language terms travel across the generations, more significant attitudes and rule-bound behaviors move from a family-of-origin to a newly emerging family system. Essentially, the family-of-origin serves as the first communication classroom. Differences in family-of-origin experiences can lead to a communication breakdown between adult partners. In the following example, a wife describes the differences in nonverbal communication in her family-of-origin from that of her husband.

It was not until I became closely involved with a second family that I became conscious of the fact that the amount and type of contact can differ greatly. Rarely, in Rob's home, will another person reach for someone else's hand, walk arm in arm, or kiss for no special reason. Hugs are reserved for comfort. When people filter into the den to watch television, one person will sit on the couch, the next on the floor, a third on a chair, and finally the last person is forced to sit on the couch. And always at the opposite end! Touching, in my home, was a natural, everyday occurrence. Usually, the family breakfast began with "good morning" hugs and kisses. Even as adults, no one ever hesitated to cuddle up next to someone else, run their hands through another person's hair, or start tickling whoever happens to be in reaching distance.

Models of relationships can act as a guide for children's behavior and influence their interpretation of others' behavior. For instance, if you have lived in a stepfamily, you may have witnessed the stress involved in integrating your stepparent's family-of-origin influences and his or her more recent adult family relationships into your system's communication patterns that already reflected family-of-origin influences.

Family-of-origin patterns have been used to study abusive or harsh parenting. Chen and Kaplan (2001) examined the continuity of supportive parenting across generations and found positive patterns. The results of their longitudinal study report modest intergenerational continuity tied to factors such as interpersonal relations, social participation, and role modeling. Although family-of-origin issues may be discussed as parent-to-child transmissions, greater emphasis has been placed on transmission across multiple generations. For example, family researchers have focused more directly on the effect of multigenerational systems, indicating some parenting and discipline patterns can be predicted from parental practices (Belsky, Jaffee, Sligo, Woodward, & Sliva, 2005). Following are the basic assumptions inherent in such an approach.

Multigenerational systems:

- Influence, and are influenced by, individuals who are born into them
- Are similar to, but more complex than, any multiperson ecosystem
- Are developmental in nature
- Contain patterns that are shared, transformed, and manifested through *intergenerational transmission*
- Impact two-parent families as the partners' heritages reflect cross-generational influences
- Contain issues that may appear only in certain contexts and may be at unconscious levels
- Have boundaries that are hierarchical in nature
- Develop functional and dysfunctional patterns based on the legacy of previous generations and here-and-now happenings. (Hoopes, 1987, pp. 198–204)

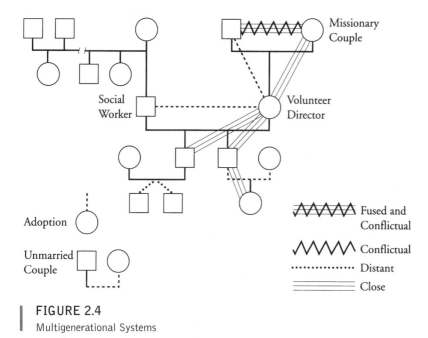

| FIGURE 2.4
Multigenerational Systems

Genograms provide one way to envision intergenerational transmissions (McGoldrick, Gerson, & Shellenberger, 1999). A genogram is a multigenerational family tree that plots familial relationships and visually records information about social relationships and biological and psychological issues in the family across three or more generations (Galvin, Bylund, & Grill, 2010).

Consider Figure 2.4, a multigenerational system genogram that contains examples of powerful parent-child relationships, a theme of service as well as flexible boundaries. In reading the genogram, men are represented by squares and women are represented by circles.

The power of multigenerational transmission is part of a puzzle that is unfolding. In the following passage, a young woman reflects on her painful experiences and insights.

I have come to learn that my behavioral problems were a reaction to my mother's alcoholism, and to her emotional distance during my infancy and childhood. Likewise, my mother's behaviors had a similar origin. Affected by her own mother's chronic depression, my mother never received the affirmation she needed and desired. Yet, having been reared by an alcoholic mother, my grandmother was in no better position to be an effective mother or role model for intimacy. With such unavailable models, the women in my family were perpetually unable to develop this essential capacity. Consequently, my own mother built our relationship from a faulty blueprint.

Family patterns are not usually so dramatic. Most relationships that significantly influence family members are of this perpetual but dormant kind: "They are part of the unchallenged and comfortable predictability of lives made up of routine, regular conversation, and assumptions that most of tomorrow will be based on the foundation of today" (Duck, 1986, p. 91). Yet, although patterns do move across generations, some change in the process. In their study of grandfather-father-son relational closeness patterns, Buerkel-Rothfuss, Fink, and Buerkel (1995) concluded, "Males use communication behaviors similar to those of their fathers and in many cases, their grandfathers, but father-son relationships may be evolving into a more positive form" (p. 80). Conversely, children also shape their parents' behavior (Olson, Defrain, & Skogrand, 2008), reflecting bidirectional interpersonal patterns.

Some of the factors used to examine multigenerational issues include the following: gender roles; managing losses; ethnic patterns of closeness and distance; factors that link individuals, such as names or physical similarities; family themes; boundary management; conflict patterns; and parenting styles. Other issues such as alcoholism (Sher, Gershuny, Peterson, & Raskin, 1997) and eating patterns and behaviors (Baker, Whisman, & Borwnell, 2000) appear to have some basis in family-of-origin messages. These patterns may emerge, consciously or unconsciously, across three or four generations. Yet, further research is needed on numerous issues, such as why some children in problematic families continue the family tradition, while others create well-functioning adult familial relationships. In his analysis of family psychosocial risk factors, Rutter (2002) states, "Some children seem to escape most serious ill effects (although that does not mean that they have been totally unaffected or unscarred) whereas others succumb to lasting psychopathology" (p. 335). In addition, mutual influence must also be considered because parents and children interact and influence each other; this occurs in a bidirectional manner as opposed to a unidirectional manner (Saphir & Chaffee, 2002).

The effects of significant traumas may be transmitted to future generations. Studies of children of Holocaust survivors identified issues faced by some of them; these included impaired self-esteem and identity problems, catastrophic expectations and preoccupation with death, anxiety, feelings of loss and increased vulnerability, exaggerated family attachments or exaggerated independence, and difficulty with intimate relationships (Kellerman, 2001). Family scholars Amato and Cheadle (2005) examined the possibility that the effects of divorce may be transmitted across the following generations.

Biological/Genetic Factors Current scientific research in biology and genetic studies will influence thinking in this area over the next decades. Many family patterns and problems have recognizable intergenerational components (Daly, et al., 1999). Some of these issues are genetically linked. Booth, Carver, and Granger (2000) proposed the importance of the following biological topics with direct links to family interaction: (1) behavioral endocrinology, (2) behavioral genetics, (3) evolutionary psychology, and (4) behavioral psychopharmacology. The impact of physiology, genetics, and evolution on interaction patterns gained attention in the past decade with renewed attention to biological contributions to individual communication practices and discussion of a communibiological paradigm (Beatty, McCroskey, & Valencic, 2001; Floyd & Haynes, 2006). Issues such as adverse or negative family relationships and their psychological health consequences have been linked to physiological factors, such as lower salivary cortisol (Kraft & Hagan, 2009). Research examining links between interaction patterns with genetics and/or physiological effects stands to contribute significantly to an understanding of family communication patterns in the future.

Although knowledge of the effects of complex sets of genes on behavior remains limited, established lines of research are exploring passive, reactive, and active influences related to behaviors of parents and children. For example, one way in which genes influence environmental risk exposure relates to their effects on children's behavior. Adoptee studies revealed that the adoptive parents of children born to, but not reared by, antisocial parents are more likely to exhibit negative forms of control than are parents of children who lack that biological risk (Rutter, 2002). The mediation occurs through the genetic effects on the children's disruptive behavior, which in turn influences their interactions with their adoptive parents who are rearing them. Animal studies suggest the quality of mothering appears to be maintained across generations not only through genetics, but also through early experiences of maternal sensory, perceptual and recognition mechanisms that affect responsiveness to offspring (Fleming, et al., 2002).

In a pioneering essay, family therapist Jeannette Kramer (1985) depicted the family-of-origin's influence on a child's view of the world.

> [The child] observes the environment he inhabits, partakes of its ambiance. He forms values and beliefs, develops assumptions about how marriages and families are and should be, and learns about life cycles, including how to handle the changes of maturation and of aging and death. He learns about power and control and about the consequences of emotions, both his own and others. He is schooled in patterns of communication: what role to take in triangles; how to handle secrets; how to respond to pressure. (p. 9)

Such a description captures the power of a child's family experiences to influence his or her entire life.

Ethnicity The role of ethnicity in multigenerational patterns often is overlooked, yet its influence can be powerful, since ethnic values and identification are retained for many generations after immigration (McGoldrick, Giordano, & Garcia-Preto, 2005). Ethnicity describes people according to their supposed common ancestry, language, and cultural ancestry. Coontz (1999) argued that ethnicity is a product not just of the traditions brought by immigrants but of the particular immigrant group's class origins and occupational skills interacting with the historically or regionally specific jobs, housing stock, and political conditions they meet (p. xvi).

Ethnic family issues may be reflected in issues such as age, gender, roles, expressiveness, birth order, separation, or individuation. For example, Italian families are known for celebrating, loving, and fighting, with value placed on cleverness, charm, graciousness, and attention to family honor. Italian families function within a network of other relatives, *gumbares* (old friends), and godparents from whom mutual support is expected. This orientation stresses parental role distinction, with the father as the undisputed head of the family and mother as the heart (Giordano, McGoldrick, & Klages, 2005).

This generalization about the Italian heritage comes into sharp contrast with descriptions of Scandinavian family patterns, which generally stress the importance of emotional control and the avoidance of open confrontation (Erickson, 2005). Within the Norwegian family, words are likely to be used sparingly; inner weaknesses are kept secret; direct conflict is avoided as aggression reveals itself through teasing, ignoring, or silence. A marriage of persons reflecting these two ethnic backgrounds has the potential for misunderstanding unless differences are addressed. Such differences may never be resolved because of the strength of the family pattern, or compromises may be necessary as the whole family is influenced by social forces.

African Americans share a communal sense of identity expressed as "We are, therefore I am" (McGoldrick, 2003, p. 240). Emphasis is placed on extended kinship bonds, African roots, strong three-generation systems, religion, and spirituality (Stewart, 2010). African American parent-child interaction patterns involve parents as cultural advisors and coaches, given their unique need to socialize children to manage situations of racial derogation (Socha, Bromley, & Kelly, 1995). African American parents tend to exhibit the "imperative mode" or directive communication with their children as a protective authority (Daniel & Daniel, 1999). Such directness does not transfer to other communication situations; many African American women learn from their family and community to avoid talking about certain health problems, such as cancer risks (Cohen, 2009).

A family's ethnic heritage may dictate norms for communication, which are maintained for generations. For example, an emphasis on keeping things "in the family," or the way in which such subjects are discussed may pass from generation to generation, reflecting individual and cultural influences. An examination of communication patterns through three generations of an extended Irish American family revealed great similarities across generations in terms of culturally predictable communication patterns (Galvin, 2007). Whereas the Irish family sets strong privacy boundaries, the following description of Arabic family life portrays a different picture.

Growing up in an Arab household, our immediate family and our extended family reflected the strong patriarchal influence and a theme of "family is family," which implied active support of many relatives. We lived by the Arabic proverb "A small house has enough room for one hundred people who love each other" and we shared joys, sorrows, money, and things among and across generations.

Although a growing number of studies address different ethnic patterns, few studies address ethnic patterns that occur as the result of remarriages and stepfamilies, or families formed through transnational adoptions (particularly of older children), or transracial domestic adoption or foster care.

Until recently, much of this research presumed family communication issues are similar across ethnic groups, therefore cultural issues have been overlooked or underrepresented. The focus on the "traditional" family has led some scholars to proclaim, "The psychology of marriage as it exists is really a psychology of European American middle class marriage" (Flanagan, et al., 2002, p. 109). Few would disagree that unique family patterns and ethnic heritage combine to create a powerful lineage that influences generations. Fortunately, recent scholarship privileges ethnicity and related family communication patterns.

The family-of-origin plays a significant role in creating and developing its members' communication patterns, tied to the primary functions of cohesion, adaptability, and the *secondary function* of images, themes, boundaries, and biosocial issues. Taken together, all these factors contribute to create a framework for examining family communication.

A FRAMEWORK FOR EXAMINING FAMILY COMMUNICATION

There are numerous approaches to analyzing the family as a system, such as looking at a family as an economic, political, or biological system. Because our concern lies with the interaction within and around the family, this text centers on the communication aspects of the family system. The following statement provides a framework for examining family communication:

> The family is a system constituted, defined, and managed through its communication. Family members regulate cohesion and adaptability to develop a collective identity through the flow of patterned, meaningful messages within a network of evolving interdependent relationships located within a multigenerational lineage and a defined cultural context.

The centrality of this definition necessitates that each segment should be explored separately:

> *The family is a system constituted, defined, and managed through its communication.*

The family may be viewed as a set of people and their relationships that, together, form a complex whole; changes in one part result in changes in other parts of the system. Essentially, family members are linked inextricably to each other; each member, and the family as a whole, reflects any change in the system. Communication—the symbolic, transactional process by which meanings are exchanged—is the means by which families are constituted and regulated.

> *Family members regulate cohesion and flexibility and enact images, themes, boundary setting, and biosocial issues to develop a collective identity . . .*

Communication facilitates a family's movement on the cohesion–adaptability axis (Figure 2.1). The way in which people exchange messages influences the form and content of their relationships. Communication and families mutually affect each other. A family's collective identity is formed through the congruence of the primary and secondary functions.

. . . through the flow of patterned, meaningful messages within a network . . .

Family members cocreate their meanings and their relational culture. Based on families-of-origin and other environmental sources (people and circumstances), each family develops its own set of meanings that become predictable as family members interact with one another using the same patterns over and over again. Such message patterns move across boundaries, define the relationships along specific networks, and determine who interacts with whom.

. . . of evolving interdependent relationships . . .

Family life is not static; both predictable, developmental changes, and unpredictable changes, or stresses, alter the system. Family relationships evolve over time as members join and leave the system and draw closer or move farther apart from each other. Family members struggle with dialectical tensions and boundary management. Yet, due to the family's systemic nature, members remain interdependent, or joined, as they deal with relational issues of intimacy, conflict, roles, power, and decision making.

. . . located within a multigenerational lineage and a defined cultural context.

Families beget families. The multigenerational lineage includes the links across multiple generations and the specific family-of-origin patterns that impact two or three generations very directly. Communication patterns move through generations, reflective of the unique individual members and their interaction practices, as well as the family's ethnic heritage(s).

Family normality or functionality may be viewed as transactional or process oriented. This perspective emphasizes attention to adaptation over the life cycle and adaptation to various contexts. Thus, issues of developmental stages and reaction to change combine with contextual issues such as ethnicity, gender, and socioeconomic status to create a culture within which families operate. Norms and expectations vary greatly across groups of families, but may remain relatively similar for families within a given cultural context. Finally, the spatial context within which a family lives its everyday life affects its functioning.

Throughout the following chapters, we will examine the concepts mentioned in this framework in order to demonstrate the powerful role communication plays in family life. They will highlight the complexity and systematic nature of family life, an often-overlooked reality as indicated in the comment below.

When you really think about it, family life is extremely complex and most of us just go through the motions every day without any reflection. I usually take for granted that most families are similar to mine. However, the more I look carefully at other family systems, the more aware I am of the differences. Perhaps families are like snowflakes, no two are ever exactly alike.

It seems appropriate to close this chapter with Handel and Whitchurch's (1994) statement, which captures the crucial nature of family interaction:

A family creates and maintains itself through its interaction, that is, through social interaction both inside and outside the family, members define their relationships to one another, and to the world beyond the family as they establish individual identities as well as a collective family identity. (p. 1)

CONCLUSION

This chapter described the communication process and proposed a connection between communication patterns and family functions. Communication was explained as a symbolic transactional process. Systems theory serves as the critical underlying theory used to understand family communication. The importance of meaning-making and managing dialectical tensions was addressed. The primary functions discussed were cohesion and flexibility, and the supporting functions include family images, themes, boundaries, and biosocial issues. The chapter concluded with a framework for analyzing family interaction.

In Review

1. Using your own family or a fictional family, identify three areas of "meaning" that would have to be explained to an outsider who was going to be a houseguest for a week. For example, what would have to be explained for the houseguest to understand how this family views the world? (E.g., teasing means Dad likes you).

2. Describe a recurring interaction pattern in a real or fictional family in terms of the predictable verbal and nonverbal messages. Describe the effect of this interaction pattern on the persons involved, or on the family as a whole (e.g., the way a teenager gets permission to take the car for the evening).

3. Give three examples of behavior that might characterize an enmeshed family and three examples of behavior that might characterize a disengaged family.

4. Using a real or fictional family, give an example of how the family moved from one point on the cohesion-flexibility grid to another point due to changes in their lives.

5. How might one of the themes in your family, or one noted in the chapter, be played out in family communication patterns? What image, boundaries, and biosocial issues might support that theme?

6. Identify three communication patterns characterized in a real or fictional stepfamily. Identify and describe how three communication patterns or three themes from a first family moved into the new family configuration or were dropped.

7. What communication patterns have been passed from your family-of-origin, representing key intergenerational transmissions? To what extent have you accepted or rejected these patterns?

KEY WORDS

Cohesion (Primary function) 30
Communication 24
Family images 38
Family themes 39
Flexibility (Primary function) 32
Intergenerational transmission 49

Metacommunication 29
Primary functions 30
Relational dialectics 36
Secondary functions 53
Transactional communication perspective 25

Family Theories

"We live our lives like chips in a kaleidoscope, always
part of patterns that are larger than ourselves and somehow
more than the sum of their parts."

—Salvador Minuchin, *Family Kaleidoscope*

The three Harrison siblings, Justin, Andy, and Beth, ages ranging from 26 to 33, live in Columbus, Ohio, sixty miles from their mother's home. Justin and his long-time partner, Rich, run a successful antiques business; Andy and his fiancée teach in the public schools; and Beth travels regularly as a consultant. Justin and Rich were pleased to see the younger siblings move near them because they enjoy many weekend activities together. These get-togethers serve as a wonderful break from their highly patterned everyday life. Recently the siblings had been sharing concerns about their 58-year-old divorced mother, Sally, who has been acting strangely for about six months—forgetting birthdays, repeating herself multiple times, and getting lost on the 60-mile drive from Granville. Each sibling noted the forgetfulness but reasoned that her stressful high school teaching schedule accounted for the situation. Recently Justin received a phone call from the principal at Sally's school, registering concern about her behavior at school. He heard reports of her leaving class and walking home, withdrawing from lunchtime interactions with friends, and forgetting parent meetings. Two days later Beth's friend called to say he met Sally on the street and she appeared to be lost. He took her home but was quite alarmed.

Last weekend the siblings' conversations centered on plans to talk with their mother about their concerns, arrange for medical tests, and discuss the possibility of closing the house in Granville and moving Sally to Columbus. Yet each sibling noted difficulties in taking time away from work to deal with all these issues. No one could imagine dealing with these multiple concerns given their career commitments. Justin reported they are preparing for their six-week European antiques-hunting trip; Andy is preparing for his wedding in three months; and Beth travels three weeks a month for work. Sally's situation threatens to create significant stress and change for everyone.

Eunjung, an international undergraduate student from Korea, encounters ongoing surprises as she begins to make American friends in her dormitory. When Eunjung hears other students on her floor talking about their conversations with their mothers, she finds herself amazed about how open they are with each other about what is going on in the family and in her friends' lives. Growing up in a traditional Korean family, she was taught to respect the distance between a child and her parents as well as the importance of saving face. Eunjung learned to avoid talking about personal family matters with her friends, as well as to withhold information about her immediate family from outsiders, even extended family members. She avoided telling her personal negative secrets to her friends because it could bring shame to her family members. Therefore, she remains silent if her comments might bring shame to herself or her family.

Although her roommate and friends talk about their parents' divorces or a parent's struggles with alcoholism, such topics are off-limits for Eunjung. In fact, sometimes it is hard to sit through the conversations because they seem so personal. An area of particular discomfort is the way her roommates talk about their grades and test scores. In Korea she learned to talk about such topics with her parents but no member of the family would discuss the topic with outsiders, especially regarding any poor academic performance. Eunjung's greatest surprise came when she heard her friends indicate that they talked about sex with their mothers. Since sexuality was seldom talked about in the Korean families she knew, Eunjung wondered what that experience would be like. When her mother calls, sometimes Eunjung will mention the topics her friends discuss just to see how her mother will react. Usually her mother reminds her to avoid joining in those conversations.

There are many ways to make sense of how a family functions, particularly how communication undergirds every aspect of family life. This chapter describes a set of theories frequently used by scholars to explore family dynamics. Although we cannot address all relevant theories, we will introduce some key theories and terminology that influence family communication research. We will focus on systems theory, symbolic interaction/social constructionism, narrative theory, dialectical theory, and communication privacy management. Understanding these theories and related concepts will help you develop your own framework for analyzing family interactions.

THE SYSTEMS PERSPECTIVE

When individuals come together to form relationships, what is created is larger and more complex than the sum of the individuals; they create a system. When individuals form families, they also create *family systems* through their interaction patterns. The systems perspective provides valuable insights into a family's communication patterns. Family systems theory, an offshoot of general systems theory (GST), provides a framework for understanding the amazing complexities of human organizations. We will focus extensively on family systems theory (Galvin, Dickson, & Marrow, 2006).

The following personal statement provides insight into how a family operates systematically and reflects the complexity of the task of examining families from a systems perspective.

Family life is incredibly subtle and complex. Everything seems tied to everything else. When our oldest daughter, Marcy, contracted spinal meningitis, the whole family reflected the strain. My second daughter and I fought more, while my husband tended to withdraw into himself, which brought me closer to my son. In their own ways, the three children became closer while our marriage became more distant. As Marcy's recovery progressed, there were more changes which affected how we relate now, even eight years later.

Everyday family behavior patterns are often subtle, almost invisible, buried in apparent predictability, yet powerful in their effects. Individuals get caught up, often unconsciously, into their family patterns, as depicted in the case of the Harrison siblings in the chapter's opening case. Unless you view individuals within their primary context, you may never fully understand their behaviors. Simply stated, a *system* is a set of components that interrelate with one another to form a whole. Due to their interconnections, if one component of the system changes, the others will change in response, which in turn affects the initial component. Therefore, a change in one part of the system affects every other part of the system.

Families do not exist in a vacuum; they live within a time period, culture, community, and experience other influences that impact them, directly, such as religion, economic status, or geographical locations. This larger context, or ecosystem, affects a family's life course. From a systems perspective, "Decontexted individuals do not exist" (Minuchin, 1984, p. 2). Persons are considered as part of an overall unit, not as individuals. Imagine a family photograph in which the members are in the background and their relationships are depicted in the foreground. Their patterns of interaction take precedence over the individuals. Therefore, understanding families involves exploring family communication patterns.

When two individuals come together in a relationship, a system is created. It is larger and more complex than the two individuals. Communication serves as the centerpiece of the system. These relationships are formed, maintained, and changed through interaction among the individuals (Duncan & Rock, 1993, p.48). Yerby (1995) captures the power of systems theory, saying:

> Systems theory has taught us to see our own and other family members' behavior as interrelated, to locate predictable patterns of interaction that seem to exert more power over the family than do any individual family members themselves, to see problems in terms of relationship struggles rather than the "fault" of one person who is "scapegoated" and "blamed" for others' pain. Most of all, systems theory has helped us to pay attention to our interdependence. (pp. 339–340)

An individual's behavior becomes more comprehensible when viewed within the context of the human system within which he or she functions and within the broader context in which the family is situated (Cowan & Cowan, 1997).

We will apply the following systems characteristics to families: interdependence, wholeness, patterns/self-regulation, interactive complexity/punctuation, openness, complex relationships, and equifinality (Watzlawick, Beavin, & Jackson, 1967; Whitchurch & Constantine, 1993; Bochner & Eisenberg, 1987; White & Klein, 2002; Galvin, Dickson, & Marrow, 2006).

Interdependence

Within any system, parts are so interrelated as to be dependent on each other for their functioning. Interdependence serves as the centerpiece of a system. In a system, the parts and the relationship between them form the whole; changes in one part will result in changes in the others. Satir (1988) described a family system as a mobile. Picture a mobile that hangs over a child's crib, with people instead of elephants or sailboats on it. As events touch one member of the family, other members reverberate in response to the change in the affected member. If a family member loses a job, wins a scholarship, marries, or joins the military, such an event affects the entire family system; the impact depends on each person's relationship with that individual. In addition, because family members are human beings, not objects, they can "pull their own strings," or make their own moves. If a daughter chooses to withdraw from the family by pulling away, she shifts other members into closer relationships. Thus, as members move toward or away from each other, all members are affected. An evolutionary model of family systems is one that incorporates the possibility of spontaneous or kaleidoscopic change (Hoffman, 1990). No matter what change a family experiences, all members are affected due to their interdependence. You may be able to pinpoint events in your own family, such as an acting-out sibling, that have influenced all members in an identifiable way. A behavior that seems problematic to the outside world may serve an important function within the family system. The following example describes this exact process as seven-year-old Judy exhibits temper tantrums and obnoxious misbehavior:

> When specifically does Judy act up and act out? From what I can piece together, this occurs when her father's distance and her mother's anxious focus on Judy reach intolerable proportions. And what is the outcome of Judy's trouble-making and tantrums? Distant Dad is roped back into the family (and is helped to become more angry than depressed), and the parents are able to pull together, temporarily united by their shared concern for their child. Judy's behavior is, in part, an attempt to solve a problem in the family. (Lerner, 1989, p. 3)

From a family systems perspective, the behavior of each family member is related to and dependent on the behavior of the others. Even in a nuclear family of four this becomes complicated. Stepfamily configurations are more complex when considering the ways members outside the immediate household affect and are affected by members outside the household (Schrodt, et al., 2007). The Harrison siblings, depicted at the beginning of the chapter, are beginning to recognize how the changes in their mother's behavior will impact their everyday life patterns directly.

Wholeness

A family systems approach assumes that the whole is greater than the sum of its parts. An integration of parts characterizes the systems model. Families exhibit

Families are characterized frequently by activities members share.

characteristics that reflect individuals and the interplay of family members. Outsiders use these to characterize the family and each member. The parts, or members, are understood in the context of that whole. The Boyer family may be characterized as humorous, religious and aggressive, yet these adjectives need not apply to each family member. Certain group characteristics may not reflect those of each individual. Wholenesss characterizes a system because behaviors emerge from the interactions of particular individuals. These are called *emergents* or *emergent properties* because they develop or appear only at the systemic level (Whitchurch & Constantine, 1993, p. 329). Conflict or affection may emerge as an inherent part of communication between specific members. A certain comment or action may trigger patterns of behavior without members' awareness. A delightful example follows.

Something wonderful and funny happens when my sister and I get together. We tend to play off each other and can finish each other's sentences, pick up the same references at the same time, and create a dynamic energy that leaves other people out. We don't do it on purpose. Rather, we just seem to "click" with each other and off we go!

Patterns/Self-Regulation

Human beings learn to coordinate their actions, creating patterns together that could not be created individually. Although coordination of actions varies dramatically across family systems, each system develops communication patterns that make life somewhat predictable. Members learn to live within a reciprocal, patterned, and repetitive world. Interaction patterns provide a lens for assessing communication behaviors within a system, because they provide the context for understanding specific behaviors. The following example describes how family members unwittingly can become stuck in a pattern.

> My older sister, Susan (a typical firstborn), managed her anxiety by overfunctioning, and I (a typical youngest) managed my anxiety by underfunctioning. Over time our positions became polarized and rigidly entrenched. The more my sister overfunctioned the more I underfunctioned, and vice versa. (Lerner, 1989, p. 28)

Communication rules constitute a special pattern. Rules are relationship agreements, often unconscious, that prescribe and limit a family member's behavior over time; they are capable of creating regularity out of chaos. Ongoing communication generates rules and is regulated by rules. Rules will be discussed further in Chapter 4.

Human systems attempt to maintain levels of constancy within an overall defined range of acceptable behavior. From a mechanistic viewpoint, a system needs to maintain some type of standard for actions, by noting deviations from the norm and correcting them when they become too significant. The function of maintaining stability in a system is called *calibration*. Calibration implies monitoring and correcting a scale. In the case of a family system, it implies checking and, if necessary, correcting the range of acceptable behaviors. On occasion, the changes happen too dramatically for a family to exert any control. But everyday life is filled with opportunities to maintain or alter family patterns. Although systems can be compared to mechanical operations, human systems are not mechanical and are capable of evolving.

Systems generate maintenance and change-promoting feedback processes. *Maintenance* feedback processes imply constancy or maintaining the standard while minimizing change. *Change-promoting* feedback processes result in recalibration of the system at a different level. You can visualize this process in the following ways. Figure 3.1a represents a system in which maintenance feedback prevents change from occurring. For example, this may happen when a teenager swears at a parent for the first time, yet the rules themselves are not totally stable.

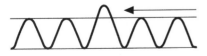
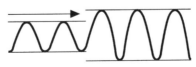

a. Maintenance Feedback
(no change)

b. Change-Promoting Feedback
(change occurs)

FIGURE 3.1
Feedback Systems

The parent may threaten, "You swear at me again and I'll ground you," or appeal to the family values, "We show each other respect even in disagreement." If the teenager becomes frightened by the threat, or apologetic for challenging the family value system, swearing may not occur again.

Figure 3.1b represents a system in which change-promoting feedback occurs. For example, if a wife cannot stop her husband's initial use of physical force, hitting may become part of their long-term conflict pattern. If she threatens him, he may refrain from hitting her again.

Change-promoting feedback processes enable the system to grow, create, innovate, and change, whereas maintenance feedback processes attempt to maintain the status quo. In the following situation, change-promoting feedback processes operate as a father responds to his son's attempts to reach greater physical closeness.

As an adult, I became very aware of the limited physical contact I had with my father. He never touched the boys, with the exception of a handshake. I determined that I wanted a greater physical closeness with him and consciously set out to change our way of relating. The first time I hugged my father was when I returned from a trip and I walked in and put my arms around him. I was nervous and tentative; he was startled and stiff, but he didn't resist. Over time I continued to greet him with hugs until we reached the point at which both of us could extend our arms to each other. I can now see my brothers developing a greater physical closeness to him also.

When a family's communication rules have been developed over time, the family is calibrated, or "set," to regulate its behavior in conformity to those rules. If one or more family members challenge the rules, the family system may be recalibrated in accordance with the new ones.

An unwritten family rule may be that a seriously ill 14-year-old is not allowed to hear the truth regarding his condition. If anyone should suggest that he has a blood disease, maintenance feedback in the form of a parental nonverbal sign or a change of subject may keep him relatively uninformed. The family is "set" not to discuss the issue with him. Yet, the rules may be changed and the system recalibrated through a variety of change-promoting feedback mechanisms. If the adolescent guesses the severity of his illness, he may confront one or more family members and insist on the truth. Once the truth has been told, he cannot return to his previous naive state. Another source of positive feedback may be a doctor who suggests that the young man's condition be discussed with him and may request the family to do so. Human systems must change and evolve in order to survive. Families constantly restructure themselves to cope with developmental stages and unpredictable crises.

The ongoing dialectical struggles of human beings keep a system in some level of flux. In addition, human systems are capable of sudden leaps to new integrations, reflecting a new evolutionary state (Yerby, 1995). The traditional calibration model needs to be modified and placed within an evolutionary framework, recognizing both types of change.

Interactive Complexity/Punctuation

Holding a systems perspective implies a move away from considering causes and effects of behavior, because systems theory maintains cause and effect are interchangeable. When you function as a member of an ongoing relational system, each of your actions serves as both a response to a previous action and a stimulus for a future action. The term *interactive complexity* implies that each act triggers new behavior as well as responds to previous behaviors, rendering pointless any attempts to assign cause and effect. In most families, patterns of behavior take on a life of their own because members' behaviors become intertwined. Family problems are seen in light of relational patterns in which all members play a part; one member is not solely to blame. This approach has been labeled an *illness-free* lens through which to view relationships (Duncan & Rock, 1993).

In order to make sense of the world, human beings tend to "punctuate" sequences of behavior. *Punctuation* refers to the interruption of the sequence of behavior at intervals in order to give it meaning or to indicate that "things started here." Interactions, like sentences, tend to be punctuated, or grouped syntactically, to create meaning. Yet punctuation may serve as a trap, leading people to assign cause and blame to individuals instead of focusing on the problematic pattern of behavior.

Confusion occurs when people punctuate behavioral sequences differently, thereby assigning varied meanings to the behaviors. A son might say, "Our trouble started when my mother became depressed," whereas the mother might indicate that the family problems started when her son began running away from home. Punctuating the cycle according to the son's interpretation implies placing blame on the mother, suggesting that "fixing" her would solve the problem. Punctuating the interaction according to the mother's view implies that the son would be at fault for running away and, if he is "fixed," the family troubles would end. It is pointless to try to locate the "cause" because, even if it could be found, the long-term pattern is what must be addressed, not an individual's past actions. Sometimes family members will "scapegoat" one person, suggesting that he or she is responsible for all the problems and removing themselves from any responsibility. Working from the idea of circular causality within the system, it seems less important to try to punctuate the system by assigning a starting point than it does to look at the act as a sequence of patterns and try to understand this ongoing process. In Figure 3.2, you can imagine the different interpretations that could emerge depending on how the cycle is punctuated. A classic example of punctuation is found in the "nag-withdraw cycle," which demonstrates the pointless nature of looking for cause and effect: "He withdraws because she nags" versus "She nags because he withdraws."

Openness

Just as there are no decontexted individuals, there are no decontexted families. Human systems include individuals, families, communities, and societies that form nested layers. Human systems need interchange with other people, ideas,

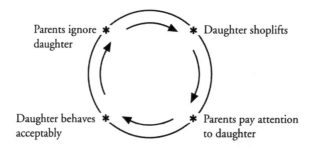

FIGURE 3.2
Circular Causality with a System

and institutions in order to remain physically and psychologically functional. Family members maintain an almost continuous interchange, within and across the family boundary to the larger ecosystem.

Each family operates within the larger ecosystem, which includes legal, educational, political, health, and economic systems, as well as extended family and friendship systems. As a small child, you depended on your family for all your immediate needs, but as you grew older you needed to interact with nonfamily members in order to function in society. Such interchange with and adaptation to the environment is critical.

Family boundary strength depends on how the family views the "outside world." A family's immediate environment may be experienced as threatening, such as when children can be shot walking to school, or supportive and nurturing, such as when neighbors create a kinship network. Individual circumstances, such as that described below, may force a family into active contact with institutions in their environment.

As the parent of a hard-of-hearing child, I am constantly managing our family's boundaries and dealing with outside systems. We deal regularly with the medical community in terms of advances that might affect Melissa's condition. The school counselor and I monitor her classroom placements. I need to keep up with legal changes to ensure that our child's rights are protected in terms of access to special programs. Finally, I am constantly aware of the support of extended family and friends who reach out to help.

Few families can insulate children totally, because schools and media expose them to a range of values and beliefs, some of which may be contrary to those held by the family. Television, the Internet, and music open worlds to children that parents may not even comprehend. Family systems rules include guidelines for maintaining and regulating relationships within the environment, but, in this rapidly changing world, families may not be able to keep pace with the technological advances.

Complex Relationships

Systems embedded in systems create a highly complex set of structures and interaction patterns and may be understood in relation to each other.

Frequently, family members are positioned on vertical dimensions reflecting dynamics of power and privilege. A traditional hierarchical view establishes parents as more powerful than children. In almost all cultures authority, respect, and power go to the older generation, and often to the males of that generation. Appropriate boundaries separate generations; when generational boundaries are blurred, confusion results, such as in the following case.

After my father moved out, I found myself playing surrogate dad to three younger sisters who needed a lot of support. I moved into the role very easily since it seemed to take pressure off my mother who was severely depressed for almost three years. At the time, I just did it. Now I wish I had not given up my adolescence so easily.

Given today's diverse family forms, the traditional hierarchical structures cannot account for multiple family experiences. Immigrant families in the United States face dramatic structural changes as young members gain power as "language brokers," or as the only English speakers. They gain power by controlling their parents' relationships to the schools and larger community.

The complexity of the family system may be seen through the multiple subsystems that contribute to the whole family's functioning. An extended family may include many smaller family units, which in turn contain subsystems. Each family system contains interpersonal systems and individual, or psychobiological, subsystems. In addition, family members interact with institutional systems, such as schools, churches, or governmental agencies.

In most cases, interpersonal subsystems change membership over time. Coalitions develop when individuals align in joint action against others. When one parent gambles, the children and the other parent may form a tight group as a means of coping with the gambler's unpredictable behavior. The coalition may develop strategies for hiding money, supporting the others in arguments, or lying to those outside the system.

Family triangles, characterized by two insiders and one outsider, represent a powerful type of coalition. Under stress two-person relationships may become unstable, so they will draw in a third to stabilize their relationship (McGoldrick, Gerson, & Shellenberger, 1999). Under stress, the insiders try to rope in the outsider to reduce the stress between them. When tensions are low, the outsider may feel isolated. Many stepfamilies struggle with these issues in early years.

I grew up in a house where my dad could not keep a job. My mother and oldest brother formed a tight relationship against him, and sometimes against everyone else. They agreed on everything and my brother became my mother's protector. Even when Dad was employed, he could not break up that coalition, and I think that was one of the reasons they got a divorce. My brother discouraged my mom from ever trusting Dad again.

Triangles often result in frustration and unhappiness for the "third" person. This is especially difficult when the triangle cuts across generations, thereby violating the appropriate boundaries, such as when a parent is aligned with a child against the other parent. A couple can triangulate a child into a scapegoat position by deflecting their marital tension onto the parent-child relationship, thereby labeling the child as the source of all family problems. A child may unwittingly learn to act out when his or her parents fight, thus deflecting their anger and keeping them together.

Equifinality

An open, adaptive family system demonstrates *equifinality*, which means that "a particular final state may be accomplished in different ways and from different starting points" (Littlejohn, 2002, p. 41). There are many ways to reach the same result. Two families may have a theme of "Family members are supportive." Yet, one family may interpret the theme to mean emotional support, whereas the other may view it as an economic issue. There are as many possible ways of reaching a goal as there are families striving for that goal.

Communication and the Systems Perspective

Communication is a key attribute of human systems. Family systems are constituted by the communication process—it is communication that creates, maintains, and changes the system's reality. Individuals in family systems behave according to the meanings they assign to each other, the family, and aspects of the environment. In most families members share relatively congruent or similar worldviews. Communication messages may be viewed as interwoven patterns of interaction that stretch through a family's history rather than as singular events.

Limitations of the Systems Perspective

Decades of thinking and research on systems theory have revealed its limitations, which include gender and individual concerns and contextual issues.

Gender Issues Systems theory has been criticized for ignoring the historical power inequality between males and females in families. A systems view does not adequately address issues such as male violence in the family and the needs of the individual (Galvin, Dickson, & Marrow, 2006). Certain feminist theorists argue that the implicit patriarchal nature of family life goes unchallenged, and an assumed equality of marital power is misleading (Hare-Mustin, 1994). A commonly cited problem area that overlaps gender and individual concerns relates to abusive families in which a systems perspective removes the individual level of responsibility. At the extreme, this suggests that a victim shares equal responsibility for the abuse.

Individual Concerns   Systems theory tends to overlook individual, or psychobiological, issues; the responsibility for problems was placed equally on the members of a troubled relationship. This resulted in inappropriate responsibility being assigned to family members for actions of individuals suffering from actual illness or having genetic predispositions to certain disorders such as manic depression or alcoholism (Broderick, 1993). A genetic predisposition may contribute to an individual member's alcoholism, which impacts not only the individual but the entire family system. Neurobiological structures underlying temperament traits and individual differences are greatly affected by genetic inheritance (McCroskey, 1997). The assumption of shared or equal responsibility can be devastating to family members who are frustrated by the problems, as indicated next.

My brother's attention deficit disorder was not fully understood in our school system and my parents were blamed for his inattention and hyperactive behavior. Over time it became clear that his acting out was a genetic inheritance; two uncles exhibited the same symptoms but they were also considered "difficult." The school personnel made my mother feel like a bad parent because they blamed Kevin's behavior on her discipline style.

Contextual Issues Looking at the family as a whole brings conceptions of interpersonal communication into greater congruence with the *interactional complexity* of family life. This perspective allows one to analyze specific behavior patterns in terms of the interpersonal context in which they occur and to understand their meaning in light of the entire family system. Parents who intuitively operate from this systemic premise are more likely to emphasize the circumstances rather than the individual child in their initial responses. Similarly teachers who hold this perspective would be looking for contextual influences on an acting-out student before moving to individual issues because they are trying to discover if the problematic behavior is a symptom of concerns in his or her family life. In contrast, some theorists argued that systems approaches can be aided by individual approaches that recognize biological components of the problem (Beatty, McCroskey, & Heisel, 1998).

SOCIAL CONSTRUCTIONISM/SYMBOLIC INTERACTION

Social construction and symbolic interaction, both interpretive theories, address the construction of meaning. Each theory emphasizes the centrality of social interaction and the joint action necessary to maintain interaction while stressing the significance of symbols, primarily language. Although these interpretive theories are often viewed as interconnected, Leeds-Hurwitz (2006) maintained they are distinct, arguing that "what separates them is that social constructionism is centrally concerned with how people make sense of the world, especially through language, and emphasizes the study of relationships; whereas symbolic interaction's central concern is making sense of the self and social roles" (p. 233). Each theory emphasizes different issues and they will be discussed separately.

Social constructionism proposes that (1) people make sense of the world by constructing their own model of the social world and how it works, and (2) language is viewed as critical to human society; therefore, conversation serves to maintain reality (Leeds-Hurwitz, 2006). Social constructionism places a unique focus on how meanings are created and negotiated *situationally* by actors, rather than significantly influenced by societal norms or expectations. For example, each family creates its own world; discourse-dependent families are formed as members constitute their family identity through language and interaction. Social constructionists believe that "the events and objects of the social world are *made* rather than *found*" (Griffin, 1997, p. 70).

According to Klein and White (1996), "The private understandings constructed by family members are based on their shared history, perspective, and interpretation of events. Dating and marriage are viewed as a process by which separate individuals 'fuse' into a common living arrangement and worldview" (p. 107). In their classic work, Berger and Kellner (1964) captured marital meaning-creation, saying, "Each partner's definition of reality must be continually correlated with the definitions of the other" (p. 224). Such correlation depends on communication. In order to form a marital system, a couple must negotiate a set of common meanings through interaction and mutual accommodation so that, eventually, the meanings for one are linked through conjoint action with the meanings of the other. Recently Holtzman (2008) explored the power of family definitions ranging from traditional (biological and/or legal) and socially expansive (i.e., non-biological and nonlegal) relationships.

Finally, families are meaning-generating systems since all social systems are created by their communication. Yerby (1995) explained the relationship between systems theory and social construction, saying:

> The assertion that families are linguistically constructed and co-constructed reflects the social constructionist view that families are meaning-generating systems and that meaning is generated through the conversation or dialogue between and among participants in a social system. The assumption is that all social systems are defined by their communication. (p. 357)

In ongoing relationships, members either develop the ability to recognize shared meanings and negotiate joint understandings through their interactions. Or, members struggle constantly with the lack of shared meanings on critical issues. One person discovers the reason his partner's belief that "having a third beer" implies a drinking problem is because her father became drunk after more than two beers. Although most family members co-construct shared meanings, perfect agreement never results. As individuals form new families or families merge through remarriage, new negotiation processes are set in motion.

Symbolic interaction emphasizes the self, meanings, and construction of self through interaction. This theory places a strong focus on social roles, assuming that (1) humans think about and act according to the meanings they attribute to their actions and contexts and (2) humans are motivated to create meanings to help them make sense of the world. Klein and White (1996) captured this view in the following example:

> A 3-year-old may show no interest in a particular toy doll. But when an older sibling plays with the doll, it suddenly takes on new interactional and situational meaning. Now, the doll is desired. The meaning of the toy is constructed by the situational interaction of the two siblings. (p. 92)

Symbolic interactionism focuses on the connection between symbols, or shared meanings, and interactions, or verbal and nonverbal communication (LaRossa & Reitzes, 1993). This approach views families as social groups; interaction fosters the development of self and group identity. The following assumptions reflect the importance of meaning for human behavior:

1. Human beings act toward things on the basis of the meanings that the things have for them.
2. Meaning arises out of the process of interaction between people.
3. Meanings are handled in and modified through an interpretive process used by the person in dealing with things he or she encounters. (LaRossa & Reitzes, p. 143)

Essentially, symbolic interaction requires paying attention to how events and experiences are interpreted by the actors (White & Klein, 2002). Meaning is negotiated through the use of language. This meaning-making process may be voluntary or involuntary, explicit or implicit, but it is always tied to language and discourse.

According to social interaction theorists, individuals and small groups are influenced by larger cultural and societal processes, and interpretation processes may be similar across groups who share similar contexts. Thus, ethnicity, gender, religion, and socioeconomic status would influence the interpretation process.

The importance of symbolic interaction from a family perspective is critical for both (1) defining families and (2) making sense out of family interaction. Thus, it is through the process of interacting together in family roles that people establish a boundary between insiders and outsiders, thereby creating their family.

Interaction among family members and the interpretation of that interaction serves as the source of meanings for each member. Partners or siblings frequently do not label the same events as fights, apologies, or invitations. How often have you heard someone say, "I apologized to you" and the other reply, "I never got an apology from you." Eventually you may hear, "I did so apologize. I took you to dinner." The issue revolves around one partner's assumption that "taking someone to dinner" means "apologizing." Enduring relationships are characterized by agreements between members as to the meaning of their interconnections. These persons develop a relationship worldview reflecting the members' symbolic interdependence.

Communication undergirds and illuminates the structure of kinship relationships. The form and content of family messages combine to create a family's view of itself and the world. Members of family systems, through their interdependence and mutual influence, create meanings and construct a reality based on their interaction patterns. These selected tenets of social constructionism and symbolic interaction will guide your thinking about the importance of families as meaning-making systems.

RELATIONAL DIALECTICS

Family relationships are not static—they are constantly in process. Dialectical theory reflects social theorist's Mikhail Bakhtin's view that social life is an open "dialogue" characterized by multiple voices and variability. This theory relies heavily on the concept of multivocality (Baxter & Braithwaite, 2008). A dialectical perspective highlights the continual tensions that relationships must manage. Relational dialectical theory asserts that meanings emerge from the struggle of different, often opposing discourses. "Looked at dialectically, relationships are defined and shaped over time by the ways in which partners manage contradictions" (Littlejohn, 2002, p. 238). The shift toward dialogue recognizes that "family life is a both/and experience—families gain their meanings from the give-and-take interplay of multiple competing themes or perspectives . . ." (Baxter, 2006, p. 131). Sometimes this is referred to as the "me-we pull," or a desire to be with one's partner or sibling at the same time one wants independence (Baxter & Montgomery, 1996). *Dialectical tensions* are reflected in questions such as: How close can we get without interfering with each other? How can we live together without hurting each other too much? These questions are indicators of the tensions in all relationships. A dialectical approach focuses on competing and opposite possibilities that exist in a relationship (Brown, Werner, & Altman, 1994). It recognizes the tension between members of a family as they negotiate and renegotiate what it means to be in a functioning relationship. Many communication scholars are interested in the contradictions of married or postmarital life (Baxter & Braithwaite, 2002; Graham, 2003; Prentice, 2009) and stepfamily life (Baxter, Braithwaite, Bryant & Wagner, 2004); fewer have applied this theory to parent-child relations (Afifi, 2003; Krusiewicz & Wood, 2001).

Communication scholars identify a range of possible dialectical tensions, including autonomy-connection, openness-closedness, and predictability-novelty (Baxter, 1990). A common struggle in almost all relationships revolves around issues of closeness and distance, sometimes called autonomy and connection, as you saw in the cohesion axis in Chapter 2. An adolescent may wish to be independent yet connected to her parents. A parent and young adult daughter may struggle with the boomerang effect as they negotiate autonomy-connection when she moves home after college (Vogl-Bauer, 2009). The openness-closedness tension refers to family members' conflicting needs to be open and expressive as well as private. Finally, the predictability-novelty tension is reflected in partners' struggles regarding a desire for constancy, ritual, and familiarity as well as a competing need for excitement and change. A dialectical approach does not mean that a relationship experiences constant overt tensions. Although at critical times relational struggles surface, more often the dialectical tensions exist in the background. In other words, "dialectics may work backstage in a relationship beyond partners' mindful awareness or ability to identify and describe them, but still contributing a sense of unsettledness or instability in the relationship" (Montgomery, 1992, p. 206).

Stepfamily members may find themselves pulled by competing forces, when members' significant dialectical dilemmas involve managing the voluntary marital relationship and the involuntary stepparent-stepchild relationship (Cissna, Cox, & Bochner, 1990). In their examination of stepparent-stepchild interaction, Baxter and colleagues (2004) focused on three underlying contradictions of this relationship. Stepchildren desired open communication with stepparents yet also resented it and they desired emotional closeness but also valued distance; they indicated a desire for power to remain with the residential parent, while also wishing the residential parent and stepparent would share authority.

It's been six years and I still can't reach some stability with my stepdaughter. Just when we seem to have made progress and are getting closer, we take four steps backward. One day she asks my advice on how to talk to her dad, and a week later she makes fun of me in front of him. Or she tells me how worried she is about her boyfriend, and the next time I ask about him, she says it's none of my business.

Although dialectical tensions are ongoing, partners or family members make efforts to manage them through a set of strategies that include the following: (1) selection, (2) segmentation, (3) neutralizing, (4) cyclic alteration, and (5) reframing (Baxter, 1990; West & Turner, 2010). *Selection* implies making choices between opposites. An older couple may choose intense togetherness to the exclusion of individual friends or interests. *Segmentation* involves denying the interdependence of the contrasting elements by uncoupling or separating them according to context or arena. Members of a family business may be close at home but distant in the workplace. *Neutralizing* implies diluting the intensity of the contrasting poles. A grandmother and granddaughter may monitor their personal sharing to keep from being closed off from each other or enmeshed with each other. *Cyclic alteration* occurs when family members choose one of the opposite poles at varying times. A mother and daughter may set aside time for each other and time to spend with individual friends; a father and daughter may be very close during her preteen years but distance themselves in early teen years. *Reframing* involves transforming a perception of the elements so the apparent contradictions are not viewed as polar opposites. A partner who used to view autonomy as the opposite of connection and now views it as a way of bringing greater closeness to the couple has reframed the tension. An athletic father may reframe his son's passion for music as providing new avenues for mutual sharing as opposed to seeing it as rejection. A dialectical approach recognizes that relationships develop and deteriorate, but it stresses the ongoing struggles characteristic of the overall life of a relationship.

Finally, a family unit may experience dialectical tensions across family boundaries as members negotiate with institutions, such as schools or courts, as well as extended family members or friends. They face contradictions such as inclusion-exclusion, conventionality-uniqueness, and revelation-concealment. Members may struggle to balance "family time" with the inclusion of friends at all family events. If family members are viewed as "weird" by community members on the basis of areas such as religious expression or artistic interests, members may try to manage that perception with contributions to schools or the community.

Clearly dialectical tensions forcefully impact family life. The essential concepts of this approach—change, connection, and contradiction—are inherent in the family's interaction. This theory emphasizes the importance of uncertainty to the continued growth of relationships and the importance of communication in creating "space for individuals and relationships to change" (Baxter & Braithwaite, 2009, p. 34).

NARRATIVE THEORY/NARRATIVE PERFORMANCE THEORY

Narrative theory and narrative performance theory represent meaning-centered approaches.

Narrative Theory

"When it comes to human lives, storytelling is sensemaking" (McAdams, 2006, p. 76). We tell each other stories to make sense of our worlds. Narrative theorist Walter Fisher maintains, "Humans are essentially storytellers" (1987, p. 64). According to narrative theory, humans experience life in narrative form and find personal meanings for their stories through interpretation, not objective observation. Similar stories may have different meanings for various tellers. Narration involves verbal and nonverbal symbolic actions, words and/or deeds, set within a sequence of events that have meaning for those who create or interpret them. As a narrator you engage in self-discovery and self-creation. The following assumptions support Fisher's (1987) narrative paradigm:

- The essential nature of humans is rooted in stories.
- People decide which stories to accept or reject, based on what makes sense or on good reasons.
- Good reasons are determined by history, biography, culture, and character.
- The standards for narrative rationality are coherence and fidelity.
- Humans experience the world as a set of stories. As they choose among them, they create and recreate their lives.

Narrative researchers do not seek objectivity. Rather they ask, "What interpretations do people construct for their lived experiences? What significance do they assign to the events and moments of their lives?" (Babrow, Kline, & Rawlins, 2005, p. 34). Two criteria determine the rational quality of a narrative and its ability to persuade or teach (Fisher, 1987). First, it must be *cohesive*—realistic, meaningful, and free of inconsistencies. Second, a narrative must display *fidelity*—appear truthful or reliable. *Narrative coherence* implies an internal consistency; all parts of the story are present and fit together. Sections of the story should not contradict each other. Overall coherence includes: (1) structural coherence, where elements flow smoothly and they are not confusing or jumbled; (2) material coherence or the degree of congruence between this story and related ones; and (3) characterological coherence or the extent to which the characters appear consistent. You experience narrative coherence when parts of the story work together; this story "fits" with other related stories and the characters are described in ways that seem consistent with what else you know about them.

Fidelity implies that a story needs direct ties to social reality in order to resonate with listeners' personal experiences and beliefs. The criterion for fidelity is "logic of good reasons." This implies truthfulness and reliability, or the sense that (1) this story appears, on the face of it, to be honest and plausible and (2) it appears to resonate with listeners' personal experiences and beliefs. For example, you find narrative characters believable when they act as you do or as you imagine you would act.

Narratives fall into overarching types: "recounting" or "accounting for" (Fisher, 1987), also described as stories/narratives and accounts (Koenig Kellas 2010). Recounting provides a history—a retelling of memories of what was experienced; accounting includes explanations or reasons for persons' behaviors or situations. Family narratives may be categorized easily into one of these types.

Narrative theorists and researchers often focus on family narratives because of their centrality to human life. For example, Dan McAdams examines narratives of generativity told in adulthood or "the adult's concern for, and commitment to promoting the welfare and development of future generations" (2006, p. 4). He concludes that adults focus most of their generativity on their families and their stories reflect this familial experience.

Family narrative scholars focus extensively on stories that recount experiences, such as births or adoptions, how we met, memorable events or ancestors' lives. Current family research explores areas such as adoption (Suter & Ballard, 2009; Docan-Morgan, 2010; Harrigan, 2010), standards for family relationships (Vangelisti, Crumley, & Baker, 1999), functions of family stories across ethnic backgrounds (Bylund, 2003), the role of aunts in family relationships (Sotirin & Elington, 2006), family members' health (Manoogian, Harter, & Denham, 2010), and stories couples tell to cover for each other (Hest, Pearson, & Child, 2006). Painful or "dark side of narratives" (Koenig Kellas, 2010) and stories that serve as accounts for behavior have received less attention. These include explanations of divorce or other failed relationships (Weber, Harvey, & Stanley, 1987) or explanations of why a spouse's ideal standards are not met (Vangelisti & Alexander, 2002).

Narrative Performance Theory

Narrative performance theory focuses on the actual performance or telling of the family stories, exploring the communicative practice of storytelling as one way of "doing family." Theorists explain their attention to the actual performance of storytelling saying, "Storytelling is participatory. In performance terms, family storytelling forms a system of shifting relationships among audiences and storytellers, narrators and characters" (Langellier & Peterson, 2006, p. 102). The strategic function of narrating serves as the theory's central concern. The narration of certain stories changes as children age, becoming an increasingly interactive storytelling performance. In her study of storytelling in families formed through international adoption, Harrigan (2010) found that adoptive mothers used artifacts, such as pictures of first meetings or a child's homeland, as an interactive tool; children often participated verbally and nonverbally in the storytelling. Over time these stories became more elaborate as the children asked questions or grew old enough to understand certain information.

The interactional work of family storytelling is ordered according to generation and gender (Langellier & Peterson, 2006). Conditions such as context and content constrain narration: for example, who is present and what is appropriate for the age or gender of those present? In addition, family storytelling operates according to norms of power and knowledge. A parent may forbid the repetition of stories that serve to ridicule a particular relative, or the older generation may tell the family immigration story because they experienced it. The right to perform certain stories may be passed down through generations according to gender.

Many families create explicit or implicit storytelling rules. These may determine who may speak or listen on a particular subject (who can tell and who can hear the "Dad got busted for speeding" story) and how such roles are determined (after Grandpa passed away, Aunt Lou and Dad may tell the immigration saga together). Rules may even address the way to present the content (respectfully, humorously), coherence (what details to include so the car accident story makes sense), and consequences (the price that is paid if Pete and Ellen use four-letter words in the telling).

Observing jointly told family stories provides insight into family identity construction. Researchers usually audiotape or videotape the family members telling narratives; these tapes are analyzed using concepts such as turn-taking, perspective-taking, and engagement. Over time, storytelling experiences may become somewhat scripted or patterned; they may be told jointly by partners, siblings, parents, and children. For example, Dickson (1995) interviewed couples who had been married more than 50 years and, in addition to analyzing the content of their responses, she focused on their storytelling patterns. One couple is described as follows: "They do not talk to each other; they consistently talk to the interviewer. . . . They rarely talk at the same time like other couples who appear more connected. . ." (pp. 45–46). Jointly shared storytelling occurs when family members construct stories through collaborative interaction. Plot, character, and setting may be developed in a way that helps assign meaning to the event(s) and to their relationships (Koenig Kellas, 2005). As family members co-construct stories they may agree or disagree, contradict or question each other, add or reject details, and correct or clarify information.

When my Uncle Jake died in Iraq his youngest son, Jack, was only 18 months old. My aunt decided that as part of the burial process we would have a long evening of storytelling about Uncle Jake so all three of his kids, but especially Jack, would remember him. It was really hard, but she collected 22 stories from relatives and friends. We laughed and cried for hours. Everyone in the family now has a copy of the CD and we will all remember Uncle Jake at special times in our lives. Even his future grandchildren will get to know Uncle Jake a little bit.

Tellers develop narrative identities and perform them for actual audiences—other people in the space and internal audiences or those people imagined to be there—a former wife, a hospitalized child—who influence the performance. Narrative performance is a fluid process. Families make sense of events and innovate meanings, they remember and forget stories and they reinterpret and emphasize what has been marginal or muted (Langellier & Peterson, 2006). Eventually both teller and listener develop their "narrative knowing" or what it is you learn from stories (McAdams, 2006).

Communication Privacy Management Theory (CPM)

Every family has its private information and secrets that are to be shared only with certain persons. Younger members learn the rules for managing family information through directions they receive from parents or other older members; different individuals establish privacy guidelines with one or more other members as new events occur that affect the family. Some members may choose to keep certain information secret from one or more family members. Communication privacy management (CPM) theory, developed by communication scholar Sandra Petronio, places communication at the core of understanding how family members negotiate private information (Petronio, 2002, 2006, 2010). This theory directly relates to the everyday family experience of managing the dialectical tensions of privacy and disclosure. Using a "boundary" metaphor to identify the border around private information, CPM theory asserts that the regulation of private information depends on the family's rule-based management system or their rules that developed over time.

This theory addresses communication management issues of ownership that control permeability and change (Petronio & Caughlin, 2006). One or more persons have *ownership* of private information and believe they have the right to *control* revealing or concealing that information. A whole family may own a secret that is not to be shared with outsiders; a pair of siblings may share a secret; or an individual may maintain a secret known to no other family member. Over time, such agreements may be changed or ignored. Boundaries may be *permeable,* or flexible, as some members share information with each other. Finally, boundaries *change* over time as circumstances lead members to include or exclude others from certain information. Privacy management, a very complex process, addresses the tension between "the need to be connected to family members while retaining a sense of autonomy apart from those members" (Petronio, 2010, p. 175).

Communication privacy management theory identifies four concepts that guide the rule management process: boundary rule formation, boundary rule usage, boundary rule coordination, and boundary turbulence (Petronio, 2002).

Boundary Rule Formation   Boundary rule formation refers to the factors that regulate the flow of information between and among others. It relies on six criteria—culture, self-esteem, gender, motivation, context, and the risk/reward ratio. *Culture* encompasses the family's global or ethnic culture. The concept of "saving face" espoused by Asian cultures may limit the negative private information that is shared with persons outside a Korean family, as depicted in the case of Eunjung and her family in the opening of this chapter. If a family's ethnic culture supports beliefs or actions which are forbidden by the local culture, such as the religious sacrifice of chickens, such information will be kept secret.

Self-esteem affects willingness to share. If one has high self-esteem, sharing negative and positive information may be comfortable; if one has low self-esteem, privacy may be prized in order to avoid rejection. One member may keep a secret from all family members because her self-esteem is low at a certain point in time. *Gender* may affect how much is shared inside or outside the family. More than males, females are socialized to create strong relationships through personal conversations; sisters or mother-daughter pairs may share more private information than brothers or father-son pairs.

A family member's *motivation,* such as to help or manipulate another member, affects privacy management. A stepfather may reveal his teenage arrest for drunken driving only when his teenage stepdaughter is getting her license as a way to help her avoid his mistake. The *context* (situation or setting) may support revealing information or make concealing desirable. A long road trip may lead an older cousin to tell her teenage cousin about her poor academic college performance as a warning, or a loud, crowded restaurant may deter a father from discussing the family's economic difficulties with his children. Finally, family members consider the *risk/reward ratio* of sharing certain information. A couple may struggle with how to discuss the husband's firm desire to remain child-free and the wife's uncertainty about this position. Continually bringing up the subject creates tension triggering the risk of disagreement, yet reaching a joint decision would provide a desirable outcome (Durham & Braithwaite, 2009).

Boundary Rule Usage   These six criteria discussed above serve to create boundary access rules that affect (1) decisions whether to talk about a particular subject or not, (2) how to talk (depth of conversation) about the subject, and (3) the timing of any discussion. Family members must consider the impact of telling certain information to a particular person. This involves considering what might be the short-term or long-term cost of the disclosure. Might it hurt another person for no reason? For example, if a woman sees her former brother-in-law holding hands with a woman in the park, should she tell her sister? If an older sister knows her brother is failing three classes in his freshman year of college should she tell her parents? Sometimes the issue involves how much information is shared. Should a ninety-year-old grandparent in a nursing home be told his granddaughter was diagnosed with terminal ovarian cancer or should he be told she received a cancer diagnosis and she is recovering well from surgery? Finally, the timing of a disclosure must be considered. If a close cousin has just suffered a miscarriage, another female cousin may postpone announcing her pregnancy for a while in order to be sensitive to the recent loss.

Additional rules may be triggered by new events. A significant drop in income may require telling children about financial problems, even though family finances have seldom been discussed. Community rumors may force an adult daughter to tell her parents about her husband's affair at work. Whereas adults may control their privacy boundaries rather easily, younger and older family members have more permeable privacy boundaries issues, due to their medical needs or their access to transportation, which may necessitate involving others. Women experiencing infertility reported their privacy boundaries became more permeable as they had to talk about delicate and sensitive topics such as sex and bodily fluids in new ways (Bute & Vik, 2010).

Boundary Rule Coordination Small or large groups of family members may co-own private information. Once an individual shares his or her private information with another person, that information is co-owned. When that happens, the co-owners may explicitly or implicitly coordinate their private boundaries. Agreements or explicit rules may be established as to how that information may be shared with others, such as when a grandfather sternly reminds his granddaughter that she is never to tell anyone that he entered the country illegally as a small child. Or the teller may assume the hearer will implicitly understand the expected level of privacy, such as when teenagers understand they should not tell others about Mom's drinking problem. Rules regarding co-ownership tend be more effective when the need for secrecy is explicitly stated and the ties between parties are strong. A third cousin may not feel as compelled to protect a secret as a sister, especially if the news is not labeled explicitly as "secret" or "private."

Boundary Turbulence Boundary turbulence arises when persons become confused as they attempt to manage multiple boundaries or when situational stresses force persons to reconsider a rule-bound agreement. Sometimes it can be as simple as an individual's assumption that "I tell my spouse everything," but the person sharing the information never imagined such an assumption. Other times people misunderstand the privacy agreement or forget that the information should be kept private. Occasionally people learn another's private information by accident, such as overhearing a phone call or receiving a misdirected e-mail, which can create a dilemma.

Privacy dilemmas develop under a range of conditions. These include: (1) The confidant may believe the teller will be harmed if the information is not revealed. A brother's drug use may escalate and the other siblings may feel compelled to tell a parent in order to get treatment for him. (2) The private information may be revealed accidentally. A member of a family business may inadvertently gain access to a parent's medical information by seeing the label on a parent's medical prescription. Or a pediatric oncologist may discuss a child's cancer diagnosis with a parent while a grandparent is in the room (Duggan & Petronio, 2009). (3) Illicit activity may be revealed by accident. A teenager may encounter e-mail information indicating that a parent is having an affair. (4) A family member may encounter information that places him or her in a dilemma—taking care of the other or oneself. A teenage niece may turn to a favorite aunt for money for an abortion; her aunt may realize that protecting her niece could jeopardize her future connections to her brother and her entire extended family, which strongly opposes abortion.

CONCLUSION

This chapter described some of the major theories that undergird family interaction. It established that a family system consists of members, relationships among them, family attributes, and an environment in which the family functions. Social constructionism and symbolic interaction theory describe meaning-making processes, which create and reflect family patterns and understandings. Narrative theory and narrative performance theory explore and demonstrate the power of story to family identity construction and meaning-making. The ongoing processes of managing dialectical tensions both within a family and between a family and the ecosystem were addressed within relational dialectical theory. Finally, the exploration of communication privacy management theory reflects the power and complexity of family boundary regulation.

In Review

1. Using the systems terminology, describe how a change in one member of a real or fictional family affected the other family members.
2. Using a real or fictional family, describe its calibrated level for acceptable conflict behaviors. Describe attempts to change this calibrated level using the concepts of maintenance or change-promoting feedback processes.
3. Relying on symbolic interactionism, describe how similar behaviors enacted by different family pairs may be interpreted in different ways.
4. Identify one or more significant narratives that serve to create family meaning (values, identity) in a real or fictional family.
5. Reflecting on a couple you know, explain how these partners attempt to manage two dialectical tensions. Give examples.
6. Describe a real or media situation in which information, thought by the family member or "information owner" to be private, became public knowledge. Explain the effect of the exposed secret on the information owner and other family members.

KEY WORDS

Boundary rule formation   75
Dialectical tensions   70
Equifinality   66
Family system   57
Interactional complexity   67
Interdependence   59

Narrative coherence   72
Narrative fidelity   72
Punctuation   63
Social constructionism   68
Symbolic interaction   69

Communication Patterns and the Creation of Family Identity

"How is one to know which patterns to look for, let alone identify,
when one is in the presence of a strange family, peering into the
gloom of its manifold transactions?"

—Lynn Hoffman

Simon Greenwald, age 86, sat stone-faced as his 52-year-old daughter, Sarah, made her recurring plea one more time. "Dad, you have to tell us about your childhood in Warsaw and your two years in the concentration camp. We need to know your story before you are no longer able to tell it. My children and Ari's children need to know that part of their heritage. Ari and I deserve to hear about that part of your life. Mother died before we were old enough to understand the importance of your stories and ask her about it." Simon, appearing anxious and depressed, responded predictably, "I do not talk about that time. It needs to stay in the past." Sara continued, "You need to get beyond the sadness and silence that you have held in all those years." After more discussion Simon finally replied, "I'll think about it. Maybe I'll write about it so I can do it my way." Sara agreed reluctantly, viewing this as one more avoidance strategy.

Four months later Simon handed a sheaf of papers to both Sarah and Ari saying, "I'll answer questions if you have any." The siblings were amazed at what they read. They learned their father and mother had met in the camp as older teenagers and vowed to search for each other, if and when they got out. Ari and Sarah had believed their parents met after the war. Their father depicted a happy childhood in Warsaw before Hitler's rise to power. Simon's older brother was killed in a resistance action. His parents died in the concentration camp. Two days later Sarah indicated that she and Ari had questions and requested to audiotape his responses. Much to her surprise Simon agreed saying, "As I wrote these words I realized that you and your brother deserved to know the truth and so should my grandchildren." Two days later Simon talked for hours at the kitchen table as the recorder captured every word. Within the next two months his grandchildren began to understand their grandparents and their family heritage in an entirely new way.

Emily wishes she could disappear on Mother's Day. Although Sharon, the woman her father married two years after her mother died, tries to be good to her, on days like this it's hard to even look at her. Emily just wants to take a walk with her mother and stop at the bookstore where her mother would select a book for her holiday present and a proud young Emily would pay for it with her babysitting money. Her brother Jake, age seven, and eight years younger, has an easier time with holidays because he was quite young when the car accident happened. He doesn't remember all the holiday rituals with her mother's relatives—the Thanksgiving family baseball game, the elaborate Christmas Eve dinner at her grandmother's, or the Fourth of July parade and barbeque. Her uncles told crazy jokes, her aunts told wonderful stories about growing up, and her grandmother taught her many of their Swedish family recipes.

Emily's family moved into Sharon's big house, about 30 miles away, and the holidays are spent with her father's family or Sharon's relatives, although Dad will drive Emily over to see her grandmother and other relatives on Christmas morning. Sometimes Emily feels as if she is the only person in her family who misses their old life. Even Jake prefers to stay with his stepbrothers to play with their toys. No one talks about Mom on her birthday or on the day she died. Sharon reminds her brother but Jake does not remember much about her. Emily fears that she will lose her precious memories of her mother.

Communicaton patterns serve as the foundation of family identity. The previous chapter examined the family from various theory perspectives; this chapter centers on the patterned meaning-making function of families. It is through communication that family members manage their everyday lives and construct their collective identity. In order to understand the significant role that meaning plays in the relational development of identity, this chapter will address (1) the formation of a family's relational culture through communication and (2) the development of those meanings through four key communication patterns: family communication rules, family secrets, family networks, and family narratives. Selected tenets of systems theory, symbolic interaction theory, and narrative theory will guide your thinking about the importance of families as meaning-making systems constructing their realities through communication.

RELATIONAL CULTURES

Each of you learns to interpret and evaluate behaviors within your family system while simultaneously creating a set of meanings that may not be understood by an outsider. Every family system creates its own worldview that reflects members' shared beliefs and meanings. Members may not identify equally with the worldview that undergirds their family's communication patterns.

Communication involves not only interchanges among family members, but also shapes and alters the structure of the family system, affecting each individual family member. Communication serves to create a relational culture, a privately transacted system of understandings reflecting the attitudes, actions, and identities of participants in a relationship. Coordinated understandings emerge from a *jointly constructed worldview* or relational culture. A *relational culture* is a "private world of rules, understandings, meanings, and patterns of acting and interpreting that partners create for their relationship" (Wood, 2007, p. 308). Relational cultures emerge from ongoing communication patterns as members build, maintain, alter, and sometimes dissolve their connections. Just as close friends and romantic pairs form relational cultures, family members also form powerful relational cultures with long-lasting effects.

Consider partners' behaviors as they develop a family system. Each must undergo a process of mutual accommodation by developing a set of patterned transactions—"ways in which each spouse triggers and monitors the behavior of the other and is, in turn, influenced by the previous behavioral sequence. These transactional patterns form an invisible web of complementary demands that regulate many family situations" (Minuchin, 1974, p. 17). To form a two-partner system, individuals must negotiate a set of common meanings. This negotiation process is both subtle and complex; some couples never effectively accomplish this task. Partners who succeeded are described below.

My parents see each other as intelligent, attractive, loving, and genuine. They don't respond well to each other when it is obvious that the other partner is trying to avoid conflict. They openly discuss problems relating to their personal relationship, inner feelings, and children because they desire to grow together through the good times and the bad times. My parents are a highly interdependent couple who value being together and experiencing life as partners yet they enjoy their separate careers and friends outside of the home. Both believe they need each other, plus their sense of independence, to make themselves spiritually whole.

Partners strive to create mutually meaningful language. Similarities in their physical and social processes assure some generalized common meanings. However, the intent of some behaviors, if not discussed, may be misinterpreted; yet, these behaviors and their interpretations become part of the relational meaning pattern. Usually, the more similar the partners' backgrounds, the less negotiation is needed. Relying on the verbal and nonverbal repertoire available, couples negotiate a set of common meanings reflecting their physical, social, and individual competencies. When behaviors are interpreted in similar ways, or interpretations are discussed and clarified, similar meanings emerge and clearer communication results.

Words play a significant role in developing a relational culture; research on distressed and non-distressed partners indicates that nonverbal behavior is also an important contributor to the relational culture. In his early work, Gottman (1979) found that distressed couples were more likely to "express their feelings, mind read, and disagree, all with negative nonverbal behavior" (pp. 467–468). In some cases they express contempt, powerfully indicated by eye rolling, sarcasm, mocking, name-calling, or belligerence (Gottman & Gottman, 2006), sometimes referred to as "the sulfuric acid of love" (Gottman, 1999, p. 47). When families add members the relational culture becomes more complex.

As a family system evolves, communication among members affects the continuously developing relationships. Over time family members come to have certain meanings within each relationship.

Our communication patterns tend to separate family members from each other, although Mom and Amy are really joined against Dad. Here's a typical example of the family in action:

Mom: *Sam, let's go to the zoo. The kids would love to see the animals.*

Dad: *I'm tired of doing what the kids want. Let's just stay home.*

Sister: *Damn, Dad, you never want to do anything that we like.*

Mom: *Amy, watch your language. Now, apologize to your father!*

Sister: *No, he doesn't care about us.*

Dad: *That's correct. I don't care! (Very serious facial expression.)*

Scott: *We always have these fights. Why do we bother being a family?*
       (Scott storms to his room.)

After living within these patterns for years, we are so used to the "moves" that as soon as one person hears the predictable opening line the entire family starts to move through the predictable script.

Well-coordinated meanings do not develop easily. Partners may struggle for years to reach similarity in interpreting and responding to each other's behaviors. Parents and children may live with serious misunderstandings throughout most of their lives as a result of communication breakdowns. For example, if two siblings sense parent favoritism, both may consciously avoid the subject, or one may resist the other's attempt to explore the subject.

COMMUNICATION PATTERNS THAT INFLUENCE FAMILY MEANINGS

Family meanings emerge through the continuous interpretation of, and response to, messages. Over time these interactions become predictable, forming communication patterns or complex sets of "moves" established through repetition that has become predictable without conscious awareness. Over time these patterns serve to create meanings and define relationships. Communication patterns emerge from the reciprocally shared verbal and nonverbal messages, recurring and predictable within family relationships; they may be altered by forces within the ecosystem or the family system itself. To fully understand how these family meanings emerge from patterns, the following areas must be explored: (1) family communication rules, (2) family secrets, (3) family communication networks, and (4) family narratives.

Family Communication Rules

When I was 15, my father had surgery on . . . to this day I don't know exactly what! When I came home from school my mother said my father had "some hospital procedures and would be home tomorrow." When my grandmother quickly became very fragile and confused, my parents refused to address it. I got the message loud and clear—never talk about a parent's or grandparent's health.

The previous example reflects a common family pattern—the communication rule. Every family develops rules for interaction and transmits them to new members. Rules are relationship agreements that prescribe and limit a family's behavior over time. *Communication rules* are "shared understandings of what communication means and what kinds of communication are appropriate in various situations" (Wood, 2007, p. 108). Every family becomes a rule-governed system; family members interact with each other in an organized, repetitive fashion, creating patterns that direct family life. Rules serve as generative mechanisms capable of creating regularity where none exists. In most cases, rules reflect patterns that have become "oughts" or "shoulds." *Relational rules* develop when people in relationships, implicitly or explicitly, develop rules unique to their connection; eventually these rules become patterned.

Because of their regularities, rules serve a powerful function in coordinating meanings for people. Through rules, family members gain a sense of shared reality and mutual understanding. Cronen, Pearce, and Harris (1979) stressed the need to coordinate joint meanings and that society relies on two types of rules, constitutive and regulative, to accomplish this coordination.

Constitutive rules define "what counts as what" as communicators construct meanings. One's family-of-origin is a primary source of such learning. "During the early years, families teach us what counts as affection (in some families, members kiss and hug but in other families, affection is not displayed overtly), and what counts as conflict (families differ in how openly and civilly they manage differences)" (Wood, 1998, p. 37). For example, in the Rosaldo family, informing others of changed plans counts as respect; in the Williams family, addressing elders formally counts as respect. *Regulative rules* prescribe acceptable communication behavior—how, when, where, and with whom to talk. For example, members of the Rosaldo family hear, "Call whenever your plans change, even if it is a small change"; Williams' family members learn, "Always greet older family members directly when you return from work or school."

Development of Rules   How did you learn these communication rules? You learned some rules explicitly, but you learned other rules implicitly. Rule formation varies on an awareness continuum, ranging from very direct, explicit, conscious relationship agreements that may have been clearly negotiated, to the implicit, unspoken, unconscious rules emerging from repeated interactions. Whereas the former are rather straightforward, the latter are extremely complex and convoluted. In some families, particular rules are negotiated directly, such as "We will never go to bed without kissing goodnight" or "We will openly discuss sex with the children." Most rules develop as a result of repeated interactions. Influential invisible rules are so much a part of the family's way of life that they are not recognized or named, but they are enforced, as indicated in the following example.

When I accidentally bring up a subject that is "taboo" when we are around other people, my mother gives me the cold stare, although she would deny it. If we are engaged in a one-on-one conversation, she ignores me or changes the subject. We've never talked about these topics or rules directly. I doubt we ever will.

Rules have great staying power. Individuals tend to carry their family rules into the families they form, implicitly combining those with their partners' family-of-origin rules. If not questioned, such rules may pass from generation to generation. Partners from families with dissimilar rules experience greater struggles than those from similar families-of-origin, forcing them to address the differences. Consider the difficulties if two people bring to their marriage the following individual rules for behavior during a family argument:

> *Partner 1:* If one person expresses strong negative emotion, the other should consider it carefully and refrain from spontaneous response. This is considered thoughtful.
> *Partner 2:* If one person expresses strong negative emotion, the other should respond with emotional supportiveness. To avoid responding would indicate rejection.

You can imagine the process of implicit and explicit rule negotiation needed in order for these two people to develop a disagreement pattern with which both feel comfortable.

Ethnic backgrounds influence family rules. When sibling conflict occurs, many Asian parents will admonish the younger child for not respecting the older sibling as well as the older child for not being a good role model. Essentially, the rule is to avoid family conflict (Lee & Mock, 2005). Members of Irish families learn to "Keep your feelings to yourself" (McGoldrick, 2005), whereas members of Polish families learn that stubbornness works unless you are fighting with a parent (Folwarski & Smolinski, 2005).

Analysis of any rule-bound system requires an understanding of the mutual influence pattern within which the rules function and which create new relational patterns. This process has been described as follows:

> No matter how well one knows the rules of communicator A, one cannot predict the logic of his/her communication with B without knowing B's rules and how they will mesh. The responsibility for good and bad communication is

thus transactive with neither A nor B alone deserving praise or blame. (Cronen, Pearce, & Harris, 1979, p. 36)

Once rules are established, changing one may be complicated and time-consuming unless the family has a flexible adaptation process and can recognize that the rule no longer serves a useful function.

Rules are maintained or changed through the negative (maintenance) or positive (growth) feedback processes discussed in systems theory. Rules may be recalibrated explicitly and implicitly as family members pass through certain developmental stages. On the other hand, rules may be openly negotiated or changed as the result of various factors, such as member dissatisfaction. A teacher's suggestion to "Encourage Patrick to stand up for his own opinions" may affect a parent's willingness to listen to a son's arguments.

Old patterns shift as the family system recalibrates itself to accept a wider variety of behaviors and people. One may hear, "I have broken the rule about not discussing sex with my mother by openly discussing my living arrangement." Some family rule changes reflect societal shifts. Family rules about sexual communication have changed over the past decades, although the expressed need for more openness is still common (Guzman, Schlehofer-Sutton, Villanueva, Stritto, Casad, et al., 2003). Even though adoption used to be highly secretive, the growth of open adoptions has made it a transparent, discussible experience (Galvin, 2003).

Most rules exist within a hierarchy. Two families may each establish the rule "Do not swear." In the Parson family, it may be a critical concern, whereas the Coopers may see it as desirable. Once you learn the family rules, you then have to figure out the importance placed on each of them.

A major source of conflict centers on breaking rules that one member may not even know exist. Such conflicts frequently arise for newlyweds or newly formed stepfamilies. In their study of topic avoidance, Guerrero and Afifi (1995) suggest that the family life cycle influences parent-child communication. For example, teenagers may exhibit verbal avoidance, thus unilaterally establishing a rule. The more conscious the rules, the greater the possibility of coordinating them at appropriate times.

Importance of Rules   Through rule-bound interaction, families enact their primary and secondary family functions. Rules set the limits of cohesion and adaptability while helping to form a family's images, themes, boundaries, and positions on biosocial issues such as power and gender. These guide further rule development. The interaction of rules and functions supports the development of a family's self-definition. Finally, rules contribute to a family's sense of satisfaction. Rules provide stability in interactions and serve to socialize younger members. Having to discover each member's response to a "hot" topic such as family money every time the subject arose would create chaos. Predictable communication patterns allow a family to carry on its functional day-to-day interactions smoothly.

Types of Communication Rules   Key questions provide a framework for looking at types of communication rules: What can be talked about? How can it be talked about? And with whom can it be talked about? (Satir, 1988). Each family's rules differ on the issues of what can be discussed. Can death, sex, salaries, drugs, and serious health problems be talked about in the Martinez family? Are there Adams family skeletons or current relatives who are never mentioned? Some topics may be forbidden under any circumstance. Most communication rules become quite clear, as explained below.

At my father's house there are lots of unspoken rules that dictate unsafe topics of conversation. It's clear that I should never mention (1) my mother, (2) the way we used to celebrate holidays, (3) my need for money, (4) my mother, (5) old family vacations, (6) my mother's relatives, (7) (8) (9) (10) my mother!

Many families limit the feelings that may be shared—especially negative feelings. Emotions such as anger, sadness, or rage may be avoided at all costs and denied whenever they begin to surface. Decision making often provides a fertile field for family rules. Are children allowed to question parental decisions, or are parents "the law," which cannot be challenged? Some families have rules that allow joint decision making through discussions, persuasion, or voting.

Over time family members learn how to talk about a particular topic or issue either directly or indirectly. In a family with an alcoholic parent, a parent or older sibling may say, "Mom's not feeling well today," but no one says, "Mom is drunk." Members tacitly agree not to deal with the real issue. Many couples never draw up a will because one or both partners cannot find a way to talk directly to each other about death. Thus, the "how" may involve vague allusions to the topic or euphemisms. Strategies involving time and place affect conversational topics. In some cases you learn not to talk about money when a parent is tired. Some topics seem to be discussed in a certain place, such as the kitchen or the car. The process of forming new systems through marriage or remarriage provides fertile ground for renegotiating each partner's rules for how to discuss a sensitive topic.

Often the rules for "who can participate, silently or actively, in the conversation" relate to biosocial issues such as age, gender, or family role. When children are small, they may be excluded from financial discussions, but as they grow older or serious financial problems arise, they are included. Sometimes unforeseen circumstances, such as death or divorce, move a child into a conversation circle that would have been denied otherwise. A 14-year-daughter of a single parent may discuss topics with her parent that would not have arisen if another adult lived in the home.

Sometimes family myths affect communication rules. Messages such as "Don't tell so and so because . . ." may create myths that prevail for years. Some grandchildren hear the following rule after the death of a grandparent: "Don't talk to Grandpa about Granny. It will make him depressed." Although this may be true for the first three months after her death, when the rule remains in place three years later, Grandpa may believe that only he misses his wife.

In order to fully appreciate the "what," "how," and "who" of a family's communication rules, it is necessary to analyze the system to see which rules are enforced in what contexts. The following set of regulative communication rules, developed within one young woman's family, indicates the interpersonal nature of rules:

- Don't disagree with Dad unless he's in a good mood.
- Do not fight with Mom about your appearance.
- Don't talk about the family's finances outside the family.
- Don't discuss sex except with siblings.
- Don't talk about Grandpa's two previous marriages.
- Never mention Aunt Bea's cancer or Tim's hearing problem.
- Family deaths are discussed only in terms of religion.
- Mother's pregnancy at marriage is never acknowledged.

The author of these rules concluded that she had learned to distinguish among people and circumstances but had not experienced very direct open communication in her family.

Metarules In addition to ordinary rules, some families have metarules, or rules about their rules. As Laing (1972) aptly stated, "There are rules against seeing the rules, and hence against seeing all the issues that arise from complying with or breaking them" (p. 106). When partners do not make a will because one or both refuses to talk about death, they may be living with an unspoken metarule "Never discuss the rule about ignoring death." Both pretend they are too busy or too young to meet with a lawyer. The following thoughtful analysis of the rules in the previous young woman's family indicates this metalevel of rule-bound behavior.

The death of my brother has spawned an entire catalogue of rules. It is unacceptable to discuss his death with family outsiders. There is a strong rule to mention him in conversation among family members where it would be appropriate. There seems to be a rule that has evolved over the past two years that it is all right for my mother, but not my father and I, to show grief in front of the family. My father and I have a sort of metarule that we ignore the rule about not showing grief to each other. I have the feeling that these rules will change when I go home this summer and help my family disassemble my brother's room.

All family members live with powerful rule-bound patterns, giving little conscious attention to most of them. Yet, they give meaning to each relationship. Rules and metarules evolve as new members enter the family and other members die, thereby increasing the complexity of communication.

Family Secrets

Secrets involve information purposefully hidden or concealed by one or more family members. The issue of family secrets emerges as one considers the link between

❚ Secrets may establish strong subgroup boundaries.

powerful family rules and taboo topics. A communication rule of alcoholic families, "Don't talk," is a way to maintain or deny the problem (Black, 2001). Family secrets are critical communication concerns because family ties are shaped "by what is shared and what is held secret by family members" (Vangelisti & Caughlin, 1997, p. 679). Making, keeping, and revealing secrets all shape a family's interaction patterns. "A secret may be silently and unknowingly passed from generation to generation like a booby-trapped heirloom" (Imber-Black, 1998, p. 4). What is considered a family secret may change over time. Whereas certain topics such as adoption, divorce, cancer, and mental illness are less stigmatized now, other issues such as being diagnosed with a genetic disease or using a sperm donor emerge (Imber-Black, 1998).

Secrets and Boundaries Secrets create or reinforce boundaries—whether between the family and the outside world or around individuals or subsystems. As discussed in Chapter 3, in her communication privacy management theory, Petronio (2002) portrays control as a boundary issue; people believe private information is owned or co-owned with others and revealing private information may make one vulnerable. Family members control an exterior boundary regulating the flow of private information, such as adoption, to those outside the family (Caughlin & Afifi, 2004), and establish internal boundaries that range from high to low permeability.

For example, in a study titled "How much did you pay for her?" Suter and Ballard (2009) described the ways adoptive parents protected their family privacy when persons outside the immediate family asked questions about their children, adopted from China, who were visibly different from their parents. Some parents indicated they would never answer questions on topics such as the cost of adoption, the child's China story or their adoption decision. Managing family secrets effectively depends on members' ability to identify who "owns" what information. An individual may believe that certain private information "belongs" to him or her and, those members who know the information, do not have the right to share it with others. If the individual's boundary is ignored, boundary turbulence will result. For example, if a new husband tells his family-of-origin that his brother-in-law has a serious drug abuse problem, his wife may be very angry because she believes she "owns" that information about her sibling.

Family secrets may be known to all immediate family members but kept from the outside world (whole family secrets), known to subgroups of the family (intrafamily secrets), or known only to an individual family member (individual secrets). Although secrets tend to be associated with something that would hurt or embarrass one or more members, some secrets protect positive information, reinforcing cohesiveness and identity. Such secrets may include funny childhood stories, inside jokes, or financial success. Even when keeping secrets is a common family practice, sometimes maintaining powerful secrets can have negative physiological consequences for the secret bearer (Pennebaker, 1990).

Types of Family Secrets

Secrets may be categorized in a variety of ways. According to Imber-Black, there are four types of family secrets: sweet, essential, toxic, and dangerous (1998, pp. 13–19). *Sweet* secrets serve the purpose of protecting fun surprises and are usually time limited. These include airline tickets to Disney World placed in a child's Christmas stocking or a cousin's surprise baby shower.

Essential secrets, which support necessary boundaries defining a relationship, may include talk about fears or insecurities, which enhances closeness and fosters the development of self and relationships. For some partners, self-disclosing conversations serve as an integral part of their relational growth. Sibling pairs may value revealing deep concerns and fears with each other.

Toxic secrets poison family relationships; key family issues and stories remain untold and unexplained. Maintaining such secrets may have chronic negative effects on problem solving, conversational repertoire, perceptions, and emotional well-being since "even when no one is in immediate physical or emotional danger, toxic secrets nonetheless sap energy, promote anxiety, burden those who know, and mystify those who don't know" (Imber-Black, 1998, p. 13). The protected alcoholism of one member may shut down vital interaction among other family members and between these members and the outside world. Avoiding issues such as affairs, drug abuse, or imprisonment may inhibit interactions about other topics. *Dangerous* secrets put their "owners" in immediate physical jeopardy or cause such severe emotional turmoil that their capacity to function is threatened. These may involve physical or sexual abuse or threats of suicide or harm to others.

Using a somewhat different approach, Vangelisti (1994b) categorized types of secrets as (1) *taboos,* or skeletons in the closet, including marital abuse, substance abuse, and illegalities; (2) *rule violations,* such as premarital pregnancy, cohabitation, and serious disobedience; and (3) *conventional* secrets, or information that is private but not "wrong," such as death, religion, and personality conflicts. Clearly, the taboo category is somewhat similar to the toxic and dangerous secrets, whereas conventional secrets are similar to the essential category. No matter how they are categorized, secrets play an important role in a family's communication patterns.

Functions of Secrets Given the commonplace nature of family secrets, a key question arises: What functions do secrets serve? In her early work on whole family secrets, Vangelisti (1994b) reports on six functions of such secrets:

1. *Bonding.* Individuals believe their family secrets increase cohesiveness among family members. The sister who intercepts her brother's school absence notices strengthens the sibling bond. Most couples' sexual rituals remain private to them. Sharing family secrets with new members, such as in-laws, acknowledges their place in the family (Serewicz, 2006).

2. *Evaluation.* Family secrets help members avoid negative judgment. Parents may hide a child's sexual preference or multiple divorces to avoid negative evaluations of the family.

3. *Maintenance.* These secrets help keep family members close while protecting them from stressors. Unusual religious practices, reliance on a sperm donor, or an unexpected inheritance may be kept a secret to prevent outside pressures. These represent attempts to prevent tension.

4. *Privacy.* Secrets are concealed because they are seen as personal and/or irrelevant to others. Family members may see income, plans for pregnancy, or payments for major purchases as none of anyone else's business.

5. *Defense.* Secrets protect information from outsiders who might use it against family members. A member's diagnosis with Huntington's disease may be kept inside the family to protect the individual and other members' genetic inheritance. Enmeshed families rely more heavily on defense secrets.

6. *Communication.* Secrets reflect a lack of open communication among family members. In families with low verbal interaction, certain topics may never surface because the family is not perceived as open or no one would know how to talk about it, such as in this example.

When one of us wants space, we may go into our bedroom, drive to the mall, or take a run alone. None of us really share too much of our private lives with one another. Our friends, social lives, and romantic lives are rarely disclosed, and if they are, it is done humorously.

The functions of family secrets have direct links to revelation choices because people who were unlikely to reveal their family secrets strongly supported functions associated with *evaluation, maintenance, privacy,* and *defense* (Vangelisti & Caughlin, 1997).

In their study of criteria for revealing family secrets, Vangelisti, Caughlin, and Timmerman (2000) identified 10 criteria linked to individuals' tendencies to reveal family secrets. Respondents who closely identified with their family secrets, viewing them as intimate or negative, were more likely to support a number of the criteria such as relational security and important reasons. A respondent's relationship to the listener was linked to the criteria he or she chose.

Secrets and Family Patterns   Secrecy links to family change. Although a secret's creation or dissolution can occur at any moment, many secrets are created or revealed at periods of intense relationship change, such as marriage, divorce, birth of a child, leaving home, or death. Secrets constructed at such key developmental points may affect the natural developmental process. "Relationships that would ordinarily change and grow become frozen in time, as the presence of a secret locks people in place" (Imber-Black, 1998, p. 10). Secrets may serve to reinforce boundaries within various family forms. Stepfamily members often share secrets with the members of their family-of-origin while concealing them from other stepfamily members (Caughlin, et al., 2000). Former partners and co-parents face the task of creating joint rules for communicating with their children about their dating and postmarital relationships since former partners often have different expectations for secrecy around this topic (Miller, 2009). Adult secrets about a family member's approaching death may create a climate in which children feel isolated (Bosticco & Thompson, 2005).

As noted earlier, multigenerational communication patterns frequently involve protecting secrets. In her study of three-generation families of Holocaust survivors, Chaitin (2002) found the *conspiracy of silence* continues to affect what survivors and their descendants can and cannot discuss because "On one hand, by not confronting the past, the grandchildren may be spared the difficulty of dealing with emotionally loaded issues. On the other hand, by avoiding the subject the grandchildren may be distancing themselves from the topic, and perhaps from their grandparents as well" (p. 395).

Family secrets impact immediate family members as well as the multigenerational family system. A hidden suicide, abortion, or prison term can affect the communication patterns of future generations. A member may struggle with questions such as: Do I have the right or responsibility to keep this a secret? Who would be injured if I reveal this secret? What is the best time or place for talking about this?

Persons affected with HIV confront painful choices as they hesitate to reveal the illness for fear of rejection, isolation, and harassment by coworkers, acquaintances, friends, and other family members (Haas, 2002). Revealing this secret within the family has great consequences and challenges. Reasons mothers decided to disclose their HIV status to their children included wanting to educate them, wanting the children to hear it from them, and wanting children to know before they became very ill. Yet some mothers opted for secrecy because, in addition to reasons of age and maturity level, they did not want their children to bear the emotional burden, to experience rejection, and to fear losing their mother (Schrimshaw & Siegel, 2002).

Relational satisfaction and secret-keeping are interlinked because "Those who were unlikely to reveal their secrets were more satisfied with their family relationships than were those who were moderately or highly likely to disclose their secrets" (Vangelisti & Caughlin, 1997, p. 694). In an essay on family secrets, Pogrebin (1992) revealed the impact of discovering her parents' lies about their marriage, saying, "I became an inveterate doubter, always peeling the onion trying to get at the truth behind the 'facts.' . . . I will never know how much it has damaged my capacity to trust" (p. 23). Family secrets link to family power patterns. Afifi and Olson (2005) examined the chilling effect of family members' concealment of secrets from one another by comparing the direct effects model with the indirect effects model. "Direct effects" suggests power in families has a direct influence—it suppresses the desire to reveal sensitive information for fear of negative consequences. In contrast, "indirect effects" suggests that power diminishes members' closeness and commitment, compelling them to conceal negative secrets. Their findings supported the direct effects model "in which coercive power created a pressure to conceal secrets in families" (p. 210). Family secrets affect family interactions, specifically how information moves between and among family members within the family's communication network.

Family Communication Networks

Family members establish patterns for connecting, referred to as *family networks*. This *communication network* creates and reflects the interactive flow of messages among family members. Some of these network systems also include persons outside the family. Family networks reflect connection as well as disconnection of members along relatively stable communication pathways. In some cases family members regulate the direction of message flow—up, down, or across the network, as well as the message recipients. Horizontal communication occurs when the persons involved represent perceived equal status or power, as when siblings share messages or when parents and children sit down and work out problems together. Vertical communication occurs when real or imagined power differences are reflected in the interaction.

Families develop communication networks to manage members' connections as well as relational tasks, such as conveying instructions, maintaining secrets, organizing activities, regulating time, and sharing resources. High member adaptability implies a wide variety of network arrangements; low adaptability implies rigid networks.

Families operate within networks that range from high technological connection to high face-to-face connection. In some families, relatives may stay in touch almost exclusively through the use of cell phones, including calling or twittering, Internet resources such as Facebook, or e-mail. Frequently these family members are spread across the country or globe so face-to-face interaction is quite limited. Other families stay in touch primarily through face-to-face interactions because members live in close proximity and, in many cases, technology costs or skill levels limit access. Most families find themselves closer to the middle of the spectrum; members rely on the most functional means of connecting at a given time.

Although two-generation networks are complicated, most current families involve multigenerational networks of even greater complexity. Such networks are

High Face/Voice Connection   High Mediated Communication

$\longleftarrow\!\!\!\!\!\!\!\!\!\longrightarrow$

highly complex, yet only key persons will relate regularly across generations. Networks also play an integral part in maintaining the roles and rules operating within the family system. Thus, networks and rules operate with mutual influence—rules may dictate the use of certain networks; networks create certain rule patterns.

Face/Voice Network Interactions   Although mediated connections increasingly impact family interactions, face-to-face and direct voice connections remain critical in family life, especially for families with children at home. These families tend to operate using interpersonal network models that include the chain, the Y, the wheel, and the all-channel.

Types of Networks   An operating *chain* network occurs when family members talk along a series of links; chains may be vertical (power-driven hierarchy) or horizontal (equal-power connection). Usually a parent figure heads a hierarchy whereby messages proceed up through the links or down from parent to an older child and on to younger ones. Requests from younger children may travel up the chain. Horizontal chains, often used for efficiency, occur when one sibling relays information to a parent or sibling who passes it on to others. If frequently used, chains keep certain members from interacting directly, although they are efficient in certain circumstances. In the *Y network*, a key person channels messages from one person on a chain to one or more other family members. In blended families with a new stepparent, the biological parent may consciously or unconsciously set up a Y network, separating the stepparent from the children. An inverted Y might involve a domineering grandmother who rules her son, who relays her wishes to his children.

The *wheel* network relies on one family member to serve as the clearinghouse for relaying messages to other family members. This position confers power and control since the key figure can filter and adapt messages positively or negatively, but puts pressure on the central figure to manage multiple messages continually. Other members maintain limited direct contact. Because only one person communicates with all the others, this person becomes critical to the ongoing family functioning. The Internet has reduced the need for such a central figure.

Mom was the center of our family network. As kids, we expected her to settle our problems with other family members. She always knew what everyone was doing and how they felt. When we left home, Mom digested the family news and relayed the information about what each of us was doing. After her death, my siblings and I have had to find new ways to keep connected. Usually we stay in contact through e-mails directed to everyone.

Messages in chain, Y, and wheel networks may become distorted as they pass from one person to another. This may help defuse some family conflicts, but misinformation could escalate others. The *all-channel* network supports exchanges between or among all family members, supporting direct interaction and maximum feedback.

Network variations occur under certain circumstances. The ends of a chain may form a circle or chains may lead toward the central figure in the wheel. Most families employ a variety of networks. When special circumstances occur, such as when a member becomes seriously ill, members establish formal patterns for keeping others informed. After a divorce, family members must establish new networks, often involving additional members, in order to maintain certain types of contact. Subgroups and coalitions directly affect the family networks. Two people on one end of a chain may support each other in all situations. Observers can frequently locate the networks in families by who has access to what information, such as secrets; revealing a toxic secret may destroy an established network pattern (Petronio, 2002).

New Media and Family Communication Networks In the twenty-first century, family networks rely heavily on mediated interactions to stay in touch. Contact occurs more frequently and in diverse ways in most families. This change reflects technological innovations as well as a shift toward more active family member connections driven by new immigrant populations and changes in parent-child relationships as offspring move toward and into adulthood.

Family connections exist within a larger network of social connections created on the Internet and other new media. Therefore, communication among family members occurs in multiple ways—through "intentional connections," such as an e-mail directed to a brother; "assumed connections," such as the belief that your in-laws will read about your China trip in the round-robin family e-mail; and "random connections" when your former sister-in-law or grandmother responds to your recent Facebook post about a workplace party.

Partnerships and families are formed and live in an increasingly wired world. Adults meet their partners through online social networks; geography and friends or family no longer dominate romantic connections (Christakis & Fowler, 2009). In 2006, 30 million adults reported knowing someone who formed a long-term relationship or marriage with someone he or she met online (Madden & Fowler, 2006).

A major Pew/Internet Life study (2008) depicted American families as "networked families" because of the wide range of communication media members use to stay connected. Most households contain multiple communication technologies: 95 percent of households formed by married/partnered adults with children had one cell phone; 80 percent of these households had multiple cell phones; and 57 percent of children (ages 7 to 17) in this group had an individual cell phone. Both spouses use the Internet at home in 76 percent of married/partnered with children households as do 84 percent of their children ages 7 to 17.

My partner and I have two sons in the same out-of-state college. I cannot imagine how we would manage without cell phones and e-mail since they are seldom in their dorm rooms and they constantly travel with the tennis team. We often catch them on the bus heading to tournaments or between classes just to check on how they are doing. It's important to keep up with their day-to-day lives—the classes, the tennis demands, and their social lives.

Couples reported contacting each other regularly during the day to coordinate their lives. More than three-quarters of children and parents connected, usually on a daily basis, on cell phones or land lines. Respondents indicated that such communication tools helped them to stay connected to family members although these contacts often blurred the lines between home and work. Study participants reported that these advanced technologies allowed their current family life to be as close, or closer, than the connections in their families-of-origin, although those with high levels of technology ownership were less likely to share meals or enjoy leisure time. In many cases, adults use technology at home for workplace reasons. Partners without children living at home tended to own less technology; single-person households reported the lowest rates of technology use.

Following family members' lives through interactional networks provides opportunities for everyday conversations, problem solving, schedule planning, tracking health issues, and sharing affection. The technological advances of the past 25 to 30 years has transformed the nature of everyday family interaction patterns.

NARRATIVES

My father was in his early twenties when he came to the United States from Taiwan, leaving behind his parents, three brothers, and two sisters. His first job was as a waiter in a Chinese restaurant. During this time the only thing my father would spend pay on was bread and bologna to feed himself on days when he did not work. He earned about $300 a month, of which he sent $200 home to repay the money he borrowed for travel. He sent $50 to his family. He used the rest for chemistry books and English classes.

My father, who became a research chemist, has told this story many times because I think he was trying to instill in us the importance of working hard for your dreams and the importance of helping your family. I will tell my children about their grandfather's struggles so they understand the importance of hard work and sacrifice.

This narrative, a powerful example of how one creates family meanings, provides family members with inspiration while carrying a clear message, "If you work hard enough, you can reach your dream." According to Wells (1986):

> Constructing stories in the mind—or storying, as it has been called—is one of the most fundamental means of making meanings. When storying becomes overt and is given expression in words, the resulting stories are one of the most effective ways of making one's own interpretation of events and ideas available to others. (p. 194)

How often have you heard comments such as "Uncle Wayne, tell us how Mom drove the car into the lake" or "My grandmother told us about the segregated school she attended while living in Alabama." Such stories give meaning to everyday life: "People grow up and walk around with their stories under their skin" (Stone, 1988, p. 6).

Narratives fall into two broad types—stories/narratives and accounts (Koenig Kellas, 2010). Stories tend to provide a history—a retelling of memories of what was experienced; these may include ancestor stories, memories of moments shared by current family members, or recounting of immediate life experiences. *Accounting* includes explanations or reasons for persons' behaviors or situations; it may include explaining why one member chose to marry or divorce or decided to join the military or retire at 60.

Occasionally family members share a master narrative—a story of extraordinary proportions that takes on the power to define what it means to be a member. Often these are linked to larger-than-life individuals who took unimaginable risks, followed a dream, or reached a seemingly unattainable goal. A master narrative, on the grand scale, may include a Holocaust story told by grandparents and passed on by grandchildren, a parent's immigration from Vietnam story, or the self-made story of a great uncle who founded the business that today employs 24 family members. In contrast, a less dramatic, but equally compelling, tale of a family member who did the "right thing," supporting three children whom his former wife would not let him see, or who exhibited commitment or drive by completing a college degree at 86. Such narratives serve as life guides for other members.

Every family develops stories that reflect its collective experience. Some stories remain too painful to voice; others serve as the centerpiece of many family gatherings. According to Stone (1988),

> A family culture makes its norms known through daily life, but it also does so through family stories which underscore . . . the essentials, like the unspoken and unadmitted family policy on marriage or illness. Or suicide, or who the family saints and sinners are, or how much anger can be expressed and by whom. (p. 7)

Stories hold a strong personal power because, "From the narrative perspective one's sense of self is the story that a person has created about herself from the totality of her experiences" (Yerby, 1993, p. 6). An individual's story brings together parts of a self into a purposeful whole (McAdams, 1993). Personal stories may "fit" with other family stories or may serve to separate a member from the family.

Stories, once voiced, develop a life of their own, assuming additional meanings beyond the first telling. One story may be embellished to turn a member into a hero; another story may be altered to save a member from embarrassment. Each retelling places a slightly different "spin" on the tale. In essence, stories do not just reflect life; stories shape life with powerful effects.

Most family members' stories are interconnected. You may be recruited into your brother's story of a childhood prank; your partner may delight in retelling your first Thanksgiving dinner disaster. Sometimes families revise a narrative in order to create a slightly different perspective. For example, a mother may reframe her son's actions as "cautious" rather than "scared."

❙ Some family stories can be told only by one key member.

Functions of Stories

Stories convey important messages to family members while serving the following key functions: (1) to remember, (2) to create belonging and family identity, (3) to teach expected behavior and deeply held values to current members or new members, (4) to develop the family culture, (5) to provide stability by connecting generations, and (6) to entertain (Stone, 2005; Koenig, Kellas, & Trees, 2006).

Family stories encourage members to remember together. Remembering connects siblings as they age, helping them recall key people or moments in their shared lives. Stories construct and reaffirm the members' identities representing part of a self-definition. Many identity stories remind members of what it means to be a Shih, a Joravsky, or a Washington. A study of 115 couples revealed 96 percent occasionally talked to their small children about their childhood; 45 percent of preschool mothers and 38 percent of preschool fathers told childhood stories at least once a week (Fiese, Hooker, Kotary, Schagler, & Rimmer, 1995).

Stories construct bridges connecting generations, creating a sense of history that gives younger members a place in the world. Family stories instruct members in the family values, or themes, and what is expected of them. Such stories contain moral lessons or practical lessons. Frequently, stories are linked to images: "Our family is a rock"; or themes, "Only your best is good enough." Stories reflecting themes such as care, togetherness, or adaptability are linked to satisfaction, whereas themes such as disregard, hostility, or chaos are negatively linked to feelings about the family (Vangelisti, Crumley, & Baker, 1999).

Stories socialize new members to the family. The prospective in-law may hear all about the family's journey from Costa Rica to Austin or about eccentric Grandpa Joe. Stepfamily members socialize each "side" to some family history because these stories serve as a connection that holds people together as they move to create their own joint stories (Collins, 1997).

Family stories remind people about who they are, helping them to see the good or bad times that contributed to current situations. Some families tell disaster stories that include surviving floods, bankruptcy, or an earthquake. Immigration stories frequently bring family heroes and risk takers alive to younger generations. Family stories also connect people to their cultures. An African American family, for instance, might use family stories to teach their children how to deal with racism (Bylund, 2003). Members of families formed through international adoption tell stories as ways to build a sense of family and a straightforward history as well as to discourage fantasies (Harrigan, 2009). Finally, family stories bring joy or laughter as members remember special times or embarrassing moments; sometimes these storytelling times can be bittersweet, such as when a cherished member becomes ill.

Now that Mom is in a nursing home and Dad comes to visit, we get them to tell us stories about camping trips, birthdays, family moves, and other childhood events. Sometimes they will have very different versions of the same story, or each remembers various pieces, or one won't remember it at all. They joke and say that in old age they "have one brain between them." Together, we get from them a fuller picture of events in our lives.

Questions Stories Answer

A family develops stories that represent its collective experience. These are frequently tied to primary and secondary family functions. Family stories often respond to questions such as the following:

- *Are parents really human?* Children love to hear stories in which parents struggle with issues of growing up or making decisions—stories that remove a parent figure from a pedestal. Some are humorous ones, such as when Mom "lost" her baby brother, and serious ones, such as a stepfather's struggle with drug addiction. Some stories may be told for the first time, when a parent self-discloses his or her youthful mistakes at the point a child is old enough to learn from such a story.
- *How did this family come to be?* Most families tell some version of "creation" stories. These may be first meetings of adult partners, birth stories, the first stepsiblings' meetings, or adoption stories. Such stories tell about how family members came to be in the family and therefore how the family came to be. Often, they are accompanied by emotional statements, such as this one.

We arrived at the airport two hours before the plane from Seoul was due to arrive, because we were too excited to stay at home. We brought Grandma and Poppa and Uncle Allen and Aunt Mary. Your father kept walking up and down the concourse and we could not get him to sit down. He had your picture and he started to tell all the people near the gate we were going to become parents when the plane arrived. Three other couples arrived to wait for their babies. We were all anxious, trying to pass the time through small talk. Finally the plane arrived, 15 minutes late, and one by one all the business passengers filed out. Finally, when it looked like there were no more people left on board, a young woman carrying a baby appeared in the doorway. She was followed by other young people with babies. When I saw the third baby I knew it was you. I started to grab you as the woman carrying you said "Dobbs." You gave me the most beautiful smile and your dad and I started to cry and laugh. We had waited two-and-a-half years for that moment.

- *How does a child become an adult in this family?* These narratives address moments or experiences when a child moves into adulthood by accomplishing some feat—beating a parent at a sport, earning more than a parent, or solving a significant family problem. These stories are poignant because they signal a passage of time and, in some cases, a role reversal between parent and child. A middle-aged adult may tell of having to care for a parent whose recent fall left her unable to live alone. A grandparent may describe how her grandson translated for the doctors when his mother had a stroke.
- *Will the family stand behind its members?* Some family stories depict strong family support, or no family support, when members face stressful times or their behavior violates family norms. You may learn that when you leave the accepted path, you will be disowned or cut off. Or learn that family members will always be there for you. These stories link to family themes and to levels of adaptability. Comments such as "No one ever mentions Aunt Ginny because she married outside our religion and Granddad disowned her" serve to answer the question, "Why don't you ever talk about Aunt Ginny?" Such stories may be told after a member is convicted of a major crime or violates a strong family value such as marrying within one's race.
- *How does the family handle adversity?* When unpredictable crises arise, such as illness or job loss, does this family pull together or does the family fall apart? How does the family cope—through cunning or through hard work? Countless immigrant stories recount heroics of ancestors battling against great odds to build a new life. Stories of family members facing illness, accidents, prejudice, or economic hardships may depict aggressive or passive responses. A study of male prostate cancer survivors revealed consistent stories of wives as health monitors, caregivers, and supporters. One man reported, "I remember standing here with my wife and crying, having my

bathrobe on in the middle of the day . . . and saying, 'It's just me and you against the whole world, honey'" (Arrington, 2005, p. 149).

- *What does it mean to be a (family name)?* This is a question of collective identity. There may be a key story that serves to capture the essence of being a Leubitz or a Watters. Family stories carry powerful messages that influence family members as they organize their lives by making decisions in accordance with the dominant narratives that tell these members who they are in the world and how they should act. Some families have a "master narrative" story that is significant because it captures what it means to be a family member.

Performing Family Stories

As you explore family stories, think about the performance element—who tells the stories, and when and where are they told?

Who Tells?   Usually storytelling is a singular experience, but frequently sibling pairs or small groups of family members tell particular stories following a predictable pattern. In her research on couple storytelling, Dickson (1995) identified three types of couples according to their performance style. Connected couples tell stories "as if they are jointly owned by both partners" (p. 36). Dialogue overlaps and partners affirm each other's words. Functional separate couples demonstrate respect, validation, and support while engaging in individual storytelling, often of unshared experiences. Dysfunctional separate couples exhibit contradiction, disagreement, and poor listening as each tells his or her stories. Couples who jointly tell more coherent and expressive stories are also more likely to have higher marital satisfaction, both at the time the story is told as well as two years later (Oppenheim, et al., 1996).

In an elaborate study of joint storytelling, Koenig Kellas (2005) videotaped 58 family triads telling stories that they told frequently and that best represented the family. The family stories addressed a wide range of themes such as accomplishment, fun, tradition, culture, togetherness/separateness, and child mischief, but the most common theme was dealing with stress. This study highlights the importance of perspective-taking among family members in explanations of family functioning and satisfaction. The author suggests that families whose members attended to and confirmed each other's perspectives during joint storytelling interactions "reported the highest feelings of family cohesion, adaptability, satisfaction, and overall family functioning" (p. 385). In a related study of making sense of difficult experiences through joint storytelling (Trees & Koenig Kellas, 2009), the authors explored how the family relational context relates to jointly enacted behaviors such as engagement, turn-taking, coherence, and perspective-taking. They found that coherence and perspective-taking emerged as important behavioral predictors of relational qualities. They speculated that members most involved in the difficult situation may engage more actively in storytelling while others listened empathically or that telling difficult stories creates a more somber and less interactive environment.

Some family members develop performance patterns whereby, on cue, one disagrees, adds the punch line, or recruits the other into the narrative. One parent may perform the bedtime ritual and become skilled at recounting key family events. An older sibling may be asked to perform the "warning" stories about troubles with drugs or drinking. Couples may jointly perform "cover stories" or stories that are constructed because there is a need to create an "explanation" to avoid conflict or hurting another's feelings, or to make one or both of the partners look good (Hest, Pearson, & Child, 2006). Family members learn to cover for each other with explanations designed to save face. Comments such as "Isabelle is in the shower and can't come to the phone" may be developed as one family member covers for another who is trying to avoid an unpleasant situation.

Family storytelling varies by gender, although women play a much more active role than men (Stone, 2005). Mothers have a tendency to introduce family stories as a way to control the topic and the timing of the stories (Ochs & Taylor, 1992). Females also hear more family stories and become more familiar with stories of previous generations. Mothers also tell stories with stronger "affiliation themes," whereas fathers tell stories with stronger "achievement" themes (Fiese, et al., 1995). In her study on parental telling of international adoption stories, Harrigan (2010) reports that only mothers responded to the call to participate and suggests that fathers' responses might offer a "richer understanding of the storytelling process"(p. 38).

When and Where?   Storytelling occurs in context. Although the traditional image of family storytelling conjures up images of holiday celebrations, many family stories are bedtime stories or stories told in response to a trigger situation, such as a bad grade or a disloyal friend. The holidays remain classic contexts for family stories. In her study of Thanksgiving rituals, Benoit and associates (1996) suggested members "chronicle" or individually update others on the recent past events in their lives and share stories at the table. Grandparents and parent generations controlled the content of talk by encouraging chronicling from younger generations and by acting as narrators. Family stories may be told at the table, on long car trips, at family parties, or in any meeting that elicits the recall. Wherever and whenever they are recounted, they carry the family meanings within them.

Family stories function to develop family solidarity and to enact family structure. Parents and grandparents usually tell the stories; frequently children become the protagonists, creating a sense of solidarity for all involved. Occasionally, the reason for recounting creates tension or heightens emotions. In their study of foster family narratives, Jacob and Borzi (1996) described how two sets of husbands and wives display degrees of emotion when discussing their experience of deciding to become foster parents. Women displayed more emotion; men remained more passive until the end of the narrative when they were active and enthusiastic.

Variations on Family Storytelling

Although storytelling occurs in most families, some families do not tell certain stories or members have lost their stories. Missing stories may be the result of family rules, painful experiences, or avoidance. In some families explicit or implicit rules develop such as "Do not mention your cousin Adam's boyfriend. Aunt Rebecca can't handle it" or "Never mention that Ashley had a brief marriage before she found Alex." Such rules may occur to protect loved ones from distress (Aunt Rebecca does not accept that Adam is gay) or support certain fictions (this is

Ashley's first marriage). In other cases, difficult or painful experiences, such as military service in a war zone, or the death of a toddler, are perceived as more than other members can handle. Finally, stories disappear as original stories are not told after a divorce (how Grandma and Grandpa fell in love) or because the teller has died or left the family. The following narrative, "Sierra's Story," was written by a foster father for his former foster daughter because he wanted her to know about a particular nine-month period in her life and no on else could tell her what she was like. He also wanted her to know she was loved during that time. He wrote the letter hoping someday she will read it or a relative will read it to her.

I'll never forget the night you first came into our lives. It was about five-thirty in the evening. Middle of December. I was at the stove making dinner when the phone rang. It was a case manager from the social service agency. "We're looking for a foster home for a nineteen-month-old girl," she said. She told me about your case and why you were in foster care. "So are you interested in taking her in?" she asked. I put my hand over the receiver and turned to my partner, Tom. "They have a nineteen-month-old girl." I repeated everything I was just told about the case. "Do we want to take her in?" "Wow," Tom said. "Yeah, I think I want to do this," he replied. "What do you think?" he asked. "I think I want to do this too," I answered. We were feeling both excited and nervous at the same time. I got back on the phone. "Yes," I said. "We'll be happy to take her in." The case manager said, "That's great. Can you pick her up at eight o'clock?" I glanced at the clock. It was less than three hours away. I put my hand back over the receiver. "Can we pick her up in a couple hours?" I asked Tom. "Sure," he said. "We can do this," he reassured me. I got back on the phone. "No problem. We'll meet you at eight." I hung up the phone. And then panic set in. We had nothing for a girl your age. Nothing. No car seat. No crib. No high chair. I wasn't even sure I knew how to change a diaper. I remember calling some of our friends who were parents and asking them all kinds of questions. What can she eat? What do we need? The couple of hours flew by and it was soon time for us to leave.

I remember driving in the snow and in the dark to pick you up at the social service agency. We walked through the front door into the lobby. There you were, this tiny little girl, all wrapped up in a big coat with your head peeking out from under the hood. We borrowed a car seat from the agency and put you in the back seat. We took your stuff, which was packed in plastic bags, and put it in the trunk. On the way home I kept glancing at you in the rearview mirror. You were beautiful. The first few days you called both me and Tom "Mama." I never thought I would be a "Mama." It was funny. We would be someplace like the grocery store and you would point to something and say, "Mama, look!" And I could see the other shoppers turning their heads and staring at us. You could tell they were wondering why this little girl was calling this man "Mama." So Tom and I talked it over and decided that I would be "Daddy" and he would be "Papa." That made you the very first one to call me "Daddy." And when you said, "I love you, Daddy" for the first time, my heart melted.

There were so many things to love about you. I really liked picking you up at daycare. No matter what you were doing or who you were playing with, you dropped everything when I walked into the room. You just got this big smile on your face. And then you would run over to me and wrap your little arms around my legs. If I was working late and you were already home, you would come running up to me as I walked through the door, yelling, "Daddy! Daddy! Daddy!" There was nothing better to come home to. We had lots of fun together. We wrestled. And jumped up and down on the bed. And played goofy games. You loved playing "Ring Around the Rosie." You called it "Ashes." You wanted to play it again and again and again. "Ashes, Daddy. Ashes," you would say. You loved to be held and you wanted to be carried everywhere. I pretty quickly learned to do everything with one hand while I held you in my other arm. You told great stories. At night we would sit on the couch and you would sit on the little bench. Sometimes you would tell us stories about your friends and what happened at daycare. "Sierra BUMP her head. Sierra cry." Most of the time you would make things up. "And I was shopping. And a monster came. And it BIT me." "Where did it bite you, Sierra?" "It bit me RIGHT HERE," you would say, holding up your hand. Half the time your stories didn't make any sense but it was so much fun to just sit there and listen to you talk . . .

Then one day we got a phone call from the social service agency. You were going back to your mom. "Back home," they said. On one hand we were happy for you. Your mom loved you a lot and she worked really hard to get you back. We liked her and wanted her to succeed. Many of the kids in foster care never return to their biological families. You were one of the lucky ones. You got to go back. But it was gonna be so hard to say goodbye to you. You had been with us for nine months. 270 days. We were completely in love with you. And the thought of saying goodbye to you and never seeing you again really hurt.

We didn't know how to explain to you what was going to happen. You were only two. I wasn't even sure you remembered a time when you lived with your mom. We kept talking about her. And how much she loved you. And how much fun it was going to be to live with her. We completely spoiled you the last few days you were with us. We let you do pretty much anything you wanted to do. We stayed up late. We ate lots of ice cream. We cherished every moment we had with you. No matter what we were doing I caught myself thinking this would be the last time for us to do it together. The last trip to the grocery store. The last time making popcorn and watching videos. The last time getting you dressed in the morning. On your very last day with us I took you and the other kids out to eat. You were asleep when we got to the restaurant. I picked you up and carried you in. While the other kids ate, I closed my eyes and held you in my arms while you slept. "This is it," I said to myself. "The last time you'll be sleeping in my arms. The last time I'll hold you like this. Just the two of us. Sierra and Daddy. For the last time."

When we dropped you off at your mom's house that night she had a little party to welcome you back. There were relatives and friends there, and she had ordered a cake and bought balloons. Papa and I thought the best thing for us to do would be to slip out without saying goodbye. We thought it would be easier that way. Easier for you, easier for us, easier for your mom. But you saw us leaving. You ran to the door and you were crying. And you were calling our names. "Daddy! Papa!" And we had to get into the car and drive away. That was so hard. It was the most difficult thing I had to do in my entire life. I kept wondering what was going through your little head. If you had any way of understanding what was happening and why we were leaving you. It still hurts to think about that day.

I don't know if you'll remember us five years from now. Ten years from now. I don't really remember anything from my life when I was two years old. But I hope there's a part of us that will always be with you. Because there's a part of you that will always be with us. Since then we've had other foster kids. And we love them very much. And we even have the opportunity to adopt some of them. But you know what, Sierra? You were our first little girl. You were the first to call me "Daddy." You were the first to win my heart. And I'll never forget you.

—Dennis Grady Patrick

CONCLUSION

This chapter explored how families develop identity through the creation of family meanings. This process involves establishing a relational culture reflective of the interactions of partners and family members. In addition, families need patterns that contribute to members' identity. These include: (1) communication rules; (2) family secrets; (3) communication networks; and (4) family stories. Each contributes to unique family meanings and each factor influences the others. As you will see throughout the book, patterns serve as the skeletal structure undergirding family life, both reflecting and determining relationships.

In Review

1. Take a position on the question: To what extent does a family-of-origin influence the communication patterns of future generations? Give examples to support your position.

2. Describe three or four communication patterns have been passed down from your family-of-origin that you believe reflect key multigenerational transmissions?

3. Identify a turning point or event in a real or fictional family's development that demonstrates specific communication rules members lived by and how those rules were maintained or changed due to the circumstance.

4. Identify a family secret in a real or fictional family. Discuss the type of secret, how it was managed communicatively, and the effect of the secret on family members.

5. Relying on a real or fictional family, describe how the most frequently used communication networks have changed over time due to developmental changes or family crises.

6. Analyze a family story and its impact on family values.

KEY WORDS

Accounts   96
All-channel networks   93
Chain network   93
Communication networks   92
Communication rules   83
Dangerous secrets   89

Joint storytelling   100
Relational cultures   80
Toxic secrets   89
Wheel network   93
Y network   93

Relational Maintenance within Families

"If love is real, it will be evident in our daily lives, in the many
ways we show we care."

—Thich Nhat Hanh

When his mother, Emma, married Christopher, Jake was angry. He and his mother had been very close since she adopted him at age four. Nine years later he resented Christopher's appearance in their lives. For two years Jake did his best to avoid him, although Christopher would talk with him about music or sports and invite Jake to go to movies. He even showed up at Jake's school concerts with his mother. Before the wedding Christopher took Jake out to lunch to talk about how much he loved Jake's mother and how he wanted to be part of Jake's life. It was a one-sided conversation; Jake didn't say much. Over the last two years Jake's resistance has broken down. Christopher appears at every music theater event at the high school as well as parent conferences. Christopher takes Jake for blueberry granola pancakes every Saturday while Emma gives piano lessons. During those breakfasts they plan events such as Emma's birthday party or a family camping trip. Last week Jake asked him to chaperone a band trip; Christopher agreed.

When Desmond was deployed to Afghanistan, his wife, Samiera, immediately started to imagine how she and the girls (ages 8, 5, and 3) would be able to stay closely connected to him for the next 18 months. Samiera decided to talk with some of the other mothers living on the Army base to learn how they managed the separation. After a week of discussions she collected a list of possibilities. She talked with the girls about what each one might wish to do. Samiera began to plan what she, herself, would do to stay close to her husband. Then she and Desmond discussed what would make him feel connected during the long separation.

Each girl decided to fill a fancy envelope with locks of her hair, photos, and drawings. Desmond decided to create tapes with stories each girl liked to hear at bedtime. Samiera planned to make a tape of readings from their wedding. Desmond planned to send monthly tapes to the girls with more stories and thoughts about them. The girls put a map of Afghanistan and a collage of Daddy pictures on the kitchen wall. Everyone also looked forward to the anticipated sporadic videophone chats and e-mail correspondence.

W hat keeps partners in a close, trusting relationship for years? How do parents and children move from a hierarchical relationship reflective of parental power, to a caring and sharing adult relationship? What explains the power of strong sibling ties in later life? Family connections, sometimes solid and sometimes fragile, depend on members' communicative efforts to create connections. Some relationships are maintained at low to moderate levels of connection for long periods; many partner and family relationships never reach deep levels of intimacy. Yet, their ties may provide strong relational satisfaction.

This chapter addresses relational maintenance. First, we will consider the concept of relational maintenance and the role of confirmation, rituals and relational currencies in actively maintaining familial ties. You may recognize that the topics addressed in the last chapter on family identity (rules, secrets, networks, and narratives) also contribute, although less directly, to relational maintenance.

RELATIONAL MAINTENANCE

Much of the time, family relationships just *are!* We live them rather than analyze them. The ordinary, routine behaviors of life carry us through each day, usually in a patterned and often unreflective way. For most families, there are good times and tough times. We *communicatively maintain* our families through everyday interactions, but, on occasion, we stop and focus on a relational connection by responding to an unpredictable crisis, strategically planning a message, or seriously considering the role of a family member in our lives.

Consider all the aspects of our lives that we attempt to maintain through routine and strategic efforts—health, cars, homes, computers, gardens, and much more. This has relevance for significant relationships because family ties need to be maintained through routines and strategic efforts. The routine behaviors include picking up a child after school or discussing your day at work. The strategic behaviors need to be more obviously nurturing, such as pleasing a partner on a birthday or apologizing after a fight. Relational maintenance usually refers to "garden variety" or everyday issues, not managing major crises (Canary, Stafford, & Semic, 2002), although occasionally a crisis must be managed.

Exactly what does *relational maintenance* mean? It is widely accepted as that "huge area where relationships continue to exist between the point of their initial development and their possible decline" (Duck, 1994, p. 45). Relational maintenance involves keeping a relationship (1) in existence, (2) in a state of connectedness, (3) in satisfactory condition, and (4) in repair (Dindia & Canary, 1993). Relational maintenance ranges from talking about everyone's day at dinner, to planning romantic birthday celebrations, to dealing with relational struggles as they occur.

How is relational maintenance accomplished? Although more may be involved, "talk is the essence of relational maintenance" because it presents "symbolic evidence to the partners that the two of them share an appreciation of the relationship and approach important experiences in similar ways" (Duck, 1994, p. 45). Talk may involve discussing individual needs, negotiating new behaviors, or forgiving another. Why does this everyday relational maintenance matter? The answer is, "People in relationships characterized by high levels of maintenance tend to stay together longer and be more satisfied" (Guerrero, Andersen, & Afifi, 2001, p. 229). Essentially, talk defines and maintains the relationship.

Relational maintenance differs across partnerships and family forms because issues are different between adults than they are between parents and children, or siblings. Marriages or partnerships involve voluntary adult relationships, whereas parent-child or sibling relationships are essentially involuntary, although most develop depth through voluntary connectedness. Adults choose whether to nurture their ties; children do not have the emotional maturity to consciously "work at" a relationship. Most relational maintenance studies focus on marriages or other adult partnerships.

Marital/Partnership Maintenance

"Maintaining high levels of satisfaction and love in marriage is problematic" (Vangelisti & Huston, 1994, p. 179). This blunt statement reflects the folk wisdom of "Over time, romance moves into reality." We will include long-term committed partnerships in our discussion because of the increasing number of unmarried persons in romantic, long-term committed relationships. Although most partnerships experience periods of intimacy, everyday life intrudes with its demands. One characteristic of enduring marriages is the ability to change over time. Relationships face predictable pressures of health concerns, money worries, and work or career demands; children, as well as older parents, may need care.

Marital maintenance has received extensive research attention. A study of the first two years of marriage concluded, "Although most spouses start with extraordinarily high levels of satisfaction and love, these feelings dwindle as time passes" (Vangelisti and Huston, 1994, p. 179). Partners develop routines and become more aware of their spouses' flaws. Eventually couples face relational reality, including disenchantment. The authors concluded, "Couples who are able to maintain strongly positive feelings toward each other over this period of adjustment may be in a particularly advantageous position to maintain their relationship over the longer haul" (p. 179). A study of couple talk revealed the daily talk behavior of satisfied couples over a week (Alberts, Yoshimura, Rabby, & Loschiavo, 2005). The 13 talk categories included: self-report, observations, back-channel comments, talk about another person, TV talk, partner's experiences, miscellaneous comments, household tasks, humor, plans, narratives, positivity, and conflict. There were variations in what was talked about during weekdays and weekends. Often, relational maintenance includes specific behaviors or activities used to sustain a desired relational definition (Canary & Stafford, 1994); this may include how a caring mother or husband might behave. Sometimes the term *relational resilience* is used to depict relational maintenance efforts. Marital resilience implies a process in which people purposefully engage in *maintenance strategies—* activities to repair, sustain, and thereby continue relationships in the ways they want them to be (Canary & Stafford, 1994). Maintenance strategies help to promote relational resilience since they prevent relationships from decaying and help to repair troubled relationships. In their early work, Stafford and Canary (1991) identified the following five maintenance strategies that contribute to romantic relational maintenance:

1. *Positivity.* Includes being cheerful and supportive; giving gifts or compliments; being upbeat when talking; and avoiding criticism. Both express pleasure regarding their involvement with one another.
2. *Openness.* Includes self-disclosure, as well as explicitly discussing the relationship and sharing thoughts and feelings about relational problems. The smaller the number of taboo or off-limit topics, the greater the openness.
3. *Assurances.* Includes stressing love, support, and commitment, implying the partners are faithful and the relationship has a future. Messages stress one's desire to remain in the relationship.
4. *Social networks.* Includes involving family and friends in activities as well as sharing interconnected networks. Social support contributes to relational stability because others are there to help.
5. *Sharing tasks.* Includes jointly performing tasks and performing one's "fair share" of the work.

The importance and intensity of these strategies vary. Assurances tend to endure over time, so the need for constant assurance is not as great as the ongoing need for positivity. In later work, these initial five categories were expanded to include (6) joint activities, (7) talk of a less intimate nature, (8) mediated communication such as e-mails, (9) avoidance (of topics of conflict), (10) antisocial behaviors such as teasing, (11) affection or displays of fondness or sexual intimacy, and (12) focus on self, such as individual spiritual growth. You will see that many of these are related to the concept of relational currencies, discussed in the following section. In her study of 179 persons, Dainton (2007) found that secure marital attachment was positively related to all five basic maintenance strategies noted above and an additional two—conflict management (using integrative strategies) and advice (sharing one's opinions with a partner).

Maintenance of gay and lesbian partnerships involves many similar romantic or marital patterns although they may experience additional stresses (Haas & Stafford, 1998). Most partners desire to live and work in environments supportive of the relationship, to be "out" in their social network, to be able to introduce the other person as one's partner, and to spend time with others who accept these relationships. A comparison of the relational maintenance practices of same-sex partners and marital partners revealed that the range of behaviors reported was quite similar with the most commonly reported behavior being "shared tasks" (Haas and Stafford, 2005). These couples differed in their ranking of the second most common behavior: same-sex couples listed meta-relational communication, or experiencing openness by discussing the state of the relationship, whereas married couples reported using positivity. Same-sex partners may emphasize meta-relational behaviors because, lacking a legal bond to hold the relationship together, they must rely on emotional commitment. When there are differences between partners about "coming out" to network members, problems can emerge (Patterson, 2000).

The crucial nature of positivity is supported by the "5 to 1 magic ratio" of positivity to negativity characteristic of stable marriages (Gottman, 1999). (This will be developed in Chapter 6.) In one of the only longitudinal examinations of marital maintenance, Weigel and Ballard-Reisch (2001) found that maintenance behaviors are used to sustain desired relational definitions and that effective use of such behaviors should predict future marital satisfaction. They also reaffirmed the importance of positivity, assurances, and similar social networks. More recently, these authors' large study of marital maintenance revealed that partners' use of maintenance behaviors are interdependent; a spouse's perception of satisfaction and commitment is associated with their own and their partner's use of maintenance behaviors (Weigel & Ballard-Reisch, 2008).

Although most studies assume persons engage in maintenance behaviors to support the relationship, this is not always the case. Ragsdale and Brandau-Brown's (2005) marital study raises the issue of individual communicator characteristics by examining issues such as self-monitoring and Machiavellianism. They raise the possibility that men, who are skilled in modifying their self-presentation, tend to emphasize positivity as an attempt to create an advantageous climate. In addition, based on a study of attachment styles of married partners, Guerrero and Bachman (2006) found that secure individuals used more assurance, romantic affection, and openness than did dismissive individuals who were uncomfortable with closeness and commitment. They concluded that "attachment plays a role in the relationship maintenance process" (p. 357). More research needs to be conducted to explore the styles of individual "relationship maintainers."

Long-distance partnerships confront special challenges. Certain strategies, such as sharing tasks and sharing social networks, do not occur frequently. If ongoing ties depend almost totally on mediated messages, difficult topics are often avoided, resulting in some level of stagnation. Yet Dainton and Aylor (2002) found that when there are at least limited opportunities for face-to-face interaction, the relationship had a good chance for ongoing relational maintenance. The pressure to have "good" times when together results in the use of more positivity; avoidance of painful or problematic topics may result in an avoidance of challenging issues.

Parent and Child Relational Maintenance

When children are small, parents create most of the consciously chosen affection messages; even a toddler learns how to delight a parent with a hug, a kiss, or a "love you." At a much later point in life, circumstances may reverse as an adult child brings favorite foods to a nursing home or a grandchild sends e-cards to a housebound grandparent. As parent and child relationships move from being highly vertical to much more horizontal, responsibility for relational maintenance becomes shared. Across many years and life stages, parents and children learn, through negotiation and some tough conversations, how to stay connected as children need more independence and develop their own preferences for how to express connectedness. Conversely, changes in parental lives may affect their desires or needs for connection. During adolescence most parents and children express differences in their needs for autonomy and connection; in later years when adult children become parents, the autonomy-connection struggles with their own parents may intensify. In some cases, midlife adults may find themselves maintaining critical ties with two or three other generations (Shellenbarger, 2005).

My father takes such good care of his mother who has suffered with Alzheimer's for many years. Every Saturday morning he picks her up at the nursing home and takes her to the local Corner Bakery for breakfast. He holds her hand from the car to the restaurant and settles her into a chair. Dad orders oatmeal for her and a muffin for himself plus two coffees in paper cups with lids. Literally, he feeds her the oatmeal while she stares into space. He also helps her to manage some of the coffee. Dad talks to Grandma about the family and sometimes he touches her hand. Then, after about 25 minutes, they head back to the car.

When family life gets complicated, relational maintenance may involve other relatives or step-relatives who assume some or all parental responsibilities for a child. In many cases, the establishment of a relational tie with a stepchild or stepparent involves a complicated set of negotiations, ranging from "What do I call you?" to "How can I build a tie with you without hurting my father?" Given that many stepfamilies are formed through voluntary ties between adults and often involuntary ties between the stepparent and stepchildren, relational maintenance may be resisted or limited. Frequently, even the form of address becomes a contested issue as it relates to establishing ties (Koenig Kellas, LeClair-Underberg, & Lamb Normand, 2008). By necessity, grandparents may assume major parental responsibilities that necessitate a renegotiation of roles and relational maintenance activities (Soliz, Lin, Anderson, & Harwood, 2006). Parent-child relational maintenance will be discussed more fully in Chapter 10.

Sibling Relational Maintenance

Sibling ties represent the longest lifetime relationships for most people, but, until recently, little was known about how these ties are maintained through communication. In an examination of the five relational maintenance behaviors noted above, Myers and his colleagues' (2001) exploration of sibling relationship revealed that, although siblings are involuntarily linked, most report having a commitment to this relationship beyond obligatory ties. In their study of 262 persons, ranging in age from 18 to 90, siblings reported using sharing tasks, such as helping each other and sharing duties most frequently, and openness least frequently. They also found that the greater the sibling liking for each other, the more they tended to use all five maintenance strategies. Sibling liking is predicted by use of positivity and networks. In addition, supportive and nurturing behaviors on the part of a parent or even an older sibling reduce the influence of negative life events on children's social adjustment (Conger & Conger, 2002). It could also be argued that sibling alliances help maintain relationships because, as the opposite of sibling rivalry, they represent a combination of efforts (Nicholson, 1999). Later Myers (2008) conducted a study of relational maintenance strategies used by 640 adult siblings ranging in age from 18 to 82; findings revealed 53 maintenance behaviors that represented five strategies: tasks, networks, avoidance of negativity, humor, and confirmation or validation of their involvement in each others' lives. Overall research in this area supports the following conclusions: (1) female siblings use relational maintenance behaviors at a higher rate than males, (2) more intimate adult siblings use these behaviors more frequently that those in congenial or apathetic relationships, (3) use of maintenance efforts in early or middle adulthood depends on the level of psychological closeness, and (4) maintenance behaviors are used more strategically than routinely. As adult siblings enact relational maintenance strategies they "provide emotional, moral and psychological support, fulfill familial responsibilities, engage in shared activities, and remain involved in each other's lives" (Myers, 2011, p. 342), as noted in the next entry.

I have six brothers and sisters, and we are spread across the country from coast to coast. We all make an effort to keep in touch with each other through e-mail, blogging, social networking, phone calls, text messages, and visits. Much of our communication is focused around certain tasks such as going in together on a gift for Mother's Day or planning a family reunion or a visit. We provide each other emotional support through the ups and downs of life, such as acceptance into graduate school, marriage, pregnancy loss, unemployment, and illness. We are also in frequent contact about less monumental things—a text to my sister to see what she thought about the final episode of our favorite TV show, an e-mail to me from a different sister with a link to a video that she thought I would like, or a quick online chat with my brother on his birthday. As far-flung as we are geographically, all of these activities help us to feel close emotionally.

Adult siblings frequently confront the challenge of keeping connected across many miles while raising their own children. Single parents confront intense pressure to provide nurturing and functional support to their children.

In certain cases, external factors support family relational maintenance. Some relationships continue, in a stagnant state, because barriers prevent dissolution. In the case of marriage, these include external barriers, such as the financial cost of ending a long-term marriage; legal complications, such as the effort involved in getting a divorce; and social barriers, the networks of people who would be upset or negatively affected by a relational breakup. Certain adult sibling or extended family relationships are maintained primarily through politely sharing rituals, such as holiday dinners or weddings.

RELATIONAL MAINTENANCE STRATEGIES

Maintaining relationships takes attention and effort. If family members take time to think about each others' lives and consciously focus on keeping their relationships strong, they are rewarded with strong ties. Although there are many ways to maintain relationships, including the selective use of some of the identity-building strategies noted in the previous chapter, three major communication strategies serve to strengthen family relationships. These include confirmation, rituals, and relational currencies.

Confirmation

Confirming messages are the cornerstone of relational maintenance. Confirmation communicates recognition and acceptance of another human being—a fundamental precondition to intimacy. Sieburg (1973) provided four criteria for such messages. A *confirming message* (1) acknowledges the other person's existence, (2) affirms the other's communication by responding relevantly to it, (3) reflects and accepts the other's self-experience, and (4) suggests a willingness to become involved with the other.

Confirming responses may be contrasted with two alternative responses: rejecting and disconfirming. Whereas *confirming responses* imply an acceptance of the other person, *rejecting responses* imply the other is wrong or unacceptable. Confirming messages *do not* necessarily suggest one person agrees with the other, but responses such as "I see" display one's regard without expressing agreement (Canary, Cody, & Manusov, 2000). Rejecting messages might include such statements as "That's really dumb" or "Don't act like a two-year-old." Disconfirming responses send the message "You do not exist." They are a direct invalidation of the person. Disconfirming responses occur when a person is ignored, talked about as if he or she is invisible, excluded from a conversation, or excluded from physical contact (Stafford & Dainton, 1994).

When my sister remarried, she and her new husband tried to pretend they did not have her 12-year-old son, Paul, living with them. Her new husband did not really want him. They would eat meals and forget to call him, plan trips and drop him with us at the last minute, and never check on his work in school. The kid was a nobody in that house. Finally, his father took him, and Paul seems much happier now.

Confirming communication is characterized by recognition, dialogue, and acceptance, which indicates a willingness to be involved.

Recognition Verbally, one may confirm another's existence by using the person's name, including him or her in conversation, or just acknowledging the individual's presence. Comments such as "I missed you" or "I'm glad to see you" serve to confirm another person's existence. Nonverbal confirmation is equally important in the recognition process. Touch, direct eye contact, and gestures also may serve to confirm another person within the norms of diverse cultures.

Dialogue Dialogue implies an interactive involvement between two people. Comments such as "Because I said so" and "You'll do it my way or not at all" do not reflect a dialogical attitude, whereas "What do you think?" or "I'm upset—can we talk about it?" open the door to dialogue and mutual exploration. Nonverbal dialogue occurs in families in which appropriate affectionate displays are mutually shared.

Acceptance   "When we feel acceptance, even though disagreed with, we do not feel tolerated; we feel loved" (Malone & Malone, 1987, p. 73). Acceptance avoids interpreting or judging one another. Rather, it lets one another be. This may involve allowing yourself to hear things you really do not want to hear or acknowledging that you understand another's perspective.

Confirming behavior often reflects cultural backgrounds and one's family-of-origin. Persons who grew up in an inexpressive family may have trouble satisfying the reassurance and recognition needs of a partner or a child. Cultural differences in the use of eye contact or touch may create a sense of disconfirmation for one partner. Family connections develop from each member's sense of acceptance. When family members continuously ignore or mistreat each other, relational maintenance remains an impossible goal. If one "learns to love by being loved," then one learns to confirm by being confirmed.

Rituals

Rituals convey a variety of meanings and messages in emotionally powerful patterns; they remind members of who they are, how much they care about each other, and they reflect a family's relational culture, as demonstrated below.

My mom and I have a ritual of taking long late-night walks together . . . whenever I come home, I can count on a walk usually every other night. We generally walk late, after we have done our own things during the day and family things in the evening. It is our chance to talk together without interruption. We tend to share our deepest secrets at this time. (Koppen, 1997, p. 11)

One thing we NEVER do is go to bed alone. Ever. I don't go upstairs and get in bed and then Robert comes up later. Or vice versa. When we go to bed, we both go to bed. Together. (Bruess & Kudak, 2008, n.p.)

Conscious repetition of actions and words creates meaning, and creates ongoing family rituals. These special meanings, enacted in repetitive form, contribute significantly to the establishment and preservation of a family's identity or relational culture. Rituals are not just pleasurable routine events; rather, rituals serve central ongoing maintenance and relational functions. They may cluster around occasions such as dinnertime, errands, vacations, or religious celebrations, or rites of passage such as birthdays, graduations, and weddings. Sometimes rituals form around less pleasurable events such as conflicts, discipline, or teasing.

Symbolic activity helps family members make sense of their lives. Thompson and Dickson (1995) asserted that rituals function as communication events; their symbolizing function leads to "sense making," which involves remembering, belonging, instructing, transitioning, and providing community.

Family rituals range from those tied to the overall culture to those known only to two or three members. They may be categorized in the following manner:

1. Family celebrations, often tied to cultural norms, include the way holidays are celebrated or that certain special events are recognized.
2. Family traditions, reflecting unique family occasions, embody patterns passed down by family-of-origin members.
3. Patterned family interactions, reflecting everyday connections, emerge out of increasingly patterned interactions usually developed implicitly (Wolin & Bennett, 1984; Baxter & Braithwaite, 2006).

A *family ritual*, broadly defined as "a voluntary, recurring patterned communication event whose jointly enacted performance by family members pays homage to what they regard as sacred, thereby producing and reproducing a family's identity and its web of social relations" (Baxter & Braithwaite, 2006, p. 262–263), connects members in meaningful ways. Although many significant family events are highly ritualized, we are particularly concerned with meaningful patterned interactions that define everyday life for partners and family members rather than culturally established holiday rituals. Therefore, although rituals and routines (patterned behavioral interactions) coexist in families, rituals may be differentiated in that they involve an ascribed meaning to ongoing patterned interactions or routines (Crespo, Davide, Costa, & Fletcher, 2008). Thus, going to bed at the same time might be a practical couple routine but consciously choosing to always go to bed together carries significant meaning.

Couple Rituals

Expressions of affection, code words for secrets, and repetitive daily or weekly experiences are signs of a developing relational culture. Carol Bruess has extensively researched relationship rituals, identifying rituals both for couples (Bruess & Kudak, 2008a) and for parents with young children (Bruess & Kudak, 2008b). Based on her earlier interview research, she reported on the following types (Bruess & Pearson, 1997, pp. 33–41).

Couple Time   This frequently enacted ritual includes three types: enjoyable activities, togetherness rituals, and escape episodes. Enjoyable activities are illustrated by the couple who reports "playing volleyball every Tuesday" or watching foreign films. Togetherness refers to times when couples simply spend time being together, such as walks after dinner. Escape episodes include rituals specifically designed to satisfy couples' needs to be alone. Escape rituals, which provide "shared time," such as a monthly overnight stay in a hotel, provide couples with a way to create boundaries around themselves.

Idiosyncratic/Symbolic   These rituals are divided into favorites, private codes, play rituals, and celebration rituals. *Favorites* include couples' favorite, often symbolic, places to go, things to eat, items to purchase or give, and activities to do. For example, one woman reported:

> His favorite cake is wicky-wacky chocolate. It's a chocolate-out-of-scratch cake, an old family recipe . . . so when I really, really, really, really like him, and he's really, really, really, really made me happy, I bake him a wicky-wacky cake. He knows I'm really happy with him when he gets a wicky-wacky cake. (p. 35)

Private codes   These include the repeated, idiosyncratic use of jointly developed words, symbols, or gestures for communicating. These have a unique and special meaning. *Play rituals* represent intimate fun in the form of couples' kidding, teasing, silliness, and/or playful bantering. *Celebrations* represent the shared manner couples develop for celebrating or acknowledging special holidays, birthdays, anniversaries, or other special events. Most involve established rules. One couple may celebrate every month's anniversary; another may have elaborate birthday surprise rituals.

Daily Routines/Tasks   These involve accomplishing everyday, mundane activities, tasks, and chores and shared daily patterns. For instance, one partner will cook while the other cleans up.

Intimacy Expressions   These rituals involve physical, symbolic, and verbal expressions of love, fondness, affection, or sexual attraction. Intimacy rituals link to relational currencies described in the next chapter.

Communication   These rituals encompass couple talk time, including the specific times and ways couples establish opportunities for talking, sharing, or staying in touch with each other such as debriefing conversations, regular cell phone calls, or text messages.

Patterns/Habits/Mannerisms   These rituals involve interactional, territorial, and/or situational patterns or habits couples develop. For example, partners may always sleep on the same side of the bed or sit in the same chairs to watch television.

Spiritual   Certain rituals serve couples' religious needs and include praying or attending spiritual worship together, saying grace before meals, or celebrating Shabbat weekly.

Rituals serve important functions in established relational partnerships; they maintain the partners' relationships and signal coupleness to the outside world. Rituals support partners' shared meanings that create a "marital culture" (Gottman & Silver, 1999). In their study of couples with children, Bruess and Kudak (2008b) identified rituals that keep partners connected while actively involved in parenting. They collected examples such as putting the kids to bed together and, after they fall asleep, sitting in the room to talk about their day or any problems, or leaving older children home alone and road biking for two hours followed by pizza and beer at a favorite restaurant. Such rituals help keep the couples highly connected.

Even daily conversations may become ritualized due to their importance. In their study of couples' daily conversations, Alberts, Yoshimura, Rabby, and Loschiavo (2005) found that satisfied couples tend to have more conflicts on the weekends while asking about each other's experiences than during the week. Their research identified 13 categories of couple conversations that might be considered routine, but not necessarily all the time. These authors raise questions about the strategic versus the routine nature of these couple conversations.

An infrequent couple ritual involves the renewal of marriage vows. After interviewing couples who participated in such a ritual, Braithwaite and Baxter (1995) suggested that couples use this ceremonial event to "weave together their past, their present and their future commitments to one another" (p. 193). This ritual serves to maintain rather than repair the relationship, while communicating ongoing commitment to each other and a larger network of family and friends. In a study of individuals engaged in a renewal ritual, Baxter and Braithwaite (2002) found the experience allowed married couples to link two different idealizations of marriage—the public marriage, experienced with a community, and the private marriage of two expressive people. Countless couple rituals exist, but often their meaning and power is overlooked.

Intergenerational Rituals

Rituals serve as a way to bond family members of all ages across generations, providing a sense of family identity and connection. Rituals frequently involve parents and children. In an attempt to apply Bruess's categories to parent-child relations, Koppen (1997) studied mother-daughter rituals. She reports, "Although mothers and daughters share an involuntary relationship unlike that of married couples, the rituals shared by many mother-daughter pairs are relatively similar in form and type to those enacted in marital relationships" (p. 3). The following is one example.

When my mom and I lived alone, we ate cold corn niblets from the can and had cereal for dinner repeatedly. But later she got married and he only likes hot corn, served on the table, etc. So, whenever he goes away or misses dinner, we revert back to our old ways, all the while making jokes about it and bonding. It evolved into a bonding event for "the girls" because it was a reminder of the past and it only involved us.

Frequently grandparents and grandchildren develop their own rituals, which provide them with special connections. These may include regular phone calls, e-mails, sleepovers, special meals, everyday care, or summer trips, as indicated by this grandchild.

Ever since I was five years old, my grandfather has taken me on a trout fishing weekend in the mountains. He rents a cabin at a fishing camp and we pack lots of food and all our gear. We spend most of the day in the streams and cook on a grill every night. Then we sit and stare at the stars and talk about life—usually this is really about me. Over the years, the conversations have changed from my baseball games to my career plans, but generally he asks and listens. He does not give much advice. Hopefully these will go on for a long time.

As families change over time, members may discontinue or change some rituals, since "people are inventing new families to live by as well as with. The old images and rituals are changing even as new ones are coming into being" (Gillis, 1996, p. 226). Sometimes the cultural changes in gender roles impact couple satisfaction with family rituals. For example, men appear to be happier when their partners report more family investment in rituals, but the more husbands reported their investment in family rituals, the less happy and close their wives were. This may occur because women view their husbands as intrusive, or find them to be critical of the plans and preparations (Crespo, Davide, Costa, & Fletcher, 2008). This is a time of much family transition, as indicated by divorce-recognition greeting cards and divorce ceremonies as well as gay-male and lesbian marriages and commitment ceremonies as the evidence of ritual adaptation.

Many blended families struggle with the place of rituals and stories in their lives. According to Baxter, Braithwaite, and Nicholson (1999), the challenge is to selectively embrace certain features of both former families while creating new ones, so that both old and new family structures can be legitimated. Successful family rituals in the blended family "hold both sides" of the contradiction between old and new family systems. Their study of stepfamily rituals reveals that (1) some unsuccessful rituals carried from the former family were perceived to threaten the new one and (2) ritual practices help well-functioning stepparents and stepchildren accept the historical roots of their blended family while constructing the new one. In her study of post-bereaved stepfamilies (ones formed after the death of a parent), Bryant (2006) identified three family forms. *Integrated* families created rituals to memorialize and celebrate that parent's life, such as taking flowers to the grave; *denial* families had no rituals acknowledging the deceased parent; and *segmented* families struggled with the presence-absence tension, often engaging in rituals that avoided acknowledgment of the deceased parent. In general, stepfamily research indicates a need for adaptive responses to old ritualized behaviors and new rituals that bond stepfamily members.

Family Ceremonials and Celebrations

Ceremonials and major special events include several rites or rituals (Trice & Beyer, 1984). Family ceremonials may include weddings, graduations, and funerals, as these are major rites of passage events celebrated in U.S. culture. Ceremonials involve elaborate preparations. Celebrating marriage with a ceremony for friends

Holiday dinners usually involve family rituals.

and family members supports newlyweds as they establish their new identity, yet partners who have cohabited for multiple years or who marry later may not strongly emphasize the social components of their marriage (Kalmijn, 2004). In addition, major cultural events such as Thanksgiving or the Fourth of July involve ritualized family celebrations. In their study of Thanksgiving rituals, Benoit and associates (1996) identified "chronicling" as the most frequently occurring verbal behavior. *Chronicling* refers to "talk about present events or those of the recent past, in which the communicator updates others by providing information about his or her life" (p. 22). Grandparents and older relatives are likely to elicit this from children; the extended kinship network participates also.

Ceremonial rituals provide unique opportunities for family members to bond with each other and significant others in their communities. Although most family members experience identification and connection through their rituals, these opportunities may not be open to everyone. Participation in ritualistic family celebrations may be limited for members of the gay and lesbian community and those facing multiple problems such as poverty and illness (McGoldrick & Carter, 2003).

Negative Rituals

Although most of the writing and research on family or couple rituals reflects members' attempts to connect and convey caring in a positive manner, some families experience painful negative rituals. A partner may obsessively engage in work rituals to gain distance and avoid relational contact. Children in alcoholic families may ritualistically water down a parent's liquor bottles (Black, 2001). Even ordinary circumstances may foster negative rituals; when a younger child mispronounces a word, an older sibling may launch into a list of the child's other verbal mistakes, or when one spouse watches televised sports, the other may complain loudly about being deserted. Partner abuse may also become ritualized such as when a wife goes out with friends and is beaten for it (Jacobson & Gottman, 1998). Incest reflects a destructive ritual played out in families. Negative rituals are difficult to identify because persons are not likely to self-report their negative experiences (Bruess, 1997).

Relational Currencies

Since as early as I remember, affection has been displayed openly in my household. I remember as a young child sitting on my father's lap every Sunday to read the comic strips with him. I always hugged my father and mother, and still do. "I love you" is still the last thing said by my parents and by me when we talk on the telephone.

One partner may make sushi to please the other, or a grandfather may e-mail his granddaughter at college. Both of these instances represent an attempt to share affection, but the meaning depends on a shared perception.

Communication behaviors that carry meaning about the affection or caring dimension of human relationships can be viewed as *relational currencies,* (Villard & Whipple, 1976), or a vocabulary of loving behaviors. Relational currencies serve as a symbolic exchange process. As family members share currencies, they form agreements about their meanings that either strengthen or limit their relationship. Many currencies arise from family-of-origin patterns because every family implicitly and explicitly teaches its members specific ways to show caring for others and to accept caring from others (Wilkinson & Grill, 2011).

Types of Currencies

Certain currencies make a direct statement; the act is the message. For example, a hug can mean "I'm glad to see you" or "I'm sad that you are leaving." Usually, the sender's intent is clear and easily interpreted. Other currencies permit a greater range of interpretation. After a family quarrel, does the arrival of flowers mean "I'm sorry, I was wrong" or "I still love you even if we don't agree on one issue"? Multiple relational currencies exist. The list that follows and is shown in Figure 5.1 presents some of the common ways family members share affection; you may mentally add to this list. Each of these currencies represents one way of sharing affection. The use of each currency must be considered within the contexts of gender, ethnicity, class, and developmental stage (McGoldrick, Giordano, & Garcia-Preto, 2005).

Positive verbal statements	Money
Self-disclosure	Food
Listening	Favors
Nonverbal affect displays	Service
Touch	Staying in touch
Sexuality	Time together
Aggression	Access rights
Gifts	

FIGURE 5.1
Sample Relational Currencies

Positive Verbal Statements   Such statements include oral and written messages indicating love, caring, praise, or support. In some households people express affection easily, saying, "I love you" directly and frequently. Other families view such directness as unacceptable, preferring to save such words for unusual situations. Within families, age, gender, and roles affect this currency.

Self-Disclosure   This currency involves self-revelation, or taking the risk of voluntarily telling another individual personal information or feelings that he or she is unlikely to discover from other sources. Johnson (2008) argued that the way to deepen a relationship involves reestablishing the emotional connection through openness. Although self-disclosure can be manipulative, generally it serves to deepen understanding between people. As a relational currency, self-disclosure is intentionally used to demonstrate trust and affection in a relationship. This currency is discussed in Chapter 6.

Listening   Good listening carries a message of involvement with, and attention to, another person. Having a partner or a parent with good listening skills builds rapport leading to the development of strong relational bonds and relational satisfaction (Gottman & DeClaire, 2001). Attentive listening may be taken for granted and the effort discounted unless the speaker is sensitive to the listener's careful attention.

Nonverbal Affect Displays   Affect displays involve spontaneous indications of affection, best characterized as one's eyes lighting up or face breaking into a smile at the sight of another, as well as a vocal shift to squeals of delight or softer more intimate tones. These nonverbal displays of affect indicate joy and comfort at being in the other's presence.

Touch   This is the language of physical intimacy. Positive physical contact carries a range of messages about friendship, concern, love, comfort, or sexual interest. It contributes to one's physical and mental well-being. Touch, a very powerful currency, often conveys feelings that a family member may not be able to put into words. In many families a member's healing touch conveys significant caring.

Sexuality For adult partners, sexuality provides a unique opportunity for intimacy. The discourse surrounding intercourse, as well as the act itself, combine to create a powerful message of affection and unique bonds. Inappropriate sexual contact can destroy family members' ties to each other. Sexuality as communication is discussed in detail in Chapter 6.

Aggression Aggressive actions, usually thought to be incompatible with affection, may serve to create an important emotional connection between members of certain families. Persons who are uncomfortable with expressing intimacy directly may rely on verbal or physical aggression as a sign of caring. Often children find teasing or poking as a way to connect to a sibling. When adults do not know how to express intimacy in constructive ways, they may use bickering, sarcasm, or belittling as their means of contact. For aggression to function as a relational currency, the target of the tease or put-down must be able to interpret these as signs of caring.

In addition to these rather personal verbal and nonverbal contacts that convey caring rather directly, other currencies may require more active interpretation in order to translate the level of caring. These include:

Gifts Presents are currencies that may be complicated by issues of cost, appropriateness, and reciprocity. "Gifts become containers for the being of the donor" (Csikszentmihalyi & Rochberg-Halton, 1981, p. 37). The process of identifying, selecting, and presenting the gift serves as part of the currency. Gifts serve as a tangible symbol of caring or remembering the other (Chapman, 2004).

Money Dollars may serve as relational currency. If money is abundant and the major currency provided by a parent, it may not convey a message of affection. To be a relational currency, money must be given or loaned as a sign of affection and not as a family or spousal obligation. In tough economic times family members may experience giving or receiving money as either an obligation or a gift.

Food A symbol of nurturing in many cultures, food has emerged as an important currency in romantic and immediate family relationships. Preparing and serving special food for a loved one serves as a major sign of affection in many relationships.

Favors Performing helpful, thoughtful acts for another are complicated by norms of reciprocity and equality. To be considered as currencies, favors must be performed willingly rather than in response to a spousal or parental order. The underlying message may be missed if the effort required by the favor is taken for granted.

Service Service implies a caring effort that has evolved into a habitual behavior. Driving the car pool to athletic events, making the family members' coffee in the morning, or maintaining the checkbook may reflect routine currencies. Such services are frequently taken for granted, thus negating the underlying message of affection.

Staying in Touch This currency implies efforts to maintain important relational ties, often across significant distances. Daily cell phone interaction between parents and college-age students frequently conveys caring. Whereas e-mail is especially useful for connecting with distant relatives, it is also used extensively to stay in touch with those nearby (Boase, Horrigan, Wellman, & Rainie, 2006). Even if the conversations are not about intimate topics, the effort to stay in touch reflects caring.

Time Together Being together, whether it is just "hanging out" or voluntarily accompanying a person on a trip or errand, carries the message "I enjoy being with you." Fathers report great tension between their desire to spend time with their children as a way of showing caring and workplace pressures (Duckworth & Buzzannell, 2009). This is a subtle currency with potential for being overlooked.

Access Rights Allowing another person to use or borrow things you value is a currency when the permission is intended as a sign of affection. It is the exclusive nature of the permission that is given only to persons one cares about that makes this a currency.

This list of currencies does not represent the "last word" on the subject. You may identify unnamed currencies that you exchange or that you have observed in family systems. For example, Fujishin (1998) suggests that "doing nothing" can be a loving and powerful message in certain relationships because it may "communicate trust in what your loved one is doing by not intervening, redirecting, evaluating, instructing, or correcting" (p. 103). Across various cultures, currencies may convey different meanings.

Meanings and Currencies

Relational satisfaction is tied to perceptions about the relational currency exchange process. Although an individual may intend to convey affection, some family members may misinterpret that person's intentions. Pipher (1996) captures this idea, saying, "Two of ten people spend their lives searching for one kind of love, when all around them there is love if only they would see" (p. 142). When meanings are shared, rewards are experienced; when meanings are missed, costs are experienced. Over time, intimate partners will create common assumptions about the importance of certain currencies as they develop high levels of symbolic interdependence.

Currencies may be exchanged with the best intentions, yet accurate interpretation occurs only when both parties can learn to speak the other's language. Consider this example:

> Each of us tends to identify as *loving* those expressions of love that are similar to our own. I may express my love . . . by touching you, being wonderfully careless with you, or simply contentedly sitting near you without speaking. You may express an equally deep love feeling by buying me a gift, cooking the veal, working longer hours to bring us more monetary freedom, or simply fixing the broken faucet. These are obviously different ways of loving. (Malone & Malone, 1987, p. 74)

The question remains, does every partner realize that a favorite dinner or a repaired computer represents an attempt to show love? Perhaps you see others as more loving if they express their affection the same ways you do. Such similarity adds to symbolic interdependence and strengthens your relational culture.

Without common meanings for relational currencies, family members may feel taken for granted or rejected. One partner may place a high value on regular sexual relations. If the other partner holds similar views, their sexual currency will be appropriately exchanged. If not, these partners struggle with communicating affection. As another example, fathers report being more affectionate with their sons than sons reported them being (Floyd & Morman, 2005). Such perceptual differences are very common.

Occasionally routine currencies may become strategic, changing their meaning (Guerrero, Andersen, & Afifi, 2001). Holding hands while taking a walk may be routine touching, but reaching for another's hand after a fight may be strategic. Such a shift frequently reflects new attention to the currency, as noted in the following comment.

My mother and I often say "I love you" in a routine way. We take the phrase for granted. But, after a fight or if something bad happens to one of us, we tend to look directly at each other and say "I really do love you" just to make sure the message gets across.

Figure 5.2 provides a way to consider how a currency's meaning might be valued by two people. In quadrant 1, both persons value the currency, which makes communication relatively direct. In quadrants 2 and 3, one party values the currency but the other does not, leading to disappointments and missed messages. In quadrant 4, neither person values the currency; the agreement helps avoid missed messages.

What happens if family members wish to share affection but seem unable to exchange the currencies desired by others? Villard and Whipple (1976) concluded that spouses with more similar affection exchange behaviors were more likely to report (1) high levels of perceived equity and (2) higher levels of relationship satisfaction, thus greater relationship reward. Interestingly, accuracy in predicting (i.e., understanding) how the other spouse used currencies did not raise satisfaction levels. For instance, knowing that your partner sends love messages through flowers does not mean that you will be more positive toward this currency if you prefer intimate talks. Individuals who were very accurate at predicting how their spouses

	Other	
	Yes	*No*
Self *Yes*	Both value the currency	You value the currency; other does not
No	You do not value the currency; other does	Neither values the currency

FIGURE 5.2
Dyadic Value of Specific Relational Currency

would respond to certain currencies still reported low marital satisfaction levels if the couple was dissimilar in their affection behaviors, as indicated in the next entry.

When my wife went through a very bad time in her work, we bumped into our differences. My caring solution was to give advice, try to help more around the house, and leave some little gifts for her. These were not having much impact. Cyndi wanted someone to listen to her—empathically listen—not a bunch of suggestions. She wanted to be hugged and she needed verbal reassurance. Fortunately, Cyndi let her needs and wants be known, and in the midst of that self-disclosing conversation a crisis was turned into an opportunity. Since that time, as I have worked to provide listening, compliments, and hugs, the bond between us has grown stronger.

Exchanging relational currencies benefits family members. High-affection communicators receive advantages in psychological, emotional, mental, social, and relational characteristics compared to low-affection communicators (Floyd, 2002). Because of their secure attachment style they receive more affection from others.

A family's levels of cohesion and adaptability interact with its relational currencies. Highly cohesive families may expect large amounts of affection displayed with regularity, whereas low-cohesion families may not provide enough affection for certain members. Families near the chaotic end of the flexibility continuum may change the type of currencies valued, whereas more rigid systems may require the consistent and exclusive use of a few specific currencies. Family themes may dictate currency exchange: "The Hatfields will stick by each other through thick and thin" requires members to provide money for hard-pressed relatives.

Because a family system evolves constantly through dialectical struggles, the personal meaning of currencies changes. Members may change their strategies for sharing affection because of new experiences, pressures, or expectations. A lost job may result in fewer gifts but more sharing and favors within a family. The process of sharing relational currencies significantly affects the intimacy attained by the family members. The more similar the exchange process, the higher the levels of relational satisfaction.

CONCLUSION

This chapter explored a range of communication practices that maintain partnered and family relationships while leading to closeness among members. It opened with an overview of relational maintenance and then discussed confirmation, rituals, and relational currencies. Family connections cannot be achieved unless members nurture their relationships through commitment.

Think about the kinds of interactions you observe in the families around you. Is most of their communication strictly functional? Do you see attempts at connecting through rituals and relational currencies? Are these people able to demonstrate an ability to touch each other comfortably? All human beings long for connectedness, but it is a rare relationship in which the members (spouses, parents and children, siblings, grandparents) consciously strive for greater sharing over long periods of time. Such mutual commitment provides rewards known only to those who put forth their best efforts.

In Review

1. Think about a partnered relationship or family that you consider a well-maintained relationship. Describe three specific examples of members' caring behaviors.
2. Identify three everyday rituals that a couple you know uses to keep in touch with each other and reaffirm their relational ties? How effective are their efforts?
3. Observe the use of confirming behaviors in a particular relationship and indicate the extent to which the receiver appears to recognize the effort. Explain how some attempts at confirmation might be taken for granted after a while.
4. Take a position on the following statement: "If you have to work at a relationship, there is something wrong with the relationship." Give your reasons for the position.
5. Analyze a significant sibling or a grandparent-grandchild relationship. Describe the efforts each person appears to make to maintain their relational ties.

KEY WORDS

Intimacy within Partnerships and Families

"Ruth, one of my dearest friends, has been married for more than fifty-five years. I once asked her to what she attributed her long marriage to Bob. She smiled and calmly said, 'The knowledge that some decades are harder than others.'"

— Randy Fujishin, *Gifts from the Heart*

Angela, the oldest of three daughters and a young valued professional at a major San Francisco bank, lives in a downtown high rise apartment building, but spends many weekends at home or hanging out with her younger sisters in the city. Her middle sister, Valeria, a star on the basketball team of a local state college, never comes home. Her other sister, Andrea, is completing her junior year in high school while working fifteen hours a week as a hostess at a local restaurant. Their mother and alcoholic father, Joseph, work as Emergency Medical Technicians on alternate schedules. Over the past 10 years the couples' fights have escalated, leaving the girls frightened and frustrated. They have encouraged their mother to leave but instead she copes by working extra hours and going out with friends. When Angela left for college she felt like she was abandoning her younger sisters; after Valeria left for college, Angela determined to save Andrea from the fighting and turmoil at home.

Currently, Angela spends weekends at her parents' home outside the city or invites Andrea to stay at her apartment. Sometimes they will watch Valeria's games and hang out together on her campus; other times they enjoy the coffee shops and events in the city. Angela spends many hours advising Andrea on the college application process; she plans to take her to visit some schools outside California in the next few months. Andrea talks about how lonely she is at home because her parents fight, and when Dad drinks, she wants to run away. Angela listens, reassuring her that, if Dad becomes abusive, Andrea must move in with her. During their hours together these sisters share dreams, plan their futures, and reassure one another that "We will always be there for each other."

Their friends talk about Max and Julie's relationship as incredibly special. Married for nine years to her college sweetheart, Julie still lights up when he enters a room. In turn, he knows just how to make her laugh. Although she worries about her father with Alzheimer's and he carries the burden of losing his younger brother in a car accident, they find ways to bring joy to each other on a daily basis.

Their rule "Never go to bed without a kiss" means that they have to settle any of their disagreements before going to sleep. Usually, it's easy but sometimes it takes an hour before that kiss. Each checks in with the other during the day, often just with a texted love message. When Max travels for business, affectionate notes appear in his suitcase; when Julie goes on her annual "Girls Weekend," flowers appear in her hotel room with a note, "Love, Me."

Life has its complications. After two years of trying to conceive a child, Julie learned that her endometriosis might prevent a pregnancy. This announcement led to long discussions about shared dreams and other routes to parenthood, and a decision to wait for a few more years before moving forward with adoption plans. Although stressful, these conversations brought them even closer together as each reaffirmed a commitment to their marriage, with or without children. Currently they are planning a wedding anniversary camping trip to the Grand Tetons where they honeymooned almost a decade ago.

Family connections, sometimes solid and sometimes fragile, depend on members' communicative efforts to create connections and intimacy. Although some relationships are maintained at low to moderate levels of connection for long periods, many family relationships reach a level of intimacy that involves sharing interpersonal emotions including love, warmth, passion, and joy (Guerrero & Anderson, 2000).

The word *intimacy* comes from the term *intimus* meaning "inner." Most individuals develop a personal sense of what intimacy means but multiple definitions exist. The term *presence*, or "being there" for another, may be understood as intimacy; it implies physical, emotional, and cognitive presence (Foley & Duck, 2006). To some intimacy means that "we can be who we are in a relationship and allow the other person to do the same" (Lerner, 1989, p. 3); to others intimacy involves a cluster of interpersonal emotions including love, warmth, passion, and joy that are tied to intimate feelings (Guerrero & Anderson, 2000). Essentially all definitions of intimacy share one important feature, "a feeling of closeness and connectedness that develops through communication between partners" (Laurenceau, Barrett, & Rovine, 2005).

Marital and family intimacy reflect many similarities. In a classic article, Feldman (1979) suggested that marital intimacy involves the following characteristics: (1) a close, familiar, and usually affectionate or loving personal relationship; (2) a detailed and deep knowledge and understanding from close personal connection or familiar experience; and (3) sexual relations (p. 70). Gottman (1994b) maintains stable couples exhibit a 5:1 ratio of positivity to negativity, evidenced by indicators such as displaying interest, affection, caring, acceptance, empathy, and joy. Intimacy research tends to focus on marriages or adult partnerships, but, with the exception of sexual relations, these characteristics apply to all family relationships. Clearly intimacy is different among siblings than between children and parents or other relatives. Family intimacy involves interpersonal devotion along intellectual, emotional, and physical dimensions, demonstrated by shared knowledge and understanding of others as well as close loving relationships appropriately reflective of developmental stages and culture. The concept of intimacy becomes a reality through partners' and family members' communication patterns.

Acceptable levels of family intimacy reflect the interactions of members as they deal with dialectical tensions over long periods of time. Relational intimacy reflects each member's past intimate experiences, current need for intimacy, perception of the other, and desire for maintaining or increasing connections within a relationship. Yet, over time, each individual experiences differing needs for and comfort with intimate ties. Schnarch (1991) argued that expectations of reciprocity promote unrealistic expectations of emotional fusion that are "alien to the acute experience of self and partner as related entities" (p. 116). Therefore, when one member of a couple feels that the intimacy is becoming too great, he or she will initiate some conflictual or withdrawal behavior to decrease the interpersonal closeness. This is a type of relational calibration. The same concept may be applied to other family relationships. Each two-person subsystem sets limits for acceptable intimacy at a given point in time. A small son and his mother may cuddle, tickle, kiss, and hug. A teenager and stepmother may discuss the adolescent's personal hopes or dreams, express affection verbally, and exchange kisses on occasion. A husband and wife develop limits for acceptable and unacceptable sexual intimacy as well as sharing feelings and showing nonverbal affection. Intimacy limits change over time; touch may become more or less important over time whereas the desire to share dreams may reappear at critical life moments. True intimacy occurs most often in two-person relationships, although there are exceptions. The comment below indicates how higher levels of intimacy can emerge after years of partnership.

After 26 years of marriage, my parents seem to have an incredibly close relationship that I haven't seen in other people. They often hold hands. They share common interests in music and theater. They just can't get enough of each other, but each has special friends and interests, which balances their intensity. Life hasn't been all that easy for them, either, yet each has helped the other cope.

Finally, intimacy is tied to overall family themes, images, boundaries and biosocial issues. Family themes that stress verbal sharing, such as "There is no need to carry secrets alone," may promote honest disclosure if a sense of support exists; if not, secrets will prevail. Viewing members as a team or a nest may convey closeness. Boundaries influence the extent to which intimacy occurs in family subsystems and how intimacy develops with those outside the immediate family. Gender-related attitudes support or restrict the capacity of members to express intimacy directly. Knowing information about another family member is not sufficient to develop intimacy. Relational growth depends on meaningful communication about that knowledge (Duck, Miell, & Miell, 1984).

The basis for all relationships lies in the members' abilities to share meanings through communication. Countless studies of enduring and/or healthy marriages or families emphasize the importance of communication as a hallmark of successful family relationships (Covey, 1997; Gottman, 1994, 1999; Foley & Duck, 2006). Marital and family intimacy develops from the base of relational maintenance behaviors, discussed in the last chapter.

In this chapter we will examine major factors that serve to undergird the development of communication-related closeness and intimacy as well as factors that threaten intimate ties. The former include commitment, self-disclosure, and sexual communication. Other factors, such as effort and sacrifice, forgiveness, and sanctification also contribute to intimacy development. Barriers include jealousy and deception. Because closeness is co-constructed in the ongoing management of both interdependence and independence, differences and struggles are inevitable.

Commitment

"If you have to work at a relationship, there's something wrong with it. A relationship is either good or it's not." These words capture a naive but common belief about marital and family relationships. How often have you heard people argue that relationships should not require attention or effort? Yet it is only through commitment that a loving relationship remains a vital part of one's life. *Commitment* implies intense singular energy directed toward sustaining a relationship. As such, it emphasizes one partnership relationship which limits other possibilities. This dual reality represents the key distinction between "commitment as the intrinsic desire to be with the partner in the future and commitment defined in terms of limits on personal choice" (Fincham, Stanley, & Beach, 2007, p. 280). In their study of marriage renewal rituals, Baxter and Braithwaite (2002) found that their couples viewed commitment as a "lifetime promise to stay in the marriage, not a fair-weather declaration to be abandoned when maintaining the relationship became effortful" (p. 103). A recent study of dating and married couples reveals that the relationships of married couples revolve around upholding the commitment made to their partners (Molden, et al., 2010). Other researchers assert that "getting married doesn't merely certify a preexisting love relationship. Marriage actually changes people's goals and behaviors" (Waite & Gallagher, 2000, p. 17). Other family relationships experience commitment differently as these do not rely on a singular tie. Siblings and other relatives may experience multiple commitments within the extended family including voluntaristic ties.

Commitment includes personal dedication and constraints (Stanley, 1998). *Personal dedication* involves one's internal devotion to the relationship, whereas *constraint commitment* refers to factors that bind people in relationships regardless of devotion. The latter include religious beliefs, promises, children, finances, and parental or social pressure. Over time, partnerships and families are held together by a combination of these types of commitments. In good times, members *want to* be connected; during rough times, members stick it out because they *ought to* do so. Under difficult conditions, they may *have to* stay together. For example, marital commitment may be very challenging when one partner becomes disabled or addicted to drugs. In his discussion of adjusting to his wife's progressive neuromuscular disease, hearing loss, and stroke, Piercy (2006) describes how his marriage changed in later life:

> When Susan and I talk together with friends, I make sure that she can follow the conversation. When we go out, I make sure she navigates the steps. Our shifting system rebalances, and we move on. (p. F13)

Adult mature commitment in intimate relationships goes deeper than an equity model of reciprocity. In such relationships "the bittersweet awareness of immutable separateness heightens the salience of intimacy" (Schnarch, 1991, p. 118) because the depth of the commitment is associated with higher relationship satisfaction and stability and with behaviors that maintain and enhance the quality of relationships (Flanagan, et al., 2002). Commitment may be the sole reason that carries people through rough times, as the following individual experienced.

There have been two times when James and I have remained together only because of outside forces—money was tight, no one else was an option, or guilt at breaking a promise. That may not be bad for 17 years but they were low points and relatively brief. Thankfully.

In her exploration of a marital life of commitment during a period of geographic separation, Diggs (2001) examined her own marriage to explore a 24-year African American marriage from inside the relationship. She captures the intensity of connection, the gender differences in emphasizing emotional versus physical presence, and concludes by suggesting that their commitment is characterized by "displays of love, and physical presence (emotional and instrumental), and dialoguing to find a connection (I *feel ya*; refocus on the person or values that keeps a couple together; and the awareness of levels or areas of unity)" (p. 25).

Intensity, repetition, explicitness, and codification support commitment talk. Certain phrases need to be repeated, and certain ideas need to be emphasized or reaffirmed. Explicitness reduces misunderstanding: "I will stand behind you even if I don't agree " or "We are brothers and that means I will support you." Such comments make the commitment quite clear. Codifying communication may be reflected in anything from love letters to a written agreement of rules for fighting to a marital contract. In the opening couple vignette, loving partners Max and Julie continuously reaffirm their love and commitment to each other in everyday meaningful ways. Parental commitment to a child, a one-sided implicit promise, emerges in the many comments or conversations reassuring one's offspring that "Daddy will always love you" or "I will always be there for you." Commitment is not always easy; words may be hard to find and say. According to Knapp and Vangelisti (2005), "The way we enact our commitment talk is at least as important, if not more so, than the content itself" (p. 297).

Although an increasing number of same-sex couples are marrying, as it is legally sanctioned in some states and not in others, some same-sex partners participate in commitment ceremonies while others enact commitment in different ways. In a recent study of 20 long-term cohabiting couples, 60 percent reported conceptualizing and forming committed relationships as they moved through the years without a ceremony (Reczek, Elliott, & Umberson, 2009). Most did not believe the commitment ceremony made a difference since it was not legal, but some respondents reported transitioning to committed unions through their many years together and being out to those around them. They did not need a ceremony to convey commitment. Yet the majority of these individuals reported desiring legal same-sex marriage.

Self-Disclosure

Intimacy is an "experiential outcome of an interpersonal, transactional, *intimacy process* reflecting two principal components: self-revealing and partner responsiveness" (Laurenceau, Barrett, & Rovine, 2005, p. 315). Such self-revealing or self-disclosures serve as a highly significant, complex, and difficult type of interpersonal communication. In an original definition, *self-disclosure* is described as occurring when one person intentionally tells another individual personal or private things about himself or herself that the other is unable to discover in a different manner. Self-disclosure involves risk on the part of the discloser, but intimacy develops only when the "other" is responsive. For the discloser to experience intimacy the listener must respond verbally or nonverbally in a manner that conveys validation, understanding, and caring (Laurenceau, Barrett, & Rovine, 2005). This creates intersubjectivity, or communicators' access to each other's thoughts and feelings (Foley & Duck, 2006), which is a prerequisite for true sharing.

Trust, the essence of which is emotional safety, serves as the foundation for self-disclosure because "trust enables you to put your deepest feelings and fears in the palm of your partner's hand, knowing they will be handled with care" (Avery, 1989, p. 27). High mutual self-disclosure is usually associated with voluntary relationships within a strong relational culture, characterized by trust, confirmation,

❙ Parent-adolescent self-disclosure paves the way for strong adult relationships.

and affection. Essentially, self-disclosure creates *mental love maps* of "the other" in a relationship (Gottman, 1999), permitting access to deeper parts of his or her life. Yet, high levels of negative self-disclosure may occur within some relationships, resulting in conflict and anger. Some cautions about high self-disclosure need to be considered, since it can be destructive, manipulative, or overwhelming to another. The cost of high levels of sharing is personal vulnerability. Satisfaction and disclosure create a curvilinear relationship; that is, relational satisfaction is greatest at moderate levels of disclosure (Littlejohn, 1992). Essentially, adult self-disclosure is coordinated through an ongoing process influenced by each individual's personal experiences, family-of-origin patterns, and the nature of the disclosure recipient.

Family Background   Family-of-origin experiences, cultural heritage, and gender set expectations that influence self-disclosing behavior. Ethnic heritage influences the amount and type of self-disclosure. For example, in many Japanese families, the degree of intimacy is prescribed by position or status; members rely heavily on nonverbal communication to share critical feelings and important messages (Shibusawa, 2005). Whereas Jewish families exhibit verbal skill and a willingness to talk about trouble and feelings, Irish families may find themselves at a loss to describe inner feelings (McGoldrick, 2005). Verbal emotional disclosure is viewed as a more feminine style of relating, whereas the more masculine style of connecting privileges sharing joint activities (Wood, 2011). Accordingly, women seem to receive more self-disclosures than do men (Pearson, West, & Turner, 1995).

Partner Relationships   Marital self-disclosure involves not only the disclosure by one partner but the listener's responses that can be perceived as supportive, understanding, accepting, or caring. Partner responsiveness is linked to the development of satisfying and close relationships. A major study of intimacy in marriage, involving spouses writing diary entries for 42 evenings, revealed that "both self-disclosure and partner disclosure significantly predicted rating of intimacy for husbands and wives on a day to day basis" (Laurenceau, Barrett, & Rovine, 2005, p. 321). These researchers found that perceptions of responsiveness to self-disclosures served as an important predictor of experiencing feelings of intimacy daily.

Partner health issues raise disclosure concerns for couples. Goldsmith (2009) suggested that the partnership context draws attention to their "interdependence as a distinctive feature of uncertainty management" (p. 205). Such circumstances confront partners with issues of empathic distress, active engagement, or discussing feelings, engaging in joint problem solving, and buffering or hiding concerns to protect the other.

High disclosure of negative feelings is related to decreased marital satisfaction. Dissatisfied marital partners often invalidate the feelings disclosed by a spouse about relational difficulties which negatively impacts marital satisfaction (Clements, Markman, Cordova, & Laurenceau, 1997). Partners who feel comfortable sharing their emotions and talking about different issues in their marriage are more satisfied (Finkenauer & Hazam, 2000). Yet, couples who insist on "No secrets" frequently discover such openness obliterates any sense of individuality (Imber-Black, 1998).

Parent-Child Relationships Parent-child disclosure has received some attention, revealing that self-disclosure does not involve all family members equally. Most mothers receive more self-disclosure than fathers (Waterman, 1979). Parents perceived as nurturing and supportive elicit more disclosure from children who find those encounters rewarding. Although older studies indicated that college students were more likely to disclose more information more honestly to same-sex best friends than to either parent (Tardy, Hosman, & Bradac, 1981), relationships between many college students and their parents have become far more open. Factors such as smaller families, a desire to remain interconnected, and constant mediated accessibility have contributed to a greater sense of partnership and openness, although this does not apply in certain cultures (Galvin, 2008). However, in some families parental privacy invasion occurs as parents and growing children struggle with autonomy and closeness-boundary conflicts (Petronio, 1994). Such invasion may be met with secrecy or confrontation. In her study of mother-daughter pairs, Miller-Day (2004) found significant differences in self-disclosure between those who were connected and those who were enmeshed. The connected pairs were more comfortable with sharing and managing boundaries appropriately. The enmeshed pairs tended to exhibit great demands for disclosure and a great need for secrecy to maintain a sense of personal identity. Although one might imagine stepfamily members would report more secrets and single-parent family members would report fewer secrets, Caughlin and colleagues (2000) report the degree of openness, number of topics, and function of secrets was consistent across stepfamilies, single-parent families, and two-parent biological families.

The nature of the disclosure topic impacts the response. An examination of parental reactions to their child's gay male or lesbian sexual orientation disclosure indicated that increasing numbers of adolescents are revealing their sexual orientation to their parents. In many cases, sadness, denial, anger, and self-blame were common parental reactions; although some mothers were supportive, the majority responded with some degree of negativity, denial, or intolerance (Willoughby, Doty, & Malik, 2008). Sometimes parents turn to children as confidants and comforters after a divorce, revealing so much personal information that discomfort results. Some divorced mothers need daughters to listen to their negative feelings about their ex-husbands, financial, and personal worries, yet this creates distress for the younger women (Koerner, Wallace, Lehman, & Raymond, 2002). Children often become anxious and worry about their parents' well-being when their parents share too much difficult information related to their divorce (Koerner, Jacobs, & Raymond, 2000).

The structural nature of the relationship also affects disclosure. In-law disclosure has the potential to affect a younger couple's marital satisfaction, although the effects are mediated by family in-group status and in-law satisfaction (Morr Serewicz, Hosmer, Ballard, & Griffin, 2008). For example, although disclosure about family information from in-laws to husbands was positively related to their wives' satisfaction, feeling part of the in-group and satisfaction with in-laws mediates the relationship between in-law disclosure and marital satisfaction for wives.

The Practice of Self-Disclosure Considering the time required to manage the functional, everyday aspects of family life, you can understand that little time or energy may be available for self-disclosure. According to Montgomery (1994), "While self-disclosure may have significant impact in close relationships, it does not occur with great frequency even between the happiest of partners" (p. 78). Finding everyday time to talk together establishes a context that supports some level of self-disclosure. Vangelisti and Banski (1993) reported that if couples hold *debriefing conversations,* or talk about how their day unfolded, partners are more likely to experience marital satisfaction. Such conversations set the groundwork for discussing riskier topics. In addition, some contexts, such as long rides in a car or a ritual of taking a walk in the evening, encourage members' disclosure. Hence, risk-taking communication is not likely to occur frequently within family life, but certain developmental or unpredictable stresses may trigger extensive amounts of personal discussion, especially if ongoing lower levels of disclosure occur regularly.

A sequence of appropriate nonverbal signals occurring in the context of verbal disclosure also contributes significantly to mutual understanding. For example, nonverbal signals may tell a husband that his wife is surprised that he is unaware of her feelings about a topic (Duck, Miell, & Miell, 1984, p. 305). Duck and colleagues proposed the term *intimation sequences* for these signals in which both partners intimate new levels of awareness within a discussion. Parents may become skilled at reading a child's facial expressions and recognizing a desire or need to talk. Thus, verbal self-disclosure and nonverbal intimation sequences are bound together in face-to face interaction.

Families create unique opportunities for self-disclosure. Joint living space provides the potential for such interaction, yet positive relationships, including trust, must exist. Parents may break a child's trust unwittingly because they discussed the child's concern with another adult, not respecting the child's privacy. Unless disclosers indicate how private certain information is to them, another person may accidentally reveal that information to others. This, as noted in the next quote, damages the relationship.

I have stopped discussing anything important with my mother because she cannot keep her mouth shut. She has told my aunt and some friends at work all about my relationship with my boyfriend, my use of birth control pills, and some of my health problems. Well, she doesn't have much to tell them now since she doesn't hear about my real concerns anymore.

Sibling disclosure increases as children age and learn to share their significant feelings as well as to protect their siblings' confidences. Young children may understand the nature of secrets, but the process of sharing oneself with another tends to emerge in adolescence. Younger adolescents' sibling disclosure occurs based on their perceptions of their relational connection to a brother or sister (Howe, Aquan-Assee, Bukowski, Lehoux, & Rinaldi, 2001). Disclosers felt positively about sharing when warmth and closeness existed in their sibling connection. As discussed in Chapter 3, communication privacy management theory holds that if self-disclosure messages are not carefully coordinated, boundary turbulence occurs. For example, when a brother reveals his sister's recent pregnancy to key relatives before his sister tells them, she may become angry.

Recent scientific and medical advances raise critical self-disclosure issues for family members. Genetic health represents a critical area of family disclosure and discussion. The proband, or first family member identified with a genetic disease, often carries the responsibility of informing other members. Issues such as gender, relationship to certain relatives, privacy rules, the nature of the disease, and culture influence such disclosures (Gaff, et al., 2007). When an individual or couple decides to use a sperm donor to achieve parenthood, decisions about disclosing to other relatives or to the child remain controversial (Golombok, MacCallum, Goodman, & Rutter, 2002).

Self-disclosure bears a direct relationship to family levels of cohesion and flexibility. An extremely cohesive family may resist members' negative self-disclosures, fearing the disclosures would threaten their connectedness, particularly if the family has a low capacity for adaptation. For example, a highly cohesive family with a theme of "We can depend only on each other" would resist negative disclosures, such as a member's desire to convert to another religion that might cause internal conflict. Families with moderate to high adaptation and cohesion capacities may cope relatively well with the effects of high levels of positive or negative self-disclosure. Essentially, "The complex dynamics of individual disclosures can contribute to the construction of a family identity" (Foley & Duck, 2006, p. 193).

Sexuality and Communication

How would you describe a sexually healthy adult partnership? For most partners, sexuality within a marital or partnership relationship involves far more than just physical performance; it involves the members' sexual identities, their history of sexual issues, their mutual perceptions of each others' needs, their feelings for their partners, the messages contained within their sexual expression, and the nature of their sexual communication. The quality of the sexual relationship affects, and is affected by, the other characteristics of intimacy—the affectionate/loving relationship and mutual knowledge of the two partners. These characteristics influence partners' overall sexual patterns as well as day-to-day sexual expressions (Ridley, Collins, Reesing, & Lucero, 2006).

How would you describe a healthy approach to sexuality within the family relationship? According to Maddock (1989), healthy sexuality reflects the balanced expression of sexuality in family structures that enhance the personal identity and sexual health of members and the system as a whole. Both parental conversations about sexuality with their children (Miller, Kotchik, Dorsey, Forehand, & Ham, 1998) and parental comfort with the area of sexuality influence the family climate.

At both the partnership and family level, sexual issues are linked directly to intimacy and communication. In fact, "communication plays an important role in the development of intimate sexuality" (Troth & Peterson, 2000, p. 195). Sex communication implies "people exchanging verbal and nonverbal messages in a mutual effort to co-create meaning about sexual beliefs, attitudes, values, and/or behavior" (Warren, 2006, p. 321). Sexuality, including sexual attitudes and behavior, may be viewed as a topic of communication, a form of communication, and a contributing factor to overall relational intimacy and satisfaction. Sprecher and McKinney (1994) suggested, "Sex is not only an act of communication or self-disclosure. Verbal and nonverbal communication is essential for the accomplishment of rewarding sexual episodes" (p. 206). Although sexuality and intimacy can be experienced as disconnected in certain relationships, we believe sexuality is directly related to intimacy in partner and family ties. In the following pages, sexuality will be explored in terms of partner communication, parent-child communication, and communication breakdowns.

The basis for a mutually intimate sexual relationship reflects each partner's orientation toward sexuality, particularly that which was learned in their families-of-origin. An individual's sexuality remains closely intertwined with his or her intrapersonal, interpersonal, and environmental systems—systems that interlock yet vary in importance according to an individual's age. The sexual dimensions of family life are tied strongly to gender identities, boundaries, and developmental change. Much of your sexual conduct was originally learned, coded, and performed on the basis of biosocial beliefs regarding gender identity learned in your family-of-origin. Most parents possess a set of gender-specific ideas about males and females developed from their childhood experiences and from "typical" behaviors of girls or boys of similar ages to their children. In addition, cultural background influences expectations about what it means to be a male or female. Personal identities include sexual/gender identity as a core component, which influences later sexual experiences.

Partner Communication As an individual develops sexual experiences and a sexual identity, his or her personal background influences these encounters, as does the partner's sexual identity. Couples establish their own patterns of sexual activity early in the relationship, and these patterns typically continue (Sprecher & McKinney, 1994). Strong connections exist between sexual desire and interpersonal affect. A 56-day couple diary study of the interpersonal affect-lust link found that mutual lust was influenced by relational affect and current relational state. Partners' lust and positive and negative affect (feelings for the partner) was associated with the other spouse's lust. On days when partners had relatively high affect toward their spouses, their spouses were also likely to experience higher lust and vice versa (Ridley, Collins, Reesing, & Lucero, 2006). Open communication becomes critical for both individuals, since a good sexual relationship depends on what is satisfying to each partner. A couple that cannot communicate effectively about many areas of their life will have difficulty developing effective communication about their sexual life. In short, "Communication in the bedroom starts in other rooms" (Schwartz, 1994, p. 74).

This sense of mutuality is enhanced by direct and honest communication between partners. Some understanding comes only through a combination of self-disclosure and sensitivity when spouses reveal their needs and desires while learning to give pleasure to the other. From another perspective, there is a distinction between monological and dialogical sex—the former being sexual experiences in which one or both partners attempt to satisfy only personal needs. Dialogical sex is characterized by mutual concern and sharing of pleasure (Wilkinson, 2006).

Some partners find it difficult to talk about their sexual relationship. Their *discourse of intercourse,* or "sexual conversation which occurs between two people prior to, during, and after sex" (Adelman, 1988, p. 1), is impoverished and ineffective. Some sexual discussions are rife with euphemisms which may serve to romanticize or confuse the message. Euphemisms serve partners well when they promote the desired erotic climate but create disappointment or distance when they replace honest dialogue. Satisfied couples report their ability to directly discuss issues of feelings about sex, desired frequency of intercourse, who initiates sex, desired foreplay, sexual techniques, or positions. They avoid "mind reading," such as "If she really loved me, she'd know I would like . . ." or "If he really loved me, he would. . . ." Metacommunication is central to intimate sexual experience. "Marital difficulties often lead to sexual difficulties (and vice versa) because of the difficulty of precluding metacommunication during sexual contact" (Schnarch, 1991, p. 98).

Partners must develop ways to engage in sexual self-disclosure. In a study of dating, MacNeil and Byers (2005) investigated two pathways between sexual self-disclosure and sexual satisfaction—expressive and instrumental. The expressive pathway implies reciprocal sexual self-disclosure contributes to relationship satisfaction, which leads to greater sexual satisfaction. The instrumental pathway implies one's own sexual self-disclosure leads to greater partner understanding of one's sexual likes and dislikes, leading to a more favorable balance of sexual costs and rewards, which promotes greater sexual satisfaction. These authors found support "for the expressive pathway for women and for the instrumental pathway for both men and women" (p. 178). They suggest that sexual disclosure by both partners may contribute more to relational and sexual satisfaction in long-term relationships than in dating relationships. Based on their history of sexual relations in a committed relationship, partners may be freer to discuss their dislikes and both partners will have a history of what is sexually satisfying to each other.

Because of their "taboos" regarding a discussion of sexual behavior, couples may rely solely on nonverbal communication to gain mutual satisfaction. Much communication around sexuality is nonverbal; it may be more romantic but it also can create more confusion (Sheehy, 1997). Some partners report a fear of using any affectionate gesture because the other spouse always sees it as an invitation to intercourse; others say their partners never initiate any sexual activity, while their partners report being ignored or rebuffed for such attempts. Mutual satisfaction at any level of sexual involvement depends on open communication between spouses, yet intercourse, according to Lederer and Jackson (1968), is special "in that it requires a higher degree of collaborative communication than any other kind of behavior exchanged between the spouses" (p. 117).

Sexual communication in the early years of a partnered relationship may not predict sexual communication decades later. Due to longevity and good health practices many individuals remain sexually active into their seventh decade or longer. Life cycle studies reveal that sexuality remains important, yet sexual expectations are altered due to developmental changes and health issues. Couples interviewed about the history of their sex lives report that they have experienced dramatic changes in sexual interest, depending on other pressures in their lives. Dual-career couples report a decline in time and desire for sexual activity. Sexuality may become more pleasurable in midlife when a couple's child-rearing burdens cease.

Across the decades some relationships face medical crises and accompanying sexual difficulties. A trauma such as a miscarriage also affects a couple's interpersonal and sexual relationships, necessitating ongoing and often difficult conversations. Yet, couples with greater self-disclosure experience higher marital adjustment (Swanson, Karmali, Powell, & Pulvermakher, 2003). Concerns, such as premature ejaculation or other performance issues, often change sexual patterns. When a male experiences this issue, reactions include performance anxiety, interpersonal alienation, and a dread of talking about sex; such experiences require couples to discuss the issue using active listening and sexual negotiation (Metz & McCarthy, 2003). Diagnosis and treatment of a partner's prostate cancer raises relational issues for many couples. Although such a diagnosis does not necessarily reduce interest in sexuality, it may heighten the need for emotional closeness and reassurance of attractiveness. Many women find themselves moving from feeling protected and cared for to a role of emotional caretaker, whereas men may feel less self-sufficient. Sexual miscommunication is common as sex is less likely to be spontaneous and may feel less romantic. It may have to be planned, which can be frustrating for many survivors and their partners (Sanders, Pedro, Bantum, & Galbraith, 2006). Talking releases some of the emotions, provides a better sense of the other's feelings, and creates a greater sense of closeness. Thus, for couples engaged in an intimate relationship, open and direct communication about sexuality may deepen their intimacy even during times of struggle.

Parent-Child Communication   Parent-child discussions of sexuality support a sense of family connectedness. Such conversations have become more open due to greater societal openness, media treatment of sexuality, concerns about sexual health, and higher levels of parental communication. Yet family members' cultural backgrounds and religious affiliations influence the extent to which such discussions occur. Research on parent-child discussions of sex reflects the tendency of mothers to discuss this topic more frequently than fathers do with their children, particularly daughters. Sons engage in far less parent-child talk about sex than daughters (Warren, 2006). Girls who talk to their mothers about sexual topics are more likely to have conservative sexual values and are less likely to have engaged in sexual activity than girls who mostly talked to their friends (Dilorio, Kelley, & Hockenberry-Eaton, 1999). For them, such conversations seem to have an impact. For example, mother-daughter discussion about condoms was associated with consistent condom use (Hutchinson, 2002). Frequently, such mother-daughter conversations present challenges; mothers and daughters may experience a dialectical tension between perceiving sex talk as natural and open and struggling with tensions leading to closeness. A recent study of mother and late adolescent daughter pair's sexual communication (Coffelt, 2010) revealed that, although mothers and daughters all described the topic as "natural," it was a challenging topic for some of them in earlier years. In addition, mothers reported being unsure about what sexual information to discuss and when to raise it.

Increasingly, fathers play a role in sexual socialization of their children. Although mothers represent the primary communicators of sexual topics with children, fathers play an important role (Hutchinson, 2002). This may occur through the discussions of sociosexual issues with daughters such as "resisting pressure for sex" and "understanding men." Some fathers predict the communication strategies males could use to convince their daughters to have sex with them. After studying father-son communication about sexuality, Lehr, Dilorio, Demi, and Facteau (2005) found permissive values were a predictor of information sharing but not a predictor of values sharing. They speculate that sharing values might lead to a son to question his father's sexual experiences, a topic the father might prefer not to discuss. In his comprehensive review of father-child sexual communication research, Wright (2009) asserted that "fathers play an important role in the sexual development of their children" (p. 223). His findings include: fathers are more likely to engage in sexual communication with sons than daughters; black and Latino fathers may engage in more sexual communication than white and Asian fathers; sexual communication varies with the amount and quality of overall father-child communication; if engaging in sexual communication is comfortable, the more likely it is to occur. Fathers are more likely to discuss sex when their children are older and in a romantic relationship. This recent research underlines the importance of father-child communication about sex.

Even when both parents become involved in sexual discussions, they are more likely to talk about sex with daughters rather than sons (Warren, 2006). Heisler (2005) asked college student–mother–father triads to recall and report on conversations about sexuality. Most participants (77 percent) could remember discussions with their parent or child, particularly on topics of morals, pregnancy, and relationships. Although mothers were predominantly responsible for sexual communication with their children, their children reported that friends were the main source of sexual information, followed by their mothers. The extent to which a family encourages or discourages talk about issues such as pregnancy, birth control, masturbation, menstrual cycles, and the initial sexual encounters of adolescents relates directly to family communication rules.

Frequently, teenagers report being more comfortable discussing sex than their parents. A study of students' attitudes about parent-child discussions on sex-related topics indicated that teenagers believe parents need to learn how to communicate supportively and empathically, even if there is disagreement. Some parents have difficulty talking with their adolescents about premarital sex because they are unsure about their own knowledge and skill, or they are concerned that bringing the topic up will encourage sexual activity and that their children will not take them seriously (Jaccard, Dittust, & Gordon, 2000). Due to their insecurities, parents rated themselves low on the list of influences on children's sexual behaviors, whereas children rated their parents high on the list (Wilson, 2004). Many parents "recognize the importance of communication and want to communicate with their children but they lacked good sexual communication role models in their own lives and are unaware of how and when to initiate sexual conversations" (Hutchinson, 2002, p. 246).

Communication researchers Clay, Warren, and Neer, developers of the Family Sex Communication Quotient (PSCQ), reported the following generalizations::

- *Satisfaction with family discussions about sex is dependent on mutual dialogue.* Children report greater satisfaction with family communication about sex when parents facilitate the conversation and help them feel comfortable raising the topic.

- *The ability to communicate supportively about sex revolves around an attitude of openness.* Teens want parents to talk *with* them, not *at* them, and to avoid preachy messages. Parents who only give instructions and commands are less effective.
- *To have the greatest impact, discussions should become part of family patterns well before children reach age 16.* Many parents put off talking about sex. Raising the topic early facilitates more frequent discussion as well as children's perceptions of their parents as effective communicators.
- *Parent-child communication about sex that is frequent and regarded as effective facilitates children's open discussion with dating partners.* Children tend to model patterns found in their home (Warren, 2006, p. 322).

Families differ greatly in their approach to sexuality. Maddock (1989) described the communication behaviors of *sexually neglectful, sexually abusive,* and *sexually healthy* families. In *sexually neglectful* families, sex is discussed seldom or never. If it must be addressed, sexual communication occurs on an abstract level so direct connection is not made between the topic and the personal experience of family members (p. 133). The avoidance appears in this entry.

My mother explained the act of sex in the most cold, mechanical, scientific, factual way she could. I was embarrassed and I couldn't look at her face after she finished. I know it was very difficult for her. Her mother had not told her anything at all, and she had let her get married and go on a honeymoon without any knowledge of what was going to happen. She made a point of saying throughout, "After marriage . . ."

Parental sexual messages communicate an underlying attitude of anxiety or displeasure, but the direct issue remains hidden. Veiled messages often continue through adolescence and into adulthood. In these families, the strong marital boundary around sexuality means that children never see their parents as sexual beings—no playful jokes, hugging, or kissing occurs in the children's presence. Therefore children may not learn that sexual expression contributes to marital intimacy or that direct expression of affection is acceptable.

In other families, the lack of any marital boundary may force children into an incestuous relationship as they are co-opted into spousal roles. A *sexually abusive* family, typically a closed, rigid system, is characterized by boundary confusion between individuals and generations. Members' communication reflects a perpetrator-victim interaction pattern, especially in cross-gender relationships, resulting in marital conflict and lack of emotional intimacy (Maddock, 1989). Yet, in both the sexually neglectful and sexually abusive families, sexual attitudes and sexual behavior are seldom addressed directly.

Sexually healthy families are characterized by (1) respect for both genders; (2) boundaries that are developmentally appropriate and support gender identities;

(3) effective and flexible communication patterns that support intimacy, including appropriate erotic expression; and (4) a shared system of culturally relevant sexual values and meanings (Maddock, 1989). Sexually healthy families communicate effectively about sex "using language that can accurately cover sexual information, reflect feelings and attitudes of members, and facilitate decision making and problem solving regarding sexual issues" (Maddock, p. 135). Sex education is accurate and set in a context of family values that is transmitted across generations. Sheehy (1997) argued that children should see their parents teasing each other and enjoying each other because parents "can make jokes, they can communicate that sexuality is sacred, because actually sex is a lot of things. It's not just one thing. And I think kids need to know and see that" (n.p.). After interviewing women in their thirties regarding their mother-daughter conversations about sex, Brock and Jennings (1993) reported that their memories were primarily of negative nonverbal messages, and limited discussion focused on warnings and rules. The women wished for openness and discussions of feelings and choices. Interestingly, most of these women excused their mothers for their silence or discomfort, but planned to do better with their own children. Warren (2006) provided suggestions for effective family communication—start talking early, include both parents and sons and daughters in the conversation, and establish a supportive environment in which mutual dialogue can occur.

Parental interaction appears to buffer adolescents from certain peer or environmental pressures about sexual activity. In her study of sexual risk communication, Hutchinson (2002) found that girls who talk to their mothers about sexual topics are more likely to have conservative sexual values and less likely to have initiated sex; girls who talk to parents about when to have sex are less influenced by peer behavior. She suggested that, although mothers are more likely to provide sexual information, fathers may provide daughters with a general understanding of men in heterosexual relationships. Hispanic-Latina women reported less parent-adolescent sexual risk communication than non-Hispanic peers.

Other Family Forms   Research on sexual communication reflects the experiences of married or romantic heterosexual pairs, yet there are variations based on partnership type that are worth noting. In their study of relationship quality for child-free lesbian couples and those with children, Koepke, Mare, and Moran (1992) found that both groups reported happy and solid relationships but that couples with children, who had been together longer, scored higher on relationship satisfaction and sexual relationship satisfaction.

Discussing one's own homosexuality with a child raises particular issues. In their study of gay and lesbian foster parents, Patrick and Palladino (2009) found that some case managers had not told the foster children that their home would have same-sex parents; some of these foster parents chose to discuss this directly with their children if they were old enough to understand. Lesbian mothers must be prepared to respond when their children insist a dad is needed to make a baby (Galvin, Turner, Patrick, & West, 2007). Some parent-child discussions include explanation of donor insemination. At the top of the next page is a journal entry by Blumenthal (1990/91) describing one of her conversations with her five-year-old son conceived through an anonymous sperm donor.

At dinner tonight Jonathon asked me to explain again why we don't know who his seed daddy is. I first explained that I didn't know a man who wanted to be a seed daddy when I wanted to have him. I also told him that I didn't want anyone to ever try to take him away from me, so I thought it would be better to have an anonymous seed daddy. When I asked him, "Does that make you feel sad?" he said, "a little." I told him we could always talk about that; "I know."

Direct parent-child communication about sexuality is not only important for healthy family functioning but for the long-term physical health of family members. Pressing issues such as sexually transmitted diseases and unplanned pregnancies necessitate such discussions. Parents need to be able to address issues of safe sex practices with their children.

In our family we did not discuss sexuality openly. When I left for college, my mother (totally unprovoked) told me that if I ever decided to go on birth control, I was never to tell her, and NOT to get it through our family doctor, but through the school health service. By doing so, she made sure she separated herself from ever discussing the topic—so much that she did not even ask me if I had ever thought of it. This is how much she wanted to avoid the subject.

Although sexuality as a form of communication conveys messages of love and affection, many spouses use their sexual encounters to carry messages of anger, domination, disappointment, or self-rejection. Often, nonsexual conflicts are played out in the bedroom because one partner believes it is the only safe way to wage a war. Unexpressed anger may appear as a "headache," tiredness, roughness, or violence during a sexual encounter.

Other Intimacy Factors

In addition to commitment, and sexual communication, partners and family members develop closeness and intimacy through members' efforts and sacrifices, willingness to forgive and sanctification.

Effort Many factors compete for attention in life. Workplace demands, homework, school, friendships, family commitments, and community responsibilities take time and effort. The nurturing of marital or family relationships often gets the time and energy that is "left over," a minimal amount at best. In most cases, this limited attention spells relational disaster. Unless familial ties receive conscious attention, relationships "go on automatic pilot" and eventually stagnate or deteriorate.

Because the family operates within larger systems including work and school, each system impacts the other. Tensions between work and home obligations often leave partners stressed and overwhelmed. This era of dual-career couples and families, commuter marriages, job losses and relocations, threatens partner and family intimacy. Developing "love maps," or actively making mental maps of one's partner's psychological world, represents a partner's significant effort to remain connected (Gottman, 1999a). Mapmakers can tell you their partner's worries and joys, dreams and hopes, their best friends, favorite movies, food and books, the names of their partner's friends and work colleagues, and what "pushes their buttons." This deep "sense of the other" allows one partner to support the other in meaningful ways when life turns painful and to mutually share celebrations when life brings joy. Writing about the effect of a first child on a marriage, Gottman (1999b) asserted that "If you don't start off with a deep knowledge of each other, it's easy for your marriage to lose its way when your lives shift so suddenly" (p. 49). Mapmakers also listen to their children, remembering the names of their best friends and teachers, their favorite foods, beloved sports heroes or music stars, current career aspirations, hobbies, fears, passions and dreams. These "cognitive maps" serve as indicators of levels of connection among family members. Only a conscious and shared determination to focus on the relationships can keep marital and family ties high on one's list of priorities. Many married couples and family members actively seek out opportunities to enrich their lives and reaffirm their commitment to protect their relationships.

Sacrifice   Sacrifice implies giving up something in order to please or assist another. It may involve a high level of commitment and effort, and a shift away from self-interest. A willingness to sacrifice your relationship demonstrates strong commitment, high relational satisfaction, and longer relationships (Flanagan, et al., 2002). Sacrifice may involve efforts such as cancelling a vacation to stay with a sick grandparent, relocating to support a partner's career, or working a second job to fund college tuitions. As shown in the opening vignette about an older sister who makes sacrifices for her younger sisters, many siblings build deep intimacy through sharing their burdens and supporting each other when parents cannot fulfill their roles effectively. Effort and sacrifice reflect a conscious commitment to a relationship.

Forgiveness   What is the relational impact of saying "I forgive you"? And what might that statement really mean? Defining *forgiveness* is difficult because of multiple meanings. Communication scholars Waldron and Kelley (2008) defined forgiveness as "a relational process whereby harmful conduct is acknowledged by one or both partners; the harmed partner extends undeserved mercy to the perceived transgressor; one or both partners experience a transformation from negative to positive psychological states, and the meaning of the relationships is renegotiated, with the possibility of reconciliation" (p. 5). Frequently, forgiveness implies an explicit renegotiation of the relationship that usually involves meta-communication.

Forgiveness appears directly related to family interactions given the long-term nature of family ties and the intensity of connections. According to Fincham and Beach (2002), "Paradoxically, those we love are the ones we are most likely to hurt and may not always be the ones with whom we communicate most effectively" (p. 239). In his study of close relationships, Kelley (1998) found that over 70 percent of respondents' motivations for forgiveness included love, restoring the relationship, and well-being of the other. He suggested that the obligatory nature of family relationships creates a sense of stability and resiliency. It seems self-evident that motivation and ability to discuss forgiveness depends on the severity of the transgressions; family reasons for forgiveness could range from an affair or physical violence to an insult or revelation of another's secret.

Because marital ties involve high emotional attachment, trust, and interdependence, some transgressions may be emotionally devastating, shaking the relationship's foundation (Waldron & Kelley, 2008). Issues such as incest, child or spousal abuse, or affairs may be unforgiveable in some relationships. Marital unwillingness to forgive may be associated with patterns of negative reciprocity because partners often hurt each other and initiate reciprocal negative messages that work against intimacy (Fincham & Beach, 2002). Parent-child forgiveness processes develop over time as the child's ability to comprehend transgressions and forgiveness changes. In extreme cases, a family member may be cut off from the entire family, or from certain relatives; frequently this occurs when the member violates a deeply held family belief or strict rule in areas such as interracial marriage, homosexuality, or religious belief. Essentially, forgoing retaliation is unlikely to increase relational intimacy; only a proactive attempt to engage a family member in reconciliation has much chance for positively increasing constructive communication and intimacy.

Sanctification Sanctification serves as a major source of relational connectedness within certain relationships. The term refers to a "psychological process through which aspects of life are perceived by people as having a spiritual character and significance" (Pargament & Mahoney, 2003, p. 221). Sanctification occurs in two ways. First, it may be a manifestation of one's images, beliefs, or experience of God; this is more common for believers in a God or deity. Second, without reference to a specific deity, a sense of transcendence, ultimate purpose, and timelessness may create a sense of the spiritual. Essentially, one position is theistically oriented, reflecting a religious tradition; the other is nontheistic and centers on attributes of the divine (Mahoney, Pargament, Murray-Swank, & Murray-Swank, 2003). Many couples view marriage as a sacred state endowed with spiritual meaning; parenthood may also be viewed as spiritual in nature. Thus, spiritual beliefs serve to sustain family relationships during difficult times.

Sanctification may serve as an "illustration of embeddedness in broader community-supported systems of meaning. . . ." (Fincham, Stanley, & Beach, 2007, p. 281). Religious affiliations influence how certain partners or parents perform their relational roles. Many weddings occur within a house of worship, conveying the couple's view of the sacred nature of these vows. Religious leaders may serve as marriage counselors providing theologically grounded guidelines for repairing marriages.

Other familial relationships may gain strength from the spiritual realm. Parents may identify their mother or father role as a sacred duty; their parenting behaviors may reflect this beliefs. For example, mothers who reported higher levels of the sanctification of parenting reported using less verbal aggression (yelling, calling names) with young children (Mahoney, Pargament, Murray-Swank, & Murray-Swank, 2003, p. 228). Attending and participating in worship services reinforces the importance of a deity to the family members.

BARRIERS TO INTIMACY

Building marital or familial intimacy involves effort and risk. For many, it is more comfortable to maintain a number of pleasant or close relationships, none involving true intimacy, than to become intensely involved with a partner, child, or other relative. Some family members establish barriers to intense relationship as a way to protect themselves from potential pain or loss.

Fears of Intimacy

Some partners and family members experience fears of intimacy, including the following: merger, exposure, attack, and abandonment (Feldman (1979, pp. 71–72). *Merger* with a loved one implies losing personal boundaries or personal identity. This occurs when the "sense of self" is poorly developed or when the "other" is very powerful. Individuals with low self-esteem who fear interpersonal *exposure* may feel threatened by being revealed as weak, inadequate, or undesirable if they get too close to another. Some individuals fear *attack* because they distrust others; many choose to protect themselves by avoiding self-disclosure. The fear of *abandonment,* the feeling of being overwhelmed and helpless when the love object is gone, may affect those who have experienced excessive traumatic separations or relational losses. To prevent helplessness their strategy is to remain distant. After taking the risk to be intimate, rejection can be devastating, resulting in reluctance to be hurt again.

Closeness is difficult to maintain. Lavee (2005) conducted a study of daily reports from 94 couples over a week containing checklists of daily hassles, interpersonal conflicts, positive/negative moods, and a measure of the sense of dyadic closeness. A sense of closeness was associated with the other spouse's level of stress. The more stress a person experienced in a certain day, the less closeness (or more distance) his or her spouse reported. The effect was stronger for men than for women. Couples who had high-quality relationships reported more closeness than did those in distressed marriages, regardless of the stress level. However, "in both happy and distressed couples, more stressful days were associated with increased dyadic distance" (p. 283). Although many individuals fear deep intimacy, even maintaining a sense of closeness is a complex process.

Jealousy

Although some partners view jealousy as a sign of affection, these feelings can turn violent or obsessive, creating a barrier to intimacy. *Jealousy* is an "aversive emotional experience characterized by feelings of anger, sadness, and fear induced by the threat or actual loss of a relationship with another person to a real or imagined rival" (DeSteno & Salovey, 1994, p. 220). Jealousy results from the perception that a treasured relationship is threatened, usually by another person. In their study of 200 couples, Andersen, Eloy, Guerrero, and Spitzberg (1995) concluded that cognitive jealousy is negatively related to relational satisfaction; constantly mulling over jealous concerns heightens tension. The tension may result in active distancing, expression of negative affect, general avoidance/denial, and violent communication/threats. Jealousy tends to erode relational connections.

Romantic jealousy is most closely associated with marital and partner relationships, although sometimes one parent feels jealous of the other's connection to a child or to another family member. Sibling jealousy reflects birth order, a redistribution of parental resources, or parental favoritism (Fitness & Duffield, 2004). One child may believe a parent shows favoritism to a sibling or new family member (Golish, 2000). A teenager may reject a sibling's new "best friend" who interferes with family time. Lucchetti and Roghaar (2001) noted the many negative consequences of parental favoritism, including increased chance of sibling rivalry, lowered self-esteem, and perceptions of declining family support.

Deception

Given that trust appears as a hallmark of intimacy, deceiving another violates their relational understanding. Most people expect family members and loved ones to be truthful as a sign of connection or relational commitment. Deception involves communicating or withholding information knowingly and intentionally for the purpose of creating a false belief. The suspicion that a partner keeps information from the spouse is strongly associated with marital dissatisfaction (Finkenauer & Hazam, 2000). When an individual in a heterosexual marriage comes out as gay, lesbian, bisexual, or transgender, the news usually overwhelms an unsuspecting spouse. In many cases the disclosure shatters the partners' core identity, facing them with a complex set of issues (Buxton, 2006). Sometimes deceptions create accidental privacy dilemmas when a member accidentally finds out information about someone in the family (Petronio, 2002). This might include discovery of a parent's affair, a cousin's death from AIDS, or a grandparent's alcoholic relapse. Some deceptions are transgressions that violate the relationship covenant, challenging certain values that are viewed as sacred, such as sexual exclusivity (Waldron & Kelley, 2008). Such cases threaten the relationship itself. Others, such as persistent secret gambling or drug use, may be resolved if the offender enters a treatment program.

MOVING FORWARD

Although many closeness and intimacy studies center on marital or parent-child relationships, multiple family types create multiple valued connections. When asked about their current relationship, lesbians and gay men reported as much satisfaction with their relationships as did heterosexual couples; the great majority describe themselves as happy. The correlates of relationship quality for lesbian and gay couples include feelings of having equal power, perceiving many attractions and few alternatives to the relationship, endorsing few dysfunctional beliefs about the relationship, and engaging in shared decision making. In his study comparing gay and lesbian cohabiting partners with married couples with children, Kurdek (2004) found that among one-half of the comparisons there was no difference in functioning. In the other areas, over 75 percent of the time gay and lesbian partners reported better functioning. He asserted there is a link between being in a close relationship and overall well-being and concludes, "Protecting same-sex relationships is tantamount to protecting the well-being of the partners involved in those relationships" (p. 896). A particular issue faced by such partnerships involves supportive networks. Certain gay and lesbian couples may find tremendous pressure to be "everything" to each other due to lack of full family support because one or both of the partners is not "out." In some cases, partners' public expressions of affection are discouraged within the family or community network.

Intimacy in stepfamilies is exceptionally complex, particularly in the early years. Issues of loyalty, guilt, and loss compound the ability of stepchildren and stepparents to develop intimate ties. Although the first few years in a stepfamily are often complicated in terms of levels of closeness, Bray and Kelly (1998) maintained that creating a strong marital bond is a key development task for all stepfamilies. Eventually many stepparent-stepchild relationships can be characterized by voluntary and deep personal interaction. In some families, members struggle with *intimacy barriers* such as favoritism or jealousy.

Single-parent families face different issues. Unmarried women with children may find more intimacy and support in their extended families, particularly in matriarchal systems, but many report difficulty in sustaining strong, intimate adult relationships due to child-raising pressures. Some children, fearing the loss of parental intimacy, sabotage a parent's efforts to develop new romantic ties. Because they do not have a partner to share their problems, joys, and decision making, single parents need to function within strong communication networks.

"Most marriages, even good ones, are gratifying in some ways and frustrating in others" (Huston, 2009, p. 318). One of life's challenges is to learn how to be yourself while you are in a significant long-term relationship with another person. In a truly intimate relationship, the "I" and the "we" coexist, to the joy of both persons. Lerner (1989) captured the link between the development of intimacy and communication. Her words serve as a fine conclusion to this chapter.

> "Being who we are" requires that we can talk openly about things that are important to us, that we take a clear position on where we stand on important emotional issues, and that we clarify the limits of what is acceptable and tolerable to us in a relationship. "Allowing the other person to do the same" means that we can stay emotionally connected to that other party who thinks, feels, and believes differently, without needing to change, convince, or fix the other. (p. 3)

CONCLUSION

This chapter explored a range of communication practices that lead to intimacy within adult partnerships and families. It also explored the close relationship between intimacy and communication, focusing on specific communication behaviors that encourage intimacy within marital and family systems: commitment, self-disclosure, and sexual communication. Commitment implies creating an unbreakable bond with another person. Family intimacy cannot be achieved unless members nurture their relationships through commitment. Self-disclosure involves intimate sharing of personal and private information with a partner or other family member as a way to build and sustain a valued relational tie. Sexuality serves as a means of communicating affection within a partnered relationship; talking about sexuality provides opportunities for intimate conversations between adult partners and important bonding conversations between parents and children. Because most people experience anxiety about intimacy, this is an ongoing and sometimes frustrating process. The barriers to intimacy may prevent certain relationships from developing their full potential.

All human beings long for intimacy, but it is a rare relationship in which family members (spouses, parents and children, siblings) consciously strive for greater sharing on significant personal topics over long periods of time. Such mutual commitment provides rewards known only to those in intimate relationships.

In Review

1. Create your own definition of marital and/or committed *partnership intimacy* and provide two examples of such relationships characterized by intimate communication.

2. Create your own definition of *family intimacy* and provide two examples of such relationships characterized by intimate communication.

3. Take a position on the following statement and defend it: A marital/partnership commitment should be broken only in cases of partner or child abuse.

4. Under what circumstances, if any, would you recommend withholding full self-disclosure of a very serious issue in a marital and/or family relationship?

5. Relying on personal observation or a media example, discuss ways you have seen an intimate adult relationship overcome jealousy or deception through forgiveness.

6. Assume you are a parent. What qualities would you advise your child to look for in a marital partnership or long-term committed partnership?

KEY WORDS

Commitment   129
Debriefing conversations   134
Family intimacy   127
Forgiveness   143
Intimacy barriers   147
Intimation sequences   134
Mental love maps   132

Sanctification   144
Self-disclosure   131
Sexually abusive families   140
Sexually healthy families   140
Sexually neglectful families   140
Sexual communication   135

Communication and Family Roles and Types

"In other words, husband, wife, parent, child, grandparent, and grandchild are names of roles that people assume as they go through life. The roles describe two things: how one person is related to another, and how this particular role is lived out."

—Virginia Satir, *The New Peoplemaking*

Rebekah is a married mother of two children, ages four and two. Before her first child, Miriam, was born, she had begun a program as a doctoral student in history at the state university. Both of her parents are professors at a college in a neighboring state and have always been very supportive and proud of their daughter following in their footsteps. Rebekah continued full-time in the program until her second child, Aaron, came along. Following Aaron's birth, Rebekah decided she needed to reduce her studies to part-time until the kids got a little older, given her husband's busy work schedule. Rebekah recognized that she really didn't need to have a career to provide for her children because her husband made enough money to support the family. However, she had such a love of history and felt a real desire to continue the program. She also wanted to be a role model for her daughter in pursuing her dreams. But even part-time has been difficult with Rebekah still taking on full responsibility for child care and managing the household. She has been discussing this with her husband.

Now Rebekah is considering quitting the program altogether, but worries what her family will think of her, especially since she is so close to completion. She feels a lot of conflict about her responsibilities: "When I'm with the kids, I am always thinking about what I should be doing in my studies; and when I'm at school or studying, I always worry that I should be with the kids," she lamented to her best friend last week.

Jarvis, age 46, is a solo parent to his son, Jamal, age 12. Jamal's mother left when he was just two years old, and Jarvis and Jamal have been on their own since then. Jarvis's mother and sister live nearby and have helped as needed, but Jarvis has prided himself for being there for Jamal as much as he can. He had often felt stretched wondering if he could provide every-thing Jamal needed. Jarvis is deeply religious, and he and Jamal attend weekly services at their local church. About a year ago, Jarvis began dating Sylvia, a woman he met at a church singles' group. As their relationship has become more serious, he has slowly begun to include Sylvia in activities that were traditionally things that he and Jamal did together, just the two of them. Jamal initially did not take to this well, but over time has seemed to adjust to having Sylvia take on a role in their family. Jarvis has been really grateful to have Sylvia around, as he was never good at what he calls the "touchy, feely stuff." He thinks that Sylvia has a nice way of providing the emotional support for Jamal that he doesn't provide very well. She has also encouraged Jamal to pursue his interest in music, often driving him to piano lessons—something that Jarvis was never able to do given his busy work schedule.

More recently, Jarvis and Sylvia have been discussing marriage, and Jarvis intends to propose fairly soon. When he explained this to Jamal, he framed the news as "something wonderful"—Jamal was going to finally have a mother! Jarvis was surprised at Jamal's intensely negative response: "She's not my mother! And she never will be my mother!"

Terminology about family roles includes terms such as *co-breadwinners, stay-at-home mom, noncustodial father, daddy track,* and *birth mother,* all of which have family interaction implications. Opinions differ widely about what it means to be in a partner, parent, sibling, grandparent, foster child, or stepchild role. Tremendous variability is found in communication across families as members interact with each other, creating patterns of role relationships. In order to explore these complex role issues and their implications for communication, this chapter will discuss (1) role definition, (2) role functions, (3) role appropriation, and (4) couple and family typologies.

ROLE DEFINITION AND DEVELOPMENT

Within families, roles are established, grown into, grown through, discussed, negotiated, worked on, and accepted or rejected. As family members mature or outside forces impact the family, roles emerge, change, or disappear. The term *role* is so widely used that it can mean very different things to different persons. In order to understand role development, you need to consider first the definitions of *roles* and then examine role expectations and role performance.

We define *family roles* as recurring patterns of behavior developed through the interaction that family members use to fulfill family functions. From a communication perspective, these expectations develop within a family system as its members create a series of shared meanings about how roles should be enacted. This perspective contrasts with theories presenting a fixed, or unchanging, view of roles. Rather than take a fixed view of a family's members, we prefer an *interactive perspective,* emphasizing the emerging aspects of roles and their behavioral regularities developed out of social interaction. Family members develop roles through dialogue with each other reflecting the transactional nature of communication. Persons with labels such as "father" or "wife" struggle with dialectical tensions as they manage the reciprocal nature of roles. According to this interactive perspective, you cannot be a stepfather without a stepchild, or a wife without a husband; in fact, you cannot be a companionable father to a child who rejects you, or be a competitive wife to a man who avoids conflict. Family members exchange interrelated behaviors—action and reaction, question and answer, request and response (Montgomery, 1994).

Today, roles are less tied to age than they were in the past, as age is no longer a predictor of life stage (Rubin, 2001). A 44-year-old female may parent a preschooler; and a 21-year-old male may do the same. Over time, family members negotiate their mutual expectations of one another, acquire role identifications, and make an emotional investment in carrying out, for example, the roles of provider or nurturer. As circumstances change, or some hopes or expectations are not realized, members may have to give up roles, a process called *role relinquishment.*

Interactive role development reflects (1) the personality, background, and role models of a person who occupies a social position, such as oldest son or stepmother, (2) the relationships in which a person interacts, (3) the changes as each family member moves through his or her life cycle or encounters life crises, (4) the effects of role performance on the family system, and (5) the extent to which a person's social/psychological identity is defined and enhanced by a particular role. For example, a woman's behavior in the role of spouse may have been very different in her first marriage than in her second, due to her own personal growth and the actions of each husband.

Roles are inextricably bound to the communication process. Family roles are developed and maintained through communication. One learns how to assume his or her place within a family from the feedback provided by other family members, such as: "I don't think we should argue in front of the children." Children are given direct instructions about how to enact the role of son or daughter in a particular household. Adults tend to use their family-of-origin history as a base from which to negotiate particular mutual roles; children develop their communicative roles through a combination of their cognitive skills, family experiences, peer relationships, and societal norms and expectations. Young family members in immigrant families sometimes feel role tension when they sense that their parents' values differ from their own desires to be Americanized.

Family roles and communication rules are strongly interrelated because each contributes to the maintenance or change of the other. Rules may structure certain role relationships, whereas particular role relationships may foster the development of certain rules. For example, such rules as "Children should not hear about family finances" or "School problems are to be settled with your mother" reinforce the roles of family members.

SPECIFIC ROLE FUNCTIONS

The concept of the family as a mobile can be applied to roles using the McMaster Model of Family Functioning (Epstein, Bishop, & Baldwin, 1982). This model focuses on discovering how the family allocates responsibilities and handles accountability for them. It examines five essential family functions that serve as a basis for necessary family roles:

1. Providing for adult sexual fulfillment and gender modeling for children
2. Providing nurturing and emotional support
3. Providing for individual development
4. Providing kinship maintenance and family management
5. Providing basic resources (Epstein, Bishop, & Baldwin, 1982)

These family functions can be categorized as instrumental (providing the resources for the family), affective (support and nurturing, adult sexual needs), and mixed (life-skill development and system upkeep). When you look at Figure 7.1, imagine

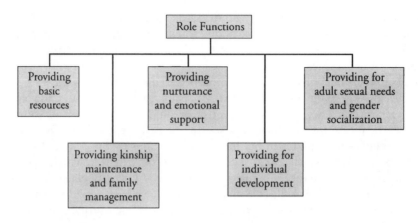

FIGURE 7.1
Family Role Functions

a mobile with the system's parts balanced by the multiple role functions operating within the family. These role functions become superimposed on the family system and its members.

Although almost all the research in this area presumes two-parent households involving a male and female parent, same-sex partners with children face many similar issues as they confront daily family life (Gianino, 2008) as do single parents and members of multigenerational households.

Providing for Gender Socialization and Sexual Needs

In a culture that provides multiple possibilities and few clear distinctions, men and women today can easily receive mixed messages. Men may hear that a woman wants a man who is expressive, gentle, nurturing, and vulnerable, yet also successful, prosperous, and capable. Women may receive similar conflicting messages regarding dependence and independence. Yet, male and female family roles are increasingly intertwined as social and economic forces impact family life.

The process of learning what it means to be male or female begins at birth. Even as newborns, males and females are handled differently and may be provided with "sex-appropriate" toys. Studies of kindergarten children show that boys are keenly aware of what masculine behaviors are expected of them and restrict their interests and activities to avoid what might be judged as feminine. Girls continue to develop feminine expectations gradually over five more years. Parents teach children about gender and physical appearance. Children learn what is "masculine" and what is "feminine" from parent comments about exercise, weight, appearance, and dress (Wood, 2011). Certain religious or political groups and cultural traditions support strong male-female distinctions, while such gender-bound distinctions appear repressive to others. Gender-based socialization may include socialization into a particular family role. For example, in considering what it means to be a son, participants in one study consistently referred to their

❚ Role development involves observing and imitating role models.

fathers, not their mothers, suggesting that sons learn how to enact that role from a male role model (Morman & Floyd, 2006).

The gender-based communication directives you received as a child come into play when you form your own family system and try to communicate effectively. For example, traditionally men were thought to disclose less about themselves than women and keep more secrets. Compared to women, men are depicted as relating more impersonally to others and see themselves as embodiments of their roles. Some men fear that talking about emotions reduces their competitive edge. If men accept a very restrictive definition of nurturing communication, they may deprive themselves and their family members of desired intimacy. Vangelisti and Banski (1993) report that husbands' expressiveness and ability to self-disclose affect both husbands' and wives' relational satisfaction more than wives' ability to be open and expressive. Current research suggests that males' roles are becoming more flexible as adult partners renegotiate their roles and males become increasingly involved in raising their children (Duckworth & Buzzannell, 2009). Yet, when married fathers lose their jobs, many fight to retain their roles as "real men" in an emasculating situation, necessitating cognitively reframing the situation while creating ways to appear to maintain a breadwinner self-concept (Buzzannell & Turner, 2003).

Wood and Inman (1993) challenged some of the early research that found women were more effective in self-disclosure via more open, expressive communication, suggesting it privileges one type of intimacy. They indicate that male self-disclosure does not reduce stress as much as it does for females; men regard practical help, mutual assistance, and companionship as better benchmarks of caring. Wood (2007a) captured the differences by suggesting that talk between women tends to be personal and disclosing, whereas men express closeness through action. These differences may be carried out in family role behaviors. Mothers share more time with daughters in meal preparation and family care projects; fathers share more time with sons in doing home repairs, yard work, car upkeep, and shopping for these activities. Same-sex couples, due to a lack of traditional marital role models, tend to negotiate responsibilities rather than rely on societal expectations or previous gender role models for their answers. Division of household tasks tends to be variable (Rothblum, 2009).

Ultimately many factors affect the way in which an individual enacts a gender role. In fact, often this process results in an individual having a very different lifestyle than that of his or her family-of-origin. One mother of an adult son wrote:

I recently received an e-mail from my son that reminded me of how his marriage is so different from mine. He wrote about his week as a "single parent" while his wife was in Los Angeles on business and how he survived the carpools and cooking. Their lifestyle amazes me, but I love to see Brian act as such a caring and active parent to their two sons.

Young adult women are more likely than young adult men to receive advice from parents that they should stop work after having children and that they should make career choices that will accommodate family (Medved, et al., 2006).

Androgyny   Androgynous people possess qualities that culture defines as masculine and feminine instead of only those assigned to one sex (Wood, 2011). This affects role performance; androgynous persons tend to be successful personally and professionally and have happier marriages than masculine-typed individuals. Androgynous family members evaluate issues on their merits or demerits, without reference to the gender of the persons involved. The androgynous person is flexible, adaptive, and capable of being both instrumental (assertive, competent, forceful, and independent) and expressive (nurturing, warm, supportive, and compassionate) depending on the demands of the situation.

Sometimes gender differences impact sexual communication. As indicated in the previous chapter, even in today's more open society, many communication breakdowns stem from an inability of couples to communicate honestly about their sexual relationship. Not only do couples have problems in their sexual communication with partners but they also have greater difficulties talking about sex with their children (Hutchinson, 2002; Wright, 2009). Rules in their current system may inhibit adult discussion, which may result in frustration, anger, or confusion as noted in this example.

If there is anything I would wish for my daughter as she enters marriage, it would be the ability to talk to her husband about sex. It was unthinkable to me that men and women could really talk about what gave them pleasure in sexual activity. My husband and I spent years in troubled silence. It took an affair, a separation, and counseling for us to be able to begin to talk about our sexual life.

If a woman cannot discuss her inhibitions about being sexually assertive, it may prevent her from being active in meeting her needs, and it may block an empathic understanding of her needs. Thus, the circle of poor communication continues.

Providing Nurturing and Support

Family members need mutual admiration, support, and reassurance. Transactionally, family happiness develops when each member meets the needs and expectations of the others. Children are socialized by parents and the community, which affect their future capability to be nurturing and supportive.

Nurturing Children   This family function incorporates communication, since it is the primary process used to transmit parental caring, values, and a sense of community to the children. Through advice, directives, and answers to questions, children learn what parents and society expect of them. Until recently, mothers had far greater contact with their children than fathers and were much more likely to contribute to the nurturing process. This is still true today, but not to the same extent as in the past. A recent study examined the way in which fathers of preschool children communicatively construct their childrearing behaviors (Golden, 2007). The results of this study reveal a "masculine concept of caregiving."

Hochschild (1997) found that employed women opted for more overtime, having discovered "a great male secret" that the workplace is nurturing because it provides an escape from home pressures of needy kids, piles of unwashed clothes, and no leftovers in the refrigerator. Historically, children usually experienced their fathers as more distant, less empathetic, and less caring, especially in verbal and nonverbal signs of love. However, fathers today spend more time with their children than fathers did in the past (Silverstein, 2002).

Men are less likely to be involved in nurturing children with special needs. Schock and colleagues (2002) report that fathers with children with mood disorders have more difficulty accepting the illness and are less likely to participate in therapy efforts. Mothers are typically the primary caregivers of children who have special needs.

Socialization for nurturing includes learning acceptable or unacceptable communication behaviors, such as yelling, lying, crying, hugging, directness, and silence. Nurturing messages vary across cultures; silence may be affirming in one and alienating in another. Sibling socialization is often overlooked, yet cross-cultural studies indicate the power of siblings in a child's learning of nurturing competence (Zukow, 1989).

In keeping with the bidirectional nature of family member influence, children can resist socialization messages. This frustrates parents, especially those in a rigid family system. Communication between parents can also become confused if the mother feels threatened when the father demonstrates to relatives and neighbors that he is capable of effective child care. It is important for children of either sex "to see their father share parenting responsibility so that society no longer idolizes motherhood and dismisses fatherhood" (Pickerd, 1998, p. 205). Likewise, the father can feel undermined in his provider role when his wife demonstrates her capabilities in a career and puts pressure on him to take more responsibility for the children (Zernike, 1998). Such struggles are communicated to children, leaving them confused.

The father role remains highly significant after divorce, separation, or out-of-marriage birth. Maintaining supportive contact on significant child-related matters has beneficial consequences for the mother and children. Single fathers are more likely than married fathers to share breakfast, home activities, and outings with their children. Single parents are challenged by not having a partner for instrumental and emotional support. Further, single parents often face economic pressures (Stewart, 2010).

Providing Support and Empathy This function, sometimes called the therapeutic function, implies a willingness to listen to another's problems and provide emotional support. Such listening must be empathic in order to give the other the understanding needed or the chance to ventilate pent-up feelings of rage, frustration, or exhaustion. This is a gift that may not be appreciated until a child becomes a parent.

My father's way is to be very calm and patient with his children. When he helped me with my homework, he would never leave until he knew I understood it completely. He would recall how hard it was to deal with math and science assignments. Now when I explain something, I try to see that my children understand because I remember the good feelings that I had when I finally understood my homework.

Empathy implies nonjudgmental understanding of what another family member is sharing. If the communication channels between family members encourage and permit the expression of open feelings, various individuals in the family can function therapeutically, which includes offering advice and questioning motives. Several important studies indicated not only how providing support and empathy is perceived by children, but how it affects them. Endres (1997) surmises that fathers create four special roles with daughters: the "Knight in Shining Armor" or dad on a pedestal; the "buddy" who sees his child as an equal and friend; the "authoritarian" who rules strictly and expects high standards of behavior; and the "shadow" who distances himself, avoiding activities with his daughter, especially communication. Daughters prefer the buddy type. A related study of father-son closeness reveals a tendency toward dissatisfaction with fathers' communication skills, their resources to demonstrate empathy, and the amount of time that they make available for communication (Fink, Buerkel-Rothfuss, & Buerkel, 1994). Another report examining mother-daughter communication from a dialectical perspective indicates that pronounced variation occurred on the autonomy-connection and openness-closedness dimensions (Pennington, 1997). Increasingly, men are spending more time with their children. Fathers with children under the age of 13 spend three hours a day with them, compared to two hours a day in 1977. Mothers spend approximately four hours a day with their children, which is similar to the 1977 figure (Galinsky, Aumann, & Bond, 2008).

Providing for Individual Development

This role function includes those tasks that each individual must fulfill in order to become self-sufficient. Individuals must simultaneously seek to sustain a "sense of uniqueness from other relationships yet the sense of commonality with other relationships" (Baxter, 1990, p. 16). Family members who do not develop this role function can easily become dependent or enmeshed in the system. A "take care of me" attitude on the part of any member diminishes the wholeness and interdependent aspects of the family system.

Family members must facilitate each other's opportunities for self-discovery and talent development. Parents perform this function in their children's formative years, but from an early age children influence one another's talents. Never underestimate how children in their play with one another develop the communication strategies they use in role situations. In communication with children, it is very important that fathers bond with their children at an early age. Men who take family leaves when the children are young take a more active, involved role as the children grow older (Hochschild, 1997). In order to avoid enmeshment, family members need messages that support or encourage making individual choices. Recognition of members' ideas creates a context for valued independence.

Providing for Maintenance and Management

Kinship Maintenance One important maintenance function involves maintaining kinship ties with the extended family network. Kinship involves sharing, participating in, and promoting the family's welfare as contacts are maintained with relatives and friends outside the family home. In short, it involves boundary management. The kinship maintenance function has direct implications for family communication because "kin-work" is the labor that enables families to endure over time (Stack & Burton, 1998). Whether one is included or excluded from family events or hears the latest family gossip signifies one's place within the family system. Although previous research indicated that kinkeepers (those who provide kinship maintenance) used the telephone frequently to keep in touch with family members (Leach & Braithwaite, 1996), today these roles are shifting as more family members use e-mail, social networking sites, and family members' blogs to create a "new connectedness"(Kennedy, Smith, Wells, & Wellman, 2008). As one mother and wife explained:

I was very reluctant to join a social networking site. I was dragged kicking and screaming by my sister but I have to say it's been a terrific tool for staying connected and reconnecting too. I love the playful exchanges and updates on all the little/regular things in daily life that really are our "lives." All of our family is far-flung so it's great to check in daily. An unexpected benefit has been improved communication with a few difficult family members, as it's the perfect tool for light-hearted interactions. It's also the perfect vehicle for me as I've never been a phone person.

Holidays are a special time for kin-related family maintenance communication. In some families, particularly highly cohesive ones, attendance at get-togethers is mandatory and only illness or great distances may be acceptable excuses. In some households, the events are painful, since "cut-off" members may be excluded, or members of low cohesive families may feel they are missing something. Stepfamilies must work to create their own rituals to provide members with a sense of identity. At holiday time, men and women share the tasks of calling, visiting, buying gifts, and attending events; women are more involved in sending cards.

Women do most of the communicating with relatives. Female partners do more of the relational maintenance, make greater use of the family kin network, and focus more energy on spending time both with friends and family (Ragsdale, 1996). Husbands maintain fewer kinship contacts with their relatives and actually have more contact with their wives' relatives (Stack & Burton, 1998). Stepfamily kinship ties are affected significantly by the attitudes of stepgrandparents; kinkeeping gender roles may change based on the new configurations (Crosbie-Burnett & McClintic, 2000). Almost all interactions with kin are concentrated in three areas: visiting, recreation, and communication by letter, phone, e-mail, and text messaging. Kinkeepers' work in maintaining family communication can take several forms including providing information, facilitating rituals, providing assistance, maintaining family relationships, and continuing a previous kinkeeper's work (Leach & Braithwaite, 1996). Women are also more likely to talk about genetic issues with extended family members (Wilson, et al., 2004) and to be the recipients of such information (Claes, et al., 2003). Ellingson and Sotirin (2010) report that aunts often take on this function, working to preserve and strengthen family bonds through kinkeeping activities, such as facilitating rituals and maintaining communication, particularly long distance.

The single-parent and blended family systems encounter special kinship concerns. For example, in divorced families, there may be special problems in communication with the ex-spouse and his or her new family. One of the ex-partners may refuse to communicate with the other; children may become pawns and resent forced separations. On occasion, children lose active contact with an entire side of their family heritage.

Family networking also varies according to family-of-origin and ethnicity. For example, Mexican men and women have equally strong relationships with their relatives. However, Mexican men networked more with other persons outside their families, whereas the women formed their strongest relationship ties within families (Falicov, 2005). In Chicano cultures, godparents (*compadrazgo*) link families and communities through friends or authorities. Although often not relatives, godparents play key roles in religious activities, such as first communion, confirmation, and marriage. They also provide nurturing and financial aid when needed, as a moral obligation (Dill, 1998).

As children move into adulthood, their relationships with their parents change. In families with multiple siblings, the quality of the relationships between the parents and the adult children may vary widely within the same family. Researchers have termed this notion that parents may have better relationships with some children than with others as "collective ambivalence" (Ward, Spitze, & Deane, 2009).

Because a family consists of persons who consider themselves to be a family, kinship ties often include extended family members bound together by caring, as noted here.

Since my immediate family is dead, and any other distant relatives on my husband's side or my side live thousands of miles away, we have worked at creating a local family. Over the years, we have developed close friends who serve as honorary aunts and uncles for the children. The highlight of our Christmas is our annual dinner when we all get together to decorate the tree and the children get to see Uncle Bernard or Aunt Lois within a family context. I feel closer to these people than to many of my blood relatives.

Such activities represent a special way to communicate the message that kinship is important. In this age in which families often live great distances from their kin or have few relatives, this idea has merit. When family members feel safe in sharing their problems, joys, and family celebrations, they reap the benefits of the kinship function.

Management of Daily Needs Other role maintenance and management functions include decision making to facilitate housekeeping, child care, recreation, and taking care of family budgets, bills, income taxes, savings, and investments. In families with dual-earner couples, men tend to spend more time than their wives working outside the home, while women do more work inside the home than do their husbands (McNeil, 2004).

One area that is prone to conflict is the division of household chores. In the case of married couples, both husbands and wives tend to see the division of household chores as less fair to wives (Grote & Clark, 2001). Wives tend to perform a greater amount of housework than husbands, regardless of the presence of children or the woman's employment status. However, in marriages where wives and husbands were both employed full-time, the gap between the amount of housework wives and husbands performed was smaller than when wives worked part-time or not at all (Grote & Clark, 2001). The changes in this area reflect active negotiation between partners, since most are creating a housekeeping system different from that in their families-of-origin. Changes in family structure through divorce creates a redefinition of roles tied to daily routines (Downs, Coleman, & Ganong, 2000). A major partner negotiation task involves coordinating duties and responsibilities with each other; 40 percent report negotiating these details daily and 26 percent indicate such negotiations occur two to three times a week (Halpin, Teixeira, Pinkus, & Daley, 2010). In commuter marriages this can be more complicated. One study revealed that although commuting wives were resisting cultural expectations by pursuing their own careers, they experienced traditional gendered expectations for housework and other family roles. For instance, wives reported needing to remind or nag their husbands to complete tasks at home (Bergen, Kirby, & McBride, 2007).

Recreation management, another role function, is defined as coordinating those things you do for relaxation, entertainment, or personal development. More husbands than wives value family recreation activities. Stereotypically, men have found a recreational niche in strong, masculine athletic behaviors (Townsend, 1998). Extremely cohesive families encourage much group recreational activity, whereas low cohesion families may not. Parental behavior telegraphs to children what is appropriate recreational behavior, and conflicts may result if a child does not measure up.

Another type of basic resource role function involves managing family members' health. Women are more likely to enact this role in different ways. For example, studies of Internet use show that women are more likely than men to search the Internet for health information (Rice, 2006).

Providing Basic Resources

Traditionally, men were expected to be the major financial providers in families, although there have always been exceptions, especially for African American women who traditionally have been expected to work outside the home to contribute to the economic resources of the family (Boushey, 2009). However, today, providing basic resources is most often a role shared by both women and men in families.

The Families and Work Institute reports that 71 percent of women with children under 18 years of age participate in the U.S. workforce (Galinsky, Aumann, & Bond, 2008). Approximately four in ten mothers are primary breadwinners, which means they earn the majority of the family's income, compared to just 12 percent in 1967. Sixty-three percent of women are either the primary breadwinner or a co-breadwinner, earning at least a quarter of the family's income, which was only 28 percent in 1967. Thirty-eight percent of working wives earn as much or more than their husbands (Boushey, 2009). In looking at trends over the past three decades, it becomes clear that this shift toward women fulfilling this role function in greater frequency has been associated with men participating more in child care, cooking, and cleaning (Galinsky, Aumann, & Bond, 2008).

A distinction is made between *dual-career couples* and *dual-earner couples*. The term *dual-career couple* refers to a pair in which each pursues full-time career advancements. By contrast, in a *dual-earner couple* both spouses work primarily for economic reasons. Obviously some couples represent both experiences.

Not surprisingly, the current economic climate and a growing cultural acceptance of both parents acting as caregivers and earners has led to stressful lifestyles. Forty-five percent of mothers and 59 percent of fathers in dual-earner couples report work-life conflict (Galinsky, Aumann, & Bond, 2008). As Boushey (2009) noted:

> At home, families cope with this day-to-day time squeeze in a variety of unsatisfactory ways. In most families today, there's no one who stays at home all day and so there's no one with the time to prepare dinner, be home when the kids get back from school, or deal with the little things of everyday life, such as accepting a UPS package or getting the refrigerator repaired. Instead of having Mom at home keeping her eye on the children after school, families face the challenge of watching over their latchkey kids from afar and worry about what their teenagers are doing after school.

Researchers who study this area have described the merging of the roles as provider/worker and family member as "*spillover*." Spillover is bidirectional; family demands can spill over into work life and work demands can spill over into family life. A divorced woman with primary parenting responsibilities for two elementary school–aged children may have spillover of her family responsibilities into her work. For example, if one of the children is sick and needs to be kept home from school, she must stay home from work to care for the child, even if she has an important meeting to attend that day. The same woman may also experience her work demands spilling over into her family life. For instance, she may take material from work home with her on the weekends to read while her children watch a movie.

A consistent line of research has addressed work and family roles. Small and Riley's (1990) research enriched a perspective on the interface between work and family roles. They examined how work spillover affects four nonwork role contexts: the parent-child relationship, the couple or marital relationship, the use of leisure time for family activities, and the home management role. Barnett, Marshall, and Pleck's (1992) research on men's multiple roles and stress focused on three key roles in men's lives: the job role, the marital role, and the parental role. The same roles and stresses exist in women's lives. More recently, Dilworth and Kingsbury (2005) examined how different generations experience spillover. Older respondents (over age 50) were more likely to report home-to-work spillover as involving care for elderly parents, while middle to younger generations reported spillover as focused on caring for children at home. However, all generations reported more negative work-to-home spillover than home-to-work spillover.

Work-family conflict and spillover may be even more of a challenge for low-income, unmarried mothers. Of these mothers, those who report high levels of work-family conflict are less likely to be employed. Work-family conflict may keep these women unemployed, or if they find jobs, make it difficult for them to maintain employment stability (Ciabatarri, 2007).

Managing the role identities of work and family can be viewed as a process of communication. Like the interactive perspective of roles explained earlier in the chapter, Golden (2002) suggests that couples create shared meanings of their roles as providers and caregivers through their communicative practices. This may come through negotiation about roles as well as regular coordination. In the Shriver Report, Maria Shriver writes that "An overwhelming majority of both men and women said they're sitting down at their kitchen tables to coordinate their family's schedules, duties, and responsibilities, including child care and elder care, at least two to three times a week" (Shriver, 2009).

In addressing the issue of managing family-to-work stress, Krouse and Affifi (2007) identified eight communication strategies mothers use for managing family spillover. These include: venting with superiors and/or with coworkers, receiving affirmation and assurances from coworkers, seeking advice from coworkers, and seeking instrumental (practical) support from supervisors.

Stepfamilies often face conflicts when the stepparent may feel that he or she has lost control of resources that go toward the stepchildren. Single parents often feel that providing economic stability has become a primary role. Providing economic support for children is a role that is often continued for a father following a divorce (Mandel and Sharlin, 2006). Solo mothers tend to work longer hours and experience more stress and less emotional support than single fathers (Gringlas & Weinraub, 1995).

The Combined Functions

Each family combines these five role functions in unique ways. For example, in a family where children have been raised and are on their own, child rearing and child socialization may no longer be important functions. Both spouses may be highly successful in their careers and devoting time to recreation and travel may be highly valued and organized by the husband. Housekeeping functions may be provided by a cleaning service. Single African American parents often face economic stresses, neighborhood safety concerns, and a need to rely on extended family members for child-care assistance. Parents may emphasize the therapeutic and providing roles (Stewart, 2010). Recreation may be more individually oriented, while kinship functions may receive limited attention. In some single-parent dual-earner families, children may be required to engage in a type or amount of activity such as sibling supervision or meal preparation. For example, an older child may assume extensive child care or housekeeping responsibilities in a busy dual-career household. In a single-parent system, children may be expected to provide therapeutic listening that might be expected of a spouse in a two-parent household.

ROLE APPROPRIATION

The key question remains: How do family members learn, demonstrate, adjust, or relinquish these role functions? The answer requires an understanding of the aspects of role appropriation. *Role appropriation* can be seen as a three-part, overlapping process involving role expectation, role enactment, and role negotiation (Stamp, 1994). Issues of role conflict also emerge. Each of these will be explored in the following section.

Role Expectations

Society provides models and norms for how certain family roles should be assumed, thus creating role expectations. Walk into any bookstore or look on a parenting Web site and you will see articles and books on how to be a good parent, grandparent, or stepparent. Media has provided many family role models through television specials, situation comedies, movies, or talk shows. Advertising reinforces stereotypes of how family members should act.

Daily life within a community also serves as a source of role expectations. When you were growing up, the neighbors and your friends probably all knew who were the "good" mothers or the "bad" kids on the block or in the community. Religious cultures and school leaders set expectations for how family members should behave. Each of you has grown up with expectations of how people should function in family roles, just as this example shows.

My mother grew up on a ranch in the Great Uinta Basin in Utah. The women in her family were extremely strong and used to doing "men's work." Again, whatever had to be done would be done by whoever was available. It didn't matter whether one was a girl or boy—all hands were necessary and looked upon as being equal in her family.

Cultural groups convey beliefs about parenting or spousal roles, which are learned by members of their community. In the Jewish tradition, the role of mother is associated with the transmission of culture and primary values; as such, it carries a particular significance and implies certain expectations (Rosen & Weltman, 2005). In their study of middle-aged and older African American women, Blee and Tickamyer (1995) reported a strong expectation of dual parenting and providing. *Familism* dominates life in Puerto Rican families: whereas women are gaining personal power by contributing financially to the household, men may suffer some loss in status if their wives work (Garcia-Preto, 2005).

In addition, role expectations also arise from significant others and complementary others. *Significant others* are those persons you view as important and who provide you with models from which you develop role expectations. Having a favorite teacher who combined a career with a family or a close friend who succeeded as a trial attorney while single-handedly raising three children may influence your role choices. Thus, part of learning roles occurs by observing and imitating *role models,* persons whose behavior serves as a guide for others (Golden, 1997).

❙ Dual-career families face constant role negotiation.

Complementary others are those who fulfill reciprocal role functions that have a direct impact on your role. During early stages of romantic relationships, men and women spend long periods of time discussing their expectations for a future spouse. "I want my wife to be home with the children until they go to school" or "I need a husband who will help parent my children from my first marriage." A future stepparent may try to explore expectations with a future stepchild; a parent and college-aged child may discuss expectations for their interaction during summer vacations.

When one parent leaves the family system, the other parent may expect a child to fulfill an emotional role of confidant or a task role of household helper. "You're the man of the house now" typifies this lowering of boundaries between parent and child subsystems and often results in communication breakdowns. This may place great pressure on the child, alienate the child from other siblings, and eventually interfere with the normal process of separating from the family at the appropriate developmental point.

Additional expectations come from each person's self-understanding. You may find that you relied on a role model or you decided that with your skills or personality you would like to be a certain kind of partner or parent. Sometimes one's role expectations clash with those of significant others, as this man reports.

Colleen and I have arguments with our parents. They expect us to produce grandchildren, but neither of us wants the responsibility of children. It has taken each of us over a decade to finish our education by paying for it on our own and working full time. We love our dog, but that doesn't guarantee we would be nurturing parents!

Role expectations are influenced by an imaginative view of yourself—the way you like to think of yourself being and acting. A father may imagine himself telling his child about the facts of life. A teenager may imagine lecturing a younger sibling on avoiding drug use. Such imaginings are not just daydreams; they serve as a rehearsal for actual performance. No matter what you imagine, until you enact your role with others, you are dealing with role expectations.

Role Enactment

Role enactment, sometimes called *role performance,* is the actual interactive behavior that defines how the role is enacted. As with role expectations, role performance is influenced by the individual's capacity for enacting the role.

Persons in complementary or opposing roles have direct bearing on how you enact your role. Have you ever tried to reason with a parent who sulks, pamper an independent grandparent, or correct a willful child? However, if two complementary family members see things in similar ways, it enhances role performance. Young adults living with their parents may believe that they should no longer be subject to curfews and notifying parents of their evening plans; this belief will be reinforced by parents who no longer ask. If a mother's advice to her adult son and his wife about caring for their sick infant is appreciated and followed, the mother will likely continue to give such advice. Thus, the way others assume their roles and comment on your role affects how you enact your role.

Additionally, your background influences your behavior. For example, if certain communication behaviors are not part of your repertoire, they cannot magically appear in a particular situation. A father may wish he could talk with his son instead of yelling at him or giving orders, but he may not know how to discuss controversial subjects with his child. Self-confidence in attempting to fulfill a role may affect behavior. A shy stepmother may not be able to express affection either verbally or nonverbally with her new stepchildren for many months. On occasion, people discover that they can function well in a role they did not expect or desire, as this woman discovered.

I was really furious when my husband quit his sales job to finish his degree. I didn't choose the role of provider and I didn't like being conscripted into it. But after a while, I got to feeling very professional and adult. Here I was supporting myself and a husband. I didn't know I had it in me.

When trying to enact both work and family roles, husbands' and wives' experiences may be somewhat different. Among a predominantly working-class sample, women's sense of balance between their work and family roles was dependent on their gender ideology. Women who had a more traditional gender ideology perceived more balance in their roles than women who had a less traditional gender ideology, but men's gender ideology did not affect their sense of balance between work and family roles (Marks, Huston, Johnson, & MacDermid, 2001). Some men attempt to enact both work and family fully, resulting in the "Superdad" role. In a study of male science and technology workers in Silicon Valley, Cooper (2000) found that "Superdads" attended to both the emotional and care needs of their families as well as investing heavily in their work, whereas other male colleagues remained in the traditional male role or chose to invest more in work when work-family pressures arose.

Choosing to enact one role may affect a person's ability to enact other roles as well. Hewlett (2002) studied how women who are highly educated and in the top 10 percent of earning power have enacted roles in their lives. At age 40, one-third of these women were childless, most not by choice. Instead, enacting the very demanding role of a consultant, lawyer, doctor, or other professional left these women with very little time to pursue relationships. In fact, Hewlett found that the more successful these women were in their careers, the less likely they were to have a partner or children. For male professionals, however, the opposite was true. The more successful they were in their careers, the more likely they were to be married with children.

Family members may have different perceptions of the way in which a role is enacted. In one study, fathers were asked to report their involvement and emotional involvement with their children. Their children's mothers (whether or not they were married to the fathers) were also asked to report on the *father's* involvement and emotional involvement with the children. Fathers reported spending 17.6 percent more time with the children than the children's mothers perceived (Mikkelson, 2008).

Role Negotiation

As individuals enact their roles, they experience a process whereby, in conjunction with others, they structure their reality and give meaning to their lives. This is called *role negotiation*. In describing the move to parenthood, Stamp (1994) concluded that, when couples become parents, "their ongoing conversation constructs, monitors, and modifies the new reality of their changed existence. Their new roles are appropriated into their overall identities" (p. 91). This critical use of conversation applies to assuming and maintaining any family role. In the case of Jarvis and his son Jamal, discussed at the beginning of the chapter, bringing a new family member into the system requires negotiation.

Once a role is assumed, the process of role enactment usually involves negotiation with those in related roles. This may involve reconstructing differences and exploring new ways to act regarding certain expectations. These role negotiations can be affected by gender. Nomaguchi and Milki (2003) report that becoming a new mother is associated with increased housework and more disagreements with spouses as compared to wives without children, although this finding did not hold true for husbands. Some gay male parents report that as same-sex couples they were free of gender role expectations and they experienced a different freedom in choosing and allowing responsibilities to evolve, partly based on personality style (Gianino, 2008).

Nippert-Eng (1996) argues that the extent to which a worker integrates his or her work role and home role is evidenced by many cultural and social acts such as calendars, eating, reading material, talk, and vacations. For example, a person who highly integrates her work and home roles might just keep one calendar with both work and family activities and keep in touch with colleagues during vacation. In contrast, a person who has not integrated these roles may have separate calendars for work and home, keep work conversations off personal topics, and rarely, if ever, bring reading material home from work.

Frequently, role negotiation involves managing interpersonal conflict when members attempt to work out their roles. Individuals may know what is expected of them in a family, but not all members perform the expected behaviors. For example, a husband and wife may have agreed early in their marriage to share the role of provider. However, after having a child, the wife may decide that she no longer wants to share that role and prefers instead to stay home with the baby. When this happens, the organizational structure in the system changes; a new kind of interdependence must evolve. When faced with difficult times, couples often have to renegotiate their previously stable agreements. In a study of 90 low-income noncustodial fathers, half of whom had been imprisoned and half of whom had criminal histories, Edin, Nelson, and Paranal (2001) found that fathers with damaged family bonds before imprisonment used prison time as an opportunity to turn their lives around and reconnect to their children—a strong role renegotiation.

Clearly, many areas of potential conflicts over roles are evident. When complementary or significant others have different expectations of the way a person should be performing a role, conflict occurs. A child or adolescent may expect far more nurturing from a parent and complain about the lack of emphasis on it. An adult son who has moved to a different country may have arguments with his mother about how frequently he can come home to visit. Some women who had been successful in their careers, and who have high-earning husbands, choose to leave their careers to raise their children, becoming part of the "opt-out revolution" (Belkin, 2003), although many of those women have returned to the workplace for economic reasons.

Role conflict may occur when a divorced parent remarries, bringing a stepparent into the family system. One study on successful stepmothers found that role ambiguities and role conflict was a common experience for stepmothers as they tried to figure out their many different role functions, such as nurturing, protecting, coordinating, and disciplining (Whiting, Smith, Barnett, & Grafsky, 2007). Stepmothers were able to resolve some of these conflicts if they had an accepting attitude, worked to resolve conflicts, and established good support systems.

Role conflict also occurs when a family member is trying to enact more than one role at the same time that seem to be incompatible with each other or difficult to enact together, such as in the example of Rebekah at the beginning of the chapter.

You have probably seen or experienced examples of role conflict in your family. For instance, a 14-year-old boy who finds out that his 17-year-old sister is sneaking out of the house at night might experience role conflict between his role as the dependable son who would tell his parents and his role as a sibling who wants his sister's approval. Frequently, grandparents who, by necessity, assume parental roles experience role conflict. Most report support groups as beneficial in managing these role conflicts (Smith, Savage-Stevens, & Fabian, 2002).

In her classic book on work-family issues entitled *The Second Shift,* Hochschild (1989) introduced the idea of "the second shift," suggesting that married women often work at taking care of house and children after putting in a full day's work on the job. In order to negotiate the role conflict that occurs from being both a provider and primary homemaker, Hochschild described how one woman would make her own meals, but not her husband's. Another woman gave up on keeping the house clean. In the ensuing decades families have found more functional ways to negotiate these role conflicts. The schedule of parents' work may also impact family functioning. A study of Canadian families found that parents working evenings, nights, and weekends was associated with worse family functioning and less effective parenting, as compared to families with parents working standard weekday times (Strazdins, et al., 2006).

Many factors may influence the border between work and family responsibilities. Campbell Clark (2000) describes a work-family border theory that helps to explain how conflict between work and family roles is increased or decreased. The theory proposes that when the domains of work and home have similar cultures and weak borders, it is easier to flow back and forth between, causing less conflict. For instance, a parent's ability to bring work home when a child is ill, but also go into the office on the weekend if needed, is an example of a weak border. However, in cases where one domain has a strong border and the other has a weak border, work-family balance is related to the domain with which a person identifies most strongly. Imagine a woman who identifies primarily as a mother, but has a job with a very strong border, such as a surgical nurse who needs to be at the hospital for her scheduled shifts. The theory explains that this mother will feel less work- family balance.

Feelings for the other person may affect the extent to which role conflict occurs. A parent may react differently to each child by basing his or her actions on the child's behavior. Conflict results when individuals struggle to maintain roles that are not appropriate to their ages or relationships as described below.

As the oldest daughter, I ended up with a great number of responsibilities and feel as if I lost a part of my own childhood. My mother was an alcoholic and my father and I almost became the "adult partners" in the house. He expected me to take care of the younger kids and to fix meals when Mom was "drying out." I hated all the work I had to do and all the responsibility. He didn't even want me to get married because he didn't know how he would cope.

Sometimes family members set aside time to discuss roles. Couples who take time to debrief and share work experiences greatly increase their relational satisfaction (Vangelisti & Banski, 1993). Certainly, increasing each partner's sense of worth affects his or her role performance and lessens conflicts.

As you will see in later chapters, predictable and unpredictable life crises affect the roles you assume and how you function in them. Unforeseen circumstances may alter life in such a way that roles change drastically from those first planned or enacted. The next section explains how couples and families can be categorized into types depending on their role behavior.

COUPLE AND FAMILY TYPOLOGIES

Couple or family typologies represent another way to explore how roles develop through family interaction. Many family researchers and therapists believe family behavior and organization can be classified into various typologies, depending on the patterns of the interactions. Typologies are useful to researchers and students of family communication because they help bring order to phenomena studied in family communication. We will discuss three couple typologies and two family typologies.

Couple-Oriented Typologies

Fitzpatrick's Couple Types An extensive attempt to classify couple types is found in Mary Anne Fitzpatrick's research (Fitzpatrick, Fallis, & Vance, 1982; Noller & Fitzpatrick, 1993; Fitzpatrick & Badzinski, 1994). In her early work, Fitzpatrick (1977, 1988) tested a large number of characteristics to find out which made a difference in maintaining couple relationships. She isolated eight significant factors that affect role enactment: (1) conflict avoidance, (2) assertiveness, (3) sharing, (4) the ideology of traditionalism, (5) the ideology of uncertainty and change, (6) temporal (time) regularity, (7) undifferentiated space, and (8) autonomy. All eight affect role enactment. Fitzpatrick designated three couple types called traditionals, separates, and independents. She also found six mixed-couple types wherein the husband and wife described their relationship differently. She found that 20 percent are traditionals, 17 percent are separates, and 22 percent are independents (1988). Thus, about 60 percent can be classified as pure types and 40 percent as mixed.

Independent types accept uncertainty and change. They pay limited attention to schedules and traditional values. Independents represent the most autonomous of the types but do considerable sharing and negotiate autonomy. Independents are more likely to conflict and to support an androgynous, flexible sex role (Fitzpatrick, 1988).

Separates differ from independents in greater conflict avoidance, more differentiated space needs, fairly regular schedules, and less sharing. In relationships, separates maintain a distance from people, even their spouses. They experience little sense of togetherness or autonomy. Separates usually oppose an androgynous sexual orientation and tend to avoid conflict (Fitzpatrick, 1988).

Traditionals uphold a fairly conventional belief system and resist change or uncertainty because it threatens their routines. This leads to a high degree of interdependence and low autonomy. They will engage in conflict but would rather avoid it. Traditionals, like separates, demonstrate strong sex-typed roles and oppose an androgynous orientation (Fitzpatrick, 1988).

The other six mixed types, which have the husband designated by the first term, are traditional/separate, separate/traditional, independent/separate, separate/independent, traditional/independent, and independent/traditional (Fitzpatrick, 1988). These are not a category of "leftovers," but represent many different couple systems (Fitzpatrick & Ritchie, 1994).

In their summary of the research, Fitzpatrick and Best (1979) reported that traditional couples were significantly higher than separate, independent, or mixed-type couples on consensus, cohesion, relational satisfaction, and expressing affection. Independents were lower on consensus, open affection to one another, and dyadic satisfaction. However, their lack of agreement on issues regarding dyadic interactions did not impair their cohesiveness. Separates were the least cohesive, but on relational issues appeared high on consensus. Separates demonstrated few expressions of affection toward their spouses and rated lower on dyadic satisfaction. In the separate/traditional category, couples had low consensus on a number of relational issues, but they were moderately cohesive. These couples claimed high satisfaction for their relationship and outwardly expressed much affection (Noller & Fitzpatrick, 1993).

Table 7.1 summarizes the ways in which couple types responded to a variety of relationship measures, including sex roles and gender perceptions. In predicting communication, you might expect that traditional families would demonstrate

TABLE 7.1

Couple Type Differences on Relational Measures

Couple Types	Marital Satisfaction	Cohesion	Consensus	Affectional Expression	Sex Roles	Psychological Gender States (Wives Only)
Traditionals	High	High	High	Moderately high	Conventional	Feminine
Independents	Low	Moderately high	Low	Low	Nonconventional	Sex-typed androgynous
Separates	Low	Low	Moderately high	Low	Conventional	Feminine sex-typed
Separates/ Traditionals	Moderately high	Moderately high	Moderately high	High	Conventional	Feminine sex-typed
Other mixed types	Moderately high	Low	Low	Moderately high	Depends on mixed type	Depends on mixed type

affection and sharing of the role functions discussed earlier in this chapter, with males and females remaining in defined positions. You could expect male dominance in attitudes and values regarding the providing, recreational, housekeeping, sex, and kinship functions, since the traditional type resists change. Because independents are more open to change, they might be more open to dual-career marriages and sharing the providing and housekeeping functions. Because independents value autonomy and avoid interdependence, individual partners may be more free in their role functions.

The potential for problems when communicating about role functions relates especially to the separates who have not resolved the interdependence/autonomy issue in their marriage. Fitzpatrick uses the label "emotionally divorced" for this type, because separates are least likely to express their feelings to their partners. Baxter (1991), in her explorations of dialectical theory, suggests that Fitzpatrick's traditionals privilege continuity over discontinuity, with independents privileging change over continuity, with separates somewhere in the middle.

Hochschild's Marital Ideology Role Types Hochschild's research on working mothers revealed three types of marital roles for dual-earner couples: traditional, transitional, and egalitarian.

Women in *traditional* couples may work, but they see themselves primarily as mothers and community members and want their husbands to identify primarily with work. Husbands in traditional couples base their identities on their work and expect their wives to manage the home.

The *transitional* husband and wife see the husband's identity as the provider. The wife identifies with home management as a role, although she also wishes to identify with her work. Transitional husbands don't mind that their wives work, but also expect them to take most of the home responsibility.

In an *egalitarian* marriage, both partners wish to jointly share home responsibilities as well as take advantage of career opportunities. Power is to be shared and each partner strives to maintain a life balance between career and family while supporting the other in this effort. The way egalitarians accomplish this may differ from couple to couple. Some might want the couple to place the most emphasis on the home or on work, whereas others expect both spouses to put joint emphasis on work and home.

As with Fitzpatrick's marital types, husbands and wives may be mixed in their types; for example, a traditionalist husband and a transitionalist wife. Hochschild (1989) also found that both husbands and wives may say one thing about their roles, yet act as if they feel another way. An example of this would be a husband who says he is egalitarian, but he expects his wife to stay home with the children each night while he goes out with his buddies because he earns more money than she does.

Hochschild's (1989) role types are not based on communication processes, yet understanding these types may be helpful when trying to understand marital communication. A dual-earner couple might argue frequently about who does the grocery shopping. To understand why they argue, it could be important to understand their gender ideology types. Perhaps the wife has an egalitarian ideology, believing that each spouse should take turns, but her transitionalist husband views grocery shopping as the wife's responsibility. Examining the couple's family-of-origin gender ideologies might also help to explain their behavior.

Gender-Organized Couple Types Other researchers have created couple types based on how gender beliefs are used to organize the relationship (Knudson-Martin & Mahoney, 2005; Cowdery & Knudson-Martin, 2005). Unlike Hochschild's work, these three couple types can be applied to dual-earner and non-dual-earner couples. *Postgender* couples are those who have made a conscious effort to move past gender as a way to organize the relationship and tasks associated with it. For example, a couple that sees each other as having equal responsibility and power in all household and child-rearing tasks would be considered *postgender. Gender-legacy* couples do not overtly recognize gender as the reason for their division of labor, but use it by default to do so. For example, if both spouses work, the wife in a gender-legacy couple may be more likely to organize her schedule to maximize her time at home. A husband, although he says he is an equal partner in child care, may describe his wife as being more "in-tune" with others' needs (Knudson-Martin & Mahoney, 2005). *Traditional* couples use gender as a conscious method of dividing labor in the relationship and see their roles, though different, as equal. Though each takes on different tasks, they see their roles as deserving equal respect.

Such use of gender also affects parenting and the construction of the role of mother. Cowdery and Knudson-Martin (2005) report that fathers in *traditional* and *gender-legacy* couples have an indirect relationship with their children that is moderated by the mother. Instead of caring for children because the children need their care, these fathers report caring for children because the mother needs a break. In contrast, *postgender* fathers have direct relational connections with their children, assuming that responsibility is shared.

Gottman's Conflict Types Gottman classifies his couple types according to the style of the conflict interactions that the couple experiences. The couple types are validating, volatile, and conflict avoiders. He found that lasting marriages existed in all three types if a "magic ratio" of five positive interactions to one negative interaction developed over time (1994a). In the *validating* type, partners respect one another's point of view on a variety of topics and, when they disagree, try to work out a compromise. This type agrees on most basic issues of sex, money, religion, and children. When they disagree about roles, they listen to one another and refrain from shouting or "hitting below the belt." The *volatile* type of couple is comfortable with disagreement and lack of harmony. Any question over roles and who does what and when leads to open conflict. They don't fight fairly, but they fight often. It tends to energize the relationship. The third type, *conflict avoiders,* abhors negative messages and goes to any length to lessen potential conflicts. Partners placate and please one another rather than meet their own needs. They walk away from arguments, often giving family members the silent treatment. They are comfortable with standoffs, and uncomfortable with rage or protest. Gottman and colleagues (2002) capture the communication differences, suggesting that volatile couples are high on immediate persuasion attempts and low on listening or validation before persuading. Validating couples listen efficiently and reflect feelings before persuading. Conflict-avoidant couples avoid persuasive attempts.

Family Typologies

Family Communication Patterns Although people often talk in general terms about the patterns of communication in a family, a typology based on specific types of family communication patterns also exists. This typology of family communication patterns is designed using two types of communication, labeled conformity orientation and conversation orientation (Koerner & Fitzpatrick, 2006). Some families' communication behavior may be characterized by one of these orientations, while other families may be divided by members who use one while others prefer the opposite. A family high on *conformity* expresses similar values and attitudes that enhance harmony. A family low on conformity expresses more varied values, attitudes, and patterns of interaction. It upholds individuality and brings out the unique personalities of family members. Family members high on the use of *conversation* have an open family system so that individuals can speak their minds easily on a whole range of conflict issues with little fear of what they say. Families low on this dimension speak out less frequently on fewer conflict issues.

Fitzpatrick and Ritchie (1994) describe four different kinds of families (consensual, pluralistic, protective, and laissez-faire) based on the family's use of either a conformity or conversation orientation in their interactions (see Figure 7.2). This typology recognizes that families can function well with different types of behaviors and that there is not just one functional way to communicate (Koerner & Fitzpatrick, 2006). *Consensual families* are high in both conversation and conformity strategies with their communication characterized by pressure for agreement, although children are encouraged to express ideas and feelings. *Pluralistic families,* high in conversation orientation and low in conformity, have open communication and emotional supportiveness in their families. *Protective families* rank low on the use of a conversational approach and high on conformity dimensions. They stress upholding family rules and avoiding conflict. *Laissez-faire families,* low

	High Conversation Orientation	*Low Conversation Orientation*
High Conformity Orientation	Consensual	Protective
Low Conformity Orientation	Pluralistic	Laissez-faire

FIGURE 7.2

Family Types Based on Family Communication Patterns

on both conformity and conversation dimensions, interact very little. In this kind of family, children may look outside the family for influence and support.

Differences also exist among family types in the motives parents have for talking to children. For example, in the two family types that are marked by a high conversation orientation (consensual and pluralistic), parents have relational motives for talking with their children, such as for pleasure or relaxation or to show affection. In the protective family types, parents are motivated to communicate with their children to seek control, although these parents also report affection as one reason they communicate with their children (Barbato, et al., 2001). In a recent study examining family communication patterns and adoption, Reuter and Koerner (2008) found that protective families and laissez-faire families were unable to lessen the adolescent adjustment risks that are associated with adoption. However, adopted adolescents in consensual and pluralistic families were no different in adjustment risks than nonadopted adolescents.

Another study examined cross-cultural differences in family communication patterns, finding that the consensual family type was most common in the United States, while the laissez-faire family type was most common in Japan. In both countries, conversation orientation was associated with communication satisfaction, while American participants reported less communication satisfaction when conformity orientation was higher (Shearman & Dunlao, 2008).

It is important to think about family communication patterns and types from a transactional perspective, as family communication patterns are developed through interaction between family members. A couple's marriage and parenting styles heavily influence family communication patterns (Koerner & Fitzpatrick, 2004), and adolescent communication also affects these patterns (Saphir & Chaffee, 2002).

Closed, Open, and Random Types Kantor and Lehr's classic work *Inside the Family* (1976) serves as the touchstone study of family types. We include it here for historical perspective. As a means of dealing with the basic family issue of separateness and connectedness, or what Kantor and Lehr call "distance regulation," they developed a six-dimensional social space grid on which family communication takes place.

All communication represents efforts by family members to gain access to targets—that is, things or ideas members want or need. Specifically, family members use two sets of dimensions. One set reaches targets of (1) affect, (2) power, and (3) meaning through the way they regulate the other set, the access to dimensions of (4) space, (5) time, and (6) energy. Using these six dimensions, Kantor and Lehr created a typology for viewing families, consisting of closed, open, and random types, acknowledging that actual families may consist of mixtures of types. The ways in which these three family types maintain their boundaries, or regulate distance through access and target dimensions, account for their differences in role enactment.

Closed families tend to regulate functions predictably with fixed boundaries. Such families interact less with the outside world. They require members to fulfill their needs and spend their time and energies within the family. Events in closed families tend to be tightly scheduled and predictable.

In the *open family,* boundaries tend to remain flexible when members are encouraged to seek experiences in the outside space and return to the family with ideas the family may use if group consensus develops. Open families seldom use censorship, force, or coercion because they believe family goals will vary, change, and be subject to negotiation. Members are more likely to concern themselves with the present, while energy is quite flexible.

Unpredictability and "do-your-own-thing" aptly describe the *random family.* The boundaries of space surrounding this family are dispersed. Family members and outsiders join in the living space based on interest or desire, or they voluntarily separate from one another without censure. Social appropriateness holds little importance for such members. Time is spent on an irregular basis. Energy in the random family fluctuates.

Table 7.2 summarizes the characteristics that Kantor and Lehr delineated for each of these family types. You may identify more closely with one of the types, or you may find that your family incorporates two of the types. You may also realize your family has shifted in typology over the years. In Figure 7.3 we present a case study of three family types. Which one or combination describes your family?

A speculative comparison can be made between Fitzpatrick's and Kantor and Lehr's research. Olson's circumplex model of cohesion and adaptability can also be integrated into their thinking. The terminology each theorist uses can be clarified by remembering that Fitzpatrick's autonomy/interdependence is similar to Olson's cohesion dimension and Kantor and Lehr's affect dimension. Adaptability as used by Olson is similar to power (measured behaviorally) in Fitzpatrick and Kantor and Lehr. Fitzpatrick's ideology refers to meaning in Kantor and Lehr's thinking but does not appear in Olson's work. Communication is included in the behavioral data collected by Fitzpatrick. In Olson's research, communication appears as an enabling dimension, and as distance regulation in Kantor and Lehr's study. Whatever the family or couple type, adults use communication strategies in their various roles that maintain their type.

TABLE 7.2

Characteristics of Family Types

Type of Family	Use of Space	Use of Time	Use of Energy
Closed	Fixed	Regular	Steady
Open	Movable	Variable	Flexible
Random	Dispersed	Irregular	Fluctuating

FIGURE 7.3

Examples of Closed, Open, and Random Families

The Closed Family: The Ward Family

Life in the seven-person Ward family is structured and predictable. Jack Ward and Lillian Ward have been married for three years. Jack was widowed for four years and brought 6-year-old twins to the stepfamily. Lillian was divorced at a young age and had three children aged 4, 7, and 9 at the time of the marriage. Her former husband has little involvement with the children. Jack and Lillian are the heads of the household and believe that family discipline is a training ground for achievement at school and financial success. Together Jack and Lillian have built a strong boundary around the marriage and family. Decisions are made at the parental level, usually announced by Jack. What the parents usually share about their private lives is revealed as a lesson to their children. Clearly, they are parents with a capital P.

In the Ward family, strong emotions are rarely expressed in public and affection is reserved for the appropriate time and place. Strong conflict is discouraged; polite disagreement is acceptable.

The Ward family themes might be expressed as follows: "Be strong, self-sufficient, and stick together" and "The family comes first." Discipline is rigorously enforced throughout the family. Failure to carry out responsibilities at any level results in a loss of privileges. The strong boundaries keep friends at a distance.

Traditions are prized in this family. Holidays involve only family members who participate in predictable rituals designed to bond the members. These are times for storytelling, praying, and being together without interference.

The Open Family: The Parker Family

Events frequently take place at the last minute in the Parker household, which consists of four members— Doris Parker and her three children aged 8, 11, and 14. Doris's work pattern is one of taking it somewhat easy on a project and then launching a big, all-night push as her deadline nears. Her office work covers a desk at home, since she often works there to finish big projects. She is frequently behind schedule due to all her commitments. Somehow key tasks are eventually done before it is absolutely too late. Doris's tardiness is not due to laziness or lack of energy; rather, it comes about because she has so much to do. The children all have responsibilities but exceptions are made around school or religious group activities.

Friends and guests are frequently brought home by both mother and children. People may drop in or telephone at any time of the day or evening without feeling uncomfortable. Every once in a while a family member declares a need for "just us" together time, a request that is always honored. For the Parker family, there is no such thing as an absolute answer to the problems that arise. There are, however, certain points of view that members generally hold to be true, one being that safety and respect for family members are critical. Decisions are group projects. The Parker family members express their affection and their differences openly and often loudly. A key theme is: "The family must be free to fight and to love!"

Members enjoy being together for holidays and birthdays, but special circumstances are recognized. Other options may be negotiated but the centrality of the family must be respected.

The Random Family: The Connor Family

Life in the four-person Connor household is sparked by multiple projects, planned and spontaneous. "Go with the flow" is the norm in the household, which is formed by Mary and David, married for 19 years, and their two teenage girls, Maggie and Michelle. Friends drop in at any time, often staying a few days or weeks, without much fuss or attention. In spite of their preference for spontaneity, the Connors are committed to huge holiday events, but rarely celebrate them in the same way from one year to another. Members are never sure who will be present or what the event will entail; there are few rituals, since repetition is not valued.

The Connor household is likely to be as cluttered with objects as it is with people. The hallway is typically strewn with clothes and the desks are piled up because the Connors are too preoccupied to take the time to tidy up routinely. The clutter is not of great significance. Clearly, it is more important that a developing school art project sits in the middle of the kitchen table than it is to impress visitors with order.

Each member complains that mealtimes do not provide a greater opportunity for emotional sharing and closeness. Yet, having a regular mealtime would interfere with each one's freedom. Therefore, the Connors often find themselves unable to ensure regular emotional connectedness. Closeness and intimacy do occur, but they occur spontaneously. When people see each other, great affection may be shared, or great conflicts may occur, if both parties are tuned in to each other. "Doing your own thing" and "Be yourself," within reasonable standards of ethics and safety, serve as the themes for this unpredictable family system.

CONCLUSION

This chapter took an interactive approach to roles, stressing the effect of family interaction on role performance. The distinction between position-oriented and person-oriented roles was developed and applied to communication. The five role functions were presented in a mobile model and explained with more emphasis placed on those roles that require more communication strategies. The development of roles takes part in a three-step process—role expectation, role enactment, and role negotiation—each of which have communication components.

Finally, the couple and family typologies, with their predictability, are viewed as sources for understanding the communication that helps to carry out role functions. A major consideration in examining roles or couple/family types is their dynamic nature, which is viewed in accordance with the personal developments and unpredictable circumstances faced by the people involved.

In Review

1. Discuss what you think will happen to roles in families by the year 2025. What directions do you see families taking in the future?
2. Compare and contrast the communication tasks required in carrying out the role functions involved in providing resources and nurturance for the family. Describe these functions in a family with which you are familiar.
3. Identify a real or fictional family that has changed over time. Note the role changes and give your reasons for these changes. What has been the effect on the system?

4. Give examples of partners you know that fit Fitzpatrick's couple types. Describe the sample communication strategies that they use.
5. Using one of the family or couple typologies for roles (for example, Fitzpatrick's, Hochschild's, Gottman's, or Knudson-Martin's), analyze your family or another real or fictional family and explain how it fits or doesn't fit the type. Cite examples of communication patterns.

KEY WORDS

Conformity orientation   173
Conversation orientation   173
Fitzpatrick's marital types   169
Gottman's conflict types   172
McMaster's family role functions   151

Role conflict   167
Role enactment   165
Role expectations   163
Role negotiation   166
Spillover   161

Power, Influence, and Decision Making in Families

"So children learn about power not just from what their parents try to teach them but also from observing their parents' interactions with them, with each other, and with other persons inside and outside the family. They learn, through trial and error and through example, which power strategies work, which ones are acceptable, and what they can get away with."

—Hilary M. Lips, *Women, Men, and Power*

When Alberto and Michael fell in love four years ago they had a series of conversations about their future, including whether they would ever become parents together. At that time Michael declared his strong desire to be a father while Alberto indicated he was open to thinking about it. By the time of their commitment ceremony, two years later, they told their guests that parenthood would be in their future—somehow. Since then they have held many conversations on the pros and cons of reaching parenthood through adoption or by using a surrogate. At first Alberto believed it would be important for one of them to have a biological link to the child, although Michael felt less strongly. But when they learned of the large financial commitment involved, that path to fatherhood seemed closed. After watching two sets of friends adopt children through a local state agency, they met with the social worker and decided to pursue adoption. The agency personnel indicated that most birth parents tended to request an open adoption, giving them some contact with the family as the child grows up. After much discussion Michael and Alberto decided to agree to an open or closed adoption and to accept a child of any ethnic or racial background. After many months they were paired with a single pregnant birthmother who desired an open adoption. At this point the two anxious men are waiting for a phone call from the agency inviting them to meet their new son.

These days the partners are discussing which of them will be the legal father because state regulations do not permit adoption by same-sex parents, and what a child would call each of them. Michael prefers Daddy whereas Alberto is considering Papa or Pops. At this point all they want to hear are the words, "Come meet your son!"

Robert groaned when he got the phone call from his mother. His father had "blown up" at his grandfather, and now his parents were not speaking to his grandparents, despite living next door to each other in the town Robert grew up in. Robert's 35 years of life had been peppered with similar fights and splits. He had not seen his aunt and uncle since he was 12 because of a falling out they had with his grandparents, and he had had a similar issue with his grandparents during his college years. Robert had just accepted that this was the way his family was, and had moved across the country when he married to get away from all of this family drama. But now, things were different. He had two young children and was planning a week-long stay in his hometown this summer. He did not want to bring his wife and his children into this family feud, and he certainly did not want to worry about having separate time with his parents and his grandparents. He had to do something!

Robert considered many courses of action. He thought about threatening his parents and grandparents that if they couldn't solve their problems, he would not come. He was the only child, and knew that they would be very sad not to see their grandchildren/great-grandchildren. But he wasn't sure he'd actually follow through on such a threat. He could try reasoning with them and explaining to them why this was going to be so difficult for him. However, he'd tried this when they'd had their last falling out and both sides were just so stubborn it didn't work. Ultimately, Robert decided to appeal to his family's minister, Pastor Michael. He called the pastor and discussed the situation with him, asking him to please help.

Who do you ask for permission to skip a family reunion? When trying to influence a sibling, do you offer to do a favor in return for another favor? When making a decision, does everyone in your family sit down together and discuss the issue or does one member make the decision and the other members go along with it? How have these responses changed over the years? In the past few years, you may have made a choice about where to enroll for college. How involved were your family members in this decision? The answers to these questions tell you something about power, influence, and decision making in your family—concepts that we address in this chapter.

As you probably realize, the concepts of power, influence, and decision making are intertwined. A mother may use her parental authority as power in order to influence her teenage daughter to clean her room, saying, "You will do it because I told you to. I'm your mother!" The Jamison family's decision to go to Disney World for summer vacation may be the result of 10-year-old Ben's persistent attempts to influence his parents and sisters. Or, a father may decide that because he paid a $400 fee for his son's martial arts class that his son cannot quit the class.

Despite how closely these concepts are connected, they are unique enough to deserve individual attention. Family members use different types of power; one family member's power does not always result in gaining influence for her or having others reach the decision she supports. As you read this chapter, think of the ways in which power, influence, and decision making have been enacted in families that you have observed.

POWER

Each family member must exercise a certain degree of power in order to gain or maintain some control over his or her life. It is almost impossible to live in a family without becoming involved in power negotiations, positive or negative, overt or subtle. Statements such as "Leave me alone," "It doesn't matter that much," or "Why should I be the one to change?" indicate how ingrained power issues are in everyday family life. The use of power produces changes that either improve or hinder family members' satisfaction. The feeling of having no power over other family members is usually unbearable, but it is also undesirable to be too openly aggressive in making power plays (Green & Elffers, 1998).

Power operates transactionally in a family. It does not belong to an individual; rather, it is a property of a relationship between two or more persons. Power should be viewed within a relationship (Dunbar, 2004). From a dialectical perspective, we view *power* by the way it uses, reduces, or increases tensions when individual family members interact with each other over goals or attempts to change others' behaviors. This dynamic perspective emphasizes change and flux. The exercise of power becomes an important factor in regulating relational tensions between closeness and distance.

Every family member's power maneuver creates a system-wide effect. As one or more members exert power or respond to others' power moves, the family system recalibrates itself. Even children exercise power since it "is an interactive quality of adults and children" (Socha & Yingling, 2010, p. 93). The system, through its adaptability mechanisms, reacts to all pressures, rebalancing to respond to the power plays and players.

Power also affects perception and behavior. The way in which one family member perceives the power dynamics helps to determine and explain the reasons for that member's actions. The same power issue may be perceived differently by every other family member. Montgomery (1992) noted how couples imitate other couples, and thus coordinate their relationship with a larger social order. Couples use their knowledge of how power operates within their relational or ethnic culture to inform them about power in their own family. In the following example, a student explains how one family member attempted to seize power.

When my parents separated and Dad left the house, my domineering grandmother became the ruling force. My mother would go along, out of respect for her age, even though she would disagree many times and secretly do what she wanted. Grandma would yell and scream if something wasn't done the way she wanted. We had no voice in her rulings. Each of us left home sooner than we might have in order to escape her domination.

The power dimension in a family system may vary greatly over time, depending on a host of factors, such as family structure, developmental stages, transitions, stresses, and the family's economic, cultural, or intellectual resources. Because the values, histories, and current socioeconomic factors of ethnic groups differ from the dominant white culture, family power processes may operate differently. For example, the older immigrant generation may use religion as a way to cope with powerlessness (McGoldrick, Giordano, & Garcia-Preto, 2005) whereas the younger generation may attain power through education. One cannot assume that all families exercise power in similar ways.

Although we discuss power, influence, and decision making together in this chapter, it is important to understand that power can affect communication in family relationships in non-influence and non-decision-making situations. Power appears in ordinary types of conversation and during intimate self-disclosure (Dunbar, 2004). In order to understand the complexity of power and its communication dynamics within family systems, you need to examine the aspects of power that impact family systems, the development of power in family systems.

Aspects of Power in Family Systems

Power can be conceptualized as having various aspects. In his classic work McDonald (1980) conceptualized power to include three important aspects, all of which affect communication: (1) power bases, (2) power processes, and (3) power outcomes.

Power Bases   The bases of family power are resources used by family members to increase their chances of exerting control in a specific situation. Resources consist of whatever is perceived as rewarding to an individual or a relationship; it is anything that one partner makes available to the other to satisfy needs or attain goals. It serves as an "agreement that gives adults the rights and responsibilities of leading family systems" (Socha & Yingling, 2010, p. 93).

McDonald's (1980) five resources are bases from which persons may derive power. They include normative, economic, affective, personal, and cognitive resources. As the case of Robert at the beginning of the chapter demonstrates, one person may have several power bases on which they may draw.

1. *Normative resources* refer to the family's values and to the cultural or societal definitions of where the authority lies. Normative definitions represent the culturally internalized expectations of how family relationships should function—the perceived role expectations and obligations of members. For example, some families' norms require that the mother have the power in managing the children's daily activities. Interestingly, in Turkish families, the higher level of education a father has, the more decreased is his perceived power in relation to his wife and son (Schonpflug, 2001). The author of this study speculated that fathers with more education operate under a more egalitarian mode in the family. In some cultures, the responsibility and power for caring for parents is given to the adult child, which impacts medical decision making.

2. *Economic resources* refer to the monetary control exerted by the breadwinner(s) and/or persons designated to make financial decisions. Economic power comes from wages earned and money saved or inherited. In some families, a breadwinning parent may refer to the household income as

"my money." Due to the recent recession, 13 percent of parents reported that a young adult moved back home, placing that person in a less powerful position (Wang & Morin, 2009). In Taiwanese marriages, the wife's resources gained from education and employment help to determine the balance of marital power (Xu & Lai, 2002).

3. *Affective resources,* related to relational currencies, reflect who in the family nurtures others and how each member in the family meets his or her needs for feeling loved or belonging to the system. For instance, a mother may withhold her normal affection from a teenaged son who broke curfew. A caring foster parent may provide her foster daughter with affection and increased self-esteem.

4. *Personal resources* refer to an individual member's characteristics such as personality, physical appearance, and role competence. They also include interpersonal factors that may cause the individual to be perceived as attractive or competent, and therefore accorded power. For example, a grandson may have the ability to make his grandparents laugh by talking in a funny voice. He soon learns that using this voice allows him to say things that otherwise would get him into trouble.

5. *Cognitive resources* refer to family members' insight, or the sense of how their power influences their own actions and affects others. It deals with using intelligence to logically determine what power options are available. Some children learn at a young age what strategies to use when trying to get what they want from different family members. Many immigrant children serve as "cultural brokers" because they speak English better than any adult relative, providing resources to older generations but dismantling the traditional family power structure (Bush, Bohon, & Kim, 2010).

No family member possesses all five of McDonald's (1980) power bases equally or uses all of them in a given situation or with a given person. Some may never be used, whereas others may be used in combination or only in certain situations or with certain other family members. It is possible for a husband to use normative and economic power resources extensively in his interactions, and simultaneously for his wife to use cognitive and affective resources regularly in her interactions. You might exert power because of your education or personal assertiveness. Your sister's power may come from her strong personality. Children in the same family might use affective and personal power resources, especially when they are younger. This process is described by the following young respondent.

I can influence Uncle Fernando. I simply have to go about it the right way! He states his ideas and expects the rest of us to agree. Then I join with my sisters and together we argue with him. We talk about what we learned in political science or history courses and, because he did not go to college, he has trouble refuting our points. Eventually we wear him down and he gives up.

Power Processes Power processes are family communication practices that affect family discussions, arguments, decision making, and especially crisis situations. Essentially the term refers to using power in family interactions (Socha & Yingling, 2010). According to McDonald (1980), these power processes are attempts to control others through influence, persuasion (discussed later in this chapter), and assertiveness. Researchers have examined the number of times people talk, how long they talk, to whom they address their comments, and how long a talk session lasts (Johnson & Vinson, 1990). Analyses of questioning, interrupting, and silence patterns led to the conclusion that family members who talk most frequently and for the longest periods of time are dominant, but those who receive the most communication are the most powerful (Berger, 1980). As you know from your own experience, the longest or loudest talker may not hold the power. Effective communicators adapt their messages to different family members. One must distinguish between the power attempts a person makes and the final outcomes.

Messages in a family are co-created as a power process by the senders and receivers. Family members may send mixed messages which are difficult to analyze accurately. When an individual says one thing but means something else, confusion results. Contradiction often appears in the nonverbal aspects of a message. In analyzing power messages, both the content and relationship dimensions must be analyzed carefully to understand family communication. A family member who acts helpless can control the other's behavior in a relationship just as effectively as another who dominates, as this respondent reports.

My sister, I think, has a great deal of power in my family because she positions herself as dependent and helpless. Everyone is supposed to help Tamika because she can't cope. I think she is highly capable, deliberately or not, of manipulating everyone to meet her needs. She preferred to remain unemployed while she was single! And, now that she has a kid, she has a very good reason not to work and to need help in every way—money, child care, home, car. My mother falls for it all the time.

Messages created by ill or dysfunctional members can also influence family power. Families with alcoholic members have learned just how powerful that member can be. Everyone may learn to tiptoe around the drinker and develop strategies to minimize the alcoholic's verbal abuse. This places the alcoholic into a central and powerful position in the family, although he or she may be talked about as weak or helpless.

My sister and I would meet at the front door to our house after school to report to each other on our father's mood. He was either in a "good" mood (sober) or a "bad" mood (drinking). Robin and I tailored our actions and plans to his mood. We learned to adapt to whatever mood and situation came our way.

Power Outcomes   The final area, family power outcomes, focuses on who makes decisions and who wins. These outcomes include decisions, solutions, new rules or procedures, emotional effects, and feelings about the decisions (Socha & Yingling, 2010). In this aspect, at least one family member gets his or her way or receives rights or privileges of leadership.

Power bases influence power outcomes. Family members who hold normative positions of authority wield the greatest power. Often, the balance of power rests with the partner who contributes the greatest economic resources. Sources of power may be tied to rewards. In her dyadic power theory, Dunbar (2004) suggested that satisfaction will be low when one partner views her power as extremely high or extremely low in relation to her partner. When partners view their power differences as moderate or small, satisfaction will be higher. A study of newlywed couples in Singapore reported that couple power tended to become equalized if prioritizing the woman's career encourages men to change role expectations, assume some household tasks, attend to their spouse, and accept partner influence (Quek & Knudson-Martin, 2008). Yet this shift is effective only when men retain the ultimate choice regarding power and their wives can influence them.

Hierarchies in the family system establish guidelines for power processes that avoid conflicts yet affect power outcomes. Family members have orchestration power and/or implementation power. *Orchestration power* means that only certain family members control family life and make critical decisions. They usually make important decisions that determine the family lifestyle. The person with orchestration power delegates unimportant and time-consuming decisions to the partner or older child who derives *implementation power* by carrying out these decisions. For example, a mother may tell her 10-year-old son to find his 6-year-old brother and tell him he needs to clean his room. In this case, the mother has the orchestration power—she made the decision that the younger child needed to clean the room. But she gave the older child the implementation power by asking him to carry that decision out.

It is important to remember that each family and each family member uses a variety of power sources relevant to their needs and personalities. Negotiation can result in mutually acceptable compromises on power issues. In some families, traditional roles, including the biosocial issue of male dominance, are clearly defined, and since no one challenges them, the family operates as if that were the only way to function.

Power Development

Due to the systemic nature of family relationships, power develops through a transactional process. An alcoholic cannot control a spouse unless the nonalcoholic spouse permits it by refusing to detach from the drama. A mother relinquishes her own personal control when she gives an "acting-out" child power over her. Only the small child who has limited means of resisting power moves must accept certain power outcomes; for example, an abused child has few means of resisting punishment. In some cultures, gender traditions limit power positions of women in families.

Spouses and Power   Marital power reflects the extent to which one spouse loves and needs the other. Marital power is often measured by looking at spouses' dependent love for one another (Loving, et al., 2004), based on the belief that the spouse with the strongest emotional involvement in the relationship is the less powerful. The spouse with the strongest feelings of attachment emerges in a less powerful position because the person with the least interest more easily controls the one who is more involved. The balance of such power in a relationship can affect how spouses respond physiologically to conflict (Loving, et al., 2004).

Couples may enter a relationship with unequal power, but the relationship can achieve balance over time, as seen in the following example.

In the beginning of our relationship, Jack, who is older, tended to dominate. He had had a previous partner for several years and when that commitment ended, he had made up his mind to be more autonomous in any future relationship. I resented being treated as if I were his former partner and assuming that we would conflict in similar situations in the same way. Now that we have been together a few years, he realizes that the past is not the present. We can make joint decisions, and both of us are much happier.

In a recent study, Vogl, et al. (2007) reported that wives tended to display more power than their husbands during problem-solving discussions, no matter which spouse brought up the topic that was being discussed.

Different authority types describe the way in which married couples divide authority. One is based on only one spouse having authority, and two describe couples with more equally divided power.

- *One-spouse dominant.* In one spouse dominant families, major areas of activity are influenced and controlled by the dominant spouse. This dominance permeates all areas of family power: the use of resources or bases, power processes, and power outcomes. One spouse demonstrates control in the system, while the other accepts such control. Thus, one spouse often orchestrates and the other implements the power.
- *Syncratic.* A syncratic relationship, characterized by much shared authority and joint decision making, implies that each partner has a strong say in all important areas. This example reveals a couple that realized the value of their syncratic relationships.

When Kurt and I married, we agreed never to make big decisions alone, and we've been able to live with that. This way we share the risks and the joys of whatever happens. It just works out best between us if we wait on deciding all important matters until we sound out the other's opinions. It's when we decide over the little things that I know that each of us respects the rights and opinions of the other.

- *Autonomic.* In the autonomic power structure, the couple divides authority; that is, the husband and wife have relatively equal authority but in different areas. Each spouse is completely responsible for specific matters. The wife might have more power over the budget, vacation plans, and choice of new home, while the husband has more power over the selection of schools, buying anything with a motor in it, and whether the family moves to another state.

Support groups for families with addicted members recognize how power transactionally affects all members. In these groups, such as Al-Anon, family members learn how to cope with some of the power maneuvers used by the alcoholic member. This includes learning how to ignore power moves that hook family members into nonproductive behaviors. Highly skewed relationships, such as extreme husband or wife dominance, experience greater violence because "partners in such marriages lack problem-solving and positive negotiation skills" (Anderson, Umberson, & Elliott, 2004, p. 631). Abusive partners aggravate one another through domineering behaviors. If both attempt control and neither submits, conflict escalates.

The degree of violence or abuse a parent experienced in his or her family-of-origin may relate to the use of coercive power in families. According to Gelles (2010), "While experiencing violence in one's family-of-origin is often correlated with later violent behavior, such experience is not the sole determining factor" (p. 127). Other factors, interpersonal, cultural, and economic, may influence violence patterns. Negative emotions in family relationships can become more intense and irrational than those in other close relationships because families are together longer in an environment with closer and more frequent contact. Because family members assume their relationships have a long future, individual members may see this as a license to violate conversational and relational norms that they would not otherwise violate (Vangelisti, 1993).

Cultural influences on marital power can also be strong. This is particularly apparent when marital couples immigrate to the United States from a more patriarchal society. In a recent study, researchers compared two groups of Chinese immigrant couples—those in which the husband had been arrested for marital violence and those in which the husband had not. Both groups had experienced a shift in marital power such that the wives had more power following immigration. In the couples where the husband had been violent, wives had gained more education than their husbands as a result of immigration. However, in the couples where there was no history of violence, both spouses had gained education and the husbands had also gained more income than their wives. The researchers concluded that the violent men may have felt the power imbalance favoring their wives more than the nonviolent men, and that they may have used physical violence to regain some of this power (Jin & Keat, 2010).

Children and Power Children need to be included in any discussion of family power because they impact family interaction. Legally and socially, parents are expected to control and be responsible for their children's behavior, yet, although children are often viewed as followers, "children function as partners with their parents in family governance" (Socha & Yingling, 2010, p. 93). Children may struggle to establish their position in the family, to gain certain resources, or to establish an identity. Their words and behaviors affect the development of family rules. In many single-parent families as well as dual-earner families, both children and adolescents assume more personal and domestic responsibilities, experiences that not only affect their power but may also enhance their maturity and self-reliance.

Sometimes children influence the interaction and outcomes of power struggles by using power plays such as interruptions or screaming. They may keep powerful information about abuse or neglect from other family members or outsiders in order to maintain the family system. Similarly, children become adept at playing one parent against the other. "Daddy said I could do it" or "If Mom was here, she'd let me" has echoed through most homes. In some families, one spouse consciously or unconsciously co-opts a child into the role of ally in order to increase the strength of his or her power. Children also gain power by forming alliances with one parent. This may be because children feel they have insufficient power to change other family members' behaviors (Vangelisti, 1994a).

Blended families often contend with issues of power and authority (Baxter, Braithwaite, Bryant, & Wagner, 2004). "She can't tell me what to do; she's not my real mother" is the kind of communication that may cause years of pain while roles and power are negotiated. Single-parent families display unique power alliances due to the presence of one adult. A child with a solo parent negotiates directly with only one adult for immediate answers and wields direct personal power. However, the same child cannot form a parent-child alliance to try to change a decision the way a child can in a two-parent family, unless the child creates an alliance with a grandparent, aunt, or uncle.

Some alliances continue in families over a period of time; others exist only for reaching a specific decision. The results of past alliances can obligate family members to feel that they must support another to repay a debt. For example, a child might think, "Leon helped me convince Dad to buy me a new bike. Now I ought to help him argue with Dad to get his own car."

Cultural differences affect power interactions in families. In Asian families most parents tend to demand filial piety, respect, and obedience from their children (Lee & Mock, 2005). The following remarks describe how the family-of-origin and cultural background influence power outcomes.

Within our Thai culture, children are taught early to defer and show respect to their elders. Given names are rarely used in conversation, except for older family members talking to younger ones. Respect for relationships is formalized verbally by the use of the term *phi* for older siblings and *nong* for younger siblings. The boy child is very important to Thai families and outranks any girl child.

Although young children exercise some power, they develop more independent power as they grow older, when they begin to demand and can handle more power within the family structure. A 6-year-old may fight for a new toy, whereas a 16-year-old fights for later curfews. Many children gain expert power through

Children engage in power struggles at very young ages.

their specialized skills. One mother reported that when her younger child wants to play Wii, she tells him to ask his older brother to set it up, because she doesn't have those skills.

As families change and move through the life cycle, the original power relationships undergo significant modification as the family network increases, fragments, or solidifies. In addition to developmental issues, other forces affect changes in power, from inflation and environmental factors to changing cultural norms. In addition, if a family faces a serious stress such as the death or serious illness of a parent or partner, the other adult may assume greater power or establish new ties with a child that involve sharing power differently.

Communication and Power

Certain family communicative acts may be used to address power issues. Because of the nature of transactional communication, these communicative acts address power only when met with a response that engages them.

Confirming, disconfirming, and rejecting can become a part of power messages when family members attempt to separate and connect in one-up, one-down subsystems. In a *one-up* position, one family member attempts to exercise more power control over one or more other members. The *one-down* member accepts from the one-up member the control implied in the messages (Escudero, Rogers, & Gutierrez, 1997).

Confirming implies acknowledgment and may be used to gain power when one tries to get another to identify with him or her, or when one tries to give rewards in order to gain power. The careful, nonjudgmental listener may wittingly or unwittingly gain power. The "silent treatment" represents a frequently used *disconfirming* behavior. One family member can put another in a one-down power position with the punishment strategy of disconfirmation. "I'll ignore him; he'll come around" represents such an effort. On the other hand, disconfirming a power message may serve as an effective method of avoiding a power struggle. The child who pretends not to hear "clean up your room" messages effectively deflects the parental power, at least for a while. *Rejecting* messages tie directly to punishment messages and are often used as control in family power plays. "I hate you" or "I don't care what you say" may effectively halt control attempts. Hample and Dallinger (1995) claimed that individuals who sense they are being berated and stressed will avoid argumentative situations. The negative conflict behaviors of displacement, denial, disqualification, distancing, and sexual withholding can also be used as rejecting power moves.

Self-disclosure serves as a major means of gaining intimacy within a relationship, but it can also be used as a power strategy when one attempts to control the other through the "information power" gained by self-disclosure. For example, when a self-disclosed affair is thrown back at a spouse during a fight ("Well, you had an affair, so how can you talk?") that person loses power.

INFLUENCE

Influence occurs when family members use their power to try to change or modify each other's behavior or beliefs. Using McDonald's (1980) conceptualization, influence is a power process; the terms *persuasion* and *control* are also used to describe this process. Influence in family communication is ever-present. Think about your last interaction with a family member and how influence was involved. Were you trying to influence a sibling to loan you some money? Did one of your parents try to persuade you to join the family for a reunion over a holiday weekend? Were you involved in a debate over an issue, trying to influence a sibling to change his or her opinion? Any parent will tell you of countless attempts to influence a child, whether it is trying to get a teenaged son to clean his room or to convince a toddler to eat her dinner. Influence is a fundamental part of everyday interactions with family members. In fact, some researchers have suggested that all communicative events can be examined for persuasive qualities (Gass & Seiter, 1999). The following section discusses the types of influence strategies family members use, who uses which strategies, and which strategies seem to be effective in producing desired change.

Types of Influence Strategies

Influencing other family members requires utilizing a set of persuasive attempts. Strategies may be characterized as direct or indirect and as unilateral or bilateral (Falbo & Peplau, 1980). *Direct* influence strategies include bargaining, reasoning, and asking; *indirect* influence strategies include hinting and withdrawal. Bargaining is an example of a bilateral or interactive strategy, whereas hinting and withdrawal are examples of unilateral strategies.

A study of dual-career couples revealed that both wives and husbands tend to use direct strategies more than indirect strategies and bilateral strategies more than unilateral strategies with their spouses (Weigel, Bennett, & Ballard-Reisch, 2006). Bilateral strategies are also used more often by children who perceive their parents to have higher power than those who perceive their parents to have lower power (Bao, et al., 2007). A study of Mexican American immigrant women and their partners found that both men and women used direct and indirect strategies, and that both sexes used bilateral strategies more frequently than unilateral strategies (Beckman, Harvey, Satre, & Walker, 1999). The only perceived difference in strategy use between the sexes was that men were more likely than women to buy gifts to influence their partners.

The sender and the receiver of the influence strategy each may perceive the strategy in different ways depending on their perspectives on the relationship (Wilson & Morgan, 2004). For example, Lauren uses a very direct strategy with her younger brother, Joel, to try to get him to carry the garbage to the street: "Joel, take out the garbage!" Lauren thinks that this strategy is perfectly appropriate as she perceives that she has more power over Joel because of her age. Joel, who does not perceive Lauren to have more power over him, finds this strategy to be face-threatening and does not comply with it. A study by Butkovic and Bratko (2007) found that high school students and their parents did not agree when asked to report the types of influence strategies they used on each other, further reinforcing the idea that senders and receivers perceive the strategies differently.

Certain influence strategies tend to be situation-specific. For instance, when making joint purchase decisions, marital and cohabiting couples more frequently used influence strategies, such as bargaining and reasoning, than other strategies, such as acting helpless and displaying negative emotions (Kirchler, 1993). Adolescents also use a variety of influence strategies when trying to persuade a parent in a purchasing decision. From interviews with adolescents and their parents, Palan and Wilkes (1997) developed a list of influence strategies that adolescents use with their parents in purchasing situations. The four major categories of these follow, with examples.

- *Bargaining.* Offering to pay for some of the item, offering to do something to get the item, reasoning with arguments, or making negotiations
- *Persuasion.* Giving opinion, asking repetitively, begging, or whining
- *Emotional.* Showing anger, pouting, "sweet-talking," or making parents feel guilty
- *Request.* Directly asking, expressing a need or a want, demanding

Family members may also use influence strategies to persuade each other to modify health behaviors. In situations where spouses are trying to influence the health behaviors of each other, Tucker and Mueller (2000) found that the most frequently used influence strategies included the following.

- *Engaging in health behavior together.* A wife who thinks her husband needs more exercise might ask him to join her on her nightly walk.

- *Discussing the health issue.* A spouse might give a newspaper or magazine article to the other spouse about a health concern or issue and then request they discuss it.
- *Requesting that the partner engage in the health behavior.* One spouse might simply ask the other spouse to quit smoking.
- *Engaging in facilitative behavior.* A husband may put a multivitamin on his wife's dinner plate or set aside money each month for her to spend on exercise classes.

The following example provides an example that includes a few of these strategies.

If I didn't cook the broccoli or cut up the cantaloupe for dinner and put it on the table, my husband would certainly revert to his bachelor diet of frozen pizza, macaroni and cheese, and fast food. I also encourage him to make doctor and dentist appointments. Sometimes I remind him that married men live longer because they have their wives to help them take care of themselves. Although I say it in a lighthearted manner, I really believe that he is healthier since marrying me.

One communication theory that helps to explain the use of influence strategies in families is goals-plans-action theory. According to Wilson and Morgan (2006), individuals form and pursue goals during their interactions with others and family members' interdependence affects these goals and plans. They provide the following example: A daughter's *goal* might be to get permission from a parent to get her ears pierced. The daughter fears her mother won't agree to this, so her *plan* is to talk to her father first so that he can discuss it with her mother. Understanding goals and plans can be a useful way to examine the influence process.

Factors Affecting Influence Strategy Use

Look back at the influence strategies explained in the last section. Which ones are you more likely to use with your family members? Most of you would probably answer, "It depends!" It depends on the outcome you are trying to attain, your closeness to, and relational history with a particular family member and on power bases that you can use in relation to that family member.

Many researchers have asked the following basic question: Do husbands and wives use influence strategies differently when trying to persuade a spouse? Traditional stereotypes of a wife nagging her husband come to mind for many people (Soule, 2001). However, in most marriages, the amount of persuasion may be similar as spouses try to influence each other. The more frequently a wife uses persuasive strategies, the more frequently her husband also does (Sexton & Perlman, 1989). When considering persuasion about health issues, wives and husband are equally likely to use influence strategies on their spouses (Tucker & Anders, 2001).

Men and women tend to be quite similar in the types of influence strategies that they use (Baxter & Bylund, 2004). Husbands' higher marital satisfaction is associated with their use of direct and bilateral influence strategies (Weigel, Bennett, & Ballard-Reisch, 2006). Kirchler's (1993) research showed that women are more likely to report using strategies that are more partner-oriented, such as offering trade-offs, whereas men are more likely to make autonomous decisions and be less cooperative. As you might expect, children's influence strategy use in purchasing decisions broadens over the years. Younger children (ages 3 to 11) are more likely to just ask for products repeatedly (Isler, Popper, & Ward, 1987), but adolescents use a range of influence strategies (Palan & Wilkes, 1997).

Although husbands' and wives' use of persuasive strategies don't differ much according to gender, personality factors may contribute to a spouse's choice of a particular influence strategy. Dual-career spouses who are less confident tend to be more likely to use indirect-unilateral influence strategies, such as withdrawing and doing their own thing, both at home and work. Dual-career wives who rate high on nurturing are more likely to use indirect-bilateral strategies, such as smiling or suggesting, at home and work (Steil & Weltman, 1992). In purchasing decisions, type of conflict, marital satisfaction, power patterns, and relationship duration all affect the choice of persuasive strategy. Traditional couples are more likely to use influence strategies that focus on the positive or negative outcomes of the decisions, whereas separate couples tend to use constraining messages. Independents are more likely to use a variety of strategies, as they rely on more power bases than traditional or separate couples (Witteman & Fitzpatrick, 1986). Couples who are more satisfied in their marital relationships are less likely to use indirect strategies in their influence attempts than are couples who are less satisfied in their marital relationships (Zvonkovic, et al., 1994).

Remember that influence strategies aren't necessarily enacted just once. Some researchers have examined the process of sequential spousal influence attempts that are often called nagging. *Nagging* is "a form of persistent persuasion that involves a persuader repeating him or herself rather than escalating to a more aggressive persuasive strategy" (Soule, 2011, p. 196). For most partners, nagging happens after one partner does not do what the other one asks. Further, spouses often report concern about the other's well-being as a reason for nagging, such as about health issues.

The sex of the parent and child and the age of the child make a difference in the types of strategies parents use in an attempt to influence their adolescent children. For example, adolescents were asked to think of a situation in which their parents were trying to get them to help with spring cleaning. Older adolescent boys reported their fathers to be more likely to use specific influence strategies, such as pre-giving (for example, first giving the child permission to stay out late) whereas younger adolescent males reported their mothers would be more likely to use pre-giving (deTurck & Miller, 1983). Conversely, children's persuasion skills depend on their ability to engage in perspective-taking or understand how another might think or feel. By age 4 many children can use multiple strategies and personalize them for a specific parent (Socha & Yingling, 2010). The culture of the family also seems to play a part in determining influence strategy use. In one cross-cultural study, researchers found American mothers to be more likely to use directive statements, such as "Bring me the toy," than did Japanese mothers (Abe & Izard, 1999).

Engaging in health behaviors together is a good influence strategy.

Influence Strategy Outcomes

If asked to think about which type of influence strategies you use with different family members and why, you would probably name a few and say, "Because they work!" When choosing an influence strategy, family members have a goal of being successful in influencing another family member. Family researchers have also been interested in which influence strategies tend to result in compliance.

In spousal persuasion, spouses who are successful in gaining compliance generally rely more on messages that focus on the activity that is being requested rather than on messages about the power or control in the relationship. They also rely on questions, direct statements, and requests (Witteman & Fitzpatrick, 1986). Strategies such as agreement, explanation, and problem solving have also been shown to be effective influence strategies (Newton & Burgoon, 1990). The choice of influence strategy may also be associated with the level of marital satisfaction the couple experiences. In a study of Israeli husbands and wives, a team of researchers found that couples that used or preferred harsher influence strategies (e.g., threatening, emphasizing obligations) had lower marital satisfaction (Schwarzwald, Koslowsky, & Izhak-Nir, 2008). Those with lower marital satisfaction were also likely to use more influence strategies in general.

In the specific realm of health behavior, effective strategies for both husbands and wives include engaging in the health behavior together, engaging in facilitative behavior, and providing emotional support (Tucker & Mueller, 2000). In another study on spouses and health behavior, Lewis and Butterfield (2007) reported that using bilateral, direct, and positive influence tactics, as well as simply a greater frequency of influence strategies, was predictive of health-enhancing behaviors.

During parents' interactions with their adolescents, effective influence strategies differ by parent gender. Mothers are successful with frequent praise and moderate levels of attempted control, and fathers are successful with moderate to high levels of attempted control (Smith, 1983). When adolescents are trying to influence their parents to purchase something, reasoning is consistently reported as one of the two most effective strategies by adolescents, their mothers, and their fathers (Palan & Wilkes, 1997). The following comment from a 15-year-old female shows how well thought out these reasoning strategies can be.

First of all, I tell my mom or dad what they *haven't* bought me lately. It gives them a guilt trip. It puts them in the right mindset, and then I go in for the kill. I say, "I need this because. . . ." And then I give three distinct reasons. I say the one that I think they'll go for first. But they have to be three distinct reasons. That way if one falls through, I can always depend on the other two.

Many older adolescents or young adults experience irresolvable conflicts because of their personal positions on certain topics or their core beliefs (Miller, 2011). Such topics or beliefs may relate to religion, money, sexuality, or values. Instead of using persuasion, these young people have learned strategies of topic avoidance, argument prevention, and withdrawal.

DECISION MAKING

Questions such as "Who should talk with Mother about our concerns about her driving" and "Where should we enroll the twins in preschool?" or "How much should we share with our families about Wei-Lin's history before we adopt her?" represent concerns that require family decision making. Family members facing family and work conflicts, as discussed in the roles chapter, often face difficult decisions as they manage these tensions. The number of children to have, whether or not one spouse should accept a promotion that requires relocation, and whether money should be spent for private school tuition represent decisions that family members make. *Decision making* is the process by which family members make choices, reach judgments, or arrive at solutions that end uncertainty. Although we will be talking about family decision making, "the extent to which families actually make decisions as a unit seems limited" (Socha & Yingling, 2010, p. 114). In actuality, most decisions occur within subgroups—two adults, a parent and two children, two grandparents and a teenage grandson.

Clearly power, influence, and decision making are closely tied together. Decision making allows differences between individual family members to be addressed. In addition, the decision-making process reflects individual differences. Family members can use power resources such as trade-offs, silence, or helpfulness as well as power processes such as influence or assertiveness processes. The decisions made in response to these efforts determine what occurs in the family system.

Decision-making processes rely on the repertoire of strategies members have developed to manage conflicting needs and desires. They help members negotiate their shifting needs for closeness and distance, novelty and predictability, as well as privacy and openness. The kind and quality of decisions affects how family roles, rules, or themes are enacted. Today's families struggle to find time to make careful decisions. The pressure on single parents and employed couples or partners with children to set aside time to engage in intelligent decision making requires prioritizing among competing demands. For example, making decisions requires a couple to take the time to debrief and shift focus from outside jobs. The more complex the family system, the more important the decision patterns, as indicated here.

Both Mom and Dad work overtime. The oldest sibling at home is in charge of decisions that involve those siblings in the house. For example, when my older brother is home, he makes decisions on who can go somewhere or what friend can come over. If he's at work, I take over. My next younger sister does the same for our youngest brother if I have something after school. It's really a problem if the younger two get into arguments because they are close in age.

Decision making, like power, is a process that belongs to the family system, not to an individual. Therefore, decision making varies greatly among families because each family negotiates about values, dreams, or resources differently. Unlike a small group that comes together to accomplish a particular task, a family has a history of continuous interaction among and between a set of interdependent individuals. Families tend to remain together even when members disagree. Even if the decision-making process results in turmoil, the family continues, although sometimes as a factional and unhappy one. This is not true of outside groups that often disband. Because family relationships are both involuntary and lengthy, members may use negative messages that ironically function to maintain the family system while reinforcing the separate identities of members (Vangelisti, 1993). A study of parent-adolescent problem solving reveals that adolescents may vent great anger over the decisions on a particular issue, but not be dissatisfied with the overall family relationship (Niedzwiecki, 1997).

Family decisions can be either instrumental or affective. *Instrumental decisions* require solving rather functional issues, such as getting a job to pay the family bills or providing transportation. Dual-career couples sitting down to map out the week's various activities for the children and their own travel schedules may involve significant instrumental decision making. Such decision making may include those outside the family, such as a babysitter. *Affective decisions* relate to decisions made based heavily on emotions or feelings. Clearly, many decisions involve affective and pragmatic arguments. For example, when parents and mental

Joint decision making reflects shared family power.

health professionals meet to discuss a child with social emotional disturbance (SED), and the family and professional team hold planning meetings, emotional and research-based arguments arise (Davis, Dollard, & Vergon, 2009). Instrumental decisions tend to be more pragmatic or basic, since "families whose functioning is disrupted by instrumental problems rarely, if ever, deal effectively with affective problems. However, families whose functioning is disrupted by affective problems may deal adequately with instrumental problems" (Epstein, Bishop, & Baldwin, 1982, p. 119).

The location of a family along the adaptability continuum (cohesion to flexibility) affects its decision-making behavior. Highly enmeshed, rigid families may pressure members to reach predictable and low-risk decisions, whereas disengaged families may have trouble sharing enough information to make reasonable decisions. The length of time together also influences decision making. Over the years, partners or families tend to develop highly predictable decision-making styles. Understanding family decision making involves examining (1) types of decision-making processes, (2) styles of decision making, (3) phases in decision making, and (4) factors that influence decision making.

Types of Decision-Making Processes

Each family has its own way of reaching decisions on issues. Decisions can be reached through use of the following levels of agreement: (1) consensus,

(2) accommodation, and (3) *de facto* decisions, each of which involves different degrees of acceptance and commitment (Turner, 1970).

Consensus   Consensus, the most democratic process, involves discussion that continues until agreement is reached. Because the desired goal is a solution acceptable to all involved, this may require compromise and flexibility. Each family member has a part in the decision and a chance for influence, making it more likely they will share the responsibility for carrying it out. Major purchases, money issues, and vacations are common topics for consensus discussions. The complexity of such decision making appears in the following example.

Every Tuesday night is family night, and everyone must be present from 7:00 until 8:00. This is the time when we make certain family decisions that affect all of us. We may make a joint decision about vacations and try to find a plan that will please everyone. We talk about who needs to be available to take care of Zak on evenings when Mom works. All six of us have to agree to go ahead with the decision.

Accommodation   Accommodation occurs when some family members consent to a decision not because they totally agree but because they believe that further discussion will be unproductive. Consent may be given with a smile or with regret. The accommodation decision requires a great deal of trading, because no one really achieves what he or she desires. For example, you may want to go to a church picnic while someone else wants to play in three ball games that weekend. This type of decision making occurs when families pressure for high cohesiveness and individual members feel they must "go along," as in this somewhat manipulative example.

It's just easier to agree with Dad and let him think his ideas are what we all want than to argue with him. He's bound to win anyway, since he controls the money. Sometimes when we humor his wishes, Mom, my sister, and I can then get our way on what we want to do—sort of a trade-off!

Sometimes family members line up on opposite sides of an issue and vote. The minority views held by losing family members might have genuine merit, but the losers accept majority rule rather than cause trouble. In *accommodation*, decisions may favor a dominant member, and less aggressive family members may develop a pattern of submitting to their wishes. Accommodative decision making encourages distance and can also enforce negative family themes and images while implementing stereotyped thinking on biosocial issues, especially in cases of male dominance.

De Facto **Decisions**   What happens when the discussion reaches an impasse? Usually, one member will go ahead and act in the absence of a clear-cut decision. This is a *de facto* decision—one made without direct family approval but nevertheless made to keep the family functioning. A fight over which video game system to buy while on sale may be continued until the sale nears an end and Mom buys one.

De facto decisions encourage family members to complain about the result, because they played either no part or a passive part in the decision. The family "decided" not to make a decision, and the family member who acts in the vacuum of that decision may have to endure complaints or a lack of enthusiasm from those who have to accept the decision. Although many families, particularly rigid ones, seem to use only one type of decision making, more flexible families vary their styles according to the issues. Critical issues may require consensus, whereas less important concerns can be resolved by a vote or a *de facto* decision.

Phases in Decision Making

Most family decision making passes through a series of phases to reach satisfactory or unsatisfactory decisions. A valuable way to consider phases is to use the family problem-solving loop developed by Kieren, Maguire, and Hurlbut (1996) (see Figure 8.1). The loop illustrates the phases of decision making developed in the somewhat circular path families take when they make decisions. It also provides for shortened loops when decision making falters. It breaks the process down into eight steps that decisions proceed through in solving problems. Remember that we are presenting this as a general model of decision making. You can certainly see how families making decisions in their everyday lives may not follow this model precisely in this order or follow all of the steps each time.

Each of the model's eight steps marks or identifies the beginning and ending of different patterns of interaction in problem solving. Note that each of the eight steps that develop the loop can be condensed into four phases based on the similarity of activity family members perform. Phase 1 includes steps 1, 2, and 3 (identification of problem, formulating a goal, and assessing resources) and is labeled identification/clarification. Phase 2, called alternatives, covers steps 4 and 5 (generation of alternatives and assessing their value). Phase 3, designated as consensus building, involves step 6 (selecting the best option). It includes the attempts individual family members make to gain support for a solution. Phase 4 relates to the decision, covering steps 7 and 8 (accepting a decision, acting on it, and evaluating it as an outcome).

Decisions are never as simple as they appear. In examining the four phases in decision making, it is important to realize that the process may be short-circuited at any point by a family member or subsystem alliance that does not agree with certain choices. A family may reach a decision by skipping some steps. It may be difficult to identify which phases are being used in problem solving because family members are doing other things simultaneously and discussing decision options intermittently. Some families tend not to be rational or to follow steps in problem solving. Once problem-solving patterns are learned, either good or bad, they are resistant to change. In their study of 40 families, Kieren, Maguire, and Hurlbut (1996) report more support for a rational rather than a random pattern

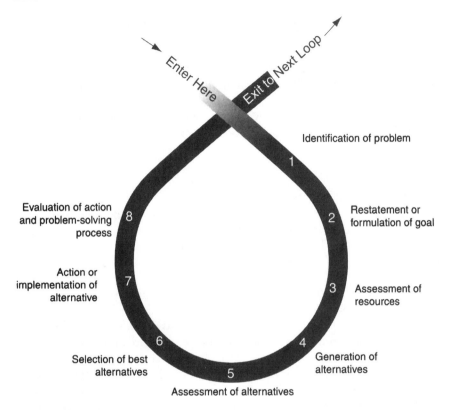

FIGURE 8.1
The Family Problem-Solving Loop

of decision making. Reflect on how this next family effectively followed decision making in terms of the loop model.

My siblings and I and our wives actually went through a formal decision-making process as we decided how to take care of our elderly mother after she was unable to live alone. We went through all kinds of hassles on topics such as nursing homes, residential facilities, and social security benefits. We had to set monetary criteria for any solution based on a percentage of our salaries and based on a location that everyone could reach. Our mother had to agree to the solution also. We agreed we could not force our solution on her. Each couple investigated different options, specific senior citizen housing options, live-in nurses, nursing homes, and specialized group homes. We finally reached two options that we could live with—a particular senior citizen facility or a nursing home. We discussed these with our mother who rejected the nursing home instantly but who agreed to the senior citizen housing facility.

This planned approach to decision making does not just happen in families. Some families become bogged down and never get beyond the first or second phase. Other families may make a tentative decision, but continue to rethink the decision. Adams (2004) studied cross-national couples and their decision-making processes about where to live. She found that although couples might decide where to live initially, this decision-making process could continue for a long time afterwards, as the decision is continually revisited in an ongoing process. Thus, in order to understand the complexity of the process, we need to examine what affects family decision making.

Factors Affecting Decision Making

The decision-making process is affected by multiple factors. In this section, we will discuss how the following affect decision making: (1) children, (2) gender influences, (3) the role of individual involvement and resources, and (4) outside influences.

The Role of Children and Adolescents

Since family-of-origin experiences affect all areas of your life, your decision-making experiences as a child impact your approach to adult decision making. In addition, your own children may affect your family's current decision-making processes. In certain circumstances, children share the leadership in decision making, especially when a child feels support from other members. For instance, Labrecque and Ricard (2001) found that children ages 9 to 12 are influential in family decision making about choosing a restaurant.

Moods of either parents or adolescents affect decision making. Niedzwiecki (1997) reported that problem solving should be postponed until participants' moods are positive or neutral. Children often respond best to positive emotional patterns of communication and perform less well when parents express negative emotions. Although negative feelings need to come out in decision making, the way in which they are treated will affect the outcomes. The "Let it all hang out" philosophy hinders family problem solving. When too many negative feelings surface during decision making, the focus shifts from problem solving to personalities.

The role of parents in adolescents' decision making remains a significant research topic. In one study of family decision making with 76 middle-class African American adolescents and their mothers, researchers found that mothers' involvement in decision making was consistently higher for conventional decisions (e.g., chores, manners) and prudential decisions (e.g., smoking cigarettes, drinking alcohol) than for other types of decisions (Smetana, Campione-Barr, & Daddis, 2004). Adolescents were more involved in personal decisions (e.g., what time to get up, what clothes to wear) than they were in other types of decisions. In viewing decisions about friends, dating, and social activities (for example), the average adolescent and mother reported that these decisions were jointly made, although over the five years the adolescent became more involved in those decisions. The researchers suggest that "parental involvement and guidance in decision making over personal issues may be very important for healthy psychosocial development" (p. 1430). A decision to move the family overseas may be a difficult one for an adolescent daughter, as shown in the following example.

When my husband and I announced to our daughters that we were considering a move to another country for my job, my older daughter was very upset. She said we would be ruining her life and that she wouldn't come with us. As we visited the country, and made plans to move, we made a consistent effort to involve her in decisions such as which bedroom she would like to have, whether to adopt a pet, and where to travel on our first vacation. Involving her in this way seemed to help her feel she had a little more control over what was happening. And now, six months later, she says she's glad we moved!

One type of family decision that children often influence is purchase decisions. Although children ages 8 to 11 may not perceive themselves as having any right to make family purchase decisions, they do try to influence them through exhibiting their knowledge about a product, using good behavior, and selecting items that they think their parents would endorse. As children feel they have successfully influenced family purchase decisions, they may expect they will have future favorable outcomes (Flurry & Burns, 2005). Cross-cultural research has shown that adolescents in both Chinese and U.S. cultures perceive themselves as being influential at both the initiation stage of purchase decision making as well as in the final decision. In comparison with research from the 1980s and 1990s, researchers comment that there may be a shift to more adolescent influence in these decisions in contemporary families (Wang, Holloway, Beatty, & Hill, 2006).

An observational study of parents and children up to 12 years old during supermarket and toy store visits found that children were most likely to try to influence their parents to purchase something for them increased until early elementary school years, and then decreased. The researchers also examined the ways in which these children tried to influence the purchase decision-making process through coercive behavior, defined as forceful or persistent verbal or nonverbal influence behavior such as begging, crying, or showing anger (Buijzen & Valkenburg, 2008). They found that coercive behavior was associated with less likelihood of being invited to participate in the purchase decision-making process and to result in purchasing the product.

The Internet has profoundly changed the way families make purchase decisions and has given the adolescent a more powerful role in these decisions. Belch, Krentler, and Willis-Flurry (2005) introduced a concept of *teen Internet mavens*. These are teenagers who "receive great personal enjoyment from surfing the Internet and use their virtual market knowledge to contribute significantly to family decision making" (p. 574). Teen Internet mavens influence the early stages of the process (such as search and information provision) more than they do the final decision.

As parents and children age, decision-making processes can take on a different meaning. Elderly parents may require caregiving decisions to be made by their adult children, which can be a difficult situation for families. Talks about preferences for caregiving may be useful to have earlier rather than later in the aging process. For mothers and adult daughters with close relationships, there may be little need to discuss the issues of future caregiving, because the mothers believe the daughters already know their preferences or because there is denial about the aging process (Pecchioni & Nussbaum, 2001).

Other families may be child-free because of decisions made by couples. Durham and Braithwaite (2009) discussed four different decision-making trajectories that lead to the spousal decision not to have children. The *accelerated-consensus* trajectory was present when spouses had similar child-free preferences, leading to a quick consensus. *Mutual negotiation* described spouses who were uncertain about family planning and had conversations over time. In some cases, a spouse who preferred to remain child-free attempted to persuade an undecided spouse to come to the child-free decision, called the *unilateral-persuasion* trajectory. Finally, the *bilateral-persuasion* trajectory involves one spouse wanting children and the other not wanting children. The spouses who wanted children had incorrectly believed that they could persuade their spouse, and though they stayed committed to the spouse, they "never committed to the child-free decision" (p. 60).

Gender Influences   A family's role ideology and biosocial beliefs determine who carries out certain decisions and tasks. Thus, in male-dominant households, the husband may take over the financial decisions, the yard, and the basement, and the wife is in charge of the household operation, kin networking, and school contacts. Wilkie, Ferree, and Ratcliff (1998) reported that conventional gender roles only significantly affect marital quality indirectly through perceptions of fairness and understanding. These two qualities of fairness and understanding would certainly impact the emotional climate in decision making in a family.

Outside factors impact decision-making styles. If men work in a participative work setting where the management encourages job autonomy, self-direction, and group problem-solving skills, they are more democratic fathers in child-parent relations, including more use of family decision making and consensus (Grimm-Thomas & Perry-Jenkins, 1993). Frequently, employed women acquire more power than their husbands in decisions about money matters. In decision making, a wife's income was found to be highly correlated with direct bargaining and reward strategies (Zvonkovic, Schmiege, & Hall, 1994). Marketers attempt to influence children to exert influence on their parents' decisions, sometimes call "pester power" (Weintraub-Austin, Hust, & Kistler, 2009).

Individual Investment and Resources   How many times have you left or avoided a family decision-making session because you did not care about the result? If you do not sense how things affect you, you are not likely to get involved, even though you will probably be affected. Parents' desire and need for a new refrigerator may not be perceived as important to a teenager. If money, or any shared resource, is scarce, decision making can become a competitive process for the limited resources. If each family member can become involved in agenda setting and has the right to raise issues and objections, the decision making prospers. Agenda-setting power rather than decision-making power better indicates marital satisfaction (Wilkie, Ferree, & Ratcliff, 1998). Discussion may be unimportant to some family members and critical to others. Personal investment in decisions varies over time with the degree of separateness or connectedness within the family system. In close relationships in which each partner has multiple role functions "individuals tacitly negotiate agreements to reciprocate support for critical components of each other's views of self or other role identities" (Stephen, 1994, p. 217).

I have learned that the best way to reach my partner with my needs is through persuasion. I suggest he consider the situation and see if he can think of some plan that will accomplish his goals with as little impact on me as possible. With a little charm thrown in, I might even venture an idea. I reveal my feelings, explain the situation as I see it, and listen to what he has to say. Then I ask for time to think about what we've said. Later, either can bring up the subject again and we'll both be better able to discuss it. Other decisions about our relationship, where there is not so much friction, are made by whoever really cares about the issue.

Reiss and Webster (2004) compared how purchase decision making differed among traditional (married heterosexual) and nontraditional (cohabiting heterosexual, gay, and lesbian partnerships). They found that across all types of couples, involvement in the purchase decision had a significant effect on the relative influence of each partner in the purchase decision making. However, the resources an individual brought to the partnership were associated with relative influence in the purchase decision making for married couples.

Outside Influences   All sorts of outside factors affect how a family makes decisions. Mom's salary, A.J.'s friends, and Miriam's teacher may all affect how a decision is resolved. Decisions within a family system often represent compromises or adaptations to other societal systems. School, corporate, and government systems impinge on families and influence decisions. For example, think of how a corporation affects family decision making. If the mother must travel, work overtime, or take customers out in the evening, the family makes decisions differently than if this were not necessary. The school-home interface requires other adjustments in decision making. Children who are responsible for themselves, filling time between the end of the school day and the time a parent arrives home, make different decisions than children greeted by a parent at the door.

Decisions forced on a family by an outside agency, such as a court, restrict individual members' choices. A tumultuous divorce or untimely death can greatly alter the decision-making processes in a family. If separating partners cannot reach decisions about money and property, attorneys and judges intervene. If there are children, decisions must be made regarding custody, visitation rights, and financial arrangements. Similarly, when a family member is seriously ill and has not made known his or her end-of-life preferences, family decisions can be difficult. In many cases, families consult experts which impact the decision making, as explained in the following example.

In this age of experts, our family was almost ripped apart as my parents tried to make decisions about how to raise my younger brother, who has a serious attention deficit disorder. My mother always wanted to follow the advice of a doctor or a teacher; my father wanted our family to make the decisions about Marcus's care. My parents were constantly disagreeing with each other and the medical and educational experts.

Health and Illness Decision making about issues surrounding health and illness can create major struggles for families. For example, a family in which the mother is diagnosed with breast cancer may face decisions surrounding the woman's treatment—deciding between a more time-consuming treatment with a slighter better prognosis and a less time-intensive treatment that will allow her to continue in her other responsibilities. Parents of male children diagnosed with fertility-threatening cancer face a decision about sperm banking before cancer treatment begins. Parents of female children and adolescents diagnosed with fertility-threatening cancer may face a decision about fertility-preserving ovarian surgery that must occur before the cancer treatment begins. Parents may have hours or days to make these decisions while confronting the overwhelming cancer diagnosis. These represent "high-stakes, emotionally charged, time-sensitive decisions with long-term implications" (Galvin, 2010, p. 98).

Decisions to undergo and complete fertility treatment among married couples may be influenced by couples' desires to make sure that they had done everything possible to have their own biological child. As one partner explained, "Because we really tried everything possible, we could let go . . . you really can't have regrets if you gave it your best shot" (Daniluk & Hurtig-Mitchell, 2003, p. 392). Other families may have to make decisions about work and family balance based on becoming caregivers for their elderly parents (Miller, Shoemaker, Willyard, & Addison, 2008).

With increased technology and medical knowledge, more and more families are facing decisions about genetic testing and the subsequent sharing of that information with other family members. Many factors will influence these decisions, including the family's privacy rules, communication patterns, and attributions and personal theories about disease and genetic risk (Gaff & Bylund, 2010).

Communication Skills in Decision Making

Each year every family member becomes involved in one or more critical decisions affecting one or more other members. Socha & Yingling (2010) argued that "especially for children, learning to make individual choices is an important part of the process of crafting their identities, discovering their likes/dislikes as well as their signature strengths" (p. 106). The more prepared members are to engage in thoughtful and well-reasoned decision making, the more effective the process will be. Family decision making can be enhanced by certain communication skills. Vuchinich and DeBaryske (1997) cited four initial items that, paraphrased in communication terms, form the basis for responsible family problem solving. They are (1) being open to allowing different family members to speak out; (2) avoiding negative messages, either verbal or nonverbal, that convey hostility; (3) seeking more than one option as a solution; and (4) communicating in clear, positive remarks focused on the problem discussed. These four relate to the phases of problem solving and styles of decision making discussed.

Many families have difficulty with disagreements when attempting to resolve problems, especially when hostile messages are sent and received. In her seminal piece on couple decision making, Krueger (1983) reported that disagreements serve as a functional part of the decision-making process, particularly when both partners use positive communication strategies to express their differences. They may acknowledge the validity of another's ideas, indicate a willingness to incorporate part of another's solution, or praise the other's past contributions. In the "give and take" of exchanges over a decision, family members establish trust and a sense of fairness and equality. Disagreeing allows for minority alliances in a family to have an input and function as a source for ideas to include in a compromise decision.

Clearly communication plays a key role in determining the outcomes of family decision making. The way in which family members use words and nonverbal cues heavily influences decision-making outcomes. The sending of mixed messages by one or more members affects decisions and may alter the cohesion and balance of the family system.

How well couples know one another's emotional responses to issues also affects decision making. Couples that were better at predicting the impact their messages had on their mates had higher positive feelings for one another (Burleson & Denton, 1997). The researchers also found that distressed couples did not have poorer communication skills than nondistressed couples; rather, stressed partners expressed many more negative intentions toward one another. Unhappy couples communicated more ill will than they demonstrated poor skills.

The following principles could help guide family members in their decision making: (1) create a sense of justice by treating family members equally, regardless of sex or power resources; (2) create a sense of autonomy by respecting each family member's rights to free choices in order to carry out actions that enhance his or her life; (3) create a sense of caring by helping other family members achieve their goals; (4) create an awareness of which decisions lead to actions and behaviors that harm family members or place them at risk; and (5) create a sense of loyalty via keeping promises and carrying out decisions mutually agreed upon. These principles should enhance the self-concepts of each family member. This complex process of decision making can be helped by experiences of a life of shared communication, as described here.

For 52 years, Lawrence and I made decisions together. We tried to spend our money as we both saw fit and discuss what was important to us. We usually shopped together for groceries, machinery, cars, and so on. Even when buying our tombstone, we looked them over and decided on one we both liked. Now he rests in front of it. We had our differences, but we always tried to see things from the other's point of view and eventually we'd resolve that problem. I miss him. We had a great life together!

CONCLUSION

This chapter presented an overview of power, influence, and decision making in the family. We discussed power bases, power processes, and power outcomes as described by McDonald's model and indicated how they affect cohesion and adaptability in family systems. There are many types of influence strategies used by family members. Use of these strategies is predicted by context, age, gender, and personality traits. Effective strategies with spouses are often direct.

Through communication interactions, power and influence are employed in decision making, often using consensus, accommodation, or *de facto* decisions. There are eight parts in four phases in the decision-making steps that families use to communicate differences, yet solve their problems. Although compromise may be required, this problem-solving process has the potential to strengthen cohesion in the family.

In Review

1. How might power affect a family's cohesion and adaptability?
2. Analyze the power resources used regularly by members of a real or fictional family. Indicate how members use communication to convey their use of these resources.
3. Analyze the types of influence strategies used by a real or fictional family. Do you see any patterns of strategy usage? Which influence strategies seem to be most effective?
4. Give specific examples of how factors such as gender, age, individual interests, or resources affected a family's decision-making process.
5. To what extent should children be part of the family's decision-making process? How can they be guided to develop the communication skills necessary to participate effectively in such discussions?
6. Using the four phases of the loop model of problem solving, analyze how a family makes a decision on an important issue. Choose your family-of-origin if you like, but feel free to select another family you know well or a family in a movie, TV show, or novel.

KEY WORDS

Accommodation decision-making process   197
Bilateral influence strategy   202
Consensus decision-making process   197
De facto decision-making process   198
Direct influence strategy   189

Indirect influence strategy   190
Power bases   181
Power outcomes   184
Power processes   183
Unilateral influence strategy   202

Communication and Family Conflict

"For many people it is hard to realize that conflict is inevitable because no two people see the world in exactly the same way. . . . Even people you love get in your way, just as you get in their way. Persons who are aware of such predictable struggles often attempt to nurture their relationships to reduce or limit the tensions."

—Kathleen Galvin, *Making Connections*

Jordan and Amanda met while working for a large Chicago-based consulting firm. Over the next two years they often found themselves assigned to the same accounts, many of which were in other cities. Frequently they would have breakfast and dinner together, with or without other team members, two or three times a week, and they soon began dating. Two years later they announced their engagement, quickly followed by their wedding. Within four years they were parents of twin daughters and Amanda chose to stay home until the twins were ready for kindergarten.

Now, three years later, Jordan and Amanda are facing a marital crisis precipitated by his relationship with Kiera, another colleague at the same firm. Jordan and Kiera have been working together on the same team for almost two years, during which time they have become close friends due to the amount of time they spend together on the road, often by themselves. Over time Jordan and Kiera have moved from discussing more trivial matters to helping each other through personal problems. Kiera's mother has been diagnosed with stage four ovarian cancer, a diagnosis that devastated Kiera because of her devotion to her mother and the realization that it may be hereditary. In addition to sharing his dreams of starting a business, Jordan has shared some of his frustrations regarding Amanda's extreme devotion to the girls which leaves him feeling increasingly invisible. In recent months Amanda became aware of Jordan and Kiera's close relationship and asked Jordan to request different accounts in order to avoid traveling with her. Jordan expressed his reluctance to do so, stating that would be bad for his chances for promotion. This is a source of daily conflict for Jordan and Amanda.

Chung Ha and Marina Revello met during sophomore year in college as dorm counselors. They became a couple during junior year. After graduation they attended the same law school, graduated, and found positions in the same city. To the joy of their families, Chung and Marina announced their engagement last Fourth of July and their wedding date of July 4th of the following year. Marina's older brother, Anthony, took a different path. He dated seriously and serially throughout college and his years in the Navy. Early last fall he fell madly in love with Michelle, a fellow officer, and proposed to her on New Year's Eve; they quickly set a wedding date of June 7th, approximately four weeks before Marina's wedding. Family fireworks followed!

Currently the Revello family is in turmoil. Marina has claimed that she "owns" this year and that Anthony and Michelle need to wait a year to marry. She is furious at the idea that they planned to upstage her wedding by marrying first, especially because they only met last fall. Michelle argues that no one can "own a year" for marriage and, given her age of 31, she wants to marry and start a family as soon as possible. In addition, she will be at sea for months after the wedding so she could not marry from August to November. Chung and Anthony, surprised and overwhelmed by the tensions, are struggling to remain in the background although each tries to support his future wife. The in-laws each support their daughters but worry about the long-term fallout between the couples. The Revello family dreads the impact on their tight-knit family unit.

Conflicts in families stem from multiple issues and are handled in a variety of ways. According to Klein and Johnson (1997), "To achieve their goals, partners engage in a variety of conflict strategies, ranging from problem-solving and compromise, to unilateral accommodation and the use of insults, threats and physical force" (p. 486). A family's themes or images influence the amount and type of conflict that develops. Family members' perceptions of conflict greatly impact how they respond to and manage disagreements. For example, if Cesar views conflict as war, he may feel the need to recruit other family soldiers to take his side; winning at any cost becomes the ultimate goal. If Lara views conflict as inevitable but unpredictable, she may feel powerless when conflict occurs. Both of these examples depict the negative connotations of conflict. However, as the opening quote suggests, there are more positive ways of viewing conflict. If a woman views conflict as a rational process, she may be able to use it as an opportunity to resolve problems and view it as a way to reach family goals (Buzzanell & Burrell, 1997).

Cultural background influences family members' attitudes toward conflict. In some cultures, open struggle is commonplace and comfortable; in other cultures, verbal expression of differences is avoided at all costs. In many Asian families, "saving face" is a priority, and preserving harmony as a social group ranks over an individual's needs to express strong feelings and inner thoughts (Lee & Mock, 2005). In contrast, in Iranian families, "fighting ensues and overt communication stops for day, weeks, or months" (Jalali, 2005), such that eventually a mediator may be required to bring about resolution. Latino families may have a strong culture of familism within which children are expected to show support and obedience to their parents, particularly their fathers (Crean, 2008). In a study of conflict in low-income Mexican families, the more supportive the mothers and the closer the children felt to their mothers, the less depression they experienced as a result of frequent parental conflicts (Dumka, Roosa, & Jackson, 1997). Furthermore, in a study of Mexican-origin adolescent siblings, researchers found that those who reported higher familism values (e.g., felt obligated to help their family and relied on their family) were more likely to use solution-oriented and nonconfrontational conflict resolution strategies (Killoren, Thayer, & Updegraff, 2008). Ultimately, individual family characteristics may account more for differences in conflict styles than culture (Oetzel, et al., 2003).

The mere absence of conflict does not mean that a family functions well. In fact, conflict avoidance can lead to negative long-term consequences (Gottman & Krokoff, 1990). One strong parent or sibling can suppress or avoid conflicts to make the family system appear to be balanced. Over time, however, such suppression can have negative effects. Dysfunctional families may get stuck in a powerful conflict cycle and devastate one or more family members, as the following quote indicates.

In our family we were not allowed to fight. My mother wouldn't tolerate it! She would say, "God only gave me two little girls and they are not going to kill one another." Arguments were cut off and we were sent to our rooms. After she died we fought most of the next 10 years! We each had so many old resentments to settle. For over two years we didn't speak! Fortunately, we relearned how to relate to one another.

It is important to consider the family context when considering conflict avoidance. As Sillars, Canary, and Tafoya (2004) stated: "Avoidance of conflict has a different meaning and consequence when it occurs in the context of a generally positive and affectionate relationship, as opposed to a context in which avoidance masks latent hostility that leaks out in various ways" (p. 423).

Although both functional and dysfunctional families experience conflict, functional families conflict more positively (Gottman, 1994a). In other words, functional family members engage in conflict when they struggle to make their differences more tolerable. The ways in which family members agree are important and the more agreement among members, the less likely that disastrous conflict will result. The ways in which family members disagree are equally important. Some battle openly, whereas others covertly harm each other. What is accepted as rational in one family may be perceived as irrational in another (Vangelisti, 1993). All family members contribute, negatively or positively, to the regulation of tensions created by conflict. For example, one young adult reported that when she and a sibling would argue as kids, her mother would make them sing their arguments to each other—which quickly turned the arguments into peals of laughter.

Conflicts also are present in many successfully functioning marriages as well as dysfunctional marriages (Gottman, 1994a). Even though all relationships have problems, successful ones include partners who have learned how to negotiate conflicts. Gottman and Krokoff (1990) found that some forms of confrontation during marital conflict precede increases in marital satisfaction. By exploring the process of conflict and how it can develop realistically or unrealistically, and by becoming aware of better communication practices to use during that process, understanding of the development and management of family conflict situations improves.

This chapter will examine the conflict process, factors related to the conflict process, unresolved conflicts, destructive conflicts, including violence, and close with a section on constructive conflict, including communication strategies for managing inevitable and often necessary family conflicts.

THE PROCESS OF CONFLICT

Family members who confront their differences are more likely to improve their relationships and experience more joint benefits that increase love and caring. Conflict may provide opportunities for valuable feedback leading to innovations that enhance adaptability and cohesiveness. Talking about a conflict may either resolve conflicts or continue them (Hocker & Wilmot, 2007). The intensity of the conflict determines the kinds of messages produced, the patterns the confrontations follow, and the interpretations placed on the communication cues (Roloff, 1996).

Conflict Defined

Conflict theory proposes that it is human nature to be self-oriented and that conflict is a confrontation about control over scarce resources (Ingoldsby, Smith, & Miller, 2004). A scare resource could be time, such as the year of a wedding as in the opening vignette about Marina and Anthony's family. From a communication perspective, interpersonal *conflict* may be viewed as "an expressed struggle between at least two interdependent parties, who perceive incompatible goals, scarce resources, and interference from the other party in achieving their goals" (Hocker & Wilmot, 2007, p. 9). Conflict may include "displaying overt mutual exchanges of intentionally hurtful behaviors" (Weiss & Dehle, 1994). As the definition states, conflict may arise as the result of a perception, such as an individual's belief that the degree of intimacy expected of him either smothers him or requires more of him than he wants to provide. Conflict may also develop over a difference in attitudes or values. Latricia, a full-time working mother, does not enjoy cooking and would prefer to go out with the family to eat pizza rather than fix dinner. Her partner values home-cooked meals. Conflict occurs when one person's behavior or desire blocks the goals of another, resulting in a "showdown" over values and resources, as each family member seeks to satisfy his or her needs—usually at some expense to the other.

The conflictual process is very complex, consisting of both individual and relational dimensions. Intrapersonal conflicts, or conflicts occurring within an individual family member, often can cause trouble with others in the family. A frustrated mother who is unhappy at work may act out the tension at home and create family struggles. In addition, family members may use conflicts in a dialectical sense to gain autonomy when they feel trapped and need to reduce connectedness. It is important to understand that not all dialectical contradictions involve conflict; those that do are referred to as *antagonistic* contradictions. Other contradictions that regulate tension are *nonantagonistic;* they do not lead to conflict. Usually these are intrapersonal in nature as "the individual experiences internally the dialectical pull between contradictory oppositions" (Werner & Baxter, 1994, p. 353). Antagonistic contradictions become externalized and result from an explicit mismatching of interests and goals of individual family members.

Conflict and Family Systems

When considering family conflict, it is important to remember that families act as systems, as discussed in Chapter 3. Because of their interdependence, a conflict between two members of the family will affect other members. Of the various subsystems in a family, the way in which marital conflict affects children has received the most attention. A review of 39 studies found that parents' conflicts influence their parenting behaviors, consequently affecting their children (Krishnakumar & Buehler, 2000). These researchers commented that "the emotions and tensions aroused during negative marital interactions are carried over into parent-child interactions" (p. 30). For instance, parents who express high hostility within their marriage also use more harsh discipline with their children and show less sensitivity, support, and love to their children. Other research has found that when spouses have conflict one day, the likelihood that they will have tense interactions with their children the next day increases (Almeida, Wethington, & Chandler, 1999).

The effects of family conflict and the way in which parents manage conflict can have profound effects on children and their relationships with family members and others, particularly as they grow older and develop their own intimate relationships. A longitudinal study of parents and adolescents found that parents' marital conflict resolution styles were related to conflict resolution styles between the parents and adolescents two years later (Van Doorn, Branje, & Meeus, 2007). A study of a racially diverse sample of families demonstrated that high levels of marital conflict in a family is related to both overt and relational aggression of young adolescents (Lindsey, Chambers, Frabutt, & Mackinnon-Lewis, 2009).

The way that parents deal with conflict within their marriage or partnership may also affect the way that their children approach conflict in their own romantic relationships. Darling and colleagues (2008) found that parents who use more positive conflict behaviors and less negative conflict behaviors have adolescents who use similar patterns with romantic partners. Similarly, a study of college students in dating relationships revealed that students who perceived higher levels of verbal aggressiveness from their parents were more likely to report higher levels of involvement as instigators and recipients of violence in their dating relationships (Palazzolo, Roberto, & Babin, 2010). This finding was particularly strong for same-sex parent-child dyads, suggesting that the strongest role model of aggressive behavior for a son is his father and a daughter is her mother. Finally, college students with secure attachment styles in their romantic relationships reported parents with lower verbal aggressive tendencies (Roberto, Carlyle, Goodall & Castle, 2009).

Conflict varies across family forms. Conflicting cohabiting couples are more likely to be abusive than dating couples of the same age. In fact, they conflict more often on a larger range of topics and are twice as abusive, particularly in longer-term relationships (Magdol, Moffitt, Capsi, & de Silva, 1998). Same-sex couples with serious conflicts or in abusive relationships may have less access to social support from others, since living a nontraditional lifestyle tends to limit access to help from family members and others who do not approve of their lifestyle. To disclose conflict problems may lead to rejection and ridicule. Another type of conflict often arises in gay and lesbian families when they have children from previous marriages, especially in the early years after divorce. This stepfamily form does not have universal acceptance which may cause conflicts at holiday times and vacations or during visits from the children, or arguments over who should have custody. Children in single-parent families and stepfamilies may be exposed to intra-household fighting within their homes and to inter-household conflicts with the biological parent living in another home. Children become tale bearers who carry stories from one home to another, which can cause conflicts.

Types of Conflict

Families experience conflict over many issues. If you have siblings, or have been around siblings, you probably realize that they can quarrel over many issues—who gets the front seat in the car, how much time can be spent on the Internet, and who gets to choose the movie for the family to watch. More serious issues in families such as a teenager using drugs, a spouse's infidelity, or a parent's alcohol addiction also lead to conflict. Technology has provided even more mediums which may cause family conflict. E-mails and text messages in particular may be used to begin arguments or continue earlier arguments. These types of communications are also prone to misunderstandings—Jon's quick reply to his wife Allison's text message may be construed by Allison as him not taking her request seriously, when Jon has just been having a stressful day at work. Gottman and DeClaire (1997) discovered that couples conflict over the same issues 69 percent of the time. They concluded that, since many conflicts arose over insolvable problems, "We need to teach couples that they'll never solve most of their problems" and that they need to "establish a dialogue" about the problems (p. 20).

In stepfamilies, conflict that results in discussion and compromise can often lead to positive change (Coleman, Fine, Ganong, Downs, & Pauk, 2001). In addition to typical family conflicts, there are also struggles unique to this family form (Coleman, et al., 2001). Conflicts over resources, space, privacy, and finances may emerge as members try to develop a family identity. One mother explained some of the conflicts that emerged with her new husband over the financial support of her son: "I think he resented it if we went on a vacation to have to pay for [my son's] plane ticket or things like that. I think he did not want to have the responsibility of [my son's] college" (p. 65).

Change may trigger uneasiness and consequently conflict. A new family member, a job loss, the trauma of a divorce, or the loss of income all impact the family system. Disturbances in family equilibrium may lead to conditions in which groups or individuals become unwilling to do what is expected of them. Family systems experience an ongoing low-level friction, since they continually change to survive and cope with conflict, either realistically or unrealistically.

Families that own a business together experience additional occasions for conflict (Klein, 2002). The following student's comment reflects some of the challenges family businesses can create.

My grandfather used some money he had earned selling a patent to open his own business. A very controlling and intelligent man, he spent a lot of time putting his business together and thus did not spend a great deal of time nurturing his relationship with my grandmother. I think that the conflict that exists between the two of them affects how they relate to their children. The overwhelming control that my grandfather had over his family created an immense amount of conflict, even though my grandfather, my uncle, my aunt, and my father all work at the family business. My uncle and my father have a great deal of conflict with my aunt because they think she does not work as hard as they do and that she (and her family) get a lot of special favors from my grandparents.

Finally, whatever the topic, some issues result in intractable or unsolvable conflicts that reappear over time to create painful and frustrating points of struggle in ongoing relationships.

Conflict Styles Model

Every family dyad or triad disagrees differently. For example, your mother and brother exhibit a conflict style different from the one you and your mother exhibit. As you grew up, you learned how to manage or survive conflicts; this learning influenced the style of the conflict strategies you tend to use. Kilmann and Thomas (1975) developed a model (Figure 9.1) to demonstrate that conflict style consists of two partially competing goals: concern for others (or cooperativeness) and concern

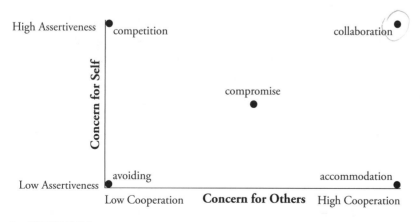

FIGURE 9.1
Conflict Styles

for self (or assertiveness). Conflict contains elements of both cooperation and assertiveness.

Competition and collaboration are at the top of the model. *Competitiveness* requires high assertiveness and going after what you want. Your concern for self is high; thus, you see conflict as a way to get what you need, regardless of another's needs or concerns. Competition becomes highly selfish if it is your only relational conflict style. It can mean "I win; you lose" too often and destroy cohesion within a family. The challenge is to compete to achieve personal goals without taking unfair advantage of other family members.

Collaboration occurs when you show concern for other family members as well as high concern for self. It often means finding an alternative or a creative solution that satisfies all parties. Collaborating depends on high trust levels and self-disclosure on the part of all members. Conflicting members must seek a solution that enables all parties to feel they have won without compromising issues vital to individual needs.

Compromise represents a solution that partially meets the needs of each member involved in the conflict. In some families, the motto is "Be wise and compromise." Such a family theme supports giving in or giving up some of one's needs. Usually it implies an equal win and loss for each member.

At the lower right of the model is *accommodation*, which occurs when you are unassertive but cooperative. It is the opposite of competition, because you meet the demands or needs of the other person but deny your own.

Finally, *avoiding* implies an unassertive and uncooperative style in which at least one member refuses to engage the issue. This may leave one partner highly frustrated because he or she cannot involve the other partner in any resolution efforts. Sometimes it is wise to use a "pick your battles" approach; other times avoiding is a powerful passive response.

This conflict style model provides a way to understand how one family member's conflict strategy affects another's response pattern. Where do you think the following example would fall on the model?

My father left my mother last year to live with someone else. I have become my mother's main support. She calls me at college almost every day demanding that I come home for all kinds of silly reasons. It's a three-hour roundtrip! Right now I can't seem to tell her to back off. So, I do whatever she wants and hope this stage will pass quickly.

The conflict style model based on Kilmann and Thomas provides one view of how families use conflict; other strategies will be discussed later.

Stages of Ongoing Conflict

Understanding how conflict develops allows you to unravel some of the complexity and position a disagreement or fight in a larger context. Families tend to experience many recurring and unresolved conflicts as certain issues arise triggered by reoccurring events or circumstances. We developed the following six stages as a

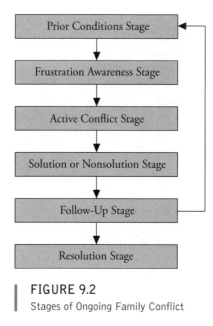

FIGURE 9.2
Stages of Ongoing Family Conflict

model for analyzing the ongoing and repetitive conflict process: prior conditions; frustration awareness; active conflict; solution or nonsolution; follow-up; and resolution stage. These are represented in Figure 9.2. As you read through this model, think about a recent conflict in your family. Did each of these stages emerge as a distinct entity or was it difficult to know when one ended and the next began?

Prior Conditions Stage   Ongoing conflict does not emerge from a vacuum. It is rooted in the history of the relationship. Prior conditions are present in the absence of active conflict but, under pressure or stress, come into play. Prior conditions that may trigger a clash include ambiguous limits on each family member's responsibilities and role expectations, ongoing competition over scarce resources such as money or affection, unhealthy dependency of one person on another, and problematic decision-making patterns. Holiday times, income tax time, drunken episodes, or the arrival of in-laws may all serve as prior conditions. Past experiences set the groundwork for tension arousal.

Frustration Awareness Stage   As a response to sensing a prior condition event, this stage involves one or more family members becoming frustrated because someone or something blocks them from satisfying a need or concern. One or more parties become aware of snappy answers, nonverbal messages in the form of slammed doors, or avoidance of eye contact. In most ongoing repetitive conflicts, it is common for nonverbal cues to appear before verbal ones. As you nonverbally become aware of the conflict, you might think, "He's really getting upset" or "I can feel myself getting tense." Certain code words or phrases also heighten tensions. For example, "You're not going to have another drink (piece of cake, cigarette) are you?" Or, "Why don't I ever have any clean clothes?"

Inaccurate perceptions can create conflict where none exists because they can trigger tensions. An incipient conflict may end at this point if one person perceives that the negative consequences outweigh the possible advantages. "Backing off" from the issue ends the immediate tension but does not remove the causes or satisfy the needs that provoked it. Sometimes tension ends through self-disclosure as one recognizes the potential for conflict: "I'm really just upset about the test tomorrow and I'm taking it out on you," or "You're right—I was selfish and I'm sorry." Also, during this stage, labeled "agenda building" by Gottman (1993), cross-complaining may begin via a series of negative messages that the involved family members are unwilling to stop. *Cross-complaining* involves meeting another's complaint or criticism with one of your own while ignoring the other's point.

Active Conflict Stage At this point, the conflict manifests itself in a series of direct overt verbal and nonverbal messages. This symbolic interchange may resemble a battleground or a calm, pointed discussion, depending on the family's rules and style of fighting. In some families, yelling signals a major fight, while yelling is commonplace in others, as noted below.

Unfortunately, my husband is the type who would rather yell. He is not always a fair fighter. When I want to talk and explain my feelings, and then give him a chance to explain his, he either goes into moody silence or explodes. I find both approaches useless.

Typically, active conflict escalates from initial statements and queries to overt fighting, bargaining, or giving an ultimatum. This may be characterized by a discernible strategy, or game plan, when one or more family members try to maneuver and convince others of the merits of an issue. The longer the conflict continues, the more the participants' behavior may raise frustrations, encourage active arguing, and increase resistance to change. Problematic couples usually escalate their conflicts by continued cross-complaining, accusations, and blaming. Functional couples tend to match positive remarks or coordinate negative with positive remarks. In one study of engaged couples, researchers found that during discussions about problems, more satisfied couples were characterized by the female's domineering statement being followed by the male's submissive statement (Heatherington, Escudero, & Friedlander, 2005).

Wives tend to have more other-directed and relationship-sensitive thoughts during active conflict; husbands are more likely to be concerned with the content of the message, their conversational role, and themselves (Sillars, Roberts, Leonard, & Dun, 2000). Thinking about the conflictual interaction in terms of a dyad (e.g., "We're getting more and more irritated," [Sillars, et al., 2000, p. 490]) is uncommon for husbands and wives. Wives and husbands also view their own communication during the conflict interaction as more favorable than the communication of their partner. One study of couples married three years or less found that a husband's or wife's expectations about the spouse's understanding and negative communication was associated with their own communication. For example, if a wife expected that in a conflict her husband would not try to understand her feelings, she was more likely to use negative communication (such as complaints and criticism) and less likely to use positive communication such as compliments and displays of affection (Sanford, 2006).

The ability of each spouse to accurately understand the emotions of the other plays an important role during active conflict. Spouses infer how the other is feeling during active conflict based on their observations of their spouse as well as their own feelings and thoughts. The presence of depressive symptoms in either husband or wife during the active conflict stage can make it difficult for the spouse to accurately assess their partner's anger (Papp, Kourous, & Cummings, 2010).

Solution or Nonsolution Stage   The active conflict stage evolves into either the temporary solution or the nonsolution stage. The solution may range from creative, constructive, and satisfactory to destructive, nonproductive, and disappointing. The solution may represent a compromise or adjustment of previously held positions. In this stage, how the conflict is managed or solved determines the outcome and whether positive or negative results follow in the immediate future. It does not *resolve* the issue.

Solutions may be considered as *conflict management.* For example, partners who struggle continually over the wife's work as an undercover police officer may argue over her inability to stay in touch with her husband while on duty. He becomes upset because he gets frightened when she does not return calls within a few hours, something that happens regularly, and he resents always being the go-to parent for problems at their son's school. The times that she has access to a safe phone or can pick up her son from school provides a short-term solution. But when the next phone call comes and she has to remain in her role, even into overtime hours, he becomes angry once again. So, although occasionally a conflict can be defused and managed with vacation days or less dangerous assignments, it is never resolved. However, if she took a desk job, the conflict would disappear.

Some conflicts move into ongoing nonsolutions: The active conflict stops but nothing is resolved. Family members live with the frustrations or angry feelings. Nonsolution brings the conflict to an impasse. In the opening vignette about Amanda and Jordan, this couple may enter into the nonsolution stage when each of them just stops talking about their problems. Obviously, communication problems can develop if too many conflicts end with nonsolutions. However, every family lives with some unresolved conflicts because the costs of an acceptable solution outweigh the advantages to one or more family members. In some families, these unresolved conflicts may become major problems, but other families may live with irresolvable disputes without a negative impact on their relationships (Roloff & Miller, 2006).

Follow-Up Stage   This stage could also be called the aftermath stage. It includes the reactions that follow the active conflict and affects future interactions, such as avoidance or conciliation without acceptance. Grudges, hurt feelings, or physical scars may fester until they lead to the beginning stage of another conflict. The house may be filled with long silences, avoidance, or formal politeness. On the other hand, the outcomes may be positive, such as increased intimacy and self-esteem or honest explorations of family values or concerns. The members may exchange apologies or communicate about the fight. This aftermath stage is linked by a feedback chain to the initial stage, because each conflict in a family is stored in the prior conditions "bank." In ongoing, unresolved conflicts, whenever the trigger or the prior conditions reoccur, the entire conflict process occurs again. This may go on for years or decades.

Resolution Stage This stage signals that a certain recurring conflict no longer exists; it no longer affects the family. For example, a husband and wife may conflict over priorities on bills to be paid. They negotiate and compromise on demands, then stick to their agreement. Time and developmental stages of each family member also affect solutions to conflicts. For example, parental conflicts over who will take Wei-Lin to school decrease or disappear after she becomes old enough to walk there by herself; the same will be true of parental conflicts over dating rules and curfews when she becomes a young adult. Conflicts over space and territory among six children competing for three bedrooms no longer require solutions when some have left home.

It is important to remember that in the model (Figure 9.2) participants may "exit" at any stage. A visitor may interrupt the frustration awareness stage and defuse the tension, at least temporarily. One or the other party may disengage from the issue, give in, or shift the focus.

Factors in Family Conflict

Family members fight with each other in different ways. Over time, most families develop rules for conflictual situations, and each pair or small group stays within their calibrated argument levels, except in unique situations when an argument may drive them beyond acceptable fighting levels or reconciling behaviors. A tearful embrace may jolt the family pattern far more than a flying frying pan. Dialectical tension generated in conflicts is not a negative force but rather a part of the ongoing dynamic interaction between opposite views and needs of family members. It can be a positive force because the "interplay of opposing tendencies serves as the driving force or catalyst of ongoing change in relationships" (Werner & Baxter, 1994, p. 351).

Patterns of Family Conflict

In their major study of conflict in early marriage, Raush, Barry, Hertel, and Swain (1974) found that although specific partners make individual contributions to the marital unit, the couple is considered a system. Their analysis revealed that the marital unit was the "most powerful source in determining interactive events" (p. 201). Couples developed their own styles of conflict, which were unique to them. Soon after marriage, the system develops its own fight style, one that often persists throughout the marriage.

In a classic study, Feldman (1979) viewed a couple's conflictual behavior as part of an intimacy-conflict cycle. Couples move away from a state of intimacy when one member becomes anxious or fearful, leading to conflict and separation.

Eventually, one partner makes an attempt to patch up the differences. The desire for intimacy draws them back together. The need to be touched, reaffirmed, comforted, and valued is a powerful conciliatory force in conflicts. At first, one partner might reject attempts to resume more positive communication, but the need for intimacy provides the motivation for repeated efforts to achieve it.

The couple's reconnection does not mean the problem between them has been resolved. Quite often, the issue has not been satisfactorily discussed or even fairly treated in the best interests of one or the other. Intimacy issues will again erupt into conflict when one partner feels threatened by the issue or aggressive enough to challenge the other. Have you heard people fighting and had the feeling you were hearing a rerun or rehearsed battle? The degree and limits of acceptable intimacy and acceptable conflict are important dimensions of a marital system's calibration. When these limits are violated, the intimacy-conflict cycle starts again.

Parts of Feldman's intimacy-conflict theory can be related to Baxter's views that individuals respond to contradictory demands by seeking to fulfill each demand separately. They do this through either cyclic alternation or segmentation responses. In *cyclic alternation,* first one partner complains or yells and the other responds. In conflict, husband and wife can "cycle or spiral between the two poles of contradiction, separating them temporally with each contradictory demand gaining fulfillment during its temporal cycle" (Werner & Baxter, 1994, p. 363). In *segmentation,* the family members try to verbally group their complaints around a conflicting point. Segmentation involves separate arenas for dealing with opposites. A couple may fight about their household finances, but when it comes to making financial decisions for the family business, the husband has complete control. These authors report that cyclic alternation and segmentation are the most frequently used responses couples enact to manage the dialectical aspects of their relationship.

One common pattern of conflict that couples engage in is called the *demand/withdraw pattern* (Caughlin & Scott, 2010). In this pattern, one spouse enacts a complaining or nagging behavior, while the other spouse withdraws, trying to avoid conflict. This can happen in a particular conflict episode, but it can also become a pattern of behavior. One spouse might nag the other about a chore that needs to be done. The more the spouse nags, the more the other withdraws, by ignoring or not answering the spouse. Substantial research has shown the association between this pattern and undesirable outcomes, including current and future marital dissatisfaction (Caughlin & Huston, 2002). Researchers have also examined the pattern of demand/withdraw in terms of parent-adolescent dyads. The most common pattern here is the parent demanding and the child withdrawing (Caughlin & Ramey, 2005). Relational dissatisfaction has been shown to be linked with the presence of this type of conflict pattern (Caughlin & Malis, 2004).

Caughlin and Scott (2010) identify four distinct types of the demand/withdraw pattern:

1. *Discuss/exit.* In this type of demand/withdraw, one partner seeks discussion of a topic and the other partner exits—either physically (by leaving the room) or communicatively ("Next topic!").

handwritten margin notes:
activity
watch video
clickers vote

demand/
withdraw

2. *Socratic question/perfunctory response.* This type of demand/withdraw is characterized by one person asking a series of questions and the other giving expected responses. It is most often seen in parent-adolescent dyads.
3. *Complain/deny.* In this type of demand/withdraw, one partner complains about a relational issue, and the other denies the legitimacy of the issue—in a sense, avoiding or denying the conflict.
4. *Criticize/defend.* This type of demand/withdraw occurs when one person states a criticism of the other, who is defensive in response.

Rules for Family Conflict

Members of family systems develop implicit and explicit rules governing the communication of conflictual messages. Jones and Gallois (1989) reported that couples generate or employ four kinds of rules in resolving their differences: (1) rules governing consideration (e.g., don't belittle me; don't blame the other unfairly; don't make me feel guilty); (2) rules governing rationality (e.g., don't raise your voice; don't get me angry; don't be so aggressive); (3) rules governing specific self-expression (e.g., let's keep to the point; let's be honest; don't exaggerate); and (4) rules governing conflict resolution (e.g., explore alternatives; make joint decisions; give reasons for your views). Rules governing conflicts differ when couples are in public or in private. The rationality rules are used more in public settings; they are also more important to husbands than to wives. However, both agree that rationality rules are the least important. These rules can become a part of coping strategies both in private and public settings on how to vent negative feelings, how to avoid conflicts, and how to find support in others.

Rules for conflicts in families with children have great variation. In some families, children cannot "talk back." In other families, children are encouraged to speak up about their feelings. In disciplining children for conflicts, the rules again vary. Some parents have rules that prohibit any hitting or verbal abuse; others believe spanking or screaming are appropriate. Couple roles frequently influence the conflict behaviors of their children, as in this example.

As a child I remember my parents referring to their rules for fighting, such as "Never go to bed mad" or "Never call the other person names." It seemed a bit silly at the time but, after the kinds of fighting I experienced in my first marriage, I made sure that my fiancé and I discussed fighting and set some rules for disagreeing before I would consider a second marriage.

Couple and Family Types and Conflict

Couple and family types, as discussed in Chapter 7, can also affect conflict patterns. As a family evolves, the system develops conflictual behaviors that characterize the group if not the individuals.

Fitzpatrick's Couple Types   The Fitzpatrick (1988) couple types, discussed in Chapter 7, demonstrate distinctive conflict behaviors. Her continued research with colleagues has strengthened her conclusions about types and conflict (Noller & Fitzpatrick, 1993; Fitzpatrick & Badzinski, 1994; Fitzpatrick & Ritchie, 1994). Traditional couples seek stability and resist change by confronting rather than avoiding conflict. However, they may avoid conflicts more than they realize. Traditionals more often collude with one another to avoid conflicts. Independents more readily accept uncertainty and change by confronting societal views on marriage in a much more direct communication style than traditionals. Independents do not run from conflicts. They resent a spouse who withdraws.

Family Communication Patterns   Family conflict depends on how much family members use two types of communication labeled *conformity orientation* and *conversation orientation* (Koerner & Fitzpatrick, 2004). Remember in Chapter 7 we referred to four types of families that are created with these two orientations (see Figure 7.2). In which kind of family did you grow up? Did your family use a conformity or conversation orientation in its conflicts? For example, if your family type was pluralistic, then children's views were heard in family disputes. There was a conversational quality about your disagreements. You could argue with Dad or your obnoxious sister. All siblings could develop verbal competence. Your parents would listen and not avoid conflicts, like a conformity-oriented family would. The interplay of these two orientations affects how family members engage in conflicts.

As you might expect, families' conversation orientation and conformity orientation affect how they deal with conflict. Families high on conformity orientation focus on avoiding conflict while families high on conversation orientation do not avoid conflict (Koerner & Fitzpatrick, 2004). More than other family types, consensual families frequently vent their negative feelings and seek outside support from friends and relatives to deal with conflicts, enabling them to better cope with negativity. Protective families conversely avoid outside social support but regularly vent negative feelings expressed in emotional outbursts (Koerner & Fitzpatrick, 1997). The importance of this study is that the results demonstrate how complex conflict dimensions are in families.

Understanding a person's family-of-origin family type may also help one understand that person's conflict behavior in romantic relationships (Koerner & Fitzpatrick, 2002). For the most part, young adults seem to approach conflict in their own romantic relationships in similar ways that their families-of-origin did. For example, persons from families with a high conformity orientation are more likely than persons from low conformity families to resist their romantic partners' aggressive moves and to engage in mutually negative behaviors with their romantic partners. Koerner and Fitzpatrick concluded that families-of-origin play an important role in socializing their children to conflict behavior.

Gottman's Conflict Types   Remember that also in Chapter 7, we discussed Gottman's conflict types (1994a). Because his typology is based on how couples conflict, it is important to revisit it. According to Gottman (1994a), a central contributing factor in marriages that do not end in divorce is the "couple's ability to resolve the conflicts that are inevitable in any relationship" (p. 28). Conflict is going to occur in marriage, and Gottman argued that expressing anger, disagreeing, and airing complaints is a very healthy activity for spouses.

As discussed previously, Gottman found couples in stable, lasting relationships to fall into one of three types. *Validating couples* agree on many important areas, and carefully pick their battles. When they do disagree, they are respectful of each other. During disagreements they validate their partners' opinions and emotions. Overall, they work together, trying to find compromise and work out their problems until they are both satisfied. *Volatile couples* are energized by conflict; they argue frequently. They may not censor comments well, believing that honesty is very important. They tend to believe marriage should emphasize individuality and partners see themselves as equals. This type of couple has marriages that tend to be passionate and exciting. *Conflict-avoiding couples* may refrain from conflict because they feel the conflict is less important than other issues. They share a marriage philosophy of acceptance of disagreement and do not feel the need to resolve conflicts. Gottman and colleagues proposed that validating, volatile, and conflict-avoidant couples can all have lasting marriages; the most important factor is not a couple's style but that the couple has a five-to-one ratio of positive to negative moments during interactions.

A recent study of 1,983 couples in committed relationships found that about one-third of participants perceived that their personal conflict style did not match their partner's conflict style. The mismatch between volatile and conflict-avoiding partners in a relationship was associated with more relationship problems and lower levels of relationship satisfaction and stability than other mismatches (Busby & Holman, 2009).

Gottman (1994a) also described two types of couples whose relationships do not tend to last: *hostile/engaged* and *hostile/detached*. The *hostile/engaged* couple is one that argues often, using sarcasm, insults, and name-calling. The *hostile/detached* couple also argues often, but individuals don't listen to one another, and stay detached and uninvolved emotionally.

Gottman has found that marriages that are in danger of moving toward separation or divorce are marked by what he calls "The Four Horsemen of the Apocalypse." These are four communication practices that "sabotage your attempts to communicate with your partner" (p. 72). Listed from least to most destructive, these are:

- *Criticism.* Criticism is sometimes confused with complaining. However, remember that complaining is thought to be healthy for a marriage. When a spouse complains, he or she is focused on the person's behavior. When a spouse criticizes, the focus is on the other person. For instance, Bridget and Liam have an ongoing disagreement about the amount of time Bridget spends working, both at the office and when she is home with the family. Bridget really likes her work and believes she can advance very quickly if she out-produces her colleagues. Liam may start out with complaints, "You worked most of the weekend again, leaving me no time to relax or do anything I enjoy." Over time, Liam's complaints may turn into criticisms: "You are so selfish, working all the time."
- *Contempt.* Contempt is considered criticism with the intention to insult and psychologically abuse the other person. Contempt may be displayed through verbal and nonverbal channels. If Bridget and Liam's conflict about

her work hours is not resolved, an argument exhibiting contempt may include Liam yelling at Bridget: "So you're the big success at the office, huh? Well, you better enjoy it, because you're the big failure at home!" Gottman proposed that contempt can be recognized when mockery, hostile humor, insults, and nonverbal behaviors such as eye-rolling are present. When contempt is present, spouses have a difficult time identifying anything positive in their partner.

- *Defensiveness.* Defensiveness is a natural response to criticism and contempt. When being attacked, spouses may use defensive techniques such as denying responsibility, making excuses, responding with a complaint about the spouse, or whining. To Liam's contempt, Bridget may respond: "Shut up! All I am doing is trying to keep up with your spending habits! If you didn't want to always buy new things, I wouldn't have to work so hard!" The major problem with defensiveness is that it prevents partners from trying to understand each other's perspective.

- *Stonewalling.* Stonewalling means the partner removes him or herself either emotionally or physically from a conversation. Spouses often think that stonewalling is a way of trying to keep things calm and not make them worse. Husbands are more likely to use this technique, and this can be particularly difficult on their wives, whose heart rates go up when their husbands stonewall them.

most destructive

Gottman pointed out that even if these behaviors are present, couples can still turn their marriages around. These are to be seen as warning signs that changes need to be made.

UNRESOLVED CONFLICT

How would you define unresolved conflict? Roloff and Miller (2006) argued that "We doubt that the cessation of arguing means the conflict has been resolved" (p. 155). Instead, these authors suggest that a sense of resolution is necessary to say a conflict is resolved. In irresolvable interpersonal conflicts, "at least one of the individuals involved believes the conflict is impossible to resolve" (Miller, 2011, p. 241). The definition of irresolvability depends on one or more perceptions that it cannot be resolved.

What happens in the family if conflict cannot be solved? The answer to this may depend on the family. "Some families may be able to live with irresolvable disputes without damaging their relationships" (Roloff & Miller, 2006, p. 155). However, in other families unresolved conflict is associated with low relationship satisfaction (Cramer, 2002). If a critical issue cannot be resolved, a loss usually occurs, which affects all members as psychological and/or physical estrangement creates and fosters some level of separation. If a child will not accept his father's remarriage or a parent will not accept a child's religious conversion, psychological and/or physical separation follows. Young family members may remain in the home but withdraw from family activities until they go away to school or establish a way to support themselves. Some members may be cut off from all contact with the family and may be treated as nonexistent, as in the following example.

When I married my husband, I was essentially making a choice between my parents and Joe. Joe is African American, and my parents said they would never speak to me again if we married. Although I knew they were angry, I thought that they would come around when we had a baby. Melissa is two years old now and my parents have never seen her. My brother and sister have been to see me, but I am "dead" as far as my parents are concerned.

Some persons become involved in irresolvable conflicts that are characterized by "a lengthy history, continued resistance and a sense of hopelessness" (Roloff, 2009, p. 341). In such cases, pessimism and frustration result. In certain relationships, unresolved conflict may lead to violence (Olson, 2002). Many unresolved partner conflicts result in divorce, or dissolution of the relationship. One or both members withdraw, seeing the ending of their formal relationships as the only logical solution. Yet, when children are involved, spouses are divorced from each other, not from their children. This means some level of ongoing interaction will continue between former spouses, often a difficult situation.

Some couples with unresolved conflicts stop short of separation because the cost of the final step may be too great; yet, the rewards of continuing to live together are few. In these cases unresolved conflict may add great tension to the entire family system. When an issue is unresolvable, it may be more functional for the family to avoid the issue and direct its communication to areas that bring cohesion (Fitzpatrick, Fallis, & Vance, 1982). Yet, over time, family members may learn to live with topics that are avoided because the pain of addressing them is too great.

When I asked my wife what she wanted for our twenty-fifth anniversary, she said, "Marriage counseling. The next 25 years have to be better than the first." I knew we had many fights, but I never knew she was that unhappy. I agreed to the counseling, and we really worked on our differences and ways of resolving them. After a few months, we were able to talk rationally about things we always fought over—money, my schedule, our youngest son. Next month we will celebrate our twenty-eighth anniversary, and I can say that the last 3 years were a lot better than the first 25.

DESTRUCTIVE CONFLICT

Some conflicts have enormously destructive outcomes. We divide destructive conflict into two types—covert (hidden) and overt (open)—discussing how families use these types to cope with conflicts. Conflict styles may range from the very covert (the burned dinner, disappearance, or cutting joke) to the very overt (hostile words, pots or fists flying). In addition, partners with highly problematic conflict patterns may be confronting many problems having no direct connection to the disagreement; these include mental disorders, drug addiction, chronic illness, and serious employment concerns (Roloff, 2009). These problems actively contribute to conflict escalation. Violence, whether in the form of verbal aggressiveness that abuses family members or physical attacks, fits under destructive conflict. It represents the worst kind of conflict. Communication is tied closely to family violence, as it affects and is affected by violence. "Violence is a form of interactive communication. It is motivated by a desire to communicate a message—often a demand for compliance" (Anderson, Umberson, & Elliott, 2004, p. 630). Destructive conflict is illustrated in the following example.

One member of our family, my 20-year-old stepson, enters the house with a barrel full of hostilities and problems. He overwhelms my wife with yelling and screaming and a string of obscenities. My reaction is to tell him to shut up and not to have anything to do with him—certainly not to do anything for him. My wife seethes until she can no longer cope; then she explodes. After a litany of verbal attacks, she retreats behind a closed bedroom door—sealing herself off from the problem.

Covert Destructive Conflict

In covert conflict, sometimes called "guerrilla warfare," feelings are hidden and messages are unclear. Sometimes family members cover up the hurt or express anger indirectly in order to preserve the balance in the system and keep the relationships intact. To cope with verbal and physical attacks in conflicts, members often use covert strategies. Covert, or hidden, conflict usually relies on one of the following five communication strategies: denial, disqualification, displacement, disengagement, and pseudomutuality. *Denial* occurs most frequently when one hears "No problem; I'm not upset" or "That's OK, I'm fine" accompanied by contradictory nonverbal signals. Sometimes acquiescence strategies such as apologizing, pleading, crying, or conceding are ways that family members discount stronger feelings and deny their deeper levels of hurt (Vangelisti & Crumley, 1998). *Disqualification* describes situations in which a person expresses anger and then discounts, or disqualifies, the angry reaction: "I'm sorry, I was upset about the money and got carried away," or "I wouldn't have gotten so upset except the baby kept me awake all night." Admittedly, these messages are valid in certain settings, but they become a disqualification when the person intends to cover the emotion rather than admit to it.

Displacement implies anger that is directed to an inappropriate person. Displacement is depicted in the story of the man whose boss yelled at him but the man could not express his anger at the boss. When he arrived home, he yelled at his wife, who grounded the teenager, who hit the fourth-grader, who tripped the baby, who kicked the dog. When a person believes anger cannot be expressed directly, the individual finds another way to vent the strong emotions. Dangerous displacement occurs when parents who cannot deal emotionally with their own differences turn a child into a scapegoat for their pent-up anger; over time he or she becomes the "acting-out" child.

Disengaged family members live within the hollow shell of relationships that used to be. Disengaged members avoid each other and express their hostility through their lack of interaction. Instead of dealing with conflict, they keep it from surfacing. Some families go to extremes to avoid conflicts, as depicted below.

My wife and I should have separated 10 years before we did. I was able to arrange my work schedule so that I came home after 11 o'clock and slept until Carmen and the kids had left in the morning. That was the only way I could remain in the relationship. We agreed to stay together until Luis graduated from high school. Now I feel as if we both lost 10 years of life, and I'm not sure the kids were any better off just because we all ate and slept in the same house.

Pseudomutuality represents the opposite of disengagement. This style of anger characterizes family members who appear to be perfect and delighted with each other because no hint of discord is ever allowed to dispel their image of perfection. Anger remains below the surface to the point that family members lose all ability to deal with it directly. Pretense remains the only possibility. Only when one member of the perfect group develops ulcers, exhibits a nervous disorder, or acts in a dysfunctional manner do the relational cracks begin to show.

Frequently, sexual interaction links to covert strategies. For some couples, sex is a weapon in guerilla warfare. Demands for, or avoidance of, sexual activity may be the most effective way of covertly expressing hostility. Sexual abuse, put-downs, excuses, and direct rejection wound others without the risk of exposing one's own strong anger. Such expressions of covert anger destroy rather than strengthen relationships.

Covert behavior links to family themes that discourage conflict or independence. Themes such as "We can depend only on each other" or "Never wash your dirty linen in public" encourages family members to hide conflicts. These covert strategies of conflict relate to the belief that conflict equals powerlessness (Buzzanell & Burrell, 1997). Family members who view themselves as victims, powerless to change or influence others, use less-threatening covert techniques to reduce conflicts.

Overt Destructive Conflict

Overt destructive conflict behaviors include hostile verbal aggression and physical aggression that can lead to violence. Domestic violence occurs when one family member imposes his or her will on another through the use of verbal abuse and often force. This violence violates acceptable social norms, but may be tolerated within a particular culture. The violent member intends to inflict pain, injury, or suffering, either psychological or physical, on other family members (Cahn & Lloyd, 1996). Threats are violent messages that warn family members that they

Sometimes partners exaggerate nonverbally as part of their fight style.

will be punished now or later if they do not comply with the wishes of the aggressive member (Roloff, 1996). Research on family violence indicates that partner abuse and parent-child abuse become a part of ongoing role relationships. In physically combative families, such behaviors occur frequently enough for children, husbands, wives, or partners to experience it as normative. Evidence suggests that when children are exposed to destructive conflict between adults, it affects their own conflict-handling behavior (Davies, Myers, Cummings, & Heindel, 1999).

Think back to the previous chapter in which we discussed power, influence, and decision making. Our discussion of overt destructive conflict is tied to those issues. Lloyd and Emery (1994) wrote that if the purpose of conflict is to meet one's own needs, and that if aggression adds to the chance of getting those needs met, the emotional and physical health of a partner becomes secondary. Some family members will win at any cost, or use aggression as power to attain the goal at the emotional expense of other family members. This power extends beyond physically abusive behaviors. Violent husbands seem to assume more of the power of decision making in their families than do nonviolent husbands (Frieze & McHugh, 1992). If the power dimensions are not equal between the sexes in the family, especially in the marital dyad, the conflicts that involve negative strategies could be attempts to more equitably balance the power domains. There are inconsistencies between men and women regarding reporting abuse. "Women often do not label their violent experiences as abusive" (Hamby, Poindexter, & Gray-Little, 1996, p. 137). Conflicts that include anger, physical abuse, and alcohol and drug use definitely do have long-term effects on women's health (Ratner, 1998). Thus, negative words and actions in conflicts can lessen family harmony. Sometimes power moves are expressed during talk about the most mundane activities, as in the next example, in which the mother asserts her expertise in shopping.

My mother always seemed to think that my father had some type of problem carrying out simple tasks. Every once in a while she would give him the shopping list to pick up a few things. When he would return home, my mother would find something that he did "wrong." For example, my dad did not get the exact meat that was on sale; he got four bags of grapefruit instead of three, or bought the wrong brand of napkins. Verbally aggressive comments such as "What is wrong with you? Are you stupid or something? Why can't you follow simple directions?" served as a spark to really set him off.

This conflict appears to address more than shopping. It may address the couple's overall inability to communicate positively with one another. Often, what couples fight about is a cover-up for larger issues.

The terms *violence* and *aggression* are often used to generally define both physical attacks and verbal attacks. Physical violence such as hitting, screaming, kicking, teasing, grabbing, and throwing objects characterize some family conflicts. Men are more likely to bully, drive dangerously, hold and shake or roughly handle a child or partner than women and children, who more often endure these painful behaviors (Marshall, 1994). Women, because they are smaller in size and have less options for leaving relationships, are at greater risk for physical injuries (Whitchurch & Pace, 1993).

Verbal attacks also can characterize family conflicts and are significant. "Words hit as hard as a fist," according to Vissing and Baily (1996, p. 87). One particular type of verbal attack is called *gunnysacking*. A gunnysack is a burlap bag and serves as a metaphor for a deadly weapon. It implies storing up grievances against someone and then dumping the whole sack of anger on that person when he or she piles on the "last straw." People who gunnysack store resentments and wield their gunnysack when a family member does that "one more thing." The offender usually retaliates, and the battle escalates. Families handle verbal attacks in different ways, one of which is described in the next example.

My husband is a workaholic. I resent that my husband does not share in the child raising. In fact, it really bothered me when he referred to his staff as his "family." It bothered me even more when his paralegal became more involved with him than we were. They went to play golf and to ballgames. I held my anger in for over a year and finally dumped all my resentments. We are at a standstill. Now he never talks about work; I resent him even more, and so the cycle goes.

In the following sections, we discuss violence and aggression in the contexts of intimate partner relationships and parent-child relationships.

Partner Destructive Conflict Destructive conflict between romantic partners is widespread. Approximately three-fourths of all couples have admitted making threats of violence to one another (Cahn & Lloyd, 1996). According to the National Research Council's Panel on Research on Violence Against Women, up to two million women are battered by an intimate partner each year (Crowell & Burgess, 1996), and 84 percent of spouse abuse victims are female (American Bar Association, 2010). But violence may be even more prevalent in couples than these numbers indicate. *Common couple violence* is defined as "the dynamic in which conflict occasionally gets 'out of hand,' leading usually to 'minor' forms of violence, and more rarely escalating into serious, sometimes even life-threatening, forms of violence" (Johnson, 1995, p. 285).

Olson (2004) emphasized the diversity of intimate aggression. Her research demonstrated that there are different types of violent couples: abusive, violent, aggressive, and combative. Abusive couples have frequent (weekly) and severe types of violence, while violent couples display very high levels of aggression bimonthly. Aggressive couples exhibit moderate levels of violence about once a month, and combative couples have episodic low-level violent episodes that are infrequent (once a year). Each of these types can be further defined by being particular to an individual or to both members of the couple.

Intimate violence involves persons of all ages. In the past decade, researchers have become more aware of intimate violence in later life or "late-onset domestic violence." This occurs when a long marriage that has been free of physical abuse unexpectedly turns violent. Triggers for this might include retirement, health problems, or disability (France, 2006).

Conflict about certain emotionally charged topics is more likely to be accompanied by physical or verbal aggression between intimate partners. When asked to describe situations in which conflict resulted in aggression, participants in one study (Olson & Golish, 2002) most frequently reported situations in which the behavior of the partner was problematic, such as drug/alcohol use, lack of motivation, or not coming home. Participants also reported life change events and the involvement of a third party (such as a past partner) to be accompanied by physical or verbal aggression. There also appears to be several different patterns in which the aggressive events occur over time. For example, some respondents reported that aggression became more severe during the course of the relationship. Others explained that aggression in their intimate relationship began as severe and declined over time. Stable patterns, cyclical patterns, and oscillating patterns (up-and-down) also were reported.

The language used by family members influences conflict outcomes. Word choice reflects the degree of emotion and reveals the amount of respect the conflicting individuals have for one another. In Marshall's (1994) study of verbal attacks, he found that 77 percent of the males and 76 percent of the females had expressed threats of violence to their partners and received almost the same percentages of threats! Emotional hate terms ("You idiot!" or "Liar") quickly escalate conflicts. In some families, swearing is an integral part of venting rage. In others, the rules do not permit swearing, but name-calling replaces it. The damage from verbal aggression is underestimated because it "can lead to serious physical, psychological, and relational problems" (Sabourin, 1996, p. 199). Put-downs heighten conflicts and slow the solution process by selecting words that describe and intensify bad feelings. The use of one-up messages represents attempts to dominate or control others. These verbal stances used by dominant family members occur whenever they feel threatened. They overreact to neutral messages if challenged (Rogers, Castleton, & Lloyd, 1996). These attacks are usually accompanied by screaming or other negative nonverbal cues. Men more often blame their wives for using verbal attacks that get out of control, whereas wives more often make excuses for their spouses being violent (Sabourin, 1996). In their study of emerging adult (18- to 25-year-olds) siblings' verbally aggressive messages, Myers & Bryant (2008) found that they used seven types of verbal aggression, although the messages did not differ in their perceived hurtfulness, intensity, and intent. The seven strategies were: name-calling, insults, withdrawal, physical acts or threats, repudiation of the relationship, negative affect (conveying hatred or dislike), and unfair comparisons between the two siblings.

Sabourin, Infante, and Rudd (1990) discovered that abusive couples exhibited significantly more reciprocity in verbally aggressive exchanges than did distressed, nonabusive control groups. For the majority of couples that used verbal aggression, conflict did not lead to physical aggression, but when it did, couples attributed it to previous verbal aggression (Roloff, 1996). Stress also increases the likelihood of verbal aggressiveness between marital or intimate partners. The ability of individuals and dyads to cope with stress is associated with less verbal aggressiveness (Bodenmann, Meuwly, Bradbury, Gmelch, & Ledermann, 2010).

Increasing numbers of studies have explored abuse in same-sex couples. Gay male and lesbian couples may use physically aggressive or occasionally violent tactics to resolve relationship conflicts. Although some patterns of conflict may be similar between heterosexual and same-sex couples, this is not always the case. The simplistic abuser-victim split observed by most professionals trained to deal with violent couples is more complicated by lesbian dynamics since certain negative behaviors may be considered more or less aggressive (Ristock, 2002), When lesbian couples have children their decisions to remain together after abuse is affected by whether or not the children were born into the relationship (Hardesty, Oswald, Khaw, Fonseca, & Chung, 2008). Thus, conflict and abuse plague same-sex as well as heterosexual couples.

In their study of violence, Cahn and Lloyd (1996) cited evidence that physical violence occurs in one of six marriages. In Sabourin's (1992) study comparing abusive couples to nonabusive couples, the abusive couples showed more imbalanced patterns of cohesion and adaptability. She found that abusive couples focused on relational issues but had no sense of intimacy between them. Abusive couples complained about each other or their children, argued over relational problems, and expressed their own feelings. Nonabusive couples were more focused on accomplishing tasks and expressed their beliefs that life is good and that cooperation is valuable. By contrast, abusive couples had these themes: "It's the same old thing; we're in a rut," "If only we had more money," "If only he/she would change." More recent research examining differences of relationship quality between women in physically abusive relationships and women in nonphysically abusive relationships (Byers, Shue, & Marshall, 2001) found women in physically abusive relationships report lower levels of relationship commitment and relationship quality as well as more verbal abuse than do women in nonphysically abusive relationships.

A power imbalance may affect how partners express or deal with conflict. A *"chilling effect,"* described by Cloven & Roloff (1993), occurred when one partner had more punitive power and the other believed they had less relational power. The less powerful partner was hesitant to complain or express grievances. This chilling effect increased when the less aggressive partner felt that the more aggressive partner was less committed to the relationship, had more alternatives, or had less dependent needs regarding the love continuing. Undoubtedly, the chilling effect exists in many marriages and leads to destructive conflict.

Unfortunately, divorce from a physically violent partner may not mark the end of the relationship, especially in cases where there are children. The typical case is the mother with custody of the children who is expected to facilitate the children's visits with the father. The mother continues to be at risk of violence and the children will undoubtedly be affected by exposure to the violence. The history of intimate violence is not always known by the courts, and even when it is, it is not often considered an important factor in visitation and custody decisions (Hardesty & Chung, 2006).

Parent-Child Destructive Conflict   In 2008, approximately 772,000 children were shown to have been victims of child abuse and neglect in the United States. Seventy-one percent of the 772,000 were neglected, 16 percent were physically abused, and 9 percent were sexually abused (U.S. Department of Health and Human Services, 2010). Clearly, child abuse is a large societal problem that has implications for the present and the future. Cahn and Lloyd (1996) reported that children who see their parents hit one another are also hit, that sons who have violent fathers become abusive to their wives, and that one in five who were sexually abused as kids repeat the abuse with their own children. However, Segrin and Flora (2005) caution that there are multiple ways of interpreting the research findings that suggest that abused children become abusers: "Most abused children do not go on to abuse their own children, but a history of child abuse greatly increases the risk of later perpetrating child abuse" (p. 354). Although this section focuses primarily on negative things that family members *do* to each other, it is also important to note that child neglect, or what parents *fail to do* for their children, can be just as severe (Segrin & Flora, 2005).

According to Wilson and Whipple (1995), "Physical child abuse is a societal tragedy of immense proportion" (p. 317). They argue that abusive parents view their children as more difficult, and therefore needing more power-assertive forms of punishment, such as threats, reprimands, whippings, and orders to comply, rather than suggestions for altering their behaviors. Abusive mothers rank the value of punishment higher than abusive dads and nonabusive couples. Abusive parents send mixed messages by failing to enforce rules consistently and then hitting or kicking children for disobeying. "Child abuse has devastating psychological and interpersonal effects on children both while they are young as well as later in life when they are at heightened risk for abusing their own children" (Segrin & Flora, 2005, p. 369). The effects of physical conflict in families takes a severe toll on members' relationships, as indicated in the following example.

As I got older and more mischievous, I became more and more familiar with the sting of my father's belt and the resultant welts and bruises that were not only across my legs and backside, but around my wrists where my father held me so I couldn't get away. Finally, when I was about 11 and tired of being embarrassed to wear shorts in gym class, and of making up stories to explain my welts, I turned on my father as he brought down the belt, caught it and tried to yank it from his hand. I was never spanked again.

An analysis of eight observational studies of parent-child interactions revealed that families with a documented history of child abuse or neglect had different interaction patterns than did families with no history of child abuse or neglect. Specifically, parental physical negative touch (e.g., hitting, slapping, spanking) was more frequent in families with documented histories of child abuse or neglect. In addition, child noncompliance was less frequent in the families with no history of child abuse or neglect (Wilson, Shi, Tirmenstein, Norris, & Rack, 2006). A social-interactional explanation for child abuse is that physically abusive parents react in an inconsistent and ineffective manner to children's noncompliance, thus using physical discipline more quickly than nonabusive parents (Wilson, Xiaowei, Tirmenstein, Norris, & Rack, 2006).

Even in situations where there is no physical abuse, mothers have more of a tendency to interact with their children in negative ways. For instance, a mother's level of child abuse potential was found to be related to how much she used affirming or soliciting behavior in interacting with her child; women who had a higher child abuse potential were less likely to use such behaviors (Wilson, Morgan, Hayes, Bylund, & Herman, 2004).

Verbal abuse or verbal aggressiveness directed from a parent to a child represents another form of child abuse. In one study, mothers who tended to be more verbally aggressive in their behaviors were also more likely to vocalize negative thoughts about their children (Wilson, Hayes, Bylund, Rack, & Herman, 2006) and to use directives to control the choice, rate, and duration of activities (Wilson, Roberts, Rack, & Delaney, 2008).

Incest represents the most extreme form of family violence. Usually cloaked in a family secret only held by the victim and the perpetrator, incest is often not revealed until adulthood, when the victim has left the family home. In their study of sexual abuse in children and adolescents, Petronio and colleagues (1996) found that victims are bound by rules enforced by those who violate them. The victims were vigilant about guarding the release of information about the abuse; they wanted to be in control of what would happen if they disclosed the truth. The authors concluded that "trust is so central in their decision to tell" (p. 196). Too many children fear they will be held accountable for any legal action, such as parental arrest, or be beaten for their disclosure of parental abuse. The increasing evidence of incest led some researchers to warn that incest occurs in families that are not classified as pathological or perceived as dysfunctional. Incest is related to family stress, and poor management of conflict certainly heightens stress. Extreme male dominance of the family, plus weakness in the mother caused by illness, disability, or sometimes death, correlates highly with rates of incest. Further, women who have been abused both in their families-of-origin and by their husbands are more likely to be forced to accept abuse, resulting in submissiveness. According to Ferguson (1996), "Perpetrators are most often fathers or father surrogates (stepfather, mother's boyfriend, uncle) and the victims are most often daughters" (p. 3).

Children are not always the victims, however. Sometimes parents are the recipients of physical or verbal abuse from their adolescent children. Parents in such situations often feel powerless to stop the abuse. They feel that they have lost the power to be a parent and that they can't turn to the legal system for help. A parent being abused by an adolescent may disengage from that child. Following a family systems perspective, it is not surprising that adolescent-parent abuse affects the parents' marital relationship as well as other family relationships (Eckstein, 2002). Finally, it should be noted that what is considered to be family physical or verbal abuse in the United States may be viewed as acceptable disciplinary behaviors in other parts of the world (McGoldrick, Giordano, & Garcia-Preto, 2005).

CONSTRUCTIVE CONFLICT

Learning skills to deal constructively with conflict can have an optimal effect on family relationships for years to come. Indeed, a couple's ability to handle conflict well can have benefits for their children. "Children who see their parents successfully resolve conflicts and share affection might be expected to feel secure about the future of their family and about their own relationships" (Cox & Harter, 2002, p. 172). When children witness such conflict resolution practices it may affect their responses to future conflicts that they encounter (Davies, et al., 1999). Additionally, among engaged couples in which male partners had experience with parental violence, there was more negative communication and negative affect expressed in their interactions (Halford, Sanders, & Behrens, 2000) than in couples where the male partner had not experienced parental violence.

In successful conflict management experiences, happy couples or children go through validation sequences (Gottman, 1979). They know they can either agree or disagree and bring out their ideas and feelings during an argument. If family members can listen to one another, they can better understand motives, opinions, and feelings. Because children are younger and have less vocabulary to use, they must have a climate in which they can participate in the disagreement, if the conflict relates to them. Children's responses to harsh messages vary greatly; some children are sensitive and will suffer immediately; others do not show any harm for a long time (Vissing & Baily, 1996). Parents can effectively model conflict management, as illustrated by the following example.

One of the things that characterizes both my parents is their willingness and ability to listen. They may not always agree with us or let us do the things we want, but no one feels like they don't care. At least we feel like they heard us, and usually they explain their responses pretty carefully if they don't agree with us. As a teenager, I was always testing my limits. I can remember arguing for hours to go on a camping trip with my male and female friends. My mother really understood what I wanted and why I wanted to go, but she made it clear that she could not permit such a move at that time. Yet I really felt that she shared my disappointment, although she stuck to her guns.

In a study of couples and argument practices, researchers found that when disagreements were negatively responded to by both partners, the couple had an unhappy relationship. Agreements and acknowledgments correlated positively with control mutuality and relational length (Canary, Weger, & Stafford, 1991). Another study reported that romantic partners who had more displays and experiences of love also dealt with conflict more constructively than romantic partners without as many displays and experiences of love (Gonzaga, Keltner, Londahl, & Smith, 2001).

Based on his research with 2,000 couples, Gottman (1994b) concluded that satisfied couples maintain a five-to-one ratio of positivity to negativity (1994). He found that it was not the way couples handled their compatibilities that prevented divorces, but how they communicated about their incompatibilities. The single positivity-to-negativity factor determined longevity, despite fighting styles that ranged from openly combative to passive-aggressive. Additionally, couples exhibiting a collaborative conflict management style (Figure 9.1) had higher marital satisfaction than couples who did not use a collaborative style (Greeff & de Bruyne, 2000).

Other studies have shown that satisfied family members often overlook conflicts or choose communication behaviors that decrease the chance of escalation (Roloff, 1987), and families that control negative emotional behaviors have an easier time of solving problems (Forgatch, 1989). In conflict, the use of direct strategies related positively to marital satisfaction. The use of indirect coercive strategies—such as complaining, criticizing, put-downs, and ignoring—led to unproductive negative conflict outcomes (Aida & Falbo, 1991).

Families appear to manage conflict creatively by recognizing that they have a twofold responsibility: to meet their individual needs and wants as well as to further the family system. This requires communicative give-and-take, resulting in compromise. These beliefs enhance flexibility and help to avoid conflicts that result from being too rigid or assuming that one family member's views must be followed. In a comparison of abusive and nonabusive mothers, Wilson and Whipple (1995) reported that nonabusive mothers exhibited flexibility by introducing more topics into discussions, giving more verbal and nonverbal instructions, and utilizing more signs of verbal and nonverbal affection. These nonabusive parents used more inductive or indirect strategies—such as time-outs, withdrawing privileges, explaining consequences, and so on—to discipline their children. If the system is flexible and differentiated, family members can more readily accommodate one another, learn new ideas from other members and themselves, and change. In a study of gay and lesbian couples and heterosexual couples, Kurdek(1994) found relationship satisfaction depended on the degree of investment in the partnership and the use of positive strategies to problem solve and resolve conflicts. Thus, a climate of validation or confirmation establishes the tone for constructive interaction.

Strategies for Constructive Conflict

Although Chapter 12 describes specific methods of improving family communication, three constructive conflict behaviors will be briefly discussed here: listening, fair fighting, and managing the physical environment.

Listening Empathic listening serves as the cornerstone of constructive conflict. Attentive listening serves to defuse conflict and helps clarify and focus the issues being debated. Empathic listening requires that one listens without judging while attempting to recognize the feelings and attitudes behind the other's remarks. A comment such as "You're really angry" or "That had to bring up all the sadness again" indicates to a family member that the other has listened yet not become trapped within his or her own emotions. Restating what one has heard another person say can be most helpful in clarifying a point or slowing the escalation of conflict. "Alex, are you saying . . .?" Asking Alex to repeat his point is another helpful approach. Some partners will go so far as to switch roles in a conflict and repeat the scene to check out the accusations. It gives one partner a chance to try out the other's feelings.

Although it may not always be a conscious strategy, the capacity to use humor and affection in the midst of a disagreement has the power to defuse the power of the argument. In their study of newlywed couples' daily interactions, Driver & Gottman (2004) found that one couples' fleeting moment of shared laughter and positive emotion "turned out to be one of the most important moments in the couple's discussion" (p. 302). The authors depicted a moment when, in the midst of an argument, the wife asked her husband about his blackened white socks and he replied with a comment about having to chase a raccoon out of the yard without having time to find shoes. The partners' ability to use positive affect in such a moment predicted future health of the relationship. After studying videotapes of 130 couples the researchers concluded that it would be difficult to teach partners to use positive affect during conflict but suggested that one partner's enthusiasm in daily moments impacts the other partner's affection during conflict.

Fair Fighting Many bitter family conflicts result from the use of unfair tactics by various members; this can be changed with a commitment to fair fighting. In a fair fight, equal time must be provided for all participants; name-calling or "below-the-belt" remarks are prohibited. In this process, family members agree on how they will disagree, including specifying shared speaking time and topic limitations. Such strategies can be used only with the mutual consent of the parties involved and the assurance that each will listen to the other's messages. Distressed couples have great difficulty in fighting fairly. They readily exchange one-for-one negative remarks and cannot cycle out of negative feedback loops. They continue blaming and fail to build on remarks that would lead to change and solve the conflict (Weiss & Dehle, 1994). An unfair example of conflict and the use of name-calling to "hit below the belt" is demonstrated in the following example.

My mother always used a lot of verbal attacks to "handle" conflict. Put-downs definitely intensified bad feelings. My mother knew the exact names to call me that really hurt. She used to call me Chubby, Fatso, and other similar words. These words only made me angrier and never settled any argument. My mother rarely used swear words when she was yelling, but if she called me those names, I would usually start swearing at her. When she went into treatment for drug abuse, the whole family got involved and through counseling we learned to avoid the "red flag" words that would set each other off.

In fair fighting, family members try to stay in the present and not bring up past fights or grievances. They specify what it is that they feel caused the conflict. Each family member takes responsibility for his or her part in the fight and does not blame the others. Jim tells his wife, "I really felt angry this evening when you told Rebecca that she didn't have to go to the church program with us. I worry that you give her more freedom than she can handle." In this approach, Jim continues to release his anger during the time granted to him by his wife. According to the rules of fair fighting, he can express his anger only verbally—no hitting or throwing things. Michelle can deny the charges Jim makes, which can lead to a careful recounting of what was said and with what intended meanings. This often helps clear the air. She can also ask for a break until later if she becomes angry and cannot listen.

Sometimes flexibility and compromise will not solve conflicts. An individual's self-image may be more important than family expectations of flexibility. Some families permit members to decide what is negotiable and nonnegotiable for them. Stating "This is not negotiable for me at this time" enables one to own his or her position and part of the problem. Speaking tentatively and including a phrase such as *"at this time"* leaves the door open for future discussion. The following is an example of a partner who works hard to resolve conflicts.

If I feel like Italian food and Roger, my husband, has his heart set on Chinese food, Chinese it is. I have never thrived on conflict, and will avoid it by settling for less, especially on "little things." In the case of a more serious conflict, I try to problem-solve. I believe that two people in conflict should never go to bed mad at each other. If the problem is big enough to cause conflict, it is worth the time and effort to solve it, for the sake of the relationship.

It goes without saying that cross-complaining defeats the purposes of fair fighting. In cross-complaining, one partner ignores the complaint of the other and counters with his or her own complaint. Both parents and children can get caught up in an endless cycle of "You did this!" followed by "But you did the same thing yesterday!"

Whatever rules or methods couples use in their fighting, the nonverbal aspects of conflict need special attention. Careful monitoring of nonverbal cues often reveals the true nature of conflict (Gottman, 1994c). Threatening gestures, rolling eyes, or refusals to look at others indicate the intensity of the conflict. Gottman observed that "nonverbal behavior discriminates distressed from nondistressed couples better than verbal behavior" (p. 469). Sometimes nonverbal cues contradict verbal statements. A receiver of such mixed messages must decide "Do I believe what I hear or what I see?" Supportive nonverbal cues may drastically reduce conflict; a soothing touch or reassuring glance has great healing powers.

Managing the Physical Environment   Choice of space may dampen certain conflicts. Sitting directly across from someone makes for easy eye contact and less chance for missing important verbal or nonverbal messages. Conflicting family members need to be aware of all the factors that can escalate a fight. Choosing an appropriate and private space lessens distractions or related problems.

One thing I have learned about fighting with my teenaged son is never to raise an argumentative issue when he is in his bedroom. Whenever we used to fight, I would go up to talk to him about school or about his jobs in the house, and five minutes after we started arguing, I would suddenly get so upset about his messy room that we would fight about that also. By now I've learned to ask him to come out or to wait until he is in another part of the house to voice a complaint.

The rewards of better-managed family conflicts are numerous. Use of positive communication practices slows the cumulative aspect of conflicts. A series of minor conflicts left unresolved can escalate into separation, divorce, or emotionless relationships. Successful resolution of conflict leads to emotional reconciliation. Effective conflict skills lead to greater appreciation for and enjoyment of each family member. The following summary of strategies for constructive conflict reflects integration of many pieces of prescriptive advice. As you will note, certain strategies are valued, but across different cultures, other strategies may be seen as more critical.

Elements of Constructive Conflict

The following descriptors characterize successful conflict management:

1. A sequential exchange takes place in which each participant has equal time to express his or her point of view.
2. Feelings are brought out appropriately, not suppressed.
3. People listen to one another with empathy and without constant interruption.

4. This conflict remains focused on the issue and does not get side-tracked into other previously unsolved conflict.
5. Family members respect differences in one another's opinions, values, and wishes.
6. Members believe that solutions are possible and that growth and development will take place.
7. Some semblance of functional rules has evolved from past conflicts.
8. Members have experience with problem solving as a process to settle differences.
9. Little power or control is exercised by one or more family members over the actions of others.

Families that are inconsistent in going through the phases of problem solving do not view a new conflict as a challenge to think creatively; rather, they resort to using old solutions. More consistent families engage all members as they search for new ways to creatively handle problems (Kieren, Maguire, & Hurlbut, 1996).

Constructive conflict management and resolution strategies seldom emerge if older family members do not model them and young people fail to learn these communication and problem-solving skills. Also, guidelines for disagreement must be culture-sensitive to be effective.

After years of researching conflict and social influence, Roloff (2009) identified practical points of conflictual practice including the following:

- Do not assume lack of argument indicates agreement.
- What you do not do matters as much as what you actually do.
- Silence does not mean the conflict is over.
- Some conflicts are intractable and serial arguing will occur.
- Serial arguments create predictable and dysfunctional repetitive patterns.

CONCLUSION

Given the many stresses families face in today's world, conflict management becomes an important critical skill. Because "whatever the stress, the more partners are able to support each other, to understand and respond empathically, the greater their marital satisfaction" (Giblin, 1994, p. 49). In this chapter, we have presented a variety of ideas about conflict. We view conflicts as inevitable, potentially rewarding, and leading to the resolution of differences within families. From a dialectic perspective, the potential for conflict is always present in families, the tension residing in the relationships and not individuals. Conflict is a dialectical force of opposites continually present in a state of fluctuation, adjustment, and change.

In Review

1. Take a position and discuss whether conflict is inevitable and necessary for the development of family relationships.

2. Using the stages of family conflict, describe a recurring conflict in a real or fictional family.
3. Interview three persons about their attitudes toward conflict that they learned in their family-of-origin and how they perceive they have learned to manage conflict today.
4. Relate examples from your own experiences with families that might agree with Gottman's conclusion that couples can encounter conflict, but the ratio needs to be five positive experiences to one negative over time if a relationship is to last.
5. Give an example of constructive conflict in a real or fictional family.

KEY WORDS

Communication and Family Developmental Stresses

"Families comprise people who have a shared history and a shared
future. They encompass the entire emotional system of at least
three, and frequently now four or even five, generations held
together by blood, legal, and/or historical ties. Relationships
with parents, siblings, and other family members go through
transitions as they move along the life cycle."

—Betty Carter and Monica McGoldrick,
The Expanded Family Life Cycle

Ashley and Tom Rybecki, parents of three teenagers, never imagined spending time in the Dean
of Students' office at Emerson High School. Last year Grace graduated with high honors,
having spent her four years intensely involved with the debate team and the student council.
She represented the school at the National Debate Tournament for three years and won the
Best Speaker award as a senior. Currently she is studying in Spain before starting college.
Dan, a senior, has played on the varsity basketball team since the middle of freshman year and
is president of the high school's community outreach program. Holly, a freshman, is in danger
of failing four classes due to attendance problems, poor test scores, and missing homework.
Although Holly was supposed to be involved in chorus and her church group, she seldom
attends, choosing to hang out at her boyfriend's house or at the park with her friends. Today's
discussion centers on how to re-engage Holly and prevent her from failing freshman year.

   As part of the discussion, Ashley recounted some experiences of the past year to Dean
Ricardo. Tom's manager assigned him to manage a big account for a client on the West Coast
for six months, necessitating weekly travel. Ashley returned to full-time nursing in order to
earn additional money for college tuition, and Tom's mother, who lives nearby, broke her hip
and still requires many hours of attention each week. Tom and Ashley find themselves holding
a painful conversation with Holly, raising questions such as "Why didn't you tell us you were in

such trouble?" "Why didn't we see what was going on?" and "Why didn't Dan tell us how bad things were?" Holly suggests that she is not one of their "star" children and that they expect too much from her.

At age 71, after 48 years of marriage, Bobby Ashford was diagnosed with stage 4 lung cancer. A smoker since his teenage years, Bobby fought the addiction for the past twenty years, always falling back into old patterns when tough times arose at the automotive garage he owned with his brother. Although he worked six days a week and sometimes on Sunday, he and his wife Sandra managed to raise three sons and, at this point, they have eight grandchildren, some of whom worked at the garage part-time while they were in school. "Gramps" is very special to everyone in the family. For the past seven months the family has struggled with the news and their emotions. Yet it is clear that time is running out.

With their doctor's guidance Bobby and Sandra investigated using hospice home care rather than having Bobby die in a hospital because they thought this would be easier on the family. The hospice staff has been coming regularly for the past three weeks, providing support to Bobby and his relatives. The grandchildren come by every day to play cards or listen to music with their grandfather. Sometimes they go through some of the old family photographs from their childhood to remember the good times, especially the vacation week at the beach each year. Sandra wanders in and out until the children and grandchildren leave. Then she sits in bed next to Bobby while knitting a blanket for their ninth grandchild who will be born next month. It's clear that Bobby is struggling more each day and that the end is near. Bobby tells her she will be alright because she is a strong woman with many people who love her.

Families change continually as time and events alter their lives; some events are developmental and predictable as passing years lead to maturation. Yet unpredictable events occur, defying usual expectations, such as family disruptions caused by poverty, severe illness, unemployment, or the termination of significant relationships. Major unforeseen events alter developmental patterns. Certain families encounter quite different experiences from other families because "life course perspectives and historical accounts of the lives of ethnic/minority families suggest that, in fact, the developmental pathways of African Americans, Hispanics, Native Americans and recent Asian American immigrants may be quite different from those of mainstream individuals" (Dilworth-Anderson & Burton, 1996, p. 326). Anytime a family or a specific member experiences a catastrophic change, communication plays a critical role in negotiating the transitions involved. Each family influences the following one, like a great chain of connections from previous generations to the present. Current family patterns will affect three or more generations.

The *developmental* perspective assumes that change occurs throughout our lives; we adapt our communication behaviors to our individual changes and the relational changes we experience as others' lives transform as well. The family mobile shifts according to the winds of developmental change and outside stressors. Every family experiences stresses at different points across the years. For example, the pressures that adolescents can place on a family system are illustrated in the following entry.

"Jesus, Mary, and Joseph, save my soul!" can be heard from the lips of my mother at least once a day. Mom thought three in diapers was bad but since has decided three teens are worse. Presently, we have three teens in Driver's Ed, three teens tying up the phone, three teens falling in and out of love. Mom threatens to run away once a day. Dad says we drive him crazy and should be locked up until we go away to college.

What has marked your family's changes? Most families acknowledge *marker events,* or the transition points in human development. A child's first steps, a bar mitzvah, a teenager's driver's license, a wedding or the birth of a baby all may mark major changes. Families that experience major outside stresses perceive unpredictable crises as significant symbols of change—winning the lottery, a parent's lung cancer surgery, or the accidental death of a sibling may symbolize a family's most significant moment of change.

Family worldviews affect members' perceptions of stresses. If one person perceives the world as chaotic, disorganized, and frequently dangerous, any change may be upsetting. Conversely, if another member views the world as predictable, and reasonably ordered, change may be perceived as manageable. How a family responds to stress depends on its organizational structure prior to the stress, its position on the cohesion-flexibility continuum, and its images, themes, boundaries and biosocial beliefs.

This chapter addresses family communication patterns related to developmental and life-course changes that are reasonably predictable; the following chapter focuses on a range of unpredictable stresses. Communication plays an important part in negotiating transitions and coping processes.

OVERVIEW OF FAMILY CHANGE

Developmental Stage and Life-Course Issues

The terms *developmental stages* and *life-course issues* are central to an understanding of change and communication in family life. Individual developmental stages refer to one's experience of critical periods of change, or life stages, until death (Erickson, 1968; Levinson, 1978; Rogers & White, 1993; Carter & McGoldrick, 2005). Sometimes these stages are referred to as *seasons* of one's life.

Communication between individuals not only reflects their environment but depends on their experiences and which life-cycle stage they are experiencing. Stress occurs when the individual's level of personal functioning cannot manage the problems in his or her social environment. The original work on developmental stages addressed only individual issues; eventually, family theorists developed life stage or developmental models of families. Early writings about the family life cycle reflected the position that "normal" couples remained intact from youthful marriage through child rearing to death in later years (Carter & McGoldrick, 2005b). Therefore, the communication components of these developmental stages were viewed as reasonably predictable.

The conception of family developmental stages has changed. Original models of family developmental stages reflected the lives of middle-class, intact, white families. Theorists believed unpredictable events, such as untimely death, divorce, or pregnancy outside marriage, prevented families from experiencing "on time" or normative life-cycle developments. Today, family theorists consider divorce or solo parenting as part of a wider view of stages. For example, Carter and McGoldrick (2005b) conceptualize divorce as an interruption or dislocation that restructures the family; rather than supporting a "straight line" model of family development, they consider it as a path with forks in the road along the way.

A *life-course approach* focusing on transitions and trajectories provides another valuable way to understand change because individual life trajectories are linked with others' trajectories, especially family members (Bianchi & Casper, 2005). The focus includes understanding "how varying events and their timing in the lives of individuals affected families in a particular historical context" (Aldous, 1990, p. 573). It includes changes in individuals, families, and social organizations over historical time. "The fluidity of family structures requires most families to deal with several family structural transitions during the life course (Price, Price, &

Like individuals, whole family systems also pass through various "seasons" of their lives.

McKenry, 2010b, p. 2). This perspective, for example, recognizes that individuals and families living in the new millennium are dealing with stresses affecting this historical period, such as environmental concerns, economic uncertainties, and concerns about adequate family medical care, globalization, new reproductive technologies, and terrorism.

Technology provides one lens through which to view how current life-course issues impact the family. Members' stress levels can be affected instantaneously via cell phones, laptops, tweets, e-mail, Blackberries and IM; posts on Facebook or other networking sites carry instantaneous news of events and people. These ever-evolving devices force attention to concerns as they occur and contribute to stress if they force people to be "on call" 24 hours a day. Laptops extend the workday; cell phones link parents and teens continuously. These technological devices have dramatically altered family life over the past decade.

A *life-course perspective* focuses on three types of *time*: individual time, generational time, and historical time. *Individual time* refers to chronological age, *generational time* refers to "family time" or the positions and roles individuals hold in families (grandmother, breadwinner), and *historical time* refers to events that occur during the era in which one lives (e.g., the Civil Rights movement; the birth of the Internet; September 11, 2001; or the Gulf oil spill). From a life-course perspective, events tend to be thought of as "on time" or "off time." Whereas most individuals marry in their twenties (traditionally viewed as on time), today, individuals may marry for the first time in their forties or choose to cohabit in a committed relationships for decades. Increasing numbers of women are becoming mothers, single or partnered, biologically or through new technologies, well into their late forties or early fifties. Many individuals will experience three or four careers before leaving the workforce, return to college multiple times to earn multiple degrees, or work until they are in their eighties. Such variations are considered "off time" compared to historical norms but they are not unique.

One way to connect the developmental-stage perspective and the life-course perspective is by adding greater diversity to the developmental perspective. For example, imagine a subcategory for 18- to 29-year-olds who remain living at home because jobs are scarce or because they returned home after failed marriages. In fact, some scholars have suggested that the later teenage years through most of the next decade should be considered a separate developmental stage (Arnett, 2004). Taking a life-course perspective suggests that when crises occur an individual family member's education, income, occupation, values, and satisfaction or dissatisfaction with life may be more significant than his or her placement within a family stage.

Future generations of families will be represented by elongated generational structures due to the recent changes in population growth in industrialized nations, another life-course factor. Bengston (2001) reported that due to increases in longevity and decreases in fertility, the population age structure in these nations has changed from a pyramid to a rectangle, creating "a family structure in which the shape is long and thin, with more family generations alive but with fewer members in the generation" (p. 5). In some countries, such as China, the effect will be an inverted pyramid as four grandparents may have only one grandchild (Greenhalgh,

2008). This creates shifts in relational interaction as elder generations compete for connections to limited numbers of grandchildren and great-grandchildren. Multi-generational bonds grow in significance as this population and its longevity will result in an increase in shared years together. No single model can reflect all family growth complexities. The life-course approach allows for more variation in under-standing stress and depicts differentiation as normal rather than as a deviation. The following represents some perspectives on family development with recognition of life-course issues, while drawing implications for family communication.

Sources of Family Stress: A Model

In their work on change in the family life cycle, Carter and McGoldrick (2005) present a model depicting the flow of stress through the family by identifying stres-sors that reflect family anxiety and affect the family system (Figure 10.1). Stressors reflect two time dimensions. The *vertical stressors* bring past and present issues to bear on the family; *horizontal stressors* represent issues that are developmental and unfolding. The vertical stressors include unique family patterns of relating that are transmitted across generations, including family attitudes, values, expectations, secrets, rules, societal pressures, and individual makeup. In other words, "These aspects of our lives are like the hand we are dealt" (Carter and McGoldrick, p. 5). The authors argue that within the same family, individual members experience and react to these stresses differently. Stress varies with the position and age of each family member. Many of these communication-related stressors were discussed earlier as the images, themes, myths, rules, boundaries, and expectations that come from the family-of-origin.

The horizontal flow in the system includes the anxiety produced by the stresses on the family as it moves across time—both the predictable (developmental stressors), the unpredictable events that disrupt the life cycle, and major historical events. Current life-event stressors interact with one another and with the vertical stressors to cause disruption in the family system. The greater the anxiety gener-ated in the family at any transition point, the more difficult the transition.

The past and present family stresses are affected by all levels of the larger sys-tems in which the family operates. These are the life course concerns—social, cul-tural, economic, and political contextual factors. One's community, family, and personal resources also contribute to the process of moving through life. This model is too complex for us to develop in two chapters, yet it gives you a sense of the enormous number of life variations experienced in the everyday world.

The developmental approach emphasizes stages, focusing on the linear pro-gression of families moving through the life cycle; increasingly more families experience a nonlinear sequence reflecting the life-course approach. Many of these families have been affected by social and structural forces such as racism, unem-ployment, technology, and poverty. As you move through phases of your individual and family existence, these forces will positively or negatively influence the process. Thus, these three major factors—vertical stressors, horizontal stressors, and system levels—taken together put a family's life cycle and its life-course position into perspective.

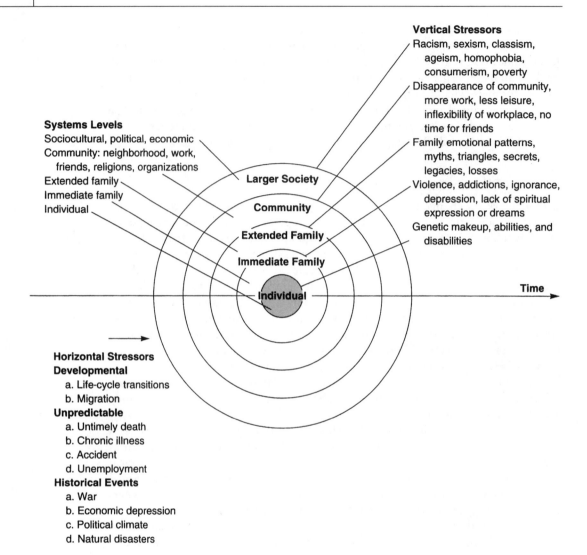

Vertical Stressors
Racism, sexism, classism,
  ageism, homophobia,
  consumerism, poverty
Disappearance of community,
  more work, less leisure,
  inflexibility of workplace, no
  time for friends
Family emotional patterns,
  myths, triangles, secrets,
  legacies, losses
Violence, addictions, ignorance,
  depression, lack of spiritual
  expression or dreams
Genetic makeup, abilities, and
  disabilities

Systems Levels
Sociocultural, political, economic
Community: neighborhood, work,
  friends, religions, organizations
Extended family
Immediate family
Individual

Larger Society

Community

Extended Family

Immediate Family

Individual

Time

Horizontal Stressors
Developmental
  a. Life-cycle transitions
  b. Migration
Unpredictable
  a. Untimely death
  b. Chronic illness
  c. Accident
  d. Unemployment
Historical Events
  a. War
  b. Economic depression
  c. Political climate
  d. Natural disasters

FIGURE 10.1
Flow of Stress Through the Family

Source: From Carter, B. & McGoldrick, M. *The Expanded Family Life Cycle,* 3/e, © 2005. Published by Allyn and Bacon, Boston, MA. Copyright © 2005 by Pearson Education. Reprinted by permission of the publisher.

FAMILY STAGES AND LIFE COURSE

Although based on the traditional life-cycle or life-stages approach, this section will integrate aspects of the life-course approach in order to broaden the discussion and recognize familial variations that affect family communication. Traditionally, family researchers applied the stage concept to whole families so that the entire system could be thought of as moving through particular stages. Experts (Carter & McGoldrick, 2005; Duvall, 1988; Hill, 1986) describe the process as including from 6 to 12 stages. Such analysis has difficulties because families consist of several individuals in different life stages at the same time. Such frameworks provide simplicity but seldom effectively account for families with numerous children or children widely spaced by age as they go through the middle stages of development. Childless partners remain overlooked.

No matter which framework is adopted, communication emerges as a critical issue across the lifespan. The following stages are most appropriately applied to the two-parent, middle-class American family life cycle. These stages, detailed by Carter and McGoldrick (2005), will be used for discussion. Table 10.1 describes the stages of the family life cycle.

Independent Life Stage

Young adulthood has received more attention in the past decade because the life experiences are more diverse than in previous generations. Although this stage seldom appears on other life-cycle lists, Carter and McGoldrick (2005) include it as an essential stage, recognizing that the young adult must come to terms with his or her family-of-origin and separating or leaving home to enter a new cycle. The unattached young adult faces developmental tasks in areas of work and relationships. These play out differently, depending on social class and ethnicity. For example, in recent years this stage has been confounded by economic stresses that keep many young adults dependent on their parents. In addition, the traditional parental separation process has been affected by changes in the separation/individuation process reflecting cultural changes. Increasing numbers of Mexican and other Latino families deemphasize offspring independence in favor of close family ties (Falicov, 2005). Recent severe economic pressures may keep young adults living at home indefinitely (Vogt, 2009).

Managing this task successfully prevents certain communication problems from developing in the stages that follow. Young people need sufficient autonomy to separate and achieve their goals independently. The goal is healthy interdependence, with the parents loosening ties and the young adults establishing themselves in the workplace, completing their education, and creating close adult friendships and peer networks. Establishing the "self" as separate yet a part of the family-of-origin remains the objective. Ideally, the young adult feels free to achieve his or her own goals and command the respect and encouragement of his or her parents, even if they might have hoped for other outcomes. Parents and children move through this stage successfully when they learn to accept separation and independence while remaining connected, tolerating difference and ambiguity in an adult child's career choice and accepting of a range of intense emotional attachments and life styles outside the family (Aylmer, 1988, p. 195). Most young people and their parents have been finding increasingly open ways to communicate throughout adolescence; at this stage adult-to-adult communication patterns emerge more fully, as seen in following example.

My older stepbrothers cannot believe that I talk with my mother at least once a day, but I've learned to treat her like a friend and I rely on her for advice. There are some things I don't talk about since she would not approve of some of my choices, but generally she serves as a good sounding board and sometimes she asks me for advice.

TABLE 10.1

The Stages of the Family Life Cycle

Family Life Cycle Stage	Emotional Process of Transition: Key Principles	Second-Order Changes in the Family Status Required to Proceed Developmentally
Leaving home: single young adults	Accepting emotional and financial responsibility for self	a. Differentiation of self in relation to family-of-origin b. Development of intimate peer relationships c. Establishment of self in respect to work and financial independence
The joining of families through marriage: the new couple	Commitment to new system	a. Formation of marital system b. Realignment of relationships with extended families and friends to include spouse
Families with young children	Accepting new members into the system	a. Adjusting marital system to make space for children b. Joining in child rearing, financial, and household tasks c. Realignment of relationships with extended family to include parenting and grandparenting roles
Families with adolescents	Increasing flexibility of family boundaries to permit children's independence and grandparents' families	a. Shifting of parent-child relationships to permit adolescents to move into and out of system b. Refocus on midlife marital and career issues c. Beginning shift toward caring for older generation
Launching children and moving on	Accepting a multitude of exits from and entries into the family system	a. Renegotiation of marital system as a dyad b. Development of adult-to-adult relationships between grown children and their parents c. Realignment of relationships to include in-laws and grandchildren d. Dealing with disabilities and death of parents (grandparents)
Families in later life	Accepting the shifting generational roles	a. Maintaining own and/or couple functioning and interests in face of physiological decline: exploration of new familial and social role options b. Support for more central role of middle generation c. Making room in the system for the wisdom and experience of the elderly, supporting the older generation without overfunctioning for them d. Dealing with loss of spouse, siblings, and other peers and preparation for death

Source: From Carter, B. & McGoldrick, M. *The Expanded Family Life Cycle,* 3/e, © 2005. Published by Allyn and Bacon, Boston, MA. Copyright © 2005 by Pearson Education. Reprinted by permission of the publisher.

Because of years of advanced schooling and a reluctance to marry early, many young adults invest in intimate peer relationships, some of which may be romantic, and begin the process of exploring deep interpersonal connections. Increasing numbers cohabit with a romantic partner without a commitment to marry. In many cases this results in "sliding" into marriage (Stanley, Rhoades, & Markman, 2006). Researchers argue that inertia, or feeling stuck, impacts the decision of long-term cohabitors to marry since it is harder to end a cohabiting relationship than a noncohabiting dating relationship (Stanley & Rhoades, 2009), thus, they slide into marriage. Conversely, noncohabitors and those who cohabit after becoming engaged make a proactive decision to marry.

Rosenfeld (2007) argued that the independent life stage "fosters a new diversity in the kinds of families young people form" (p. 2), including interracial and same-sex unions that have become more visible and increasingly accepted and single pregnancy at all ages. Interracial marriages continue to rise, as more diverse educational systems bring young people of varied backgrounds into contact. The timing of "coming out" has changed in the gay and lesbian communities. Although "coming out" occurs gradually, about two-thirds of gay or lesbian individuals report having first come out by age 18 (Kaiser Family Foundation, 2001). Many experienced major family stress as they attempted to negotiate their identity and continued presence within the immediate and extended family network. Young people usually come out to mothers before fathers. Although the rate of teen pregnancy is lower than a decade ago, many young adults in their teens or twenties continue to live at home because they are single parents. Increasing numbers of African American and Latino young women are single parents.

Partners

Although many young people remain single or cohabit for years before deciding to marry and others remain in partnered unions indefinitely, sometimes involving a commitment ceremony, some move rather quickly into a marital relationship (Surra, Gray, Cottle, & Boettcher, 2004). A small number remains single throughout their lives.

Marriage or committed partnership affects not only the two individuals involved but their extended families as well as future generations. The couple negotiates a new relational definition, with many other subsystems: parents, siblings, grandparents, nieces and nephews, and friends. Marriage, however, is no longer the defining marker of entering adulthood nor is it the highly predictable event it used to be. Spending time together in a long-term relationship serves a critical function because "the decision to marry is a prediction about how one person's life with another person will evolve in the future based on how it has evolved in the past" (Yerby, Buerkel-Rothfuss, & Bochner, 1990, p. 98).

Partners creating a long-term relationship must resolve three developmental challenges in order to achieve satisfaction in later stages: commitment, power, and closeness. *Commitment* requires each to make the other his or her primary partner and loosen their ties to parents, siblings, and friends. *Power* reflects the dialectical tension between full self-determination and the yielding of power to a partner to strengthen the relationship. *Closeness* involves establishing a balance between separation and attachment that is mutually satisfying for the couple. In this early stage, partners continue to develop rules for distance regulation as they negotiate a mutually satisfying level of interpersonal togetherness. Over time partners revisit the issue of what is an acceptable or unacceptable interpersonal distance, as the following example illustrates.

Sometimes I feel like a piece of Swiss cheese—full of holes. I grew up in a non-touching, often violent family. I realize I hunger for touch and affection. I can cuddle and hold my partner for long periods of time, but he gets uneasy after a while. We have struggled to reach a point where both of us are comfortable and feel our needs are met.

Based on their review of premarital relationship stability, Cate, Levin, and Richmond (2002) developed a commitment model that includes intimacy-oriented relationship behaviors of self-disclosure, frequency of interaction, diversity of interaction, impact of interaction, and sexual intimacy. Involvement over time leads to deeper levels of connection. Partners establish communication boundaries: If certain topics, feelings, or actions frighten or offend the other, rules are developed governing their communication patterns if such concerns arise. Frequently verbal and nonverbal symbols indicate a deepening relationship. "Girlfriend" may be replaced with "partner" or "fiancé." Significant jewelry is exchanged; invitations to special family events such as holiday dinners, are extended. This may differ for some same-sex partners for which the deepening of the relationship may be hidden from relatives or coworkers. As you read the following example, think of the way it would happen in your family.

In my family, we always knew that relationships were serious when the annual family reunion time arrived. If you brought someone, you were expected to formally introduce this person to each member of the clan. However, you didn't choose to go through this ritual, and take all the teasing that followed, unless an engagement was imminent.

The act of bonding, or institutionalizing, the relationship changes the nature of many relationships. Some parents may not be prepared for the separation issues involved. Each family faces the questions of realignment wondering: "How willing are we to accept this new person as an in-law?" Couples must confront the following issues that need to be discussed: spending time with friends, desires for children, sexual needs, career goals and related educational plans, religious participation, money management, housing, in-laws, and acceptable conflict behaviors. Extended family members may become involved. In some cultures, such as Asian Indian Muslim and Christian, marriage brings together families, not just individuals.

Many of these young couples' lives involve extensive involvement within a strong hierarchical extended family (Almeida, 2005). The communication event—the actual ritualized wedding or partnership ceremony—serves as a sign of formal bonding to the outside world. For some couples, a wedding ceremony, representing ethnic customs, also serves as a symbol of negotiating intercultural differences (Leeds-Hurwitz, 2002).

Marriages between young adults involve certain predictable tasks such as (1) separating further from the families-of-origin; (2) negotiating roles, rules, and relationships; and (3) investing in a new relationship. This is a period of unconscious negotiation between the couple and their families-of-origin regarding how the old and new systems will relate to each other. Sometimes marriage holds surprises even when couples have known each other a long time and lived together, as noted in the following example.

I had known my husband since childhood, and we dated since our junior year. Our parents knew each other and we attended the same church, yet we had some real difficulties in the first years of our marriage. We had lived together for six months but I had difficulty in the following areas: First, still learning to live with my husband's habits; second, trying to be a full-time employee and a homemaker; third, deciding at which family's house to celebrate holidays; fourth, telling my husband when I was angry; and fifth, dealing with my husband's mother who kept dropping in unexpectedly.

In some cultures, the task of separating from one's family-of-origin does not occur. In Mexican families parent-child connectedness may remain more powerful than the marital bond; the eldest son and mother bond is particularly strong. Therefore, mothers may remain an integral figure in a young couple's life (Falicov, 2005).

The initial stage of marriage involves trying on the roles of "husband" and "wife" or "partner"—a shift even for those who cohabited for a long time—and holding conversations about the committed relationship. Even a formal commitment ceremony represents a new way of conceiving the partnership; many couples report a deeper sense of "we-ness." Social networks may shift as partners renegotiate issues of time together, with joint friends, and with individual friends. Some partners view marriage as "a solution to life's problems such as loneliness, work/career uncertainty, or extended family difficulties" (Carter & McGoldrick, 2005, p. 232). Because the mother-in-law and daughter-in-law relationship tends to be viewed as the most turbulent tie, although sons-in-law have potentially problematic in-law relationships also (Rittenour & Soliz, 2009), these now-formal links require attention and discussion. After entering a committed relationship, formally or informally, same-sex partners often struggle with similar extended family issues.

Partners' ability to invest in their new relationship relates directly to the quality of their communication. This is a time of investing in their relationship through deeper self-disclosure and open sexual communication. Time, energy, and risk-taking nourish the relationship and establish a range of acceptable intimacy for the system. The previous descriptions assume a two-person relationship. Increasingly marriages involve a woman who has a child or is pregnant with one, frequently fathered by her new husband. In such cases investing in the marital relationship becomes more complicated because the partners are starting out as a group of three or more.

Couple conflict patterns tend to establish themselves within the first two years of marriage and demonstrate great stability; a greater proportion of communication is devoted to marital conflicts that gradually surface (Sillars & Wilmot, 1989). Usually, the balance of power between partners is established early in the marriage based on decision-making behaviors and role performance.

A life-course approach recognizes that marriage may be delayed, follow the birth of one or more children, or never occur. Because of legal restrictions, racism, unemployment, welfare rules, and poverty, many couples follow a nonlinear path of relationship development. Such families construct "developmental pathways in which the timing and ordering of life course transitions such as marriage and childbearing are not comparable to mainstream patterns" (Dilworth-Anderson & Burton, 1996, p. 328).

Most couples eventually become a three-person system, with pregnancy heralding the transition to a new stage. Yet the past decade witnessed the "decoupling" of marriage and childbearing and a continuing increase in nonmarital childbearing (Smock & Greenland, 2010). Same-sex partners face a complicated road as they consider adoption or biological parenthood. When gay males and lesbians choose parenthood they face unique decisions. For example, lesbian partners confront questions such as: How will we become parents? If we use donor insemination, who will be the biological mother? (Chabot & Ames, 2004). Gay males must decide to use one man's sperm or mix their sperm so it is unknown which one is the biological father (Berkowitz & Marsiglio, 2007). In addition, increasing numbers of single women in their thirties and forties are choosing solo parenthood by means of adoption or known or unknown sperm donors (Hertz, 2006).

The period before the children began to arrive was a critical point. If we had not established a really strong, trusting relationship in those first two years, we would have drifted totally apart in the next 23 years of child rearing. We lost most of our time together. If I had it to do over, I would have waited five years before having children, to share who we really were before we tried to deal with who the four new people in our lives were.

Families with Children

The transition to parenthood challenges most new fathers and mothers. Partner communication shifts dramatically as the new role requires significant time and energy. While three phases are discussed here, remember that each family will experience each phase differently, depending on its size, age of its members, and adult family configuration. The three phases are:

- Family with first child
- Family with preschool children (3 to 6 years, possibly with younger siblings)
- Family with school-aged children (oldest child 6 to 12 years, possibly with younger siblings)

A key dynamic characterizing parent-child interaction is the bidirectional nature of this relationship—parents and children experience a mutual influence process (Saphir & Chaffee, 2002). Parents grow and change as a result of their new roles while their children learn and grow from their interactions with their parents.

Although the life course differs for single parents, gays or lesbians with children, and unmarried cohabitors, they will go through variations of these same phases of experience. Therefore, single parents will tend to rely on relatives or hired child-care resources in order to remain employed. Gay male partners find themselves attempting to identify significant female figures to serve as female role models for their children; lesbian couples tend to seek out significant males to play a role in children's lives (Galvin & Patrick, 2009).

Given the complexities of parent-child interactions, the following sections can only highlight certain communication issues.

❙ Parents play a major role in developing a child's communication competence.

Family with First Child   Parenthood occurs later in life than in earlier decades because the age at first marriage has steadily increased. Yet approximately one-third of children, as noted in Chapter 1, an increasing number of children are born to single mothers. Some youths go from adolescence right into adult status as parents, thus speeding up their whole life-course trajectory. Pregnant teens turn their mothers into grandmothers as young as age 30. Typical adolescent communication issues of dating or choosing the right college are replaced with talk about breast-feeding, how to manage school, and supporting the baby. Such stresses complicate partnerships. Couples who entered parenthood before marriage or soon after marriage reported lower marital quality prior to becoming parents than couples who had their baby "on time" or "delayed" (Helms-Erickson, 2001).

No matter when a first pregnancy occurs, significant changes in a couple's relationship follows. When a couple desires a child and the pregnancy is uncomplicated, this time may involve much intimate communication and long-range planning, yet subtle communication changes occur, particularly in conflict patterns.

Three factors that influence couples during the transition to parenthood are their views on parental responsibilities and restrictions, the gratification child rearing holds for them as a couple, and their own marital intimacy and stability. New parents facing this transition "need to renegotiate the reality of their marriage due to both the presence of the child and to their transformed presence with one another with the addition of a new role" (Stamp, 1994, p. 109). To date, much more is known about the role of mothering across childhood and adolescence; less is known about what "kinds" of fathers matter (Crosnoe & Cavanagh, 2010), although the study of fathers is a growth area.

If you have ever lived with a newborn baby, you are well aware how one extremely small person can change an entire household. "There is a gradual decline from the emotional high experienced initially to a state more tempered by negative as well as positive feelings" (Sillars and Wilmot, 1989, p. 233). A key question arises: To what extent is there psychological space in the environment for a child? Children can be born into a relational environment that has psychological space for them, has no psychological space for them, or has a vacuum the child is expected to fill. *Psychological space* refers to the capacity of parents to focus on a child's needs and desires, often limiting their ability to focus on personal or couple needs and desires. Adoptive parents tend to have much greater psychological space because the child has been desired for a long period of time. An unexpected pregnancy may surprise and challenge a middle-age couple who married later in life and did not expect to become pregnant. When a child arrives and the pair becomes a triad, alliances or subsystems may emerge. No longer can all members receive undivided attention at the same time.

New parents must deal with the following communication-related tasks: (1) renegotiating roles, (2) transmitting culture while establishing a community of experiences, and (3) developing the child's communication competence. Moderately flexible families are likely to weather this period more easily than do rigid or chaotic family systems.

Partners' ability to focus on each other declines during early parenthood. New parents may feel inept or exhausted. Whereas women traditionally have assumed the major responsibility for baby care, increasingly fathers are sharing part of the efforts, as indicated in Chapter 7. Even so, mothers may become depressed or overwhelmed with caring for an infant and recovering from child-birth. Partners' plans for how employment responsibilities will be managed factor actively into who engages in child care and how it is accomplished. In their study of new parenting, Huston and Holmes (2004) reported that parenthood expands the workload at home. The arrival of a child increased the number of family-related activities carried out on any given day. For example, new fathers increased their participation in tasks from 1.9 to 2.4 a day and new mothers increased from 3.9 to 5.3 a day. The more husbands thought their wives viewed them as compe-tent, the more husbands contributed to both housework and child care. Increas-ingly, couples with careers tend to delay parenthood. A study of "*on-time*" (becoming a father by age 23) or "*off-time*" (becoming a father after age 40) reveals that late-time fathers are more involved with their children, forming more affective ties with them (Cooney, Pedersen, Indelicato, & Palkovitz, 1993, p. 213). Based on the life-course perspective, late fathers are more able than early fathers to be active parents because their careers are more established and they may have more flexibility at work.

Couple intimacy certainly changes with the birth of a child. Female sexual desire remains low for a period of time; both partners tend to be exhausted from the added responsibilities. Yet, although these parents have limited time for main-taining their adult connections, Huston and Holmes (2004) found that new par-ents tended to laugh together, hug and kiss, and discuss feelings about as often as comparable nonparent partners.

The first child represents a link to posterity and continuation of the family name and heritage—a potentially heavy burden. Naming the child becomes a com-munication event. Names may serve to link family generations or reflect parental dreams. Although families face a decision regarding what a child will call his or her parents and grandparents, gay and lesbian couples face the more complicated decision of what their child should call each of them, such as Daddy and Papa or Mommy and Ema (Chabot & Ames, 2004).

When you think about your future children, or the children you have, what aspects of your family background would you wish to pass on to them? Do you wish they could experience the same type of Passover Seders or Christmas dinners you did as a child? Would you want them to have a strong Pakistani or Chinese identity? What games, songs, or stories would you teach them? An example of struggling with transmission of culture follows.

The birth of our first child revived our ties to our childhood. I suddenly recited nursery rhymes and sang songs I forgot I even knew. I started to talk about sending him to camp because everyone in my family went to camp every summer. Onyi began to make fancy decorated cookies and little cakes that she remembered from her childhood. We both had many Christmas rituals from childhood that we wanted our son to experience.

For many people, a child represents a link to the past and the future and a sense of immortality. Once a couple becomes a triad, certain dormant issues may arise—particularly unresolved ones. The child's future religious affiliation may become a contentious issue. A father's unfulfilled dreams may be transferred to his son. Spousal conflicts arise over what is to be "passed down." The transmission of both the cultural heritage and the family's own heritage may create a complicated communicative task, as this observer reports.

It was amazing for me to watch my sister and her husband with their first child. After almost 25 years, my sister could remember so many of the songs that our mother sang to us as little ones. She and Lee took great pleasure in creating new words and expressions from things that Jonathan did. They set certain patterns for birthday parties, established Friday nights as "family night," and began to take Jonathan to museums, children's theater, and library storybook programs together. They created their own three-person world.

Young parents who develop an independent lifestyle often feel a sudden urge for greater connections with parents, grandparents, and other relatives. Appropriate family and friend boundaries usually require careful negotiation.

Some young unmarried mothers depend on their parents for providing housing and sharing child care. These unmarried mothers and their parents follow different life-course trajectories than a traditional couple with occasional help from the child's grandparents. Some grandparents welcome this; others feel guilty that their own children cannot take care of themselves or "their kids." Often, the unmarried mother at ages 14 to 16 has a working mother somewhere between the ages of 30 and 35 and the great-grandparents have to shoulder the child-care responsibilities. Some new parents remain "on the margins" of their child's life. In her study of low-income black fathers, Hamer (2007) distinguished between two types of fathers—those who were just "fathers," or baby-makers who did not care for their children, and those who were "daddies" and "expressed love, provided social support and companionship, and made their children a central part of their lives" (p. 439). Most of her respondents fell somewhere in the middle. Their ability to parent actively was affected by circumstances such as substance abuse, illegal employment, incarceration, and contention between themselves and the baby's mother.

Parents serve as their children's first communication models, eliciting babies' responses over time. The moment of birth exposes the child to the world of interpersonal contacts, beginning a powerful parent-child bonding process through physical contact, facial/eye contact, and reciprocal vocal stimulation. Most new parents respond to crying babies intuitively by cradling, rocking, or soothing the child (Socha & Yingling, 2010). Parental warmth, support, sensitive responses, and children's temperament and signaling interrelate to create parent-child connections (Peterson, Madden-Derdich, & Leonard, 2000).

A child makes its first contact with the world through touch, and this becomes an essential source of comfort, security, and warmth. The first few months mark the critical beginning of a child's interpersonal learning. A child's personality is being formed in the earliest interchanges with nurturing parents. Children begin to respond to words at age 6 or 7 months; by 9 or 10 months, they can understand a few words and will begin to use language soon thereafter. Parents set the stage for positive interpersonal development by verbally and nonverbally communicating to a child the feeling of being recognized and loved. From a communication perspective, "Couples do not become parents just by virtue of having a child: parenthood is constituted and maintained through conversation" (Stamp, 1994, p. 109). Such conversations occur between partners and between parent and child. Eventually, conversations include stories: birth narratives for biological children and entrance narratives for adopted children (Harrigan, 2010) that reveal a child's identity and family events surrounding his or her arrival.

Most partners experience significant life changes. Mothers tend to experience a dramatic transition after a child's birth; fathers may experience a more dramatic transition to parenthood after the first six months. Whereas fathers expected changes in the early period, such as changes in a partner's body or availability, they are faced with a different reality when things don't shift back as easily as they expected (Huston & Holmes, 2004). Fathers are more likely to confront pressures to remain consistent in their workplace commitments than mothers who have maternity leaves and, in many cases, reduced or altered work expectations. Same-sex partners need to negotiate role responsibilities because they are not presented with strong societal expectations. In cases of open adoption, the adoptive parents will begin to establish the patterns of contact with their child's birth mother or family.

Family with Small Children The preschool family (two- to six-year-old child) experiences less pressure than in the previous period. Parents have learned to cope with a growing child. Barring physical or psychological complications, the former baby now walks, talks, feeds, and entertains himself or herself for longer periods of time.

Three- and four-year-olds exhibit well-developed language skills. A four-year-old may produce well over 2,000 different words, probably understands many more, and can identify tasks and expectations according to gender. Children at this age begin to develop more sophisticated persuasive strategies for gaining such ends as later bedtimes or favorite foods; in many cases children can use multiple strategies to reach their goals. (Socha & Yingling, 2010). And most children over 18 months use negation quite effectively, starting with NO! As children become more independent, parents may directly influence their language acquisition skills through enrichment activities such as reading, role playing, and storytelling. Media increasingly impact children at this age. In addition to watching children's television shows and DVDs, or playing with computerized toys, in many households or day care situations children spend time on the computer, with or without a parent, playing educational games or beginning to participate in e-mail with a grandparent or other older members of the family. Family economic resources directly affect access to these opportunities.

Communication with children differs according to the family's use of restricted or elaborated speech codes, reflecting whether the family tends to be position oriented or person oriented. (This was described in Chapter 1). A child in a position-oriented family learns to rely on a prescribed, or restricted, range of communication behaviors; the child in a person-oriented family is encouraged to use a greater, or elaborated, range of communicative behaviors. These families differ in the degree to which the child is provided with verbalized reasons for performing or not performing certain functions at certain times with certain individuals. Persons growing up in a household where things are done "because I am your father and I say so" do not gain experience in extended conversation or adapting to the unique individuals involved. Elaborated speech codes also prepare children to interact with a wider range of persons outside the family.

Eventually, first-born children may have to incorporate siblings into their world. The arrival of a second or third child moves the triad to a four- or five-person system and places greater stress on the parents. Additional children trigger a birth-order effect, which interacts with sex roles to affect parent-child interaction. You may have heard characteristics attributed to various people because "She is the middle child" or "He is the baby of the family." There appear to be differences in parent-child communication based on sex and position (Sulloway, 1996). Furthermore, each additional child limits the amount of time and contact each child has with the parents and the parents have with each other. Single parents often struggle to find time for themselves. These years set the foundation for a child's ties to many extended family members. For example, children may begin to interact regularly with aunts, establishing a connection that may increase in depth as the years pass or that may be reinvented when the child is closer to young adulthood (Sotirin & Ellingson, 2006).

Sibling competition develops as the family grows. It is more prevalent when children are close in age and the same gender because they have to share parental attention. The sibling relationship is predictably the longest shared familial relationship. It is typically seen as moving from "closeness in early life, distance in middle life, and back to closeness in later life" (Nussbaum, Pecchioni, Baringer, & Kundrat, 2002, p. 379).

A comparison of parenting and children's social, psychological, and academic success across varied family structures revealed that biological or adoptive parents in never-divorced families used more positive parenting and co-parenting practices than did single-parent or cohabiting couples. Children in intact families showed higher levels of adjustment (Bronstein, Clauson, Stoll, & Abrams, 1993). The pressures of parenting are captured in the following example.

Angie was three years old when Gwen was born, and it was a very hard period for her and therefore for us. Angie changed from being a self-sufficient, happy child to a whining clinger who sucked her thumb and started to wet her pants again. Jimmy and I had to work very hard to spend "special" time with her, to praise her, and to let her "help" with the baby when she wanted to. Luckily, Gwen was an easy baby, so we could make the time to interact with Angie the way she needed us to.

The example illustrates why parents need direct communication with an older child or children before the next baby's birth or adoption and during the months that follow. Siblings three or more years older are more likely to treat the baby with affection and interest, because they are more oriented to children their own age and less threatened by the new arrival. A sibling closer in age may engage in aggressive and selfish acts toward the baby.

In the three- to six-year-old stage, children begin to communicate on their own with the outside world. Some attend preschool. At five or six years old, most enter kindergarten. From their young peers, children learn about friendship and establish relationships outside the family. Children's interactions with one another vary in response to each other's gender and social characteristics such as dominance or shyness. By age two most children distinguish boys from girls and within two more years they identify behaviors and tasks according to gender (Garcia-Preto, 2005).

Cultural differences impact communication development. A study of Mexican and African American working mothers reported the difficulty in finding day-care providers who do not racially insult their children or put them down for their cultural differences. Speaking Spanish was often not permitted by the caretakers (Uttal, 1998). This reality affected communication and required the mothers to reduce stress by explaining to their children "about race relations with white society and how to navigate them" (p. 605). African American parents have an additional task of preparing children to deal with racial derogation (Ferguson, 1999); these parents often rely on an imperative communication style to protect their children from racism (Daniel & Daniel, 1999). Finally, how parents talk about play differs across cultures. Whereas European mothers use talk to describe their play with a child ("Push the green tractor back to Daddy"), African mothers focus more on social relationships than objects ("Your Daddy will get that for you") (Socha & Yingling, 2010).

Family with School-Aged Children   The school-aged family experiences new communication struggles as children become even more connected to the outside world. The family system overlaps continuously with other social systems—educational, religious, and community. Even families with strong boundaries experience increasing outside influences. Schools introduce children to a wider world of ideas, beliefs, and values, while potentially challenging their families' ways. Some parents find communicating with school personnel in support of a child's learning to be highly stressful; the amount and type of homework can create nightly stress, especially for working parents (Wingard, 2009). Parents from diverse cultural backgrounds may face special challenges; school personnel vary in their perceptions of how Hispanic and African American parents can become involved with their children's education (Cooper, 2006). An educator's lack of cultural sensitivity may result in family alienation or lack of direct involvement in a child's education. Some schools and communities will welcome the diverse family forms represented by their local students; if that is not the case, children will be faced with messages that discount or challenge their family experiences.

Given that one in five children in the United States is an immigrant or child of an immigrant, special demands are placed on both parents and children to mediate the family-school relationship. Parents must strive to overcome the language barrier because "without the ability to communicate parents felt helpless, alienated, and unable to advocate on behalf of their children" (Perriera, Chapman, & Stein, 2006). On the other hand, many school-aged children have become "family translators" or "cultural brokers," a role that creates a significant power shift.

School-aged children spend many hours away from family influences. In addition to school-related activities, religious organizations provide educational and recreational events. Organizations such as the Girl Scouts and Boy Scouts of America, dance troupes, chess clubs, sports leagues, and Boys & Girls Clubs compete for family members' time; some organizations may encourage parental involvement whereas others may attempt to set clear parental boundaries. In their study of parent communication and child athletic involvement, Turman, Zimmerman, and Dobesh (2009) interviewed parents about their experience. Respondents talked about how other parents tried to "butter up" the coaches for favoritism, and how coaches tried to set boundaries on the coach-parent relationships. During this period of growth, most children experience strong peer pressures, which may conflict with parental views. Often, family conflict develops because the child feels compelled to please friends rather than parents. Mothers who take time to communicate with their children and listen empathically to them when disciplining or comforting tend to have children who are less rejected by their peers and more frequently chosen as companions (Burleson, Delia, & Applegate, 1992).

During this period children develop additional communication skills. Negotiation and priority setting become important aspects of child-parent communication. Children's use of persuasive message strategies increase as they age. Kline and Clinton (1998) reported that children ages 5 to 8 use one to two different arguments in beginning to create persuasive messages; children ages 9 to 12 create two to four arguments; and children ages 13 and older used three or more arguments. Summarizing studies of children's speech, they report five- to six-year-olds used more pleading, sulking, threats, and requests. Between third grade and eleventh grade, children increasingly use more compromises, arguments that advance their views, more appeals to what they think society expects, and more deliberation about competing alternatives. "Second and third graders use unilateral or coercive strategies such as threats, punishments or appealing to adult authority. Fourth and fifth graders are more likely to use reciprocal strategies such as interpersonal bribes, coordinated teamwork or attempts to convince the other that he/she is wrong" (p. 121). Children become increasingly competent at producing messages adapted to their listeners and creating counterarguments. During this period, a child's communication competence increasingly impacts parental decision making.

During the school years, the family identity as a unit reaches its peak. Members can enjoy a range of joint activities, bringing richness to the intimacy of the family relationship. Due to the intense activity level, some partners neglect their own relationship or use the children as an excuse to avoid dealing with marital problems. Children living in two households due to custody arrangements experience unique challenges as they must ensure that all school materials are in the right household while continuously adapting to two different family lifestyles.

Media use impacts member role reversals in families with school-aged children because "new media and technologies are often introduced through the younger generations, whose swift adoption of these technologies and wholesale reliance on them in their daily communication behaviors forces older family members to adopt the technologies to maintain communication ties" (Bryant & Bryant, 2006, p. 300). This can be especially problematic if older family members cannot adapt. A recent national Pew study of families and technology revealed that in married-with-children households, 89 percent own multiple cell phones, 55 percent own two or more computers, and 65 percent contain a husband, wife, and child (aged 7 to 17) who all use the Internet (Kennedy, Smith, Wells, & Wellman, 2008). Other family configurations reported lower levels of involvement with technology. This study found that "a majority of adults say technology allows their family life today to be as close, or closer than their families were when they grew up" (p. v).

Families with Adolescents

Most family systems change significantly as younger members enter adolescence. Some parents send the message to their teenagers to "hurry up and grow up," promoting this agenda by allowing early dating, relaxed curfews, and dressing like adults. Other parents encourage the opposite, with an attitude "You're only young once; enjoy it." Adolescents experience dramatic physical, sexual, and emotional changes. Physical maturation experiences differ biologically; some children begin puberty very early while others are off-time. Some adolescents become pregnant, drop out of school, or become involved in drugs, essentially shortening the adolescent development phase. A 15-year-old school dropout without a job or a 16-year-old mother face different stresses than those who do not confront such complications. Although previous research characterized this period as tumultuous for parents and children, current research takes a more nuanced approach; "cultural factors and socioeconomic forces greatly affect how families define this stage of development (Garcia-Preto, 2005, p. 274).

Child and parent bidirectional influence processes become particularly obvious during adolescence. Hormonal changes impact moods, aggression, and feelings of self-worth, all of which affect parental interaction processes. In his review of adolescents' impact on parental development, Farrell (2000) asserted that adolescent development affects immediate states such as mood, distress level, or well-being as well as sense of identity and generativity. At least in some cases, a child's adolescence coincides with parental midlife issues, a challenging combination. For example, in a study of family bonds and emotional well-being in families with teenagers, fathers reported higher emotional well-being while being with other family members than when being alone, whereas mothers did not report the same experience (Vandeleur, Jeanpretre, & Perrez, 2010). At a time when children may need less connection, fathers appear to benefit from strong connections.

Highly functional parent-teen relationships depend on open communication. The more open the communication, the greater sense of equity that is expressed in mother-adolescent relationships (Vogl-Bauer & Kalbfleisch, 1997). Teenagers who view their parents positively are more likely to be open in their communication about topics that are sexually risky and are likely to discuss sensitive issues more frequently (LePoire, 2006). In addition, the more parents are aware of their adolescents' moods and refrain from forcing discussions or decisions during a negative period, the more positive are the eventual outcomes (Niedzwiecki, 1997). Family communication that supports mutual sensitivity and a gradual separation eases the transition.

Teenagers experience struggles as they cope with change and individuation particularly in areas of sexuality, identity, autonomy, and friendships. For most adolescents, prior interest in same-sex friendships switches to a growing interest in the opposite sex: "Keep out" signs appear on doors; phone calls become private. Teenagers establish strong boundaries around certain topics in relation to parents (Guerrero & Afifi, 1995). Stronger physical and psychological boundaries, which thereby limit communication with some or all family members, are established.

Adolescent self-esteem affects family relationships. Teenagers care greatly about what peers, parents, and other adults think of them. Through communication interactions, adolescents gain a sense of their own identity. Teens express concerns about identity protection and managing the outcomes of their remarks (Manning, 1996). They trust people who keep personal information private. For African American adolescents, racial esteem is the primary predictor of self-esteem. Diggs (1994) reported, "Parental communication, particularly mothers' remarks about self and race, is of greater relative importance than peer's communication in shaping the self-worth of children at the young adolescent stage" (p. 2).

Based on her experience counseling adolescents, Garcia-Preto (2005) concluded that "girls are more likely to let parents know what they are feeling by yelling, while boys are more avoidant and tend to deal with situations by leaving the field" (p. 280). Fink, Buerkel-Rothfuss, and Buerkel (1994) reported that fathers' negative behaviors of verbal aggression, high control, lack of involvement with their families, and personal dysfunction can damage father-son communication. Obviously, the relational dialectics of closeness and distance with parents affect stress. The need for privacy often accompanies the search for identity, as illustrated here.

I grew up in a home where doors were always open, and people knew each other's business. I remember going through a terrible period starting at the end of junior high when I hated sharing a room with my sister. I would spend hours alone sitting on my bed listening to music with the door shut, and if anyone came in, I would have a fit. I even locked my sister out a number of times.

A major task of adolescence involves loosening family bonds while strengthening bonds with peers. If the family atmosphere is warm and supportive, adolescents successfully negotiate differences with their parents (Reuter & Conger, 1995). If the atmosphere is hostile and coercive, adolescents rebel, conflicts escalate, and disagreements remain unresolved. Reuter and Conger's four-year study of adolescents found that behaviors affecting family communication in the first year escalated by year four. Negative strategies increased in negative families and positive strategies increased in positive families. Stress was much higher and more frequent in families with overly dominant, demanding, and coercive parents. The quality of parent-child relationships prior to adolescence foreshadowed their behaviors during adolescence. The authors concluded that "families entering adolescence showing a straightforward communication, attentive listening, and warmth tended to remain at highest levels of warm interaction one year later" (p. 446). Using data from the Sloan 500 Family Study, Snyder (2007) analyzed parents of adolescents' answers to the question "What does quality time mean to you?" Their responses fell into three categories according to parent types: structured planning parents, time available parents, and child-centered parents. Those in the last category described quality time as "the intimate heart-to-heart talks they had with their children" (Synder, p. 331). Whether parents talked about sharing moments during errands or having an evening conversation routine, the interactions needed to be personal, nurturing, and focused. As revealed in the opening vignette, the availability of parents, such as the Rybeckis, may differ across time. A need to care for an aging parent or to return to work may result in less time for one child than for other children.

Adolescence is characterized by higher conflict than earlier stages: teens report that 40 percent of their daily conflicts occur with a sibling or a parent (Roloff & Miller, 2006). The process of creating a self-identity leads to increased conflict and decreased closeness with parents, especially for girls (Lauer & Lauer, 2009). Parents and teens frequently interpret the conflicts differently, with finances becoming a more important issue; conflicts with girls tend to be less difficult to resolve than those with boys (Roloff & Miller, 2006). Conflicts occur most frequently over simple items, such as chores and appearance, rather than over bigger issues, such as drugs and sex. If a child has a positive perception of parental communication, there is a greater likelihood of a positive relationship and positive self-image (Bollis-Pecci & Webb, 1997). The more time parents spend with adolescents, the more frequent but shorter the conflicts (Vuchinich, Teachman, & Crosby, 1991).

Some adolescents may be drawn into parental conflicts. In their study of adolescent triangulation into parental conflict, Fosco and Grych (2010) revealed that "when interparental conflict is persistent, hostile, and unresolved, adolescents are more likely to be drawn into the arguments." (p. 264). This leads adolescents to blame themselves for the conflict or to feel responsible for solving their parents' problems. Neither alternative serves a teenager well.

Personal decision making provides a sense of autonomy for teenagers. Between the ages of 13 and 19 adolescents undergo an individuation process leading to self-reliance accompanied by a desire to make up their own minds. By asserting their developing talents to speak out, work, or perform tasks without constant help and supervision, adolescents signal their maturity and competence.

The adolescent's struggles to work through developmental tasks of sexuality, identity, and autonomy send reverberations throughout the family system. The sexual awakening of their children has a powerful effect on many parents. The upsurge in sexual thoughts and feelings serve as an undercurrent to many interactions that may make parents uneasy because they are forced to consider their child as a sexual being. Opposite-gender parents and children may experience a new distance between them as a response to the power of the incest taboo in society. Unfortunately, in many families this results in the end of nonverbal affection, as illustrated in this example.

I will never forget being hurt as a teenager when my father totally changed the way he acted toward me. We used to have a real "buddy" relationship. We would spend lots of time together; we would wrestle, fool around, and I adored him. Suddenly, he became really distant, and I could not understand whether I had done something. But I did not feel I could talk about it either. Now that I am older, I can see the same pattern happening with my two younger sisters. Obviously, he has a personal rule that when your daughter starts to develop breasts, you have to back off. Now I can understand that it hurts him as much as it hurts us.

Parents and children of the same gender may face internal conflicts if they perceive a major contrast between their children's budding sexuality and their own sexual identity. Such conflicts are tied to the parents' stages of development and negative self-evaluations. Because facing this issue would be uncomfortable, such perceptions may result in conflict over more "acceptable" issues such as friends, money, independence, or responsibility. For gay and lesbian adolescents, this is the time they are likely to label and understand their sexual orientation and face questions and fears about the coming-out process. Estimates suggest that 40 to 75 percent of young gay men and lesbians have disclosed their sexual identity to their mother and 30 to 55 percent to their father (Savin-Williams & Esterberg, 2000).

When considering adolescents raised by same-sex parents, Patterson's research (2009) revealed that female teenagers raised in same-sex partner households reported that factors such as adolescent adjustment and qualities of peer and family relationships did not differ significantly from adolescents raised in opposite-sex parent homes. For such adolescents, the quality of parent-adolescent relationships, rather than family form, is associated with adolescent adjustment.

Opportunities for time spent together between parents and children decreases in a linear form during the period from preadolescence through adolescence. Although perceptions of warm and supportive relationships continue over that time "both adolescents and parents report less frequent expressions of positive emotions and more frequent expressions of negative emotions" (Laursen & Collins, 2004, pp. 338–339). In stepfamilies, a close, nonconflictual stepfather-stepchild relationship improves adolescent well-being, especially when the teenager has a nonconflictual relationship with his or her mother (Yuan & Hamilton, 2006).

Adolescents and parents struggle with open communication. Parents report difficulty detecting deceptions by their children, partly because children vary in their communication strategies that include lies. Sometimes it is a "no-win" experience, since some parents will perceive incomplete answers as lying while others see complete information as a sign of deception (Grady, 1997). Adolescents are more likely to accept parental guidelines when they have clear, open lines of communication and feel that their parents respect their values. Only after some adolescents achieve adulthood and independence do they feel close to their parents again.

Economic concerns place significant stress on families, affecting members' communication. In recent years these stresses have escalated. An increasing number of adolescents have experienced homelessness; many older adolescents are postponing their college careers in order to earn money to help out at home. Many families are living apart because the primary breadwinner found a job in a different location but the family cannot move. Countless serious family conversations accompanied these changes. Family culture also interacts with economics. For example, in dual-earner Puerto Rican families when both parents are at work, the young adolescent daughters may be required to take over household responsibilities, including the care of siblings (Toro-Morn, 1998). The teenagers experience an abbreviated adolescence because they must communicate as adults in order to manage the house and protect their siblings.

Launching Children and Midlife

The period when older children leave home often coincides with parental midlife, signaling another family reorganization. Although midlife definitions very greatly (Fingerman, Nussbaum, & Birditt, 2004), it is likely to encompass the late thirties to the mid-fifties. Midlife experiences include (1) transition of parent-child relationships to adult-adult relationships; (2) changes in partnership functioning or single parent experiences; (3) expansion of the family to include new in-laws and grandchildren, biological, adopted, or stepchildren; (4) opportunities to resolve relationships with aging parents; and (5) opportunities to revitalize sibling ties. Each of these transitional tasks affects the entire family system.

During this period parents move from being responsible for their children to a sense of mutual responsibility between caring adults. In highly communal role-bound cultures in which parents and children retain a more position-oriented relationship, the parent-child relationship will experience minimal change. When young adults live on their own, especially if they are self-supporting, they assume the responsibilities of adulthood, including significant decision making. For some young people this process actively begins with a move to the college campus; for others, it may occur later as they enter the workplace or attend a local college while living at home. The launching stage becomes a time of clearing out the childhood bedrooms, sending along the extra coffeepot or dishes, and letting go of the predictable daily interactions at breakfast or bedtime that tied parents and siblings into a close, interactive system. When this separation takes place without significant struggle, parent-child communication usually remains open and flexible. Frequent contact with parents and siblings via cell phones, texts, e-mails, or visits maintains family links. Specific conversation topics involve managing money, negotiating living space, making career decisions, maintaining good health habits, or staying in contact.

Since I've been in college, I call home nearly every day. If I sense that my mother is upset about something and I ask about it, she will say, "Oh, don't you worry about it. It's not your problem; you don't live here anymore." That upsets me, because I still feel I am part of the family. Other times she will call me three times a day because of something my brother did.

The high cost of living makes leaving home difficult. As noted in Chapter 1, many college students are living at home or returning home to live after college due to economic pressures. Many married children who are divorcing return home as single parents for the same reason. The countertrend involves young people leaving home to live independently prior to marriage, with increasing numbers entering cohabiting relationships. More midlife adults are intimately involved with their children's lives than in the previous generation.

Unforeseen stresses may arise during midlife. Many adults serve as caregivers to both their older children and one or both of their parents or their partner's parents. Although few actually face the overwhelming task of ongoing caretaking of both generations, many encounter crisis situations, such as a parent's heart surgery, when the competing needs become overwhelming, especially if the caretaker is employed (Fingerman, Nussbaum, & Birditt, 2004). As the elongated generational structure becomes the norm, grandparents and even great-grandparents may rely on the two younger generations for emotional, physical, or financial support. Parental support of grown children appears ongoing in many cases; this includes listening and emotional support, advice, and practical financial assistance (Fingerman, Miller, Birdett, & Zarit, 2009). Not surprisingly, younger children tend to receive more overall support, high achieving offspring receive less tangible communication support (e.g., listening or companionship), and children with problems receive more material support.

Some parents force departures before their children feel ready, often resulting in hard feelings, conflict, and resentment. Many parents downsize their living space while others remarry or cohabit now that they feel free to do so. In some communities or cultures, departure is expected; in others, daughters may remain home indefinitely.

Major changes occur in many husband-wife relationships or partnerships after children leave as opportunities for increased adult intimacy present themselves. Mothers whose children are preparing to leave home are seldom enthusiastic. Fathers with fewer children report greater unhappiness over their departures than do fathers with more children. Also, older fathers react more strongly than younger fathers. It is only after the children are gone that the second honeymoon occurs—for some couples. Single parents may experience even more dramatic shifts; especially those who "placed" their relational lives "on hold" to raise children; others find their personal life–parental responsibility struggles diminish significantly. The amount of stress experienced is related to the parent-child relationship prior to the transition. Aquilino (1997) found that "earlier levels of closeness and conflict set the stage for intergenerational solidarity in adulthood" (p. 683).

Stresses vary greatly. Most parents successfully launch their children, but a significant number have their plans thwarted by significant responsibilities for their children or grandchildren. In offering shelter and care, they repeat an earlier part of their life trajectory—parenting. Others experience "getting younger while getting older" as "age is no longer a predictor of life stage for a very large number of Americans" (Rubin, 2001, p. 62). Due to technological advances, some women in their forties are having their first children, 50-year-olds are electing cosmetic surgery to look 10 years younger, and 60-year-olds are jogging daily. Therefore, a predictable midlife transition does not exist.

Spouses who focused intensively on their children for so many years may find themselves unconnected. Partners sensing a distance may feel unable, or unwilling, to attempt a reconnection. For many couples, the readjustment to a viable, two-person entity requires hard work. Divorces occur frequently in this midlife transition period. The challenge for some spouses is reflected in the following example.

When the children left, I discovered myself living with essentially a mute man. We hadn't realized that for years we had talked little to one another—that most of our communication was with or about the children. Since we both worked, we always took vacations with the kids, and kept busy chasing after kids' activities; we never had time for ourselves. Now I've got time to talk, and I have to compete with TV—that's the "other woman" in my house.

By this point in time, parents and their adult children have negotiated, and may continue to negotiate, issues such as privacy rights and the management of intergenerational boundaries (Cooney, 1997). Adult children and parents may continue to engage in conflict. Adult children reported that most conflicts with their elderly parents resulted from the parents' unwillingness to provide assistance and accept the child's autonomy, whereas parents may resist their self-assigned authority (Dickson, Christian, & Remmo, 2004).

Grandparenting is becoming more common, given increased longevity and the rise in single parents and same-sex parents. A 30-year-old adult has a 75 percent chance of having at least one living grandparent (Soliz, et al., 2006). Children in blended families may experience up to eight grandparent figures. Given the reality of a mobile society, some grandparents and grandchildren experience limited face-to-face contacts. Conversely, many grandparents take on participatory roles in modern families, particularly in situations of divorce and dual-career marriages.

Today, grandparents may range in age from 30 to 90-plus; grandchildren range in age from newborns to retirees. The performance of grandparenting reflects the connections between the grandparent and parent generation. When adult children become parents, this may serve as an opportunity for reconnection and healing in some families; the younger generation may have a new understanding and appreciation of what parents do (Walsh, 1999). Ties to in-laws may be impacted by the arrival of children. According to Videon (2005), "Relationships with children-in-law were more strongly associated with qualities of ties to grandchildren than relationships with the grandparents' own children" (p. 118).

Assuming the title of grandparent opens the door for unique family communication experiences. Grandparents may play many different roles depending on geographical location, amount of available time, connections to the parents, and the level of responsibility they have for their grandchildren. Their role contributions include spending pleasurable time with the child, providing financial support for grandchildren or their parents, extending emotional support during divorce or parental separation, or assisting with the caretaking of a child with special needs (Soliz, Lin, Anderson, & Harwood, 2006). These interpersonal roles may vary across the years.

Grandparents and grandchildren who interact frequently express feelings of closeness; some grandparents experience continuity, and grandchildren develop increased self-identity through storytelling and oral history. Grandparents provide access to a grandchild's ancestry and the family's roots. Through conversation and storytelling, the intergenerational transmission of family lore and history is passed down. Grandmothers are more likely to talk about family relationships and family history, whereas grandfathers are more likely to discuss historical issues and health issues (Nussbaum & Bettini, 1994). Grandparenthood provides an opportunity for meaningful interaction, while it usually does not entail the responsibilities, obligations, or conflicts of parenthood. Stress can result if grandparents are drawn into parental conflicts. Occasionally, grandparents act as an emotional refuge for children in a strife-torn family, serving as supporters and listeners. Geographically separated grandparents and grandchildren have greater opportunities to communicate regularly today due to technology; many seniors' prime motivation for going online is to connect with their children and grandchildren, rather than with friends (Wired Seniors, 2001). Video conferencing permits grandparents and grandchildren to interact face-to-face on a daily basis. Multiple factors affect how grandparents play their roles, such as age, gender, and culture. Off-time grandparents have varied experiences: those who are young may resist the title and role, whereas very old grandparents may not be capable of active engagement in the role (Soliz, et al., 2006). Maternal grandparents tend to have closer relationships and more communication with their grandchildren than paternal grandparents (Williams & Nussbaum, 2001). Although most communication research focuses on what family stories grandparents pass down, Fowler and Soliz (2009) examined how young adult grandchildren react when grandparents' engage in painful disclosures with them. They found that less satisfying grandparent-grandchild relationships are predicted by the discomfort such disclosures produce for some grandchildren. Again this raises the issue of significant bidirectional communication between a much older adult and a young adult.

Cultural expectations affect grandparent involvement. In certain cultures, grandparents are expected to assume a major role in child rearing. In most African American families, older family members play many roles—adviser, mediator, financial supporter, health resource, and transmitter of culture. "Grandparents often have relationships with their grandchildren that are as close as, if not closer than, the relationships they have with their own adult children" (Hines, 1999, p. 339). A study of African American, Latina, and white grandmothers raising or helping to raise grandchildren revealed that Latina grandmothers had higher satisfaction than the other grandmothers when they co-parented with a parent in the household; African American grandparents experienced higher life satisfaction when they had custodial rather than co-parenting situations (Goodman & Silverstein, 2006). Such cross-generational contact provides opportunities for extended transmission of culture and for development of a sense of family history.

Midlife brings its challenges and its joys. In spite of the decisions about major life changes and the pressures of launching children, this period can be a time of happiness and growth. Children entering adulthood are often wonderful companions and supporters as adult-to-adult sharing increases. Partners and single parents have the opportunity to focus on renewing old relationships or creating new ones.

Families in Later Life

Family relationships continue to be significant throughout later life. During this time approximately one-third of men and over one-half of women live alone. Most parents live near at least one adult child. Total isolation is rare. As family members grow older, they tend to rank their happiness higher, the more frequently they interact with relatives (Ishii-Kuntz, 1994). Because people live longer today, more adults ages 65 to 69 now work because they wish to do so, or fear that they will not have enough money for health care. If they have to work and care for their grandchildren, stress increases.

Older family members face self-identity issues related to retirement, health concerns, interpersonal needs (especially if they lose a spouse), and their mortality. Some couples experience "re-entry" problems when one or both return to the home after retiring and remain there 24 hours of most days. The increased contact may lead to a deepening of the relationship or result in friction from the forced closeness. However, a survey of over 900 couples revealed that marital conflict is unaffected by husbands' and wives' transition to retirement but wives' continued employment appears associated with greater conflict (Davey & Szinovacz, 2004). In a large study of Dutch retirees, Van Solinge and Henkens (2005) found that the preretirement concerns about marital conflict predicted the problems that developed as partners entered retirement. Many men adapt less well to unstructured time and rely on their wives for regular companionship; many women report a frustration at their loss of independence in these circumstances. As reflected in the adage "For better or worse but not for lunch," many women resent male intrusion into their established social life with female friends. Some retired persons undergo significant losses of professional identities and self-definitions, such as that of doctor or provider. Losing the workplace's social communication network places increased pressure for intimacy on retirees' partners or children. Some retirees face different communication challenges since, as noted earlier, many live alone. Women reach out during midlife and beyond, using communication strategies to extend and multiply friendships, whereas men rarely make new friends. As a result men tend to become more emotionally dependent on their wives (Sheehy, 1998).

For some, the later years serve as a time of rejuvenation. Established couples now have time to enjoy each other and, if financially secure, to enjoy hobbies and travel. Individuals who put their lives on hold to raise children may find new partners. Additionally, "living apart together" (LAT), or living a partnered life while maintaining both residences, represents a growing trend among widowed, divorced, separated, and ever-single men and women in their sixties into their nineties (Levaro, 2009). Although many older individuals show little interest in forming a new partnered relationship, an increasing number seek committed companionship in nonmarital unions. In many cases such individuals choose not to marry for pragmatic reasons, such as losing a deceased spouse's pension. For some, maintaining separate residences allows them to balance their involvement with adult children and grandchildren with a loving adult relationship.

During old age, many family relationships are emotionally important even if there is limited face-to-face contact, as these ties are sustained by memories of intense interaction (Bedford & Blieszner, 1997). New technologies provide greater opportunities to bridge the distance gap. For example, 34 percent of Americans aged 65 and over go

| Later life conversations and communication contribute to an individual's well-being.

online; by age 70 only 28 percent go online (Fox, 2006). Yet this reveals a significant shift in the past decade and as more men and women retire they will bring their computer skills from the workplace into retirement. Many Internet-skilled seniors stay in touch with family members, shop, and search for health information online.

Family members' health and declining strength further impacts family communication. Ill health strains a couple's physical, mental, and financial resources, creating a need for nurturing communication from other family members. Weiss (1997) cataloged a list of physical changes in many aging adults: vision declines and lenses thicken; ears lose the ability to detect higher-pitched tones and, later in life, low pitches; senses of smell and taste grow duller; skin grows thinner; muscles waste and fat accumulates around the waist; and so on. Such changes contribute to a loss of self-esteem, increased stress, and communication frustrations, making individuals reluctant to initiate personal contacts. Listeners may become impatient with an older person's infirmities.

Communication among family members becomes increasingly important at this stage. Many older family members engage in the "elder function," or the sharing of the accumulated wisdom of their lives with younger people, usually family members. There is a need to feel useful to the rising generations, and, for many older persons, satisfaction comes from imparting historical information or spinning stories designed to guide the younger listener. Reminiscing serves as a coping mechanism, to maintain self-esteem, to feel loved, to gain self-awareness, or to see oneself in a larger historical context. Oral history can enrich a family, especially its members' sense of their family-of-origin, while giving elderly members a chance to communicate to those they love, helped raise, or even hurt at some point in time. Some need to "set the record straight" or to let go of past marital disappointments in order to make peace with previous life events (Dickson, Christian, & Remmo, 2004). More older people are writing their memoirs, not for publication but because they "want to leave a record of their lives for future generations" (Harker, 1997, p. 32). The importance of this storytelling is demonstrated below.

I'm glad my dad, Bill, lived past 75. Only then did we come to terms with one another. Long after he retired, he mellowed, had a stroke, and became approachable. He talked about the depression, the war years, and the struggle to pay for the farm. Finally I sensed what had made him so tough and noncommunicative.

During this period older family members depend on their children or other younger family members for attention, affection, and mutual aid. In addition, many seniors find support from their siblings, with whom they engage in reminiscing, storytelling, providing emotional support, and sharing mutual aid. Sister-sister pairs usually sustain the most contact, followed by sister-brother pairs; brother-brother pairs have the least amount of contact (Mikkelson, 2006).

Although many older persons see their children with some regularity, many are prevented from maintaining the interpersonal contacts they desire due to concerns of economics, safety, geography, and health. Rising costs of living restrict travel and entertainment; many urban senior citizens do not feel safe travelling home from evening meetings or social activities. Inflation has increased stress on older Americans as more fall below the poverty level; this tends to impact elderly women, African Americans, Hispanics, and single persons most frequently.

Many couples confront the serious illness of one of the partners. In some cases full or partial recovery is a strong possibility; in other cases, one member faces a terminal disease or chronic decline due to dementia. Either situation alters their marital interaction. In her study of couples in which one partner is dealing with cancer, Imes (2006) reported the development of a "new normal" status, a term her respondents use to describe the relational status. They reported that things went back to "normal," but their use of this term indicated an acceptance of the cancer event and a return to many routine behaviors, at the same time recognizing their new roles and altered communication behaviors. These couples struggled with role shifts in areas of partnership, health, identity, health awareness, and managing community support. They also negotiated the extent to which they avoided or discussed the cancer-related topic as well as the manner in which they did so. Similarly, wives of elderly husbands with adult dementia confront living in the ambiguous state of "married widowhood" (Baxter, Braithwaite, Golish, & Olson, 2002). These women faced a redefinition of their marital relationships as they watched the husbands they knew slip away; they were present physically but not emotionally or mentally. The wives developed a range of coping mechanisms, such as relying on nonverbal communication, working hard to interpret the limited communication cues, relying on the nursing home staff for information, or limiting contact with their partner. Single ill, elderly adults need more support than some elderly partnered adults when one of them is a reasonably healthy spouse. Yet, a partner may "overfocus on the other's disability to avoid facing his or her own vulnerability, anxiety, or longing to be taken care of" (Rolland, 2005, p. 314). When needed, elder care is most often carried out by daughters. The care-giving daughter is more likely to be divorced, widowed, or never married (Weldon, 1998).

The loss of an elderly family member may be seen as on-time within the life course, but this does not diminish the grief. Functional families find ways to acknowledge death as a normal and appropriate topic throughout life; therefore, an aging member's potential death can be openly addressed in these families. The death of an elderly relative frequently forces family members to confront end-of-life decision making (Hoppough & Ames, 2001). Families participate in approximately 70 percent to 80 percent of end-of-life decisions in hospital intensive care units (Pochard, et. al., 2001). In many cases, one designated member has been prepared to make do not resuscitate orders, if appropriate, and to engage in discussions with other members and the health care team (Galvin & DiDomenico, 2009). As depicted in the second opening vignette describing the Ashford family, more individuals and families are choosing a hospice approach to death, which permits family members to interact with a loved one in a setting that supports the natural process of letting go without a continuation of heroic measures to keep the loved one alive. Although death remains a difficult or taboo topic in many families, others, particularly those with strong ties to an ethnic heritage, are able to confront the issue directly and realistically. For example, within Mexican American families, events surrounding death bring a family together to express emotions freely, reinforce family cohesiveness, and involve members of all ages sharing support for each other and participating in related rituals with each other (Martinez, 2001).

After the death of a spouse or partner, the grieving other must face the reality of living as a single person. Working through the grief period, such individuals may make great demands on friends or family members who are resentful of, or unprepared for, such pressures. The surviving member of a couple has to renegotiate roles and boundaries as he or she attempts to create or maintain interpersonal contacts. It is important that older family members have a say in their care and be a part of all communication that concerns them as long as possible.

Much to the surprise of their adult children, after a couple of years many former partners enter new relationships although remarriage, which occurs more frequently for men than for women (Walsh, 2005). The importance of dating or living apart together is growing, but not necessarily as a prelude to marriage. Interpersonal motives for dating include meeting possible mates, exchanging intimacies, remaining socially active, interacting with the opposite sex, engaging in sex, and maintaining a stable identity. Remarriages are relatively rare, although more common for those of a younger age and experiencing greater unhappiness as a single person.

Eventually, an elderly person must confront his or her own death. Many families resist addressing the issue directly with an elderly member, yet relationships that include discussion of death and that provide direct emotional support are more helpful. Family members—particularly adult children—may face their own crises as they try to (1) acknowledge the loss of the generation separating them from death, (2) make sense of the experience, (3) anticipate shifts in the family formation, and (4) deal with their own feelings of impending loss. Often, these concerns get in the way of saying farewell in a direct and meaningful manner. True "final conversations" involving talk, interactions, or nonverbal messages may occur when it is understood that one person is dying (Keeley & Yingling, 2007). Such moments help to convey love, caring, gratitude, and forgiveness that bring comfort and closure to the family members engaged in such interactions.

TRANSITIONS BETWEEN STAGES

Although each of these stages holds life-changing experiences and opportunities for functional and meaningful communication, it is important to highlight the importance of transitions between these developmental stages because the instability of these periods often triggers highly meaningful family interactions. Functional families manage these predictable changes through ongoing conversations about their experiences as well as finding ways to recognize and support each other. These families experience the transitions with temporary, but not permanent, stress resulting from the transition. Functional families experience transitions as challenging and at times, unpleasant events, but not as long-lasting negative influences. Transitions into marriage or the birth of a child, for example, affect family functioning, but usually the family progresses through them as a normal maturation process. Transitions out of marriage—such as divorce, desertion, or death, or the loss or serious illness of a member—have negative effects and cause higher stress over longer periods of time. Functional families exhibit adaptive capacities that support them through very rough times.

Individual transitions tend to involve periods of oscillations, movements forward and backward, until the new behavior becomes more routine (Breunlin, Schwarts, & Kune-Karrer, 2001). Just as a child does not suddenly stop crawling when she begins to walk, a father does not stop setting rules when he starts to relax them. Family relationships are characterized by variability as each shift is negotiated. Only after a new pattern has begun to take hold can one let go of an old pattern. Even well into adulthood, moments of significant change or crisis arise when a young adult female reverts to being a little girl or a midlife male acts like a teenager for a short time.

Variations on typical transitions are increasingly common. Such variations include gay or lesbian marriage or formal commitments, family formation through reproductive technologies, adoption of older children, foster parenting, remarriage to a former spouse, or the termination of cohabiting partnerships. These moments need their own adapted rituals symbolizing family connectedness and support (Imber-Black, 1999).

Problematic families tend to include members who fail to make these transitions at the appropriate times in their lives, thus creating imbalance in their family systems. These members, often confronting serious psychological or physical issues, may remain stuck at a certain developmental stage, unable to move on. They are "off course" in proceeding through expected changes in the life cycle stages. These affected families experience a piling-up effect, with one or more members stuck at the same stage. Sometimes these same family members experience external stresses (crime, bankruptcy, or devastating divorce) and, as a result of these circumstances, they become even less able to cope.

The changes in family life over decades are accompanied by changes in the communication characteristics of each stage. In some families, communication among members remains vibrant across the years; in other families, communication fulfills a sense of obligation. A recent survey of 500 British couples found that after one year of marriage couples engaged in 40 minutes of conversation during a one-hour dinner. After 20 years, they spent 21 minutes talking and after 30 years, only 16 minutes. Those married for 50 years spent three minutes in conversation (Zazlow, 2010). Clearly communication diminishes over time in many relationships; the only hope is that meaningful conversation continues.

There are great variations in how families cope with developmental stresses. Some families experience a roller-coaster effect with little relief, especially when multiple stressors accumulate. As they struggle with change and transitions, most persons experience life in its immediate moments, often losing sight of the larger process. Eventually, the movement across the life span becomes lost in its moments.

CONCLUSION

This chapter provided an overview of the effects of developmental stresses on communication within families and how these affect the life course. Some stresses may come from outside the family system, while others are created within the family system, but all affect the family. After indicating how individuals move through a life cycle, the chapter focused on a stage model for intact U.S. families. The stages included are (1) single young adults, (2) partners, (3) families with children, (4) families with adolescents, (5) launching children and midlife, and (6) families in later life. As families move through the years, each generation faces predictable developmental issues as couples marry, beget children, and live through stages of child development superimposed on their own adult developmental changes. As children leave home to form new systems, their parents face the middle years and adjustment issues. The cohesion-adaptability axis overlays each family system's personal growth, while themes, images, and biosocial beliefs may be challenged as the years pass. Throughout the chapter, research has been included on how the individual's life course can be altered by the on-time or off-

time sequencing of life cycle or developmental stages.

The entire family developmental process is extremely complex and challenging. Achieving the developmental tasks in each stage represents accomplishment and psychological growth for each family member in his or her life course. Stress gets expressed in the intrapersonal and interpersonal communication that follows as the family member struggles for balance in the dialectical tension between self needs and family system needs.

In Review

1. Reflecting on your own family or one you know well, compare and contrast how the traditional stages of development were affected by life-course issues. Cite three examples of on-time and off-time events that altered the life course.

2. Discuss what impact different cultural backgrounds have on the communication in various stages of development on children and parents. To what extent might an Asian

American, Hispanic, African American, or Native American heritage (pick one) influence two or three developmental issues?

3. Imagining your own family or a family you know well, provide examples of verbal or nonverbal communication patterns that seemed commonplace at different developmental stages in the family life cycle. Focus on parent-child or sibling patterns.

4. Relying on your own family or a family you have observed, describe how a couple or partners have dealt with the communication tasks of incorporating a child into their system and dealing with the following communication-related issues: (a) renegotiating roles, (b) transmitting culture, (c) establishing a community of experiences, and (d) developing the child's communication competence.

5. What key qualities appear to characterize family communication during the period when one or more adolescents are living within the household?

6. Describe three ways in which communication is affected by the departure of young adults during the launching stage in either two-parent systems or in single-parent systems.

7. Compare and contrast communication patterns you have observed in the interactions between middle-aged and older family members in two families. To what extent were reminiscing, reflection, and sorting out important to members at these stages?

KEY TERMS

Family Communication and Unpredictable Stress

"The loss of a child is one abyss from which few families return. Some claw their way again toward the light, perhaps finding a narrow ledge where, in time, memory can shed its skin of pain. Others dwell in darkness forever."

—Nicholas Evans, *The Loop*

Erin and Luke Johnson were excited to be expecting their third child. On the day they went for their 20-week ultrasound, they had no idea how profoundly everything would change. They were shocked to learn that their unborn daughter had spina bifida, a birth defect that involves the incomplete development of the spinal cord. Erin thought that every dream she had for her life and her family and children had changed. She couldn't eat, she couldn't sleep, and she couldn't stop crying. The way she felt about the little girl inside of her had changed so quickly. Erin and Luke wanted to hope for the best, but there were so many unanswered questions and terrifying statistics. All of a sudden, the Internet became the scariest place in the world.

As time went on, Erin and Luke found hope. They talked to family members, relied on their faith, and came to believe that their daughter was going to come to them exactly how God wanted her to come to them. They found support online from other parents, and learned about a clinical trial for prenatal surgery and that gave them purpose as they moved forward through the next few weeks. One year later, their daughter is a happy baby and doing much better than anyone had expected.

Adelina Perez had just started her junior year of college when she received a phone call from her mother telling her that she and her father had separated and were planning to file for divorce. Adelina was devastated and particularly sad for her mother, whom she knew had always tried her best to make the marriage work. She'd known that her parents had problems—both Adelina and her brother Ethan had heard their parents fighting on many occasions. But she always thought they would work it out and stay together. Ethan had just started his freshman year of college. Adelina realized that her parents had stayed together until she and her brother were out of the house.

Adelina had many talks with her mother over the next few months, and became, in a sense, her mother's confidant. There were many things her mother told her that she wished she hadn't known—about her father's infidelity, his emotional abuse toward her mother, and their financial problems. Her relationship with her father, which was never good to begin with, became more and more distant. Ethan continued to keep in contact with both their father and mother. Adelina's relationship with her own boyfriend of two years, Elliott, also began to deteriorate as Adelina began to have doubts of whether she could trust Elliott.

"I never thought we would have to deal with something like this." These words have been spoken by countless family members as they faced unexpected challenges, such as home foreclosures, loss of employment, loss of property in natural disasters, and the death of a loved one. Family members may live in dread of some situations, such as losing a father to a stroke, hearing a mother has relapsed into alcoholism, dealing with a father's deployment, or having a young son experience a recurrence of his cancer. This chapter addresses what happens to a family system when events occur for which the members have little or no warning and how communication functions in such circumstances.

Unpredictable stresses are brought about by events or circumstances that disrupt life patterns but cannot be foreseen from either a developmental or life-course perspective. Usually they result from significant negative occurrences, the "slings and arrows of outrageous fortune," or shocks to the system. Such stresses involve losses such as untimely death, divorce, economic challenges, or serious illness or injury. Some positive events—such as a large inheritance, wedding, promotion, or the rediscovery of long-lost relatives—may also stress the system. Mmari and colleagues (2009) have noted how the return of a parent from war, seemingly a positive event, can be confusing for adolescents as they adjust to having two parents again and become reacquainted with the parent who was deployed. In recent years, some theorists have distinguished between stress and trauma, suggesting that stresses can be managed whereas trauma "is a stress so great and unexpected that it cannot be defended against, coped with or managed" (Boss, 2006. p. 35). For example, a mother's breast cancer surgery may be considered a serious stressor whereas a brother's suicide can devastate the family. Such a critical, major loss would be considered a trauma. Yet, it is difficult to predict with accuracy the effect of major stressors on a particular family.

Sometimes family members experience *ambiguous loss,* one characterized by high uncertainty regarding personal relationships (Boss, 1999). There are two types of ambiguous loss, one in which "people are perceived by family members as physically absent but psychologically present," and the other in which "a person is perceived as physically present but psychologically absent" (Boss, 1999, pp. 8–9). The first instance includes missing soldiers, runaways, or kidnapped children; the second instance includes people with addictions, closed head injuries, or Alzheimer's disease. Such losses are often referred to as "frozen grief" because they limit the grieving process due to the uncertainties involved. Families of those killed in the World Trade Center collapse struggled with the physical loss of a member without verification of their death and no body to bury. The absence of a body delayed or altered the usual ceremonies, such as a funeral mass or sitting shiva, and loved ones found it difficult to start grieving because it might be considered disloyal (Boss, 2001). Ambiguous loss is considered the most stressful type of loss because "It defies resolution and creates long term confusion about who is in or out of a particular couple or family" (Boss, 2006, p. xvii).

Crises occur when a family lacks the resources to cope or when "family demands significantly exceed their capabilities" (Patterson, 2002, p. 351). All families undergo some degree of strain or stress. *Strain* can be defined as that tension or difficulty sensed by family members which indicates that change is needed in their relationships and their family environment. *Stressor events,* discussed in this chapter, are characterized by unexpectedness, greater intensity, longer duration, and their undesirability and serious effects (Lavee, Sharlin, & Katz, 1996). Think about the stresses of a family dealing for over 20 years with what became a fatal illness for three of their members as described in this example.

There were nine children in our family, and three had muscular dystrophy. I remember how hard it was for Mom to accept their illness. She wouldn't talk about it within the family. Her rule was that it was better not discussed, yet I would find her crying at unpredictable times. We all learned how to cope from Marilyn, Dan, and Virginia. Communication reached a tense stage when Marilyn was the first to die. We sensed the fear and panic in Dan and Virginia. It took time to get them to talk about these fears and finally, near their own deaths, they would joke about who was going next. All of this was strictly among Dan and Virginia and myself. Mom, Dad, and the rest couldn't handle any humor on the subject. I feel they would like to have shared these feelings with all of us, but some of the living in our family put great distance between themselves and those who were dying.

The previous chapter contains a model of family stressors (Figure 10.1) and a description of the developmental stresses a family faces. This chapter focuses on those that are unpredictable and which may appear as either horizontal or vertical stressors. It examines (1) coping with unpredictable stress (including the stressors), a model for coping, and the stages of crisis, and (2) communication patterns for coping with stresses such as death, illness, disability, divorce, and remarriage. It also links these stressors to the systems or the life-course frame of the model.

UNPREDICTABLE STRESS AND FAMILY COPING PATTERNS

Stress involves a physiological response to stressors—events or situations that are seen as either powerful negative or positive forces. Individuals or family members under stress experience physiological and psychological changes as their heightened anxiety affects their coping patterns. Systems under stress tend to fall into predictable patterns, some functional and some dysfunctional, as the members try to cope. As you might imagine, what is a major stressor to one family may be a minor stressor to another. What one family or family member does to reduce tension differs greatly from another family's or individual's strategies. In order to appreciate the processes of coping, the family stressors, models of coping, and stages of crisis must be examined.

Stressors

Family researchers have examined stresses and crises for over 50 years. In his classic longitudinal study of families of World War II soldiers, Hill (1949) identified family disruptions that cause crises. These include (1) the coming apart of the family due to the death of a member; (2) the addition of new or returning family members; (3) the sense of disgrace, which may result from infidelity, alcoholism, or nonsupport; and (4) a combination of the above, which could include suicide, imprisonment, homicide, or mental illness. Other stressors such as drug abuse, handgun violence, job loss, and teenage suicide are more prevalent today. Major stresses throw a family system out of its normal balance and precipitate long-term change. When a stress arises that affects members at multiple stages of the life span, the stress is compounded (Afifi & Nussbaum, 2006). The new stepfather who is trying to develop ties to a hostile stepdaughter while managing the early stages of a parent's dementia will experience severe stress, which will affect other family members. Although everyone knows that death is inevitable, that accidents happen daily, and that serious illnesses can affect anyone, the actual occurrence of these events brings challenges that test the limits of endurance. These struggles affect all family members.

How well a family copes depends on several factors. In his early, classic work, Bain (1978) claimed a family's coping capacity was tied to four factors: (1) the number of previous stressors the members had faced in recent years, (2) the degree of role change involved in coping, (3) the social support available to members, and (4) the institutional support available to members. Past experiences with crises prepare family members to understand new crises when they occur, but they may also retraumatize family members. The piling up of sad, unpredictable events affects coping, as does the amount of recovery time between shocks to the system. For example, the severe illness of a child is likely to be very difficult for a family who has recently dealt with major financial or marital problems. It may cause greater strain if a parent has to change roles, such as giving up a career to care for the child. Support from friends and family members who assist physically or offer empathy lessens the stress. The support needs to meet the affected person's need. Emotional support is the type of social support most desired by cancer patients and most strongly linked to adjustment (Helgeson & Cohen, 1999). Yet, often a family or one of its members needs to acknowledge the need for support and not assume people will know what is needed or how to respond. The following observation by a teacher attests to the importance of support at the time of crisis.

| The unexpected death of a key family member sends a family into shock and role confusion.

As a teacher, I watch a few students' families undergo divorce each year. The ones who seem to cope reasonably well with the pain are those that have some resources to bring to the process. Usually this is the family that has strong extended family members or neighborhood friends and the family that tells the school or church what is going on. In short, this family lets people in on the pain—asks for some help.

The family stress literature emphasizes the possible productive outcomes of dealing with stress as well as the difficulties inherent in such a process. Certainly some families fare better during stressful situations than others. Researchers use the word *resilience* to refer to a family's ability to "do well in the face of adversity" (Patterson, 2002, p. 350). Couples who suffer through the loss of a child and are able to build intimacy during the grieving process, rather than growing more distant, would be considered a resilient family. Quality of life factors affect resilience (Patterson, 2002). Living in poverty or in a violent neighborhood affects a family's ability to be resilient. Resilient low- to low-middle–income families are characterized by internal strengths complemented by community support services, religious programs, and a sense of belonging to the community.

Family Stress Model

Each family exhibits unique coping behaviors. _Coping_ implies "the central mechanism through which family stressors, demands, and strains are eliminated, managed, or adapted to" (McCubbin, Patterson, Cauble, Wilson, & Warwick, 1983, p. 359). The primary model currently used to understand family crises evolved from Hill's (1949) original model, which proposed that:

> A [the stressor event], interacting with B [the family's crisis-meeting resources], interacting with C [the family's definition of the event], produces X [the crisis]. (McCubbin & Patterson, 1983b, p. 6)

The stressor, _a,_ represents a life event or transition that has the potential to change a family's social system—indeed, its life course. Such events as the loss of a job, untimely death, unexpected military deployment, serious illness, or a major win in the lottery may fall into this category. A stressor event itself is not positive or negative; it is neutral until the family members place their interpretations on it (Ingoldsby, Smith, & Miller, 2004). The _b_ factor represents the resources a family can use to manage the stressor and avoid creating a crisis; these include money, friends, time and space, or problem-solving skills. A family's levels of cohesion and adaptability influence their access to, and use of, resources. Resources may come from individuals, family members, and the community (McCubbin & Patterson, 1985). For example, if a child wanders away from home, community and family member resources are needed to conduct thorough searches of the area. If a child contracts swine flu, the local doctor becomes a key resource. The _c_ factor represents the importance a family attaches to the stressor. For example, in one family, a diagnosis of a member's juvenile diabetes might overwhelm the entire system, whereas another family might cope relatively well, perceiving the diabetes as a manageable disease, one not likely to alter their lives drastically. The view of the family and the families-of-origin of the stressor influences the perception of crisis. For example, a three-generation family that has never experienced a divorce may define a young granddaughter's marital separation as a severe crisis. A multigenerational system with a history of divorce may see the separation as sad, but not as a crisis. Together, _a, b,_ and _c_ contribute to the experience of stress that is unique to each family, depending on its background, resources, and interpretation of the event. The _x_ factor represents the amount of disruptiveness that occurs to the system. It is characterized by "the family's inability to restore stability and by the continuous pressure to make changes in the family structure and patterns of interaction" (McCubbin & Patterson, 1983b, p. 10). Not all stressors lead to a crisis.

McCubbin and Patterson (1983a) developed a Double _ABCX_ model based on Hill's original work that incorporates postcrisis variables (Figure 11.1), or the next stages of coping. Although Hill's _ABCX_ model focused on precrisis areas, the Double _ABCX_ model incorporates the family's efforts to recover over time. In this model, the _aA_ factor includes not only the immediate stressor (e.g., death) but also the demands or changes that may emerge from individual system's members, the system as a whole, and the extended system. McCubbin and Patterson suggest that the _aA_ factor includes (1) the initial stressor and its hardships, (2) normative transitions, (3) prior strains, (4) the consequences of the system's coping attempts, and

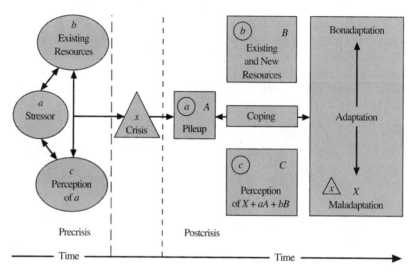

FIGURE 11.1
The Double ABCX Model

(5) ambiguity. Imagine, for example, the death of a man, age 36, with a wife and three daughters, ages 6, 10, and 14. When a young father dies, the system must deal with the immediate loss as well as potential economic uncertainty and changes in the mother's role. In addition, a child's developmental stage may require the family to cope with an adolescent's need for independence. The new stress is compounded by any prior strains, such as mother-daughter conflicts. A consequence of the family's attempts to cope may lead to new stresses. For example, if the mother takes a full-time job, it may keep her from meeting her daughters' needs for support at home. Finally, ambiguity might be caused by the confusion of new roles now that the father died. In the future the mother may remarry; change becomes expected. Thus, *aA* is broader than the original conception of *a*.

The *bB* factor represents the family's ability to meet its needs. Over time a family relies on existing and new resources. Existing resources reflect a family's background. In the case of death, these may include the ways in which a family coped in the past when the father was gone on long business trips. The expanded family resources emerge from the crisis itself. A widow may create new resources by studying accounting, which leads to a well-paying position, or by joining a widows' self-help group. The emerging social systems are a critical element in the *bB* factor.

The *cC* factor refers to the ways in which a family interprets a crisis, including both the meaning the family gives to the stressor event and to the added stressors caused by the original crisis. When a young father dies, a family must cope with that event and its meaning. If the mother believes she has lost her only chance at happiness in life, her perceptions will strongly influence her recovery and the attitudes of her children. Family members must also interpret the changes in finances, changes in the mother's role, and how the entire family is affected. In families who manage such a situation well, members adapt to changes in responsibilities and provide support to one another. Families who have difficulty coping find themselves overwhelmed, with little sense of hope or opportunity for growth.

The xX factor represents the effect of the family's adaptation on the individual, family, and community levels. Family adaptation is achieved "through reciprocal relationships where the demands of one of these units are met by the capabilities of another so as to achieve a 'balance' of interaction" (McCubbin & Patterson, 1983a, p. 19). If a member's demands are too great for the family's capabilities, there will be an imbalance. There will also be imbalance if the family demands more than the community is capable of providing. Conversely the family and workplace demands may create an imbalance by expecting too much of one person. The positive end of the outcomes continuum, called *bonadaptation,* is characterized by balance between (1) member and family and (2) family and community. The negative end, or *maladaptation,* reflects imbalance or severe losses for the family. Disruptions may be resolved eventually in positive or negative ways. The whole family system reacts to the crisis, even down to its youngest member, as shown in the following story.

Fifteen years ago our son, Mitch, came home to die. He had lived an independent life since his AIDS diagnosis four years earlier, but the shadow of the crisis was always there—waiting. My top priority was to help him. Our first grandchild, Hannah, was 2 years old when her uncle came home to die. She had been coming to our house every Wednesday since she was an infant. Hannah had her own room that was fixed up just for her. Because of Mitch's needs, the visits stopped. Weeks later she came over with her mommy only to find all of her toys had been replaced by hospital equipment. The expression on that little face was one of complete bewilderment. We tried to say and do all of the right things but Hannah was angry with her Grandma for a long time.

Many variations on this model developed over the years. Olson (1997) refined this stress model by developing a multisystem assessment of stress and health (MASH), which focused on four areas of life (individual, work, couple, and family), creating a biopsychological approach that measures the relationships between stress, coping, system variables, and adaptation in the four areas of life. Other approaches to understanding stress in families include the risk and resiliency theoretical perspective and the family strengths or asset-based approach to understanding coping (Afifi & Nussbaum, 2006).

All unpredictable stresses affect cohesion and adaptability. A family with a high capacity for adaptation and above-average cohesion is likely to weather stressor events more easily than families who are rigid and disengaged. Adaptable and open families are more likely to use and benefit from social supports in their community. In their study of how Army families adapted when a member was deployed to a war zone, Pittman, Kerpelman, and McFayden (2004) found that greater unit support was strongly tied to a sense of community, which was linked to family adaptation to the stress. More adaptable families exhibit the capacity to discover alternative ways of relating and can adjust their communication behavior to encompass a stressor. But this is not easy.

Families with rigid boundaries may be unable to cope adequately when severe external stresses occur. *Boundary ambiguity* increases stress. This term refers to the degree of uncertainty in family members' perceptions of who "belongs" and who is expected to function in various roles, as well as the degree of openness regarding who is allowed to help. By limiting open communication with such institutions as hospitals or schools, members deprive themselves of information and emotional support. Boundaries that prevent friends or extended family from knowing about the problem reduce the number of resources available to support a family through a critical period.

Seemingly positive events can create great stress. Most immigrants in the United States chose to move to a new country, viewing it as a positive change for their family. Often potential stresses are minimized. A survey of over a thousand immigrants to the Minneapolis–St. Paul area found that most experienced significant stresses over a long period of time, including adapting to a new language, separation from family and friends, health problems, financial problems, finding and keeping a job, and homesickness and isolation (Mattessich, 2001). Even developmental changes create stress. Family members may find it painful to cope with a much-loved child's departure for college. Great joys may be accompanied by great losses.

The picture is not entirely negative, however. On occasion, communication improves when the family manages a major crisis. In her study of dialectical tensions in families with a stroke survivor, Pawlowski (2006) found that survivors experienced more open communication with their family members and believed these relationships were closer now than before the stroke. Families of childhood cancer survivors reported positive outcomes from the experience in addition to the stresses and anxiety. The study of childhood cancer survivors an average of 17 years away from treatment and their parents revealed that talking about the experience was emotionally beneficial and healing. Communicating with each other helped them move on (Galvin, Grill, Arntson, & Kinahan, in press).

Communication plays a central role in the resolution of such stresses and contributes specifically to the family's movement through stages of stress reaction. In some families, members use direct verbal messages to explore options, negotiate needs, express feelings, and reduce tension. In other families, the members' stress may be apparent through the nonverbal messages that indicate their anxiety, fear, or anger. As part of the family's coping pattern, members constantly interpret each others' verbal and nonverbal messages, which inform their responses.

Stages of Family Crisis

In any crisis situation, members go through a process of managing the loss, grief, or chaos. Depending on the circumstance, these stages may last from a few days to several months or years. Stages may be evident in the case of a death, divorce, or news of an incurable illness, but in any crisis, most family members experience a progression of feelings from denial to eventual acceptance. Sometimes a member becomes stuck in the coping process, never reaching the final stage. Yet, since equifinality suggests that no two families view a crisis in the same way, each family will move through the process in a different way. The following stages approximate the process of grieving significant losses. These stages were developed as a response to understanding losses surrounding death, but have since been applied to a range of losses, because all changes involve loss and all losses require change (Goldsworthy, 2005). Although the stages may follow one another, they may overlap, and some may be repeated a number of times.

1. Shock resulting in numbness, disbelief, or denial
2. Recoil resulting in anger, confusion, blaming, guilt, and bargaining
3. Depression
4. Reorganization resulting in acceptance and recovery (Kubler-Ross, 1970; Mederer & Hill, 1983; Worden, 1991).

After a critical life event, moving through such stages usually results in transformation of the family system. Persons may find themselves more separated from, or connected to, different members and experience a shift in adaptability patterns. Members' communication reflects and aids progress through the stages. Understanding the process allows an individual to analyze others' progress through the stages or to be more understanding of one's own behavior and personal progress.

Shock/Denial   At the *shock stage,* family members tend to deny the event or its seriousness. Comments such as "It can't be true," or "It's a mistake," are accompanied by nonverbal behavior, such as awkward attempts at smiles and encouragement with a terminally ill person or spending money lavishly when the paycheck has been cut off. Most persons move from this stage, exhibiting behaviors that indicate a recognition of reality. Family members acknowledge their grief and feel the pain of the loss. Withdrawal or quietness characterizes the communication of those who find it hard to cry. The news of the crisis begins to take on fuller meanings, such as "Mom will never be the same." Denial is transformed into an intense desire to recapture what has been lost, especially in the case of a family death, illness, or severe injury. It tends to occur more powerfully after a shock rather than an expected loss. This may lead to actions that deny reality: for example, "I keep expecting to see her walking down the street" or "I still automatically set the table for five people and then I catch myself."

Recoil   After the initial blow, family members may move into the *recoil stage* of blaming, anger, and bargaining. Blaming often takes place as the grieving family members seek reasons for what has happened. This may include blaming the self ("I was too trusting" or "I never should have left town") or blaming others ("It's his own fault" or "The doctors never told us the truth soon enough"). Such reactions may be interspersed with feelings of "It's not fair." Anger may be directed at the event or person most directly involved or may be displaced onto others, such as family members, friends, or coworkers. Attempts at real or imagined bargains may occur ("If I take a cut in pay, they could hire me back" or "If you come back, I'll stop gambling forever"). Thoughts that the world is unfair, that God has been cruel to let this happen, fill the minds of individual family members and then are communicated to one another.

Depression   Frequently members experience some level of depression; an overwhelming sadness permeates the family members' thinking. Whereas anger is directed outward, depression is directed inward. Usually, family members need to talk about what has happened. In fact, they often retell the crisis story over and over. This represents a normal and healthy response, especially for families experiencing a long period of suffering because of death, incurable illness, permanent injuries, a long jail sentence, or mental breakdown. People outside the family often fail to understand the sad person's need to talk and may attempt to avoid the subject, not recognizing that support may involve just listening.

Reorganization   Grief-stricken individuals usually move on to what is described as a "turning point." It may be a moment of recognizing the finality of the event or of realizing one must move ahead with life. Graham (1997) studied the communication between divorced spouses and identified eleven turning points in which it changed, usually from negative to more positive over time. A frequent pattern that she labeled as "gradual relational progress" meant that the partners through "trial and error eventually figure out how to proceed in the new relationship." Usually, a decision marks the turning event. It may be to sell a failing business, put away the pictures that serve as daily reminders, go on a date, or join a self-help group. This decision signals that the individual has moved into the fourth crisis stage—reorganization of events in his or her life to effect a recovery. This stage is characterized by family members' taking charge of their lives and making the necessary changes forced on them by the crisis.

   If crisis emotions could be diagrammed, the line would descend to the lowest point with depression. The descent begins with the impact of the news and continues the decline with some upward movement in the recoil stage that diminishes as reality returns. After a descent into depression, most people move upward toward recovery (Figure 11.2).

   Throughout this process, communication serves to link family members as they share their reactions. It also links one or more family members to outside

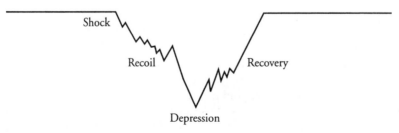

FIGURE 11.2
Linear Scale of Emotions during Crisis

sources of institutional or social support. If family members become cut off from support or cannot talk about their loss, they may become stuck, unable to complete the process and reach acceptance.

When a family experiences an ambiguous loss, these stages cannot be fully completed. Members struggle with how to move on because a long-term coma victim may wake up or a missing soldier may return. Eventually most members learn to normalize the ambivalence in order to move on. "Resiliency depends on knowing that the ambivalence from the ambiguous loss is normal and can be managed" (Boss, 2006). The next section will consider some common types of family crises and communication issues involved with each.

COMMUNICATION AND SPECIFIC CRISES

Communication patterns and networks shift dramatically when members face major life crises. Interaction becomes unpredictable as individuals withdraw into silence, explode into anger, or resort to constant talking as a way to handle stress or grief. This section focuses on major crises that have been studied extensively. However, remember that less dramatic events, such as moving or losing a job, also disrupts the family system by altering dreams or plans and introducing new tensions into the family. A crisis may force parents and their children to rely on different relationship maintenance strategies as dialectical tensions shift and the strategies that worked previously no longer address the situation (Baxter & Dindia, 1990). The crisis event can force open discussion among members or expose a family to public scrutiny, as in the case of a suicide, cyberbullying attack, or drug arrest. The triggering event may create closeness and connection as the family attempts some sort of a united front in order to cope and support one another, or members may withdraw from each other due to disagreements or pain. Variations in the predictability-novelty dialectical tension in individual family members' communication may be exacerbated when the crisis demands a response from each family member. Following we discuss four types of specific crises: untimely death, disability, separation and divorce, and separation in military families.

Untimely Death

The finality of death is an emotionally overwhelming crisis for most families. Although the death of any family member carries with it a sense of grief, the death of an elderly person who has lived a full life does not generate the anger aroused by untimely death, nor does it carry the potential for major role changes for most family members. However, the untimely death of a younger or middle-aged family member is a major crisis for many families. Surviving partners or children are not prepared for the loss or the role changes. The death of a single parent raises highly complicated issues. Sudden death, such as a car accident, provides family members no opportunity to say farewell or resolve relationship issues with the individual. Untimely death throws a family into severe shock, often resulting in prolonged mourning across many years (McGoldrick & Walsh, 2005).

Communication patterns range from the highly intense and emotional to the very superficial and denial oriented. Communication rules influence how members talk to each other about the loss. Religious beliefs and cultural patterns affect the grieving practices; grief may be unrestrained, as in Greek families where women may express intense sorrow at funeral ceremonies (Killian & Agathangelou, 2005). Irish families may experience a mix of celebration and sorrow, reflecting the deceased's move to a better world (McGoldrick, 2005). Dying persons and their family members often resort to a two-sided pretense that "everything is going to be all right." Critically ill persons or their family members may search for and continue to enroll in clinical trials, hoping to find something that will save the loved one. Family members in their own grief may deny the diagnosis of a terminal illness. This has been called "conspiracies of silence," where family members avoid talking about the prognosis because they fear it will result in a loss of hope and worsen the illness (Gueguen, Bylund, Brown, Levin, & Kissane, 2009). They shield the dying from such knowledge and develop communication rules to support this fiction. Frequently, the dying member knows the truth, and then pretends not to know it, in order to protect other family members. Sometimes family rules block the dying family member from dealing with all his or her feelings, as well as with immediate fears and loneliness. Some dying members resent the dishonesty involved, as explained here.

I will never forget my uncle complaining bitterly two days before he died about his family treating him like a helpless child and insisting he would recover whenever he started to talk about dying or his fear of never leaving the hospital. I was only 14 and did not fully understand what he was trying to tell me at the time, but I never forgot his pain or anger as he tried to explain the feeling of dying without emotional support.

A pioneer in the study of death and dying, Elizabeth Kübler-Ross (1970), suggested that death should be regarded as an "intrinsic part of life" and discussed openly like other events in family life, especially since almost all terminally ill patients are aware of it. The question should change from "Do I tell?" to "How do I share the information?" If a family confronts the issue openly, all members can go through preparatory grief together, which facilitates the later bereavement process. As the process continues, patients and loved ones may attempt to strike bargains—silently or openly. Finally, the loneliness, fears, and practical concerns may be addressed; these may range from "What is really on the other side?" to "How will they cope in school without my help?"

Dying persons need empathic listeners who do not deny their reality. Although watching a person die can be devastating to the family members, terminal illness (unlike sudden death) does provide the family members with an opportunity to resolve relationship issues and to say "final goodbyes." One man's experience facing the death of his partner is exemplified below.

We had been together for several years as partners-in-life. We knew that each of us cared for the other but we had intimacy issues because we found it difficult as two men to talk about what we really felt about one another, our relationship, and our kids from previous marriages. His illness changed all that! We began to have long talks late into the night, pouring out all the things we had never said, and trying to say what needed to be said about a future I would face alone. He not only helped me to accept his leaving, but he reconnected with all his siblings and his mother, in deeper, more meaningful ways. They all came for a weekend three weeks before he died and I made a two-hour video of each of them reminiscing about happy and sad times in their lives. Each told him what his life had meant to them and he did the same. He wanted this tape to be his gift of remembrance. Never was communication better or easier for him and those he loved than in his last few months!

Frequently, family members have a chance to talk with the dying member following confirmation of a terminal illness. These "final conversations" include "all the moments of talking, touching, and spending time with the Dying" (Keeley & Yingling, 2007, p. 2). Based on interviews, primarily with surviving family members, Keeley (2004) found three themes of love that characterized such conversations: affirmation of love, communication of love as a bridge to reconciliation, expressing altruistic love through the sacrifice of caring for the dying loved one.

After the death of a family member, the remaining relatives experience an ongoing bereavement process. An unexpected death, either by accident or illness, throws a family into an initial state of shock. Eventually, the shock wears off and the bereavement process begins. The event traumatizes the family, even in cases in which members know of an impending death. The survivors experience anger and depression. Approximately 5 percent of widows or widowers become severely depressed, while 10 to 17 percent become depressed to a clinically significant degree (Walsh, 2005, p. 316). Adolescents may withdraw from family and friends after a sibling's death and refuse to discuss their feelings (McGoldrick & Walsh, 2005). Family members may express regrets about unspoken issues: "If only I had told him how much I loved him." Unforeseen circumstances may arise that present communication challenges. A member's death may become a family secret because it is too painful to address; stories of the deceased may be excluded from conversation, or answering a question about the number of children in the family may confound a grieving parent (Bosticco & Thompson, 2005).

When persons choose their own death through suicide, many of their preparatory messages are denied; their attempts to communicate suicide plans go unrecognized until after the event. Parents of young people are advised to watch for behaviors such as talking about suicide, giving away possessions, acting abnormally cheerful after depression, and losing appetite. Suicidal elderly family members may exhibit depression, withdrawal, isolation, changes in sleep patterns, lower self-image, and prolonged bereavement. However, many relatives refuse to interpret these messages as they are intended.

The coping process varies according to the position that the deceased filled in the family system. The death of a young parent with children leaves a surviving partner or parent yearning for the missing family member, while at the same time assisting the children through the crisis without total withdrawal into personal grief. Parents who have lost a child to an accident, suicide, or homicide most frequently report using private prayer and church attendance to help them grieve (Murphy, Johnson, Lohan, & Tapper, 2002). A death by homicide appears to be most directly related to post-traumatic stress disorder, grief and despair (Murray, et al., 2010), and is a particularly critical issue given the number of young people who encounter multiple shooting deaths of relatives. The extended family system also experiences stress when a child dies. This young mother was bothered by her older brothers' response after the death of her infant daughter.

When they came to visit at Christmas, they didn't even ask to see her grave. I wanted them to go and be a part of it. I guess I don't know how I would be if it happened to someone else and I didn't experience it, but it just frustrated me a lot because it was like she never existed to them. I think it took them by surprise that we talked about her so openly. I guess that scared them because they didn't know how to react.

The death of a child devastates a family. It carries with it the loss of parental dreams of their child graduating, marrying, and having children, thus violating the natural order of life—the belief that children outlive parents. "A child's death affects every aspect of a parent's life and the marital relationship in particular" (Toller & Braithwaite, 2009, p. 257). In a study of the dialectical contradictions faced by bereaved parents, Toller and Braithwaite found that they experienced a dialectical contradiction between trying to grieve the child's death together and separately. Although wishing to help the other, each parent grieved differently, complicating a very difficult process. Over time, and painfully, couples learned to accept their differences and to compromise on each other's needs. Although both parents experienced needs for openness and closedness, these needs differed in terms of valuing verbal or nonverbal communication, the role of others in the process, and acceptance of each other's way of communicating about the child's death. In a related study, Toller (2008) examined how parents constructed their identities following the death of a child. Respondents faced issues of being "a parent without a child to parent" and being "an insider and an outsider." Over time, some parents chose to tend the gravesite and celebrate the child's birthday as a way to continue to nurture the lost child. Parents also had to negotiate with other family members and friends on issues, such as talking about their child, as they moved on.

Death disrupts a family system: couples may separate and sometimes divorce. Siblings may experience great stress and pressure. Adolescents who lose their siblings in a sudden, violent death experience a painful and complex grieving process for up to two years (Lohan & Murphy, 2002). In some cases, members experience disenfranchised grief—grief that exists although society may not recognize the relationship—at the death of a former spouse, a foster parent or a stepparent (Murray, Johnson, Lohan, & Tapper, 2010). Many family members experience a return of sadness or withdrawal on the anniversaries of deaths. Such dates, as well as significant holidays, act as markers of loss, with memories surfacing with great force.

Miscarriage is a special case of death, and the intensity of grief following miscarriage can be similar to other losses. Unlike other deaths there is "no publicly acknowledged person to bury or established rituals to structure mourning and gain support" (Brier, 2008, p. 451). Family therapists and counselors often have not been trained to help women and their partners deal with miscarriage (Sperry & Sperry, 2004). Women and men may not have ample opportunities to discuss their loss and feelings about the miscarriage, as early pregnancies are often kept secret. Research has shown that grief decreases over time and with a subsequent pregnancy (Brier, 2008). Although grief may subside over time, it may never really go away completely, as experienced by the following mother.

When my daughter was 2 years old, I became pregnant again. My husband and I were thrilled to be adding another child to our family. A miscarriage at 8 weeks followed and we were very distressed. A few months later I became pregnant with our second daughter. A son followed soon after. A few months ago I was watching a movie in which the main character has a miscarriage. I immediately started crying uncontrollably and had to stop watching the movie. Both my husband and I were surprised at the intensity of my sadness. Here it was, 3 years and 2 kids later, and I was still mourning the loss of the pregnancy.

Culture plays a significant role in how a family deals with death. In general, African American families, Irish families, and Italian families believe in a "good" send-off. White Anglo-Saxon Protestant families may limit their emotional expression. Puerto Rican families, especially the female members, suffer publicly. Jewish families, reflecting a tradition of shared suffering, tend to deal openly and directly with death. Chinese families believe a "good death" includes relatives surrounding the dying person. Cultures with rituals for dealing with death, a strong sense of community and tolerance of verbal expressions, provide members with greater support. In addition, religion or spirituality can offer meaning about death and provide comfort and support (McGoldrick & Walsh, 1999).

Illness or Disability

Members of families with a seriously ill or disabled member confront the need for meaningful coping processes. In families where a member has suffered a stroke, the Double *ABCX* model has been shown to be useful in understanding the family's experience (Clark, 1999). There is a strong relationship between family stress and family illnesses. Those families that demonstrated hardiness—a personality construct composed of control, challenge, and commitment—handled stress far better than those families that did not possess it. Coping with a child's disability, disease, or serious accident requires major adjustments involving physical and emotional energy. The immediate disruption of the family in no way equals the long-term drain on family resources and energies required to help the affected family member deal with what may be a lifelong situation.

The mourning process that families may undergo when a member is diagnosed with a serious illness or disability may be similar to stages of coping with death. These include impact, denial, grief, focusing outward, and closure, each with a communication condition. At the *impact* stage the family learns of a member's condition. Anxiety and tension characterize this period; family members respond in a disorganized manner. The family can absorb very little information and has very limited responses. Husbands of women diagnosed with breast cancer have reported feeling "struck by lightning" or wondering "why God would single her out" (Zahlis & Lewis, 2010). Usually, the *denial* stage follows, carrying with it a sense of disbelief and distorted expectations. Parents may reject the diagnosis of a child's cancer, finding themselves unable to hear what others are saying about the problem. Anger and sadness characterize the *grief*. Parents do not dream of giving birth to a child with health difficulties, and adult children may be devastated at their mother's loss of memory as Alzheimer's disease sets in. Parents question why this happened to their child. Children question why their sibling has to suffer. They may blame each other for the difficulty and isolate themselves from interacting with friends or extended family, effectively preventing open and supportive communication. Eventually, parents move toward the *focusing outward* stage, beginning a process of seeking information, discussing options, asking for help, expressing feelings, or forming a support group. In the case of Erin and Luke Johnson at the beginning of the chapter, this happened as they began to work to get Erin admitted to a prenatal clinical trial. Signs of relief are evident as the family moves toward dealing with the issues. The *closure* stage represents reconciliation with reality and a sense of adaptation to the child's needs. The family pulls together and adjusts in ways that allow the members of the altered system to move forward and to communicate directly about its concerns. A study of family caregivers of cancer patients showed that they had returned to normal levels of quality of life at two years postdiagnosis (Kim & Spillers, 2010).

Illness impacts the entire family system. Many adults who become ill also have older parents who are affected by their adult child's condition. These parents do not get the same help in coping with their child's illness as the child's spouse and children do, often being left to cope with their feelings alone (Gilbar & Refaeli, 2000). Following the onset of a chronic disease, it is typical for a patient to assume a central position in the family. This shift in focus, if continued over a longer period of time, affects the marital relationship and other parent-child relationships. Parents who are forced to focus on a sick and demanding child have little time or energy to deal with each other. In two-parent homes, a mother's disability leads to less parental school involvement and a less enriching home environment (Hogan, Shandra, & Msall, 2007). Even when a child develops a disease that can be managed effectively, parents and siblings are impacted. A study of siblings of a diabetic young person revealed that their sisters and brothers evidenced specific diabetes knowledge, awareness of related medical terminology, and diabetes management skills. In addition, their sense of immortality was affected (Pavlik, 2004). In many situations, families must spend a great deal of time with a child in the hospital or in doctors' offices. In a pediatric intensive care unit, parents expressed a desire for communication that would foster family normalcy, respect family rights, and strengthen the family as a whole (Tomlinson, Swiggum, & Harbaugh, 1999).

Disability and illness put stress on marriages, usually in negative ways. In fact, research reveals a high divorce rate among people with children with disabilities (Braithwaite & Thompson, 2000). One child's disability makes the parents' choice to have another child more difficult. Couples with disabled children have reported their inability to go to certain places or do certain things together. They may confront greater dialectical tension between predictability and novelty than before. The stresses are heightened when single mothers have the main responsibility for their disabled children.

As also illustrated in the case of Erin and Luke Johnson, some marriages do well despite the stress of illness or disability. Other marriages may struggle. One study examined marriages in which one spouse had chronic heart failure, a life-threatening condition where the body has limited ability to maintain normal blood circulation (Benazon, Foster, & Coyne, 2006). Researchers found that in these marriages, there were high levels of satisfaction and infrequent occurrences of criticism or hostility. In cases where a partner has been diagnosed with lung cancer, the other spouse's blaming of the partner for behaviors which led to the lung cancer was significantly associated with depressive symptoms for both the patient and the caregiver (Siminoff, Wilson-Genderson, & Baker, 2010).

In another study, some husbands reported that their wives' breast cancer had strengthened their relationship, while others found it negatively affected their relationship (Zahlis & Lewis, 2010). Those who found it to negatively affect their relationship cited communication difficulties such as the wife not wanting to talk about it, talking being difficult because of the serious nature of the illness, and feeling that talking didn't get them anywhere.

Siblings are significantly affected by a brother's or sister's illness or disability. Research on sibling response indicates that siblings may have a surprising lack of information about the disability. This lack of information may confuse siblings in the following ways: They may feel responsible for the condition, wonder if they are susceptible to it, experience confusion about how to talk about it with others, and feel overwhelmed by anger, hurt, or guilt (Seligman & Darling, 2007).

A study of the siblings of children with Down syndrome revealed that many siblings have a positive experience in living in such a family. These siblings had above-average self-concepts, were socially competent, and had low numbers of behavior problems. Siblings did better in families that had less demands, more resources, and better coping and problem-solving skills. The siblings in the study stated that they had learned patience, love, and courage from their siblings with Down syndrome (Van Riper, 2000). Parents attribute about twice as much of their stress to a child with a disability than they attribute to the youngest sibling in the family without a disability (Baxter, Cummins, & Yiolitis, 2000). Siblings may have to adjust to whole new interaction patterns, as shown here.

A child with special needs significantly alters family communication patterns.

A year-and-a-half ago, my brother, Steve, suffered a paralyzing head injury when he swerved his motorcycle to miss a dog. He dreams of driving his Chevy pickup again but he knows he might live the rest of his life in a nursing home. When asked when he expects to get out, his eyes go blank. "Never," he says. My father discourages such talk. "Now if you work real hard you might get your legs going again, right?" he says. Steve's eyes grow red. "OK," he replies and stares at the wall. It pains me to see him like this.

As in the Double *ABCX* model described earlier, the family organizes its current resources at the outset of the crisis and then attempts to develop new resources to carry them through the crisis. Those with less economic resources may struggle the most. One study documented how single, low-income, and immigrant fathers who were primary medical caretakers for their children may be at highest risk for difficulty coping (Wolff, Pak, Meeske, Worden, & Katz, 2002).

Individuals with a disability indicate that they wish to be acknowledged as persons first, especially with outsiders, and then hope to keep the focus on the relationship rather than the disability (Braithwaite, 1991). The frustrations involved are revealed in the following example.

I certainly knew I had multiple sclerosis! I knew that if I started using a wheelchair, I would lose more than I would gain, including a feeling of control over my life and my disease. I had difficulty with steps, and not all buildings had friendly ramps. I left for classes a half hour early. I pulled myself up the steps slowly, using the railing for support. Too often I would be stopped and would have to listen to remarks that internally sounded like "Oh, Janet, you poor thing." I resented the intrusions—it may have been a beautiful day and I was thinking about the novel I read for my English literature class, and these clods had to remind me that I was a cripple!

The ability of family members to communicate in a direct and supportive manner directly influences the coping process. The availability of support from the extended family members varies greatly, especially when the family with a severely ill member lives miles or states away. In a study of intergenerational help within Mexican American families, Dietz (1995) reported strong support for taking care of the elderly when ill. Also affecting the coping process may be the social support the family perceives that it has. In a study of families with a child who is diagnosed with congenital heart disease, the more social support a parent perceived, the higher level of coping he or she reported (Tak & McCubbin, 2002).

A few common types of illness that families face are Alzheimer's disease, addiction, cancer, and mental illness. The type of illness affects the ability to cope. A particularly difficult situation that many families encounter is when a family member is diagnosed with Alzheimer's disease. Spouses of men and women who are in nursing homes and have Alzheimer's make sense of their marriage to the affected spouse in different ways. Some continue to strongly view their relationship with their spouse as a couple, while some spouses consider themselves to be "married widows" (Baxter, Braithwaite, Golish, & Olson, 2002). Others fall in various places on the continuum between those two (Kaplan, 2001).

When a woman has breast cancer, she as well as her family members have to adjust to changes. Families that were more flexible, could balance family and illness needs, and had prior ability to cope with stress had more positive outcomes in cases of breast cancer (Radina & Armer, 2001). The roles of husbands of women with breast cancer are affected at home and work, especially when the wives are unable to perform tasks at home that they once did and when the family has children (Hilton, Crawford, & Tarko, 2000). In families with school-aged children, a mother's diagnosis with breast cancer can put particular stresses on the father as he takes on additional roles and communicates with the children about their mother's disease. One study found that although mothers typically were the first to tell the children about their diagnosis, the fathers described strategies they used to help the children cope, such as giving them information, providing opportunities for them to talk about it, and ensuring that the schools knew about the situation (Forrest, Plumb, Zieland, & Stein, 2009). In some families, there may be disagreement between the parents on how much information to give and when to give it.

Another form of illness that impacts the family is addiction to drugs or alcohol. Alcoholism distorts a family's patterns of behavior and communication, affecting all members (Hudak, Krestan, & Bepko, 2005). If one or more members are addicted, the entire family tends to develop a verbal pattern to cope with the problem. Such families are characterized by the rules "Don't talk, don't trust, don't feel" (Black, 2001). The questions arise—What do you tell? When do you openly seek help and end the secrecy? How do you communicate with a family member who is in an altered mental state while under the influence of alcohol or drugs? The stress in such families is monumental. In a study of communication between alcoholic parents and their children, Menees (1996) revealed that the coping strategy of "venting" improved the children's self-esteem. If they can vent their feelings about their parents' drinking, they maintain better self-esteem because venting serves as a protective factor and reduces stress. The closed boundaries of most alcoholic families inhibit recovery and support.

Mental illness can also have a profound effect on family functioning. Research has examined how both children's and parents' mental illness affects family functioning. For instance, families of adolescents with bipolar disorder have been found to have lower levels of cohesion and adaptability and more conflict than families with healthy adolescents (Sullivan & Miklowitz, 2010). Adolescent children of parents with a history of depression are more likely to use coping strategies that allow them to adapt to the environment, rather than to avoid or try to change the reality of their parents' illness. These coping strategies include positive thinking, acceptance, and distraction (Jaser, Champion, Reeslund, et al., 2007). The effect on children may be more profound when the parent with mental illness is a mother rather than a father. A recent study examined cases where either a mother or father of a young adult had a mental illness. Young adults with mentally ill mothers reported more mental health symptoms, more loneliness, and less overall psychological well-being than young adults without parents with mental illness. There was no difference between young adults with mentally ill fathers and those with mentally healthy parents (Abraham & Stein, 2010).

Separation and Divorce

Separation and divorce, variations in the family life course, are transitional crises that create emotional and practical upheaval. In most cases, there tends to be two phases—the separation and legalization phase and the settling into the single-parent family form. These phases usually overlap to some degree (Carter & McGoldrick, 2005). Divorce tends to be the result of unhappiness and problems that have developed over time, not just the result of one negative occurrence in the marriage (Hetherington & Kelly, 2002). A systemic view of divorce assumes that both parents contributed to the dissolution of the marriage, although specific individual issues such as addiction, abuse, or severe mental or physical health problems may be presented by one partner. Problematic or negative communication patterns, such as negativity, stonewalling, aggressiveness, and demand-withdraw patterns are risk factors for divorce (Amato, 1996).

Although postdivorce families often are referred to as single-parent families headed by females, most fathers tend to remain active in a parental role (Stewart, et al., 1997). Parents remain linked through their children and must find ways to function as an ongoing altered family system in which former partners function as co-parents. Increasingly, the resulting binuclear family reflects three key qualities that contribute to the well-being of children: a child's basic psychological and economic needs are met; extended family or predivorce close friendship relations are maintained; and parents exhibit mutual cooperation and support around child-oriented concerns (Ahrons, 2005).

Separation and divorce processes resemble a mourning pattern. At some point, each partner mourns the loss of the relationship, although one may have emotionally separated from the other years before the divorce became a reality. Initially, spouses may deny that anything is really wrong and communicate to children or others that "Our problems aren't all that serious" or "Daddy will be back soon, so don't tell anyone he's gone." As the reality of separation takes hold, anger, bargaining, and depression intermingle. Attempts at reconciliation may occur. Social integration helps to minimize divorce rates; membership in religious groups and having children serve as integrating factors (Lauer & Lauer, 2009). Painful accusations and negative conflict are often heightened by the adversarial positions required in legal divorce proceedings. Many individuals experience depression, which reflects the sense of loss and/or rejection, often accompanied by great loneliness and a sense of failure (Hetherington & Kelly, 2002). Divorce pressures are intensified by the predictable and problematic withdrawal of social support; a "community divorce" occurs when each of the partners leaves one community of friends and relations and enters another, a process that may include loneliness and isolation for a period of time (Lauer & Lauer, 2009, p. 342). Old friends may be afraid to "take sides," or they act as if divorce might be contagious.

According to Knapp and Vangelisti (2005), a relationship that is coming apart is characterized by (1) a recognition of differences, (2) an experience of constricted communication, (3) a sense of stagnation, (4) a pattern of avoidance, and, finally, (5) the immediate or protracted experience of termination. During these stages divorcing partners interact in ways that create increasing physical and psychological distance. A complicating factor is that most parents, while trying to separate from each other, still attempt to stay connected with their children. "Many post marital couples struggle with the necessity of maintaining a relationship with a person whom they have chosen to no longer be married to. It seems that the desire and responsibility one might feel to stay connected to one's former spouse is fraught with contradiction" (Graham & Edwards, 2002, p. 14). There are few accepted rituals or rites of passage to help divorcing partners to mourn their losses or begin their healing (Ahrons, 2005).

Divorce tends to have adverse effects on children (Amato, 2001; Waite & Gallagher, 2000). Although divorce is often a badly needed fresh start for the parents, divorce is a much different experience for the child (Wallerstein, Lewis, & Blakeslee, 2000). Children are often affected by their parents' marital problems long before and long after the divorce; detrimental psychological and academic effects on children may occur from about three years before to three years after the divorce (Sun & Li, 2002). Over time, the family system recalibrates itself to establish an altered course, including the development of new communication patterns. The presence of siblings may ease the transition because they protect each other from parents' attempts to hook them into the struggle, share the "care" of a distraught parent, and support each other (Hines, 1997). Indeed, siblings often become closer after a divorce and their close relationships frequently carry over into adulthood (Wallerstein, et al., 2000).

However, many children pay a long-term price for their parents' decision to divorce. In their analysis of links between divorce in the grandparent generation and the outcomes in the grandchild generation, Amato and Cheadle (2005) found that "divorce has consequences for subsequent generations, including individuals who were not yet born at the time of the divorce" (p. 191). Taking a life course approach, they documented the transmission of family problems across three generations. They found that for some families, divorce in the grandparent generation (G1) had the potential to affect educational attainment, marital stability, and parent-child tension in the next generation (G2). In turn, problems in that generation affected the grandchild generation (G3) in terms of lower educational attainment, an increase in marital strife, and weakened bonds with parents. The authors are careful to provide limitations on their findings, such as a lack of information about marital discord or parent-child tensions in G1, and other, unreported stresses or family transitions may have influenced the outcomes.

Most children experience confusion and chaos when parents divorce. The following example illustrates what may happen if those fears are not addressed.

When my parents divorced, although it was a relief from the fighting and constant tension, I experienced a sense of loss and many new fears about their future as well as my own. As a child who experienced divorce, I was expected to "bounce back." I was just expected to adapt, but without being given time to express grief. I repressed these feelings and fears, and since they were never really addressed, they resurfaced now, years later, to haunt me.

Wallerstein and colleagues (2000) studied the long-term effects of divorce on children which carry into adulthood. In their study of adults, who they had first met during their parents' divorces many years earlier, the authors found the following. First, children who grew up in divorced families didn't have happy memories of play as did those who grew up in intact families. "Instead of caring about who finds who in a game of hide-and-seek or who is at bat in the local softball game, children of divorce have other, more pressing concerns. Is Mom all right? Is Dad going to pick me up tonight? Can I bring my new friend over to the house to play if no one is home?" (p. 19). Second, those who grew up in intact families were much more likely to be able to tell the story of their parents' courtship than those from divorced families. Third, children from intact families also received more financial support through their college years. Wallerstein and colleagues concluded that growing up is harder in a divorced family than in an intact family. However, the researchers described adult children of divorce who created good lives for themselves with happy marriages, children, and successful careers.

Few divorcing parents have appropriate conversations with their children about the divorce for a variety of reasons. The parents often do not have information about how to have such a conversation, the parents may be angry, and they are often overwhelmed. "This means that the child, especially the preschool child, often learns about the divorce in the most traumatic way possible when she wakes up one morning to find that her father and his belongings have vanished into thin air" (Wallerstein, et al., 2000, p. 47). Parents who felt they did not have control over the divorce stressors (e.g., the other parent's behavior) are more likely to make inappropriate disclosures to a child about the divorce than parents who felt they did have control (Affifi, McManus, Hutchinson, & Baker, 2007).

Frequently children are informed about the divorce but not encouraged to discuss their concerns. Whereas loss through death involves a socially expected mourning period, there is no sanctioned mourning period for the loss of the "family that was." Children need support at the time of divorce and during the postcrisis period. Divorce forces a division of parental assets, and messages about the availability of money suddenly become frequent. Children who have never been concerned about family resources are faced with new realities—a smaller home, sharing rooms, moving, fewer vacations, less clothing, and so on (Ono, 1998).

One recent study asked participants to recall their experiences of being told about their parents' divorce and how they felt about these experiences (Gumina, 2009). Five themes of good communication about the decision to divorce emerged:

1. Both parents should talk about the decision with the child/children
2. Parents should avoid negative communication about the other in front of the children
3. Emphasize that it is not the child's/children's fault
4. Do not give unnecessary or specific details about the reasons for divorce
5. Invite the children to respond or ask questions

Usually one parent, most often the mother, is named the custodial parent, although increasing numbers of fathers receive custody of children. The term *coparenting* is used to describe what has been thought to be the ideal parenting relationship after divorce and is seen to involve both parents in decision making about children. "Coparents maintain a cooperative and constructive relationship with their former partner and opt to prioritize their children's welfare over their own discord" (Gasper, Stolberg, Macie, & Williams, 2008, p. 273). Coparenting has been shown to be an important factor in young adult adjustment outcomes (Gasper, et al., 2008).

Divorce and adjustment to life after divorce are often influenced by the emotional climate of the marriage (Hetherington & Kelly, 2002). The transition to a postdivorce family involves managing multiple issues. Orderly separations, as opposed to abrupt and chaotic ones, are characterized by good management and firm relationship boundaries, or a clear understanding of how separated spouses will interact (Ahrons, 2000). Little is known about specific aspects of interparental patterns of conflict and negative disclosure in such families (Afifi & McManus, 2006). Yet it is clear that members need to coordinate their privacy rules in order to function effectively; for example, children may learn to avoid talking about one parent in front of the other because parents become upset or angry at the disclosures (Golish & Caughlin, 2002).

In postdivorce families who perceive themselves to be strong or moderately strong, in other words resilient, shared family time was important in contributing to their communal coping, relational maintenance, and growth-oriented change (e.g., creating new family rituals) (Hutchinson, Afifi, & Krause, 2007).

Usually, communication between former spouses becomes less conflictual in the years following a divorce. Lorenz and colleagues (1997) reported that divorcing mothers experience a piling up of stressful events and depressive symptoms right after the divorce but they diminish over the next three years. In comparison to a married sample, however, divorced women reported a higher number of stressful events and depressive symptoms at the end of the multiyear study. There are many models for postdivorce partners. Ahrons (2000) identified five types of arrangements: perfect pals, cooperative colleagues, angry associates, fiery foes, and dissolved duos; over time about half the divorced parent pairs become part of the cooperative colleagues group.

Women find talk to be helpful in dealing with divorce during the first year following it. Men, however, are less likely to talk about it. Hetherington and Kelly (2002) suggested that this is because men have lost the person to whom they disclosed the most—their wives. Because of stress from the divorce, men and women experience more health problems in the early years after divorce, including depression, alcoholism, sleep disorders, and pneumonia. However, women who were previously in hostile marriages or distant marriages frequently had improved health (Hetherington & Kelly, 2002).

Mothers talk to their daughters about a range of topics following divorce, including personal accomplishments, hopes for future, or feelings of happiness about being a parent. More problematic topics, such as negative feelings about the daughter's father, financial concerns, and child support payments have been shown to be associated with a poorer mother-daughter relationship quality (Luedemann, Ehrenberg, & Hunter, 2006).

Divorce is seen as a risk to preserving a strong father-child bond. The importance of the nonresidential father's relationship with his children should not be overlooked. Stone (2006) found three important influences on the quality of the father-child relationship after divorce. These are: (1) a father's view of his own role as being important; (2) a father's belief in his abilities to be an effective parent; and (3) the belief that the mother is not an effective parent. Young adults whose parents divorced when the children were between the ages of 8 and 15 reported lower levels of father involvement, father nurturance, and less frequent verbal and physical contact with fathers compared to young adults from intact families (Peters & Ehrenberg, 2008).

Although it is impossible to remove all the negative aspects of divorce stress on children and their communication, parents can certainly reduce the stress. If neither parent uses the child as a go-between, nor encourages "tattletale" behavior, opportunities for conflict are reduced. If each supports the other's discipline, the child cannot play one against the other. When dads depart, there is evidence that boys suffer more than girls. They display more behavioral and school problems (Mott, Kowaleski-Jones, & Menaghan, 1997). In addition, when marital quality, including communication, deteriorates, children have difficulty in maintaining relationships with both parents and, as a result, develop closer ties to one parent. *Parental alienation* occurs when one parent tries to distance a child from the other parent, although this can occur in both intact and divorced families and is associated with negative feelings toward the parent who is attempting the alienation (Mone & Biringen, 2006).

The communication between adolescents and their parents can have an effect on the adolescents' coping. One study asked adolescents and their custodial parents about their communication about divorce-related stressors (Affifi, Huber, & Ohs, 2006). The researchers found that adolescents who were more skilled or comfortable having discussions with their custodial parent about divorce-related stressors were able to cope more positively with the divorce. Further, the custodial parents' communication was associated with children's ability to cope with the divorce, such that parents who did not communicate well with the adolescent were more likely to have adolescents who were not coping positively.

Eventually many of these divorced parents and their children find themselves as members of a stepfamily, married, or cohabiting. Just as there are many variations on living as divorced partners, there are many variations of stepfamily life. Multiple pathways are represented in the quest to reach the point of "feeling like a family"; the five developmental trajectories that have been identified represent diverse communicative patterns and include variations in openness and rituals. These trajectories are: accelerated, prolonged, declining, stagnating, and high-amplitude turbulent (Braithwaite, Olson, Golish, Soukup, & Turman, 2001).

Military Families: A Special Case of Separation

A different, but profound, type of separation exists when a member of a family is deployed to war, often for multiple and extended periods of time. This has specific effects on parent-child relationships and partner relationships. A recent study of children from military families found that the children reported emotional difficulties at higher levels than in the general population (Chandra, et al., 2009). The longer a parent was separated from the family due to deployment, the more severe were the children's emotional difficulties.

Couples who are separated by war learn to enact relational maintenance strategies that help them cope with the separation and uncertainty. A recent study of wives of deployed U.S. service members found three different types of relational maintenance strategies used by the couples. First, intrapersonal maintenance strategies included journaling, positive thinking, and prayer. Mediated partner strategies were the second type of maintenance strategies and included activities such as e-mail, webcam, care packages, future talk, and affection and intimacy. Third, wives reported that social and family support helped in maintaining relationships (Merolla, 2010). Couples' dialectical tensions when the husband is deployed include certainty-uncertainty during predeployment, autonomy-connection during deployment, and openness-closedness after the husband returns home (Sahlstein, 2010).

Support and Communication

Throughout any of these crises the family's capacity for open communication, reflective of its levels of cohesion and adaptation and its images, themes, boundaries, and biosocial beliefs, determines how the system will weather the strain.

low cohesion

rigidity

A family with low cohesion may fragment under pressure, unless such pressure can link the unconnected members. A family with limited adaptability faces a painful time, since such crises force change on the system and the lives of each member. A family whose images and themes allow outside involvement in family affairs may use its flexible boundaries to find institutional and social support. A family with rigid biosocial beliefs faces difficult challenges if key family figures are lost or injured and others are not permitted to assume some of their role responsibilities. How much social support family members receive in crises depends on how much support they have given one another prior to the crises.

Some family members may use *protective buffering* to try to reduce distress in other family members by protecting them from becoming upset or being burdened. Protective buffering is achieved through hiding worries and concerns and avoiding disagreements (Manne, et al., 2007). In a study of couples where the wife has breast cancer, the use of such techniques has been shown to cause more distress, but only in relationships where marital satisfaction is reported.

Coping Strategies Every family undergoes periods of unpredictable stress. Many of these stresses are not as immediately critical as death, illness, or divorce, but they do eat away at members' resources and affect coping strategies. Burr, Klein, and Associates (1994) view stress as a multifaceted phenomenon with multiple causes and coping strategies. Their research indicates that families deal with stress in a sequential process, trying Level I coping strategies first, and if these fail, moving on to Level II and III strategies (see Table 11.1).

When a stress occurs, a family will first try to use a Level I process by perhaps changing the family rules or role expectations. In a case where a child is consistently wetting the bed, this might include meeting with a therapist. If families are struggling with financial issues, they may agree to quit using credit cards. Or, if one partner takes on new responsibilities at work, the other may need to increase responsibilities at home. If any of these changes work, the family proceeds into a period of recovery. If changing the rules and more superficial aspects of the family's operation fails, then the family seeks more basic or meta-level changes at Level II.

Level II changes involve a middle level of abstraction, one that alters the system in fundamentally different ways. For example, at Level II, the family may need

---

TABLE 11.1

Coping Strategies Sequence

Level	Strategy
I	Change or adapt existing rules, ways of doing things, rearranging responsibilities to address the stress.
II	Change metarules (rules about rules) so that new areas of rules are created to address the stress.
III	Change the basic assumptions about life; reorder value structure to address stress.

to change metarules about how their rules are made and by whom. For instance, in a family where the parents have divorced, a Level II strategy would include talking about decision making in the family, changing the way Mom as a single parent directs the family now, modifying the way the family makes and changes rules, and replacing competitive strategies with cooperative ones.

If Level II strategies fail to reduce the stresses to a comfortable point for the family's well-being, the need arises for more abstract Level III coping strategies—ones that entail attempts to change the fundamental values or philosophies of life that govern the family. Changes at this level require communication about what being a member in a particular family means and how members can enhance one another's lives by participating more effectively within the system they have created. Level III refers to highly abstract processes that seek to make changes in the family's beliefs, paradigms, and values to reduce stress. At Level III, the family will question its basic beliefs and try to decide if members can change in any way to accommodate the negative effects of stress. For instance, a family may strongly believe that children should be raised by a father and mother. When a single, 40-year-old female family member makes the decision to use a sperm donor to become pregnant, her parents may initially react with disapproval. However, as the pregnancy and subsequent birth take place, they may gradually accept their daughter's wishes and realize that their role as grandparents will be important to the child, ultimately giving emotional support to the daughter and baby. Other examples of Level III changes might be a family changing religions or connecting to kinship networks after ignoring them for years.

Many predictable and unpredictable stresses will be handled easily by families using Level I coping strategies. Some significant stresses will force the family system to adopt new, creative, and possibly painful ways. Members have less experience in creating new coping strategies, and thus creating Levels II and III strategies is difficult and requires trial and error.

Family members, immediate and extended, serve as critical supports when one or more members face a crisis. These internal social relationships aid in maintaining the well-being of members both physically and psychologically (Sieber, Edwards, Kallenberg, & Patterson, 2006). Other members may engage in new health behaviors (diet, health monitoring) with the patient or may engage in critical psychological behaviors such as forgiving or listening.

Support Groups Negative stresses—such as alcoholism, drug abuse, child abuse, economic reversals, job transfers, and suicides—take their toll on a family's emotional resources. A stress, such as divorce, reduces the family's support systems at the same time that the family members' pain is increasing. Without a strong communication network, the individuals—forced to rely on themselves—may become alienated or severely depressed. Even seemingly positive experiences such as raising a gifted child, achieving a high-powered position, adopting a child, or receiving large sums of money, can stress the system. In order to understand a family's coping capacity, a family's immediate and postcrisis resources, especially support networks, must be understood.

In a society characterized by mobility and smaller families, persons are finding interpersonal support from others who share similar experiences and pain. Groups such as Alcoholics Anonymous or support groups for parents who have lost a child can make a real difference in coping. The Internet has increased the possibilities for persons and families to find support. Internet-based support groups can be particularly important to those dealing with rare diseases or who are uncomfortable with face-to-face disclosures (Albrecht & Goldsmith, 2003). Participation in social support groups for cancer patients has been shown to reduce social isolation and negative moods, including depression and cancer-related trauma (Im, et al., 2007). In all cases, self-help groups rely on members' communication as a healing process, an important way to share and receive comfort.

CONCLUSION

This chapter examined communication and unpredictable life stresses. Specifically, it focused on (1) the process of dealing with unpredictable stresses and (2) communication during certain major stressful life events, such as death, illness or disability, and divorce. Over the years, every family system encounters external stress from crisis situations as well as stress from developmental change. The system's ability to cope effectively with stress depends on a number of factors, such as the number of recent stresses, role changes, and social and institutional support. The Double *ABCX* model provides an effective explanation of family coping because it focuses on precrisis and postcrisis variables. Death, illness, and divorce necessarily alter family systems over long periods of time. Communication may facilitate or restrict a family's coping procedures. In most families, sharing of information and feelings can lower the stress level. The family with flexible boundaries has the capacity to accept support and the potential for surviving crises more effectively than families who close themselves off from others. Many family members find support through membership in self-help organizations.

In Review

1. Using a real or fictional family, analyze the effects on the family of a severe stress that impacted one member (e.g., drug problem, serious car accident, or severe illness).

2. Using the same example of family stress, compare and contrast an analysis of the problem according to the *ABCX* model and the Double *ABCX* model.

3. Describe how a "happy event" has brought high levels of stress to a family with which you are familiar.

4. How do different cultural and/or religious attitudes toward death aid or restrict the mourning process for surviving family members?

5. What guidelines for communication would you recommend to spouses who have children and are about to separate?

6. Using Baxter's concepts of dialectical tensions in relationships, discuss with examples how you think crises affect openness-closedness, predictability-novelty, and autonomy-connectedness in a family system.

7. Give examples of Level I, II, and III coping strategies that reflect how families cope with crises.

KEY WORDS

Ambiguous loss   277
Bonadaptation   283
Boundary ambiguity   284
Coparenting   299
Coping   278

Double ABCX model   281
Maladaption   283
Protective buffering   302
Stages of family crisis   284
Stressor events   278

Family Communication and Well-Being

"Good families—even great families—are off track 90 percent
of the time! The key is that they have a sense of destination.
They know what the 'track' looks like. And they keep coming
back to it time and time again. . . . With regard to our families,
it doesn't make any difference if we are off target or even if our
family is a mess. The hope lies in the vision and in the plan and
in the courage to keep coming back time and time again."

—Stephen R. Covey, *The Seven Habits of Highly Effective Families*

After two years of failed diagnoses, Drew's doctor suggested he get tested for hemochromatosis, a little known genetic disease that attacks the organs but, if caught in time, can be managed indefinitely by ongoing blood transfusions. After the diagnosis, the genetic counselor recommended that Drew inform his family members, particularly his two siblings, about his diagnosis because they were at an increased risk for being affected by it also. His sister Alisha lived in the same city and he saw her regularly; his brother lived across the country and they seldom were in contact. Although it seemed to be a straightforward task, Drew hesitated for months, worrying about health insurance or the reactions of colleagues if they knew, until his partner, Molly, started to pressure him to alert his relatives.

After more weeks of stalling, Drew finally sent his sister a short e-mail, although he did not go into much detail on the subject. Alisha immediately called Molly to ask if this weird-sounding disease was serious. Molly provided information about hemochromatosis, sent Alisha to a medical Web site and explained that if Alisha tested positive, she could control the disease indefinitely. The next week, upon Alisha's request, Drew met Alisha for lunch and they talked about hemochromatosis and the process of testing. During this lunch, Drew asked Alisha to call their sister-in law, Charlene, to inform their brother Kevin about the disease. Within a day Alisha passed on the news.

After nine years of marriage, two full-time jobs, and two small children, Angeli and Dante had fallen into a set of everyday rhythms that kept the household and family running. Every weekday started at 5:45 a.m. with packing lunches, getting the kids dressed, driving to daycare, and heading to the warehouse or office. In the evenings things went in reverse, with dinner, baths, and bedtime stories carrying the couple into an hour of staring at the television. Every Saturday meant cleaning, shopping, and playing with the kids and a Netflix movie. Sunday morning involved church attendance before spending the afternoon with Angeli's parents. Angeli and Dante rarely had time alone, and going out without the children was saved for birthdays or anniversaries.

Despite feeling like she had everything she had wanted—two children, good employment, a nice home, two cars, and a couple of family vacations each year—Angeli found herself growing increasingly dissatisfied with her life and her marriage. After a number of conversations in which Angeli claimed she hardly knew Dante anymore, the couple decided to go on a Marriage Encounter weekend with other church couples in order to find some time to be together and talk about their relationship and their lives. Angeli's parents agreed to watch the children. On Friday evening the couple arrived at a retreat center for the opening session. By Saturday evening Dante and Angeli had heard five leader-couples talk about how they learned to make positive changes in their marriages. They also held private writing sessions and conversations on a series of issues that affected their marriage. Both partners were looking forward to the final Sunday sessions. One year later, Dante and Angeli have made strides to improve their marriage. They set aside a monthly date night where they go out alone, take a few minutes every night for debriefing conversations, and try to be more affectionate with each other.

How do members of well-functioning families live, grow, and relate to each other year after year? How do they cope with problems and changes? To what extent can family members create new communication patterns, develop healthy ways of loving, fighting, or making decisions? How do these communication practices contribute to family well-being?

In the previous chapters, we have introduced and described many of the important theories and models that help to explain family communication concepts and processes. Throughout these chapters we have referred to outcomes associated with family communication, particularly relationship satisfaction. This final chapter explores the connections between family communication and family members' well-being. Defined broadly, the term "well-being" has to do with family members' quality of life (Segrin, 2006).

Many people believe that life happens *to* them, that they have no ability to improve their relationships. Such individuals are *reactors*, taking no responsibility for their part in a problem or for changing relationships. Other persons serve as *actors*, believing they can make personal changes and co-create desirable relational change. The differences between a reactor and an actor are captured in the following example.

"That's the way I am. Take me or leave me" was the common comment of my first husband. He believed that if you had to work on a relationship there was something wrong with it. Needless to say, after a few years we dissolved the marriage. Now I am engaged to a man who wants to talk and think about how to keep a relationship growing over a lifetime. We have even had some premarital counseling to explore important issues before the marriage. Life is very different when both people are open to change.

Family members have the potential to grow in chosen directions, although such growth may require great risk, effort, and pain. The systems perspective implies that whenever change is attempted by some members, it may be resisted by other members who wish to keep their system in balance no matter how painful that balance is. It is difficult, although not impossible, for an individual to initiate lasting change in the system; change is more easily accomplished when most or all members are committed to an alternative way of relating. Also, it is a challenge for members of the system to recognize certain negative patterns in which they play a part. It may take a third party or clearheaded, objective analysis to recognize a destructive pattern. Change depends on one's ability to discover the meanings underlying one's own actions and that of other family members. According to Gottman's "Sound Marital House Theory," change is a process of creating shared, symbolic meaning through dreams, narratives, myths, and metaphors (Gottman, Ryan, Carrère, & Erley, 2002). Because there is no "one right way" for all families to behave, the members of each family have to discover what works well for their system by sharing dreams and stories.

Throughout this book we have focused primarily on functional families, rather than severely troubled ones, recognizing that every functional family experiences alternating periods of ease and distress. Therefore, families fall on a continuum ranging from severely dysfunctional to optimally functional. Although few families remain at the optimally functional point indefinitely due to tensions caused by developmental or unpredictable stresses, many do remain within the functional to optimal range over long periods of time. How do these families maintain their state of well-being? The following sections will attempt to answer that question by exploring (1) the interrelationship of family members' physical health status and health practices and communication, (2) family capacity for holding difficult conversations, (3) personal, instructional, and therapeutic approaches for creating and maintaining effective communication within families, and (4) final perspectives on family communication and well-being.

FAMILY COMMUNICATION AND PHYSICAL WELL-BEING

Think about the family in which you grew up. What were the rules about health behaviors? Perhaps your parents said, "Clean your plate if you want dessert." Maybe yours was a household in which you were expected to try new types of food. Or perhaps your parents let you eat what you wanted. In some families, a child may stay home from school if she says she doesn't feel well, while in others, a high temperature may be required. As you reached adolescence, your parents may have established a new set of rules focused on reducing health risk behaviors, possibly including rules about alcohol and drug use, smoking, and sexual activity. Over the years, you have also likely experienced the illness and perhaps the death of a family member. The communication in your family that surrounded these events likely has helped to shape your thoughts about health and illness.

These are just a few examples of the interrelationships between family communication and health. As Bylund and Duck stated: "Throughout the lifespan, the everyday interactions among family members have the potential to have a tremendous impact on individuals' construction of health, talk about health, participation in health care systems, enactment of healthy or unhealthy behaviors, and health status" (2004, p. 5). To this we add that individuals' health, illness, and healthy or unhealthy behaviors also have an impact on family members' communication. There is a mutual influence between health and family communication.

Health Status

Family researchers have been particularly interested in marital relationships and marital partners' health status for many years. In general, married adults are healthier than unmarried adults and have lower mortality rates. This may be because married people have more resources, more support, and behave in less risky ways. Or it may be because people who are healthier are more likely to get married and stay married (Waite & Gallagher, 2000). The benefit of being married is not equal, though. Husbands gain greater health benefits from marriage than do wives, in part because of wives' greater tendencies to attempt to manage their husbands' health habits. Also, wives are likely to have more people in their support system, whereas husbands usually name their wives as their primary confidant (Kiecolt-Glaser & Newton, 2001).

Despite the overall benefit of marriage on health, it is important to recognize that marital quality also plays a role. Unhappily married persons are generally less healthy than those who are unmarried. The quality of married couples' interactions can have a profound effect on their health. Factors such as spousal conflict, spousal over-involvement, and inequality in decision making can contribute to poorer health. Conflict in particular seems to have more of a negative effect on wives' health than on husbands' health. In studies where researchers have asked husbands and wives to have a discussion about a topic that they have conflict over, spouses' blood pressure and heart rates tend to increase, with the wives having the greater increases (Kiecolt-Glaser & Newton, 2001). When both spouses in a marriage have a tendency to suppress their anger, their mortality risk may be greater (Harburg, et al., 2008). Family distress and conflict can affect the health and health habits of both adults and children in families (Jones, Beach, & Jackson, 2004; Michael, Torres, & Seeman, 2007).

The fact that a good quality marriage provides a health benefit makes sense when you consider that those persons who are socially isolated have worse health than those who have meaningful relationships. Marriage frequently provides a stable and consistent guard against social isolation, bringing with it the health-enhancing benefits of a relationship. Whether or not someone is married, however, they can still be healthy and have meaningful relationships with partners, family, and friends.

Influencing Health Behaviors

Family communication may impact family members' health through communication about health-promoting behaviors (e.g., nutrition, exercising) and health risk reduction behaviors (e.g., quitting smoking, practicing safe sex). For example, farmers are at a particular risk for developing skin cancer because of the time they spend in the sun, and communication from their families can be an important factor in their health risk prevention behaviors (Parrott & Lemieux, 2003). Chapter 8 contained examples of how spouses might use influence strategies to modify the other's health behaviors. Here we focus on other ways that family communication might affect family members' health behaviors.

The content of health promotion and risk reduction communication is tied closely to developmental issues in the family. For example, when a couple becomes new parents, one health promoting behavior for the infant can be how long the mother breastfeeds. Researchers found that how strongly the male partner thinks that his partner should breastfeed influences the mother's breastfeeding behaviors. They point out, "These women behaved more in accordance with what their partners thought they should do than with what they had originally intended to do" (Rempel & Rempel, 2004, p. 107).

As children grow older, health promotion and risk reduction discussions may change. For adolescents and young adult children, parents' communications about health issues often focus on risky behaviors such as smoking, drinking alcohol, using other drugs, and engaging in sexual activity. They may use "abstinence rules" or "contingency rules" (Baxter, Bylund, Imes, & Routsong, 2009). An example of an abstinence rule is "Don't drink alcohol until you are 21," while a contingency rule is "But if you do drink, don't drive." Baxter and colleagues found that parents and their adolescent offspring reported abstinence and contingency rules were used for both alcohol and risky sexual behaviors. However, very few contingency rules about tobacco were reported. Miller-Day (2008) found that

❙ Parents teach their children about health-promoting behaviors in many ways.

using a strategy of "no-tolerance" may be the most effective in preventing substance abuse. Parents also play an important role in encouraging adolescents to use health-promoting behaviors such as exercise, good nutrition, and sun protection (Bylund, Baxter, Imes, & Wolf, 2010).

One way to view family health communication is to look at the rules that families have about health behaviors and how these rules guide family members' actions. In families that are considered to have high expressiveness, members experience a lot of freedom to express opinions and room for individuality. In contrast, families who rate high on expressiveness (similar to the conversation-orientation discussed in Chapter 7) rate lower on compliance to health rules, articulation of health rules, and consequences of violating health rules. Parents in these families seem to value individual decision making, with less focus on a rule-based system. However, in families that emphasize conformity to authority (similar to conformity-orientation), adolescents and parents recall *family health rules* in similar ways. These families seem to have a shared understanding of health rules. Finally, families that are conflict avoidant (similar to conformity-orientation) tend to hold all children in a family accountable to the same health rules, perhaps to avoid claims of favoritism from siblings (Baxter, Bylund, Imes, & Schieve, 2005).

Family health rules are seldom stated explicitly in a one-time sit-down conversation between parent and child. Two-thirds of parents and offspring report not having those types of conversations, but instead engaging in ongoing conversations about alcohol and drug use. Content in such discussions may include expressions of disapproval, warnings about the dangers of use, and the potential health consequences (Miller-Day & Dodd, 2004). Parents' targeted and frequent conversations with their children about alcohol have been associated with less likelihood of alcohol use (Miller-Day & Kam, 2010).

Overall parent-child communication may have a more indirect influence on children's substance use. Families with regular conflict tend to have children who are more likely to use drugs. Adolescents who engage in demand/withdraw conflict patterns with their parents are more likely to have lower self-esteem and high alcohol and drug use. This is true whether the conflict is about allowance, cleaning one's room, or alcohol and drug use (Caughlin & Malis, 2004).

In some families, persuasive messages about health behaviors may increase after a cancer diagnosis. These persuasive messages might come from the person diagnosed with cancer or from a family member. For example, 94 percent of patients recently diagnosed with skin cancer reported having at least one or two discussions with family members about skin cancer risk since their diagnosis (Hay, et al., 2005). Another study showed that in families in which one member had been diagnosed with melanoma, those that were characterized by high cohesiveness and adaptability reported more frequently discussing melanoma with family members (Harris, Hay, Kuniyuki, Asgan, Press, & Bowen, in press). In addition, melanoma patients may make decisions about which family members they think are at risk, and then target their discussions toward those family members (Hay, et al., 2009). Patients with cancer might be particularly well-positioned to help family or friends quit smoking (Garces, et al., 2010). In one study, researchers interviewed prostate cancer patients and their wives three different times across an eight-month period following prostate cancer treatment. Surprisingly, wives' attempts to influence their husbands to engage in certain health behaviors were associated with less healthy behaviors and lower psychological well-being. There are a couple of possible reasons for this: Husbands may react negatively to these influence attempts by not enacting the behaviors or wives may be more likely to attempt to influence less healthy husbands (Helgeson, Novak, Lepore, & Eton, 2004).

Family Communication and Health Care Interactions

Think about your own experiences going to the doctor as a child. There was a socialization process happening as your parents or older siblings taught you how to communicate with doctors, nurses, and other health care professionals. While you were quite young, your parents probably did most of the communicating, but as you grew older, you probably became more active in communicating your complaints and symptoms to the doctor. Many young adults can recall when they were first allowed to go to the doctor alone. A study of African American women found that most sought gynecological health care as an adolescent based upon their mother's recommendation (Warren-Jeanpiere, Miller, & Warren, 2010).

Family members often act as informal "*health care advocates*" for each other by attending each other's doctor's appointments. When patients are seriously ill, these family members serve an important function by asking questions and helping patients to recall information later. In one study of consultations with an oncologist where bad news was given, 86 percent of patients had at least one companion (family member or friend) present with them. These companions asked more questions than the patient did on average (Eggly, et al., 2006). Sometimes family members must act as an interpreter for the patient and doctor. As noted previously, in certain immigrant families, children are usually the bilingual members of the family and frequently have to take on this role, creating a generational reversal.

Although having a companion present in an interaction may be helpful for information recall and emotional support, some dialectical issues of privacy also can emerge (Petronio, et al., 2004). For example, imagine two adolescent brothers who went to a party they weren't supposed to attend when their parents were out of town. The younger brother, Rob, got in a fight at the party and sprained his wrist. When his older brother Mark took him to the family doctor the next day, Mark told the doctor how Rob sprained his wrist, even though Rob wanted to come up with a different explanation, as he was worried the family doctor would tell his mother.

As children reach adolescence, privacy issues may emerge when the pediatrician asks the adolescent about health risk behaviors while the parent is in the room and the adolescent is faced with lying to the doctor or revealing private information about her behaviors. In some cases physicians request time alone with adolescent patients to discuss making life healthy choices and to provide the patient with privacy to raise personal concerns. Most parents agree to such requests.

Illness and Family Communication

The illness of a family member can have a profound effect on the family system. Families' communication patterns and practices are often affected by such illness.

The content of conversations, the rules of communication, and frequency of conflict may be drastically altered when a family member becomes seriously ill. In this section we briefly present some of the family communication issues that emerge when a family member is diagnosed with a serious disease or suffers a stroke.

Every year, hundreds of thousands of families are affected by cancer. In 2010, it was expected that 1,529,560 new cases of cancer will be diagnosed in the United States (Cancer Facts & Figures, 2010). Children whose parents are diagnosed with advanced cancer are affected in all aspects of their lives (Kennedy & Lloyd-Williams, 2009). As these families face a diagnosis of cancer in one of their family members, their conversations may focus on describing, explaining, and informing others about the cancer status. Some family members find themselves serving as an intermediary between other family members and the doctors, explaining what doctors have told them. In doing so, they learn to speak the "language of uncertainty regarding cancer" (Beach & Good, 2004, p. 28). Young or adolescent children may find this new language of cancer to be difficult, as the following quote indicates.

We found out that my mom had cancer the same day that the orthopedist removed a cast from my leg after 8 long weeks. As a sixteen-year-old, I was already walking a fine line between teenager and adult in all aspects of my life, but that distinction became even more blurry when "the Big C" entered my house. That afternoon, the conversation in our family room shifted from talk of celebratory ice cream to medical appointment-making with no end in sight. It was clear in that moment that life had changed. I had always prided myself on the fact that my parents treated me like an adult, sharing family news and decisions with me, but when they tried to do this with my mom's disease, I think we were all surprised that there were many things I just wasn't ready to hear. This made it hard for my parents to decide what to share with me and hard for me to decide what of my "normal" life to share with them.

Many families are faced with the diagnosis of a chronic or life-threatening disease of a child, such as childhood cancer. Communication surrounding this disease can be very difficult but can also have a tremendous impact on the child's well-being. For example, parent-child communication seems to impact a child's experience of pain and distress during cancer treatments. Children whose parents used normalizing and supportive communication with them during potentially painful cancer treatments had less pain and distress than those whose parents used invalidating communication with them (Cline, et al., 2006).

Helping children to understand and make sense of illness (whether their own or another family member's) is important to effective family communication. Discussing illness with children needs to be tailored to their developmental stage. Children's ideas about the causes of disease mature over time and are correlated with a child's developmental stage. A very young child (2 years old) would not even consider the how or why of disease. A child who is 3 to 7 years old may begin to think in terms of disease being contagious, realizing that if Dad has a cold, you might have a cold too. So a child this age may think that since Grandpa has cancer, he might "catch" cancer too. Children who are 8 to 11 years of age begin to understand that the source of an illness can be external or from within the body. By 12 years of age, children are able to understand the cause of disease as a body's process and explain it in terms of organs (Koopman, Baars, Chaplin, & Zwinderman, 2004).

Often, family members are required to take on the role of the caregiver. Having a family member who gives supportive communication and care can lessen the burden of being ill (Segrin & Flora, 2006). It may also benefit family relationships. For example, stroke survivors reported spending more time with spousal caregivers and having more open communication and greater appreciation for family relationships after their stroke (Pawlowski, 2006). However, becoming a caregiver can be a stressful situation, as the caregiver may feel ill-equipped to handle the time demands, physical demands, emotional burdens, and financial costs (Pecchioni, Thompson, & Anderson, 2006). When caring for a relative who has Alzheimer's, family members may become frustrated by their communication with the ill family member (Segrin & Flora, 2006). Older caregivers of a sick spouse face an increased risk of death (Christakis & Allison, 2006). In many cases, caregivers become so overwhelmed that it is important for them to seek support as well. Interventions for caregivers can be helpful and appreciated as they learn how to take better care of themselves and interact with others in similar situations (Schure, et al., 2006).

If you think about this change in roles from a family systems perspective, it is easy to see the impact that an illness requiring a family caregiver can have on the family system. Open and frequent communication about the changes taking place in the family may be helpful in absorbing some of the shock to the family system.

DIFFICULT CONVERSATIONS ON CURRENT ISSUES

In a world characterized by the explosion and dissemination of new knowledge, family members confront the challenge of talking with each other about new, complex, and sometimes emotionally charged topics. Although each past generation has experienced such challenges, the ongoing knowledge explosion requires that parents and children need to be able to discuss new complicated and challenging issues as they arise. They need to be able to engage in difficult conversations on current concerns. The following section explores three topics that have emerged in recent years that have major significance for everyday life in many families. The first one, talking about genetics in families, focuses specifically on disclosing and discussing genetic disease, a topic made possible only by advances in scientific research, including the groundbreaking Human Genome Project. The second one, talking about money, has long been a topic of family conversation, at least in theory. However, in many families serious discussions of money do not usually include young or even adult children. The recent economic downturn and worldwide financial instability makes understanding and discussions of family finances a critical topic. The third one involves a reversal of the traditional parent-dominated information model, discussions of cutting-edge advances in digital technology belong more to the younger generations. Children and adolescents may enter technological worlds that their parents do not fully comprehend and are unable to discuss. These new and exciting worlds as well as related safety concerns necessitate that family members hold conversations about members' use of digital technology.

Genetic Heritage and Family Risk

Recent technological advances make it possible for family members to be tested for multiple hereditary genetic diseases. The Human Genome Project, completed in 2003, opened the door to a wealth of genetic information. Increasingly, family members will be faced with the delicate task of communicating with each other about their genetic heritage, and in stepfamilies or adoptive families multiple genetic heritages must be acknowledged. These often difficult conversations, unimaginable 15 years ago, will become critical in managing family members' health. Family discussions about genetic risk may center on identifying who is at risk, deciding whether and how to disclose this risk to family members, and supporting family members who are dealing with undesirable or painful genetic knowledge (Galvin, 2006c).

Disclosure Genetic counselors frequently interact only with one individual, or sometimes with a small number of family members, and, given their professional code of conduct, they are seldom in a position to alert other members about the family's genetic inheritance and the risks other family members may face. The *proband,* or the first person in the family to be diagnosed with the genetic condition, has a major impact on when or if family members learn about their risk and, furthermore, if they decide to get tested. For example, a study on family communication about hereditary hemochromatosis found that a contributing factor in getting tested was an affected sibling's or other family member's communication (Bylund, Galvin, Dunet, & Reyes, in press). Probands may choose to disclose results to encourage relatives to get tested, obtain emotional support, and get advice about medical decisions. But probands may avoid sharing genetic information when they believe this might lead to a difficult encounter. Such a situation appears in the opening vignette in which Drew attempts to avoid direct conversation with his brother, Kevin, and instead relies on his partner, Molly, to convery the news of his diagnosis with hemochromatosis. Avoiding disclosure frequently occurs when the disease is perceived as highly devastating or deadly, the relational history with the person has been problematic, or the disease is not manageable (Galvin & Grill, 2009). A proband may be willing to tell a relative about a diagnosis that, if caught early, can be managed. But a proband may not be willing to share a diagnosis of Huntington's disease because of its devastating effects and the lack of treatment options.

Disclosure is also difficult if the genetic information must be conveyed within already problematic family relationships. A family's communication patterns and norms become set from years of interaction. Cohesive families may respond better to these discussions (McCann, in press), whereas families with significant rifts may struggle with such news. Some family members may refuse to listen to the proband or give subtle cues that they don't want to discuss this topic (Gaff, et al., 2007).

Emotionally distant relationships and little contact may prevent this information from being passed on (McGivern, et al., 2004). Sometimes probands deliberately avoid conversation, choosing instead to send an e-mail or post the news to a family Web site. Finally, when the news could be devastating, such as a diagnosis of hereditary forms of breast or ovarian cancer, a proband may be reluctant to pass on the news. In the case of Huntington's disease a proband may remain silent, choosing instead to monitor family members, scanning the environment for threatening clues of the disease in a relative, before choosing to address the issue.

Two main styles of disclosing genetic testing information are *pragmatism* and *prevarication*. A proband who uses a pragmatic style will disclose the information actively and practically. Someone who calls or sends an e-mail to his siblings to tell them of his recent genetic test and suggests that they get tested enacts the pragmatic style. On the other hand, a proband who uses a prevarication style would try to find the "right moment" to disclose the information. Such a person using this style would look for opportunities within normal events, such as a family gathering. However, this attempt to find the right moment may take months or even years (Forrest, et al., 2003).

Experts recommend that probands follow certain steps when conveying genetic risk information to family members. First, probands should start by identifying who, how, and where to tell. To continue, they should find out how much these family members already know about this genetic risk and how much they want to know. Probands should then share the genetic test information and respond to family members' emotions. Finally, they should refer family members to a genetic counselor and share other materials with them (Daly, et al., 2001). Family members need each others' support throughout the process of testing (Koehly, 2008). Genetic counselors and other health-care providers have been urged to explore and address family communication issues in their meetings with clients (Gaff, Galvin, & Bylund, 2010).

High proportions of patients going for genetic testing report an intention to tell their family members (Clarke, et al., 2005). For example, in a study of 329 women being tested for the BRCA1 or BRCA2 mutations for hereditary breast cancer, 98 percent reported before their genetic test that they intended to tell at least one of their adult first-degree relatives (e.g., sibling, parent, or offspring) about their test result; 63 percent reported that they would tell all of these relatives (Barsevick, et al., 2008). However, in reality, this information is not always passed on, resulting in a decision to engage in *passive nondisclosure* (Gaff, Collins, Symes, & Halliday, 2005). Why does passive nondisclosure happen? Gaff and colleagues (2007) suggested that nondisclosure needs to be examined on a case by case basis, recognizing the many possible causes that may prevent disclosure, some of which are discussed above. Probands find themselves in a very difficult position; they must find a balance between causing the potential psychological harm the information may inflict on a family member and providing critical information that could have important health consequences (Gaff, 2007).

Discussion Family members' ongoing discussions about genetic risk are difficult, and may not occur, for several reasons. Some types of diseases may be more difficult to discuss than others. For example, one study compared families' experiences talking about genetic testing for Huntington's disease, a condition that causes brain cells to degenerate, with other families' experiences talking about genetic testing for hereditary breast and ovarian cancer (HBOC). Findings revealed that family members tested for Huntington's disease were less forthcoming with information than family members being tested for HBOC (Hamilton, Bowers, & Williams, 2005). In their study of the impact of genetic testing for Huntington's disease on a particular family and members' interactions, Sobel and Cowan (2003) reported that members experienced significant loss and grief. Siblings found themselves split along lines of those who carried the gene and those who did not. Members who learned they did not carry the gene felt as if they had lost membership in the family because they were excluded from meaningful and emotional conversations. The diversity of members' responses to their test results led to distancing and silence.

Talking to children about genetic testing can be difficult for many reasons (Sullivan & McConkie-Rosell, 2010). In cases of genetic risk for breast and ovarian cancer, the offspring usually are not encouraged to be tested until they are 25 years old. Those who get tested may react differently—some may find the tests confirm what they already thought, while others may be devastated by their diagnosis. Some may search for more information on the Internet, from other family members, or through health-care providers. Offspring report both positive and negative aspects of knowing. For instance, advantages include being able to change health behavior and being aware of future genetic testing and surgical opportunities. Disadvantages include worrying about or developing a fatalistic attitude toward developing cancer (Bradbury, et al., 2009).

Issues of privacy and conflict may arise when one member of the family gains genetic information and another wants to remain unaware. Imagine a family with Lynn, a 58-year-old mother diagnosed with early-stage breast cancer. After discussing her family history of breast cancer with her oncologist, Lynn decides to be tested for a genetic condition that is often present in women with family histories of breast cancer. Lynn discusses this decision with her daughters, Julianne, 28, and Meg, 32, and invites them to meet with the genetic counselor and be tested as well. Meg agrees, but Julianne declines saying she would rather not know. Both Lynn and Meg test positive for the genetic condition, which means the possibility that Julianne has the genetic condition is increased. Lynn and Meg are now faced with the conflicting desires of wanting to respect Julianne's wishes by not disclosing this information and wanting to give Julianne information about cancer prevention.

As studies on the results of the Human Genome Project continue to unfold, and more family members choose to receive their genetic profile, family discussion of genetics will increase. Partners will share genetic information with each other in order to determine what, if any, genetic disorder may present itself in their biological child. They may also discuss the use of in vitro fertilization (IVF) to create embryos which can be tested for certain genetic disorders. The future holds the potential for many difficult family conversations related to genetic inheritances.

Money and Financial Stress

"Bankruptcy, short sale, foreclosure"—such terms have entered dinner conversations in many homes. Traditionally, the topic of family finances has been viewed as an adult topic, one to be discussed between husbands and wives, adult partners, or household adults such as a mother and grandmother. Many adolescent or adult children do not know how much money their parents make or how much money the family has in savings. This may occur because money tends to be equated with power, self-esteem, and success and failure. Money is used as a "way of showing off, wielding power, and creating an image—a persona for an individual" (Jellinek & Beresin, 2008, p. 249). Therefore, talking about money outside the family becomes complicated; frequently children hear a communication rule, "Do not talk about our family's money outside the family." Talking about money inside the family also presents challenges. According to Jellinek and Beresin (2008), "Virtually every interpersonal dynamic—controlling, restrictive, aggressive, secretive, guilt-inducing, ambivalent, generative, altruistic—can be manifested in how money is used in families (p. 251). In other words, family money is a potent and challenging topic.

Until the last quarter of the twentieth century, family money was a highly gendered issue; an adult male's family identity was linked to the breadwinner role. In recent decades, however, female careers and earning power have changed. Sixty-three percent of women are either the primary breadwinner or a co-breadwinner, earning at least a quarter of the family's income. Additionally, 38 percent of wives earn as much or more than their husbands (Boushey, 2009). Today, couples' ability to adapt to a situation in which the man earns less than the woman depends a great deal on the examples set by their parents. According to Wood (2005), "Men and women who had mothers who were successful in the paid labor force see a woman's career success as consistent with femininity" (p. 183).

The meaning of money varies across ethnicity and culture. In more individualistic cultures, money is managed within nuclear households with limited expectations of sharing with extended family members. In more collectivist cultures, money is viewed as an extended family resource; wealthier members have responsibilities to share some of their earnings with other relatives, such as when a niece needs money for college or medical treatment. In many African American families, resources are shared within social networks providing direct and in-kind assistance that softens financial strain (Lincoln, 2007). These different approaches may create tension in intercultural partnerships such as the one depicted below.

My husband grew up in a middle class white family with parents who provided well for them. I grew up in an African American extended family in which everyone helped everyone out. In addition to providing for their own children, those who succeeded were expected to help nieces or nephews whose families were less well-off. Carl and I argue a lot about how much of "our" money or "my" money goes to my younger relatives for tuition or special educational programs. His nieces and nephews get Christmas and birthday presents but we do not take any responsibility for their education.

Over the past decade most families experienced multiple economic challenges. You may have heard friends or relatives expressing anxiety about their financial state or your family may have suffered serious financial setbacks. The media reported the rising number of homeless families, the return of young adults to their parents' homes, the loss of employment by parents in well-established careers, the struggles of recent college graduates to find employment, and the additional workplace stresses faced by those fortunate enough to remain employed. Many families were totally unprepared for an economic downturn; members who had never talked with each other about family finances or family financial planning were confronted with challenging conversations.

Adult family members confronted discussing issues such as sending children to less expensive colleges and universities, setting ground rules for twenty-something adults moving back home, assessing whether to help a brother's family with the mortgage, and trying to cut out "extras" ranging from giving up the second car to eating out. In some cases, family members discussed whether to declare bankruptcy. Conversations included topics such as closing out credit cards, living without health insurance, and going on a staycation rather than a vacation (Mckee-Ryan, Song, Wanberg, & Kinicki, 2005).

Because economic stress affects individual well-being and indirectly influences family interaction (Conger, et al., 1990), such conversations tend to address multiple family stresses. Partner or parental unemployment frequently results in depression, role anxiety, strained family relationships, and low self-esteem. Social networks change as resources diminish, altering social activities and social support. Increasing economic stress results in rising family tensions which lead to diminished family relational quality and family disruption (Bartholomae & Fox, 2010).

Gender stresses tend to complicate the issues. When unemployment occurs, traditional gender socialization may be upended. Losing the role of breadwinner or co-breadwinner leaves many males upset and depressed; conversely, females, even those with employment, may find themselves stressed at assuming the sole breadwinner role (Gudmunson, Beutler, Israelsen, McCoy, & Hill, 2007).

Furthermore, financial strain increases the incidence of couple disagreements, fighting, and decreases their quality time together. A study of the link between financial strain and marital instability involving almost 5,000 married couples revealed that "couple financial strain contributed strongly and *evenly* to increases in husband's emotional distress and wife's emotional distress" (Gudmunson, Beutler, Israelsen, McCoy, & Hill, 2007, p. 371). Although couples were quite similar in terms of how they assessed their financial situation, their disagreements were strongly linked to increased couple fighting and decreased quality time together. The lack of couple quality time, compounded by the need to work extra hours or work nontraditional hours, was significantly linked to marital instability.

Not only does partner interaction suffer during times of economic instability but parenting tends to decline. When parents are stressed by economic threats and losses they exhibit lower levels of involvement with, and supportiveness of, their children (Gudmunson, Beutler, Israelsen, McCoy, & Hill, 2007). Many suffer from exhaustion, often from working extra hours, or depression leading to low energy and high distractibility. In these difficult economic circumstances, parental warmth and affective support declines (Mistry, Lowe, Remers, & Chien, 2008), as depicted in the next example.

My father was laid off from his position as a computer engineer over a year ago. My parents resisted talking about it with us but we watched as he went on interview after interview with no luck. Eventually my mother went back to heavy drinking because of the worry and pressure on her to beg for extra hours at her job. They began to have terrible fights after we went to bed. Right now he is in a final round of interviews for an administrative position. If he does not get it, I don't know how they will cope.

Impact on Future Family Interactions   Throughout the past decade media and family professionals stressed the need for adult family members to talk with each other and their children about financial matters. You may have participated in such discussions. Depending on a family's life stage, discussions might involve middle-aged adults talking with their older parents about their financial status and needs; middle-aged parents sharing their financial status with their young adult or adolescent children as well as providing guidance about ways to manage their money; or young adult parents talking with children about saving and the importance of managing money.

Although celebrity experts, television shows, magazine articles, and trade books provide countless suggestions on managing money, these ideas need to be discussed openly by family members, sometimes in conjunction with a financial adviser. Additionally, many adults seek professional advice about communicating with family members. Some suggestions for partners' discussions include talking about feelings such as fear, loss, and guilt, and talking about your experience without blaming your partner. Middle-aged persons are advised to talk with their older parents about their financial status, asking questions such as "How much do you have—and is it enough?" and "Have you made long-term care arrangements?" (Max, 2009).

Some parents resist talking with their children about finances because they do not wish to worry them. A recent study of 420 college students revealed that parents had a moderately significant influence on their financial attitudes and behaviors but did not have a an effect on their financial knowledge (Jorgensen & Savla, 2010), indicating a need for parents to learn how to discuss, teach, and model financial principles to their children. Yet, the 2007 study by the Michael Cohen Group of the feelings of teenagers regarding the nation's economy revealed that two-thirds of the respondents believed the economic crisis is having or will have a negative impact on their families (Tugend, 2008). When talking with children, parents are advised to answer children's questions with as much information as they can handle. Popular advice to parents from work-family expert Ellen Galinsky includes to avoid using certain terminology with small children such as "fired" because it may raise images of guns and shooting, and when telling children the difficulties, also discuss the coping strategies that will be used (Abel, 2010).

Most experts remind adult family members that money does not determine a child's happiness. When asking adults in family workshops to go on a "journey of happy memories" from childhood, John DeFrain, an expert in family strengths, found that "adults rarely recall something that cost a lot of money" (Olson, DeFrain, & Skogrand, 2008, p. 345). Instead they remember holiday traditions,

Friday night rituals, doing chores together, or vacations. Serious discussions about family money are often difficult but they are necessary for the financial education of children and the management or resolution of family financial issues.

Digital Competence

Individuals living in a networked world can be categorized as digital natives, digital settlers, and digital immigrants (Palfrey & Gasser, 2008). The concept of digital natives and digital immigrants, labels coined by Marc Prensky (2001), emerged from conversations on generational differences and the digital world. *Digital natives* are continuously connected by technology; they think and process information differently from previous generations because they are native speakers of the language of technology. Although *digital settlers* grew up in an analog world, they have become sophisticated in their use of technology though they also rely heavily on analog communication. *Digital immigrants* are those who were not born into the digital age and who have not adapted easily to new technologies. They may have learned to use e-mail or to go to social networking sites, but live much or all of their lives offline. Although not all younger people are digital natives, a culture defined by age and interaction with information technologies, the number of such natives is increasing exponentially.

Many families have members who represent each category of digital connection, which may lead to communication breakdowns or generational competence reversals. Although Palfrey and Gasseer (2008) argue that "the more often 'significant adults' talk to young people about their experiences online (and occasionally monitor what they are doing), the less likely the youth are to engage in risky behavior" (p. 101). In many homes those conversations do not occur because parents are unprepared to discuss these issues. Risky behavior may include disclosing personal information, meeting up offline with online acquaintances, sharing photos with strangers, or bullying peers.

Parents of digital natives worry that their children are at risk for cyberbullying (Palfrey & Glasser, 2008), but many feel helpless to prevent it. *Cyberbullying*, or deliberate and repeated harm inflicted through phones and computers, presents serious challenges to young people and their families. Cyberbullying includes activities such as harassment, posting false rumors on social networking sites, creating offensive Web sites, or repeatedly killing a player's avatar (Whitaker & Bushman, 2009). In recent years the media has provided numerous examples of adolescent suicides attributed to cyberspace bullying; the phenomenon has become so prevalent that the term "cyberbullicide" was coined to describe "suicide directly or indirectly influenced by experiences with online aggression" (Hinduja & Patchin, 2009, n.p.). Cyberbullying represents a particularly dangerous form of harm because, in contrast to former decades when home provided sanctuary from taunting peers, cyberbullying has become a 24/7 experience for many preadolescents and adolescents. A study of 2,000 middle school students reported that 20 percent of respondents indicated seriously thinking about attempting suicide due to cyberbullying (Hinduja & Patchin, 2009). The students reported the most frequent form of cyberbullying involved posting "something online about another person to make others laugh," whereas cyber victims chose receiving "an upsetting email from someone

Parents can monitor their children's online activities.

you know." Cyberbullying victims were almost twice as likely to have attempted or considered suicide compared to youth who had not experienced cyberbullying. In many cyberbullying cases parents expect schools to provide justice and protection for their children, although school district discipline codes seldom address authority over student cell phones or home computers (Hoffman, 2010). Many parents do not discuss these issues with their children or ask their children if they have witnessed or experienced such interactions.

Another important, but less dramatic, concern involves sharing personal and family information through new technologies. In traditional face-to-face communication, conversations are relatively secure, but that level of privacy does not exist in an Internet-connected world (Grill, 2010). Family members run the risk of sharing each other's news, or violating their communication privacy, as e-mails are forwarded, posts are shared, and members of every generation use Facebook, MySpace, or other social networking sites. The size of the potential audience for private family information is staggering. For example, Facebook has more than 400 million active users; an average user has 130 friends, some of whom are family members (Facebook.com, 2010). In recent years increasing numbers of older people have joined

Facebook, often requesting to friend grandchildren or other younger relatives. In many cases this results in younger relatives changing their privacy settings.

In their national survey of parental mediation of children's Internet use, Livingstone and Helsper (2008) examined parental attempts to regulate their children's media use in order to maximize the advantages of the online environment by using strategies such as rule-making, restrictions, co-viewing, or co-using. They found that co-use was widespread; two-thirds of parents discuss Internet use with their children, almost half watch the screen, and about a third remain physically close when a child is online. Although parental involvement had some impact, one major exception was the ban on giving out personal information online involving buying, filling out forms, and taking quizzes. The study reported that the characteristics of the children determined the incidence of their online risks. Older boys with high skill levels were at the greatest online risk. The authors concluded that "the relative ineffectiveness of parental mediation in reducing risks is consistent with other recent research on children's Internet use" (n.p.).

Not all parents, grandparents, or guardians are able to use the technology well enough to understand these issues or hold meaningful conversations about dangerous online behavior. In some families, older siblings or cousins go online to see what a young relative posted, such as looking at a Facebook page to see if any information could be used to cyberbully them (Hinduja & Patchin, 2010).

Another technology-related issue with dangerous implications for younger family members involves "*sexting*," or the sending of text messages with pictures of children or teens that are naked or engaged in sexual acts (American Academy of Pediatrics, 2009). Sexting has emerged as a serious problem for many young people and their families. In addition to causing emotional pain, and cited as the cause of suicide for a few young people, this activity has serious legal consequences. As part of an online panel study (AP-MTV Digital Abuse Study, 2009) researchers interviewed 1,247 respondents ages 14 to 24. Results indicated that 3 in 10 young people have been involved in some type of naked texting (the incidence overall is higher among 18 to 24-year-olds and 14 to 17-year-olds). Researchers found that 29 percent reported receiving messages "with sexual words or images" by text or on the Internet. One in 10 had shared a naked image of themselves. Nearly 1 in 5 recipients of such texts reported passing them on to someone else. Approximately 30 percent reported sharing sexts as a joke or to be funny. Most reported not considering the risks and implications of such behavior. A survey developed by the National Campaign to Prevent Teen and Unplanned Pregnancy and CosmoGirl.com (2008) found similar results. It appears that many parents do not know about this practice or do not believe their children would participate in such a practice. Little is known about actual parent-child communication regarding sexting.

Parents need to communicate with their children and adolescents about their online lives. They need to see their children's profiles on Facebook or other social networking sites as well as stay abreast of cyber trends, such a bullying or sexting. Only then will parents be able to talk with their children and provide guidance regarding digital experiences. As more parents become digital natives and digital settlers, more family conversations about these difficult topics will occur.

APPROACHES FOR IMPROVING FAMILY COMMUNICATION

If you believed that communication in your family should be improved, would you be willing to talk with other family members about the communication problems or participate in a structured improvement program? As families go through predictable developmental stresses as well as unpredictable stresses, frequently members do not know how to move forward effectively. Strategies designed to suport positive family change exist on a continuum ranging from personal through instructional to therapeutic approaches. Most of the personal and instructional approaches are designed for functional partnerships or families whose members wish to make changes in their relationships or to find ways to manage a particularly stressful situation. Therapeutic approaches are designed to aid a couple or a family in coping with a serious problem or repair a troubled relationship.

Personal Approaches

Many partnerships or whole family systems attempt to change their relational communication patterns through personal efforts. Personal approaches include (1) seeking education, such as that found through books or the media; (2) engaging in conscious negotiation with partners or family members; (3) establishing ongoing meetings for family members; and (4) obtaining support from friends or members of a supportive network.

Personal Education A perusal of bookstore shelves, videos, or Web sites reveals countless resources devoted to improving family relationships, parenting skills, and the ability to deal with relational change. There are checklists, rules, and prescriptions for improving family meetings, sexual communication, and approaches to conflict. The "checkup" stands as a cornerstone concept of the personal approach to improving partner or family communication. Family members are encouraged to call for a conversation on the question "How are we doing?"

Personal Negotiation In many families, members discuss and plan new ways to communicate or to solve problems. Partners attempt to identify recurring "trouble spots" in their relationship and plan how to avoid them. Members may learn to recognize times when intimacy or conflict is too threatening and to find ways to acknowledge this. Some families create and practice their own rules for fair fighting.

Parents may consciously attempt to defuse high-anxiety moments by engaging in emotion coaching—trying to listen empathically or helping a child verbally label his or her emotions (Gottman & DeClaire, 1997). Parents and children may risk sharing their feelings when silence would be more comfortable but less effective. Significant change involves ongoing communication efforts. One discussion seldom results in permanent change, as demonstrated in the following example.

In my own marriage, my wife and I have been using two mechanisms to serve as a kind of checkup on our marital relations. First, we have learned to communicate both the negative and the positive feelings we have. Second, we sit down together with no outside distractions and, while maintaining eye contact, express our innermost feelings or our current concerns. We each try very hard to listen rather than judge the other. This ritual is a special part of our relationship.

How do conversations about change actually start? Sometimes one or more family members express their nagging feelings that things could be better. They may encounter new ideas or models for relationships through the media, friends, or religious and educational experiences. Then they take the risk of trying out new behaviors and evaluating their effectiveness, an approach that involves ongoing mutual cooperation.

Instead of having a conversation, an individual family member may choose to change his or her behavior, hoping that this change will encourage another family member to do the same. From a systems perspective, it is easy to imagine how one member's change in communication may result in another family member's change as well, although these individual efforts may be met with strong resistance. The following quote from a young adult illustrates how she used this strategy to change communication in her family.

My father, although being very caring and supportive, has always been the type to only rarely express his love verbally. While in college, my younger sister and I were talking about this and we realized that maybe we didn't say "I love you" very often to him. So we decided to see if we could encourage some change. Whenever we talked on the phone with Dad from then on we would end our conversation with "Love you!" or "I love you." At first Dad would just respond with a pause followed by "Goodbye," but soon he began saying, "We love you" (meaning he and Mom) before hanging up. Still, that was a good change and we were happy to hear it. He still rarely says, "I love you," but according to our other siblings he ends phone calls with "Love you" to them as well.

Ongoing Time Commitments One marital or family change strategy involves instituting "couple time," or "family meetings." Members agree to come together regularly in order to solve problems and improve relationships. Members at all stages of family development agree to reserve times to "really talk." Some families find their topics emerge easily and directly, such as during regular debriefing conversations; others prefer to use a guidebook that prescribes topics or provides questions or discussion material.

Family meetings or family councils create opportunities for all family members to address mutual concerns. Such experiences provide children with important practice in discussion and decision making. Many religious groups recommend such meetings. Within the Family Home Evening program developed by the Church of Jesus Christ of Latter-day Saints, church members are encouraged to set aside one night a week to be together as a family, spending time in religious study and family activities (Building a Strong Family, 2010). Topics of discussion include building a strong family, honesty, and compiling family history, as well as religious subjects. Other religious groups support similar programs.

Support Networks   In an era when the extended family is increasingly inaccessible, individuals, couples, and families are creating informal or formal support systems to help them face family problems. Informal support networks, such as friends or members of a faith community, provide adequate support for some families. Talking about family issues may help put things into perspective, serve as a point of emotional release, or help rebuild a marriage (Faith and Marriage Ministries, 2010). Sometimes the support groups become a kind of extended network of friends who provide the caring that biological families cannot or will not provide (Weston, 1993). A personal testimonial to such a group follows.

For eight months I have participated in a divorce recovery group through our church and it has helped me with parenting my three sons and coping with my ex-husband's remarriage. This group has saved my sanity more than once and I have reached some important insights about loss and change.

Instructional Approaches

My husband and I are team leaders for the Jewish Marriage Encounter, and we keep trying to tell our friends that every marriage should have an "annual checkup." People spend thousands of dollars on "preventive maintenance" for their cars, teeth, bodies, and homes, but how much do we spend either in dollars, effort, or time to have a marital examination? Too often in attempting to get couples to attend on Encounter weekend I am told, "Our marriage is OK" or "We don't need to go on any weekend, as we have no problems." I am both angry and sad at such blindness, stupidity, and fear. There is not a marriage existing that does not have some problems, and if they are not attended to, they will get bigger.

The above statement captures the underlying philosophy of one instructional approach. There has been a significant growth in marital and family enrichment programs designed to instruct individuals, couples, and whole family systems. Generally their purpose is educational and they do not involve counseling. Frequently, they are referred to as psychoeducational approaches (Lebow, 1997).

Cole and Cole (1993) defined *marriage and family enrichment programs* as:

> The process of assisting couples and families who have relatively healthy relationships in the development of interpersonal skills that will enable them to enhance and add to individual couple and family strengths, develop more effective strategies for dealing with difficulties, and learn to view their relationships as growing and changing rather than static. (p. 525)

Morgaine (1992) viewed instructional programs as "inoculating" functional families with facts, skills, and information to help prevent disasters. Today, countless national and local programs assist married or cohabiting partners as well as parents and children to improve their relational lives, including their communication skills and practices (Smart Marriages, 2010).

Marital/Partner Enrichment Programs Multiple national organizations offer marriage enrichment programs. These programs, which began in the 1950s and 1960s, are designed to enhance couple growth. Most programs insist that partners attend together. Communication skills appear as the core of most of these marital enrichment efforts (Arcus, 1995). These programs challenge the reluctance of partners to discuss their relationship. Most persons who attend enrichment programs are self-referred and self-screened. Potential participants receive the message: "If your marriage is in serious trouble, our program is not for you. We are designed to help good relationships become better."

Many professionals believe that enrichment programs are not desirable options for distressed couples. Yet deMaria (2005) found that of 129 married couples who had participated in marital enrichment programs in the United States and Canada, 93 percent of the couples were distressed and highly dissatisfied with their relationship. Despite this, couples maintained feelings of secure attachment and romantic love to some degree, which may explain why they chose to attend an enrichment program, leading to the suggestion that professionals need to rethink their beliefs on who should enroll in these programs.

Although numerous systems-oriented marital and family enrichment programs emphasize communication, only a few representative ones will be described. The most well-known and frequently attended marital enrichment programs include the Couple Communication Program, Marriage Encounter programs, PAIRS (Practical Application of Intimate Relationship Skills), Relationship Enhancement (RE), and the Prevention and Relationship Enhancement Program (PREP).

The Marriage Encounter, a weekend program sponsored by World Wide Marriage Encounter and conducted by a leadership team consisting of three couples and a religious leader, follows a simple pattern. Team members provide the information and modeling designed to facilitate each participating couple's private dialogue. Through a series of nine talks, team members reveal personal and intimate information to encourage participants to do the same when alone. After each talk couples separate to write individual responses to the issues raised by the talk. Each partner must write his or her feelings about the topic before they come together for a private dialogue using each other's written responses as a starting point. Although the program began within the Catholic faith, almost all religious traditions offer a version (WWME, 2010). The second opening vignette depicts Angeli and Dante who spent so much time involved in working and taking care of their children that they had little time or energy to focus on their marriage. Their decision to attend a Marriage Encounter weekend was one step toward taking care of their relationship.

The Prevention and Relationship Enhancement Program (PREP) represents a research-based skills approach. The program is designed to teach couples better communication and conflict strategies, assist them in clarifying and evaluating expectations, promote understanding of their choices reflecting commitment, and enhance the positive bonding in the relationship (Jakubowski, Milne, Brunner & Miller, 2004).

The Couple Communication Program, developed by communication scholars, attempts to increase self, partner, and relationship awareness. Focus is placed on the development of clear, direct, and open communication in order to reduce stress. Communication skills are developed and practiced during four weekly meetings.

Finally, PREPARE/ENRICH is a customized couple online assessment designed to reveal a couple's strengths and areas of growth. It was designed for premarital counseling, although some counselors use the program with couples. This program, developed by David Olson and colleagues, is grounded in the circumplex model of family functioning and includes three inventories and guidelines for counselor/leader training.

In addition, the Gottman Institute provides multiple enrichment programs. One two-day program, the Art and Science of Love, claims that couples will learn how to (1) foster respect, affection, and closeness, (2) build and share a deeper connection with each other's inner world, (3) keep conflict discussions calm, (4) break through and resolve conflict gridlock, and (5) strengthen and maintain the gains in the relationship. Participant couples are assured that no public disclosure or discussion is involved. All work is done as a couple (www.gottman.com/54740/ couples-workshops.html).

These well-known programs represent only a few of the many options available. Some specialty programs address issues of premarital couples (Engaged Encounter), troubled couples (Retrouvaille), sexuality (Passionate Marriage), or remarriage (Personal Reflections). Making a case for premarital enrichment programs, Stanley (2001) presented four benefits: (1) fostering couple deliberation, (2) sending a message that marriage matters, (3) helping couples learn about supports they may use later, and (4) lowering the risk of disasters or divorce for some couples. Descriptions of these major marital enrichment programs indicate that communication plays a central place within each. Interpersonal skills may be taught through modeling, role playing, lecture, guided feedback, and readings.

Family Enrichment Programs   Programs for encouraging entire families or parents and children to examine and improve their relationships have developed more slowly. One widely known program is STEP (Systematic Training for Effective Parenting), a set of eight-week online classes, which was developed by the American Guidance Service (AGS). Based on Adlerian psychology, STEP focuses on the goals of children's behavior, the natural and logical consequence of the behavior, and good versus responsible parenting practices. The program stresses active listening, I-messages, and family meetings.

Specialized programs for stepfamilies are aimed at normalizing the stepfamily experience and developing communication skills to enhance stepfamily life. The Stepfamily Association of America promotes local support groups and educational programs for stepfamily members. One established program is Smart Steps for Adults and Children in Stepfamilies, a 12-hour course with a focus on communication for children ages 6 to 16 and adult stepfamily members.

Government and educational institutions have entered the family enrichment area in response to divorce rates and child neglect or abuse. Many states provide incentives for couples to take premarital education classes or to participate in counseling before divorcing. Although some states have tried to make these activities mandatory, they have not succeeded (Brotherson & Duncan, 2004). Additionally, many high schools offer life skills classes that include parenting and communication units. Increasing numbers of community organizations offer parent management training programs with communication components (Webster-Stratton, 1997).

Secondary prevention efforts are increasing also as more schools, communities, and therapists respond to perceived needs. Frequently, these are directed at disruptive behavior problems. For example, the Fast-Track multisite demonstration project focuses on school children at risk for conduct disorder by engaging families in programs designed to improve parenting and parent-teacher interaction (Pinsof & Hambright, 2002). Some of the challenges facing effective relationship education include making it more accessible, integrating it more with community initiatives to gain support, broadening program formats, and expanding programs to address relationships outside of marriage (Halford, 2004).

Appraisal of Enrichment Programs   Given the range and type of programs, as well as the diversity of communication content and skills built into these programs, questions have been raised regarding their effectiveness. The limited research that does exist focuses primarily on marital programs. Burleson and Denton (1997) concluded that "the relationship between communication skills and marital satisfaction is not simple and straightforward" (p. 884), based on their finding that skills and satisfaction were positively associated in nondistressed couples. Other research found that the skills must be combined with a desire or spirit of goodwill to motivate partners to use them appropriately (Renick, Blumberg, & Markman, 1992). Additional factors that need to be studied include the length of the training's effectiveness, skill maintenance, and nature of the participants.

A review of 13 specific marital enrichment programs (Jakubowski, Milne, Brunner, & Milner, 2004) led the authors to conclude that "only four programs could be considered 'efficacious.' Three were found to be 'possibly efficacious,' and six were considered empirically untested" (p. 528). The authors conducted a rigorous evaluation of selected published research. The four programs rated as efficacious (producing or capable of producing the desired effect) were the Prevention and Relationship Enhancement Program (PREP), Relationship Enhancement (RE), the Couple Communication Program (CC), and Strategic Hope-Focused Enrichment. One of the largest and oldest programs, Marriage Encounter, has served countless couples, yet few empirical studies have been published on its effectiveness. Similarly, although Gottman's Survival Kit (Gottman & Gottman, 1999) was developed based on a strong research tradition, it remains underresearched.

Another evaluative review (Balswick & Balswick, 2007) covered a wide range of programs for their quality and research base concerning issues such as program content, user friendliness, teaching materials, exercises, gender roles, and the degree to which the program reflects a biblical or theological perspective. These authors, who watched program videos and read all the teaching materials and student materials, concluded that much variation existed among programs. A key unifying focus was learning good communication and conflict resolution skills. Typical programs addressed issues including children, sex, money, in-laws, religon, roles, and personality differences. They noted a difference between programs built on biblical texts and those built on social science research, concluding that it was necessary to develop marital enrichment programs "that are based on an integration of the best empirical studies on marriage, social science literature, outcome researh on program effectivenss and a comprehensive use of biblical truth as a foundation for marriage" (n.p.).

Overall, research on these programs does not attribute undisputed success to their efforts. Responding to the need for better assessment methods, Gottman and colleagues have initiated proximal change experiments with couples as a way of gathering empirical evidence for effective marital interventions. In these experiments, a married couple has one conflict discussion before a brief intervention and one conflict discussion after an intervention. The success of the intervention is assessed by the improvement in the couple's communication in the second conflict discussion. The researchers believe that by using brief interventions, researchers can better understand which interventions affect different marital communication behaviors. In one study, couples were randomized into one of five interventions, with the pre- and post-intervention conflict discussions video recorded. Many of the interventions did result in an improvement in the second conflict interactions (Gottman, Ryan, Swanson, & Swanson, 2005).

One longitudinal study has evaluated the impact of an enrichment education program for couples that experienced parenthood for the first time (Shapiro & Gottman, 2005). Couples were assessed in the last trimester of pregnancy before attending a two-day enrichment workshop that addressed issues such as "What is the transition to parenthood like?" "What are the warning signs of marital meltdown?" and "Understanding marital communication." Couples were assessed again when the baby was three months old and when the baby was one year old. Compared to a control group, couples that experienced this enrichment program had higher marital quality, lower postpartum depression, and lower hostile affect during conflict.

Research on the long-term effectiveness of marital and family enrichment programs is too limited to draw secure conclusions. However, Stanley (2001), a PREP developer, argued that "there are clear advantages in terms of interaction quality for couples taking the more empirically-based, skills-oriented training" (p. 278). Scholars have called for, and contributed to, studies of enrichment program effectiveness but there is much work left to do. Family communication scholars may develop primary intervention programs and partner with therapists to create secondary intervention-level programs.

A key question remains: To what extent does communication skill level determine marital satisfaction? Some studies indicated that low-skilled couples are just as happy and satisfied with their marriages as high-skilled couples, a finding that

Burleson (1998) speculated may arise from ethnic differences or lack of awareness of such skills. Burleson and Denton (1997) maintained there was a problem with the naïve assumption that deficient communication skills was the cause of many marital communication problems. They identified other possible contributing factors—skill type, marital distress, gender, and analytical unit (self, couple)—that may impact the situation. The distressed couple mantra "We just can't communicate" cannot be addressed by simplistic skill training. Additional research needs to be conducted on communication-oriented enrichment programs.

Therapeutic Approaches

Partners or families experiencing severe relational pain or crisis are most effectively served by therapy. A vast body of family-oriented therapeutic literature exists (Nichols, 2008; Pinsof & Wynne, 1995); this section only introduces the concept of *family therapy*. Individual therapy has long been an established approach to dealing with personal problems or illnesses. For those families experiencing a severe crisis or living in long-term dysfunctional patterns, therapeutic interventions may be warranted. The one-to-one, counselor-client relationship remains one valid therapeutic approach, but when a relational system encounters difficulties, family or systems counseling presents an appropriate approach.

Exactly what does family therapy entail? The goal of family therapy is to identify family patterns that contribute to a behavior disorder or mental illness and help family members break those habits. Family therapy involves discussion and problem-solving sessions with the family. Some of these sessions may involve group, couple, or one-on-one sessions. In family therapy, the web of interpersonal relationships is examined and, ideally, communication is strengthened within the family (Medicine.Net.com, 2004). A description of a family therapy experience follows.

Two years ago, my family went into therapy because my younger brother was flunking school and shoplifting and his treatment center required the entire family to become involved in the treatment program. The therapist stressed that Chris's acting out was a family problem, not just Chris's problem. After a few months we were able to understand our patterns of family interaction that "fed" Chris's problem. The therapy forced my mother and stepfather to deal with some problems in their marriage that they had ignored and allowed us to make enough changes that Chris could return to high school and control the shoplifting.

The family therapy movement developed as a result of research and clinical advances of the 1950s, including hospital psychiatry, group dynamics, interpersonal psychiatry, the child guidance movement, research in communication and schizophrenia, and marriage counseling. Communication issues emerged as a key feature of the family therapy movement because many of these pioneers, most

A couple often gains insight into their problems when a third party helps to clarify issues.

notably Virginia Satir, focused explicit attention on communication patterns. Early family therapy practices relied heavily on systems theory's assumptions about change and context. Once therapists encountered the whole family system, they realized that often the difficulties of the "problem" member served to stabilize the system and deflect attention from key family issues and that increased parental collaboration served as an effective strategy for breaking up the strong parent-child coalition (Olson, 2000, p. 163). Therefore, problems of individual members must be examined within their family context. Furthermore, attention must be paid to how communication among family members affects members' alliances.

Family communication practices and patterns frequently play a role in therapy. After interviewing counselors about couples' communication problems, Vangelisti (1994a) reported that the most frequently noted communication problems included failing to take the other's perspective when listening, blaming the other for negative occurrences, and criticizing the other. Counselors believed that communication problems resulted from patterns taught to individuals by their families-of-origin. A majority of counselors viewed communication as a manifestation of more fundamental difficulties; only one-quarter viewed communication as the central issue. Olson (2000) argued that although increasing positive communication skills of couples and families can facilitate change, it is a necessary but not sufficient condition to alter a family's cohesion and adaptability. An important therapeutic goal is to provide members with skills to negotiate system change over time.

Family therapy approaches have influenced the development of programs designed for the treatment of drug and alcohol abuse, eating disorders, major illness, and sexual abuse. Problem-centered family therapy raises the question: "What prevents the patient system from solving the presenting problem?" (Pinsof, 1995, p. 7). The integrative problem-solving approach encompasses the contexts of family-community, couple, and the individual. It relies on a range of orientations involving behavioral, biobehavioral, experiential, family origin, psychodynamic, and self-psychology (Pinsof, 1995).

Currently family therapists struggle with issues of culture and gender and their effects on the treatment process. The growing number of culturally diverse families who need the services of family therapists has led to increasing interest in cross-cultural family norms and treatment approaches (McGoldrick, Giordano, & Garcia-Preto, 2005). Cross-cultural family relationships encounter differences in such areas as attitudes toward marriage, male-female roles, and the significance of extended family. Although few therapists can demonstrate expertise in communication patterns of multiple cultures, it is essential for therapists to be open to cultural variability and the relativity of their own values (Hines, et al., 2005).

Some critics suggest that family therapy has been grounded in beliefs about gender and sexual orientation that limit relational flexibility. Knudson-Martin and Laughlin (2005) argued that family therapy should use a relationship model that is founded on equality, not gender. Therapists are encouraged to examine myths that partners hold about male and female roles. For example, a heterosexual couple may present with the husband's complaint that his wife is too busy to give him attention, whereas she asserts that her responsibilities at home and for her aging parents take all her time and energy. A therapist who operates from an equality model (a postgender approach) would focus on the value of the wife's responsibilities and how the husband might also make contributions more equally in that realm. This type of approach would make the problem the couple's problem, rather than just the wife's problem (Knudson-Martin & Laughlin).

The past decades witnessed an increase in research addressing the overall effectiveness of family therapy and specific issues of unique approaches (Goldenberg & Goldenberg, 2008; Gottman, Ryan, Carrère, & Erley, 2002). In a review of therapeutic research, Lebow and Gurman (1996) included the following points: Family therapy is at least as helpful as more traditional, individual approaches; troubled couples relationships is the area in which a wide range of systemic approaches have been validated as effective; and family therapy engages difficult individuals to engage. They conclude that although there are many positive findings, some of the treatment effects lose hold over time and there are many underresearched areas. Gottman and colleagues (2002) argued that marital therapy remains relatively uninformed by empirical research, relying instead on clinical history. Research revealed that although marital therapy creates significant short-term effects, there is a high relapse factor over time. Those who show improvement are likely to be less distressed, more emotionally engaged, and show less negative affect. Ongoing research in family therapy will continue to inform therapeutic practice.

In order to change the current communication patterns within your family system, many options are open to you, ranging from individual approaches to the involvement of all members. Communication can be improved; families can grow through effort, time, and struggle. Relationships take work to maintain, and communication stands at the core of that process. The effort required is worthwhile since ultimately it is our loving connections that give life meaning (Wallerstein & Blakeslee, 1995). Intimate relationships encourage members to enlarge their visions of life and diminish their preoccupation with self. We are at our most considerate, most loving, and most selfless within the orbit of a well-functioning family.

Final Perspectives

Just as there is no one right way to be a family, there is no one family scholar who has all the answers. Each scholar reflects his or her own professional and personal orientation to family life. Historical perspectives tend to be descriptive, reflecting few cultural or structural variations. Henry (1973), in his classic work on family functioning, identified seven characteristics of family psychopathology. A reversed wording of his findings would lead to the following characteristics of well-functioning families: (1) interactions are patterned and meaningful, (2) there is more compassion and less cruelty, (3) persons are not scapegoats because problems are identified with the appropriate persons, (4) members exhibit appropriate self-restraint, (5) boundaries are clear, (6) life includes joy and humor, and (7) misperceptions are minimal. Virginia Satir (1988) maintained that untroubled and nurturing families demonstrate the following: "Self-worth is high; communication is direct, clear, specific, and honest; rules are flexible, human, appropriate, and subject to change; and the linking to society is open and hopeful" (p. 4). Bochner and Eisenberg (1987) suggested that the following features are characteristic of optimal family functioning: (1) Strong sense of *trust*; members rarely take oppositional attitudes and avoid blaming each other; (2) *Enjoyment*; optimal families are spontaneous, witty, and humorous; (3) *Lack of preoccupation* with themselves; they do not overanalyze their problems looking for hidden motives, life is not taken too seriously; and (4) *Maintenance of conventional boundaries* reflecting a strong parental coalition and clear sense of hierarchy (p. 559).

Today, countless trade books, television shows, CDs, and DVDs, provide advice on "How to Have a Healthy Partnership" and "How to Create a Happy Family." Most of the highly popular advice literature, based on expert opinion and research, supports the positions of academic researchers but presents the ideas in more readable and prescriptive language. Although stepfamily material has been available in popular literature for two decades, few popular resources were available for same-sex partners and parents until quite recently. Now, titles such as *The Kid, Gay Dads, Out of the Ordinary,* and *The Complete Lesbian and Gay Parenting Guide* appear in chain bookstores.

You can recognize the value of these ideas as well as the need to be more inclusive of family diversity. Well-functioning families must be understood within their cultural and structural contexts. Communication patterns in a well-functioning Hispanic stepfamily may differ from that in an African American single-parent family system. Open communication may not be possible or desirable for every family, as noted here.

My family struggles with the concept of openness because although my two siblings and I were born in China, our parents moved to Michigan when we were young. We grew up in a Western culture surrounded by families who talked about everything and expressed differences directly. My parents were raised to honor the wishes of their elders and not to question or argue about adult decisions. It has been very hard for them to adjust to open and direct communication patterns. We all struggle between the "new" way and the "old" way.

Low-income families, an often overlooked population in academic studies of well-functioning families, face challenges such as existing on public assistance, struggling with health problems, and dangerous living conditions. In spite of these challenges, however, many low-income families demonstrate family strengths, including good communication and problem-solving skills. These skills lead to positive outcomes such as meeting needs and providing activities for children that will help them succeed (Orthner, Jones-Sanpei, & Williamson, 2004).

Our Personal Views

As the authors of this book, we hold strong beliefs about well-functioning families. Our beliefs may be stated as follows:

> *A healthy family recognizes the interdependence of all members and attempts to provide for the growth of the system as a whole, as well as the individual members involved. These families develop a capacity for adaptation and cohesion that avoids functioning at an extreme level. Members welcome each life stage and attempt to adapt to variations in their family forms. Individuals seek to find joy while living in the present and creating a personal and familial support network. Healthy families exhibit levels of connection that permit members to feel cared for but not smothered. Family members make an effort to understand the underlying meanings of other members' communication. All members find a sense of connections in the family's stories, rituals, and cultural heritages.*

Our beliefs have been influenced by our research, counseling and teaching experiences, where we are repeatedly reminded of families who lack the necessary communication skills to negotiate their difficulties and an inability to understand another member's perspective. Meaningful family connections require consistent nurturing. In most families, day-to-day routines overwhelm members' lives, resulting in primarily functional rather than nurturing communication patterns. Families profit from taking time to ask, "How are we doing as a family?" and "How can we improve our communication?" Well-functioning families are able to engage in metacommunication—they are able to talk about how members relate to each other and how, if necessary, the current communication patterns could be strengthened. Finally, strong families have learned the values of communication, commitment, caring, and change.

We leave you with the following jazz ensemble metaphor, which captures the dynamics of a well-functioning family.

> I like to think of the family as a jazz ensemble, where members move with the flow of what's happening around them, looking for a harmony of sorts, playing off one another, going solo at times, always respecting the talents and surprises surrounding them. Standards, yes. Expectations, always. But everyone moving with the "feel" of the moment and one another. Anyone at anytime can say or shout, "This isn't working!" and can challenge other members toward a different beat or movement or settle into a silence that regenerates spontaneous creativity and energy. We do know "family" isn't a lonely drum in the distance or a plaintive flute on an empty stage. Family is found in the creative energy and interplay of its members. (Wilkinson, 1998)

CONCLUSION

This chapter explored perspectives and research addressing family communication and well-being. *Well-being* included family members' ability to communicate about physical health, capacity to hold difficult conversations on challenging topics, and willingness to engage in individual or structured enrichment experiences or couple or family therapy to strengthen their relationships. These family members have the capacity to profoundly affect each other's health through their attempts to persuade each other to adopt healthy behaviors, their interactions with health care providers, and their family communication when a member is ill. Such families exhibit the capacity to engage in difficult conversations in order to ensure the health and well-being of members. It is imperative that families learn to talk about tough topics such as their shared genetic heritage, their economic challenges, and members' risky involvement in digital participation in dangerous practices. Finally, family members must be willing to consider engaging in strategies for improving marital and family communication, including personal actions, instructional programs, and therapeutic interventions. Such willingness demonstrates a level of commitment and openness to change, forcing participants to move beyond daily life patterns in order to reflect on and improve their family experience.

In Review

1. In what ways should family communication about health change over the lifespan?
2. Identify and explain three effective and three ineffective ways for family members to influence each other's health.
3. How would you describe communication in a well-functioning family? Answer within a context of a specific developmental stage, culture, and family form (e.g., a two-parent, Chinese family with adolescents).
4. Analyze the prescriptions for marital or parent-child communication found in a popular book or magazine article. Evaluate the effectiveness of the advice based on your understanding of family systems and communication patterns.
5. What goals and criteria would you establish for a successful marriage or family enrichment program with a communication focus? Briefly describe the audience you envision (e.g., a stepfamily with school-aged children).
6. Take a position on the following question: To what extent should couples or parents be required by religious or civic institutions to engage in family enrichment workshops or family therapy?
7. In what ways would you predict that family therapy would differ across two ethnic groups?

8. Select a specific issue within the difficult conversations areas of genetics or money. Explain how you might suggest to a family you know how an adult member could address the topic meaningfully with other members.

9. Identify strategies that parents might use to stay abreast of digital media advances and ways they can effectively address their concerns with their children.

KEY WORDS

Cyberbullying   320
Digital immigrant   320
Digital native   320
Digital settler   320
Family health rules   310
Family therapy   330
Health care advocate   311

Marriage enrichment programs   326
Marital support networks   327
Pragmatic style of disclosure (genetics)   315
Prevaricating style of disclosure   315
Proband   314
Sexting   322

BIBLIOGRAPHY

Abe, J. A. A., & Izard, C. E. (1999). Compliance, noncompliance strategies, and the correlates of compliance in 5-year-old Japanese and American children. *Social Development, 8*(1), 1–20.

Abel, K. (2010). When parents lose a job: Talking to kids about layoffs. *Family Education Network.* Retrieved from http://life.familyeducation.com/money-and-kids/communication/29623.html.

Abraham, K. M. & Stein, C. H. (2010). Staying connected: Young adults' felt obligation toward parents with and without mental illness. *Journal of Family Psychology, 24*(2), 125–134.

Ackerman, N. J. (1989). The family with adolescents. In E. Carter & M. McGoldrick (Eds.), *The family life cycle: A framework for family therapy*. New York: Gardner Press.

Adams, J. (2004). "This is not where I belong!" The emotional, ongoing and collective aspects of couples' decision making about where to live. *Journal of Comparative Family Studies, 35*(3), 459–484.

Adelman, A., Chadwick, K., & Baerger, D. (1996). Marital quality of black and white adults over the life course. *Journal of Social and Personal Relationships, 13*, 361–384.

Adelman, M. (1988, November). *Sustaining passion: Eroticism and safe sex talk*. Paper presented at the meeting of the Speech Communication Association, New Orleans, LA.

Afifi, T. D. (2003). "Feeling caught" in stepfamilies: Managing boundary turbulence through appropriate privacy coordination rules. *Journal of Social and Personal Relationships, 20*, 729–756.

Affifi, T. D. Huber, F. N., & Ohs, J. (2006). Parents' and adolescents' communication with each other about divorce-related stressors and its impact on their ability to cope positively with the divorce. *Journal of Divorce and Remarriage, 45*(1), 1–30.

Afifi, T. D. & Keith, S. (2004). A risk and resiliency model of ambiguous loss in postdivorce stepfamilies. *Journal of Family Communication, 4*, 65–98.

Afifi, T. D. & McManus, T. (2006). Investigating privacy boundaries: Communication in post-divorce families. In K. Floyd & M. T. Morman (Eds.), *Widening the family circle: New research on family communication* (pp. 171–187). Thousand Oaks, CA: Sage.

Affifi, T. D. McManus, T., Hutchinson, S., & Baker, B. (2007). Inappropriate parental divorce disclosures, the factors that prompt them, and their impact on parents' and adolescents' well-being. *Communication Monographs, 74*, 78–102.

Afifi, T. D. & Nussbaum, J. (2006). Stress and adaptation theories: Families across the life span. In D. O. Braithwaite & L. A. Baxter (Eds.), *Engaging theories in family communication: Multiple perspectives* (pp. 276–292). Thousand Oaks, CA: Sage.

Afifi, T. D. & Olson, L. (2005). The chilling effect in families and pressure to conceal secrets. *Communication Monographs, 72*, 192–216.

Afifi, T. D. & Schrodt, P. (2003). "Feeling caught" as a mediator of adolescents' and young adults' avoidance and satisfaction with their parents in divorced and non-divorced households. *Communication Monographs, 70*, 142–173.

Ahlander, N. R. & Bahr, K. S. (1995). Beyond drudgery, power, and equity: Toward an expanded discourse on the moral dimensions of housework in families. *Journal of Marriage and the Family, 57*, 54–68.

Ahrons, C. R. (2000). Divorce: An unscheduled family transition. In B. Carter & M. McGoldrick (Eds.), *The expanded family life cycle: Individual, family and social perspectives* (3rd ed., pp. 381–398). Boston, MA: Allyn & Bacon.

Aida, Y. & Falbo, T. (1991). Relationships between marital satisfaction, resources and power strategies. *Sex Roles, 41*, 43–50.

Alba, R. (1990). *Ethnic identity: The transformation of white America*. New Haven, CT: Yale University Press.

Alberts, J. K. (1988). An analysis of couples' conversational complaints. *Communication Monographs, 55*, 184–196.

Alberts, J. K., Yoshimura, C. G., Rabby, M., & Loschiavo, R. (2005). Mapping the topography of couples' daily conversation. *Journal of Social and Personal Relationships, 22,* 299–322.

Albrecht, T. L. & Goldsmith, D. J. (2003). Social support, social networks, and health. In T. L. Thompson, A. M. Dorsey, K. I. Miller, & R. Parrott (Eds.), *Handbook of Health Communication,* (pp. 263–284). Mahwah, NJ: Lawrence Erlbaum.

Aldridge, H. (1994, April). *Adrift in a sea of words: An examination of the connection between gender, audiences, and argument.* Paper presented at the meeting of the Central States Communication Association, St. Paul, MN.

Alexander, A., Kang, S., & Kim, Y. (2006). Cyberkids: The influence of mediation and motivation on children's use of and attitudes toward the Internet. In L. H. Turner & R. West (Eds.), *The family communication sourcebook* (pp. 315–334). Thousand Oaks, CA: Sage.

Allen, K. R. & Demo, D. H. (1995). The families of lesbians and gay men: A new frontier in family research. *Journal of Marriage and the Family, 57,* 111–127.

Allen, K. R. & Wilcox, K. L. (2000). Gay/lesbian families over the life course. In S. J. Price, P. C. McKenry, & M. J. Murphy (Eds.), *Families across time: A life course perspective* (pp. 51–63). Los Angeles, CA: Roxbury.

Allen, M. & Burrell, N. (1996). Comparing the impact of homosexual and heterosexual parents on children: Meta-analysis of existing research. *Journal of Homosexuality, 32,* 19–35.

Almeida, D. M., Wethington, E., & Chandler, A. L. (1999). Daily transmission of tensions between marital dyads and parent-child dyads. *Journal of Marriage and the Family, 61,* 49–61.

Almeida, T. (2005). Asian Indian families. In M. McGoldrick, J. Giordano, & N. Garcia-Preto (Eds.), *Ethnicity and family therapy* (3rd ed., pp. 377–394). New York: The Guilford Press.

Amato, P. R. (2001). Children of divorce in the 1990's. *Journal of Family Psychology, 15,* 355–370.

Amato, P. R. (1996). Explaining the intergenerational transmission of divorce. *Journal of Marriage and the Family, 58,* 628–640.

Amato, P. R., & Booth, A. (1996). A prospective study of divorce and parent-child relationships. *Journal of Marriage and the Family, 59,* 356–365.

Amato, P. R. & Cheadle, J. (2005). The long reach of divorce: Divorce and child well-being across three generations. *Journal of Marriage and the Family, 67,* 191–206.

Amato, P. R., & Rezacs, S. (1994). Contact with non-resident parents, interpersonal conflict, and children's behavior. *Journal of Family Issues, 15,* 191–207.

Amato, P. R., & Rogers, S. L. (1997). A longitudinal study of marital problems and subsequent divorce. *Journal of Marriage and the Family, 59,* 612–624.

Ambry, M. K. (1993). Recipes for marriage. *American Demographics, 15,* 30–38.

American Academy of Pediatrics. (2009). Help kids with cell phones get the message: Say no to "sexting."*AAP News,* 30:26. Retrieved from http://aapnews.aappublications.org/cgi/content/full/30/8/26-d.

American Bar Association, Commission on Domestic Violence. (2010). *Survey of Recent Statistics.* Retrieved from http://new.abanet.org/domestic violence/Pages/Statistics.aspx#prevalence.

American Cancer Society. (2006). *Estimated new cancer cases and deaths by sex for all sites, U.S.* Retrieved from http://www.cancer.org.

American Community Survey. (2009). *Same-sex couples in the 2008 American community survey.* Retrieved from http://www.law.ucla.edu/williamsinstitute/pdf/ACS2008_WEBPOST_FINAL.pdf

American Community Survey. (2008). *Statistical portrait of Hispanics in the United States, 2008.* Retrieved from http://pewhispanic.org/files/factsheets/hispanics2008/Table%201.pdf

Andersen, P. A., Eloy, S. V., Guerrero, L. K., & Spitzberg, B. H. (l995). Romantic jealousy and relational satisfaction: A look at the impact of jealousy experience and expression. *Communication Reports, 8,* 77–85.

Anderson, K. L. (1997). Gender, status, and domestic violence: An integration of feminist and family violence approaches. *Journal of Marriage and the Family, 59,* 655– 669.

Anderson, K. L., Umberson, D., & Elliott, S. (2004). Violence and abuse in families. In A. Vangelisti (Ed.), *Handbook of family communication* (pp. 629–649). Mahwah, NJ: Lawrence Erlbaum.

Aquilino, W. S. (1997). From adolescent to young adult: A prospective study of parent-child relations during the transition to adulthood. *Journal of Marriage and the Family, 60,* 678–686.

Arnett, J. J. (2004). *Emerging adulthood: The winding road from the late teens through the twenties.* New York: Oxford University Press.

Arp, D. & Arp, C. (1996). *The second half of marriage.* New York: Zondervan.

Arrington, M. I. (2005). "She's right behind me all the way": An analysis of prostate cancer narratives and changes in family relationships. *Journal of Family Communication, 5,* 141–162.

Art & Science of Love: Weekend Workshops for Couples. (2010). Retrieved from http://www.gottman.com/54740/566065/Couples-Workshops/The-Art-and-Science-of-Love—LIVE-workshop.html.

Avery, C. (1989). How do you build intimacy in an age of divorce? *Psychology Today, 23,* 27–31.

Aylmer, R. (1988). The launching of the single young adult. In B. Carter & M. McGoldrick (Eds.), *The changing family life cycle: A framework for family therapy* (2nd ed., pp. 191–208). New York: Gardner Press.

Babrow, A. S., Kline, K. N., & Rawlins, W. K. (2005). Narrating problems and problematizing narratives: Linking problematic integration and narrative theory in telling stories about our health. In L. M. Harter, P. M. Japp, & C. S. Beck (Eds.), *Narratives, health and healing: Communication, research and practice* (pp. 31–52). Mahwah, NJ: Lawrence Erlbaum.

Bain, A. (1978). The capacity of families to cope with transitions: A theoretical essay. *Human Relations, 31,* 675–688.

Baker, C. W., Whisman, M. A., & Brownell, K. D. (2000). Studying intergenerational transmission of eating, attitudes and behaviors: Methodological and conceptual questions. *Health Psychology, 19,* 376–381.

Balswick, J. & Balswick, J. (2007). *Marriage enrichment program evaluation.* Retrieved from www.baylor.edu/content/services/document.php/41412.pdf.

Bao, Y., Fern, E. F., & Sheng, S. (2007). Parental style and adolescent influence in family consumption decisions: An integrative approach. *Journal of Business Research, 60,* 672–680.

Barbato, C. A., Graham, E. E., & Perse, E. M. (2001, April). *Communicating in the family: An examination of the relationship of family communication climate and interpersonal communication motives.* Paper presented at the meeting of the Central States Communication Association, Atlanta, GA.

Barnett, R., Kibria, N., Baruch, G. K., & Pleck, J. H. (1991). Adult daughter-parent relationships and their associations with daughters: Subjective well-being and psychological distress. *Journal of Marriage and the Family, 53,* 29–42.

Barnett, R., Marshall, N., & Pleck, J. (1992). Men's multiple roles and their relationship to men's psychological distress. *Journal of Marriage and the Family, 54,* 358–367.

Barsevick, A. M., Montgomery, K. R., Ross, E. A., Egleston, B. L., Bingler, R., Malick, J., & Miller, S. M., et al. (2008). Intention to communicate BRCA1/ BRCA2 genetic test results to the family. *Journal of Family Psychology, 22,* 300–312.

Bartholet, E. (1993). *Family bonds: Adoption and the practice of parenting.* New York: Houghton Mifflin.

Bartholomae, S. & Fox, J. (2010). Economic stress and families. In S. J. Price, C. A. Price, & P. C. McKenry (Eds.), *Families and change: Coping with stressful events and transitions* (4th ed., pp. 185–209). Los Angeles, CA: Sage.

Baxter, C., Cummins, R. A., & Yiolitis, L. (2000). Parental stress attributed to family members with and without disability: A longitudinal study. *Journal of Intellectual & Developmental Disability, 25*(2), 105–118.

Baxter, L. A. (1991, November). *Bakhtin's ghost: Dialectical communication in relationships.* Paper presented at the meeting of the Speech Communication Association, Atlanta, GA.

Baxter, L. A. (2006). Relational dialectics theory: Multivocal dialogues of family communication. In D. O. Braithwaite & L. A. Baxter (Eds.), *Engaging theories in family communication* (pp. 130–145). Thousand Oaks, CA: Sage.

Baxter, L. A. & Braithwaite, D. O. (2002). Performing marriage: Marriage renewal rituals as cultural performance. *Southern Communication Journal, 67,* 94–109.

Baxter, L. A., & Braithwaite, D. O. (2006). Family rituals. In L. H. Turner & R. West (Eds.), *The family communication sourcebook* (pp. 259–280). Thousand Oaks, CA: Sage.

Baxter, L. A. & Braithwaite, D. O. (2008). Relational dialectics theory: Crafting meaning from competing discourses. In L. A. Baxter & D. O. Braithwaite (Eds.), *Engaging theories in interpersonal communication: Multiple perspectives* (pp. 349–361). Thousand Oaks, CA: Sage.

Baxter, L. A., Braithwaite, D. O., Bryant, L., & Wagner, A. (2004). Stepchildren's perceptions of the contradictions in communication with stepparents. *Journal of Social and Personal Relationships, 21*, 447–467.

Baxter, L. A., Braithwaite, D. O., Golish, T. D., & Olson, L. N. (2002). Contradictions of interaction for wives of elderly husbands with adult dementia. *Journal of Applied Communication Research, 30*, 1–26.

Baxter, L. A., Braithwaite, D. O., & Nicholson, J. H. (1999). Turning points in the development of blended families. *Journal of Personal and Social Relationships, 16*, 291–313.

Baxter, L. A., & Bylund, C. L. (2004). Social influence in close relationships. In J. Seiter & R. Gass (Eds.), *Perspectives on persuasion, social influence, and compliance gaining* (pp. 317–336). Boston, MA: Allyn & Bacon.

Baxter, L. A., Bylund, C. L., Imes, R., & Routsong, T. (2009). Parent-child perceptions of parental behavioral control through rule-setting for risky health choices during adolescence. *Journal of Family Communication, 9*, 251–271.

Baxter, L. A., Bylund, C. L., Imes, R. S., & Routsong, T. (2006, November). *Relationships between family rule structures and adolescents' risky behaviors: Abstinence and contingency rules about sex, tobacco, alcohol and drugs.* Paper presented at the meeting of the National Communication Association, San Antonio, TX.

Baxter, L. A., Bylund, C. L., Imes, R. S., & Schieve, D. M. (2005). Family communication environments and rule-based social control of adolescents' healthy lifestyle choices. *Journal of Family Communication, 5*, 209–227.

Baxter, L. A., & Dindia, K. (1990). Marital partners' perceptions of marital maintenance strategies. *Journal of Social and Personal Relationships, 7*, 187–208.

Baxter, L. A., & Montgomery, B. M. (1996). *Relating: Dialogues and dialectics.* New York: Guilford Press.

Beach, W. A., & Good, J. S. (2004). Uncertain family trajectories: Interactional consequences of cancer diagnosis, treatment, and prognosis. *Journal of Social and Personal Relationships, 21*, 8–32.

Beatty, M. J., & McCroskey, J. C. (1998). Interpersonal communication as temperamental expression: A communibiological paradigm. In J. C. McCroskey, J. A. Daly, M. M. Martin, & M. J. Beatty (Eds.), *Communication and personality: Trait perspectives.* Cresskill, NJ: Hampton Press.

Beatty, M. J., McCroskey, J. C., & Heisel, A. D. (1998). Communication apprehension as temperamental expression: A communibiological paradigm. *Communication Monographs, 64*, 197–219.

Beatty, M. J., McCroskey, J. C., & Valencic, K. M. (2001). *The biology of communication: A communibiological perspective.* Cresskill, NJ: Hampton Press.

Beckman, L. J., Harvey, S. M., Satre S. J., & Walker, M. A. (1999). Cultural beliefs about social influence strategies of Mexican immigrant women and their heterosexual partners. *Sex Roles, 40*(11/12), 871–892.

Bedford, V. H., & Blieszner, R. (1997). Personal relationships in later-life families. In S. Duck (Ed.), *Handbook of personal relationships* (2nd ed., pp. 523–539). New York: John Wiley & Sons.

Belch, M. A., Krentler, K. A., & Willis-Flurry, L. A. (2005). Teen Internet mavens: Influence in family decision making. *Journal of Business Research, 58*, 569–575.

Belkin, L. (2003, October 26). The opt-out revolution. *New York Times Magazine*, 42–47, 58, 85–86.

Belsky, J., Jaffee, S. R., Sligo, J., Woodward, L., & Silva, P. A. (2005). Intergenerational transmission of warm-sensitive-stimulating parenting: A prospective study of mothers and fathers of 3-year-olds. *Child Development, 76*, 384–396.

Benazon, N. R., Foster, M. D., & Coyne, J. C. (2006). Expressed emotion, adaptation, and patient survival among couples coping with chronic heart failure. *Journal of Family Psychology, 20*, 328–334.

Bengston, V. L. (2001). Beyond the nuclear family: The increasing importance of multigenerational bonds. *Journal of Marriage and the Family, 63*, 1–16.

Benoit, P. J., Kennedy, K. A., Waters, R., Hinton, S., Drew, S., & Daniels, F. (1996, November). *Food, football, and family talk: Thanksgiving rituals in families.* Paper presented at the meeting of the Speech Communication Association, San Diego, CA.

Berger, P. & Kellner, H. (1964). Marriage and the construction of reality: An exercise in the microconstruction of knowledge. *Diogenes, 46*, 1–25.

Berkowitz, D. & Marsiglio, W. (2007). Gay men: Negotiating procreative, father, and family identities. *Journal of Marriage and the Family, 69,* 366–381.

Beutler, I., Burr, W., Bahr, K., & Herrin, D. (1988). The family realm: Theoretical contributions for understanding its uniqueness. *Journal of Marriage and the Family, 51,* 805–815.

Bianchi, S. M., & Casper, L. M. (2005). Explanations of family change: A family demographic perspective. In V. L. Bengston, A. C. Acock, K. R. Allen, P. Dilworth-Anderson, & D. M. Klein (Eds.), *Sourcebook of family theory & research* (pp. 93–117). Thousand Oaks, CA: Sage.

Bielski, V. (1996, March–April). Our magnificent obsession. *Family Therapy Networker,* 22–35.

Black, C. (2001). *It will never happen to me* (2nd ed.). Center City, MN: Hazelden.

Blau, F. D., Ferber, M. A., & Winkler, A. E. (1997). *The economics of women, men and work* (3rd ed.). Upper Saddle River, NJ: Prentice-Hall.

Blee, K. M., & Tickamyer, A. T. (1995). Racial differences in men's attitudes about women's gender roles. *Journal of Marriage and the Family, 57,* 21–30.

Blumenthal, A. (1990–91). Scrambled eggs and seed daddies: Conversations with my son. *Empathy: Gay and Lesbian Advocacy Research Project, 2,* 2.

Boase, J., Horrigan, J. B., Wellman, B., & Rainie, L. (2006). *The strength of Internet ties.* Retrieved from the Pew Internet and American Life Project, Web site: www.pewinternet.org.

Bochner, A. P., & Eisenberg, E. (1987). Family process: System perspectives. In C. Berger and S. Chaffee (Eds.), *Handbook of communication science* (pp. 540–563). Beverly Hills, CA: Sage.

Bodenmann, G., Meuwly, N., Bradbury, T. N., Gmelch, S. & Ledermann, T. (2010). Stress, anger, and verbal aggression in intimate relationships: Moderating effects of individual and dyadic coping. *Journal of Social and Personal Relationships, 27,* 408–424.

Bollis-Pecci, T. S., & Webb, L. M. (1997, November). *The Memphis family perceptions instrument: Tests for validity and reliability.* Paper presented at the meeting of the National Communication Association, Chicago, IL.

Bonebright, A., Clay, D., & Ankenmann, R. D. (2000). The relationship of workaholism with work-life conflict, life satisfaction, and purpose in life. *Journal of Counseling Psychology, 47*(4), 469–477.

Booth, A., & Amato, P. R. (1994). Parental marital quality, parental divorce. *Journal of Marriage and the Family, 56,* 21–34.

Booth, A., Carver, K., & Granger, D. (2000). Biosocial perspectives on the family. *Journal of Marriage and the Family, 62,* 1018–1034.

Boss, P. (1999). *Ambiguous loss: Learning to live with unresolved grief.* Cambridge, MA: Harvard University Press.

Boss, P. (2001, December). Ambiguous loss: Frozen grief in the wake of the WTC catastrophe. *Family Focus* (pp. F12–F13). National Council of Family Relations.

Boss, P. (2006). *Loss, trauma and resilience: Therapeutic work with ambiguous loss.* New York: W. W. Norton.

Bosticco, C., & Thompson, T. (2005). The role of communication and story telling in the family grieving process. *Journal of Family Communication, 5,* 255–278.

Boushey, H. (2009). The new breadwinners. *The Shriver Report: A study by Maria Shriver and the Center for American Progress.* Retrieved from http://www.awomansnation.com/economy.php.

Bradbury, A. R., Patrick-Miller, L., Pawlowski, K., Ibe, C. N., Cummings, S. A., Hlubocky, F., Olopade, O. I., & Daugherty, C. K., et al. (2009). Learning of your parent's BRCA mutation during adolescence or early adulthood: A study of offspring experiences. *Psycho-Oncology, 18,* 200–208.

Braithwaite, D. O. (1991). Just how much did that wheelchair cost? Management of privacy boundaries by persons with disabilities. *Western Journal of Speech Communication, 55,* 254–274.

Braithwaite, D. O., & Baxter, L. A. (1995). "I do" again: The relational dialectics of renewing marriage vows. *Journal of Social and Personal Relationships, 12,* 177–198.

Braithwaite, D. O., & Baxter, L. A. (2006). "You're my parent but you're not": Dialectic tensions in stepchildren's perceptions about communication with the nonresidential parent. *Journal of Applied Communication Research, 34*(1), 30–48.

Braithwaite, D. O., Olson, L. N., Golish, T. D., Soukup, C., & Turman, P. (2001). "Becoming a family": Developmental processes represented in blended family discourse. *Journal of Applied Communication Research, 29,* 221–247.

Braithwaite, D. O., Schrodt, P., & Baxter, L. A. (2006). Understudied and misunderstood: Communication in stepfamily relationships. In K. Floyd & M. T. Morman (Eds.), *Widening the family circle: New research on family communication* (pp. 153–170). Thousand Oaks, CA: Sage.

Braithwaite, D. O., & Thompson, T. L. (2000). Communication and disability research: A productive past and a bright future. In D. O. Braithwaite & T. L. Thompson (Eds.), *Handbook of communication and people with disabilities* (pp. 507–515). Mahwah, NJ: Lawrence Erlbaum.

Bray, J. H. & Kelly, J. (1998). *Stepfamilies: Love, marriage and parenting in the first decade*. New York: Broadway Books.

Breunlin, D. C., Schwartz R. C., & Kune-Karrer, B. M. (2001). *Metaframeworks: Transcending the models of family therapy* (2nd ed.). San Francisco, CA: Jossey-Bass.

Brier, N. (2008). Grief following miscarriage: A comprehensive review of the literature. *Journal of Women's Health, 17,* 451–464.

Brock, L. & Jennings, G. (1993). What daughters in their 30s wish their mothers had told them. *Family Relations, 42,* 61–65.

Bronstein, P., Clauson, J., Stoll, M. F., & Abrams, C. L. (1993). Parenting behavior and children's social, psychological and academic adjustment in diverse family structures. *Family Relations, 42,* 268–276.

Brothers, J. (1998, June). Are you caught in the middle? *Parade,* 4–7.

Brubaker, T., & Roberto, K. (1993). Family life education for the later years. *Family Relations, 42,* 212–221.

Bruess, C. J. (1994). *Bare-chested hugs and tough guy nights: Examining the form and function of interpersonal rituals in marriage and friendship.* Unpublished doctoral dissertation, Ohio University, Athens, Ohio.

Bruess, C. J. (1997). *Interview in family communication.* Teleclass, available from PBS Adult Learning Satellite Service, 1320 Braddock Pl., Alexandria, VA.

Bruess, C. J. & Kudak, A. D. H. (2008a). *What happy couples do: The loving little rituals of romance.* Minneapolis, MN: Fairview Press.

Bruess, C. J. & Kudak, A. D. H. (2008b). *What happy parents do: The loving little rituals of a child-proof marriage.* Minneapolis, MN: Fairview Press.

Bruess, C. J., & Pearson, J. C. (1997). Interpersonal rituals in marriage and adult friendship. *Communication Monographs, 66,* 25–46.

Bryant, J. A., & Bryant, J. (2006). Implications of living in a wired family: New directions in family and media research. In L. H. Turner & R. West (Eds.), *The family communication sourcebook* (pp. 297–314). Thousand Oaks, CA: Sage.

Bryant, L. E. (2006). Ritual (in)activity in postbereaved stepfamilies. In L. H. Turner & R. West (Eds.), *The family communication sourcebook* (pp. 281–293). Thousand Oaks, CA: Sage.

Buehler, C., Betz, P., Ryan, C., & Trotter, B. (1992). Description and evaluation of the orientation for divorcing parents: Implications for post divorce prevention programs. *Family Relations, 41*(2), 154–162.

Buijzen, M. & Valkenburg, P. M. (2008). Observing purchase-related parent-child communication in retail environments: A developmental and socialization perspective. *Human Communication Research, 34*(1), 50–69.

Building a strong family. (2010). Retrieved from http://lds.org/hf/display/0,16783,4209-1,00.html.

Bullock, C. & Foegen, A. (2002). Constructive conflict resolution for students with behavioral disorders. *Behavioral Disorders, 27*(3), 289–295.

Burleson, B. R. (1998). Similarities in social skills: Interpersonal attraction and the development of personal relationships. In J. S. Trent (Ed.), *Communication: Views from the helm for the 21st century* (pp. 77–84). Boston, CA: Allyn & Bacon.

Burleson, B. R., Delia, J., & Applegate, J. (1992). Effects of maternal communication and children's social-cognitive and communication skills on children's acceptance by the peer group. *Family Relations, 41,* 264–272.

Burleson, B. R., & Denton, W. H. (1997). The relationship between communication skill and marital satisfaction: Some moderating effects. *Journal of Marriage and the Family, 59,* 884–902.

Burr, W. R., Klein, S., & Associates. (1994). *Reexamining family stress.* Thousand Oaks, CA: Sage.

Busby, D. M. & Holman, T. B. (2009). Perceived match or mismatch on the Gottman conflict styles: Associations with relationship outcome variables. *Family Process, 48,* 531–545.

Bush, K. R., Bohon, S. A., & Kim, H. K. (2010). Adaptation among immigrant families: Resources and barriers. In S. J. Price, C. A. Price, & P. C. McKenry (Eds.), *Families and change: Coping with stressful events and transitions* (4th ed., pp. 285–310). Los Angeles, CA: Sage.

Bute, J. J. & Tennley, A. V. (2010). Privacy management as unfinished business: Shifting boundaries in the context of infertility. *Communication Studies, 61,* 1–20.

Butkovic, A. & Bratko, D. (2007). Family study of manipulation tactics. *Personality and Individual Differences, 43,* 791–801.

Buxton, A. P. (2006). When a spouse comes out: Impact on the heterosexual partner. *Sexual Addiction and Compulsivity, 13,* 317–332.

Buzzanell, P. M., & Burrell, N. A. (1997). Family and workplace conflicts: Examining metaphorical conflict schemas and expressions across context and sex. *Human Communication Research, 24*(1), 109–146.

Buzzanell. P. M. & Turner, L. H. (2003). Emotion work revealed by job loss discourse backgrounding-foregrounding of feelings, construction of normalcy, and (re)instituting of traditional masculinities. *Journal of Applied Communication Research, 31,* 27–57.

Byers, L. A., Shue, C. K., & Marshall, L. L. (2001, November). *The interplay of violence, relationship quality, commitment, and communication in relationships: An examination of the dyad and the family.* Paper presented at the meeting of the National Communication Association, Atlanta, GA.

Bylund, C. L. (2003). Ethnic diversity and family stories. *Journal of Family Communication, 3,* 215–236.

Bylund, C. L., Baxter, L. A., Imes, R. S., & Wolf, B. (2010). Parental rule socialization for preventive health and adolescent rule compliance. *Family Relations, 59,* 1–13.

Bylund, C. L., & Duck, S. (2004). The everyday interplay between family relationships and family members' health. *Journal of Social and Personal Relationships, 21*(1), 5–7.

Bylund, C. L., Galvin, K. M., Dunet, D. O., & Reyes, M. (in press). Using the extended health belief model to understand siblings' perceptions of risk for hereditary hemochromatosis. *Patient Education and Counseling.*

Cahn, D. D., & Lloyd, S. A. (1996). *Family violence from a communication perspective.* Thousand Oaks, CA: Sage.

Canary, D. J., Cody, M. J., & Manusov., V. L. (2000). *Interpersonal communication: A goals-based approach* (2nd ed.). Boston, MA: Bedford/St. Martin's.

Canary, D. J., & Stafford, L. (1994). Maintaining relationships through strategic and routine interaction. In D. J. Canary & L. Stafford (Eds.), *Communication and relational maintenance* (pp. 3–22). San Diego, CA: Academic Press.

Canary, D. J., Stafford, L., & Semic, B. A. (2002). A panel study of the associations between maintenance strategies and relational characteristics. *Journal of Marriage and the Family, 64,* 395–406.

Canary, D. J., Weger, H., & Stafford, L. (1991). Couples' argument sequences and their associations with relational characteristics. *Western Journal of Speech Communication, 55,* 159–179.

Cancer Facts & Figures. (2010). *American Cancer Society.* Atlanta, GA: American Cancer Society.

Cappella, J. N. (1991). The biological origins of automated patterns on human interaction. *Communication Theory, 1,* 4–35.

Carp, E. W. (1998). *Family matters: Secrecy and disclosure in the history of adoption.* Cambridge, MA: Harvard University Press.

Carter, B., & McGoldrick, M. (2005a). The divorce cycle: A major variation in the American family life cycle. In B. Carter & M. McGoldrick (Eds.), *The expanded family life cycle: Individual, family and social perspectives* (3rd ed., pp. 373–398). Boston, MA: Allyn & Bacon.

Carter, B. & McGoldrick, M. (2005b). Overview: The expanded family life cycle: Individual, family, and social perspectives. In B. Carter & M. McGoldrick (Eds.), *The expanded family life cycle: Individual, family and social perspectives* (3rd ed., pp. 1–26). Boston, MA: Allyn & Bacon.

Caughlin, J. P. & Huston, T. L. (2002). A contextual analysis of the association between demand/withdraw and marital satisfaction. *Personal Relationships, 9,* 95–119.

Caughlin, J. P. & Ramey, M. E. (2005). The demand/withdraw pattern of communication in parent-adolescent dyads. *Personal Relationships, 12,* 337–356.

Caughlin, J. P. & Scott, A. M. (2010). Toward a communication theory of the demand/withdraw pattern of interaction in interpersonal relationships. In S. Smith & S. R. Wilson (Eds.), *New directions in interpersonal communication* (pp. 180–200). Thousand Oaks, CA: Sage.

Cate, R. M., Levin L. A., & Richmond, L. S. (2002). Premarital relationship stability: A review of recent research. *Journal of Social and Personal Relationships, 19,* 261–284.

Caughlin, J. P. (2002). The demand/withdraw pattern of communication as a predictor of marital satisfaction over time. *Human Communication Research, 28*(1), 49–85.

Caughlin, J. P., & Afifi, T. D. (2004). When is topic avoidance unsatisfying? A more complete investigation into the underlying links between avoidance and dissatisfaction in parent-child and dating relationships. *Human Communication Research, 30,* 479–513.

Caughlin, J. P., Golish, T. D., Olson, L. N., Sargent, J. E., Cook, J. S., & Petronio, S. (2000). Intrafamily secrets in various family configurations: A communication boundary management perspective. *Communication Studies, 51,* 116–134.

Caughlin, J. P., & Malis, R. S. (2004). Demand/withdraw communication between parents and adolescents: Connections with self-esteem and substance abuse. *Journal of Social and Personal Relationships, 21*(1), 125–148.

Caughlin, J. P., & Vangelisti, A. L. (2000). An individual difference explanation of why married couples engage in the demand/withdraw pattern of conflict. *Journal of Social and Personal Relationships, 17*(4–5), 523–551.

Cawyer, C. S., & Smith-Dupre, A. (1995). Communicating social support: Identifying supportive episodes in an HIV/AIDS support group. *Communication Quarterly, 43,* 243–358.

CDC (2009). Assisted reproductive technology: Home. Retrieved from http://www.cdc.gov/art/

CDC. (2010). *Health, United States, 2009.* Retrieved from http://www.cdc.gov/nchs/pressroom/10newreleases/hus09.htm

Chabot, J. M., & Ames, B. D. (2004). It wasn't "Let's get pregnant and go do it": Decision making in lesbian couples planning motherhood via donor insemination. *Family Relations, 53,* 348–356.

Chaitin, J. (2002). Issues and interpersonal values among three generations in families of Holocaust survivors. *Journal of Social and Personal Relationships, 19,* 379–402.

Chandra , A., Lara-Cinisomo, S., Jaycox, L. H., Tanielian, T., Burns, R. M., Ruder, T., & Han, B. (2009). Children on the homefront: The experience of children from military families. *Pediatrics, 125,* 16–25.

Chapman, G. (2004). *The five love languages: How to express heartfelt commitment to your mate.* Chicago, IL: Northfield Press.

Chelsey, N. (2005). Blurring boundaries: Linking technology use, spillover, individual distress, and family satisfaction. *Journal of Marriage and the Family, 67,* 1237–1248.

Chen, Z., & Kaplan, H. B. (2001). Intergenerational transmission of constructive parenting. *Journal of Marriage and the Family, 63,* 17–31.

Childress, H. (2004). Teenagers, territory and the appropriation of space. *Childhood, 11,* 195–205.

Christakis, N. A., & Allison, P. D. (2006). Mortality after the hospitalization of a spouse. *New England Journal of Medicine, 4,* 2190–2191.

Christakis, N. A. & Fowler, J. H. (2009). *Connected: The surprising power of our social networks and how they shape our lives.* New York: Little, Brown.

Ciabatarri, T. (2007). Single mothers, social capital, and work-family conflict. *Journal of Family Issues, 28,* 34–60.

Cissna, K. H., Cox, D. E., & Bochner, A. P. (1990). The dialectic of marital and parental relationships within the stepfamily. *Communication Monographs, 57,* 45–61.

Claes, E., Evers-Kiebooms, G., Boogaerts, A., Decruyenaere, M., Denayer, L., & Legius, E. (2003). Communication with close and distant relatives in the context of genetic testing for hereditary breast and ovarian cancer in cancer patients. *American Journal of Medical Genetics Part C, 116,* 11–19.

Clark, M. S. (1999). The double ABCX model of family crisis as a representation of family functioning after rehabilitation from stroke. *Psychology, Health and Medicine, 4*(2), 203–220.

Clark, S. C. (2000). Work/family border theory: A new theory of work/family balance. *Human Relations, 53*(6), 747–770.

Clarke, A., Richards, M., Kerzin-Storrar, L., Halliday, J., Young, M. A., Simpson, S. A., . . . Forest, K. (2005). Genetic professionals' reports of nondisclosure of genetic risk information within families. *European Journal of Human Genetics, 13*(5), 556–62.

Clements, M. L., Cordova, A. D., Markman, H. J., & Laurenceau, J-P. (1997). The erosion of marital satisfaction over time and how to prevent it. In S. R. Sternberg & M. Hojjat (Eds.), *Satisfaction in close relationships* (pp. 335–355). New York: Guilford Press.

Cline, K. (1989). The politics of intimacy: Costs and benefits determining disclosure intimacy in male-female dyads. *Journal of Social and Personal Relationships, 6,* 5–20.

Cline, R. J. W., Harper, F. W. K., Penner, L. A., Peterson, A. M., Taub, J. W., & Albrecht, T. L. (2006). Parent communication and child pain and distress during painful pediatric cancer treatments. *Social Science and Medicine, 63*(4), 883–898.

Cloven, D. H., & Roloff, M. I. (1993). The chilling effect of aggressive potential on the expression of complaints in intimate relationships. *Communication Monographs, 60*(660), 199–219.

Coffelt, T. A. (2010). Is sexual communication challenging between mothers and daughters? *Journal of Family Communication, 10,* 116–130.

Cohen, E. L. (2009). Naming and claiming cancer among African American women: An application of problematic integration theory. *Journal of Applied Communication Research, 37,* 397–417.

Cole, C. L., & Cole, A. L. (1999). Marriage enrichment and prevention really works: Interpersonal competence training to maintain and enhance relationships. *Family Relations, 48,* 273–276.

Coleman, M., Fine, M. A., Ganong, L. H., Downs, K. J. M., & Pauk, N. (2001). When you're not the Brady Bunch: Identifying perceived conflicts and resolution strategies in stepfamilies. *Personal Relationships, 8,* 55–73.

Coleman, M., Ganong, L., & Fine, M. (2000). Reinvestigating remarriage: Another decade of progress. *Journal of Marriage and the Family, 62,* 1288–1307.

Coleman, M., Ganong, L., & Fine, M. (2004). Communication in stepfamilies. In A. Vangelisti (Ed.), *Handbook of family communication* (pp. 215–232). Mahwah, NJ: Lawrence Erlbaum.

Collins, R. (1997). *Interview in family communication.* Teleclass, available from PBS Adult Learning Satellite Service, 1320 Braddock Pl., Alexandria, VA.

Coltrane, S. (2007). Fathering: Paradoxes, contradictions and dilemmas. In S. J. Ferguson (Ed.), *Shifting the center: Understanding contemporary families* (3rd ed., pp. 416–431). Boston, MA: McGraw-Hill.

Conger, R. D., & Conger, K. J. (2002). Resilience in midwestern families: Selected findings from the first decade of a prospective longitudinal study. *Journal of Marriage and the Family, 64,* 361–373.

Conger, R. D., Elder, G. H., Jr., Lorenz, F. O., Conger, K. J., Simons, R. L., Whitbeck, L. B., . . . Melby, J. N. (1990). Linking economic hardship to marital quality and instability. *Journal of Marriage and Family, 52*(2), 643–656.

Cooney, T. M. (1997). Parent-child relations across adulthood. In S. Duck (Ed.), *Handbook of personal relationships: Theory, research and interventions* (pp. 451–468). New York: John Wiley & Sons.

Coontz, S. (1996, May–June). Where are the good old days? *Modern Maturity,* 36–43.

Coontz, S. (1999). Introduction. In S. Coontz, M. Parson, & G. Raley (Eds.), *American families: A multicultural reader* (pp. ix–xxxiii). New York: Routledge.

Coontz, S. (2005). *Marriage, a history.* New York: Viking.

Cooper, M. (2000). Being the "go-to-guy": Fatherhood, masculinity, and the organization of work in Silicon Valley. *Qualitative Sociology, 23,* 379–405.

Cooper, P. J. (2006). Family-school relationships: Theoretical perspectives and concerns. In L. H. Turner & R. West (Eds.), *The family communication sourcebook* (pp. 405–423). Thousand Oaks, CA: Sage.

Covey, S. R. (1997). *The 7 habits of highly effective families.* New York, NY: Golden Books.

Cowan, C. P., & Cowan, P. A. (1997). Working with couples during stressful transitions. In S. Dreman (Ed.), *The family on the threshold of the 21st century.* Mahwah, NJ: Lawrence Erlbaum.

Cowdery, R. S., & Knudson-Martin, C. (2005). The construction of motherhood: Tasks, relational connection, and gender equality. *Family Relations, 54,* 335–345.

Cox, M. J., & Harter, K. S. M. (2002). The road ahead for research on marital and family dynamics. In J. P. McHale & W. S. Grolnick (Eds.), *Retrospect and prospect in the psychological study of families* (pp. 167–188). Mahwah, NJ: Lawrence Erlbaum.

Cramer, D. (2002). Linking conflict management behaviours and relational satisfaction: The intervening role of conflict outcome satisfaction. *Journal of Social and Personal Relationships, 19*(3), 425–432.

Crean, H. F. (2008). Conflict in the Latino parent-youth dyad: The role of emotional support from the opposite parent. *Journal of Family Psychology, 22,* 484–493.

Crespo, C., Davide, I. N., Costa, M. E., & Fletcher, G. J. O. (2008). Family rituals in married couples: Links with attachment, relationship quality, and closeness. *Personal Relationships, 15,* 191–203.

Cronen, V., Pearce, W. B., & Harris, L. (1979). The logic of the coordinated management of meaning: A rules-based approach to the first course in inter-personal communication. *Communication Education, 23,* 22–38.

Crosbie-Burnett, M., & McClintic, K. (2000). Remarried families over the life course. In S. J. Price, P. C. McKenry, & M. J. Murphy (Eds.), *Families across time: A life course perspective* (pp. 37–50). Los Angeles, CA: Roxbury.

Crowell, N. A., & Burgess, A. W. (1996). *Understanding violence against women.* Washington, DC: National Academies Press.

Dainton, M. (2007). Attachment and marital maintenance. *Communication Quarterly, 55*(3), 283–298.

Dainton, M. & Aylor, B. (2002). A relational uncertainty analysis of jealousy, trust, and maintenance in long-distance versus geographically close relationships. *Communication Quarterly, 49,* 172–188.

Dainton, M., Stafford, L., & McNeilis, K. S. (1992, October). *The maintenance of relationships through the use of routine behaviors.* Paper presented at the meeting of the Speech Communication Association, Chicago, IL.

Daly, K. J., & Beaton, J. (2005). Through the lens of time: How families live in and through time. In V. Bengston, A. Acock, K. R. Allen, P. Dilworth-Anderson, & D. M. Klein (Eds.), *Sourcebook of family theory and research* (pp. 241–262). Thousand Oaks, CA: Sage.

Daly, M., Farmer, J., Harrop-Stein, C., Montgomery, S., Itzen, M., Costalas, J. W., Rogatko, A. (1999). Exploring family relationships in cancer risk counseling using the genogram. *Cancer, Epidemiology, Biomarkers and Prevention, 8,* 393–398.

Daly, M. B., Barsevick, A., Miller, S. M., Buckman, R., Costalas, J., Montgomery, S., & Bingler, R. (2001). Communicating genetic test results to the family: A six-step, skills-building strategy. *Family Community Health, 24,* 13–26.

Daniel, J., & Daniel, J. (1999). African-American child rearing: The context of the hot stove. In T. H. Socha & R. C. Diggs (Eds.), *Communication, race and family: Exploring communication in black, white, and biracial families* (pp. 25–43). Mahwah, NJ: Lawrence Erlbaum.

Daniluk, J. C. & Hurtig-Mitchell, J. (2003). Themes of hope and healing: Infertile couples' experiences of adoption. *Journal of Counseling and Development, 81,* 389–399.

Darling, N., Cohan, C. L., Burns, A., & Thompson, L. (2008). Within-family conflict behaviors as predictors of conflict in adolescent romantic relations. *Journal of Adolescence, 31,* 671–690.

Davey, A., & Szinovacz, M. E. (2004). Dimensions of marital quality and retirement. *Journal of Family Issues, 25,* 431–464.

David, C. S., Dollard, N., & Vergon, K. S. (2009). The role of communication in child-parent-provider interaction in a children's mental health system of care. In T. J. Socha & G. H. Stamp (Eds.), *Parents and children communicating with society: Managing relationships outside of the home* (pp. 133–153). New York: Routledge.

Davies, P. T., Myers, R. L., Cummings, E. M., & Heindel, S. (1999). Adult conflict history and children's subsequent responses to conflict: An experimental test. *Journal of Family Psychology, 13*(4), 610–628.

DeFrain, J., & Stinnett, N. (1985). *Secrets of strong families.* Boston, MA: Little, Brown.

DeGenova, M. K., Rice, F. P. (2005). *Intimate relationships, marriages, and families* (6th ed.). New York: McGraw-Hill.

deHoyos, G. (1989). Person in environment: A tri-level practice model. *Social Casework, 70*(3), 131–138.

Delaney, K. J. (2005, November. 26–27). Big mother is watching. *The Wall Street Journal,* pp. A1, A6.

DeMaria, R. M. (2005). Distressed couples and marriage education. *Family Relations, 54,* 242–253.

DeMaris, A. (2001). The influence of intimate violence on transitions out of cohabitation. *Journal of Marriage and the Family, 63,* 235–246.

DeSteno, D. A., & Salovey, P. (1994). Jealousy in close relationships: Multiple perspectives on the green-eyed monster. In A. L. Weber & J. H. Harvey (Eds.), *Perspectives on close relationships* (pp. 217–242). Boston, MA: Allyn & Bacon.

deTurck, M. A., & Miller, G. R. (1983). Adolescent perceptions of parental persuasive message strategies. *Journal of Marriage and the Family, 45*(3), 543–552.

Dickson, F. C. (1995). The best is yet to be: Research on long-lasting marriages. In J. T. Wood & S. Duck (Eds.), *Understudied relationships* (pp. 22–50). Thousand Oaks, CA: Sage.

Dickson, F. C., Christian, A., & Remmo, C. J. (2004). An exploration of the marital and family issues of the later-life adult. In A. L. Vangelisti (Ed.), *Handbook of family communication* (pp. 153–174). Mahwah, NJ: Lawrence Erlbaum.

Dickson, F. C., & Walker, K. L. (2001, Summer). The expression of emotion in later-life married men.

Qualitative Research Reports in Communication, 66–71.

Dietz, T. L. (1995). Patterns of intergenerational assistance within the Mexican-American family. *Journal of Family Issues, 16,* 344–356.

Diggs, R. C. (2001, November). *Searching for commitment with a radical(izing) method: The experiences of an African-American long-distance married couple.* Paper presented at National Communication Association Convention, Atlanta, GA.

DiGiulio, J. F. (1992). Early widowhood: An atypical transition. *Journal of Mental Health Counseling, 14,* 97–109.

Dill, B. (1998). Fictive kin, paper sons, and *compadrazgo:* Women of color and the struggle for family survival. In K. V. Hansen & A. I. Garey (Eds.), *Families in the U.S.* (pp. 431–445). Philadelphia, PA: Temple University Press.

Dilorio, C., Kelley, M., & Hockenberry-Eaton, M. (1999). Communication about sexual issues: Mothers, fathers and friends. *Journal of Adolescent Health, 24,* 181–189.

Dilworth, J. E. L. & Kingsbury, N. (2005) Home-to-job spillover for generation X, boomers, and matures: A comparison. *Journal of Family and Economic Issues, 26*(2), 267–281.

Dilworth-Anderson, P., & Burton, L. M. (1996). Rethinking family development: Critical conceptual issues in the study of diverse groups. *Journal of Social and Personal Relationships, 13,* 325–334.

Dindia, K., Fitzpatrick, M. A., & Kenny, D. A. (1997). Self-disclosure in spouse and stranger interaction: A social relations analysis. *Human Communication Research, 23,* 388–412.

Dinero, R., Conger, R., Shaver, P., Widaman, K., & Larsen-Rife, D. (2008). Influence of family of origin and adult romantic partners on romantic attachment security. *Journal of Family Psychology, 22,* 622–632.

Doherty, W. J., & Carlson, B. Z. (2002). *Putting family first: Successful strategies for reclaiming family life in a hurry-up world.* New York: Henry Holt.

Downs, K. J., Coleman, M., & Ganong, L. (2000). Divorced families over the life course. In S. J. Price, P. C. McKenry, & M. J. Murphy (Eds.), *Families across time: A life course perspective* (pp. 24–36). Los Angeles, CA: Roxbury.

Driver, J. L. & Gottman, J. M. (2004). Daily marital interactions and positive affect during marital conflict among newlywed couples. *Family Process, 43,* 301–314.

Duck, S. (1986). *Human relationships: An introduction to social psychology.* London: Sage.

Duck, S. (1994). Steady as (s)he goes: Relational maintenance as a shared meaning system. In D. J. Canary & L. Stafford (Eds.), *Communication and relational maintenance* (pp. 45–60). San Diego, CA: Academic Press.

Duck, S., Miell, D., & Miell, D. (1984). Relationship growth and decline. In H. Sypher & J. Applegate (Eds.), *Communication by children and adults* (pp. 292–312). Beverly Hills, CA: Sage.

Duckworth, J. & Buzzannell, P. (2009). Constructing work-life balance and fatherhood: Men's framing of the meanings of *both* work *and* family. *Communication Studies, 60*(5), 558–573.

Duggan, A. & Petronio, S. (2009). When your child is in crisis. In T. J. Socha & G. H. Stamp (Eds.), *Parents and children communicating with society: Managing relationships outside of the home* (pp. 117–132). New York: Routledge.

Dumka, L. E., Roosa, M. W., & Jackson, K. M. (1997). Risk, conflict, mothers' parenting, and children's adjustment in low-income, Mexican immigrant, and Mexican American families. *Journal of Marriage and the Family, 59,* 309–323.

Dunbar, N. E. (2004). Dyadic power theory: Constructing a communication-based theory of relational power. *Journal of Family Communication, 4,* 235–248.

Duncan, B. L., & Rock, J. W. (1993, January–February). Saving relationships: The power of the unpredictable. *Psychology Today,* 46–51, 86, 95.

Dunlop, R. (1978). *Helping the bereaved.* Bowie, MD: Charles Press.

Dunstan, F., Weaver, N., Araya, R., Bell, T., Lannon, S., Lewis, C., Patterson, J., . . . Palmer, S. (2005). An observation tool to assist with the assessment of urban residential environments. *Journal of Environmental Psychology, 24,* 293–305.

Durham, W. & Braithwaite, D. O. (2009). Communication privacy management within the family-planning trajectories of voluntarily child-free couples. *Journal of Family Communication, 9,* 43–65.

Duvall, E. (1988). Family development's first forty years. *Family Relations, 37,* 127–134.

Eckstein, N. J. (2002). *Adolescent-to-parent abuse: A communicative analysis of conflict processes present in verbal, physical, or emotional abuse of parents.* Unpublished dissertation, University of Nebraska–Lincoln.

Edin, K., Nelson, T., & Paranal, R. (2001). Fatherhood and incarceration as potential turning points in the criminal careers of unskilled men. Institute for Policy Research, Northwestern University, Evanston, IL. WP-01-02.

Edwards, T. (2009). As baby boomers age, fewer families have children under 18 at home. *U.S. Census Bureau News.* Retrieved from http://www.census.gov/Press-Release/www/releases/archives/families_households/013378.html.

Eggly, S., Penner, L. A., Greene, M., Harper, F. W. K., Ruckdeschel, J. C., & Albrecht, T. L. (2006). Information seeking during "bad news" oncology interactions: Question asking by patients and their companions. *Social Science and Medicine, 63*(11), 2974–2985.

EHRC. (2009). *Working better: Fathers, family and work—contemporary perspectives.* Retrieved from http://www.equalityhumanrights.com/media-centre/2009/october/fathers-struggling-to-balance-work-and-family/

Ellingson, L. L. & Sotirin, P. (2010). Aunting: Cultural practices that sustain family and community life. Waco, TX: Baylor University Press.

Endres, T. G. (1997). Father-daughter dramas: A Q-investigation of rhetorical visions. *Journal of Applied Communication Research, 25,* 317–340.

Ennett, S. T., Bauman, K. E., Foshee, V. A., Pemberton, M., & Hicks, K. A. (2001). Parent-child communication about adolescent tobacco and alcohol use: What do parents say and does it affect youth behavior? *Journal of Marriage and the Family, 63,* 48–62.

Epstein, N. B., Bishop, D. S., & Baldwin, L. M. (1982). McMaster model of family functioning. In F. Walsh (Ed.), *Normal family processes* (pp. 115–141). New York: Guilford Press.

Erickson, B. M. (2005). Scandinavian families: Plain and simple. In M. McGoldrick, J. Giordano, & N. Garcia-Preto (Eds.), *Ethnicity and family therapy* (3rd ed., pp. 641–653). New York: Guilford Press.

Erikson, E. H. (1968). *Identity, youth, and crisis.* New York: W. W. Norton.

Escudero, V., Rogers, L. E., & Gutierrez E. (1997). Patterns of relational control and nonverbal affect in clinic and nonclinic couples. *Journal of Social and Personal Relationship, 14,* 5–29.

Facebook.com (2010). Retrieved from www.facebook.com.

Fadiman, A. (1997). *The spirit catches you and you fall down.* New York: Farrar, Straus & Giroux.

Falbo, T., & Peplau, L. A. (1980). Power strategies in intimate relationships. *Journal of Personality and Social Psychology, 38,* 618–628.

Faith and Marriage Ministries. (2010). Retrieved from http://faithandmarriageministries.org.

Falicov, C. J. (2005). Mexican families. In M. McGoldrick, J. Giordano, & N. Garcia-Preto (Eds.), *Ethnicity and family therapy.* (3rd ed., pp. 229–41). New York: Guilford Press.

"Family chats." (1998, February). *American Demographics,* 37.

Farrell, M. P. (2000). Adolescents' effects on the psychological functioning and adult development of their parents. *Family Science Review, 13,* 10–18.

Feldman, L. B. (1979). Marital conflict and marital intimacy: An integrative psychodynamic-behavioral systemic model. *Family Process, 18,* 69–78.

Fenigstein, A., & Peltz, R. (2002). Distress over the infidelity of a child's spouse: A crucial test of evolutionary and socialization hypotheses. *Personal Relationships, 9,* 301–312.

Ferguson, S. M. (1996, November). *From nightmares to peace: A case study of sexual abuse recovery using a pre-critical thinking approach.* Paper presented at the meeting of the Speech Communication Association, San Diego, CA.

Ferguson, S. M. (1997, November). *Children's attitudes toward parental dating: An empirical inquiry into contemporary family lifestyles.* Paper presented at the meeting of the National Communication Association, Chicago, IL.

Fields, J. (2004). America's families and living arrangements: 2003. *In Current Population Reports* (pp. 20–53). Washington, DC: U.S. Census Bureau.

Fiese, B. H. (2005). Time and time again: A critical look at order in family life. In V. Bengston, A. Acock, K. R. Allen, P. Dilworth-Anderson, & D. M. Klein (Eds.), *Sourcebook of family theory and research* (pp. 258–260). Thousand Oaks, CA: Sage.

Fiese, B. H., Hooker, K. A., Kotary, L., Schagler, J., & Rimmer, M. (1995). Family stories in the early stages of parenthood. *Journal of Marriage and the Family, 57,* 763–770.

Fincham, F. D., & Beach, S. R. (2002). Forgiveness in marriage: Implications for psychological aggression and constructive communication. *Personal Relationships, 9,* 239–251.

Fincham, F. D. & Beach, S. (2010). Of memes and marriage: Toward a positive relationship science. *Journal of Family Theory and Review, 2,* 4–24.

Fincham, F. D., Stanley, S. M., & Beach, S. R. H. (2007). Transformative processes in marriage: An analysis of emerging trends. *Journal of Marriage and Family, 69,* 275–292.

Fingerman, K., Miller, L., Birditt, K., & Zarit, S. (2009). Giving to the good and needy: Parental support of grown children. *Journal of Marriage and Family, 71,* 1220–1233.

Fingerman, K. L. (1998). Tight lips: Aging mothers' and their adult daughters' responses to interpersonal tensions in their relationship. *Personal Relationships, 5,* 121–138.

Fingerman, K. L. (2001). "We had a nice little chat": Age and generational differences in mothers' and daughters' descriptions of enjoyable visits. *Journal of Gerontology: Psychological Sciences, 55,* 95–106.

Fingerman, K. L. (2004). The role of offspring and in-laws in grandparents' ties to their grandchildren. *Journal of Family Issues, 25,* 1026–1049.

Fingerman, K. L., Nussbaum, J., & Birditt, K. S. (2004). Keeping all five balls in the air: Juggling family communication at midlife. In A. L. Vangelisti (Ed.), *Handbook of family communication* (pp. 135–152). Mahwah, NJ: Lawrence Erlbaum.

Fink, D. S., Buerkel-Rothfuss, N. L., & Buerkel, R. A. (1994, November). *Father-son relational closeness: The role of attribution-making in reducing the impact of bad behavior.* Paper presented at the meeting of the Speech Communication Association, New Orleans, LA.

Finkenauer, C., & Hazam, H. (2000). Disclosure and secrecy in marriage: Do both contribute to marital satisfaction? *Journal of Social and Personal Relationships, 17,* 245–263.

Fisher, C., & Miller-Day, M. (2006). Communication over the life span: The mother–adult daughter relationship. In K. Floyd & M. T. Morman (Eds.), *Widening the family circle* (pp. 3–19). Thousand Oaks, CA: Sage.

Fisher, T. D. (1986). Parent-child communication about sex and young adolescents' sexual knowledge and attitudes. *Adolescence, 16,* 517–527.

Fisher, W. R. (1987). *Human communication as narration: Toward a philosophy of reason, value and action.* Columbia, SC: University of South Carolina Press.

Fitness, J., & Duffield, J. (2004). Emotion and communication in families. In A. L. Vangelisti (Ed.), *Handbook of family communication* (pp. 473–494). Mahwah, NJ: Lawrence Erlbaum.

Fitzpatrick, M. A. (1977). A typological approach to communication in relationships. In B. Rubin (Ed.), *Communication yearbook I* (pp. 263–275). New Brunswick, NJ: Transaction Press.

Fitzpatrick, M. A. (1987). Marital interaction. In C. Berger & S. Chaffee (Eds.), *Handbook of communication science* (pp. 564–618). Newbury Park, CA: Sage.

Fitzpatrick, M. A. (1988). *Between husbands and wives.* Beverly Hills, CA: Sage.

Fitzpatrick, M. A. (1998). Interpersonal communication on the Starship Enterprise: Resilience, stability, and change in relationships in the twenty-first century. In J. S. Trent (Ed.), *Communication: Views from the helm for the 21st century* (pp. 41–46). Boston, MA: Allyn & Bacon.

Fitzpatrick, M. A., & Badzinski, D. M. (1994). All in the family: Interpersonal communication in kin relationships. In M. L. Knapp & G. L. Miller (Eds.), *Handbook of interpersonal communication* (2nd ed., pp. 726–771). Thousand Oaks, CA: Sage.

Fitzpatrick, M. A., & Best, P. (1979). Dyadic adjustment in relational types: Consensus, cohesion, affectional expression, and satisfaction in enduring relationships. *Communication Monographs, 46,* 165–178.

Fitzpatrick, M. A., Fallis, S., & Vance, L. (1982). Multifunctional coding of conflict resolution strategies in marital dyads. *Family Relations, 31,* 61–70.

Fitzpatrick, M. A., & Ritchie, L. D. (1994). Communication schemata within the family: Multiple perspectives on family interaction. *Human Communication Research, 20,* 275–301.

Flanagan, K. M., Clements, M. L., Whitton, S. W., Portney, M. J., Randall, D. W., & Markman, H. J. (2002). Retrospect and prospect in the psychological study of marital and couple relationships. In J. P. McHale & W. S. Grolnick (Eds.), *Retrospect and prospect in the psychological study of families* (pp. 99–128). Mahwah, NJ: Lawrence Erlbaum.

Fleming, A. S., Kraemer, G. W., Gonzalez, A., Loric, V., Rees, S., & Melo, A. (2002). Mothering begets mothering: The transmission of behavior and its neurobiology across generations. *Pharmacology, Biochemistry and Behavior, 73,* 61–75.

Floyd, K. (1996). Communicating closeness among siblings: An application of the gendered closeness perspective. *Communication Research Reports, 13,* 27–34.

Floyd, K. (2002). Human affection exchange: V. Attributes of the highly affectionate. *Communication Quarterly, 50,* 135–152.

Floyd, K., & Haynes, M. T. (2006). The theory of natural selection: An evolutionary approach to family communication. In D. O. Braithwaite & L. A. Baxter (Eds.), *Engaging theories in family communication* (pp. 325–340). Thousand Oaks, CA: Sage.

Floyd, K., Mikkelson, A. C., & Judd, J. (2006). Defining the family through relationships. In L. H. Turner & R. West (Eds.), *The family communication sourcebook* (pp. 21–39). Thousand Oaks, CA: Sage.

Floyd, K., & Morman, M. T. (2005) Fathers' and sons' reports of fathers' affectionate communication: Implications of a naïve theory of affection. *Journal of Personal and Social Relationships, 22,* 99–109.

Flurry, L. A., & Burns, A. C. (2003). Children's influence in purchase decisions: A social power theory approach. *Journal of Business Research, 58,* 593–601.

Foley, M. K. & Duck, S. (2006). "That Dear Octopus": A family-based model of intimacy. In L., H. Turner & R. West (Eds.), *The family communication sourcebook* (pp. 183–199). Thousand Oaks, CA: Sage.

Folwarski, J. & Smolinski, J. (2005). Polish families. In M. McGoldrick, J. Giordano, & N. Garcia-Preto (Eds.), *Ethnicity and Family Therapy* (3rd ed., pp. 741–755). New York: Guilford Press.

Forgatch, M. (1989). Patterns and outcomes in family problem solving: The disrupting effect of negative emotion. *Journal of Marriage and the Family, 51,* 115–124.

Forrest, G., Plumb, C., Zieland, S., & Stein, A. (2009). Breast cancer in young families: A qualitative interview study of fathers and their role and communication with their children following the diagnosis of maternal breast cancer. *Psycho-Oncology, 18,* 96–103.

Forrest, K., Simpson, S. A., Wilson, B. J., van Teijlingen, E. R., McKee, L., Haites, N., & Mathews, E. 2003). To tell or not to tell: Barriers and facilitators in family communication about genetic risk. *Clinical Genetics, 64,* 317–326.

Fosco, G. M. & Grych, J. H. (2010). Adolescent triangulation into parental conflicts: Longitudinal implications for appraisals and adolescent-parent relations. *Journal of Marriage and Family, 72,* 254–266.

Fowler, C. & Soliz, J. (2009) Responses of young adult grandchildren to grandparents' painful self-disclosures. *Journal of Language and Social Psychology, 29.* Retrieved from http://jlsp.sagepub.com.

Fox, S. (2006, April). *Data memo.* Retrieved from the Pew Internet and American Life Project, Web site: http:// www.perinternet.org/pdfs/ PIP_Wired_ Senior_2006,memo.pdf.

France, D. (2006, January–February). "And then he hit me." *AARP Magazine,* 61–63, 76–77, 81–83.

Friedman E. H. (1988). Systems and ceremonies: A family view of rites of passage. In B. Carter & M. McGoldrick (Eds.), *The changing family life cycle* (2nd ed., pp. 119–147). New York: Gardner Press.

Frieze, I. H., & McHugh, M. C. (1992). Power and influence strategies in violent and nonviolent marriages. *Psychology of Women Quarterly, 16,* 449–465.

Fry, R. & Passel, J. (2009). *Latino children: A majority are U.S.-born offspring of immigrants.* Retrieved from http://pewhispanic.org/reports/report.php?ReportID=110.

Fujishin, R. (1998). *Gifts from the heart.* San Francisco, CA: Acada Books.

Fulmer, R. (1999). Becoming an adult. In B. Carter & M. McGoldrick (Eds.), *The expanded family life cycle* (3rd ed., pp. 215–230). Boston, MA: Allyn & Bacon.

Gaff, C. L. & Bylund, C. L. (Eds.). (2010). *Family communication about genetics: Theory and practice.* New York: Oxford University Press.

Gaff, C. L., Clarke, A. J., Atkinson, P., Sivel, P., Elwyn, G., Iredahl, R., . . . Edwards, A. (2007). Process and outcome in communication of genetic information within families: A systematic review. *European Journal of Human Genetics, 15,* 999–1011.

Gaff, C. L., Collins, V., Symes, T., & Halliday, J. (2005). Facilitating family communication about predictive genetic testing: Probands' perceptions. *Journal of Genetic Counseling, 14,* 133–140.

Gaff, C. L., Galvin, K. M., & Bylund, C. L. (2010). Facilitating family communication about genetics. In C. L. Gaff & C. L. Bylund (Eds.), *Family communication about genetics: Theory and practice* (pp. 243–272). Oxford, England: Oxford University Press.

Galinsky, E. (1999). *Ask the children.* New York: William Morrow.

Galinsky, E., Aumann, K., & Bond, J. T. (2008). *The times are changing: Gender and generation at work*. Retrieved from Families and Work Institute Web site: www.familiesandwork.org.

Galvin, K. (2003). International and transracial adoption: A communication research agenda. *Journal of Family Communication, 3*, 237–253.

Galvin, K. (2006). Gender and family interaction: Dress rehearsal for an improvisation? In B. J. Dow & J. T. Wood (Eds.), *The sage handbook on gender and communication* (pp. 41–55). Thousand Oaks, CA: Sage.

Galvin, K. M. (2004). The family of the future: What do we face? In A. L. Vangelisti (Ed.), *Handbook of family communication* (pp. 675–697). Mahwah, NJ: Lawrence Erlbaum.

Galvin, K. M. (2006a). Diversity's impact on defining the family: Discourse dependence and identity. In L. H. Turner & R. West (Eds.), *The family communication sourcebook* (pp. 3–19). Thousand Oaks, CA: Sage.

Galvin, K. M. (2006b). Joined by hearts and words: Adoptive family relationships. In K. Floyd & M. T. Morman (Eds.), *Widening the family circle: New research on family communication* (pp. 137–152). Thousand Oaks, CA: Sage.

Galvin, K. M. (2008, September). Helicopter parents. Presentation to Lake County Counselors Association, Grayslake, IL.

Galvin, K. M., Bylund, C. L., Dunet, D., & Reyes, S. (2006, November). *Sibling communication about genetic risk of hemochromatosis: Using the health belief model to understand sibling decision-making about testing.* Presentation to the National Communication Association Conference, San Antonio, TX.

Galvin, K. M., Bylund, C. L., & Grill, B. (2007). Genograms: Construction and interpretation. Retrieved from http://www.genograms.org

Galvin, K. M., Dickson, F. C., & Marrow, S. K. (2006). Systems theory: Patterns and (w)holes in family communication. In D. O. Braithwaite & L. A. Baxter (Eds.), *The family communication sourcebook* (pp. 309–324). Thousand Oaks, CA: Sage.

Galvin, K. M., Turner, L. H., Patrick, D. G., & West, R. (2007, November). Difficult conversations: The experience of same-sex partners. Paper presented at the National Communication Association Convention, Chicago, IL.

Galvin, K. M. (2007). It's not all blarney: Intergenerational transmission of communication patterns in Irish American families. In P. Cooper, C. Calloway-Thomas, & C. Simonds (Eds.), *Intercultural communication: A text with readings* (pp. 172–192). Boston, MA: Allyn & Bacon.

Galvin, K. M., & DiDomenico. S. (2009, November). High stakes, emotionally charged health decisions: New directions for family communication and group communication scholars. Paper presented at the National Communication Association Conference, Chicago, IL.

Galvin, K. M. & Grill, L. H. (2009). Opening up the conversation on genetics and genomics in families: The space for communication scholars. In C. S. Beck (Ed.), *Communication Yearbook, 33* (pp. 213–257). New York: Routledge.

Galvin, K. M. & Patrick, D. (2009, November). Gay male partners achieving parenthood: Stories of communicative complexities and challenges. Paper presented at the National Communication Association Conference, Chicago, IL.

Galvin, K. M. (2010). Deliberation in a contested medical context: Developing a framework to aid family decision making when an adolescent son faces fertility-threatening cancer. In D. S. Gouran (Ed.), The functions of argument and social context (pp. 98–106). *Selected papers from the 16th biennial conference on argumentation.* Washington, DC: National Communication Association.

Galvin, K. M., Bylund, C. L., & Grill, B. (2010). *Genograms: Constructing and interpreting interaction patterns.* Retrieved from http://www.genograms.org/.

Galvin, K. M., Grill, L. H., Arntson, P. H., & Kinahan, K. (in press). Experiences of parents and adult survivors of childhood cancer an average of 16 years after diagnosis. In F. Dickson & L. Webb (Eds.), *Families and stress.* Cresskill, NJ: Hampton Press.

Gangotena, M. (1997). The rhetoric of *la familia* among Mexican Americans. In A. Gonzalez, M. Houston & V. Chen (Eds.), *Our voices: Essays in culture, ethnicity, and communication* (2nd ed., pp. 70–83). Los Angeles, CA: Roxbury.

Garces, Y., Pattern C. A., Sinicope, P. S., Decker P. A., Offord, K. P., & Brown, P. D., et al. (2010). Willingness of cancer patients to help family members to quit smoking. *Psycho-Oncology.* Retrieved from www.interscience.wiley.com.

Garcia-Preto, N. (2005a). Puerto Rican families. In M. McGoldrick, J. Giordano, & N. Garcia-Preto (Eds.), *Ethnicity and family therapy* (3rd ed., pp. 242–255). New York: Guilford Press.

Garcia-Preto, N. (2005b). Transformation of the family system during adolescence. In B. Carter & M. McGoldrick (Eds.), *The expanded family life cycle: Individual, family and social perspectives.* (3rd ed., pp. 274–286). Boston, MA: Allyn & Bacon.

Gasper, J. A. F., Stolberg, A. L., Macie, K. M., & Williams, L. J. (2008). Coparenting in intact and divorced families: Its impact on young adult adjustment. *Journal of Divorce and Remarriage, 49*(3), 272–290.

Gass, R. H., & Seiter, S. J. (1999). *Persuasion, social influence, and compliance-gaining.* Boston, MA: Allyn & Bacon.

Gelles, R. J. (2010). Violence, abuse, and neglect in families and intimate relationships. In S. J. Price, C. A. Price, & P. C. McKenry (Eds.), *Families and change: Coping with stressful events and transitions* (4th ed., pp. 119–139). Los Angeles, CA: Sage.

Gianino, M. (2008). Adaptation and transformation: The transition to adoptive parenthood for gay male couples. *Journal of GLBT Family Studies, 4*(2), 205–243.

Gilbar, O., & Refaeli, R. (2000). The relationship between adult cancer patients' adjustment to the illness and that of their parents. *Families, Systems and Health: The Journal of Collaborative Family Healthcare Association, 18*(1), 5–17.

Gillis, J. R. (1996). *A world of their own making: Myth, ritual and the quest for family values.* New York: HarperCollins.

Giordano, J., McGoldrick, M., & Klages, J. G. (2005). Italian families. In M. McGoldrick, J. Giordano, & N. Garcia-Preto (Eds.), *Ethnicity and family therapy* (3rd ed., pp. 616–628). New York: Guilford Press.

Golden, A. (1997). *Juggling work and family: The effects of modernity on the communicative management of multiple roles.* Paper presented at the meeting of the National Communication Association, Chicago, IL.

Golden, A. G. (2002). Speaking of work and family: Spousal collaboration on defining role-identities and developing shared meanings. *Southern Communication Journal, 67,* 122–141.

Golden, A. G. (2007). Fathers' frames for childrearing: Evidence toward a "masculine concept of caregiving." *Journal of Family Communication, 7*(4), 265–285.

Goldenberg, I. & Goldenberg, H. (2008). *Family therapy: An overview* (7th ed.). Belmont, CA: Thomson, Brooks/Cole.

Goldner, V., Penn, P., Sheinberg, M., & Walker G. (1990). Love and violence: Gender paradoxes in volatile attachments. *Family Process, 29,* 343–364.

Goldsmith, D. J. (2009). Uncertainty and communication in couples coping with serious illness. In T. D. Affifi & W. A. Affifi (Eds.), *Uncertainty, information managements, and disclosure decisions: Theories and applications* (pp. 203–225). New York: Routledge.

Goldsworthy, K. K. (2005). Grief and loss theory in social work practice: All changes involve loss, just as all losses require change. *Australian Social Work, 58,* 167–178.

Golish, T. D. (2000). Changes in closeness between adult children and their parents: A turning point analysis. *Communication Reports, 13,* 79–97.

Golish, T. D., & Caughlin, J. (2002). "I'd rather not talk about it": Adolescents' and young adults' use of topic avoidance in stepfamilies. *Journal of Applied Communication Research, 30,* 78–106.

Golombok, A., MacCallum, F., Goodman, E., & Rutter, M. (2002). Families with children conceived by donor insemination: A follow-up at age twelve. *Child Development, 73,* 952–968.

Gonzaga, G. C., Keltner, D., Londahl, E. A., & Smith, M. D. (2001). Love and the commitment problem in romantic relations and friendship. *Journal of Personality and Social Psychology, 81*(2), 247–262.

Goodman, C. C. & Silverstein, M. (2006). Grandmothers raising grandchildren: Ethnic and racial differences in well-being among custodial and coparenting families. *Journal of Family Issues, 27*(11), 1605–1626.

Gotcher, J. M. (1993). The effects of family communication on psychological adjustment of cancer patients. *Journal of Applied Communication Research, 21,* 176–188.

Gottman, J., Ryan, K., Swanson, C., & Swanson, K. (2005). Proximal change experiments with couples: A methodology for empirically building a science of effective intervention for changing couples' interaction. *Journal of Family Communication, 5*(3), 163–190.

Gottman, J. M. (1979). *Marital interaction: Experimental investigations.* New York: Academic Press.

Gottman, J. M. (1993). The roles of conflict engagement, escalation of avoidance in marital interaction: A longitudinal view of five types of couples. *Journal of Consulting and Clinical Psychology, 61,* 6–15.

Gottman, J. M. (1994). *What predicts divorce?* Hillsdale, NJ: Lawrence Erlbaum.

Gottman, J. M. (1999). *The marriage clinic: A scientifically based marital therapy*. New York: W. W. Norton.

Gottman, J. M., & DeClaire, J. (1997). *The heart of parenting*. New York: Simon & Schuster.

Gottman, J. M., & Krokoff, L. J. (1990). Complex statistics are not always clearer than simple statistics: A reply to Woody and Costenzo. *Journal of Consulting and Clinical Psychology, 58,* 502–505.

Gottman, J. M. & Gottman, J. S. (with DeClaire, J.) (2006). *10 lessons to transform your marriage.* New York: Crown Publishers.

Gottman, J. M. & Gottman, J. S. (1999). The marriage survival kit: A research-based marital therapy. In R. Berger & M. Hannah (Eds.), *Preventive approaches in couples therapy* (pp. 304–330). Philadelphia, PA: Brunner/Mazel.

Gottman, J. M., & Silver, N. (1999). *The seven principles for making marriage work.* New York: Three Rivers Press.

Grady, D. P. (1997, November). *Conversation strategies for detecting deception: An analysis of parent-adolescent child interactions.* Paper presented at the meeting of the National Communication Association, Chicago, IL.

Graham, E. E. (1997). Turning points and commitment in post-divorce relationships. *Communication Monographs, 64,* 350–368.

Graham, E. E. (2003). Dialectical contradictions in postmarital relationships. *Journal of Family Communication, 3,* 193–214.

Graham, E. E., & Edwards, A. P. (2002, November). *Dialectic characteristics and shadow realities in postmarital relationships.* Paper presented at the meeting of the National Communication Association. New Orleans, LA.

Grall, T. (2009). Custodial mothers and fathers and their child support: 2007. *In Current population reports.* Washington, DC: U.S. Census Bureau.

Greeff, A. P., & de Bruyne, T. (2000). Conflict management style and marital satisfaction. *Journal of Sex and Marital Therapy, 26,* 221–224.

Green, R., & Elffers, J. (1998). The laws of power. *Utne Reader, 1,* 78–85.

Greenhalgh, S. (2008). *Just one child: Science and policy in Deng's China.* Berkeley, CA: University of California Press.

Griffin, E. (1997). *A first look at communication theory* (3rd ed.). New York: McGraw-Hill.

Grill, B. D. (2011). From telex to twitter: Relational communication skills for a wireless world. In K.M. Galvin (Ed.), *Making Connections: Readings in Relational Communication* (pp. 89–96). New York: Oxford University Press.

Grimm-Thomas, K., & Perry-Jenkins, M. (1993). All in a day's work: Job experiences, self-esteem and fathering in working-class families. *Family Relations, 42,* 174–181.

Gringlas, M., & Weinraub, M. (1995). The more things change . . . single parenting revisited. *Journal of Family Issues, 16,* 29–52.

Gross, J. (2006, February 9). Aging at home: For a lucky few, a wish come true. *New York Times,* pp. D1, D8.

Grote, N. K., & Clark, M. S. (2001). Perceiving unfairness in the family: Cause or consequence of marital distress? *Journal of Personality and Social Psychology, 80,* 281–293.

Grzywacz, J. G., Almeida, D. M., & McDonald, D. A. (2002). Spillover and daily reports of work and family stress in the adult labor force. *Family Relations, 51,* 28–36.

Gudmunson, C. G., Beutler, I. F., Israelsen, C. L., McCoy, J. K., & Hill, E. J. (2007). Linking financial strain to marital instability: Examining the roles of emotional distress and marital interaction. *Journal of Family Economic Issues, 28,* 357–376.

Gueguen, J. A., Bylund, C. L., Brown, R. F., Levin, T., & Kissane, D.W. (2009). Conducting family meetings in palliative care: Themes, techniques and preliminary evaluation of a communication skills module. *Palliative and Supportive Care, 7*(2), 171–179.

Guerney, B. G. (1977). *Relationship enhancement: Skill training programs for therapy, problem prevention, and enrichment.* San Francisco, CA: Jossey-Bass.

Guerrero, L. K., & Afifi, W. (1995). What parents don't know: Topic avoidance in parent-child relationships. In T. J. Socha & G. H. Stamp (Eds.), *Parents, children and communication* (pp. 219–245). Mahwah, NJ: Lawrence Erlbaum.

Guerrero, L. K., Andersen, P. A., & Afifi, W. A. (2001). *Close encounters: Communicating in relationships.* Mountain View, CA: Mayfield.

Guerrero, L. K., & Bachman, G. F. (2006). Association among relational maintenance behaviors, attachment-style categories, and attachment dimensions. *Communication Studies, 57,* 341–361.

Gumina, J. M. (2009). Communication of the decision to divorce: A retrospective qualitative study. *Journal of Divorce and Remarriage, 50*(3), 220–232.

Guzman, B. L., Schlehofer-Sutton, M. M., Villanueva, C. M., Dello Stritto, M. E., Casad, B. J., & Feria, A. (2003). Let's talk about sex: How comfortable discussions about sex impact teen sexual behavior. *Journal of Health Communication, 8*, 583–598.

Haas, S. (2002). Social support as relationship maintenance in gay male couples coping with HIV or AIDS. *Journal of Social and Personal Relationships, 19*, 87–111.

Haas, S. M., & Stafford, L. (1998). An initial examination of maintenance behaviors in gay and lesbian relationships. *Journal of Social and Personal Relationships, 15*, 846–855.

Haas, S. M., & Stafford, L. (2005). Maintenance behaviors in same-sex and marital relationships: A matched sample comparison. *Journal of Family Communication, 5*, 43–60.

Hafen, M., Jr. & Crane, D. R. (2003). When marital interaction and intervention researchers arrive at different points of view: The active listening controversy. *Journal of Family Therapy, 25*, 4–14.

Halford, W. K., Sanders, M. R., & Behrens, B. C. (2000). Repeating the errors of our parents? Family-of-origin spouse violence and observed conflict management in enraged couples. *Family Process, 39*(2), 219–235.

Halpin, J., Teixeira, R., Pinkus, S., & Daley, K. (2009). Battle of the sexes gives way to negotiations. *The Shriver Report: A study by Maria Shriver and the Center for American Progress.* Retrieved from http://www.awomansnation.com/americanPeople.php.

Hamby, S. L., Poindexter, V. C., & Gray-Little, B. (1996). Four measures of partner violence: Construct similarity and classification differences. *Journal of Marriage and the Family, 58*, 127–139.

Hamer, J. (2007). What it means to be Daddy: Fatherhood for black men living away from their children. In S. J. Ferguson (Ed.), *Shifting the center: Understanding contemporary families* (3rd ed., pp. 431–446). Boston, MA: McGraw-Hill.

Hamilton, B. E., Ventura, S. J., Martin, J. A., & Sutton, P. D. (2004). *Final births for 2004.* Retrieved from http://www.cdc.gov/nchs/products/pubs/pubd/hestats/finalbirths04/finalbirths04.htm

Hamilton, R. J., Bowers, B. J., & Williams, J. K. (2005, first quarter). Disclosing genetic test results to family members. *Journal of Nursing Scholarship*, 18–24.

Hample, D., & Dallinger, J. (1995). A Lewian perspective on taking conflict personally: Revision, refinement, and validation of the instrument. *Communication Quarterly, 43*, 297–319.

Handel, G., & Whitchurch, G. (Eds.). (1994). *The psychological interior of the family.* Hawthorne, NY: Aldine de Gruyter.

Harburg, E., Kaciroti, N., Gleiberman, L., Julius, M., & Schork, A. (2008). Marital pair anger-coping types may act as an entity to affect mortality: Preliminary findings from a prospective study (Tecumseh, Michigan, 1971–1988). *Journal of Family Communication, 8*, 44–61.

Hardesty, J. L., & Chung, G. H. (2006). Intimate partner violence, parental violence, parental divorce, and child custody: Directions for intervention and future research. *Family Relations, 55*, 200–210.

Hardesty, J. L., Oswald, R. F., Khaw, L., Fonseca, D., & Chung, G. C. (2008). Lesbian mothering in the context of intimate partner violence. *Journal of Lesbian Studies, 12*, 191–210.

Hare-Mustin, R. (1994). Discourses in a mirrored room: A postmodern analysis of therapy. *Family Process, 33*, 19–36.

Harevan, T. (1982). American families in transition: Historical perspective on change. In F. Walsh (Ed.), *Normal family processes* (pp. 446–465). New York: Guilford Press.

Harker, C. (1997, Autumn). Life-saving stories. *Iowa Alumni Quarterly*, 32–34.

Harrigan, M. M. (2009). The contradictions of identity-work for parents of visibly adopted children. *Journal of Social and Personal Relationships, 26*, 634–658.

Harrigan, M. M. (2010). Exploring the narrative process: An analysis of the adoption stories mothers tell their internationally adopted children. *Journal of Family Communication, 10*, 24–39.

Harris, J., Hay, J., Kuniyki, A., Maryam, A., Press, N., & Deborah, B. (2010). Using a family systems approach to investigate cancer risk communication within melanoma families. *Psycho-Oncology, 19*, 1102–1111.

Harris, J. R. (1998). *The nurture assumption: Why children turn out the way they do; parents matter less than you think and peers matter more.* Boston, MA: Free Press.

Harter, L. M., Japp, P. M., & Beck, C. S. (2005). Vital problematics of narrative theorizing about health and healing. In L. M. Harter, P. M. Japp, & C. S. Beck (Eds.), *Narratives, health and healing: Communication, research and practice* (pp. 7–29). Mahwah, NJ: Lawrence Erlbaum.

Hay, J., Shuk, E., Zapolska, J., Ostroff, J., Lischewski, J., Brady, M., & Berwick, M. (2009). Family communications patterns after melanoma diagnosis. *Journal of Family Communication, 9,* 209–232.

Hay, J., Ostroff, J., Martin, A., Serle, N., Soma, S., Mujumdar, U., & Berwick, M. (2005). Skin cancer risk discussions in melanoma-affected families. *Journal of Cancer Education, 20,* 240–246.

Hayes, R. L. (1994). The legacy of Lawrence Kohlberg: Implications for counseling and human development. *Journal of Counseling/Development, 72,* 261–267.

Heatherington, L., Escudero, V., & Friedlander, M. L. (2005). Couple interaction during problem discussions: Toward an integrative methodology. *Journal of Family Communication, 5*(3), 191–207.

Heaton, T. B., & Jacobson, C. K. (1994). Race differences in changing family demographics in the 1980s. *Journal of Family Issues, 15,* 290–308.

Heisler, J. M. (2005). Family communication about sex: Parents and college-aged offspring recall discussion topics, satisfaction, and parental involvement. *Journal of Family Communication, 5,* 295–312.

Helgeson, V. S., & Cohen, S. (1999). Social support and adjustment to cancer: Reconciling descriptive, correlational and intervention research. In R. M. Suinn & G. R. VandenBos (Eds.), *Cancer patients and their families* (pp. 53–79). Washington, DC: American Psychological Association.

Helgeson, V. S., Novak, S. A., Lepore, S. J., & Eton, D. T. (2004). Spouse social control efforts: Relations to health behavior and well-being among men with prostate cancer. *Journal of Social and Personal Relationships, 21*(1), 53–68.

Helms-Erickson, H. (2001). Marital quality ten years after the transition to parenthood: Implications of the timing of parenthood and the division of housework. *Journal of Marriage and the Family, 63,* 1099–1110.

Henry, J. (1973). *Pathways to madness.* New York: Vintage Books.

Hess, R., & Handel, G. (1959). *Family worlds.* Chicago, IL: University of Chicago Press.

Hest, T. L., Pearson, J. C., & Child, J. T. (2006). Cover stories as family communication practice. In L. H. Turner & R. West (Eds.), *The family communication sourcebook* (pp. 129–142). Thousand Oaks, CA: Sage.

Hetherington, E. M. (1987). Family relations six years after divorce. In K. Pasley & M. Inhinger-Tallman (Eds.), *Remarriage and stepparenting: Current research* (pp. 185–205). New York: Guilford Press.

Hetherington, E. M., & Kelly, J. (2002). *For better or for worse: Divorce reconsidered.* New York: W. W. Norton.

Hewlett, S. A. (2002). *Creating a life: Professional women and the quest for children.* New York: Talk Mirimax Books.

Hiedemann, B., Suhomlinova, O., & O'Rand, A. M. (1998). Economic independence, economic status, and empty nest in midlife marital disruption. *Journal of Marriage and the Family, 21,* 219–231.

Hill, R. (1949). *Families under stress: Adjustment to the crises of war separation and reunion.* New York: Harper & Brothers.

Hill, R. (1986). Life cycle stages for types of single parent families: Of family development theory. *Family Relations, 35,* 19–29.

Hilton, B. A., Crawford, J. A., & Tarko, M. A. (2000). Men's perspectives on individual and family coping with their wives' breast cancer and chemotherapy. *Western Journal of Nursing Research, 22*(4), 438–459.

Hinchliff, S., & Gott, M. (2004). Intimacy, commitment, and adaptation: Sexual relationships within long-term marriages. *Journal of Social and Personal Relationships, 21,* 595–609.

Hindjua, S. & Patchin, J. W. (2009). *Cyberbullying and suicide.* Cyberbulllying Research Center. Retrieved from www.cyberbullying.us.

Hindjua, S. & Patchin, J. W. (2010). *Ten ideas for youth to educate their community about cyberbullying.* Cyberbulllying Research Center. Retrieved from www.cyberbullying.us.

Hines, A. M. (1997). Divorce-related transitions, adolescent development, and the role of the parent-child relationship: A review of the literature. *Journal of Marriage and the Family, 59,* 375–388.

Hines, P. M. (1999). The family life cycle of African-American families living in poverty. In B. Carter & M. McGoldrick (Eds.), *The expanded family life cycle* (3rd ed., pp. 327– 345). Boston, MA: Allyn & Bacon.

Hines, P. M. & Boyd-Franklin, N. (2005). African American families. In M. McGoldrick, J. Giordano, & N. Garcia-Preto (Eds.), *Ethnicity and family therapy* (3rd ed., pp. 77–100). New York: Guilford Press.

Hines, P. M., Preto, N. G., McGoldrick, M., Almeida, R., & Weltman, S. (2005). Culture and the family life cycle. In B. Carter & M. McGoldrick (Eds.), *The expanded family life cycle* (pp. 88–105). Boston, MA: Allyn & Bacon.

Ho, D. Y. F. (1989). Continuity of variation in Chinese patterns of socialization. *Journal of Marriage and the Family, 51,* 149–163.

Hochschild, A. (1989). *The second shift.* New York: Avon Books.

Hochschild, A. (1997, April 10). There's no place like work: Americans say they want more time with their families; The truth is, they'd rather be at the office. *New York Times Magazine,* 51–55, 81–84.

Hocker, J. L, & Wilmot, W. (1998). *Interpersonal conflict.* Dubuque, IA: Wm. C. Brown.

Hof, L., & Miller, W. R. (1983). *Marriage enrichment.* Bowie, MD: Brady/Prentice-Hall.

Hoffman, J. (2010, June 28). Online bullies pull schools into the fray. *New York Times,* pp. A1, A12–A13.

Hoffman, L. (1990). Constructing realities: The art of lenses. *Family Process, 29*(1), 1–12.

Hogan, D. P., Shandra, C. L., & Msall, M. E. (2007). Family developmental risk factors among adolescents with disabilities and children of parents with disabilities. *Journal of Adolescence, 30,* 1001–1019.

Hohn, C. (1987). The family life cycle: Needed extension of the concept. In T. K. Burch & K. W. Wachter (Eds.), *Family demography: Methods and their application* (pp. 156–180). New York: Oxford University Press.

Holtzman, M. (2008). Defining family: Young adults' perceptions of the parent-child bond. *Journal of Family Communication, 8,* 1–6.

Honeycutt, J. M. (1997, November). *Typological differences in predicting marital happiness from oral history behaviors and imagined interactions.* Paper presented at the meeting of the National Communication Association, Chicago, IL.

Hoopes, M. (1987). Multigenerational systems: Basic assumptions. *American Journal of Family Therapy, 15,* 195–205.

Hoppe-Nagao, A., & Ting-Toomey, S. (2002). Relational dialectics and management strategies in marital couples. *Southern Communication Journal, 67*(20), 142–159.

Hoppough, S. K., & Ames, B. (2001). Death as normative in family life. In *Family focus on. . . . death and dying* (pp. F1–F2). Minneapolis, MN: National Council on Family Relations.

Horwitz, J., & Tognoli, J. (1982). Role of home in adult development: Women and men living alone describe their residential histories. *Family Relations, 31,* 335–341.

Howe, N., Aquan-Assee, J., Bukowski, W. M., Lehous, P. M., & Rinaldi, C. M. (2001). Siblings as confidants: Emotional understanding, relationship warmth, and sibling self-disclosure. *Social Development, 10,* 439–454.

Hudak, J., Krestan, J. A., & Bepko, C. (2005). Alcohol problems and the family life cycle. In B. Carter & M. McGoldrick (Eds.), *The expanded family life cycle: Individual, family and social perspectives* (3rd ed., pp. 455–469). Boston, MA: Allyn & Bacon.

Hughes, C., Lerman, C., Schwartz, M., Peshkin, B. N., Wenzel, L., Narod, S., . . . Main, D. (2002). All in the family: Evaluation of the process and content of sisters' communication about BRCA1 and BRCA2 genetic test results. *American Journal of Medical Genetics, 107,* 143–150.

Huston, T. L. (2009). What's love got to do with it? Why some marriages succeed and others fail. *Personal Relationships, 16,* 301–327.

Huston, T. L. & Holmes, E. K. (2004). Becoming parents: An exploration of the marital and family issues of the later-life adult. In A. L. Vangelisti (Ed.), *Handbook of family communication* (pp. 105–133). Mahwah, NJ: Lawrence Erlbaum.

Hutchinson, M. K. (2002). The influence of sexual risk communication between parents and daughters on sexual risk behaviors. *Family Relations, 51,* 238–247.

Hutchinson, S. L., Afifi, T., & Krause, S. (2007). The family that plays together fares better. *Journal of Divorce and Remarriage, 46*(3), 21–48.

Im, E., Chee, W., Liu, Y., Lim, H. J., Guevara, E., Tsai, H. M., et al. (2007). Characteristics of cancer patients in Internet cancer support groups. *Computers, Informatics and Nursing, 25,* 334–343.

Imber-Black, E. (1993). Secrets in families and family therapy: An overview. In E. Imber-Black (Ed.), *Secrets in families and family therapy* (pp. 369–386). New York: Guilford Press.

Imber-Black, E. (1996). Idiosyncratic life cycle transitions and therapeutic rituals. In B. Carter & M. McGoldrick (Eds.), *The changing family life cycle* (2nd ed., pp. 149–189). New York: Gardner Press.

Imber-Black, E. (1998). *The secret life of families.* New York: Bantam Books.

Imber-Black, E. (1999). Creating meaningful rituals for new life cycle transitions. In B. Carter & M. McGoldrick (Eds.), *The expanded family life cycle* (3rd ed., pp. 202–214). Boston, MA: Allyn & Bacon.

Imes, R. S. (2006, April). *"Everything's the same, except it's different": Communicatively negotiating the new normalcy in the post-treatment cancer stage of long time marriages.* Paper presented at the Kentucky Conference on Health Communication, Lexington, KY.

Ingoldsby, B. R., Smith, S. R., & Miller, J. E. (2004). *Exploring family theories.* Los Angeles, CA: Roxbury Publishing.

Isler, L., Popper, T., & Ward, S. (1987, October–November). Children's purchase requests and parental responses. *Journal of Advertising Research, 27,* 28–39.

Jaccard, J., Dittust, P. J., & Gordon, V. V. (2000). Parent-adolescent communication about premarital sex: Factors associated with the extent of communication. *Journal of Adolescent Research, 15,* 187–208.

Jacob, A., & Borzi, M. G. (1996, April). *Foster families and the co-construction of shared experiences: A narrative approach.* Paper presented at the meeting of the Central States Communication Association, Chicago, IL.

Jacobson, N. S., & Gottman, J. M. (1998). *When men batter women: New insights into ending abusive relationships.* New York: Simon & Schuster.

Jakubowski, S. F., Milne, E. P., Brunner, H., & Miller, R. B. (2004). A review of empirically supported marital enrichment programs. *Family Relations, 53,* 528–536.

Jalali, B. (2005). Iranian families. In M. McGoldrick, J. Giordano, & N. Garcia-Preto (Eds.), *Ethnicity and family therapy.* (3rd ed., pp. 451–467). New York: Guilford Press.

Jaser, S. S., Champion, J. E., Reeslund, K. L., Keller, G., Merchant, M. J., Benson, M., & Compas, B. E. (2007). Cross-situational coping with peer and family stressors in adolescent offspring of depressed parents. *Journal of Adolescence, 30,* 917–932.

Jellinek, M. S., & Beresin, E. (2008, March). Money talks: Becoming more comfortable with understanding a family's finances. *Journal of the*

American Academy of Child and Adolescent Psychiatry, 47(3), 249–253.

Jin, X. C., & Keat, J. E. (2010). The effects of change in spousal power on intimate partner violence among Chinese immigrants. *Journal of Interpersonal Violence, 25,* 610–625.

Johnson, C., & Vinson, L. (1990). Placement and frequency of powerless talk and impression formation. *Communication Quarterly, 28,* 325–333.

Johnson, M. P. (1995). Patriarchal terrorism and common couple violence: Two forms of violence against women. *Journal of Marriage and the Family, 57,* 283–294.

Johnson, S. (2008). *Hold me tight: Seven conversations for a lifetime of love.* Boston, MA: Little, Brown.

Jones, D. J., Beach, S. R., & Jackson, H. (2004). Family influences on health: A framework to organize research and guide intervention. In A. Vangelisti (Ed.), *Handbook of family communication* (pp. 647–672). Mahwah, NJ: Lawrence Erlbaum.

Jones, E., & Gallois, C. (1989). Spouses, impressions of rules for communication in public and private marital conflicts. *Journal of Marriage and the Family, 51,* 957–967.

Jorgenson, J., & Bochner, A. P. (2004). Imagining families through stories and rituals. In A. Vangelisti (Ed.), *Handbook of Family Communication* (pp. 513–538). Mahwah, NJ: Lawrence Erlbaum.

Kaiser Family Foundation. (2001). *A report on the experiences of lesbians, gays and bisexuals in America and the public's views on issues and policies related to sexual orientation.* Retrieved from http://www.kff.org

Kaiser Family Foundation. (2006). *The media family: Electronic media in the lives of infants, toddlers, preschoolers and their parents.* Retrieved from http://www.kff.org/entmedia/7500.cfm

Kalmijn, M. (2004). Marriage rituals as reinforcers of role transitions: An analysis of weddings in the Netherlands. *Journal of Marriage and Family, 66,* 582–594.

Kanter, R. M. (1977). *Men and women of the corporation.* New York: Basic Books.

Kantor, D., & Lehr, W. (1976). *Inside the family.* San Francisco, CA: Jossey-Bass.

Kaplan, L. (2001). A couplehood typology for spouses of institutionalized persons with Alzheimer's disease: Perceptions of "We"–"I". *Family Relations, 50*(1), 87–98.

Keeley, M. (2004). Final conversations: Messages of love. *Qualitative Research Reports in Communication, 1*, 34–40.

Keeley, M. & Yingling, J. M. (2007). *Final conversations*. Acton, MA: Vander-Wyk & Burnham.

Kellerman, N. P. (2001). Transmission of Holocaust trauma—An integrative view. *Psychiatry, 64*, 256–267.

Kelley, D. (1998). The communication of forgiveness. *Communication Studies, 49*, 255–271.

Kellogg, T. (1990). *Broken toys, broken dreams: Understanding and healing boundaries codependence, compulsion and family relationships.* Amherst, MA: BRAT Publishing.

Kelly, D., & Sequeira, D. L. (1997). Understanding family functioning in a changed America. *Communication Studies, 48*, 93–108.

Kelly, D., & Warshafsky, L. (1987). *Partner abuse in gay male and lesbian couples.* Paper presented at the Third National Conference for Family Violence Researchers, Durham, NC.

Kennedy, T. L. M., Smith, A., Wells, A. T., & Wellman (2008). *Networked families*. Retrieved from the Pew Internet and American Life Project Web site: www.pewinternet.com.

Kennedy, V., Lloyd–Williams, M. (2009). How children cope when a parent has advanced cancer. *Psycho-Oncology, 18*, 886–892.

Kiecolt-Glaser, J. K., & Newton, T. L. (2001). Marriage: His and hers. *Psychological Bulletin, 127*(4), 472–503.

Kieren, D. K., Maguire, T. O., & Hurlbut, N. (1996). A marker method to test a phasing hypothesis in family problem-solving interaction. *Journal of Marriage and the Family, 58*, 442–455.

Killian, K. D. & Agathengelou, A. M. (2005). Greek families. In M. McGoldrick, J. Giordano, & N. Garcia-Preto (Eds.), *Ethnicity and family therapy* (3rd ed., pp. 573–585). New York: Guilford.

Killoren, S. E., Thayer, S. M., & Updegraff, K. A. (2008). Conflict resolution between Mexican origin adolescent siblings. *Journal of Marriage and the Family, 70*, 1200–1212.

Kilmann, R., & Thomas, K. (1975). Interpersonal conflict handling behavior as reflections of Jungian personality dimensions. *Psychological Reports, 37*, 971–980.

Kim, Y. & Spillers, R. L. (2010). Quality of life of family caregivers at 2 years after a relative's cancer diagnosis. *Psycho-Oncology, 19*, 431–440.

Kirchler, E. (1988). Marital happiness and interaction in everyday surroundings. *Journal of Social and Personal Relationships, 5*, 375–382.

Kirchler, E. (1993). Spouses' joint purchase decisions: Determinants of influence tactics for muddling through the process. *Journal of Economic Psychology, 14*(2), 405–438.

Klein, D. M., & White, J. M. (1996). *Family theories: An introduction.* Thousand Oaks, CA: Sage.

Klein, K. E. (2002, March 21). When it's all in the family. *Business Week Online.*

Klein, R. C. A., & Johnson, M. J. (1997). Strategies of couple conflict. In S. Duck (Ed.), *Handbook of personal relationships: Theory, research and interventions* (pp. 307–324). New York: John Wiley & Sons.

Kline, S. L., & Clinton, B. L. (1998). Developments in children's persuasive message practices. *Communication Education, 47*, 120–136.

Knapp, M. L., & Vangelisti, A. L. (2005). *Interpersonal communication and human relationships* (5th ed). Boston, MA: Allyn & Bacon.

Knudson-Martin, C., & Laughlin, M. J. (2005). Gender and sexual orientation in family therapy: Toward a postgender approach. *Family Relations, 54*, 101–115.

Knudson-Martin, C., & Mahoney, A. R. (2005). Moving beyond gender: Processes that create relationship equality. *Journal of Marital and Family Therapy, 2*, 235–246.

Koehly, L. M., Peters, J. A., Kuhn, N., Hoskins, L., Letocha, A., Kenen, R., . . . Greene, M. H. (2008). Sisters in hereditary breast and ovarian cancer families: Communal coping, social integration, and psychological well-being. *Psycho-Oncology, 17*, 812–821.

Koenig Kellas, J. (2005). Family ties: Communicating identity through jointly told stories. *Communication Monographs, 72*, 365–389.

Koenig Kellas, J. (2010). Narrating family: Introduction to the special issue of narratives and storytelling in the family. *Journal of Family Communication, 10*, 1–6.

Koenig Kellas, J., LeClair-Underberg, C., & Lamb Normand, E. (2008). Stepfamily address terms: "Sometimes they mean something and sometimes they don't." *Journal of Family Communication, 8*, 238–263.

Koenig Kellas, J., & Trees, A. R. (2006). Finding meaning in difficult family experiences: Sense-making and interaction processes during joint family storytelling. *Journal of Family Communication, 6,* 49–76.

Koenig Kellas, J. & Trees, A. R. (2009). Telling tales: Enacting family relationships in joint storytelling about difficult family experiences. *Western Journal of Communication, 73,* 91–111.

Koepke, L., Mare, J., & Moran, P. (1992, April). Relationship quality in a sample of lesbian couples with children and child free. *Family Relations, 41,* 224–229.

Koerner, A. F., & Fitzpatrick, M. A. (1997). Family type and conflict: The impact on conversation orientation and conformity orientation on conflict in the family. *Communication Studies, 48,* 59–74.

Koerner, A. F., & Fitzpatrick, M. A. (2002). You never leave your family in a fight: The impact of family of origin on conflict behavior in romantic relationships. *Communication Studies, 53*(3), 234–251.

Koerner, A. F., & Fitzpatrick, M. A. (2004). Communication in intact families. In A. Vangelisti (Ed.), *Handbook of family communication* (pp. 177–195). Mahwah, NJ: Lawrence Erlbaum.

Koerner, A. F., & Fitzpatrick, M. A. (2006). Family communication patterns theory: A social cognitive approach. In D. O. Braithwaite and L. A. Baxter (Eds.), *Engaging theories in family communication: Multiple perspectives* (pp. 50–65). Thousand Oaks, CA: Sage.

Koerner, S. S., Jacobs, S. L., & Raymond, M. (2000). When mothers turn to their adolescent daughters: Predicting daughters' vulnerability to negative adjustment outcomes. *Family Relations, 49,* 301–309.

Koerner, S. S., Wallace, S., Lehman, S. J., & Raymond, M. (2002). Mother-to-daughter disclosure after divorce: Are there costs and benefits? *Journal of Child and Family Studies, 11,* 469–483.

Koesten, J., Miller, K. I., & Hummert, M. L. (2001). Family communication, self-efficacy, and white female adolescents' risk behavior. *Journal of Family Communication, 2*(1), 7–27.

Kohlberg, L. (1969). Stage and sequence: The cognitive developmental approach to socialization. In D. Goshen (Ed.), *Handbook of socialization theory and research* (pp. 347–480). Chicago, IL: Rand McNally.

Koopman, H. M., Baars, R. M., Chaplin, J., & Zwinderman, K. H. (2004). Illness through the eyes of a child: The development of children's understanding of the causes of illness. *Patient Education and Counseling, 55,* 363–370.

Koppen, M. M. (1997). *Exploring the typology of mother-daughter rituals.* Unpublished paper presented at Northwestern University, Evanston, IL.

Kramer, J. (1985). *Family interfaces: Transgenerational patterns.* New York: Brunner-Mazel.

Kreider, R. (2005). Number, timing, and duration of marriages and divorces: 2001. In *Current population reports.* Washington, DC: U.S. Census Bureau.

Kreider, R. & Elliot, D. (2009). America's families and living arrangements: 2007. In *current population reports.* Washington, DC: U.S. Census Bureau.

Kreider, R. M. (2003, October). Adopted children and stepchildren: 2000 (CENSR-6RV). In *Census 2000 special reports.* Washington, DC: U.S. Census Bureau. Retrieved from http://www.census.gov/prod/2003oubs/censr-6.pdf.

Kreider, R. M., & Simmons, T. (2003, October) Marital Status: 2000. In *Census 2000 brief.* Washington, DC: U.S. Census Bureau. Retrieved from http://www.census.gov/prod/2003pubs/c2kbr-30.pdf.

Krishnakumar, A., & Buehler, C. (2000). Interparental conflict and parenting behaviors: A meta-analytic review. *Family Relations, 49*(1), 25–44.

Krouse, S. S. & Afifi, T. D. (2007). Family-to-work spillover stress: Coping communicatively in the workplace. *Journal of Family Communication, 7,* 85–122.

Krueger, D. L. (1983). Pragmatics of dyadic decision making: A sequential analysis of communication patterns. *Western Journal of Speech Communication, 47,* 99–117.

Krusiewicz, E. S., & Wood, J. T. (2001). "He was our child from the moment we walked in that room": Entrance stories of adoptive parents. *Journal of Social and Personal Relationships, 18,* 785–803.

Kübler-Ross, E. (1970). *On death and dying.* New York: Macmillan.

Kurdek, L. A. (1991). The relations between reported well-being and divorce history, availability of a proximate adult, and gender. *Journal of Marriage and the Family, 53,* 71–78.

Kurdek, L. A. (1994). Conflict resolution styles in gay, lesbian, heterosexual nonparent and heterosexual parent couples. *Journal of Marriage and the Family, 56*(3), 705–722.

Kurdek, L. A. (2004). Are gay and lesbian cohabiting couples *really* different from heterosexual married couples? *Journal of Marriage and the Family, 66,* 880–900.

Labrecque, J., & Ricard, L. (2001). Children's influence on family decision-making: A restaurant study. *Journal of Business Research, 54*(2), 173–176.

Laing, R. D. (1972). *The politics of the family.* New York: Vintage Books.

Langellier, K. M. (2002). Performing family stories, forming cultural identity: Franco American memere stories. *Communication Studies, 53*(1), 56–73.

Langellier, K. M., & Peterson, E. E. (2006). Narrative performance theory: Telling stories, doing family. In D. O. Braithwaite & L. A. Baxter (Eds.), *Engaging theories in family communication: Multiple perspectives* (pp. 99–114). Thousand Oaks, CA: Sage.

LaRossa, R., & Reitzes, D. (1993). Symbolic interactionism and family studies. In P. G. Boss, W. J. Doherty, R. La Rossa, W. R. Schumm, & S. K. Steinmetz (Eds.), *Sourcebook of family theory and methods* (pp. 135–163). New York: Plenum Press.

Lauer, R. H., & Lauer, J. C. (2009). *Marriage and family: The quest for intimacy* (7th ed.). Boston, MA: McGraw-Hill.

Laurenceau, J-P., Feldman-Barrett, L., & Rovine, M. J. (2005). The interpersonal process model of intimacy in marriage: A daily-diary and multilevel modeling approach. *Journal of Family Psychology, 13,* 314–323.

Laursen, B., & Collins, W. A. (2004). Parent-child communication during adolescence. In A. L. Vangelisti (Ed.), *Handbook of family communication* (pp. 333–348). Mahwah, NJ: Lawrence Erlbaum.

Lavaro, L. B. (2009). Living together or living apart together: New choices for old lovers. *Family focus on . . . cohabitation* (Issue FF42, pp. FF9-F10). Minneapolis, MN: National Council on Family Relations.

Lavee, L., Sharlin, S., & Katz, R. (1996). The effect of parenting stress on marital quality: An integrated mother-father model. *Journal of Family Issues, 17,* 114–135.

Lavee, Y. (2005). Couples under stress: Studying change in dyadic closeness and distance. In V. L. Bengston, A. C. Acock, K. R. Allen, P. Dilworth-Anderson, & D. M. Klein (Eds.), *Sourcebook of family theory and research* (pp. 281–283). Thousand Oaks, CA: Sage.

Le Poire, B. (2006). Commentary on Part C. In K. Floyd & M. T. Morman (Eds.), *Widening the family circle: New research on family communication* (pp. 189–192). Thousand Oaks, CA: Sage.

Leach, M. S., & Braithwaite, D. O. (1996). A binding tie: Supportive communication of family kinkeepers. *Journal of Applied Communication Research, 24,* 200–215.

Lebow, J., & Gurman, A. S. (1996). Making a difference: A new research review offers good news to couples and family therapists. *The Family Networker, 20,* 69–76.

Lee, E. & Mock, M. R. (2005). Asian families: An overview. In M. McGoldrick, J. Giordano, & N. Garcia-Preto (Eds.), *Ethnicity and Family Therapy* (3rd ed., pp. 269–289). New York: Guilford Press.

Lee, T. R., Mancini, F. A., & Maxwell, J. W. (1990). Sibling relationships in adulthood: Contact patterns and motivations. *Journal of Marriage and the Family, 52,* 431–440.

Leeds-Hurwitz, W. (2002). *Wedding as text: Communicating cultural identities through ritual.* Mahwah, NJ: Lawrence Erlbaum.

Leeds-Hurwitz, W. (2006). Social theories: Social constructionism and symbolic interactionism. In D. O. Braithwaite & L. A. Baxter (Eds.), *The family communication sourcebook* (pp. 229–242). Thousand Oaks, CA: Sage.

Lehr, S. T., Dilorio, C., Demi, A. S., & Facteau, J. (2005). Predictors of father-son communication about sexuality. *Journal of Sex Research, 2,* 119–129.

Levinson, D. (1978). *The seasons of a man's life.* New York: Ballantine Books.

Lewis, M. A. & Butterfield, R. M. (2007). Social control in marital relationships: Effect of one's partner on health behaviors. *Social Control in Marital Relationships, 37,* 289–319.

Lincoln, K. D. (2007). Financial strain, negative interactions, and mastery: Pathways to mental health among older African Americans. *Journal of Black Psychology, 33*(4), 439–462.

Lindsey, E. W., Chambers, J. C., Frabutt, J. M., & Mackinnon-Lewis, C. (2009). Marital conflict and adolescents' peer aggression: The mediating and moderating role of mother-child emotional reciprocity. *Family Relations, 58,* 593–606.

Littlejohn, S. (1992). *Theories of human communication* (4th ed.). Belmont, CA: Wadsworth.

Littlejohn, S. W. (2002). *Theories of human communication* (7th ed.). Belmont, CA: Wadsworth/Thomson Learning.

Livingstone, S. & Helsper, E. J. (2008, December 1). Parental mediation of children's Internet use. *Journal of Broadcasting and Electronic Media.* Retrieved from http://www.allbusiness.com/society-social-families-children-family/11764547-1.html.

Lloyd, S., & Emery, B. (1994). Physically aggressive conflict in romantic relationships. In D. Cahn (Ed.), *Conflict in personal relationships* (pp. 27–46). Hillsdale, NJ: Lawrence Erlbaum.

Lohan, J. A., & Murphy, S. A. (2002). Parents' perceptions of adolescent sibling grief responses after an adolescent or young adult child's sudden, violent death. *Omega, 44*(3), 195–213.

Lollock, L. (2000, March). The foreign-born population in the United States. In *Current population reports.* Washington, DC: U.S. Census Bureau.

Lorenz, F. O., Simons, R. L., Conger, R. D., Elder, R. H., Johnson, C., & Chao, W. (1997). Married and recently divorced mothers' stressful events and distress: Tracing change across time. *Journal of Marriage and the Family, 59,* 219–232.

Loving, T. J., Hefner, K. L., Kiecolt-Glaser, J. K., Glaser, R., & Malarkety, W. B. (2004). Stress hormone changes and marital conflict: Spouses' relative power makes a difference. *Journal of Marriage and Family, 66,* 595–612.

Lucchetti, A. E., & Roghaar, L. A. (2001, November). *The dark side of families: Communicating favoritism to children.* Paper presented at the meeting of the National Communication Association, Atlanta, GA.

Luecken, L. J., Kraft, A. J., & Hagan, M. (2009). Negative relationships in the family-of-origin predict attenuated cortisol in emerging adults. *Hormones and Behavior, 55,* 412–417.

Luedemann, M. B., Ehrenberg, M. F., & Hunter, M. A. (2006). Mothers' discussions with daughters following divorce. *Journal of Divorce and Remarriage, 46*(1 & 2), 29–55.

Lum, L. (2006). Handling "helicopter parents." *Diverse Issues in Higher Education, 23*(20), 43–46.

MacNeil, S., & Byers, E. S. (2005). Dyadic assessment of sexual self-disclosure and sexual satisfaction in heterosexual dating couples. *Journal of Social and Personal Relationships, 22,* 169–181.

Madden, M. & Lenhart, A. (2006). *Online dating.* Retrieved from the Pew Internet and American Life Project Web site: http://www.pewinternet.org/pdfs/PIP_Daring.pdf.

Maddock, J. (1989). Healthy family sexuality: Positive principles for educators and clinicians. *Family Relations, 38,* 130–136.

Mahoney, A., Pargament, K. I., Murray-Swank, A., & Murray-Swank, N. (2003). Religion and the sanctification of family relationships. *Review of Religious Research, 22*(3), 220–236.

Mandel, S. & Sharlin, S. A. (2006). The non-custodial father: His involvement in his children's lives and the connection between his role and the ex-wife's, child's, and father's perception of that role. *Journal of Divorce and Remarriage, 45,* 79–95.

Manne, S. L., Norton, T. R., Ostroff, J. S., Winkel, G., Fox, K., & Grana, G. (2007). Protective buffering and psychological distress among couples coping with breast cancer: The moderating role of relationship satisfaction. *Journal of Family Psychology, 21,* 380–388.

Manning, L. M. (1996, November). *Adolescent's communication concerns.* Paper presented at the meeting of the National Communication Association, San Diego, CA.

Manoogian, M. M., Harter, L. M., & Denham, S. A. (2010). The storied nature of health legacies in the familial experience of Type 2 diabetes. *Journal of Family Communication, 10,* 40–56.

March, K., & Miall, C. (2000). Adoption as a family form. *Family Relations, 49,* 359–362.

Markowitz, L. (1994). The cross-currents of multiculturalism. *Family Therapy Networker, 18*(4), 18–27, 69.

Marks, S. R., Huston, T. L., Johnson, E. M., & MacDermid, S. M. (2001). Role balance among white married couples. *Journal of Marriage and Family, 63,* 1083–1098.

Marshall, L., & Rose, P. (1988). Family-of-origin violence and courtship abuse. *Journal of Counseling and Development, 66,* 414–418.

Martin, J., Hecht, M., & Larkey, L. (1994). Conversational improvement strategies for inter-ethnic communication: African-American and European American perspectives. *Communication Monographs, 61*(3), 237–255.

Martinez, E. A. (2001). Death: A family event for Mexican-Americans. In *Family focus on . . . death and dying* (Issue FF12). Minneapolis, MN: National Council on Family Relations.

Mason Bergen, K., Kirby, E., & McBride, M. C. (2007). "How do you get two houses cleaned?": Accomplishing family caregiving in commuter marriages. *Journal of Family Communication, 7,* 287–307.

Mattessich, P. (2001, June). Pressure points: Factors related to stress in a survey of immigrants. *Family focus on . . . stress* (pp. F14–F15). Minneapolis, MN: National Council of Family Relations.

Max, S. (2009, September). How to talk money with Mom and Dad. *Money, 31–32.*

McAdams, D. (1993). *Stories we live by: Personal myths and the making of the self.* New York: William Morrow.

McAdams, D. P. (2006). *The redemptive self: Stories Americans live by.* New York: Oxford University Press.

McCann, S., MacAuley, D., Barnett, Y., Bunting, B., Bradley, A., Jeffers, L., & Morrison, P. J., (2009, November). Family communication, genetic testing and colonoscopy screening in hereditary non-polyposis colon cancer: A qualitative study. *Psycho-Oncology, 18(11),* 1208–1215.

McCroskey, J. C. (1997, November). *Why we communicate the ways we do: A communibiological perspective.* The Carroll C. Arnold Distinguished Lecture presented at the meeting of the National Communication Association, Chicago, IL.

McCubbin, H. I., & Patterson, J. (1983a). The family stress process: The double ABCX model of adjustment and adaptation. In H. McCubbin, M. Sussman, & J. Patterson (Eds.), *Social stress and the family: Advances and developments in family stress theory and research* (pp. 7–37). New York: Haworth Press.

McCubbin, H. I., & Patterson, J. M. (1983b). Family transitions: Adaptation to stress. In H. I. McCubbin & C. R. Figley (Eds.), *Coping with normative transitions* (Vol. 1, pp. 5–25). New York: Brunner/Mazel.

McCubbin, H. I., & Patterson, J. M. (1985). Adolescent stress, coping, and adaptation: A normative family perspective. In G. K. Leigh & G. W. Peterson (Eds.), *Adolescents in families* (pp. 256–276). Cincinnati, OH: Southwestern.

McCubbin, H. I., Patterson, J. M., Cauble, A. E., Wilson, W. R., & Warwick, W. (1983). CHIP— Coping Health Inventory for Parents: An assessment of parental coping patterns in the case of the chronically ill. *Journal of Marriage and the Family, 45,* 359–370.

McGivern, B., Everett, J., Yager, G. G., Baumiller, R. C., Hafertepen, A., & Saal, H. M. (2004). Family communication about positive BRCA1 and BRCA2 genetic test results. *Genetics in Medicine, 6(6),* 503–509.

McGoldrick, M. (1995). *You can go home again: Reconnecting with your family.* New York: W. W. Norton.

McGoldrick, M. (2003). Culture: A challenge to concepts of normality. In F. Walsh (Ed.), *Normal family processes: Growing diversity and complexity* (3rd ed., pp. 235–259). New York: Guilford Press.

McGoldrick, M. (2005a). Becoming a couple. In B. Carter & M. McGoldrick (Eds.), *The expanded family life cycle: Individual, family and social perspectives* (3rd ed., pp. 231–248). New York: Allyn & Bacon.

McGoldrick, M. & Carter, B. (2003). The family life cycle. In F. Walsh (Ed.), *Normal family processes: Growing diversity and complexity* (pp. 375–398). New York: Guilford Press.

McGoldrick, M., & Gerson, R. (1985). *Genograms in family assessment.* New York: W. W. Norton.

McGoldrick, M., Gerson, R., & Shellenberger, S. (1999). *Genograms: Assessment and intervention.* New York: W. W. Norton.

McGoldrick, M., Giordano, J., & Garcia-Preto, N. (2005a). *Ethnicity and family therapy* (3rd ed.). New York: Guilford Press.

McGoldrick, M., Giordano, J., & Garcia-Preto, N. (2005b). Overview: Ethnicity and family therapy. In M. McGoldrick, J. Giordano, & N. Garcia-Preto (Eds.), *Ethnicity and family therapy* (3rd ed., pp. 1–40). New York: Guilford Press.

McGoldrick, M., & Walsh, F. (1999). Death and the family life cycle. In B. Carter & M. C. Goldrick (Eds.), *The expanded family life cycle* (3rd ed., pp. 185–201). Boston, MA: Allyn & Bacon.

McGoldrick, M., & Walsh, F. (2005). Death and the family life cycle. In B. Carter & M. McGoldrick (Eds.), *The expanded family life cycle: Individual, family and social perspectives* (3rd ed., pp. 185–201). Boston, MA: Allyn & Bacon.

McKee-Ryan, F. M., Song, Z., Wanberg, C. R., & Kinicki, A. J. (2005). Psychological and physical well-being during unemployment: A meta-analytic study. *Journal of Applied Psychology, 90*(1) 53–76.

McNeil, D. G., Jr. (2004, September 19). Culture or chromosomes? Real men don't clean bathrooms. *New York Times,* sec. 4, p. 3.

McNulty, J. K. & Karney, B. R. (2004). Positive expectations in the early years of marriage: Should couples expect the best or brace for the worst? *Journal of Personality and Social Psychology, 86,* 729–743.

Mederer, H., & Hill, R. (1983). Cultural transitions over the family span: Theory and research. In H. McCubbin, M. B. Sussman, & J. M. Patterson (Eds.), *Social stress and the family* (pp. 39–60). New York: Haworth Press.

Medved, C. E., Brogan, S. M., McClanahan, A. M., Morris, J. F., & Shepherd, G. J. (2006). Family and work socializing communication: Messages, gender, and ideological implications. *Journal of Family Communication, 6,* 161–180.

Mercier, L. R., & Harold, R. D. (2003). At the interface: Lesbian-parent families and their children's schools. *Children and Schools, 25,* 35–47.

Merolla, A. J. (2010). Relational maintenance during military deployment: Perspectives of wives of deployed U.S. soldiers. *Journal of Applied Communication Research, 38*(1), 4–26.

Metz, M. E. & McCarthy, B. W. (2003). *Coping with premature ejaculation: How to overcome PE, please your partner and have great sex.* Oakland, CA: New Harbinger Publications.

Michael, K. C., Torres., A., & Seemann, E. A. (2007). Adolescents' health habits, coping styles and self-concept are predicted by exposure to inter-parental conflict. *Journal of Divorce and Marriage, 48,* 155–174.

Mikkelson, A. C. (2006). Communication among peers: Adult sibling relationships. In K. Floyd & M. T. Morman (Eds.), *Widening the family circle: New research on family communication* (pp. 21–35). Thousand Oaks, CA.

Mikkelson, K. S. (2008). He said, she said: Comparing mother and father reports of father involvement. *Journal of Marriage and Family, 70*(3), 613–624.

Miller, A. E. (2009). Revealing and concealing post-marital dating information: Divorced coparents' privacy rule development and boundary coordination processes. *Journal of Family Communication, 9,* 135–149.

Miller, C. W. (2011). Irresolvable interpersonal conflicts: Students' perceptions of common topics, possible reasons for persistence, and communication patterns. In K. M. Galvin (Ed.), *Making connections: Readings in relational communication* (5th ed., pp. 240–247). New York: Oxford University Press.

Miller, K. I., Shoemaker, M. M, Wilyard, J., & Addison, P. (2008). Providing care for elderly parents: A structurational approach to family caregiver identity. *Journal of Family Communication, 8,* 19–43.

Miller, K. S., Kotchick, B. A., Dorsey, S., Forehand, R., & Ham, A. Y. (1998). Family communication about sex: What are people saying and are their adolescents listening? *Family Planning Perspectives, 30*(5), 218–222, 235.

Miller-Day, M. (2004). *Communication among grandmothers, mothers, and adult daughters: A qualitative study of maternal relationships.* Mahwah, NJ: Lawrence Erlbaum.

Miller-Day, M., & Dodd, A.H. (2004). Toward a descriptive model of parent-offspring communication about alcohol and other drugs. *Journal of Social and Personal Relationships, 21*(1), 69–91.

Miller-Day, M. (2008). Talking to youth about drugs: What do late adolescents say about parental strategies? *Family Relations, 51,* 1–12.

Miller-Day, M. & Kam, J. A. (2010). More than just openness: Developing and validating a measure of targeted parent-child communication about alcohol. *Health Communication, 25,* 293–302.

Minow, M. (1998). Redefining families: Who's in and who's out? In K. V. Hansen & A. I. Garey (Eds.), *Families in the U.S.* (pp. 7–19). Philadelphia, PA: Temple University Press.

Minuchin, S. (1974). *Families and family therapy.* Cambridge, MA: Harvard University Press.

Minuchin, S. (1984). *Family kaleidoscope.* Cambridge, MA: Harvard University Press.

Mistry, R. S., Lowe, E. D., Remers, A. D., & Chien, N. (2008). Explaining the family economic stress model: Insights from a mixed methods approach. *Journal of Marriage and Family, 70,* 196–209.

Mmari, K., Roche, K. M., Sudhinaraset, M., & Blum, R. (2009). When a parent goes off to war: Exploring the issues faced by adolescents and their families. *Youth and Society, 40,* 455–475.

Mogelonsky, M. (1997, January). Reconfirming the American dream (house). *American Demographics, 19*, 30–36.

Mone, J. G. & Biringen, Z. (2006). Perceived parent-child alienation. *Journal of Divorce and Remarriage, 45*(3), 131–156.

Montgomery, B. M. (1992). Communication as the interface between couples and culture. In S. Deeter (Ed.), *Communication Yearbook, 15* (pp. 476–508). Newbury Park, CA: Sage.

Moore, J. (2000). Placing home in context. *Journal of Environmental Psychology, 20*, 207–217.

Moorman, S. A., Booth, A., & Fingerman, K. L. (2006). Women's romantic relationships after widowhood. *Journal of Family Issues, 27*, 1281–1304.

Morgan, C. V. (2009). *Intermarriage across race and ethnicity among immigrants.* El Paso, TX: LFB Scholarly Publishing.

Morman, M. T., & Floyd, K. (2006). The good son: Men's perceptions of the characteristics of sonhood. In K. Floyd & M. T. Morman (Eds.), *Widening the family circle: New research on family communication* (pp. 37–55). Thousand Oaks, CA: Sage.

Morr Serewicz, M. C., Hosmer, R., Ballard, R. L., & Griffin, R. A. (2008). Disclosure from in-laws and the quality of in-law and marital relationships. *Communication Quarterly, 56*, 427–444.

Mosher, W. D., Chandra, A., & Jones, J. (2005, September 15). Sexual behavior and selected health measures: Men and women 15–44 years of age, United States, 2002. *Advance data from vital and health statistics: No. 362.* Hyattsville, MD: National Center for Health Statistics.

Mott, F. L., Kowaleski-Jones, L., & Menaghan, E. G. (1997). Paternal absence and child behavior: Does a child's gender make a difference? *Journal of Marriage and the Family, 59*, 103–118.

Murphy, S. A., Johnson, L. C., Lohan, J., & Tapper, V. J. (2002). Bereaved parents' use of individual, family, and community resources 4 to 60 months after a child's violent death. *Family and Community Health, 25*(1), 71–82.

Murray, C. I., Toth, K., Larsen, B., & Moulton, S. (2010). Death, dying, and grief in families. In S. J. Price, C. A. Price, & P. C. McKenry (Eds.), *Families and change: Coping with stressful events and transitions* (4th ed., pp. 73–95). Los Angeles, CA: Sage.

Myers, S. A. (2008, November). *An investigation of relational maintenance across the adult sibling lifespan.* Paper presented at the meeting of the National Communication Association, San Diego, CA.

Myers, S. A. & Bryant, L. E. (2008). Emerging adult and siblings' use of verbally aggressive messages as hurtful messages. *Communication Quarterly, 56*, 268–283.

Myers, S. A., & Members of COM 200. (2001). Relational maintenance behaviors in the sibling relationship. *Communication Quarterly, 49*, 19–34.

Myers, S. A., Schrodt, P., & Rittenour, C. E. (2006). The impact of parents' use of hurtful messages on adult children's self-esteem and educational motivation. In L. H. Turner & R. West (Eds.), *The family communication sourcebook* (pp. 425–445). Thousand Oaks, CA: Sage.

National Campaign to Prevent Teen and Unplanned Pregnancy & CosmoGirl.com. (2008). *Sex and tech: Results from a survey of teens and young adults.* Retrieved from http:// www.thenationalcampaign.org/sextech/PDF/SexTech_ Summary.pdf.

National Council on Family Relations. (1998). Annual Report. Minneapolis, MA.

Newton, D. A., & Burgoon, J. K. (1990). The use and consequences of verbal influence strategies during interpersonal disagreements. *Human Communication Research, 16*(4), 477–518.

Nichols, M. P. (2008). *Family therapy: Concepts and methods* (8th ed.). Boston, MA: Allyn & Bacon.

Nicholson, J. H. (1999, November). *Sibling alliance rules.* Paper presented at the annual meeting of the National Communication Association, Chicago, IL.

Niedzwiecki, C. K. (1997, November). *The influence of affect and attribution on the outcome of parent-adolescent communication in decision-making.* Paper presented at the meeting of the National Communication Association, Chicago, IL.

Nippert-Eng, C. E. (1996). *Home and work: Negotiating boundaries through everyday life.* Chicago, IL: University of Chicago Press.

Noller, P., Atkin, S., Feeney, J. A., & Peterson, C. (2006). Family conflict and adolescents. In L. H. Turner & R. West (Eds.), *The family communication sourcebook* (pp. 165–812). Thousand Oaks, CA: Sage.

Nomaguchi, K. M., & Milki, M. A. (2003). Costs and rewards of children: The effects of becoming a parent on adults' lives. *Journal of Marriage and Family, 65*, 356–374.

Noone, R. (1989). Systems thinking and differentiation of self. *Center for Family Communication Consultation Review, 1*(1).

Nussbaum, J. F., & Bettini, L. (2004). Shared stories of the grandparent-grandchild relationship. *International Journal of Aging and Human Development, 39,* 67–80.

Nussbaum, J. F., Pecchioni, L. L., Baringer, D. K., & Kundrat, A. L. (2002). Lifespan communication. In W. B. Gudykinst (Ed.), *Communication yearbook, 26* (pp. 366–389). Mahwah, NJ: Lawrence Erlbaum.

Ochs, E., & Taylor, C. (1992). Family narrative as political activity. *Discourse and Society, 3*(3), 301–340.

Oetzel, J., Ting-Toomey, S., Chew-Sanchez, M. I., Harris, R., Wilcox, R., & Stumpf, S. (2003). Face and facework in conflicts with parents and siblings: A cross-cultural comparison of Germans, Japanese, Mexicans, and U.S. Americans. *Journal of Family Communication, 3,* 69–93.

Olson, D. H. (1997). Family stress and coping: A multisystem perspective. In S. Dreman (Ed.), *The family on the threshold of the 21st century* (pp. 259–282). Mahwah, NJ: Lawrence Erlbaum.

Olson, D. H. (2000). Circumplex model of marital and family systems. *Family focus on . . . death and dying* (p. F4). Minneapolis, MN: National Council on Family Relations.

Olson, D., H., DeFrain, J., & Skogrand, L. (2008). *Marriages and Families: Intimacy, Diversity, and Strengths* (6th ed.). Boston, MA: McGraw-Hill.

Olson, D. H., Russell, C., & Sprenkle, D. (Eds.). (1983). *Circumplex model: Systematic assessment and treatment of families.* New York: Haworth Press.

Olson, D. H., Sprenkle, D., & Russell, C. (1979). Circumplex model of marital and family systems: Cohesion and adaptability dimensions, family types, and clinical applications. *Family Process, 18,* 3–28.

Olson, L. N. (2002). Exploring "common couple violence" in heterosexual romantic relationships. *Western Journal of Communication, 66*(1), 104–128.

Olson, L. N. (2004). Relational control-motivated aggression: A theoretically-based typology of intimate violence. *Journal of Family Communication, 4* (3 & 4), 209–233.

Olson, L. N., & Golish, T. D. (2002). Topics of conflict and patterns of aggression in romantic relationships. *Southern Communication Journal, 67*(2), 180–200.

Ono, H. (1998). Husbands' and wives' resources and marital dissolution. *Journal of Marriage and the Family, 60,* 674–689.

Oppenheim, D., Wamboldt, F. S., Gavin, L. A., Renouf, A. G., & Emde, R. N. (1996). Couples' co-construction of the story of their child's birth: Associations with marital adaptation. *Journal of Narrative and Life History, 6*(1), 1–21.

Orthner, D. K., Jones-Sanpei, H., & Williamson, S. (2004). The resilience and strengths of low-income families. *Journal of Customer Services, 53,* 159–167.

Palan, K. M., & Wilkes, R. E. (1997). Adolescent-parent interaction in family decision making. *Journal of Consumer Research, 24*(2), 159–169.

Palazzolo, K. E., Roberto, A. J., & Babin, E. A. (2010). The relationship between parents' verbal aggression and young adult children's intimate partner violence victimization and perpetration. *Health Communication, 25,* 357–364.

Palfrey, J. & Gasser, U. (2008). *Born digital: Understanding the first generation of digital natives.* New York: Basic Books.

Papp, L. M., Kourous, C. D., & Cummings, E. M. (2010). Emotions in marital conflict interactions: Empathic accuracy, assumed similarity, and the moderating context of depressive symptoms. *Journal of Social and Personal Relationships, 27,* 367–387.

Papp, P. (1983). *The process of change.* New York: Guilford Press.

Parental E-mail: A hot ticket on college campuses. *PC Week, 14,* 131.

Parkes, C. M. (1997). Conclusions II: Attachments and losses in cross-cultural perspective. In C. M. Parkes, P. Laungani, & B. Young (Eds.), *Death and bereavement across cultures* (pp. 233–243). New York: Routledge.

Parrott, R., & Lemieux, R. (2003). When the worlds of work and wellness collide: The role of familial support on skin cancer control. *Journal of Family Communication, 3*(3), 95–106.

Pasley, K. & Lee, M. (2010). Stress and coping within the context of stepfamily life. In Price, S., Price, C., & McKenry, P. (Eds.), *Families and change: Coping with stressful events and transitions* (4th ed., pp. 235–262). Los Angeles, CA: Sage.

Patrick, D. & Palladino, J. (2009). The community interactions of gay and lesbian foster parents. In T. J. Socha & G. H. Stamp (Eds.), *Parents and children communicating with society: Managing relationships outside of the home* (pp. 323–342). New York: Routledge.

Patterson, C. J. (2009). Lesbian and gay parents and their children: A social science perspective. In D. A. Hope (Ed.), *Contemporary perspectives on lesbian, gay, and bisexual identities* (pp. 141–182). New York: Springer.

Patterson, J. M. (2002). Integrating family resilience and family stress theory. *Journal of Marriage and Family, 64,* 349–360.

Pavlik, L. (2004). *The effect of a sibling's diabetes on a non-diabetic sibling: A communicative approach.* Unpublished honors thesis, Northwestern University, Evanston, IL.

Pawlowski, D. R. (2006). Dialectical tensions in families experiencing acute health issues: Stroke survivors' perceptions. In L. H. Turner & R. West (Eds.), *The family communication sourcebook* (pp. 468–489). Thousand Oaks, CA: Sage.

Pawlowski, D. R., Thilborger, C., & Cieloha-Meekins, J. (2001). Prisons, old cars, and Christmas trees: A metaphoric analysis of familial communication. *Communication Studies, 52,* 180–196.

Pearson, J. C., West, R., & Turner, L. H. (1995). *Gender and communication.* Madison, WI: Brown & Benchmark.

Pecchioni, L. L., & Nussbaum, J. F. (2001). Mother-adult daughter discussions of caregiving prior to dependency: Exploring concepts among European-American women. *Journal of Family Communication, 1,* 133–149.

Pecchioni, L. L., Thompson, T. L., & Anderson, D. J. (2006). Interrelations between family communication and health communication. In L. H. Turner and R. West (Eds.), *The family communication sourcebook* (pp. 447–468). Thousand Oaks, CA: Sage.

Peddle, N., & Wang, C. (2001). *Current trends in child abuse prevention, reporting and fatalities: The 1999 fifty-state survey.* Retrieved from http://www.prevent-child abuse. org/learnmore/research docs/199950 survey. pdf

Pennebaker, J. W. (1990). *Opening up: The healing power of confiding in others.* New York: William Morrow.

Pennington, B. A., (1997, November). *Pecked to death by ducks: Managing dialectical tensions in the mother–adolescent daughter relationship.* Paper presented at the meeting of the National Communication Association, Chicago, IL.

Pennington, B. A., & Turner, L. H. (2004). Playground or training ground? The function of talk

in African American and European American mother-daughter dyads. In P. M. Buzzanell, H. Sterk, & L. H. Turner (Eds.), *Gender in applied communication contexts* (pp. 275–294). Thousand Oaks, CA: Sage.

Perreira, K. M., Chapman, M. I., & Stein, G. L. (2006). Becoming an American parent: Overcoming challenges and finding strength in a new immigrant Latino community. *Journal of Family Issues, 27,* 1383–1414.

Perry, Y. V., & Doherty, W. J. (2005). Viewing time through the eyes of overscheduled children and their unconnected families. In V. Bengston, A. Acock, K. R. Allen, P. Dilworth-Anderson, & D. M. Klein (Eds.), *Sourcebook of family theory and research* (pp. 255–257). Thousand Oaks, CA: Sage.

Peters , B. & Ehrenberg, M. F. (2008). The influence of parental separation and divorce on father-child relationships. *Journal of Divorce and Remarriage, 49*(1), 78–109.

Peterson, G., Madden-Derdich, D., & Leonard, S. A. (2000). Parent-child relations across the life course. In S. J. Prece, P. C. McKenry, & M. J. Murphy (Eds.), *Families across time: A life course perspective* (pp. 187–203). Los Angeles, CA: Roxbury.

Petronio, S. (1994). Privacy binds in family interactions: The case of parental privacy invasion. In W. R. Cupach & B. H. Spitzberg (Eds.), *The dark side of interpersonal communication* (pp. 241–257). Mahwah, NJ: Lawrence Erlbaum.

Petronio, S. (2002). *Boundaries of privacy: Dialectics of disclosure.* Albany: State University of New York Press.

Petronio, S. (2004). Road to developing communication privacy management theory: Narrative in progress, please stand by. *Journal of Family Communication, 4,* 193–207.

Petronio, S. (2006). Impact of medical mistakes: Navigating work-family boundaries for physicians and their families. *Communication Monographs, 73*(4), 462–467.

Petronio, S., & Caughlin, J. P. (2006). Communication privacy management theory: Understanding families. In D. O. Braithwaite & L. A. Baxter (Eds.), *Engaging theories in family communication: Multiple perspectives* (pp. 35–49). Thousand Oaks: Sage.

Petronio. S., & Jones, S. N. (2006). When "friendly advice" becomes a privacy dilemma for pregnant couples: Applying communication privacy management theory. In L. H. Turner & R. West (Eds.), *The family communication sourcebook* (pp. 201–218). Thousand Oaks, CA: Sage.

Petronio, S., Reeder, H. M., Hecht, M. L., & Mon't Ros-Mendoza, T. (1996). Disclosure of sexual abuse by children and adolescents. *Journal of Applied Communication Research, 24,* 181–199.

Petronio, S., Sargent, J., Andea, L., Reganis, P., & Cichocki, D. (2004). Family and friends as healthcare advocates: Dilemmas of confidentiality and privacy. *Journal of Social and Personal Relationships, 21*(1), 33–52.

Pew Research Center. (2006). *Guess who's coming to dinner.* Retrieved from http:// pewresearch.org

Pew Research Center (2009a). *Majority continues to support civil unions: Most still oppose same-sex marriage.* Retrieved from http://people-press.org/report/553/same-sex-marriage

Pew Research Center (2009b). *Millennials: A portrait of generation next.* Retrieved from the Pew Internet and American Life Project Web site: www.pewinternet.org

Pew Research Center (2010). *The return of the multi-generational family household.* Retrieved from http://pewresearch.org/pubs/1528/multi-generational-family-household

Pickerd, M. (1998). Fatherhood in contemporary society. *Family Relations, 47,* 205–208.

Piercy, F. (2006). Disability and marital interaction: A few personal reflections. *Family focus on . . . special needs and disabilities (*Issue FF31). Minneapolis, MN: National Council on Family Relations.

Pinsof, W. M. (1995). *Integrative problem-centered therapy.* New York: Basic Books.

Pinsof, W. M., & Hambright, A. B. (2002). Toward prevention and clinical relevance: A preventive intervention model for family therapy research and practice. In H. Liddle, D. Santisteban, R. Levant, & J. Bray (Eds.), *Family psychology: Science-based intervention* (pp. 177–195). Washington, DC: American Psychological Association.

Pinsof, W. M., & Wynne, L. (Eds.). (1995). *Journal of Marital and Family Therapy, 21.*

Pipher, M. (1996). *The shelter of each other: Rebuilding our families.* New York: Ballantine Books.

Pistole, M. C. (1994). Adult attachment styles: Some thoughts on closeness-distance struggles. *Family Process, 33*(2), 147–159.

Pittman, J. F., Kerpelman, J. L., & McFadyen, J. M. (2004). Internal and external adaptation in Army families: Lessons from Operations Desert Shield and Desert Storm. *Family Relations, 53,* 249–260.

Pochard, F., Azoulay, E., Chevret, S., Lemaire, F., Hubert, P., Canoui, P., Grassin, M., et al. (2001). Symptoms of anxiety and depression in family members of intensive care unit patients: Ethical hypothesis regarding decision-making capacity. *Critical Care Medicine, 29,* 1893–1897.

Pogrebin, L. (1992, November 29). To tell the truth. *New York Times Magazine,* 22–23.

Pollan, M. (1997, December 14). Town-building is no Mickey Mouse operation. *New York Times Magazine,* 56–63, 76–81, 88.

Prensky, M. (2001, October). On the horizon. *MCB University Press, 9(5).* Retrieved from http://facebook.com/pages/Not-posting-personal-problems-or-family-issues-in status-updates.com.

Prentice, C. (2009). Relational dialectics among in-laws. *Journal of Family Communication, 94,* 67–89.

Preto, N. G. (1999). Transformation of the family system during adolescence. In B. Carter & M. McGoldrick (Eds.), *The expanded family life cycle* (2nd ed., pp. 274–286). Boston, MA: Allyn & Bacon.

Price, S. J., McKenry, P. C., & Murphy, M. J. (2000). *Families across time: A life course perspective.* Los Angeles, CA: Roxbury.

Price, S. J., Price, C. A., & McKenry, P. C. (2010a). *Families and change: Coping with stressful events and transitions* (4th ed.). Los Angeles, CA: Sage.

Price, S. J., Price, C. A., & McKenry, P. C. (2010b). Families coping with change: A conceptual overview. In *Families and change: Coping with stressful events and transitions* (4th ed., pp. 1–23). Los Angeles, CA: Sage.

Primus, W. E. (2002, November). *Child living arrangements by race and income: A preliminary analysis.* Washington, DC: Center on Budget and Policy Priorities.

Putney, N. M., & Bengston, V. L. (2001). Families, intergenerational relationships, and kinkeeping in midlife. In M. E. Lachman (Ed.), *Handbook of midlife development* (pp. 528–570). New York: John Wiley & Sons.

Quek, K. M-T. & Knudson-Martin, C. (2008). Reshaping marital power: How dual-career newlywed couples create equality in Singapore. *Journal of Social and Personal Relationships, 25,* 511–532.

Quittner, J. (2002, July 9). Where will they live? *Advocate,* 27–25.

Radina, M. E., & Armer, J. M. (2001). Post–breast cancer lymphedema and the family: A qualitative investigation of families coping with chronic illness. *Journal of Family Nursing, 7*(3), 281–299.

Ragsdale, J. D. (1996). Gender, satisfaction level, and the use of relational maintenance strategies in marriage. *Communication Monographs, 63,* 354–369.

Ragsdale, J. D. & Brandau-Brown, F. E. (2005). Individual differences in the use of relational maintenance strategies in marriage. *Journal of Family Communication, 5,* 61–75.

Ratner, P. A. (1998). Modeling acts of aggression and dominance as wife abuse and exploring adverse health effects. *Journal of Marriage and the Family, 60,* 453–465.

Raush, H. L., Barry, W. A., Hertel, R. K., & Swain, M. A. (1974). *Communication conflict and marriage.* San Francisco, CA: Jossey-Bass.

Reczek, C., Elliot, S., & Umberson, D. (2009). Commitment without marriage: Union formation among long-term same-sex couples. *Journal of Family Issues, 30,* 738-756.

Reid, J. S. (1986). Social interactional patterns in families of abused and non-abused children. In C. Zahn-Waxler, E. M. Cummings, & R. Ianotti (Eds.), *In Biological and social origins* (pp. 238–257). Cambridge, UK: Cambridge University Press.

Reilly, T., Entwisle, D., & Doering, S. (1987). Socialization into parenthood: A longitudinal study of the development of self-evaluation. *Journal of Marriage and the Family, 49*(2), 295–309.

Reiss, M. C., & Webster, C. (2004). An examination of established antecedents of power in purchase decision making: Married and nontraditional couples. *Journal of Applied Social Psychology, 34,* 9, 1825–1845.

Reitz, M., & Watson, K. W. (1992). *Adoption and the family system.* New York: Guilford Press.

Rempel, L. A., & Rempel, J. K. (2004). Partner influence on health behavior decision-making: Increasing breastfeeding duration. *Journal of Social and Personal Relationship, 21*(1), 92–111.

Renzetti, C. (1989). Building a second closet: Third party responses to victims of lesbian partner abuse. *Family Relations, 38,* 157–163.

Rice, R. E. (2006). Influences, usage, and outcomes of Internet health information searching: Multivariate results from the Pew surveys. *International Journal of Medical Informatics, 75,* 8–28.

Ridley, M. C., Collins, D. M., Reesing, A. L., & Lucero, A. A. (2006). The ebb and flow of marital lust: A relational approach. *Journal of Sex Research, 43*(2), 144–153.

Ristock, J. L. (2002). *No more secrets: Violence in lesbian relationships.* New York: Routledge.

Rittenour, C. & Soliz, J. (2009). Communicative and relational dimensions of shared family identity and relational intentions in mother-in-law/daughter-in-law research. *Western Journal of Communication, 73,* 67–90.

Roberto, A. J., Carlyle, K. E., Goodall, C. E., & Castle, J. D. (2009). The relationship between parents' verbal aggressiveness and responsiveness and young adult children's attachment style and relational satisfaction with parents. *Journal of Family Communication, 9,* 90–106.

Robinson, L., & Blanton, P. (1993). Marital strengths in enduring marriages. *Family Relations, 42,* 38–45.

Rogers, R., & White, J. (1993). Family development theory. In P. Boss, W. Doherty, R. LaRossa, W. Shumm, & S. Steimmetz (Eds.), *Sourcebook of family theories and methods* (pp. 225–254). New York: Plenum Press.

Rolland, J. S. (2005). Chronic illness and the family life cycle. In B. Carter and M. McGoldrick (Eds.), *The expanded family life cycle: Individual, family, and social perspectives* (3rd ed., pp. 492–511). Boston, MA: Allyn & Bacon.

Roloff, M. (1987). Communication conflict. In C. Berger & S. Chafee (Eds.), *Handbook of communication science* (pp. 484–534). Beverly Hills, CA: Sage.

Roloff, M. (1996). The catalyst hypothesis: Condition under which coercive communication leads to physical aggression. In D. Cahn & S. Floyd (Eds.), *Family violence from a communication perspective* (pp. 20–36). Thousand Oaks, CA: Sage.

Roloff, M. E. (2009). Links between conflict management research and practice. *Journal of Applied Communication Research, 37,* 339–348.

Roloff, M. E., & Miller, C. W. (2006). Mulling about family conflict and communication: What we know and what we need to know. In L. H. Turner & R. West (Eds.), *The family communication sourcebook* (pp. 143–164). Thousand Oaks, CA: Sage.

Rosen, E. J. & Weltman, S. F. (2005). Jewish families: An overview. In M. McGoldrick, J. Giordano, & N. Garcia-Preto (Eds.), *Ethnicity and family therapy* (3rd ed., pp. 667–679). New York: Guilford Press.

Rosenbaum, J. (1995). Beat the clock. *American Health, 14*(10), 70–74.

Rosenfeld, M. J. (2007). *The age of independence: Interracial unions, same-sex unions, and the changing American family*. Cambridge, MA: Harvard University Press.

Rosenfeld, R. (1986). U.S. farm women: Their participation in farm work and decision making. *Work and Occupations, 13*, 179–202.

Rothbloom, E. D. (2009). An overview of same-sex couples in relationships: An area still at sea. In D. Hope (Ed.), *Contemporary perspectives on lesbian, gay and bisexual identities* (pp. 113–139). New York: Springer.

Rubin, L. (2001). Getting younger while getting older: Building families at midlife. In R. Hertz & N. L. Marshall (Eds.), *Working families* (pp. 58–71). Berkeley, CA: University of California Press.

Rueter, M. & Koerner, A. (2008). The effect of family communication patterns on adopted adolescent adjustment. *Journal of Marriage and the Family, 70*(3), 715–727.

Rutter, M. (2002). Family influences on behavior and development: Challenges for the future. In J. P. McHale & W. S. Grolnick (Eds.), *Retrospect and prospect in the psychological study of families* (pp. 321–351). Mahwah, NJ: Lawrence Erlbaum.

Sabourin, T. (1994). *The role of negative reciprocity in spouse abuse: A relational control analysis*. Cincinnati, OH: Dept. of Communication, University of Cincinnati.

Sahlstein, E., Maguire, K. C., & Timmerman, L. (2010). Contradictions and praxis contextualized by wartime deployment: Wives' perspectives revealed through relational dialectics. *Communication Monographs, 76*, 421–442.

Sanders, S., Pedro, L.W., Bantum, E., & Galbraith, M. E. (2006). Couples surviving prostate cancer: Long-term intimacy needs and concerns following treatment. *Clinical Journal of Oncology Nursing, 10*, 503–508.

Sanderson, B., & Kurdek, L. A. (1993). Race and gender as moderator variables in predicting relationship satisfaction and relationship commitment in a sample of dating heterosexual couples. *Family Relations, 42*, 263–267.

Sanford, K. (2006). Communication during marital conflict: When couples alter their appraisal, they change their behavior. *Journal of Family Psychology, 20*, 256–265.

Saphir, M. N., & Chaffee, S. H. (2002). Adolescents' contributions to family communication patterns. *Human Communication Research, 28*(1), 86–108.

Satir, V. (1988). *The new peoplemaking*. Mountain View, CA: Science and Behavior Books.

Savin-Williams, R. C., & Esterberg, K. G. (2000). Lesbian, gay, and bisexual families. In D. H. Demo, K. R. Allen, & M. Fine (Eds.), *Handbook of family diversity* (pp. 197–214). New York: Oxford University Press.

Scanzoni, J., & Polonko, K. (1980). A conceptual approach to explicit marital negotiation. *Journal of Marriage and the Family, 42*, 31–44.

Schmidt, L., Holstein, B., Christensen, U., & Boivin, J. (2005). Communication and coping as predictors of fertility problem stress: Cohort study of 816 participants who did not achieve a delivery after 12 months of fertility treatment. *Human Reproduction, 20*, 3248–3256.

Schnarch, C. M. (1991). *Constructing the sexual crucible: An integration of sexual and marital therapy*. New York: W. W. Norton.

Schock, A. M., Gavazzi, S. M., Fristad, M. A., & Goldberg-Arnold, J. S. (2002). The role of father participation in the treatment of childhood mood disorders. *Family Relations, 51*, 230–237.

Schonpflug, U. (2001). Decision-making influence in the family: A comparison of Turkish families in Germany and in Turkey. *Journal of Comparative Family Studies, 19*, 219–230.

Schrimshaw, E. W., & Siegel, K. (2002). HIV-infected mothers' disclosure to their uninfected children: Rates, reasons, and reactions. *Journal of Social and Personal Relationships, 19*, 19–43.

Schrodt, P. (2005). Family communication schemata and the circumplex model of family functioning. *Western Journal of Communication, 69*, 359–376.

Schrodt, P., Braithwaite, D. O., Soliz, J., Tye-Williams, S., Miller, A., Normand, E. L., & Harrigan, M. M. (2007). An examination of everyday talk in stepfamily systems. *Western Journal of Communication, 71*, 216–234.

Schure, L. M., van den Heuvel, E. T. P., Stewart, R. E., Sanderman, R., de Witte, L. P., & Meyboom-de Jong, B. (2006). Beyond stroke: Description and evaluation of an effective intervention to support family caregivers of stroke patients. *Patient Education and Counseling, 62*, 46–55.

Schwartz, P. (1994). *Peer marriage*. New York: Free Press.

Schwartz, S. J., & Liddle, H. A. (2001). The transmission of psychopathology from parents to offspring: Development and treatment in context. *Family Relations, 50*, 301–307.

Schwarzwald, J., Koslowsky, M., & Izhak-Nir, E. B. (2008). Gender role ideology as a moderator of the relationship between social power tactics and marital satisfaction. *Sex Roles, 59*, 657–669.

Scott, J. (2002, February 7). Foreign born in U.S. at record high. *New York Times*, p. A18.

Segrin, C. (2006). Family interactions and well-being: Integrative perspectives. *Journal of Family Communication, 6*(1), 3–21.

Segrin, C., & Flora, J. (2005). *Family communication*. Mahwah, NJ: Lawrence Erlbaum.

Seligman, M. (1988). Psychotherapy with siblings of disabled children. In M. Kahn & L. Lewis (Eds.), *Siblings in therapy: Life span and clinical issues* (pp. 167–189). New York: W. W. Norton.

Seligman, M. & Darling, M. B. (2007). *Ordinary families, special children: A systems approach to childhood disability* (2nd ed.). New York: Guilford Press.

Serewicz, M. C. M. (2006). Getting along with the in-laws: Relationships with parents-in-law. In K. Floyd & M. K. Morman (Eds.), *Widening the family circle* (pp. 101–116). Thousand Oaks, CA: Sage.

Sexton, C. S., & Perlman, D. S. (1989). Couples' career orientation, gender role orientation, and perceived equity as determinants of marital power. *Journal of Marriage and the Family, 51*(4), 933–941.

Shapiro, A. F., & Gottman, J. M. (2005). Effects on marriage of a psycho-communicative-educational intervention with couples undergoing the transition to parenthood, evaluation at 1-year post intervention. *Journal of Family Communication, 5*(1), 1–24.

Shearman, S. M. & Dumlao, R. (2008). A cross-cultural comparison of communication patterns and conflict between young adults and parents. *Journal of Family Communication, 8*, 186–211.

Sheehy, G. (1998, April 26). How to age well. *Parade*, 4–5.

Shellenbarger, S. (2002, February 13). Americans are spending so much time in cars, living takes a back seat. *Wall Street Journal*, p. B6.

Shellenbarger, S. (2005). *The breaking point: How female midlife crisis is transforming today's women*. New York: Henry Holt and Co.

Sher, K., Gershuny, B., Peterson, L., & Raskin, G. (1997). The role of childhood stressors in the intergenerational transmission of alcohol use disorders. *Journal of Studies on Alcohol, 58*, 414–427.

Shibusawa, T. (2005). Japanese families: An overview. In M. McGoldrick, J. Giordano, & N. Garcia-Preto, (Eds.), *Ethnicity and Family Therapy* (3rd ed., pp. 339–348). New York: Guilford Press.

Shin, H. & Kominski, R. (2010). Language use in the United States: 2007. *American Community Survey Reports*. Washington, DC: U.S. Census Bureau.

Shreve, B., & Kunkel, M. (1991). Self-psychology, shame and adolescent suicide: Theoretical and practical considerations. *Journal of Counseling and Development, 69*, 305–312.

Shriver, M. (2009). Times are changing: Gender and generation at work and home. *The Shriver Report: A study by Maria Shriver and the Center for American Progress*. Retrieved from http://www.familiesandwork.org/site/research/reports/Times_Are_Changing.pdf.

Sieber, W. J., Edwards, T. M., Kallenberg, G. A., & Patterson, J. E. (2006). Maximizing patients' health through engagement with families. In D. R. Crane & E. S. Marshall (Eds.), *Handbook of families and health* (pp. 438–450). Thousand Oaks, CA: Sage.

Sieburg, E. (1973). *Interpersonal confirmation: A paradigm for conceptualization and measurement*. Paper presented at the meeting of the International Communication Association, Montreal, Quebec. (ERIC document No. ED 098 634 1975.)

Sillars, A., Canary, D. J., & Tafoya, M. (2004). Communication, conflict, and the quality of family relationships. In A. Vangelisti (Ed.), *Handbook of family communication* (pp. 413–446). Mahwah, NJ: Lawrence Erlbaum.

Sillars, A., Roberts, L. J., Leonard, K. E., & Dun, T. (2000). Cognition during marital conflict: The relationship of thought and talk. *Journal of Social and Personal Relationships, 17*, 479–502.

Sillars, A. L. (1995). Communication and family culture. In M. A. Fitzpatrick & A. L. Vangelisti (Eds.), *Explaining family interactions* (pp. 375–399). Thousand Oaks, CA: Sage.

Sillars, A. L., & Wilmot, W. (1989). Marital communication across the life span. In J. Nussbaum (Ed.), *Life-span communication: Narrative processes* (pp. 225–254). Hillsdale, NJ: Lawrence Erlbaum.

Silverstein, L. B. (2002). Fathers and families. In J. P. McHale & W. S. Grolnick (Eds.), *Retrospect and prospect in the psychological study of families* (pp. 35–64). Mahwah, NJ: Lawrence Erlbaum.

Silverstein, M., & Bengston, V. L. (1997). Intergenerational solidarity and the structure of adult child-parent relationships in American families. *American Journal of Sociology, 103,* 429–460.

Siminoff, L. A., Wilson-Genderson, M., & Baker, S. (2010, December). Depressive symptoms in lung cancer patients and their family caregivers and the influence of family environment. *Psycho-Oncology, 19(12),* 1285–1293.

Simmons, T., & O'Connell, M. (2003, February). Married-couple and unmarried-partner households: 2000. *Census 2000 special reports.* Retrieved from http://www.census.gov/prod/2003pubs/censr-5.pdf

Simms, M., Fortuny, K., & Henderson, E. (2009). *Racial and ethnic disparities among low-income families.* Retrieved from Urban Institute Web site: www.urban.org.

Small, S., & Riley, D. (1990). Toward a multidimensional assessment of work spillover into family life. *Journal of Marriage and the Family, 52,* 51–61.

Smart Marriages. (2010). Retrieved from www.smartmarriages.com.

Smetana, J. G., Campione-Barr, N., & Daddis, C. (2004). Longitudinal development of family decision making: Defining healthy behavioral autonomy for middle-class African American adolescents. *Child Development, 75,* 1418–1434.

Smith, G. C., Savage-Stevens, S. E., & Fabian E. S. (2002). How caregiving grandparents view support groups for children in their care. *Family Relations, 51,* 274–281.

Smith, T. E. (1983). Adolescent reactions to attempted parental control and influence techniques. *Journal of Marriage and the Family, 45*(3), 533–542.

Smits, J., Ultee, W., & Lammers, J. (1996). Effects of occupational status differences between spouses on the wife's labor force participation and occupational achievement: Findings from 12 European countries. *Journal of Marriage and the Family, 58,* 101–115.

Snyder, K. A. (2007). A vocabulary of motives: Understanding how parents define quality time. *Journal of Marriage and the Family, 69,* 320–340.

Sobel, S. & Cowan, B. C. (2003). Ambiguous loss and disenfranchised grief: The impact of DNA predictive testing on the family as a system. *Family Process, 42*(1), 47–57.

Socha, T. J. & Stamp, G. H. (2009). *Parents and children communicating with society: Managing relationships outside of the home.* New York: Routledge.

Socha, T. J. & Yingling, J. (2010). *Families communicating with children.* Malden, MA: Polity.

Socha, T. J., Bromley, J., & Kelly, B. (1995). Invisible parents and children: Exploring African-American parent-child communication. In T. J. Socha & G. H. Stamp (Eds.), *Parents, children and communication: Frontiers of theory and research* (pp. 127–145). Mahwah, NJ: Lawrence Erlbaum.

Soliz, J. E., Lin, M., Anderson, K., & Harwood, J. (2006). Friends and allies: Communication in grandparent-grandchild relationships. In K. Floyd & M. T. Morman, (Eds.), *Widening the family circle* (pp. 65–79). Thousand Oaks, CA: Sage.

Sotirin, P. J., & Ellington, L. L. (2006). The "other" women in family life: Aunt/niece/nephew communication. In K. Floyd & M. T. Morman (Eds.), *Widening the family circle* (pp. 81–99). Thousand Oaks, CA: Sage.

Soule, K. P. (2011). The what, when, who, and why of nagging in interpersonal relationships. In K. M. Galvin (Ed.), *Making connections* (5th ed., pp. 193–199). New York: Oxford University Press.

Sperry, P. & Sperry, L. (2004). The family experience of loss associated with miscarriage and ectopic pregnancy. *Family Journal, 12,* 401–404.

Sprecher, S., & McKinney, K. (1994). Sexuality in close relationships. In A. Weber & J. Harvey (Eds.), *Perspectives in close relationships* (pp. 193–216). Boston, MA: Allyn & Bacon.

Stack, C., & Burton, L. (1998). Kinscripts. In K. V. Hansen & A. I. Garey (Eds.), *Families in the U.S.* (pp. 431–445). Philadelphia, PA: Temple University Press.

Stanley, S. M. & Rhoades, G. K. (2009). "Sliding vs. deciding": Understanding a mystery. *Family focus on . . . cohabitation* (Issue FF42, pp. F1–F4). Minneapolis, MN: National Council on Family Relations.

Stanley, S. M., Rhoades, G. K., & Markman, H. J. (2006). Sliding vs. deciding: Inertia and the premarital cohabitation effect. *Family Relations, 55,* 499–509.

Stafford, L. (2004). Communication competencies and sociocultural priorities of middle childhood. In A. L. Vangelisti (Ed.), *Handbook of family communication* (pp. 311–332). Mahwah, NJ: Lawrence Erlbaum.

Stafford, L., & Canary, D. J. (1991). Maintenance strategies and romance relationship type, gender and relational characteristics. *Journal of Social and Personal Relationships, 8,* 217–242.

Staley, S. M., Whitton, S. W., & Markman, H. J. (2004). Maybe I do: Interpersonal commitment and premarital or nonmarital cohabitation. *Journal of Family Issues, 25,* 496–519.

Stamp, G. H. (1994). The appropriation of the parental role through communication during the transition to parenthood. *Communication Monographs, 61,* 89–112.

Stanley, S. M. (1998). *The heart of commitment: Compelling research that reveals the secrets of lifelong intimate marriage.* Nashville, TN: Nelson.

Stanley, S. M. (2001). Making a case for premarital education. *Family Relations, 50,* 272–280.

Stanley, S. M., Markman, H. J., & Leber, B. D. (1997). Strengthening marriages and preventing divorce. *Family Relations, 44,* 368–376.

Steffenmeier, R. H. (1982). A role model of the transition to parenthood. *Journal of Marriage and the Family, 44,* 319–334.

Steier, F. (1989). Toward a radical and ecological constructivist approach to family communication. *Journal of Applied Communication Research, 17,* 1–26.

Steil, J. M., & Weltman, K. (1992). Influence strategies at home and at work: A study of sixty dual-career couples. *Journal of Social and Personal Relationships, 9,* 65–88.

Stepfamily Solutions. (2010). *The 21st century family: The stepfamily.* Retrieved from http://www.stepfamilysolutions.com/statistics.asp.

Stephen, T., & Enholm, D. (1987). On linguistic and social forms: Correspondences between metaphoric and intimate relationships. *Western Journal of Speech Communication, 51,* 329–344.

Stewart, A. J., Copeland, A. P., Chester, N. L., Malley, J. E., & Barenbaum, N. B. (1997). *Separating together: How divorce transforms families.* New York: Guilford Press.

Stewart, P. E. (2010). Stress and coping in African American families. In S. J. Price, C. A. Price, & P. C. McKenry (Eds.), *Families and change: Coping with stressful events and transitions* (4th ed., pp. 311–331). Los Angeles, CA: Sage.

Stinnett, N., & DeFrain, J. (1985). *Secrets of strong families.* Boston, MA: Little, Brown.

Stone, E. (2005). *Black sheep and kissing cousins: How our family stories shape us.* New Brunswick, NJ: Transaction.

Straus, M. A. (1979). Measuring intrafamily conflict and violence: The conflict tactics (C.T. scales). *Journal of Marriage and the Family, 41,* 75–88.

Straus, M. A., & Gelles, R. J. (1986). Societal change and change in family violence from 1975 to 1985 as revealed by two national surveys. *Journal of Marriage and the Family, 48,* 465–479.

Straus, M. A., Hamby, S. L., Finekelhor, D., Moore, D. W., & Runyan, D. (1998). Identification of child maltreatment with the parent-child conflict tactics scales: Development and psychometric data for a national sample of American parents. *Child Abuse and Neglect, 22*(4), 249–270.

Strazdins, L., Clements, M. S., Korda, R. J., Broom, D. H., & D'Souza, R. M. (2006). Unsociable work? Nonstandard work schedules, family relationships, and children's well-being. *Journal of Marriage and the Family, 68,* 394–410.

Sullivan, A. E. & Miklowitz, D. J. (2010). Family functioning among adolescents with bipolar disorder. *Journal of Family Psychology, 24*(1), 60–61.

Sullivan, J. & McConkie-Rosell, A. (2010). Helping parents talk to their children. In C. L. Gaff & C. L. Bylund (Eds.), *Family communication about genetics: Theory and practice* (pp. 227–242). Oxford, England: Oxford University Press.

Sulloway, F. J. (1996). *Born to rebel: Birth order, family dynamics, and creative lives.* New York: Pantheon.

Sun, Y., & Li, Y. (2002). Children's well-being during parents' marital disruption process: A pooled time-series analysis. *Journal of Marriage and the Family, 64*(2), 472–488.

Surra, C. A., Gray, C. R., Cottle, N., & Boettcher, T. M. J. (2004). In A. L. Vangelisti (Ed.), *Handbook of family communication* (pp. 53–82). Mahwah, NJ: Lawrence Erlbaum.

Suter, E. A. & Ballard, R. L. (2009). "How much did you pay for her?": Decision-making criteria underlying adoptive parents' responses to inappropriate remarks. *Journal of Family Communication, 9,* 107–125.

Swanson, K. M., Karmali, Z. A., Powell, S. H., & Pulvermakher, E. (2003). Miscarriage effects on couples' interpersonal and sexual relationships during the first year after loss: Women's perceptions. *Psychosomatic Medicine, 65*, 902–910.

Tak, Y. R., & McCubbin, M. (2002). Family stress, perceived social support and coping following the diagnosis of a child's congenital heart disease. *Journal of Advanced Nursing, 39*(2), 190–198.

Tardy, C., Hosman, L., & Bradac, J. (1981). Disclosing self to friends and family: A reexamining of initial questions. *Communication Quarterly, 29*, 263–268.

Tejada-Vera, B., & Sutton, P. D. (2009). Births, marriages, divorces, and deaths: Provisional data for 2008. National vital statistics reports, 57(19). Hyattsville, MD: National Center for Health Statistics.

Thilborger, C. (1998, April). *Metaphorical perceptions of familial communication: Where gender differences are really more than skin deep.* Paper presented at the meeting of the Central State Communication Association, Chicago, IL.

A Thin Line. (2009). *AP-MTV Digital Abuse Study.* Retrieved from http://www.athinline.org/ MTV-AP_Digital_Abuse_Study_Executive_ Summary.pdf.

Thompson, D. C., & Dickson, F. (1995, November). *Family rituals as communicative events: A grounded theory.* Paper presented at the annual meeting of the Speech Communication Association, San Antonio, TX.

Times will begin reporting gay couples' ceremonies. (2002, August 18). *New York Times,* The Sunday Styles Section, p. 23.

Toller, P. W. (2008). Bereaved parents' negotiation of identity following the death of a child. *Communication Studies, 59*, 306–321.

Toller, P. W. & Braithwaite, D. O. (2009). Grieving together and apart: Bereaved parents' contradictions of marital interaction. *Journal of Applied Communication Research, 37*, 257–277.

Tomlinson, P. S., Swiggum, P., & Harbaugh, B. L. (1999). Identification of nurse-family intervention sites to decrease health-related family boundary ambiguity in PICU. *Issues in Comprehensive Pediatric Nursing, 22*, 27–47.

Toro-Morn, M. (1998). Gender, class, family and migration: Puerto Rican women in Chicago. In K. Hansen & A. Garey (Eds.), *Families in the U.S.* (pp. 190–199). Philadelphia, PA: Temple University Press.

Townsend, N. (1998). Fathers and sons: Men's experience and the reproduction of fatherhood. In K. V. Hansen & A. I. Garey (Eds.), *Families in the U.S.* (pp. 364–376). Philadelphia, PA: Temple University Press.

Trice, H. M., & Beyer, J. M. (1984). Studying organizational cultures through rites and ceremonies. *Academy of Management Review, 9*, 653–669.

Troth, A., & Peterson, C. C. (2000). Factors predicting safe-sex talk and condom use in early sexual relationships. *Health Communication, 12*, 195–218.

Trujillo, N. (1998). In search of Naunny's grave. *Text and Performance Quarterly, 18*(4) 344–368.

Tucker, J. S., & Anders, S. L. (2001). Social control of health behaviors in marriage. *Journal of Applied Social Psychology, 31*(3), 467–485.

Tucker, J. S., & Mueller, J. S. (2000). Spouses' social control of health behaviors: Use and effectiveness of specific strategies. *Personality and Social Psychology Bulletin, 26*(9), 1120–1130.

Tugend, A. (2008, November 8). Breaking financial bad news to the children. *New York Times,* p. B5.

Turman, P. D., Zimmerman, A., & Dobesh, B. (2009). Parent-talk and sport participation: Interaction between parents, children, and coaches regarding level of play in sports. In T. J. Socha & G. H. Stamp (Eds.), *Parents and children communicating with society: Maintaining relationships outside of home* (pp. 171–188). New York: Routledge.

Turner, R. H. (1970). Conflict and harmony. *Family interaction* (pp. 135–163). New York: John Wiley & Sons.

Udry, J. R., & Campbell, B. (Eds.). (1994). *Sexuality across the life course.* Chicago, IL: University of Chicago Press.

United States Census Bureau. (2002, January 17). *World Population Profile: 1998—Highlights.* Retrieved from http://www.census.gov/ipc/www/ wp98001.html.

United States Census Bureau. (2005). *Income stable, poverty rate increases, percentage of Americans without health insurance unchanged.* Retrieved from http://www.census.gov/Press-Release/www/ releases/archives/income_wealth/005647.html.

United States Census Bureau. (2006, August 10). *Unmarried and Single Americans Week: Sept 17–23, 2006.* Retrieved from http://www.census.

gov/Press Release/www/releases/archives/families_house holds/006840.html.

United States Census Bureau. (2007). *Most people make only one trip down the aisle, but first marriage shorter, Census Bureau reports.* Retrieved from http://www.census.gov/Press-Release/www/releases/archives/marital_status_living_arrangements/ 010624.html.

United States Census Bureau. (2008). *Black (African-American) history month: February 2009.* Retrieved from http://www.census.gov/Press-Release/www/releases/archives/facts_for_features_special_editions/013007.html.

United States Census Bureau. (2009). *Opposite sex unmarried couples by presence of biological children/1 under 18, and age, earnings, education, and race and Hispanic origin/2 of both partners: 2009.* Retrieved from http://www.census.gov/population/socdemo/hh-fam/cps2009/tabUC3-all.xls.

United States Census Bureau. (2010). *Marriages and divorce rates by country: 1980 to 2007.* Retrieved from http://www.census.gov/compendia/statab/2010/tables/10s1300.pdf.

United States Department of Health and Human Services. Child Welfare Information Gateway. Retrieved June 9, 2010, at http://www.childwelfare.gov/can/prevalence/.

Uttal, L. (1998). Racial safety and cultural maintenance: The child care concerns of employed mothers. In K. V. Hansen & A. I. Garey (Eds.), *Families in the U.S.* (pp. 597–618). Philadelphia, PA: Temple University Press.

Van Doorn, M. D., Branje, S. J. T., & Meeus, W. H. J. (2007). Longitudinal transmission of conflict resolution styles from marital relationships to adolescent-parent relationships. *Journal of Family Psychology, 21,* 426–434.

Van Riper, M. (2000). Family variables associated with well-being in siblings of children with Down syndrome. *Journal of Family Nursing, 6*(3), 267–286.

Van Solange, H. & Henkens, K. (2005). Couples' adjustment to retirement: A multi-actor panel study. *Journal of Gerontology, 60B,* 511–520.

Vandeleur, C. L., Jeanpretre, N., & Perrez, M. (2009). Cohesion, satisfaction with family bonds, and emotional well-being in families with adolescents. *Journal of Marriage and Family, 71,* 1205–1219.

Vandivere, S. & Malm, K. (2009). *Adoption USA: A chartbook based on the 2007 national survey of adoptive parents.* Washington, D.C.: U.S. Department of Health and Human Services.

Vangelisti, A. L. (1994a). Couples' communication problems: The counselor's perspective. *Journal of Applied Communication Research, 22,* 106–126.

Vangelisti, A. L. (1994b). Family secrets: Forms, functions, and correlates. *Journal of Social and Personal Relationships, 11,* 113–135.

Vangelisti, A. L., & Alexander, A. L. (2002). Coping with disappointment in marriage: When partners' standards are unmet. In P. Noller & J. A. Feeney (Eds.), *Understanding marriage: Development in the study of couple interaction* (pp. 201–227). New York: Cambridge University Press.

Vangelisti, A. L., & Banski, M. A. (1993). Couples, debriefing conversations: The impact of gender, occupation and demographic characteristics. *Family Relations, 42,* 149–157.

Vangelisti, A. L., & Caughlin, J. (1997). Revealing family secrets: The influence of topic function and relationships. *Journal of Social and Personal Relationships, 14*(5), 679–705.

Vangelisti, A. L., Caughlin, J. P., & Timmerman, L. (2000, November). *Criteria for revealing family secrets.* Paper presented at the meeting of National Communication Association, Seattle, WA.

Vangelisti, A. L., & Crumley, L. (1998). Reactions to messages that hurt: The influence of relational contexts. *Communication Monographs, 65,* 173–196.

Vangelisti, A. L., Crumley, L. P., & Baker, J. L. (1999). Family portraits: Stories as standards for family relationships. *Journal of Social and Personal Relationships, 3,* 335–368.

Vangelisti, A. L., & Huston, T. L. (1994). Maintaining marital satisfaction and love. In D. J. Canary & L. Stafford (Eds.), *Communication and relational maintenance* (pp. 165–186). San Diego, CA: Academic Press.

Videon, Y. M. (2005). Parent-child relations and children's psychological well-being. *Journal of Family Issues, 26,* 55–78.

Villard, K., & Whipple, L. (1976). *Beginnings in relational communication.* New York: John Wiley & Sons.

Vissing, Y., & Baily, W. (1996). Parent-to-child verbal aggression. In D. Cahn & S. Lloyd (Eds.), *Family violence from a communication perspective* (pp. 85–107). Thousand Oaks, CA: Sage.

Vogl, D. L., Murphy, M., Werner-Wilson, R. J., Cutrona, C. E. & Seeman, J. (2007). Sex differences in the use of demand and withdraw behavior in marriage: Examining the social structure hypothesis. *Journal of Counseling Psychology, 54*(2), 165–177.

Vogl-Bauer, S. (2009). When the world comes home: Examining internal and external influences on communication exchanges between parents and their boomerang children. In T. J. Socha & G. H. Stamp (Eds.), *Parents and children communicating with society: Managing relationships outside of the home* (pp. 285–304). New York: Routledge.

Vogl-Bauer, S. M., & Kalbfleisch, P. J. (1997, November). *The impact of perceived equity on parent/adolescent communication strategy usage and relational outcomes.* Paper presented at the meeting of the National Communication Association, Chicago, IL.

Vogt, P. (2009). Live with your parents after graduation? *Monster 2009 Annual Entry-Level Job Outlook.* Retrieved from http://career-advice. monster.com/job-search/getting-started/live-with-parents-after-graduation/article.aspx.

Vogt Yuan, A. S. & Hamilton, H. A. (2006). Stepfather involvement and adolescent well-being: Do mothers and nonresidential fathers matter? *Journal of Family Issues, 27,* 1191–1213.

Vuchinich, S., & DeBaryske, B. D. (1997). Factor structure and predictive validity of questionnaire reports on family problem solving. *Journal of Marriage and the Family, 59,* 915–927.

Vuchinich, S., Ozretich, R. A., Pratt, C. C., & Kneedler, B. (2002). Problem-solving communication in foster families and birth families. *Child Welfare, 81*(4), 571–594.

Vuchinich, S., Teachman, J., & Crosby, L. (1991). Families and hazard rates that change over time: Some methodological issues in analyzing transitions. *Journal of Marriage and the Family, 53,* 898–912.

Waite, L. J., & Gallagher, M. (2000). *The case for marriage.* New York: Doubleday.

Waldron, V. R. & Kelley, D. L. (2008). *Communicating forgiveness.* Los Angeles, CA: Sage.

Waldron, V. R., & Kelley, D. L. (2005). Forgiving communication as a response to relational transgressions. *Journal of Social and Personal Relationships, 6,* 723–742.

Wallerstein, J. S., Lewis, J. M., & Blakeslee, S. (2000). *The unexpected legacy of divorce: A 25 year landmark study.* New York: Hyperion.

Walsh, F. (1993). Conceptualization of normal family processes. In F. Walsh (Ed.), *Normal family processes* (2nd ed., pp. 3–69). New York: Guilford Press.

Walsh, F. (2005). Families in later life: Challenges and opportunities. In B. Carter & M. McGoldrick (Eds.), *The expanded family life cycle: Individual, family and social perspectives* (3rd ed., pp. 307–326). New York: Allyn & Bacon.

Wamboldt, F., & Reiss, D. (1989). Defining a family heritage and a new relationship identity: Two central tasks in the making of a marriage. *Family Process, 28,* 317–335.

Wang, Q. (2005, July). Disability and American families: 2000. *Census 2000 special reports.* Washington, DC: U.S. Census Bureau.

Wang, S., Holloway, B. B., Beatty, S. E., & Hill, W. W. (2006). Adolescent influence in family purchase decisions: An update and cross-national extensions. *Journal of Business Research, 60,* 1117–1124.

Wang, W. & Morin, R. (2009). *Home for the holidays . . . and every other day.* Pew Research Center. Retrieved from Pew Research Center Web site: http://pewsocialtrends.org.

Ward, R. A., Spitze, G., & Deane, G. (2009). The more the merrier? Multiple parent–adult child relations. *Journal of Marriage and Family, 71*(1), 161–173.

Warren, C. (1995). Parent-child communication about sex. In T. J. Socha & G. H. Stamp (Eds.), *Parents, children and communication: Frontiers of theory and research* (pp. 173–201). Mahwah, NJ: Lawrence Erlbaum.

Warren, C. (2003). Communicating about sex with parents and partners. In K. M. Galvin & P. J. Cooper (Eds.), *Making connections: Readings in relational communication* (3rd ed., pp. 317–324). Los Angeles, CA: Roxbury.

Warren-Jeanpiere, L., Miller, K., & Warren, A. (2010). African American women's retrospective perceptions of the intergenerational transfer of gynecological health care information received from mothers: Implications for families and providers. *Journal of Family Communication, 2,* 81–98.

Waterman, J. (1979). Family patterns of self-disclosure. In G. Chelune & Associates (Eds.), *Self-disclosure* (pp. 225–242). San Francisco, CA: Jossey-Bass.

Watzlawick, P., Beavin, J., & Jackson, D. D. (1967). *Pragmatics of human communication.* New York: W. W. Norton.

Webster-Stratton, C. (1997). From parent training to community building. *Families and Society, 78,* 156–171.

Weigel, D. J. & Ballard-Reisch, D. S. (2001). The impact of relational maintenance behaviors on marital satisfaction: A longitudinal analysis. *Journal of Family Communication, 1,* 265–279.

Weigel, D. J. & Ballard-Reisch, D. S. (2008). Relational maintenance, satisfaction, and commitment in marriages: An actor-partner analysis. *Journal of Family Communication, 8,* 212–229.

Weigel, D. J., Bennett, K. K., & Ballard-Reisch, D. (2006). Influence strategies in marriage: Self and partner links between equity, strategy use, and marital satisfaction and commitment. *Journal of Family Communication, 6,* 77–95.

Weintraub-Austin, E., Hust, S. J. T., & Listler, M. E. (2009). Arming parents with strategies to affect children's interactions with commercial interests. In T. J. Socha & G. H. Stamp (Eds.), *Parents and children communicating with society: Managing relationships outside of the home* (pp. 133–153). New York: Routledge.

Weiss, R. (1997, November 10). Aging: New answers to old questions. *National Geographic, 31.*

Weiss, R., & Dehle, C. (1994). Cognitive behavioral perspectives on marital conflict. In D. Cahn (Ed.), *Conflict in personal relationships* (pp. 95–116). Hillsdale, NJ: Lawrence Erlbaum.

Weldon, M. (1997, July 20). Many new moms feel guilt, anger. *Chicago Tribune,* sec. 13, p. 3.

Weldon, M. (1998, January 11). Elderly care usually falls to daughters. *Chicago Tribune,* sec. 13, p. 3.

Wells, B. (1986). *The meaning makers.* Portsmouth, NH: Heineman.

Werner, C., Altman, I., & Brown, B. (1992). A transactional approach to interpersonal relations: Physical environment, social context and temporal qualities. *Journal of Social and Personal Relationships, 9,* 287–323.

West, R., & Turner, L. H. (2007). *Introducing communication theory: Analysis and application* (3rd ed.). New York: McGraw-Hill.

West, R., & Turner, L. H. (2010). *Understanding interpersonal communication: Making choices in changing times.* Boston, MA: Cengage Learning.

Weston, K. (1993). *Families we choose.* New York: Columbia University Press.

"What constitutes a family?" (1992, July–August). *Public Opinion and Demographic Report,* 101.

Whitaker, J. L. & Bushman, B. J. (2009). Online dangers: Keeping children and adolescents safe. *Washington and Lee Law Journal.* Retrieved from http://law.wlu.ed/deptimages/Law%20Review/66-3WhitakerBushmanOnline.pdf.

Whitchurch, G., & Constantine, L. (1993). Systems theory. In P. Boss, W. J. Doherty, R. LaRossa, W. R. Schumm, & S. K. Steinmetz (Eds.), *Sourcebook of family theories and methods* (pp. 325–352). New York: Plenum Press.

Whitchurch, G., & Dickson, F. C. (1999). Family communication. In M. B. Sussman, S. K. Steinmetz, & G. W. Peterson (Eds.), *Handbook of marriage and the family* (2nd ed., pp. 687–704). New York: Plenum Press.

White, J. M., & Klein, D. M. (2002). *Family theories* (2nd ed.). Thousand Oaks, CA: Sage.

White, L., & Rogers, S. J. (2000). Economic circumstances and family outcomes: A review of the 1990's. *Journal of Marriage and the Family, 62,* 1035–1051.

Whiteside, M. F. (1989). Family rituals as a key to kinship connections in remarried families. *Family Relations, 38,* 34–39.

Whiting, J. B, Smith, D., Barnett, T., & Grafsky, E. (2007). Overcoming the Cinderella myth: A mixed methods study of successful stepmothers. *Journal of Divorce and Remarriage, 47,* 95–109.

Whitton, S. W., Waldinger, R. J., Schulz, M. S., Allen, J. P., Crowell, J. A., & Hauser, M. A. (2008). Prospective associations from family-of-origin interactions to adult marital interactions and relationship adjustment. *Journal of Family Psychology, 22*(2), 274–286.

Widenfelt, B. V., Hosman, C., Schaap, C., & van der Staak, C. (1996). The prevention of relationship distress for couples at risk: A controlled evaluation with nine-month and two-year follows. *Family Relations, 45,* 156–165.

Wight, V., Chau, M., & Aratani, Y. (2010). Who are America's poor children? The official story. *National Center for Children in Poverty.* New York: Columbia University.

Wilcox, B. (Ed.), & Marquardt, E. (Assoc. Ed.) (2009). *The state of our unions: Marriages in America 2009. Social indicators of marital health and wellbeing.* University of Virginia: The National Marriage Project.

Wilkie, J. R., Ferree, M. M., & Ratcliff, K. S. (1998). Gender and fairness: Marital satisfaction in two-earner couples. *Journal of Marriage and the Family, 60,* 577–594.

Wilkinson, C. A. (1998). *Family communication* [Video class]. University Park, IL: Governors State University.

Wilkinson, C. A. & Grill, L. H. (2011). Expressing affection: A vocabulary of loving messages. In K. M. Galvin (Ed.), *Making Connections* (5th ed., pp. 164–173). New York: Oxford University Press.

Williams, A., & Nussbaum, J. F. (2001). *Intergenerational communication across the lifespan.* Mahwah, NJ: Lawrence Erlbaum.

Willoughby, B. L. B., Doty, N. D., & Malik, N. M. (2008). Parental reactions to their child's sexual orientation disclosure: A family stress perspective. *Parenting: Science and Practice, 8,* 70–91.

Wilmot, W. W. (1987). *Dyadic communication* (3rd ed.). New York: Random House.

Wilmot, W. W. & Hocker, J. L. (2007). *Interpersonal Conflict* (7th ed.) New York: McGraw-Hill.

Wilson, B. J., Forrest, K., Van Teijlingen, E. R., McKee, L., Haites, N., Matthews, E., & Simpson, S. A. (2004). Family communication about genetic risk: The little that is known. *Community Genetics, 7,* 15–24.

Wilson, P. M. (2004). 1994: Forming a partnership between parents and sexuality educators: Reflections of a parent advocate. *SIECUS Report, 32,* 6–8.

Wilson, S., Hayes, J., Bylund C., Rack, J., & Herman, A. (2006). Mothers' trait verbal aggressiveness and child abuse potential. *Journal of Family Communication, 6,* 279–296.

Wilson, S., & Morgan, W. (2004). Persuasion in families. In A. Vangelisti (Ed.), *Handbook of family communication* (pp. 447–471). Mahwah, NJ: Lawrence Erlbaum.

Wilson, S. R. & Morgan, W. M. (2006). Goals-plans-action theories: Theories of goals, plans and planning processes in families. In D. O. Braithwaite and L. A. Baxter (Eds.), *Engaging theories in family communication: Multiple perspectives* (pp. 66–81). Thousand Oaks, CA: Sage.

Wilson, S. R., Morgan, W. M., Hayes, J., Bylund, C., & Herman, A. (2004). Mothers' child abuse potential as a predictor of maternal and child behaviors during play-time interactions. *Communication Monographs, 71*(4), 395–421.

Wilson, S. R., Roberts, F., Rack, J. J., & Delaney, J. E. (2008). Mothers' trait verbal aggressiveness as a predictor of maternal and child behavior during playtime interactions. *Human Communication Research, 34*(3), 392–422.

Wilson, S. R., Shi, X., Tirmenstein, L., Norris, A., & Rack, J. J. (2006). Parental physical negative touch and child noncompliance in abusive, neglectful, and comparison families: A meta-analysis of observational studies. In L. H. Turner & R. West (Eds.), *The family communication sourcebook* (pp. 237–258). Thousand Oaks, CA: Sage.

Wilson, S. R., & Whipple, E. E. (1995). Communication, discipline, and physical child abuse. In T. Socha & G. Stamp (Eds.), *Parents, children, and communication: Frontiers in theory and research* (pp. 299–317). Hillsdale, NJ: Lawrence Erlbaum.

Wilson, S. R., Xiaowei, S., Tirmenstein, L., Norris, A., & Rack, J. J. (2006). Parental physical negative touch and child noncompliance in abusive, neglectful, and comparison families: A meta-analysis of observational studies. In L. H. Turner & R. West (Eds.), *The family communication sourcebook* (pp. 237–258). Thousand Oaks, CA: Sage.

Wingard, L. (2009). Communicating about homework at home and school. In T. J. Socha & G. H. Stamp (Eds.), *Parents and children communicating with society: Maintaining relationships outside of home* (pp. 81–104). New York: Routledge.

Wired seniors: A fervent few, inspired by family ties. (2001, September 9). Retrieved from the Pew Internet and American Life Project Web site: www.pewinternet.org

Witteman, H., & Fitzpatrick, M. A. (1986). Compliance-gaining in marital interaction: Power bases, processes, and outcomes. *Communication Monographs, 53*(2), 130–143.

Wolff, J., Pak, J., Meeske, K., Worden, J. W., & Katz, E. (2002). Challenges and coping styles of fathers as primary medical caregivers: A multicultural qualitative study. *Journal of Psychosocial Oncology, 28*(2), 202–217.

Wolin, S. J., & Bennett, L. A. (1984). Family rituals. *Family Process, 23,* 401–420.

Wood, J. T. (1998). *But I thought you meant . . . Misunderstandings in human communication.* Mountain View, CA: Mayfield.

Wood, J. T. (2011). *Gendered lives: Communication, gender, and culture* (9th ed.). Boston, MA: Cengage Learning.

Worden, J. W. (1991). *Grief counseling and grief therapy: A handbook for the mental health practitioner* (2nd ed.). London: Springer.

World Wide Marriage Encounter. (2010). Retrieved from http://www.wwme.org/.

Wright, P. J. (2009). Father-child sexual communication in the United States: A review and synthesis. *Journal of Family Communication, 9,* 233–250.

Xu, X., & Lai, S. (2002). Resources, gender ideologies and marital power. *Journal of Family Issues, 23*(2), 209–245.

Yerby, J. (1993, November). *Co-constructing alternative stories: Narrative approaches in the family therapy literature.* Paper presented at the meeting of the Speech Communication Association, Miami, FL.

Zahlis, E. H. & Lewis, F. M. (2010). Coming to grips with breast cancer: The spouse's experience with his wife's first six months. *Journal of Psychosocial Oncology, 28*(1), 79–97.

Zaslow, J. (2010, June 3). 'Til 40 years do us part. *Wall Street Journal,* D1, p. 3.

Zernike, K. (1998, June 21). Feminism has created progress, but man, oh, man, look what else. *Chicago Tribune.* Retrieved from http://articles.chicagotribune.com/1998-06-21/features/9806210422_1_men-and-masculinity-dads-million-man-march.

Zukow, P. G. (1989). *Sibling interaction across cultures: Theoretical and methodological issues.* New York: Springer-Verlag.

Zvonkovic, A. M., Schmiege, C. J., & Hall, L. D. (1994). Influence strategies used when couples make work-family decisions and their importance for marital satisfaction. *Family Relations, 43*(2), 182–188.

PHOTO CREDITS

NAME INDEX

SUBJECT INDEX